济南统计年鉴

JINAN STATISTICAL YEARBOOK

2021

（总第39期 NO.39）

济 南 市 统 计 局
国家统计局济南调查队 编

Jinan Municipal Bureau of Statistics
NBS Survey Office In Jinan

图书在版编目（CIP）数据

济南统计年鉴. 2021 = Jinan Statistical Yearbook 2021 : 汉英对照 / 济南市统计局，国家统计局济南调查队编 . -- 北京 : 中国统计出版社，2021.8
ISBN 978-7-5037-9507-7

Ⅰ. ①济… Ⅱ. ①济… ②国… Ⅲ. ①统计资料—济南—2021—年鉴—汉、英 Ⅳ. ①C832.521-54

中国版本图书馆 CIP 数据核字（2021）第 117548 号

济南统计年鉴—2021

作　　者 / 济南市统计局　国家统计局济南调查队
责任编辑 / 钟钰
装帧设计 / 山东麦德森文化传媒有限公司
出版发行 / 中国统计出版社有限公司
地　　址 / 北京市丰台区西三环南路甲 6 号
邮政编码 / 100073
电　　话 / 邮购（010）63376909　书店（010）68783171
网　　址 / http://www.zgtjcbs.com
印　　刷 / 山东麦德森文化传媒有限公司
经　　销 / 新华书店
开　　本 / 890mm×1240mm　1/16
字　　数 / 244 千字
印　　张 / 26.25
版　　别 / 2021 年 8 月第 1 版
版　　次 / 2021 年 8 月第 1 次印刷
定　　价 / 396.00 元　Price:396.00yuan(RMB)

如有印装差错，由本社发行部调换。

编辑委员会及编辑工作人员

Editorial Board and Editorial Staff

编 辑 说 明

一、《济南统计年鉴－2021》是一部全面反映济南市国民经济和社会发展情况的资料性统计年刊。本书收录了济南市及所辖县、区 2020 年经济和社会发展各方面大量的统计数据，以及历史重要年份的主要统计数据，是认识和研究济南市情、经济和社会发展，制定宏观政策、指导工作的重要工具书。

二、本年鉴以丰富、翔实的统计资料为主，辅以直观的统计图、特载，全面反映了济南市国民经济和社会发展状况。全书统计资料共分为二十二个部分，即：1. 行政区划；2. 人口；3. 综合；4. 国民经济核算；5. 劳动就业；6. 固定资产投资；7. 城市公用事业和环境保护；8. 财政和金融保险；9. 物价；10. 人民生活；11. 农业；12. 工业；13. 建筑业；14. 运输与邮电；15. 国内贸易；16. 对外贸易与国际旅游；17. 科技；18. 教育与文化；19. 体育卫生；20. 民政司法和其他；特载和附录。各篇末附有《主要统计指标解释》，对主要统计指标的含义、统计范围、统计方法以及历史变动情况作了简要说明。

三、本年鉴中使用的度量衡均采用国际统一标准计量单位，统计口径除特别注明外，均包括济南市区、平阴县、商河县。资料取自济南市统计局、国家统计局济南调查队及有关部门的统计报表。

四、本年鉴中部分数据合计数或相对数由于计量单位取舍不同而产生的计算误差，均未做机械调整。

五、本年鉴表中的符号使用说明：

"空格"表示该项统计指标数据不足本表最小单位数、数据不详或无该项数据；

"-"表示无此项事实；

"#"表示其中的主要项；

"*"或"①"表示本表下有注解。

《济南统计年鉴》自出版以来，受到了社会各界的关心和支持，对此我们深表感谢。同时，欢迎使用《济南统计年鉴－2021》，敬请广大读者提出宝贵意见。帮助我们进一步提高统计年鉴编辑工作，更好的为社会各界服务，谢谢！（网址：http://jntj.jinan.gov.cn/）

编　者

2021 年 8 月

EDITOR'S NOTES

Ⅰ . *Jinan Statistical Yearbook 2021* is a statistical reference book published yearly that comprehensively reflects the development of Jinan' s national economy and society. With a vast amount of statistical data on various aspects of economic and social development in Jinan and the counties and districts under its jurisdiction in 2020, as well as the main statistical data of important historical years, the yearbook is an important reference book for people to understand and study Jinan and its economic and social development, for government to formulate macro policies and guidance work.

Ⅱ . The *yearbook* is centered on rich and detailed statistical data with intuitive statistical charts and special articles added, comprehensively reflecting Jinan' s economic and social development. Statistical data of the yearbook contains 22 parts, namely:1. Division of Administrative Areas;2. Population;3. General Survey;4. National Accounts;5. Labor and Employment;6. Investment in Fixed Assets;7. Urban Public Utilities and Environmental Protection;8. Government Finance and Financial Insurance;9. Prices;10. People's Livelihood;11.Agriculture;12. Industry;13. Construction;14. Transportation, Post and Telecommunications;15. Domestic Trade;16. Foreign trade and International Tourism;17. Science and Technology;18. Education and Culture;19. Sports and Public Health;20. Social Welfare Civil Administration and Justice; Special Published and Appendices. We edit Exploratory Notes on Main statistical Indicators at the end of every article, briefly explaining the meaning, statistical scope, methods and historical changes of the main statistical indicators.

Ⅲ . The units of measurement used in this yearbook are internationally unified and standard measurement units. The statistical caliber includes Jinan City, Pingyin County and Shanghe County unless otherwise noted. The data in this yearbook are from the statistical reports of Jinan Municipal Bureau of Statistics, Jinan Investigation Team of National Bureau of Statistics and relevant departments.

Ⅳ . The statistical discrepancies caused by the unit of measurement in the total or relative numbers of some data in this yearbook are not adjusted.

Ⅴ . Notations used in this yearbook:

"Blank Space" indicates that the statistical index data is not large enough to be measured with the smallest unit in this table, or data are unknown or not available;

"–" means that there is no such fact;

"#" indicates the main item;

"*" or "①" means there are annotations in this table.

Since its publication, *Jinan Statistical Yearbook* has received the concern and support of all sectors of society, for which we are deeply grateful. At the same time, welcome to use *Jinan Statistical Yearbook 2021* and offer valuable suggestions, so as to help us further improve the editing of statistical yearbooks and better serve all sectors of society, thank you! (Website: http://jntj.jinan.gov.cn/)

Editor

August 2021

目　录

特载　Special Report

一　行政区划　Divisions of Administrative Areas

二　人　口　Population

三 综 合 General Survey

四 国民经济核算 National Accounts

五 劳动就业 Labor and Employment

六 固定资产投资 Investment in Fixed Assets

七　城市公用事业和环境保护 Urban Public Utilities and Environmental Protection

八　财政和金融保险 Government Finance and Financial Insurance

九 物 价 Price

十 人民生活 People's Livelihood

十一 农 业 Agriculture

十二 工 业 Industry

十三 建筑业 Construction

十四 运输与邮电 Transportation Post and Telecommunication

十五 国内贸易 Domestic Trade

十六　对外贸易与国际旅游　Foreign Trade and International Tourism

十七　科　技　Science and Technology

十八　教育与文化　Education and Culture

十九　体育与卫生　Sports and Public Health

二十 民政、司法和其他
Social Welfare Civil Administration and Others

附 录 Appendix

特载

SPECIAL REPORT

特载 -1

济南概况

济南市位于山东省中部，地理位置介于北纬36° 01′ 至 37° 32′、东经116° 11′ 至117° 44′之间，面积10244平方公里。南依泰山，北跨黄河，地处鲁中南低山丘陵与鲁西北冲积平原的交接带上，地势南高北低，依次为低山丘陵、山前倾斜平原和黄河冲积平原。境内河流较多，河流分属黄河、小清河、海河三大水系。湖泊有大明湖、白云湖等。济南属于暖温带大陆性季风气候区，四季分明，日照充分，年平均气温13.6℃，年平均降水量614.0毫米。

济南矿产资源丰富，主要有铁、煤、花岗石、耐火粘土以及铜、钾、铂、钴等多种有色金属、稀有金属和非金属。特别是石灰岩品位高、储量大。花岗石中的黑色花岗石，质地纯正，为国内独有。有植物149科，1175种和变种。陆栖野生动物211种。南部山区盛产苹果、黄梨、柿子、核桃、山楂、板栗等，并产有远志、丹参、野菊、香附等多种药材。北部沿黄河的平原地带，大枣也有很高的产量。济南种植和养殖资源也相当丰富，有多种粮食作物、经济作物以及家禽、家畜、水产品等。这些资源为济南城乡建设和经济发展储备了一定的物质基础。

济南自然景色秀丽，名胜古迹众多，是中国历史文化名城之一。尤以泉水遍布、清冽甘美而闻名于世，有“济南泉水甲天下”和“泉城”之美誉。主要风景名胜有趵突泉、黑虎泉、珍珠泉、五龙潭、百脉泉五大泉群，大明湖、千佛山、龙洞、灵岩寺、五峰山、华山、城子崖龙山文化遗址、孝堂山汉代郭氏祠、隋代四门塔、唐代龙虎塔、九顶塔以及抢救挖掘的洛庄汉墓、野生动物世界、红叶谷生态旅游区等供人们观赏游览。

济南辖历下、市中、槐荫、天桥、历城、长清、章丘、济阳、莱芜、钢城十区和平阴、商河二县。2020年，全市地区生产总值10140.9亿元，比上年增长4.9%。户籍总人口806.7万人。第七次全国人口普查显示，济南市常住人口920.24万人。济南又是一个多民族聚居的城市，除汉族外，主要有回、满、苗、蒙古、壮、朝鲜等55个少数民族。

济南是国务院公布的历史文化名城。因地处古四渎之一“济水”（故道为今黄河所据）之南而得名。据史学家考证，早在公元前45世纪之前，已有人类在此繁衍、生息。传说东夷族的首领舜，曾躬耕于济南历山（今千佛山）之下。2600多年前，就建有城郭，最早出现史册上的名称为“泺”（《春秋左传》），系因济南诸泉汇为泺水，故名。春秋战国时代，济南属齐国，称“泺”“鞍”“历下”等邑，为齐国西南边陲重镇。西汉始置济南郡，公元前164年设立济南国。公元前154年又废国改郡。东汉建武十七年（公元41年），济南郡复称济南国。宋代至道三年(公元997 年)，分全国为15路，济南属京东路，为齐州（《宋史》）。徽宗政和六年（公元1116年），齐州升为济南府，辖历城等五县，治所设历城，为府治之始。自明代以来，一直是山东省的省会。 1929年7月设济南市至今。1928年4月至1937年底，日本帝国主义先后二次侵占了济南，济南人民深受暴虐的民族压迫和经济掠夺，致使大部分工厂倒闭，无辜同胞惨遭杀戮。1945年8月，日寇投降后，国民党反动派又进行强盗式的劫收，城市又遭到了摧残蹂躏，民生凋敝，物价飞涨，古城一片萧条。1948年 9月24日，济南获得解放，这座古城终于回到了人民的怀抱，开始了她新的历史时期。

新中国建立后，济南市始终是中国东部沿海经济大省—山东省省会。是全国副省级城市之一，环渤海地区南翼的中心城市，是全省的政治、经济、文化、教育、交通和科技中心，是山东半岛城市群和济南都市圈核心城市。2017年，荣膺“全国文明城市”称号，跨入全国文明城市行列。2018年12月26日，国务院批复同意山东省调整济南市莱芜市行政区划，撤销莱芜市，将其所辖区域划归济南市管辖。济南是全国区域性金融中心，2020年年末金融机构本外币各项存款余额达21065.0亿元，各项贷款余额20720.2亿元。

济南是山东省铁路、公路、航空的交通枢纽，京沪、胶济铁路在市区交汇，北连北京、天津，南接南京、上海、福州，东达港口城市青岛、烟台。济南为京沪高铁沿线5个始发终到站之一。济南机场是经国家批准的国际空港，有通往北京、上海、香港、澳门、广州、深圳、福州、厦门、西安、武汉、哈尔滨、珠海、海口等城市的208条空中航线，通航城市91个。“济青高速”“济聊高速”与“京福高速”在济南交汇，从而形成了辐射全省、连接全国的高速公路系统省内中心、全国区域性枢纽的格局。济南基本形成了铁路、航空、公路立体构造，联结全省、全国和海外的现代交通网络。

Special Report-1

Introduction of Jinan

Jinan is located in the middle of Shandong Province with an area of 10,244 km2. The geographic position is between 36° 01′ N ~ 37° 32′ N and 116° 11′ E ~ 117° 44′ E with the Mount Tai land in the south and Yellow River plain in the north. Jinan City is located at the junction of low mountains and hills in the middle and south of Shandong Province and alluvial plain in the northwest of Shandong Province. The terrain in the south is higher than that in the north, featuring low mountains and hills, sloping plain in front of mountains and Yellow River alluvial plain. Jinan mainly enjoys many rivers under the Yellow River, Xiaoqinghe River and Haihe River systems. The lakes here are Daming Lake, Baiyun Lake, etc. Jinan City is in the temperate continental monsoon climate zone. Jinan City has four distinctive seasons with sufficient sunlight hours. The annual average temperature is 13.6℃, the annual amount of precipitation is 614.0 mm.

Jinan has abundant mineral resources, mainly including various non-ferrous metals, rare metals and non-metals, such as the iron, coal, granite, fire clay and copper, kalium, platinum and cobalt, etc. In particular, the limestone has large reserves with high grade. The texture of black granite is pure and unique in China. There are 149 families of plants, 1175 species and varieties. There are 211 species of terrestrial wild animals. The apple, yellow pear, persimmon, walnut, hawthorn and Chinese chestnut, etc. are rich and the polygala tenuifolia, Salvia, chrysanthemum indicum and rhizoma cyperi, etc. medicinal materials are produced in the southern mountain area. The output of Chinese-date is very high in the flat-bottomed land along the Yellow River in the north. Jinan has rather abundant planting and breeding resources with various grain crops, economic crops and poultry, livestock and aquatic products, etc. These resources reserve a certain of material basis for the urban and rural development and economic development of Jinan.

As one of China's famous historical and cultural cities, Jinan has beautiful natural scenery and many scenic spots and historical sites. It is especially famous for clear and luscious springs and enjoys good reputations of "Jinan Springs Are the Best in the World" and "Spring City". The main scenic spots are Baotu Spring, Heihu Spring, Pearl Spring, Five Dragon Pool, Five Groups of Baimai Spring, Daming Lake, Qianfo Mountain, Dragon Cave, Lingyan Temple, Five Mountain, Mount Hua, Chengziya Longshan Cultural Site, Stone Memorial Hall at Guos' Temple on Xiaotang Mountain, Sui Dynasty Pagoda of Four Gates, Tang Dynasty Dragon Tiger Tower, Jiuding Tower and Luozhuang Han Tombs through rescue and excavation, newly-built Wildlife World and Red Leaves Canyon, etc. for viewing and sightseeing.

Now, Jinan City has jurisdiction over ten districts of Lixia, Shizhong, Huaiyin, Tianqiao, Licheng, Changqing, Zhangqiu, Jiyang, Laiwu and Gangcheng and two counties of Pingyin and Shanghe. In 2020, local GDP of Jinan city reached RMB 1014.09 billion, with an increase of 4.9 % over that of the previous year; The total registered population was 8.067 million. The 7th National Census indicates that the number of permanent residents in Jinan City is 9.2024 million.Jinan is a city inhabited by multiple nationalities which mainly include 55 ethnic minorities, such as Hui, Man, Miao, Mongol, Zhuang and Korean, etc., in addition to Han.

Jinan is a famous historic and cultural city listed by the State Council. It is named after its location at the south of "Jishui River" (now occupied by the Yellow River), one of four ancient channels. According to the historians textual research, human beings had lived here long before 45th Century B.C. Legend has it that Shun, the leader of Dongyi Tribal Groups, farmed at the foot of Mount Li once(Qianfo Mountain today). More than 2600 years ago, the city walls had been built. It was named as "Luo" first appeared in history annals (Zuo's Commentary). Because Jinan springs converge to the Luoshui River, hence the name is gained. Jinan was the State of Qi in the warring state period, named "Luo", "An" and "Lixia" counties. It was in a key position in the southwest of the State of Qi. In the Western Han Dynasty, Jinan was changed Jinan Prefecture. The State of Jinan was set up in 164 B.C. Then it was changed into the County of Jinan in 154 B.C. In the 17th year of Jianwu Period of the Eastern Han Dynasty (41 A.D.), Jinan was renamed the State of Jinan. The whole state was divided into 15 regions in Emperor Taizong Zhidao 3th year (997 A.D.), Jinan belonged to Jingdong Region, named Qizhou (History of the Song Dynasty). Qizhou was promoted to Jinan Palace in Emperor Huizong Zhenghe 6th year (1116 A.D.), governing five countries of Licheng, etc. with the seat in Licheng. It is the provincial capital of Shandong Province all the time since the Ming Dynasty. Jinan City was set up in Jul. 1929 to this day. The Japanese imperialist successively occupied Jinan for two times at the end of Apr. 1928 to 1937. Jinan people are deeply influenced by tyrannical national oppression economic plundering. Most of the factories closed down and innocent compatriots are massacred in cold blood. In Aug. 1945, KMT reactionaries took over the city like bandits upon surrender of Japanese aggressors. The city was destroyed and devastated again. The people live in destitution, the prices are soaring and the city was in the great depression. On Sep. 24, 1948, Jinan was liberated and finally returned to the people's arms, starting her new historical period.

Jinan is always the provincial capital of Shandong Province which is the coastal economic big province of East China after the founding of new China. It is one of sub-provincial cities around the country, central city of Circum-Bohai Sea Region South Wing, the center of the whole Province in politics, economics, culture, education, transportation and science and technology and the core city of Shandong Peninsula Urban Agglomerations and Jinan Metropolitan Circle. In 2017, it was awarded as the title of "National Civilized City" and stepped into the national civilized city list. The State Council approved Shandong Province adjusted the administrative division of Laiwu city in Jinan, cancelled Laiwu City and incorporated its jurisdiction under the jurisdiction of Jinan. Jinan is the regional financial center around the country. The outstanding of deposits of local and foreign currencies for the financial institutions at the end of 2020 was RMB 2.1065 trillion and the loan balance was RMB 2.0720 trillion.

It is the transportation junction of Shandong railway, highway and aviation. Beijing-Shanghai Railway and Jiaozhou-Jinan Railway converge at the city, connecting Beijing and Tianjin in the north, Nanjing, Shanghai and Fuzhou in the South and port cities of Qingdao and Yantai in the east. Jinan is one of 5 starting-terminating stations along Beijing-Shanghai High-Speed Railway. Jinan Airport is an international airport with 208 airways approach to Beijing, Shanghai, Hong Kong, Macao, Guangzhou, Shenzhen, Fuzhou, Xiamen, Xi'an, Wuhan, Harbin, Zhuhai and Haikou, etc. and 91 destinations. "Jinan-Qingdao Expressway", "Jinan-Liaocheng Expressway" and "Beijing-Taibei Expressway" converge at Jinan, thus forming the provincial central and national regional hub pattern of expressway system which radiates the whole province and connects the whole nation. Jinan basically forms the stereometric structure of railway, aviation and highway and modern traffic network that connects the whole province, the whole nation and foreign countries.

2020年济南市
国民经济和社会发展统计公报[1]

济 南 市 统 计 局
国家统计局济南调查队

2020年，面对错综复杂的经济形势，特别是新冠肺炎疫情严重冲击，在市委、市政府坚强领导下，全市上下坚持以习近平新时代中国特色社会主义思想为指导，全面贯彻党的十九大和十九届二中、三中、四中、五中全会精神，坚决落实习近平总书记对山东、对济南工作的重要指示要求，按照省委、省政府对省会建设提出的新目标、新定位，主动融入、服从服务黄河流域生态保护和高质量发展重大国家战略，统筹推进疫情防控和经济社会发展，扎实做好“六稳”工作，全面落实“六保”任务，全市经济稳步回升、逐季向好，全年地区生产总值迈上万亿新台阶，高质量发展加速起势，“十三五”实现圆满收官，全面建成小康社会取得历史性、决定性成就，实现经济实力城市能级新跨越，为新时代现代化强省会建设奠定了坚实基础。

一、综合

初步核算，全年全市地区生产总值[2]10140.9亿元，比上年增长4.9%。分产业看，第一产业增加值361.7亿元，增长2.2%；第二产业增加值3530.7亿元，增长7.0%；第三产业增加值6248.6亿元，增长3.7%。三次产业构成为3.6：34.8：61.6。分季度看，一季度实现2027.0亿元，下降4.4%；二季度实现2502.7亿元，增长5.1%；三季度实现2718.7亿元，增长7.1%；四季度实现2892.5亿元，增长8.8%。

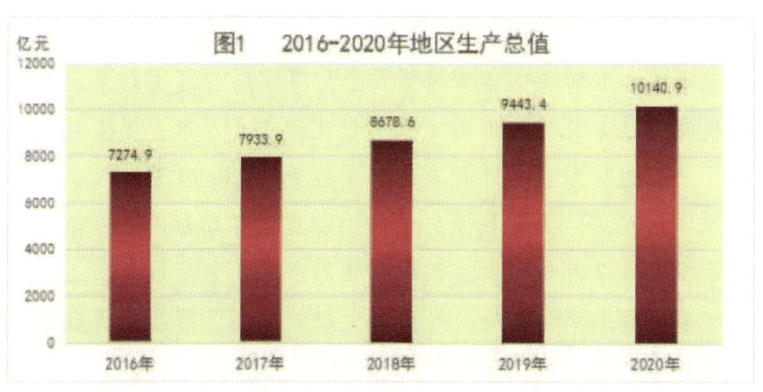

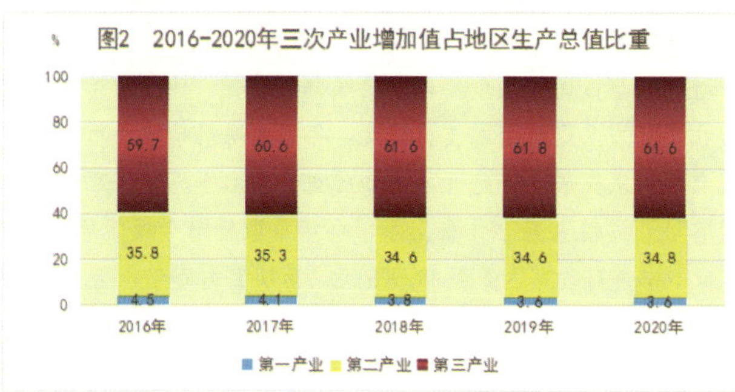

全年新增城镇就业16.3万人，超额完成15万人左右的预期目标，年末城镇登记失业率2.03%，低于3%左右的预期目标。

全年居民消费价格指数（CPI）上涨2.4%，涨幅比上年缩小0.9个百分点，保供稳价成效凸显，八大类商品“两涨一平五降”。新建商品住宅销售价格指数环比涨幅基本保持稳定。

表1 2020年居民消费价格比上年涨跌幅度

指 标	比上年增长（%）
居民消费价格指数	2.4
食品烟酒	9.9
衣着	-0.1
居住	-1.5
生活用品及服务	-0.6
交通和通信	-4.3
教育文化和娱乐	-0.4
医疗保健	0
其他用品和服务	8.6

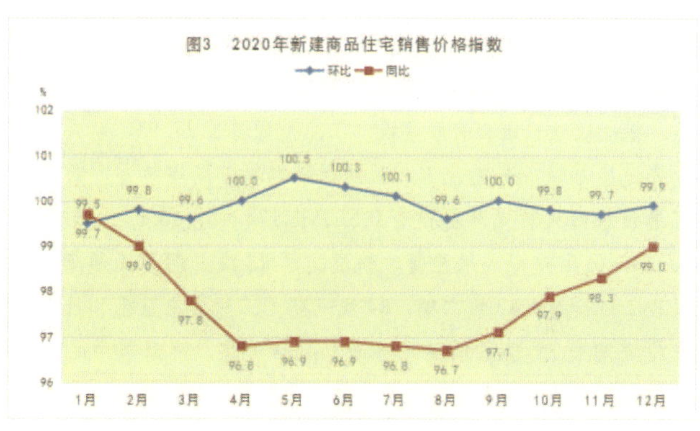

二、重点工作

重点改革有序推进。重大战略落地实施。黄河流域生态保护和高质量发展国家战略行动加快实施，城市发展战略规划编制完成，国土空间总体规划、重点区域专项规划编制取得积极进展。新旧动能转换起步区列入国家《黄河流域生态保护和高质量发展规划纲要》。山东自贸试验区济南片区形成60余项制度创新成果，累计新注册企业1.8万余家、总量突破7万家。建立健全省会经济圈一体化发展工作机制，省市一体化推进济南加快发展工作成效显著。体制机制改革精准发力。省级以上开发区体制机制改革基本完成，全市开发区实行“党工委（管委会）+公司”管理体制，内设机构数量压缩51.4%。深化国资国企改革，全力推进落实国企改革三年行动计划，市属国有企业完成混改项目25个。营商环境持续优化。深入推进“一次办好”改革，商事登记实现全城通办、跨市通办、跨省通办，涉企事项100%容缺受理，高分通过政务服务标准化国家试点验收。开放活力持续提升。创新对外合作模式，跨境电商综试区综合服务平台搭建完成，线下产业园区建设初具规模。全年组织展会107场，展览面积超180万平方米，济南商贸服务型国家物流枢纽和济南国家骨干冷链物流基地成功获批。积极推进省会人才特区建设，与133名海内外院士建立合作关系，新增国家级人才工程人选4人，泰山系列人才工程人选37人，新引进泉城“5150”人才（团队）79个，支持泉城产业领军人才（团队）43个。全省首个“人才贷”金融服务窗口落地，在副省级以上城市中第1个全面放开落户限制，成功创建全国第20家、省内第2家国家级人力资源服务产业园，全市人才资源总量突破200万。

动能转换质效进一步提高。工业新动能加快成长。工业强市战略深入实施，规模以上工业增加值增速领跑全国主要城市。规模以上工业装备制造业实现增加值比上年增长24.3%，拉动全市规模以上工业增长9个百分点；高技术制造业实现增加值增长22.2%，营业收入总额突破千亿大关，增长20.8%。高端产品快速增长，高端产品服务器产量超过140万台，增长35.2%。消费结构优化升级。升级类产品势头良好，全年限额以上单位零售额中，新能源汽车实现零售额20.1亿元，增长47.6%，智能家用电器和音像器材类实现零售额29.9亿元，增长113.2%，体育娱乐用品类实现零售额6.8亿元，增长26.4%。线上消费快速增长，限额以上单位通过公共网络实现零售额136.8亿元，增长19.2%，线上消费成为消费品市场企稳回升的生力军。投资拉动量质齐升。产业项目亮点频现，莱钢集团新旧动能转换系统优化升级改造项目、重汽集团智能网联（新能源）重卡项目等一批优质项目正在有序建设。工业投资增长27.9%，新兴产业投资进度加快，高端化工、新能源新材料、高端装备、新一代信息技术四大新兴产业投资分别增长174.4%、66.6%、48.6%、30.2%。民生投资成果显著，轨道交通R3线一期竣工通车，R2线竣工试运行，R3线二期、R4线一期开工建设。卫生和社会工作投资增长59.6%，树兰（济南）国际医院、济南市中心医院（东院区）、济钢森林公园正在建设。服务业新动能不断增强。现代服务业[3]实现增加值3843.4亿元，增长7.1%，占服务业比重为61.5%。规模以上服务业实现营业收入2412.2亿元，下降3.0%。规模以上服务业中新兴行业保持较快增长，高技术服务业带动作用增强，营业收入比上年增长14.3%，占规模以上服务业比重为33.8%。其中，互联网和相关服务业、专业技术服务业分别增长89.3%、18.7%。物流运力提升，邮政业、多式联运和运输代理业分别增长35.9%、31.5%。绿色转型成效显著。随着煤炭、钢铁等行业去产能不断推进，原煤生产明显下降，全年原煤生产比上年减少73.7万吨。能源消费更加低碳清洁，规模以上工业煤炭消费比上年减少253.7万吨。节能降耗成效显著，初步核算，万元GDP能耗比上年下降7.5%，完成当年节能降耗目标任务。创新驱动作用增强。“四新”经济增加值占比超过36%，保持全省领先水平，“四新”经济投资占比较上年提高4个百分点。新认定高新技术企业1427家，总数达到3029家，其中，规模以上工业高新技术企业达到1014家，比上年净增59家；实现产值占全市规模以上工业比重为55.3%，比上年提高4.1个百分点。R&D经费投入[4]225.5亿元，占GDP比重为2.4%。中科院济南科创城建设加快推进，新增省级工程实验室48家，省级新型研发机构48家，省级创新创业共同体8家，省级技术创新中心12家，济南高新区获批建设国家级双创示范基地。

“三农”工作取得新成效。全力建设美丽宜居乡村。建成6个市级田园综合体，农村人居环境整治三年行动圆满收官，农村饮水安全两年攻坚行动全面完成，39个省级美丽乡村示范村、105个乡村振兴齐鲁样板村和123个区县级示范村全面建成。积极引导农用地经营权有序流转。全市土地流转面积126.9万亩，比上年增长22.9%；参与土地流转农户27.9万户，增长21.9%。流向家庭农场、农村合作社土地分别增长46%和40.2%。全力巩固脱贫攻坚成果。1006个贫困村脱贫成效进一步巩固提升，贫困人口稳定实现“两不愁三保障”和饮水安全，基本医保、慢病帮扶和大病报销实现全覆盖，贫困学生资助政策从学前教育到高等教育高标准全覆盖。

“六稳”“六保”落实有效。稳就业保民生成效突出。发放稳岗补贴6.35亿元、稳定岗位123.3万个。23件为民办实事全面完成，企业退休人员基本养老金待遇、城乡居民基本养老保险基础养老金标准进一步提升。稳外贸稳投资稳预期进展良好。进出口总额同比增长22.9%，创近五年新高，新增外贸进出口实绩企业950家。开行欧亚班列542列，新开通国际（地区）航线12条，济南章锦综保区封关运行，济南综保区进出口额增长1.4倍。市场主体活力增强。全力落实助企纾困政策，新增减税降费328亿元，市场主体总量突破130万户，规模以上企业（“四上”企业）总量首次历史性突破10000家。粮食能源供给保持稳定。全年粮食总播种面积比上年增加1.7万亩，总产量提升5.3万吨，均达到历史较高水平。全年规模以上企业发电量276.7亿千瓦时，风力、太阳能、垃圾等新能源发电持续向好。产业链供应链保障平稳。打通产业链供应链卡点堵点，保障重点行业和产品生产。规模以上工业41个大类行业中，23个行业实现增长，增长面为56.1%，增加值合计占比71.1%，行业增长面与占比水平今年以来持续稳定扩张。稳金融保基层运转扎实有力。财政金融支撑稳定，年末金融机构本外币存、贷款余额双双突破2万亿元，达到历史最高水平。与国家开发银行签订开发性金融合作备忘录，全年争取新增专项债券401.3亿元，中央财政直达资金49.9亿元，落实直达资金分配、拨付、监控三个“一竿子插到底”工作机制，迅速将资金直达基层。

三、农业

农业经济综合保障能力不断增强。全年农林牧渔业总产值 671.7 亿元，比上年增长 2.6%；农林牧渔业增加值 380.3 亿元，增长 2.3%。粮食总产量 290.8 万吨，增长 1.9%；蔬菜总产量 673.7 万吨，增长 0.4%；油料总产量 6.8 万吨，增长 3.7%；水果总产量 63.2 万吨，增长 0.4%。

表 2 2020 年主要农产品种植面积和产量

指　标	单位	面积 / 产量	比上年增长 (%)
粮食总播种面积	万亩	720.7	0.2
棉花种植面积	万亩	5.3	-7.9
油料种植面积	万亩	27.2	-5.7
蔬菜种植面积	万亩	147.9	-1.7
实有果园面积	万亩	59.2	1.5
粮食总产量	万吨	290.8	1.9
棉花产量	万吨	0.4	-22.0
油料产量	万吨	6.8	3.7
蔬菜产量	万吨	673.7	0.4
水果产量	万吨	63.2	0.4

特色农产品发展良好。以长清茶叶、章丘大葱、莱芜生姜、仁风西瓜、曲堤黄瓜等为代表的特色农产品声名远扬，稳定了疫情期间的市场供应，也带来了良好的经济效益。2020 年全市茶叶产量 61.2 万公斤，大葱 74.3 万吨，生姜 29.4 万吨，西瓜 29.2 万吨，黄瓜 107.8 万吨。

化肥、农药使用量逐年下降。全年化肥使用量（折纯）20.50 万吨，比上年减少 4.6%；农药使用量 0.32 万吨，比上年减少 7.1%，农业节本增效成果明显。

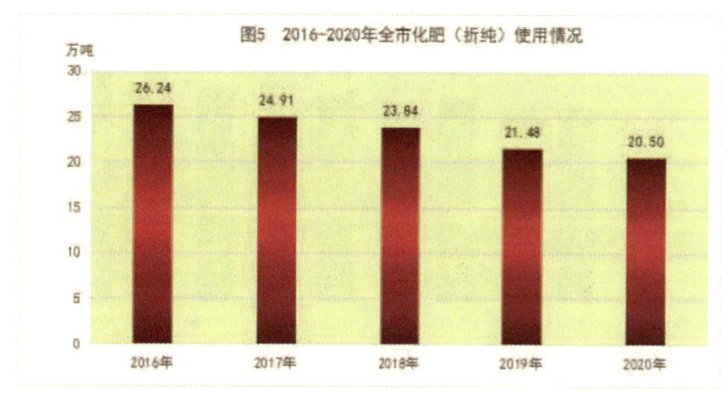

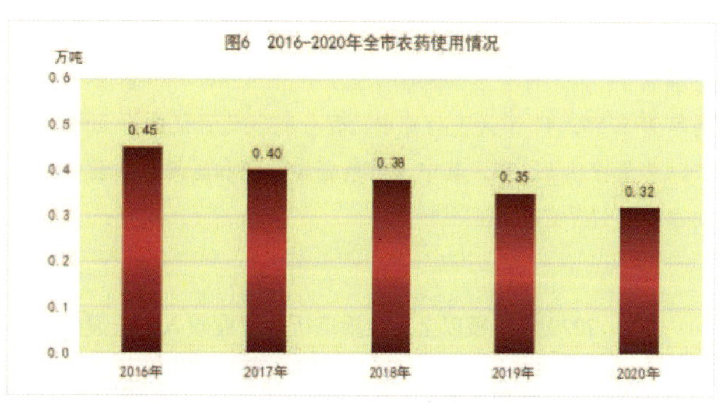

肉蛋奶供应基本稳定。全年生猪出栏 157.0 万头，肉产量 12.8 万吨；牛出栏 9.0 万头，肉产量 2.1 万吨，牛奶产量 41.4 万吨；羊出栏 86.9 万头，肉产量 1.5 万吨；禽肉产量 7.4 万吨，禽蛋产量 27.5 万吨。全年水产品产量 1.3 万吨。

全年完成造林面积 1.1 万公顷，森林抚育面积 966 公顷，建设生态廊道 151 公里、绿道 133.8 公里，绿化黄河堤防淤背区 2531 亩。创建市级绿化模范村 100 个，创建全国森林康养基地试点建设单位 26 家，省乡村林场 3 家。

现代高效农业发展较好。全市现代高效农业增加值 56.7 亿元，比上年增长 18.5%，提高 8.9 个百分点，现代高效农业增加值占农林牧渔业增加值比重 14.9%，比上年提高 1.6 个百分点。市级以上农业产业化龙头企业 480 家，其中国家级 8 家，省级 72 家；家庭农场 5960 个；农民专业合作社 10626 家，当年新增 2705 家。国家级畜禽养殖标准化示范场 2 个，新增 1 个，市级畜禽养殖标准化示范场 30 个，新增 6 个。

四、工业和建筑业

全年全部工业增加值 2360.5 亿元，比上年增长 8.2%。规模以上工业增加值增长 12.2%，分经济类型看，公有制经济增长 9.5%，非公有制经济增长 14.1%；分轻重工业看，轻工业增长 12.3%，重工业增长 12.2%。全市规模以上工业六大重点行业中，汽车制造业增长 77.9%，医药制造业增长 31.3%，计算机通信制造业增长 20.3%，黑色金属压延加工业增长 8%，石油煤炭加工业、非金属矿物制品业分别下降 9.9%、11.1%。

全年规模以上工业企业完成营业收入7387.8亿元，比上年增长14.3%，利润总额407.3亿元，增长40.6%，营业收入利润率为5.5%。41个大类行业中，营业收入超百亿的行业达到15个，总量占比92.7%。其中，黑色金属冶炼和压延加工业、汽车制造业超过千亿规模。

表3 2020年规模以上工业重点行业营业收入增长速度

行业名称	比上年增长（%）
黑色金属冶炼和压延加工业	7.5
汽车制造业	63.1
计算机、通信和其他电子设备制造业	17.2
非金属矿物制品业	-14.0
电气机械和器材制造业	15.8
通用设备制造业	0.3
石油、煤炭及其他燃料加工业	-17.1
金属制品业	7.9
化学原料和化学制品制造业	13.9
医药制造业	28.7
专用设备制造业	15.7
电力、热力生产和供应业	-2.7
食品制造业	6.4

全年规模以上工业产品产销率为98.7%。所生产的174种大类产品中，有94种产品产量实现增长，增长面为54.0%。其中，增幅超过30%的产品有37种，占比为21.3%，比上年提高7.5个百分点。生产载货汽车39.4万辆，增长92.7%，汽车用发动机、汽车仪器仪表分别增长74.7%、55.4%。光缆、工业机器人、高温合金分别增长50.1%、24.6% 、13.4%。

表4 2020年规模以上工业企业[5]主要产品产量及增长速度

产品名称	单位	产量	比上年增长(%)
鲜、冷藏肉	万吨	15.1	2.4
乳制品	万吨	49.0	1.4
饮料酒	万千升	26.8	-13.0
合成氨（无水氨）	万吨	60.0	-13.5
聚丙烯树脂	万吨	11.6	0.8
初级形态塑料	万吨	15.9	-5.8
中成药	吨	6038.2	69.5
水泥	万吨	1328.2	6.9
石墨及碳素制品	万吨	172.7	-4.1
钢材	万吨	2336.5	2.3
锻件	万吨	113.6	13.0
粉末冶金零件	万吨	1.3	-2.2
发动机	万千瓦	6167.1	72.1
数控金属切削机床	台	670	-34.0
气动元件	万件	1464.6	-12.6
矿山专用设备	万吨	6.4	9.0
工业机器人	套	1960	24.6
载货汽车	万辆	39.4	92.7
铁路货车	辆	3418	-35.6
变压器	万千伏安	13645.4	-11.9
太阳能电池（光伏电池）	万千瓦	36.2	-35.0
电子计算机整机	万台	144.9	34.8
服务器	万台	143.5	35.2
集成电路	万块	889.2	-43.0
发电量	亿千瓦时	276.7	-6.0

全年建筑业增加值1181.8亿元，比上年增长3.9%，占GDP比重11.7%。房屋施工面积达到17089.9万平方米。主营业务为建筑业、具有总承包和专业承包资质的、有工作量的建筑业企业1033家，比上年增加168家。实现建筑业总产值3748.1

亿元，增长 6.7%。其中，国有及国有控股企业产值 2842.9 亿元，增长 10.3%。签订合同额 9823.0 亿元，增长 17.0%。其中，本年新签合同额 5531.7 亿元，增长 22.0%。

图8 2016-2020年建筑业总产值

五、固定资产投资

全年固定资产投资比上年增长 4.0%。分产业看，第一产业投资增长 12.0%，第二产业投资增长 27.3%，第三产业投资增长 0.4%。重点领域中，民间投资增长 3.9%，基础设施投资增长 13.5%。年末亿元以上固定资产投资项目（不含房地产）1343 个，增加 235 个，其中，五十亿元以上项目 36 个，比上年增加 4 个。中国航天科技园（济南）项目进度为 43.9%，莱钢集团新旧动能转换系统优化升级改造项目进度 38%，树兰（济南）国际医院项目进度 35.4%，济南至莱芜高速铁路进度 25.1%。

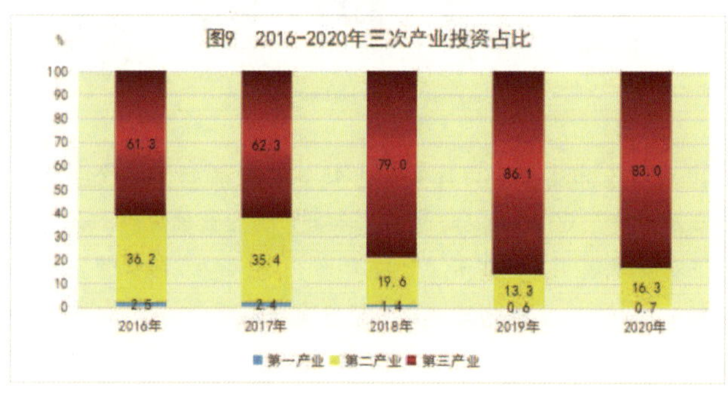

图9 2016-2020年三次产业投资占比

全年房地产开发完成投资 1707.6 亿元，增长 8.3%，其中，住宅完成投资 1204.3 亿元，增长 6.0%。房屋施工面积 10353.0 万平方米，增长 3.7%，其中，住宅施工面积 6700.9 万平方米，增长 2.7%。房屋竣工面积 1273.0 万平方米，增长 19.0%，其中，住宅竣工面积 913.6 万平方米，增长 18.5%。商品房销售面积 1335.7 万平方米，增长 7.2%，其中，住宅销售面积 1145.2 万平方米，增长 12.2%。商品房销售额 1571.9 亿元，增长 13.8%，其中，住宅销售额 1406.5 亿元，增长 19.8%。

六、国内贸易

全年社会消费品零售总额 4469.1 亿元，比上年增长 1.1%。其中，商品零售 3858.4 亿元，增长 2.6%；餐饮收入 610.7 亿元，下降 7.2%。分城乡看，城镇社会消费品零售额 4013.2 亿元，增长 1.2%；乡村社会消费品零售额 455.9 亿元，增长 0.5%。限额以上单位[6]实现零售额 1504.2 亿元，下降 0.9%。

图10 2016-2020年社会消费品零售总额

限额以上单位商品零售额中，粮油、食品类 156.4 亿元，增长 7.0%；家用电器和音像器材类 85.6 亿元，增长 6.7%；汽车类 477.2 亿元，增长 7.4%。

表 5 2020 年限额以上批发和零售业单位主要商品零售额及增长速度

商品类别	零售额（亿元）	比上年增长（%）
粮油、食品类	156.4	7.0
饮料类	13.1	1.8
烟酒类	33.1	33.0
服装、鞋帽、针纺织品类	91.3	-19.2
化妆品类	32.3	0
金银珠宝类	32.7	-13.7
日用品类	38.1	-5.6
家用电器和音像器材类	85.6	6.7
中西药品类	56.9	15.4
文化办公用品类	47.1	4.6
通讯器材类	67.5	2.6
石油及制品类	183.5	-14.3
汽车类	477.2	7.4

七、开放型经济

全年货物进出口总额 1382.7 亿元，同比增长 22.9%。其中，出口 755 亿元，增长 17.2%；进口 627.6 亿元，增长 30.7%。出口市场中，对欧洲国家和地区出口增长 34.4%，对韩国、日本出口分别增长 19% 和 12.4%，对美国出口增长 19.9%，对“一带一路”沿线国家和地区出口增长 15.9%。主要出口商品中，机电产品出口 406 亿元，增长 11%；高新技术产品出口 145.3 亿元，增长 59.3%；农产品出口 67.7 亿元，增长 28.7%，防疫物资出口 40.5 亿元，增长 868.8%。全年经济外向度 13.6%，比上年提高 1.9 个百分点。

全年实际使用外资 19.2 亿美元，比上年下降 14.2%。其中，制造业使用外资 1.5 亿美元，三产使用外资 14.6 亿美元。全年实现合同外资额 58.5 亿美元，下降 14.4%。新批外商投资项目 203 个，总投资过亿美元的项目 34 个，合同外资 39.9 亿美元。

全年对外承包工程新签合同额 44.0 亿美元，比上年下降 23.2%；完成营业额 42.7 亿美元，增长 4.5%；备案设立境外企业（机构）77 家，实际投资 19.1 亿美元，增长 72.7%。派出各类劳务人员 11966 人，增长 48.7%。

八、交通、邮电和旅游

全市年末公路通车里程数 18117.2 公里，比上年增长 2.0%。其中，境内高速公路里程数 737.8 公里，增长 12.9%。公路客运量 1209 万人，下降 62.7%；旅客周转量 17.1 亿人公里，下降 68.4%。公路货运量 2.8 亿吨，增长 0.4%；货运周转量 562.4 亿吨公里，增长 0.2%[7]。年末拥有民用机动车 313.9 万辆，其中，民用汽车 279.4 万辆，增长 8.1%。公交线路 650 条，比上年增加 54 条，线路总长度 13204.7 公里，增加 2397.5 公里，旅客运输量 5.3 亿人次，减少 3.2 亿人次。全年累计完成航班起降 10.2 万架次，下降 21.2%；旅客吞吐量 1238.5 万人次，下降 29.5%；货邮吞吐量 14.7 万吨，增长 8.4%。

全年邮政行业业务收入（不包括邮政储蓄银行直接营业收入）85.1 亿元，比上年增长 22.4%；业务总量 146.5 亿元，增长 28.6%。快递服务企业业务收入 66.8 亿元，增长 19.2%；业务量 6.5 亿件，增长 26.3%。年末移动电话用户 1154.1 万户，其中，4G 电话用户 922.7 万户，增长 3.8%。宽带网用户 445.5 万户，增长 7.7%。

全年接待国内外游客 6048.8 万人次，恢复至上年水平的 60.3%。其中，接待国内游客 6037.9 万人次，接待入境游客 10.9 万人次。实现旅游总收入 702.8 亿元，恢复至上年水平的 54.6%。其中，国内旅游收入 700.5 亿元，入境旅游收入 3322.0 万美元。A 级景区 86 家，其中，5A 级旅游景区 1 家，4A 级旅游景区 16 家。省级旅游度假区 2 家。

九、财政和金融

全年一般公共预算收入 906.1 亿元，比上年增长 3.6%，可比增长 7.2%。其中，税收收入 696.6 亿元，下降 0.5%，占一般公共预算收入比重为 76.9%。一般公共预算支出 1288.4 亿元，增长 7.6%。其中，教育支出 213.4 亿元，增长 14.7%；社会保障和就业支出 176.3 亿元，增长 8.0%；城乡社区支出 281.6 亿元，增长 11.7%。

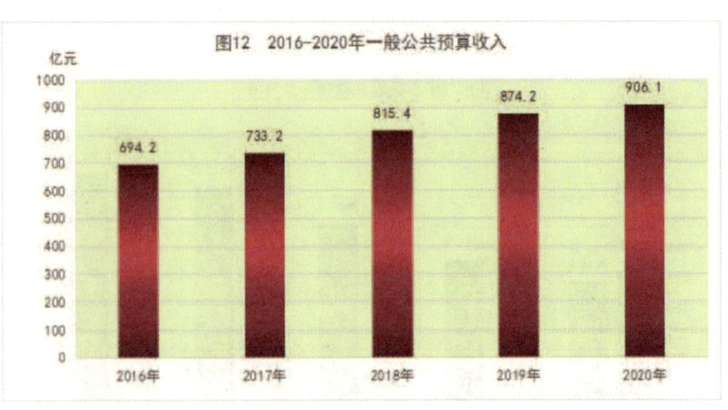

年末金融机构本外币各项存款余额 21065.0 亿元，比上年增长 13.0%；金融机构本外币各项贷款余额 20720.2 亿元，增长 10.4%。法人金融机构 41 家，其中，银行 20 家，保险公司 3 家，证券公司 1 家，期货公司 1 家，财务公司 11 家，信托公司 1 家，汽车金融 1 家，金融租赁 2 家，金融科技 1 家。

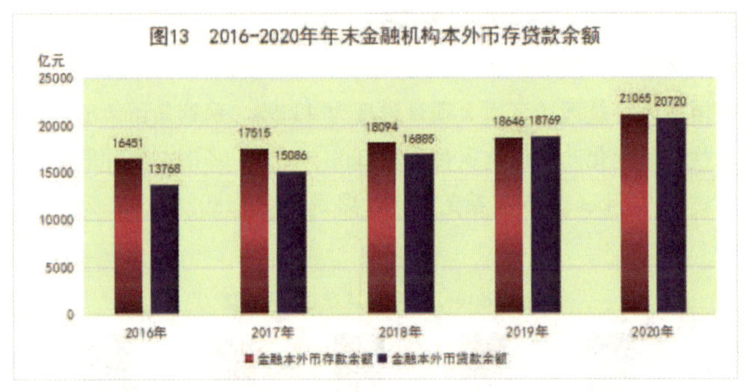

年末全市上市公司数量达到 45 家，股票 47 只，全年新增上市及过会企业 11 家，超过前三年上市企业数量总和。全年完成证券交易额 4.8 万亿元，比上年增长 31.0%；期货营业部交易额 11 万亿元，增长 38.6%；新增直接融资 2269.5 亿元，增长 12.2%。年末全市在中国证券投资基金业协会登记的私募基金管理机构 190 家，管理基金 435 只，管理基金规模 993.2 亿元，增长 24.5%。

全市保险业实现保费收入 628.0 亿元，比上年增长 18.0%。其中，财产险 125.6 亿元，增长 6.9%；人身险 502.5 亿元，增长 21.1%。各项赔款与给付 160.3 亿元，增长 31.5%。

十、科技、教育、文化、卫生和体育事业

全年万人有效发明专利拥有量 33.2 件，比上年增长 13.4%。技术合同实现交易额 337.8 亿元，增长 21.3%。全市获国家科技进步二等奖 2 项，省科技进步一等奖 6 项、二等奖 37 项。专利申请量 69642 件，其中发明专利申请量 19859 件。专利授权量 40903 件，其中发明专利授权量 5827 件。全市国家知识产权示范企业、优势企业共计 80 家。

全市开工新建、改扩建中小学校（幼儿园）144 所，普惠性幼儿园覆盖率达到 87%，义务教育阶段集团化建设率达到 85.2%。全面实施市校融合发展战略，开展校地合作 85 项，围绕

重点产业设置特色优势学科专业51个，签约引进高等教育项目25个。

表6　2020年教育事业基本情况

学校类别	学校数量（所）	在校生（万人）	专任教师（人）
驻济高等学校	52	89.85	42202
中等职业学校（不含技工学校）	41	6.28	3642
普通中学	320	39.84	34796
小学	666	57.01	37219
特殊教育学校	13	0.13	545

年末国有艺术表演团体14个，文化馆（站）174个，公共博物馆13个，档案馆17个，公共图书馆14个。市级以上文物保护单位435处，其中国家级30处。城市可统计票房数字影院64家，观众481.25万人次，票房收入1.75亿元。年末广播人口混合覆盖率99.7%，电视人口混合覆盖率99.3%。新建泉城书房12处，基层综合性文化服务中心覆盖率100%。

年末拥有卫生机构7514个，比上年增加27个，其中，医院、卫生院343个。卫生机构床位6.9万张，增长3.4%。各类卫生技术人员10.2万人，增长4.7%；执业（助理）医师4.0万人，增长5.0%。

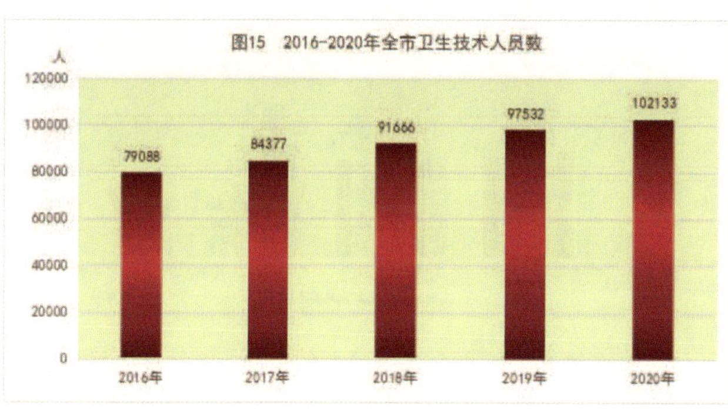

全年新成立体育社会组织8个，培训社会体育指导员3364人。组织各类全民健身活动（赛事）385次，参与人数225万人次（含线上活动）。获省级及以上金牌407枚，银牌264枚，铜牌336枚。组织举办第六届全国大众冰雪季暨首届泉城冰雪运动嘉年华活动、第八届济南国际泉水节龙舟赛等大型赛事，举办第八届中国济南冬季畅游泉水国际公开赛，来自30个国家、102支代表队、1195名冬泳选手参赛，创历史新高。

十一、能源、环境、城市建设[8]和安全生产

绿色低碳能源体系建设取得积极进展。煤炭消费压减工作成效显著，规模以上工业煤炭消费2769.5万吨，下降8.4%；天然气消费8.0亿立方米，增长19.4%，煤减气增，清洁能源消费占比逐步提高。规模以上工业能源加工转换效率比上年提高0.5个百分点，其中炼焦效率提高2.9个百分点，供热效率提高0.9个百分点，炼油效率提高0.1个百分点。新能源生产方兴未艾，规模以上企业风力发电7.6亿千瓦时，增长1.7%，占发电总量的2.8%；太阳能发电1.4亿千瓦时，增长1.3%，占发电总量的0.5%；垃圾发电6.9亿千瓦时，增长23.5%，占发电总量的2.5%。

表7　规模以上（限额以上）企业能源生产情况

指标	累计	比上年增长（%）
原煤（万吨）	82.4	-47.2
发电量（亿千瓦时）	276.7	-6.0
火力发电量（亿千瓦时）	267.7	-6.2
风力发电量（亿千瓦时）	7.6	1.7
太阳能发电量（亿千瓦时）	1.4	1.3

表8　规模以上工业能源消费情况

指标	累计	比上年增长（%）
煤炭（万吨）	2769.5	-8.4
天然气消费量（亿立方米）	8.0	19.4
焦炭（万吨）	1026.7	11.6
汽油（万吨）	0.5	36.7
柴油（万吨）	3.9	7.3

全市用电稳步增长。全社会用电433.9亿千瓦时，比上年增长4.4%，其中，居民生活用电79.7亿千瓦时，增长5.4%。分产业看，第一产业用电3.3亿千瓦时，增长10.9%；第二产业用电248.6亿千瓦时，增长6.3%，其中，工业用电239.6亿千瓦时，增长6.1%；第三产业用电102.3亿千瓦时，下降0.9%。

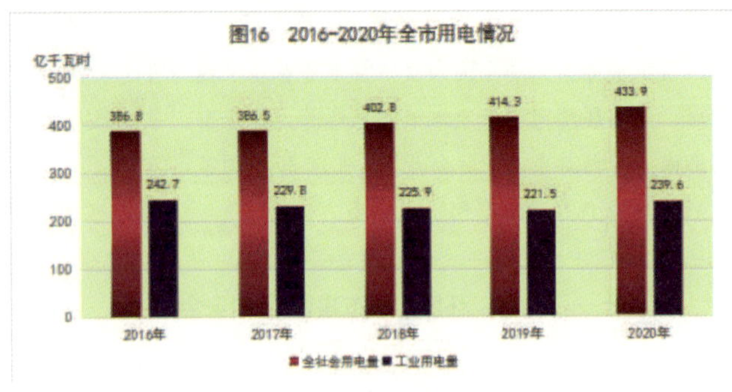

图16 2016-2020年全市用电情况

表9 2020年全市用电情况

指 标	累计用电（亿千瓦时）	比上年增长（%）
全社会用电	433.9	4.4
城乡居民生活用电	79.7	5.4
第一产业	3.3	10.9
第二产业	248.6	6.3
工 业	239.6	6.1
第三产业	102.3	-0.9

全年市区空气质量良好以上天数达到227天，城区环境空气中可吸入颗粒物（PM_{10}）年均浓度86微克/立方米，细颗粒物（$PM_{2.5}$）47微克/立方米，二氧化硫12微克/立方米，二氧化氮35微克/立方米。小清河出境断面辛丰庄化学需氧量浓度21.6毫克/升，小清河出境断面辛丰庄氨氮浓度0.83毫克/升。区域环境噪声昼间平均等效声级54.4分贝，市区道路交通噪声平均等效声级69.1分贝。

年末城市建成区面积839.7平方公里，比上年增加79.1平方公里。建成区绿化覆盖率40.7%，人均公园绿地面积13.1平方米。全年天然气供气量16.2亿立方米，增长12.5%；液化石油气供气量3.8万吨，下降15.7%。集中供热面积27739.7万平方米，增长6.4%。自来水供水量4.5亿吨，增长1.6%。垃圾无害化处理率100%。

全年刑事案件立案32965件。破获当年刑事案件21565件。受理社会治安案件68614件。

全市共发生各类生产安全事故293起、死亡192人，分别比上年下降36.2%、26.4%，实现了事故起数、死亡人数“双下降”，安全生产形势总体平稳。

十二、居民生活和社会保障

全年城镇居民人均可支配收入53329元，比上年增长2.7%；城镇居民人均生活消费支出34391元，增长2.8%。农村居民人均可支配收入20432元，增长5.0%；农村居民人均生活消费支出12947元，增长5.3%。城乡居民收入比由上年的2.67：1缩小为2.61：1。城镇居民恩格尔系数[9]23.5%，农村居民恩格尔系数30.4%。

图17 2016-2020年居民人均可支配收入

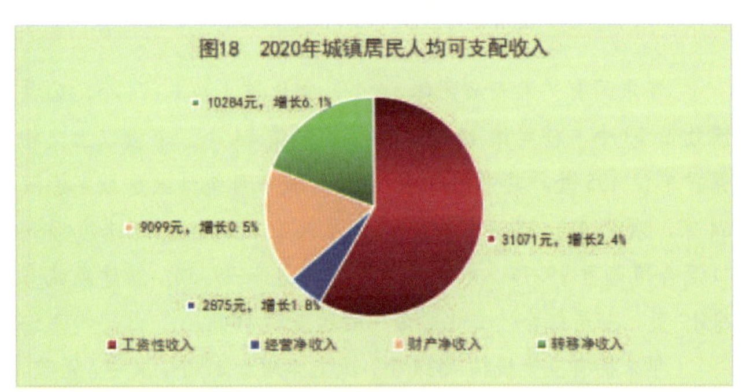

图18 2020年城镇居民人均可支配收入

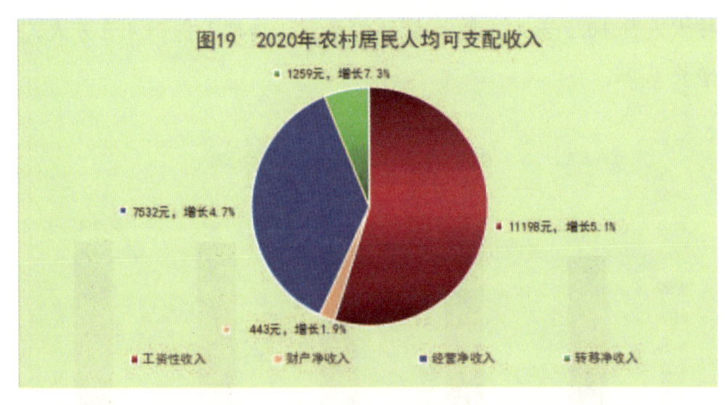

图19 2020年农村居民人均可支配收入

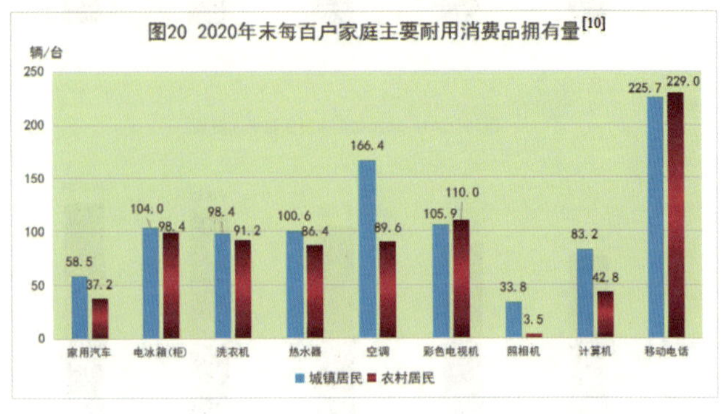

图20 2020年末每百户家庭主要耐用消费品拥有量[10]

年末城镇职工基本养老保险参保人数437.3万人，比上年增加29万人；职工医疗保险参保人数313.5万人，增加25.5万人；失业保险参保人数213.6万人，增加23.9万人；工伤保险参保人数278.6万人，增加16万人；生育保险参保人数213.1

万人，增加 11.9 万人。居民养老保险和医疗保险参保人数分别达到 302.7 万人和 507.6 万人。

城市居民最低生活保障标准由上年每月 685 元提高到 821 元，保障城镇居民 0.96 万户、1.4 万人，发放保障金及各类补贴 1.3 亿元；农村居民最低生活保障标准由上年每月 457 元提高到 614 元，保障农村居民 5.87 万户、8.4 万人，发放保障金及各类补贴 4.9 亿元。城市特困人员基本生活标准由上年每月 1028 元提高到 1232 元，农村特困人员基本生活标准由上年每月 594 元提高到 1071 元，城市特困保障 682 人，农村特困保障 1.37 万人，共发放特困供养救助金及补贴 1.43 亿元。照料护理标准按照自理、半自理和完全不能自理人员分三种档次，自理标准由 191 元 / 月提高到 210 元 / 月，半自理标准由 318.3 元 / 月提高到 350 元 / 月，完全不能自理人员标准由 637 元 / 月提高到 700 元 / 月。市中区、槐荫区、天桥区、历城区、济南高新区五区实现了城乡社会救助标准一体化。

全市共有救助管理站 3 处，济南市未成年人救助保护中心 1 处。培训残疾人 7445 人次，安置残疾人员就业 3209 人，帮扶救助残疾人投入资金 2.5 亿元。

注释:

[1] 2020 年统计数据为统计快报数或初步核算数，正式数据以出版的《济南统计年鉴 - 2021》为准。部分数据因四舍五入影响，存在总计与分项合计不等情况。

[2] 全市地区生产总值、各产业增加值绝对数按现价计算，增长速度按不变价格计算。根据第四次全国经济普查结果，对国内生产总值、各产业增加值等相关指标的历史数据进行了修订。

[3] 现代服务业包括：信息传输、软件和信息技术服务业，金融业，房地产业，租赁和商务服务业，科学研究和技术服务业，水利、环境和公共设施管理业，居民服务、修理和其他服务业，教育，卫生和社会工作，文化、体育和娱乐业。

[4] R&D 经费投入相关指标错年使用 2019 年数据。

[5] 规模以上工业企业指年主营业务收入 2000 万元及以上的工业法人单位。

[6] 限额以上单位是指年主营业务收入 2000 万元及以上的批发业单位、500 万元及以上的零售业单位、200 万元及以上的住宿和餐饮业单位。单位包括法人企业、产业活动单位和个体户。

[7] 2019 年交通运输部组织开展道路货物运输量专项调查，对公路货运数据进行重新核算，2019 年和 2020 年公路货运量数据统一采用核算后的新数据。

[8] 城市建设指标来源于住建部城市建设统计年报，为初步上报数，口径为包含两县的整个济南地区。

[9] 恩格尔系数是指食品支出在消费支出中的比重。

[10] 数据来自于住户收支与生活状况调查。

资料来源：本公报中改革相关数据来自市委改革办、发展改革部门；人才数据来自组织部门；扶贫数据来自市扶贫开发领导小组办公室；教育数据来自教育部门；科技数据来自科技部门；电信相关数据来自工业和信息化部门；户籍、社会治安、民用机动车数据来自公安部门；城乡最低生活保障、特困人员救助供养相关数据来自民政部门；财政、减税降费数据来自财政部门；城镇新增就业、登记失业率、城镇职工保险参保数据来自人力资源社会保障部门；环境保护相关数据来自生态环境部门；城市建设相关数据来自住房和城乡建设部门；公路里程、公交数据、公路运输、航空运输数据来自交通运输部门；邮政、快递数据来自邮政管理部门；水产品产量、农业数据来自农业农村部门；林业数据来自园林和林业部门；进出口、展会、新设境外企业、外派劳务人员数据来自商务部门；旅游、文化数据来自文化和旅游部门；卫生数据来自卫生健康部门；安全生产数据来自应急管理部门；国资国企数据来自国有资产管理部门；知识产权数据来自市场监管部门；市场主体数据来自行政审批服务部门；体育数据来自体育部门；医疗保险类数据来自医疗保障部门；金融数据来自地方金融管理部门；招商引资、园区、外资数据来自投资促进部门；物流数据来自口岸物流部门；残疾人保障数据来自残联；居民收入与支出数据、恩格尔系数、价格指数、粮食数据、城乡家庭主要耐用消费品拥有量来自国家统计局济南调查队；自由贸易试验区济南片区建设数据来自中国（山东）自由贸易试验区济南片区管委会；济南综合保税区数据来自济南综合保税区管理委员会；其他数据均来自市统计局。

STATISTICAL COMMUNIQUÉ OF THE JINAN MUNICIPAL ON THE 2020 NATIONAL ECONOMIC AND SOCIAL DEVELOPMENT [1]

Jinan Municipal Bureau of Statistics
NBS Survey Office in Jinan

In 2020, under the complicated economic situations, especially with great impacts of COVID–19 crisis, Jinan City fully adhered to the guidance of Xi Jinping Thought on Socialism with Chinese Characteristics for a New Era, under the firm leadership of the Jinan Municipal Party Committee and the Jinan Municipal People' s Government, comprehensively carried out the spirits of the 19th National Congress of the CPC, the Second Plenary Session of the 19th CPC Central Committee, the Third Plenary Session of the 19th CPC Central Committee, the Fourth Plenary Session of the 19th CPC Central Committee and the Fifth Plenary Session of the 19th CPC Central Committee, and stoutly implemented the principles of General Secretary Xi Jinping' s important speeches and instructions during his inspection tour to Shandong Province and Jinan City. According to the new targets and new positions for the construction of the provincial capital raised by the Provincial Party Committee and Provincial Government, we actively integrated into, followed and served the major national strategies of the ecological conservation and high–quality development of the Yellow River Basin. We coordinated to advance the epidemic prevention and control as well as promote economic and social development, concentrate on ensuring the stability on the six fronts and security in the six areas. On this basis, the economic situations throughout the city were gradually resumed and went up by each quarter, the annual GDP reached a new level of over one trillion yuan, the high–quality development was accelerated. Moreover, the "13th Five–Year Plan" was successfully completed, the construction of a moderately prosperous society ("Xiaokang") has made historical and conclusive achievements, the economic strength and municipal energy level have achieved a new leap, laying a solid foundation for the construction of a modernized provincial capital in the new era.

I. General

According to preliminary calculations, the regional GDP [2] of the whole city throughout the year was RMB 1014.09 billion, increased by 4.9% over the previous year. By each industry, the increment of the primary industry was RMB 36.17 billion, increased by 2.2%; the increment of the secondary industry was RMB 353.07 billion, increased by 7.0%; the increment of the tertiary industry was RMB 624.86 billion, increased by 3.7%. The proportion of these three industries is 3.6: 34.8: 61.6. By each quarter, we achieved RMB 202.70 billion in the first quarter, decreased by 4.4%; RMB 250.27 billion in the second quarter, increased by 5.1%; RMB 271.87 billion in the third quarter, increased by 7.1%; RMB 289.25 billion in the fourth quarter, increased by 8.8%.

Figure 1 Gross Domestic Product Between 2016–2020

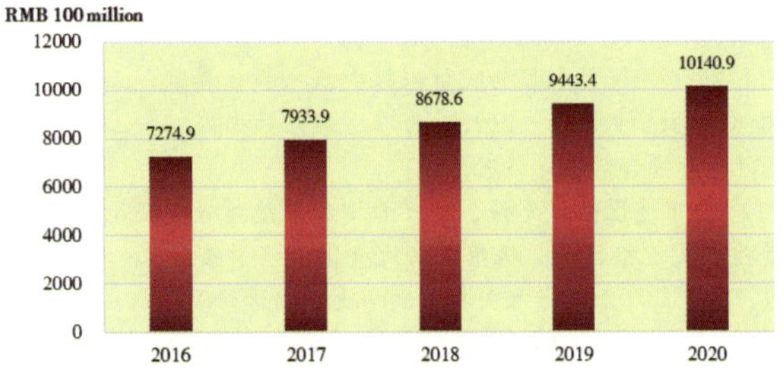

RMB 100 million
12000
10000
8000
6000
4000
2000
0
7274.9
7933.9
8678.6
9443.4
10140.9
2016
2017
2018
2019
2020

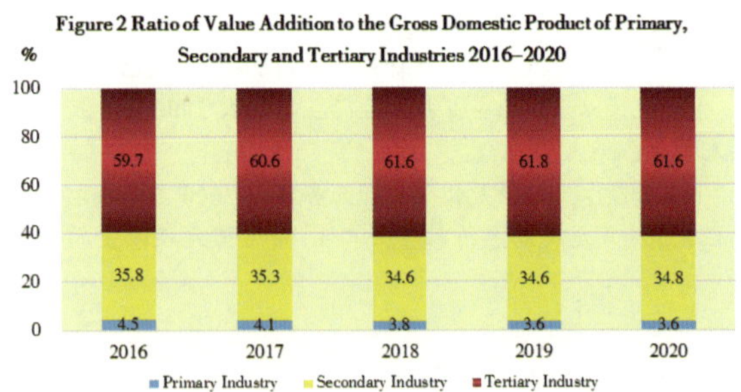

Figure 2 Ratio of Value Addition to the Gross Domestic Product of Primary, Secondary and Tertiary Industries 2016–2020

The urban employed population throughout the year was increased by 163,000, surpassing the expected target of around 150,000. The registered urban unemployment rate at the end of the year was 2.03%, lower than the expected target of around 3%.

The consumer price index (CPI) throughout the year increased by 2.4%, with the increment 0.9 percentage points lower than that of the previous year. The supply guarantee and price stability effects were significant, and among eight categories of commodities, "two categories increased, one category in the parity, five categories decreased" . The month–on–month increase in the sales price index of newly–built commercial residential buildings remained basically stable.

Table 1 Year-on-Year Growth/Decrease Rate of Consumer Prices Index In 2020

Index	Year-on-year growth Rate(%)
Consumer price index	2.4
Food,Tobacco and liquor	9.9
Clothing and Footwear	-0.1
Housing	-1.5
Household Equipments, Furnishings and Services	-0.6
Transport and Communications	-4.3
Education, Culture and Recreation	-0.4
Health Care and Medical Services	0
Miscellaneous Goods and Services	8.6

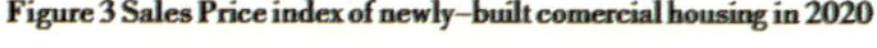
Figure 3 Sales Price index of newly-built comercial housing in 2020

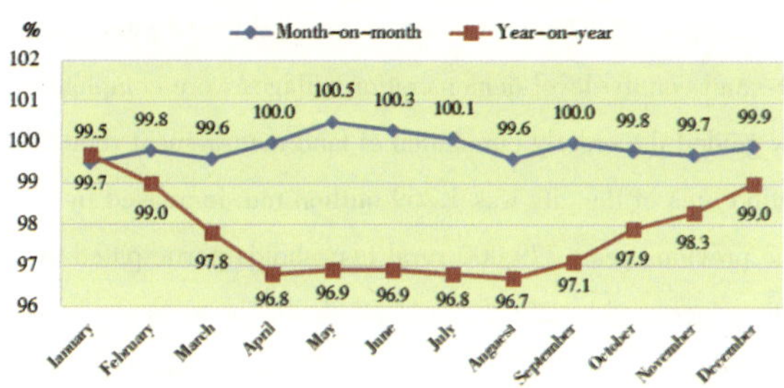

II. Key Work

Key reforms were carried out in an orderly manner. Major strategies were implemented. Our city accelerated the implementation of the national strategic actions on ecological conservation and high-quality development of the Yellow River Basin.The strategic plan for urban development was prepared, and positive progress was made in formulating the general plan for territorial space and the special plan for key regions. The early adopting areas for replacing old growth drivers with new ones have been listed in the Planning Outlines of the ecological conservation and high-quality development of the Yellow River Basin. In the Jinan Area of Shandong Pilot Free Trade Zone, more than 60 institutional innovations have been achieved, the number of newly registered enterprises and of all registered enterprises has reached more than 18,000 and 70,000, respectively. The integrated development mechanism of provincial economic circle was established and improved, and the integration of provinces and cities was remarkable in accelerating the development of Jinan City. **Precise efforts have been made to reform the institutions and mechanisms.** Reforms of the institutions and mechanisms in the development zones at or above the provincial level have been basically completed. The "Party Working Committee (Management Committee) + Company" management system has been implemented in the development zones throughout the city, and the number of internal institutions has been reduced by 51.4%. We deepened the reform of state-owned assets and enterprises, and took all the resources to advance and implement the three-year action plan for the reform of state-owned enterprises. We have completed 25 mixed reform projects in municipally state-owned enterprises. **The business environment continued to be improved.** We further advanced the reform of "doing it well once" services such that the business registration is now available throughout the city, across cities and across provinces, and enterprise-related items are 100% accepted with the tolerance of defects. In this point, we have passed the acceptance inspection of the national pilot project of government service standardization with high marks. **The waves of opening up continued to go up.** We have made innovations in foreign cooperation models, completed the construction of the comprehensive service platform for cross-border E-commerce pilot zones, and began to build the offline industrial parks. We organized 107 exhibitions throughout the year, and the exhibition area exceeded 1.8 million square meters. Jinan National Logistics Hub for Business Service and Jinan Key National Cold Chain Logistics Base were successfully approved. We have actively promoted the construction of provincial talent special zones, established the cooperative relationship with 133 academicians at home and abroad, added 4 candidates for national talent program, 37 candidates for Taishan series talent program, introduced 79 "5150" talents (teams) into the City of Spring, and supported 43 leading talents (teams) in each industry of the City of Spring. The first "talent loan" financial service window throughout the province has been implemented. Jinan City becomes the first city above the deputy provincial level to fully release the restrictions on residence settlement. In addition, we have successfully established the 20th and the second national human resources service industrial park throughout the country and province, respectively, and the total number of human resources in the city has exceeded 2 million.

Transformation from old growth drivers to new ones has been further improved in the quality and efficiency. The development of new industrial growth drivers has been accelerated. The strategy for strengthening the city by industry was thoroughly implemented, and the growth rate of the added value of the industries above the designated size was in the leading position among major cities in China. The added value of industrial equipment manufacturing industry above the designated size increased by 24.3% over the previous year, driving the growth of industries above the designated size by 9 percentage points throughout the city; The high-tech manufacturing sector achieved the 22.2% growth in the added value, and its total operating revenue exceeded RMB 100 billion, increased by 20.8%. High-end products went up rapidly, and the output of high-end servers exceeded 1.4 million units, increased by 35.2%. The consumption structure was improved and upgraded. Upgraded products saw a good momentum. In the annual retail sales of units above the quota, the retail sales of new-energy vehicles reached RMB 2.01 billion, increased by 47.6%; the retail sales of intelligent home appliances and audio-video equipment reached RMB 2.99 billion, increased by 113.2%; and the retail sales of sports and entertainment goods reached

RMB 680 million, increased by 26.4%. Online consumption went up rapidly. The retail sales of units above the quota reached RMB 13.68 billion via public networks, increased by 19.2%. Online consumption became an enabler in the stable recovery of the consumer goods market. **Investment boosts up both quantity and quality.** Amazing industrial projects frequently emerged. A number of high-quality projects are under construction in an orderly manner, including Laigang Group' s optimization, upgrading and renovation project of transformation from old growth drivers to new ones, and CNHTC Intelligent Network (New Energy) Heavy Truck Project. Investments in industries rose by 27.9%. Investments in emerging industries were accelerated, and investments in high-end chemicals, new energy and new materials, high-end equipment, and new-generation information technology increased by 174.4%, 66.6%, 48.6% and 30.2%, respectively. Investments in people' s wellbeing have achieved remarkable results. The first phase of Rail Transit Line R3 was completed and opened to traffic, Line R2 was completed and put into the trial operation, the second phase of Line R3 and the first phase of Line R4 were commenced. The investments in health and social work increased by 59.6%, and the Shulan (Jinan) International Hospital, Jinan Central Hospital (East Branch) and Jigang Forest Park are under the construction. **New growth drivers of the service sector were constantly enhanced.** The modern service industry[3] has achieved the added value of RMB 384.34 billion, increased by 7.1%, accounting for 61.5% of the service industry. The operating income of service industries above the designated size reached RMB 241.22 billion, decreased by 3.0%. Emerging industries in the service sectors above the designated size maintained the rapid growth. High-tech service industries enhanced their driving effects, and its operating revenue increased by 14.3% over the previous year, accounting for 33.8% of the service sector above the designated size. The Internet, related services and professional technology services grew by 89.3% and 18.7%, respectively. Logistics capacity was improved, and the postal service, multimodal transport and transport agency increased by 35.9% and 31.5%, respectively. **The green transformation has achieved remarkable results.** As the coal, steel and other industries made progress in cutting the overcapacity, the production of raw coal has greatly reduced, and the annual production of raw coal decreased by 737,000 tons compared with the previous year. Energy consumption became more low-carbon and cleaner, and coal consumption in the industries above the designated size was 2.537 million tons lower than that of the previous year. Significant results have been achieved in energy conservation and consumption reduction. According to preliminary calculations, energy consumption per RMB 10,000 of GDP decreased by 7.5% over the previous year, meeting the energy conservation and consumption reduction targets for the year. The driving effects of innovations were enhanced. The added value of "four new" economy accounted for more than 36%, holding the leading level throughout the province, and investment rate of the "four new" economy was increased by 4 percentage points. There were 1,427 newly recognized high-tech enterprises, and the total number was 3,029. High-tech enterprises in industries above the designated size reached 1,014, with a net increase of 59 over the previous year. The realized output value accounted for 55.3% of the industries above the designated size in the city, with an increase of 4.1 percentage points over the previous year. The R&D investment[4] was RMB 22.55 billion, accounting for 2.4% of GDP. The construction of Jinan Science and Technology Innovation City under the Chinese Academy of Sciences has been accelerated. There were 48 new provincial-level engineering laboratories, 48 new provincial-level research and development institutions, 8 provincial-level innovation and entrepreneurship communities, and 12 provincial-level technology innovation centers. Jinan High-tech Zone has been approved to construct the national demonstration base for business startups and innovation.

New progress was made in our work related to agriculture, rural areas and farmers. We made every effort to build the beautiful and livable countryside. Six city-level pastoral complexes were completed, the three-year action to improve the rural living environment was successfully completed, and the two-year campaign to improve rural drinking water safety was completed. 39 provincial-level demonstration villages for beautiful villages, 105 Qilu model villages for rural revitalization, and 123 district- and county-level demonstration villages were completed. **We actively guided the orderly circulation of land management rights.** Land circulation area of the city was 1.269 million mu, increased by 22.9% over the previous year; 279,000 rural households participated in land circulation, increased by 21.9%. The land circulation to family farms and rural cooperatives increased by 46% and 40.2%, respectively. We took all the resources to enhance our achievements in poverty alleviation. Poverty alleviation in 1,006 poverty-stricken villages has been enhanced and improved. Now people living in poverty enjoy "two assurances and three guarantees", and have access to basic medical insurance, assistance for chronic diseases, and reimbursement for serious diseases. The financial aid policy for poor students covers everything from pre-school education to higher education.

The "stability on the six fronts and security in the six areas" were implemented effectively. Remarkable progress was made in maintaining employment and ensuring people's wellbeing. The subsidy of RMB 635 million was provided to ensure job stability and covered 1.233 million jobs. We completed 23 practical projects that were performed for the people, and further raised basic pension benefits for enterprise retirees and basic old-age insurance and basic pension benefits for urban and rural residents. **Great progress has been made in stabilizing foreign trade and investment as well as expected development.** Total import and export volume increased by 22.9% year on year, the highest in nearly five years, and 950 new import and export enterprises were registered. There were 542 new Eurasian trains in operation, 12 new international (regional) routes were opened. The Jinan Zhangjin Comprehensive Bonded Zone was running, and the import and export volume of the zone increased by 1.4 times. **Market entities became more dynamic.** We took all the resources to implement policies to assist enterprises and rescue them for difficulties, and the amount of taxes and fees reduction increased by RMB 32.8 billion. The total number of market entities exceeded 1.3 million, and the number of enterprises above the designated size ("four top" enterprises) historically exceeded 10,000 for the first time. **Grain and energy supply remained stable.** The total annual sown area of grains increased by 17,000 mu over the previous year, and the total output increased by 53,000 tons, both reaching historic high levels. The electricity generation by enterprises above the designated size was 27.67 billion kilowatt-hours, and the power generated by wind, solar, waste and other new energy sources continued to grow. **Industrial chains and supply chains remained stable.** We solved problems in the industrial chain and supply chain to ensure the production of key industries and products. In the 41 industries above the designated size, 23 industries achieved the growth, with the growth area of 56.1% and the added value accounting for 71.1%. The growth area and the share level of the industry have been expanded steadily since this year. **We made solid and effective efforts to ensure financial stability and ensure community-level operation.** Fiscal and financial support was stable. At the end of the year, the outstanding domestic and foreign currency deposits and loans of financial institutions exceeded RMB 2 trillion, reaching the highest. We signed the memorandum of understanding on development financial cooperation with the China Development Bank, and increased RMB 40.13 billion of special bonds and RMB4.99 billion of direct funds from the central government throughout the year. We implemented the three "thoroughly" working mechanisms of direct funds allocation, appropriation and monitoring, and quickly distributed funds to the grass-roots level.

III. Agriculture

The ability to provide comprehensive support for the agricultural economy has been continuously improved. The total output value of agriculture, forestry, animal husbandry and fishery throughout the year was RMB 67.17 billion, increased by 2.6% over the previous year. The added value of agriculture, forestry, animal husbandry and fishery was RMB 38.03 billion, increased by 2.3%. The total output of grains reached 2.908 million tons, increased by 1.9%; The total output of vegetables reached 6.737 million tons, increased by 0.4%; The total output of oil plants was 68,000 tons, increased by 3.7%; The total output of fruits was 632,000 tons, increased by 0.4%.

Figure 4 Gross Output of Grains Between 2016-2020

10,000 tons

Year	2016	2017	2018	2019	2020
Output	298.4	281.0	276.9	285.5	290.8

Table 2 Plantation Area and Yield of Main Agricultural Products in 2020

Index	Unit	Area/ Yield	Year-on-year Growth rate (%)
Gross plantation area of grain crops	10 000 mu	720.7	0.2
Plantation area of cotton	10 000 mu	5.3	-7.9
Plantation area of oil plants	10 000 mu	27.2	-5.7
Plantation area of vegetables	10 000 mu	147.9	-1.7
Area of existing orchards	10 000 mu	59.2	1.5
Gross output of grain	10 000 tons	290.8	1.9
Yield of cotton	10 000 tons	0.4	-22.0
Yield of oil plants	10 000 tons	6.8	3.7
Yield of vegetables	10 000 tons	673.7	0.4
Yield of fruits	10 000 tons	63.2	0.4

Characteristic agricultural products saw great development. The characteristic agricultural products represented by Changqing tea, Zhangqiu green onion, Laiwu ginger, Renfeng watermelon, Qudi cucumber and others became well-known, stabilizing the market supply during the epidemic period, and also bringing good economic benefits. In 2020, the output of tea throughout the city was 612,000 kilograms, 743,000 tons of green onion, 294,000 tons of ginger, 292,000 tons of watermelon and 1.078 million tons of cucumber.

The use of chemical fertilizers and pesticides decreased year by year. The annual use of chemical fertilizer (discounted) was 205,000 tons, reduced by 4.6% over the previous year. The usage of pesticides was 3,200 tons, reduced by 7.1% over the previous year. Remarkable achievements were made in saving costs and increasing agricultural efficiency.

Figure 5 Unitilization quantity of chemical fertilizer (converting to the pure) of the whole city between 2016-2020

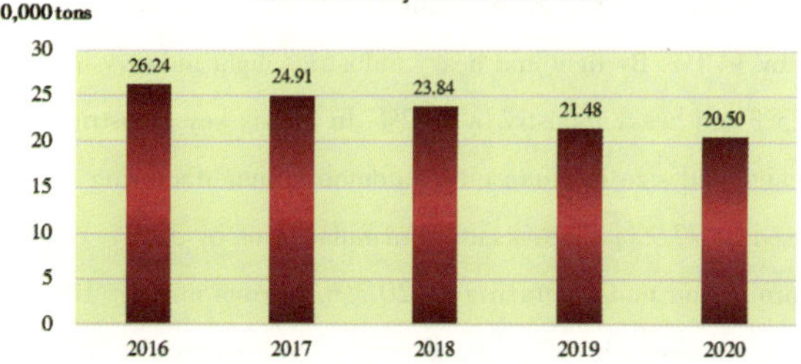

Figure 6 Application quantity of pesticise of the whole city between 2016-2020

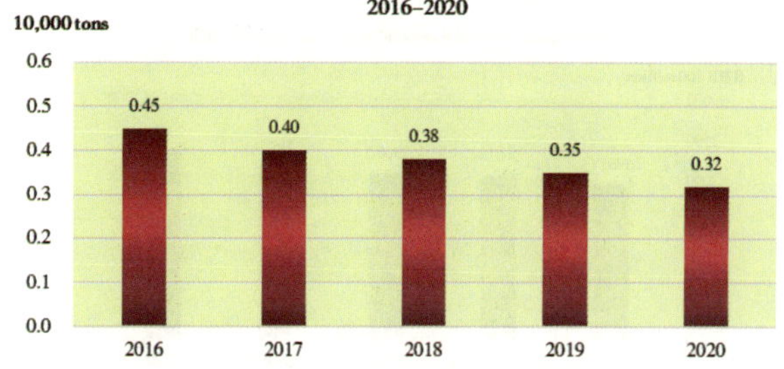

The supply of meat, eggs and milk was basically stable. Throughout the year, 1.57 million pigs were harvested and 128,000 tons of meat were produced. A total of 90, 000 heads of cattle were harvested, with the output of 21, 000 tons of meat and 414, 000 tons of milk. 869,000 sheep were harvested, and the output of meat was 15,000 tons. 74,000 tons of poultry meat and 275,000 tons of eggs were produced. The annual output of aquatic products was 13,000 tons.

The afforestation area reached 11,000 hectares and forest cultivated area of 966 hectares, 151 kilometers of ecological corridors and 133.8 kilometers of greenways were built, and 2,531 mu of silting area on the Yellow River embankment was greened. 100 municipal-level greening model villages, 26 national pilot construction units of forest health and conservation bases, and 3 provincial rural forest farms have been established.

Modern and efficient agriculture saw great development. The added value of modern and efficient agriculture throughout the city was RMB 5.67 billion, increased by 18.5% over the previous year and risen by 8.9 percentage points compared with the previous year. The added value of modern and efficient agriculture accounted for 14.9% of the added value of agriculture, forestry, animal husbandry and fishery, increased by 1.6 percentage points over the previous year. There are 480 leading agricultural industrialization enterprises at or above the municipal level, including 8 at the national level and 72 at the provincial level; There are 5,960 family farms and 10,626 specialized farmer cooperatives, including 2,705 newly established ones that year. In addition, the city has 2 state-level livestock and poultry breeding standardization demonstration farm including 1 new one, 30municipal livestock and poultry breeding standardization demonstration farms including 6 new ones.

IV. Industry and Construction Industry

The total annual added value of the industries was RMB 236.05 billion, with an increase of 8.2% over the previous year. The added value of industries above the designated size rose by 12.2%. By the economic type, the public sector of the economy rose by 9.5% and the non-public sector by 14.1%. By light and heavy industries, light industry increased by 12.3% and heavy industry by 12.2%. In the six key industries above the designated size in Jinan city, automobile manufacturing industry increased by 77.9%, pharmaceutical manufacturing by 31.3%, computer communication manufacturing by 20.3%, ferrous metal rolling and processing industry by 8%, oil and coal processing industry and non-metallic mineral products industry by9.9% and 11.1%, respectively.

Figure 7 Gross industrial value addition between 2016-2020

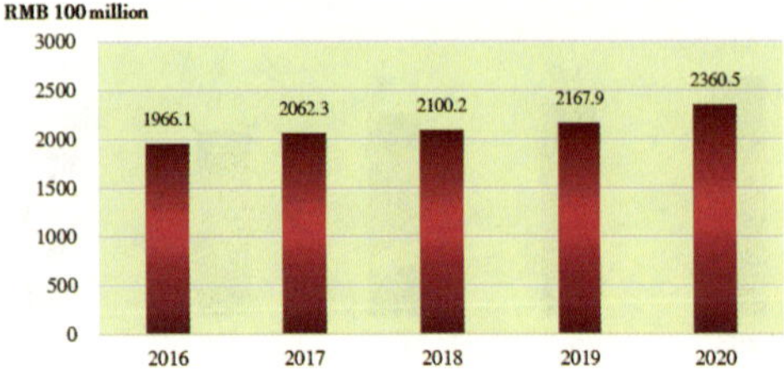

The operating income of industrial enterprises above the designated size throughout the year was RMB 738.78 billion, increased by 14.3% over the previous year. The total profit was RMB 40.73 billion, increased by 40.6%, and operating profit margin was 5.5%. Among 41 sectors of industries, 15 industries achieved an operating income of more than RMB 10 billion, accounting for 92.7%. Of those, the ferrous metal smelting and rolling processing industry and the automobile manufacturing industry exceeded RMB 100 billion.

Table 3 Operation Revenue Growth Rate of Above-Scale Key Industrial Sectors

Industry	Year-on-year Increase Rate(%)
Manufacture and Processing of Ferrous Metals	7.5
Manufacture of Automotive	63.1
Manufacture of Computer, Communications and Other Electronic Equipment	17.2
Manufacture of Non-metallic Mineral Products	-14.0
Manufacture of Electrical Machinery & Equipment	15.8
Manufacture of General Purpose Machinery	0.3
Processing of Petroleum, Coal and Other Fuels	-17.1
Manufacture of Metal Products	7.9
Manufacture of Chemical Raw Material and Chemical Products	13.9
Manufacture of Medicines	28.7
Manufacture of Special Purpose Machinery	15.7
Production and Supply of Electric Power and Heat Power	-2.7
Manufacture of Foods	6.4

The annual output-sales ratio of industrial products above the designated size was 98.7%. Among 174 categories of products, the output of 94 kinds of products increased, accounting for 54.0%. Among them, 37 kinds of products increased by more than 30%, accounting for 21.3%, increased 7.5 percentage points over the previous year. A total of 394,000 trucks were produced, increased by 92.7%, and motor engines for automobiles and instruments for automobiles increased by 74.7% and 55.4%, respectively. Fiber optic cable, industrial robots and superalloys increased by 50.1%, 24.6 % and 13.4 %, respectively.

Table 4 Output and growth rate of main products of above-scale key industrial enterprises[5] in 2020

Product Designation	Unit	Yield	Year-on-year growth rate (%)
Fresh, chilled meat	10 000 tons	15.1	2.4

Product Designation	Unit	Yield	Year-on-year growth rate (%)
Dairy products	10 000 tons	49.0	1.4
Alcoholic beverages	10 000 kiloliter	26.8	-13.0
Synthetic ammonia (anhydrous ammonia)	10 000 tons	60.0	-13.5
Polypropylene resin	10 000 tons	11.6	0.8
Plastics in primary form	10 000 tons	15.9	-5.8
Chinese patent medicines	ton	6038.2	69.5
Cement	10 000 tons	1328.2	6.9
Graphite and carbon products	10 000 tons	172.7	-4.1
Steel	10 000 tons	2336.5	2.3
Forging piece	10 000 tons	113.6	13.0
Powder metallurgy parts	10 000 tons	1.3	-2.2
Engine	10 000 kw	6167.1	72.1
CNC metal cutting machine tools	unit	670	-34.0
Pneumatic components	10 000 unit	1464.6	-12.6
Mining equipment	10 000 tons	6.4	9.0
Industrial robot	unit	1960	24.6
Truck	10 000 unit	39.4	92.7
Railway wagon	unit	3418	-35.6
Transformer	10 000 kva	13645.4	-11.9
Solar cell(photovoltaic cell)	10 000 kw	36.2	-35.0
Complete electronic computer set	10 000 unit	144.9	34.8
Servers	10 000 unit	143.5	35.2
Integrated circuit (IC)	10 000 unit	889.2	-43.0
Generating capacity	100 million kwh	276.7	-6.0

The added value of the construction industry in 2020 was RMB 118.18 billion yuan, increased by 3.9% over the previous year and accounting for 11.7% of GDP. The construction area of houses reached 170.899 million square meters. There were 1,033 construction enterprises with the construction works in their main business, general contracting and professional contracting qualifications and quantities of works, increased by 168 over the previous year. The total output value of the construction industry reached RMB 374.81 billion, with an increase of 6.7%. The output value of state-owned and state-holding enterprises was RMB 284.29 billion, increased by 10.3%. The value of contracts signed reached RMB 982.30 billion, increased by 17.0%. Newly signed contracts this year reached RMB 553.17 billion, increased by 22.0%.

Figure 8 Gross Product of Construction Industry Between 2016–2020

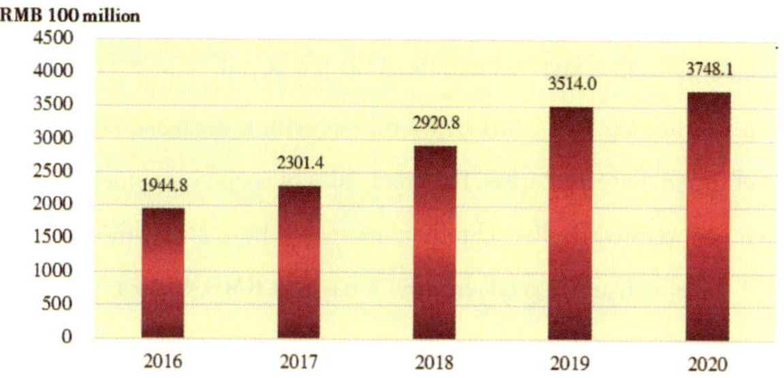

V. Fixed Asset Investment

The annual fixed asset investment increased by 4.0% over the previous year. By each industry, investment in the primary industry rose by 12.0%, secondary industry by 27.3% and tertiary industry by 0.4%. In key areas, private investment rose by 3.9% and infrastructure investment by 13.5%. At the end of the year, there were 1,343 fixed asset investment projects (excluding real estate) equivalent to over RMB 100 million, with an increase of 235, including 36 projects worth more than RMB 5 billion, increased by 4 over the previous year. The progress of the China Aerospace Science and Technology Park (Jinan) project was 43.9%, the Laigang Group's optimization and upgrading of the new and old drivers conversion system project was advanced by 38%, the Shulan (Jinan) International Hospital project by 35.4% and the Jinan-Laiwu high-speed railway by 25.1%.

Figure 9 Investment Proportion of the Primary, Secondary and Tertiary Industry 2016–2020

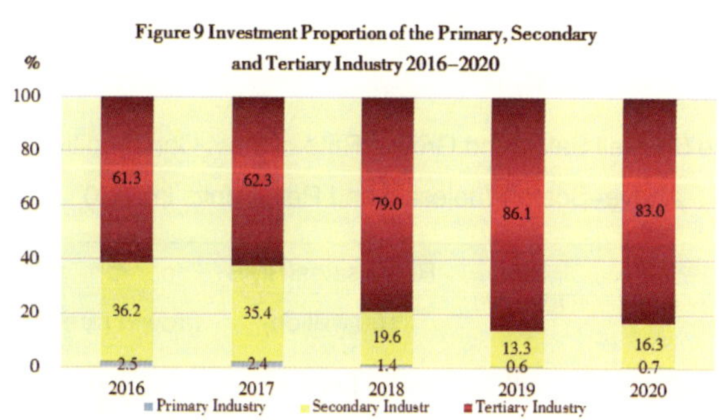

The completed investment in the real estate development reached RMB 170.76 billion in 2020, with an increase of 8.3%. Of those, the completed residential investment was RMB 120.43 billion, increased by 6.0%. The construction area of buildings reached 103.530 million square meters, increased by 3.7%. The residential construction area was 67.009 million square meters, with an increase of 2.7%. The area of as-built buildings was 12.730 million square meters, increased by 19.0%. Of those, the completed residential area was 9.136 million square meters, with an increase of 18.5%. The sales area of commercial residential buildings was 13.357 million square meters, with an increase of 7.2%. Of those, the residential sales area was 11.452 million square meters, increased by

12.2%. The sales volume of commercial residential buildings was RMB 157.19 billion, increased by 13.8%, including residential sales of RMB 140.65 billion, with an increase of 19.8%.

VI. Domestic Trade

The total annual retail sales of social consumer goods were RMB 446.91 billion, increased by 1.1% over the previous year. The retail sales of commodity were RMB 385.84 billion, with a growth rate of 2.6%%; the revenue of catering was RMB 61.07 billion, with a decrease of 7.2%. In terms of urban and rural areas, the retail sales of social consumer goods in urban areas were RMB 401.32 billion, increased by 1.2%; while the retail sales of social consumer goods in rural areas was RMB 45.59 billion, with an increase of 0.5%. Units above the designated size [6] have achieved the retail sales of RMB 150.42 billion, with a decrease of 0.9%.

Figure 10 Retail Sale of Consumer Goods Between 2016-2020

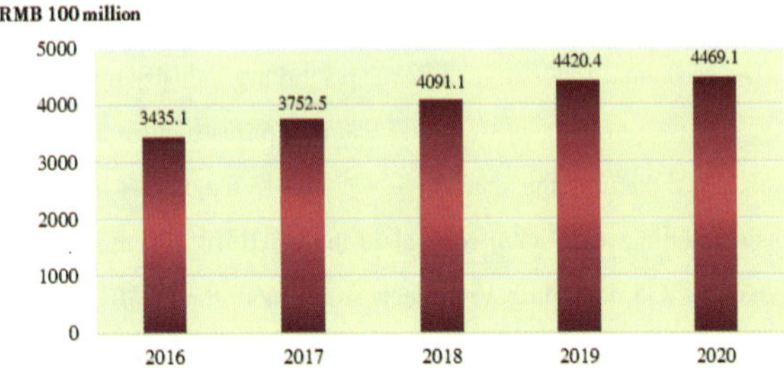

For units above the designated size, the retail sales of grain, oil and food products were RMB 15.64 billion, with an increase of 7.0%; those of household appliances and audio and video equipment were RMB 8.56 billion, with an increase of 6.7%; and those of automobiles were RMB 47.72 billion, increased by 7.4%.

Table 5 Retail Sales and Growth Rate of Main Commodities Of Above-Scale Wholesale and Retail Units in 2020

Category of commodities	Retail sales(RMB 100 million)	Year-on-year growth rate (%)
Grain and oils, food stuff	156.4	7.0
Beverage	13.1	1.8
Liquor & tobacco	33.1	33.0
Clothing, shoes and hats, textiles etc.	91.3	-19.2
Cosmetics	32.3	0
Gold, silver and jewelry	32.7	-13.7
Daily necessities	38.1	-5.6
Household appliances and phonotape & videotape apparatus	85.6	6.7
Chinese and western medicines	56.9	15.4
Stationery	47.1	4.6
Communication equipment	67.5	2.6
Petroleum and derivatives	183.5	-14.3
Automobile	477.2	7.4

VII. Open Economy

The total imports and exports of goods throughout the year reached RMB 138.27 billion, with the year-on-year growth of 22.9%. Among them, the export amount was RMB 75.5 billion, increased by 17.2%; the import amount was RMB 62.76 billion, increase by 30.7%. In the export market, exports to countries and regions in Europe increased by 34.4%, exports to South Korea and Japan increased by 19% and 12.4% respectively, while exports to the United States increased by 19.9%. Exports to countries and regions in the "Belt and Road" increased by 15.9%. Among the main commodities for exports, the export amount of mechanical and electrical products was RMB 40.6 billion, with an increase of 11%; the export volume of high-tech products was RMB 14.53 billion, increased by 59.3%; the export volume of agricultural products was RMB 6.77billion, with an increase of 28.7%, and the export volume of epidemic prevention supplies was RMB 4.05 billion, increased by 868.8%. The economic extroversion throughout the year was 13.6%, increased by 1.9 percentage points over the previous year.

Figure 11 Total Value of Imports and Exports Between 2016-2020

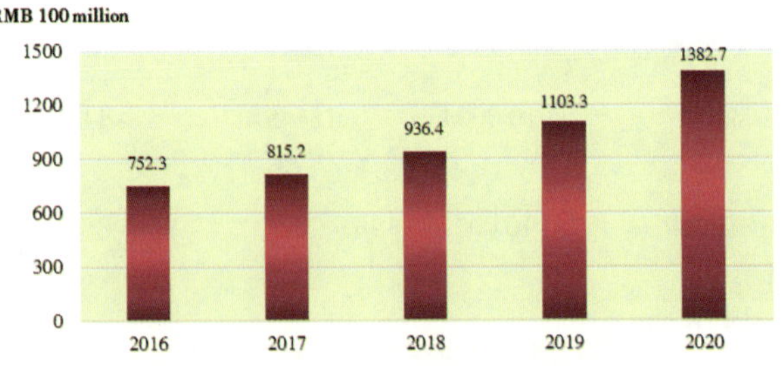

The actual use of foreign capital was ¥1.92 billion, decreased by 14.2% over the previous year. Among them, ¥150 million was used in manufacturing and ¥1.46 billion in the tertiary industry. The contracted foreign capital reached ¥5.85 billion, decreased by 14.4%. A total of new 203 foreign-funded projects were approved, including 34 projects with a total investment of over ¥100 million, with a contracted foreign investment of ¥3.99 billion.

The total annual value of newly signed contracts for overseas projects was ¥4.40 billion, decreased by 23.2% over the previous year; The completed turnover reached ¥ 4.27 billion, increased by 4.5%; A total of 77 overseas enterprises (institutions) were registered and established, and the actual investment amounted to ¥1.91 billion, increased by 72.7%. A total of 11,966 workers in various types were dispatched, with an increase of 48.7%.

VIII. Traffic, Post and Communications and Tourism

The mileage of highways opened to traffic reached 18117.2 kilometers at the end of the year, increased by 2.0% over the previous year. The length of expressways reached 737.8 kilometers, with an increase of 12.9%. The passenger capacity of highways was 12.09 million, decreased by 62.7%; passenger turnover was 1.71 billion person-kilometers, decreased by 68.4%. The freight volume of highways was 280 million tons, with an increase of 0.4%; freight turnover was 56.24 billion ton-km, with an increase of 0.2%[7]. There were 3.139 million of civilian motor vehicles at the end of the year, including 2.794 million of civilian cars. There were 650 bus lines at the end of the year, with an increase of 54; the total length of the lines was 13204.7 kilometers, with an increase of 2397.5 kilometers; the passenger transport volume was 530 million persons, with a decrease of 320 million persons. Jinan Airport has completed a total of 102,000 sorties, with a decrease of 21.2%; passenger throughput of 12.385 million persons, decreased by 29.5%; cargo and mail throughput of 147,000 tons, with an increase of 8.4%.

The business income of the postal industry (excluding the direct operating income of the Postal Savings Bank of China) in 2020 totaled RMB 8.51 billion, with an increase of 22.4%; the total business volume achieved RMB 14.65 billion, increased by 28.6%. The business income of express service enterprises reached RMB 6.68 billion, with an increase of 19.2%; the business volume was 650 million pieces, increased by 26.3%. There were 11.541 million of mobile phone users at the end of the year, including 9.227 million of 4G phone users, increased by 3.8%. There were 4.455 million wide-band network users, increased by 7.7%.

The number of domestic and foreign tourists was 60.488 million persons throughout the year, accounting for 60.3% of the last year. A total of 60.379 million domestic tourists were received, while 109,000 inbound tourists were received. The total tourism revenue reached RMB 70.28 billion, accounting for 54.6% of the last year. Domestic tourism revenue totaled RMB 70.05 billion, and inbound tourism revenue was USD 33.220 million. There were 86 A-level tourist attractions, including 1 5A-level scenic spot and 16 4A-level scenic spots as well as 2 tourist resorts above the provincial level.

IX. Fiscal and Financial Industry

The annual general public budget revenue reached RMB 90.61 billion, increased by 3.6% over the previous year, with the comparable increase of 7.2%. The tax revenue totaled RMB 69.66 billion, with a decrease of 0.5%, accounting for 76.9% of general public budget revenue. The general public budget expenditure was RMB 128.84 billion, with an increase of 7. 6%. Of those, education expenditure reached RMB 21.34 billion, with an increase of 14.7%; social security and employment expenditures were RMB 17.63 billion, with an increase of 8.0%; expenditures of urban and rural communities reached RMB 28.16 billion, increased by 11.7%.

Figure 12 General Pubilic Budget Revenue Between 2016-2020

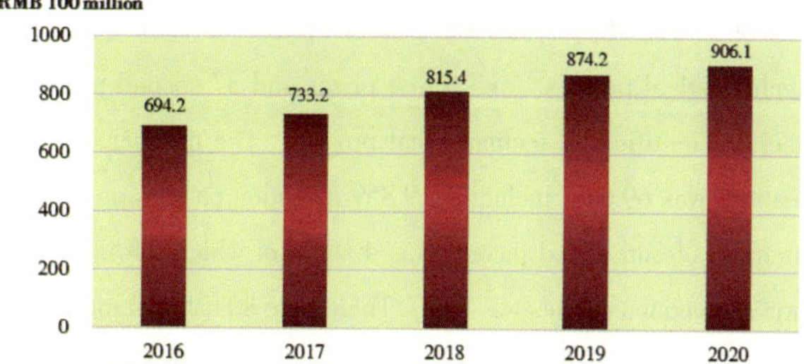

At the end of the year, the balance of deposits in local and foreign currencies of financial institutions was RMB 2,106.50 billion, increased by 13.0% over the previous year. The outstanding loans in local and foreign currencies of financial institutions reached RMB 2,072.02 billion, increased by 10.4%. There were 41 legal person financial institutions, including 20 banks, 3 insurance companies, 1 securities company, 1 futures company, 11 finance companies, 1 trust company, 1 auto finance company, 2 financial leasing companies and 1 financial technology company.

Figure 13 The Ending Balance of all Deposits and Loans in RMB and Foreign Currencies of Financial Institutions Between 2016-2020

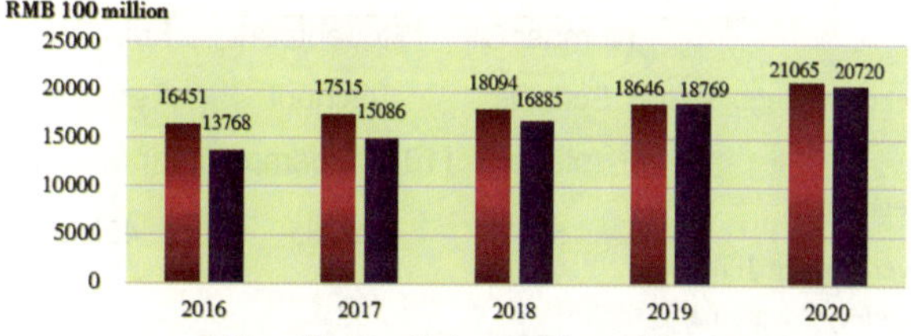

At the end of the year, the number of listed companies in Jinan city reached 45, offering 47 stocks, and there were 11 newly listed companies and those submitting IPO application and passing the review in the whole year, exceeding the total number of listed companies in the previous three years. The annual turnover of securities was RMB 4.8 trillion, increased by 31.0% over the previous year. The annual turnover of the futures business department was RMB 11 trillion, increased by 38.6%; The new direct financing amount was RMB 226.95 billion, increased by 12.2%. By the end of the year, there were 190 private equity fund management institutions registered with AMAC, with 435 funds under management, and the scale of funds under management reached RMB 99.32 billion, with an increase of 24.5%.

The insurance industry throughout the city realized the premium income of RMB 62.80 billion, with an increase of 18.0% over the previous year. Among them, property insurance was RMB 12.56 billion, increased by 6.9%; personal insurance of RMB 50.25 billion, increased by 21.1%. Indemnity payments and payments totaled RMB 16.03 billion, increased by 31.5%.

X. Science and Technology, Education, Culture, Health and Sports

The number of valid invention patents per 10,000 people throughout the year was 33.2, increased by 13.4% over the previous year. The transaction value of technology contracts was RMB 33.78 billion, with an increase of 21.3%. The city has won 2 second prizes for national scientific and technological progress, and 6 first prizes and 37 second prizes for provincial scientific and technological progress. The number of patent applications was 69,642, including 19,859 invention patent applications. The number of authorized patents was 40,903, of which the number of authorized invention patents was 5,827. There were 80 national intellectual property demonstration enterprises and competitive enterprises in Jinan City.

The construction, renovation and expansion of 144 primary and secondary schools (kindergartens) in Jinan City were commenced, the coverage rate of universal kindergartens reached 87%, and the construction rate of collectivized compulsory education reached 85.2%. We fully implemented the integrated development strategy of municipal schools, carried out 85 school-local cooperation projects, set up 51 specialties with distinctive advantages centered on key industries, and signed contracts to introduce 25 higher education projects.

Table 6 Basic Status of Educational Business in 2020

School Categories	Number Of Schools (place)	Students At School (10 000 persons)	Full-Time Teachers (person)
Colleges and Universities in Ji'nan	52	89.85	42202
Secondary vocational schools (excluding technician training schools)	41	6.28	3642
Ordinary secondary schools	320	39.84	34796
Elementary schools	666	57.01	37219
Special schools	13	0.13	545

At the end of the year, there were 14 state-owned art performance groups, 174 cultural centers (stations), 13 public museums, 17 archives, and 14 public libraries. There were 435 cultural relics protection units above the city level, including 30 ones at the national level. The city had 65 box office digital cinemas, containing 4,812,500 viewers, and with box office revenue of RMB 175 million. At the end of the year, the mixed coverage rate of radio population was 99.7%, and the mixed coverage rate of TV population was 99.3%. Besides, 12 "Study Rooms of Spring City" have been built, and the coverage rate of the primary-level comprehensive cultural service centers reached 100%.

At the end of the year, there were 7,514 health institutions, with an increase of 27 over the previous year. There were 343 hospitals and health centers. There were 69,000 beds in health institutions, with an increase of 3.4%. There were 102,000 health professionals, with an increase of 4.7%; and 40,000 licensed (assistant) physicians, with an increase of 5.0%.

Figure 14 Number of health agencies in the whole city between 2016-2020

Unit
9000
8000
7000
6000
5000
4000
3000
2000
1000
0
7017 7058 7343 7487 7514
2016 2017 2018 2019 2020

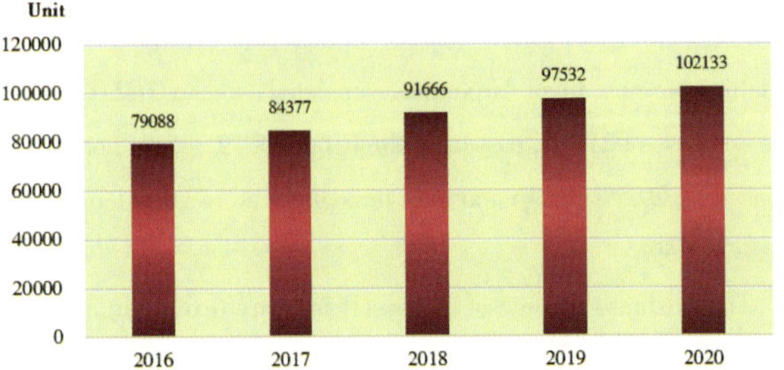

Figure 15 Number of health workers in the whole city between 2016-2020

Statistically, 8 new social sports organizations were established throughout the year, and 3,364 social sports instructors were trained. We have organized 385 general fitness activities (events), with 2.25 million of participants. We won 407 provincial and above gold medals, 264 silver medals, and 336 bronze medals. We successfully held a number of large international events, such as the Sixth National Public Ice and Snow Season and the First Ice and Snow Sports Carnival in the City of QuanCheng, the 8th Jinan International Spring Festival Dragon Boat Race. The 8th China Jinan Winter Spring Swimming International Open Championship was held, and 1,195 winter swimming participants came from 30 countries, 102 representative teams, reaching the highest level in the history.

XI. Energy, Environment, City Construction[8] and Safety Production

Great progress was made in developing the green and low-carbon energy system. Significant progress was made in reducing coal consumption, with coal consumption of industries above the designated size of 27.695 million tons, reduced by 8.4%; Natural gas consumption reached 800 million cubic meters, increased by19.4 percent, with coal consumption decreased and gas consumption increased, and clean energy consumption gradually increased. The efficiency of energy processing and conversion in industries above the designated size increased by 0.5 percentage points over the previous year, including the efficiency of coking by 2.9 percentage points, the efficiency of heating by 0.9 percentage points and the efficiency of oil refining by 0.1 percentage points. New energy production is rising. Wind power generation by enterprises above the designated size reached

760 million kWh, increased 1.7% and accounting for 2.8% of the total power generation. Solar power generation reached 140 million kWh, increased by 1.3% and accounting for 0.5% of the total power generation. Waste power generation reached 690 million kWh, increased by 23.5%, accounting for 2.5% of the total power generation.

Table 7 Energy Production Status of Above-Scale (Above Norm) Enterprises

Index	Accumulated	Year-To-Year Growth Rate(%)
Raw coal (10 000 tons)	82.4	-47.2
Generating capacity (100 million kwh)	276.7	-6.0
Thermal power (100 million kwh)	267.7	-6.2
Wind power (100 million kwh)	7.6	1.7
Solar power (100 million kwh)	1.4	1.3

Table 8 Energy Resources Consumption of Above-sized Industrial Enterprises

Index	Accumulated	Year-to-year growth rate (%)
Coal (10 000 tons)	2769.5	-8.4
Natural gas consumption (100 million cu.m)	8.0	19.4
Coke (10 000 tons)	1026.7	11.6
Gasoline (10 000 tons)	0.5	36.7
Diesel (10 000 tons)	3.9	7.3

The electricity consumption increased steadily throughout the city. The electricity consumption of the whole society was 43.39 billion kWh, with an increase of 4.4% over the previous year. The household electricity consumption was 7.97 billion kWh, with an increase of 5.4%. By each industry, the primary industry consumed 330 million kWh of electricity, increased by 10.9%. Electricity consumption for the secondary industry was 24.86 billion kWh, increased by 6.3%, of which industrial electricity consumption was 23.96 billion kWh, increased by 6.1%; Electricity consumption in the tertiary industry was 10.23 billion kWh, reduced by 0.9%.

Figure 16 Electricity Consumption Between 2016-2020

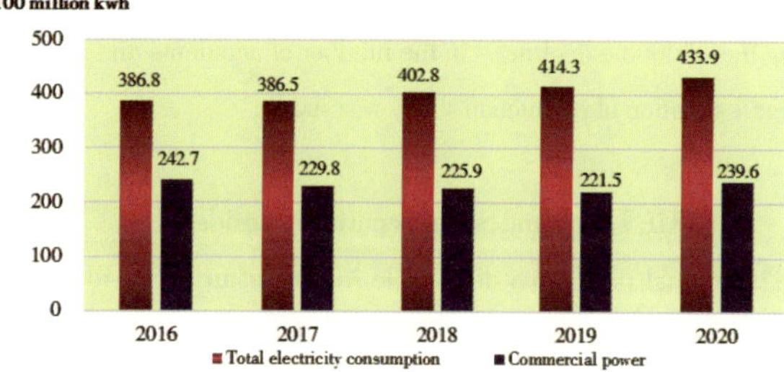

Table 9 Electricity Utilization of the Whole City in 2020

Index	Accumulated Power Consumption (100 million kwh)	Year-to-year Growth Rate (%)
Electricity utilization of the society at large	433.9	4.4
Electricity consumption of urban and rural residents	79.7	5.4
Primary industry	3.3	10.9
Secondary industry	248.6	6.3
Industry	239.6	6.1
Tertiary industry	102.3	-0.9

The number of days with good air quality or above in urban areas throughout the city reached 227. The average annual concentration of PM_{10}, $PM_{2.5}$, SO_2 and NO_2 in air in urban areas was 86 micrograms/m3, 47 micrograms/m3, 12 micrograms/m3 and 35 micrograms/m3, respectively. There were fracture surfaces on the. The concentration of chemical oxygen demand in Xinfengzhuang at Xiaoqinghe River fracture surface was 21.6 mg/L, and the concentration of ammonia nitrogen in Xinfengzhuang at Xiaoqinghe River fracture surface was 0.83 mg/L. The average daytime equivalent sound level of regional environmental noise was 54.4 dB, and that of urban road traffic noise was 69.1 dB.

At the end of the year, the urban built-up area reached 839.7 square kilometers, increased by 79.1 square kilometers over the previous year. The green coverage rate of the built-up area is 40.7%, and the per capita green area of parks was 13.1 square meters. The annual supply of natural gas was 1.62 billion cubic meters, with an increase of 12.5%; the supply of liquefied petroleum gas was 38,000 tons, decreased by 15.7%. The area of central heating was 277.397 million square meters, with an increase of 6.4%. The tap water supply counted 450 million tons, with an increase of 1.6%. The harmless treatment rate of garbage reached 100%.

In the whole year, 32,965 criminal cases were filed. A total of 21,565 criminal cases were handled that year and 68,614 Public order cases were accepted.

There were 293 production safety accidents and 192 fatalities throughout the year in the city, dropped by 36.2% and 26.4%, respectively, realizing the "double decline" in the number of accidents and fatalities. The overall situation of production safety was stable.

XII. Living and Social Security of Residents

The annual per capita disposable income of urban residents was RMB 53,329, increased by 2.7% over the previous year; and the per capita living consumption expenditure of urban residents was RMB 34,391, with an increase of 2.8%. The per capita disposable income of rural residents was RMB 20,432, with an increase of 5.0%; the per capita living consumption expenditure of rural residents was RMB 12,947, with a growth rate of 5.3%. The income ratio of urban and rural residents decreased from 2.67: 1 in the previous year to 2.61:1. Engel coefficient of urban residents[9] was 23.5%, while that of rural residents was 30.4%.

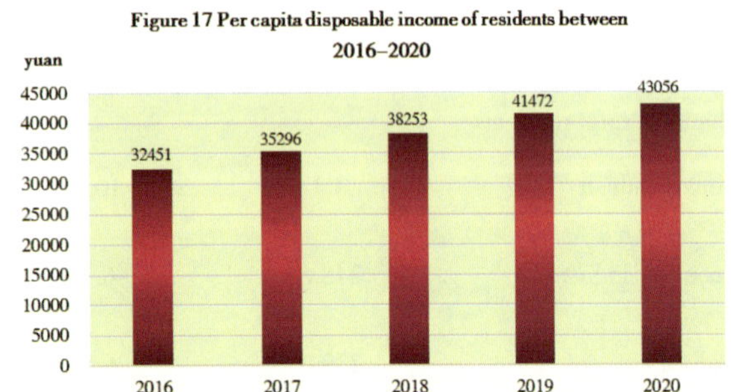

Figure 17 Per capita disposable income of residents between 2016-2020

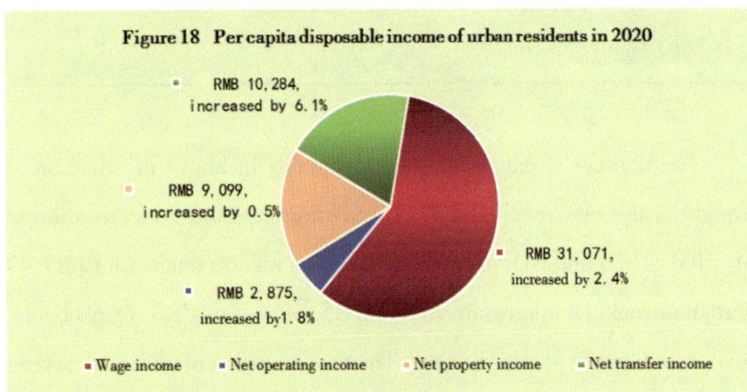

Figure 18 Per capita disposable income of urban residents in 2020

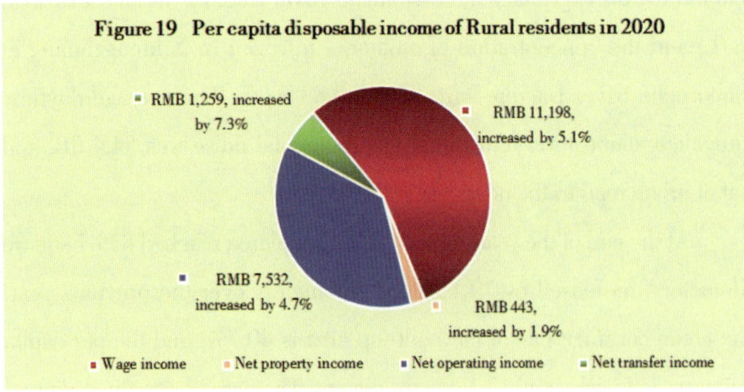

Figure 19 Per capita disposable income of Rural residents in 2020

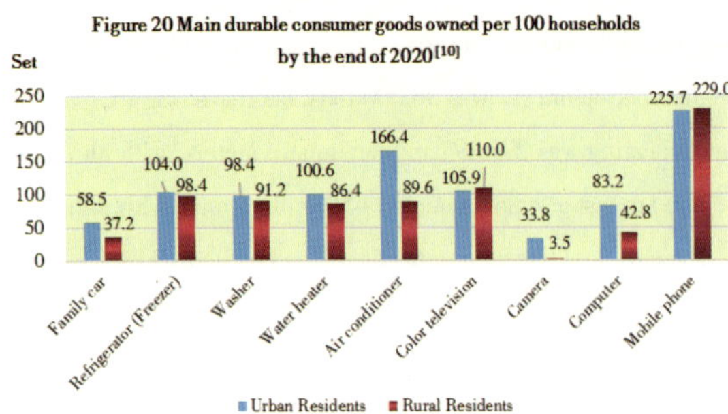

Figure 20 Main durable consumer goods owned per 100 households by the end of 2020[10]

At the end of the year, the number of urban employees participating in basic endowment insurance was 4.373 million, with an increase of 290,000; the number of employees participating in medical insurance was 3.135 million, increased by 255,000 persons; the number of participants in unemployment insurance was 2.136 million with an increase of 239,000 persons; the number of employees participating in work injury insurance was 2.786 million, increased by 160,000 persons; the number of people participating in maternity insurance was 2.131 million, with an increase of 119,000 persons. The number of residents participating in pension insurance and medical insurance reached 3.027 million and 5.076 million, respectively.

The minimum living allowance standard of urban residents was raised from RMB 685 per capita per month in the last year to RMB 821. There were 9600 urban resident households and 14,000 persons entitled to the urban minimum living allowance and subsidies totaling RMB 130 million. The minimum living allowance standard in rural areas has been raised from RMB 457 per person per month in the last year to RMB 614, and 58,700 rural households and 84,000 rural residents under the rural minimum living security, with a minimum living allowance and various subsidies of RMB 490 million. The basic living standard of the extremely poor persons in urban areas increased from RMB 1,028 per month in the last year to RMB 1,232, and the basic living standard of the extremely poor persons in rural areas increased from RMB 594 per month in the last year to RMB 1,071; There were 682 urban residents under the extremely poor allowance security and 13,700 rural residents under the extremely poor allowance security, and the support allowance and subsidies for the extremely poor persons were RMB 143 million. The care and nursing standards were divided into three levels according to self-care, semi-self-care and completely unable to self-care. The standard allowance for the self-care increased from RMB 191/month to RMB 210/month, the standard allowance for the semi-self-care increased from RMB 318.3/month to RMB 350/month, and the allowance for persons completely unable to self-care increased from RMB 637/month to RMB 700/month. Shizhong District, Huaiyin District, Tianqiao District, Licheng District and Jinan High-tech Zone have realized the integration of urban and rural social assistance standards.

There were 3 rescue management stations and 1 protection center for vagrant minors in the city. We have trained 7,445 persons with disabilities, placed 3,209 disabled persons in employment, and invested RMB 250 million in helping and assisting persons with disabilities.

Notes:

[1] Statistics data in 2020 are statistical bulletin or preliminary accounting data, and the official data are subject to the published Jinan Statistical Yearbook-2021. Due to the effect of rounding, partial data are not equal in the total and itemized total.

[2] The city gross regional product and the absolute amount of the value added of various industries are calculated on current price, while the growth rate is calculated at a constant price. Based on the results of the fourth national

economic census, historical data on relevant indicators, such as GDP and the added value of industries have been revised.

[3] Modern service industry includes: Information transmission, software and IT, financial industry, real estate, leasing and business services, scientific research and technology services, water conservancy, environment and management of public facility, residential service, repair and other services, education, health and social work, culture, sports and entertainment.

[4] The related indexes of R&D expenditure input uses the data of 2019.

[5] Industrial enterprises above designated size refer to industrial legal entities with annual prime business revenue of RMB 20.000.000 and above.

[6] Units above quota refer to wholesale enterprises with annual prime business revenue of RMB 20,000,000 and above, retail enterprises with annual prime business revenue of RMB 5,000,000 and above, and accommodation and catering enterprises with annual prime business revenue of RMB 2.000.000 and above. Unit includes corporate enterprises, industrial activity units and self-employed business.

[7] In 2019, the Ministry of Transport organized the special survey on road freight traffic volume to recalculate the road freight traffic data, and road freight traffic volumes in 2019 and 2020 are subject to new data.

[8] The urban construction index is derived from the urban construction statistical annual report of the Ministry of Housing and Urban-Rural Development, which is a preliminary report and covers the whole Jinan area including two counties.

[9] Engel's Coefficient refers to the proportion of food expenditure in consumption expenditure.

[10] The data is from the survey of household income and expenditure and living conditions.

Source of data: The data on the reforms in this communique come from the Reform Office and the Development and Reform Commission under the Municipal Committee; the talent data come from the organization departments; the poverty alleviation data come from the Municipal Poverty Alleviation and Development Leading Group Office; the education data come from the education departments; the science and technology data come from the science and technology department; telecommunications-related data comes from the industry and information department; household registration, social of security and civil motor vehicle data come from the public security department; data on urban and rural minimum living allowance, and the assistance and support of rural people in extreme poverty come from the civil affairs department; data on the finances and taxes and fees reduction come from the financial department; new urban jobs, registered unemployment rate, urban employee insurance participation data come from the human resources and social security department; environmental protection data come from the ecological environment department; urban construction data come from the urban and rural construction department; highways mileage, bus data, road transportation, and air transportation data come from the transportation department; post and express data come from the postal administration department; aquatic product output and agricultural data come from the agricultural and rural departments; forestry data come from the garden and forestry department; data on import and export, exhibitions, newly established overseas enterprises and expatriates come from the commerce departments; tourism and cultural data come from the culture and tourism departments; health data come from the health departments; safety production data come from the emergency management departments; data on state-owned assets and enterprises come from the state-owned asset management department; data on intellectual property come from the market supervision departments; data on market entities come from the administrative approval service departments; sports data come from sports departments; medical insurance data from medical security departments; financial data come from local financial management departments; data on investment and business introduction, parks and foreign capital come from investment promotion departments; logistics data come from port logistics departments; data on the guarantee of the disabled come from the Disabled Persons' Federation; data on residents' income and expenditure, Engel coefficient, price index, grain data and holding quantity of major durable consumer goods in urban and rural households come from the NBS Survey Office in Jinan; the construction data of the Jinan area of the free trade pilot zone comes from Jinan Area of the China (Shandong) Pilot Free Trade Zone; data on Jinan Comprehensive Bonded Zone come from the Management Committee of Jinan Comprehensive Bonded Zone; Other data come from the Municipal Bureau of Statistics.

2020 年的济南
Jinan in 2020

10140.9
地区生产总值（亿元）
Gross Domestic Product
(100 million yuan)

61.6
第三产业比重 (%)
Proportion of Tertiary
Industry(%)

920.24
常住人口（万人）
Permanent Population
(10 000 persons)
第七次全国人口普查数据
Data from The 7th National Census

960.1
一般公共预算收入（亿元）
General Pubilic Budget
Revenue(100 million yuan)

4.0
全社会固定资产投资增长幅度 (%)
Growth Rate Total Investment in
Fixed Assets(%)

199.9
海关进出口总额（亿美元）
Total Value of Imports and
Exports(100 million USD)

110199
人均地区生产总值（元）
Per Capita Gross Domestic
Product(yuan)

53329
城镇居民人均可支配收入（元）
Per Capita Disposable Income of
Urban Inhabitant(yuan)

4469.1
社会消费品零售总额（亿元）
Total Retail Sale of Consumer
Goods(100 million yuan)

20432
农村居民人均可支配收入（元）
Per Capita Disposable Income of
Rural Inhabitant(yuan)

102.4
居民消费价格指数 (%)
Consumer Price Index(%)

济南一日
A Day in Jinan

每日创造
Daily Production

24756.8

一般公共预算收入
（万元 / 天）
General Pubilic Budget Revenue
(10 000 yuan/day)

35213.1

一般公共预算支出
（万元 / 天）
General Public Budget Expenditure
(10 000 yuan/day)

5461.1

海关进出口总额
（万美元 / 天）
Total Value of Imports and Exports
(10 000 USD/day)

297

入境游客人数
（人次 / 天）
Number of Inbound Tourists
(person-time/day)

9.1

旅游外汇收入
（万美元 / 天）
Foreign Exchange Income of Tourism
(10 000 USD/day)

9881.4
第一产业（万元 / 天）
Primary Industry(10 000 yuan/day)

277074.0
地区生产总值（万元 / 天）
Gross Domestic Product (10 000 yuan/day)

96466.4
第二产业（万元 / 天）
Secondary Industry(10 000 yuan/day)

170726.2
第三产业（万元 / 天）
Tertiary Industry(10 000 yuan/day)

33033

公路客运量
（人 / 天）
Highways Passenger Traffic
(person/day)

33839

民航客运量
（人 / 天）
Civil Aviation Passenger Traffic
(person/day)

1077

生产汽车
（辆 / 天）
Automobile Manufacturing
(unit/day)

7560

发电量
（万千瓦时 / 天）
Power Generating Capacity
(10 000 kwh/day)

18408

蔬菜产量
（吨 / 天）
Output of Vegetables
(ton/day)

7946

粮食产量
（吨 / 天）
Output of Grain Crops
(ton/day)

13176

原油加工量
（吨 / 天）
Crude Processing Volume
(ton/day)

3921

生产服务器
（台 / 天）
Server Manufacturing
(unit/day)

每日生活
Daily Life

229
出生人口
（人 / 天）
Population of Birth
(person/day)

160
死亡人口
（人 / 天）
Population of Death
(person/day)

2177.2
城乡居民生活用电量
（万千瓦时 / 天）
Household Electricity Consumption of Urban and Rural Residents
(10 000 kwh/day)

138
登记结婚
（对 / 天）
Registered Marriages
(couple/day)

296
城镇非私营单位在岗职工平均工资
（元 / 天）
Average Wages of On-post Staff in Urban Non Private Entities(yuan/day)

100
离婚
（对 / 天）
Divorces
(couple/day)

146
城镇居民人均可支配收入
（元 / 天）
Per Capita Disposable Income of Urban Inhabitant(yuan/day)

123.5
自来水供水量
（万吨 / 天）
Volume of Water Supply
(10 000 tons/day)

105382.8
批发零售业零售额
（万元 / 天）
Total Retail Sale of Wholesale and Retail Trades (10 000 yuan/day)

696.9
住宿业零售额（万元 / 天）
Total Retail Sale of Accommodation
(10 000 yuan/day)

16027.8
餐饮业零售额（万元 / 天）
Total Retail Sale of Catering Industry
(10 000 yuan/day)

122107.5
社会消费品零售总额（万元/天）
Total Retail Sale of Consumer Goods
(10 000 yuan/day)

94
城镇居民人均生活消费支出
（元 / 天）
Per Capita Consumer Expenditure of Urban Inhabitant(yuan/day)

440.0
天然气供气量
（万立方米 / 天）
Total Natural Gas Supply
(10 000 cu.m/day)

7596
生活垃圾清运量
（吨 / 天）
Domestic Waste Removed and Transported(ton/day)

35
农村居民人均生活消费支出
（元 / 天）
Per Capita Consumer Expenditure of Rural Inhabitant(yuan/day)

56
农村居民人均可支配收入
（元 / 天）
Per Capita Disposable Income of Rural Inhabitant(yuan/day)

综 合
General Survey

地区生产总值（亿元）
Gross Domestic Product (100 million yuan)

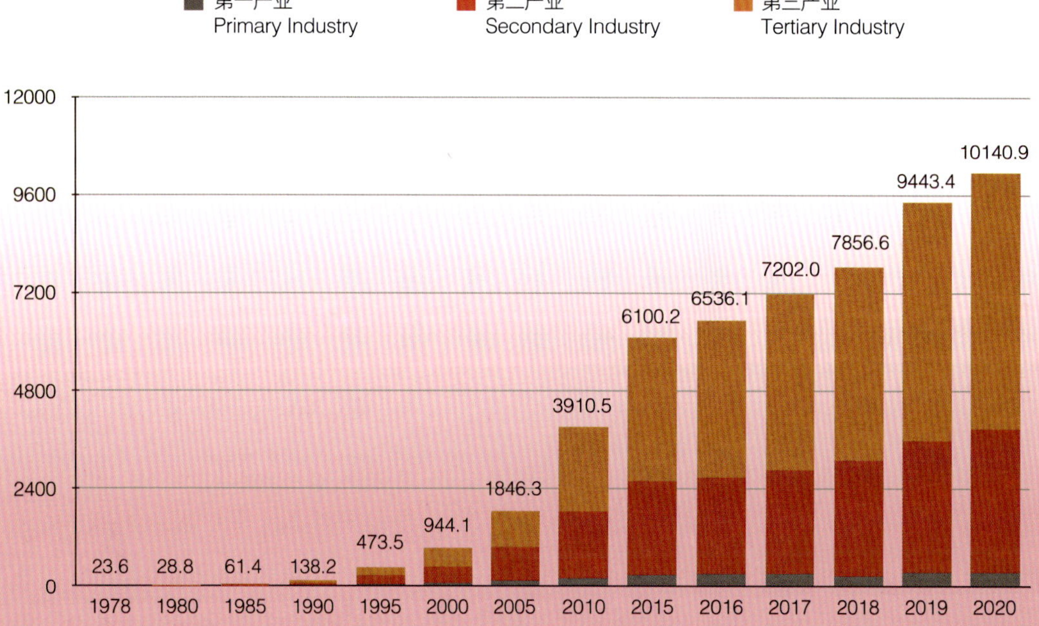

人均地区生产总值（元）
Per Capita Gross Domestic Product (yuan)

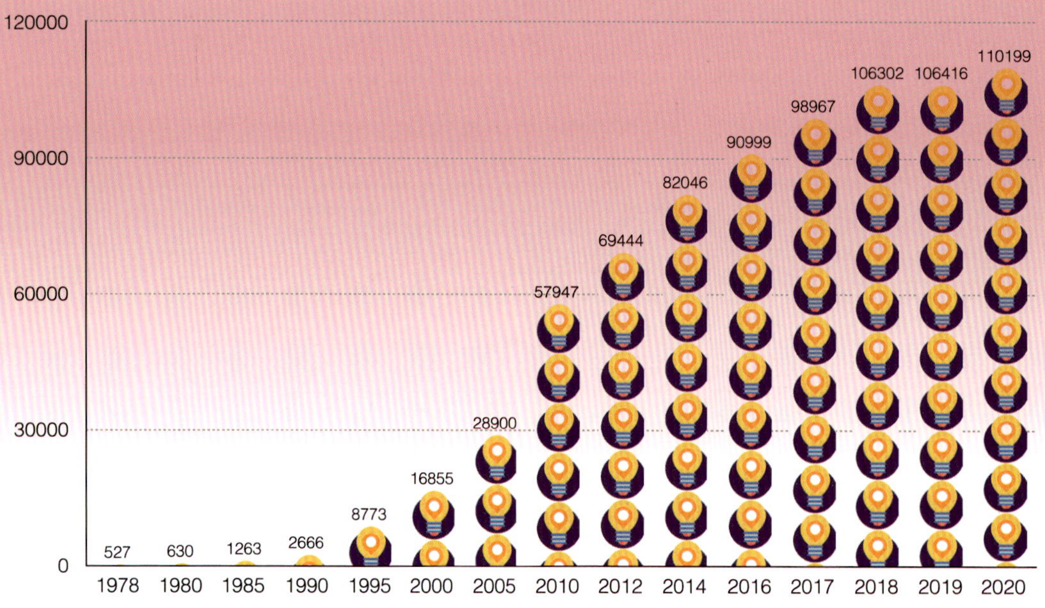

人口 Population

年末户籍总人口（万人）
Registered Population Year-end (10 000 persons)

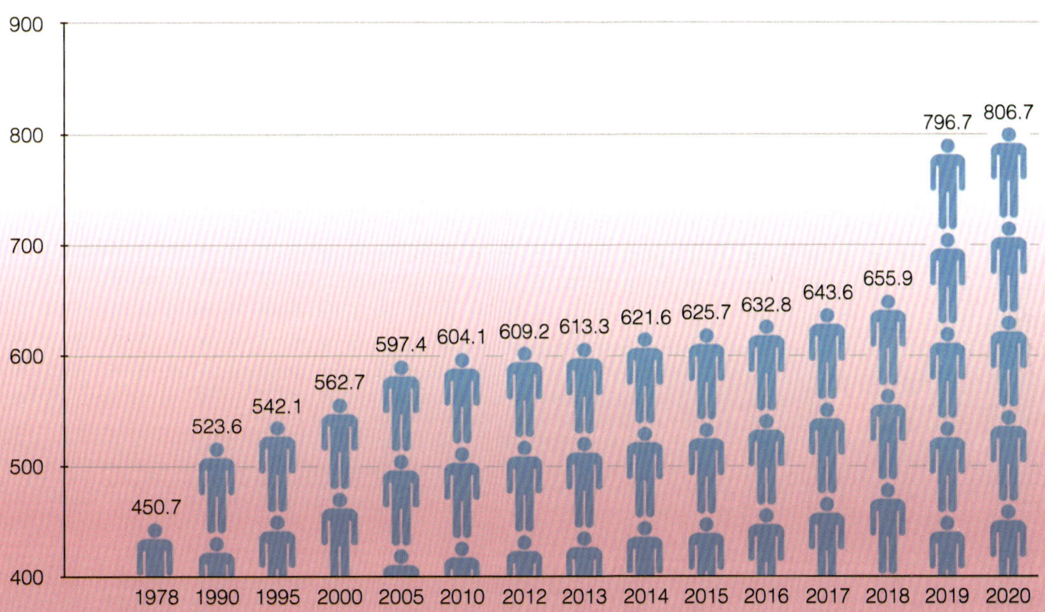

人口自然变动情况（‰）
Natural Changes of Population (‰)

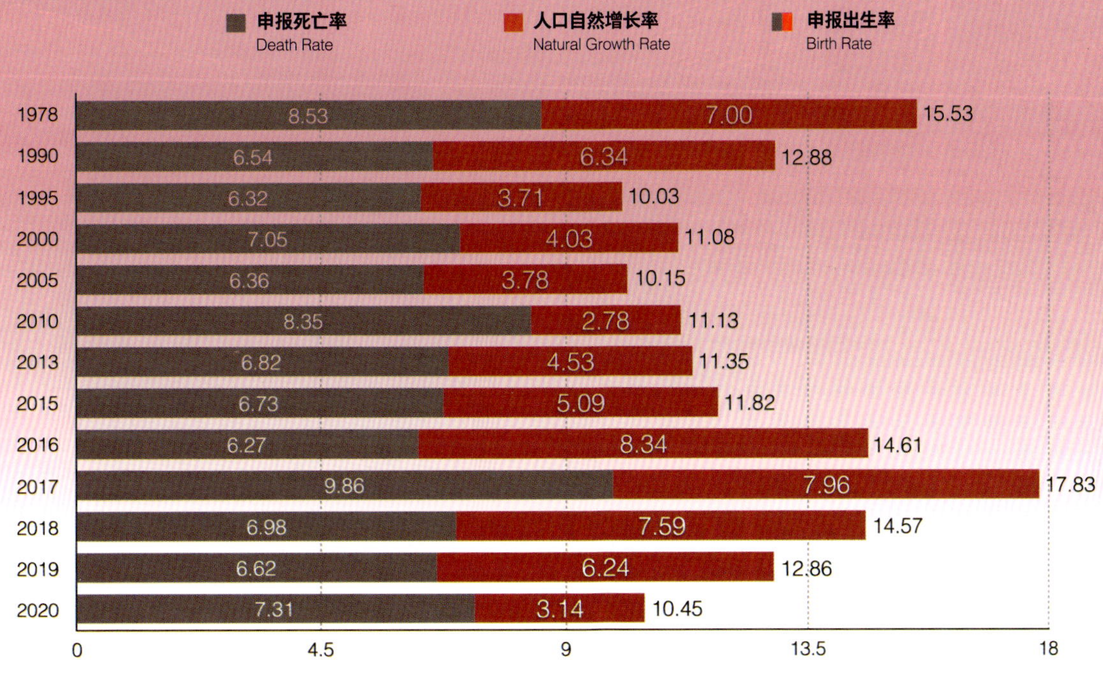

就 业
Employment

全社会从业人员（万人）
Total Employed Persons (10 000 persons)

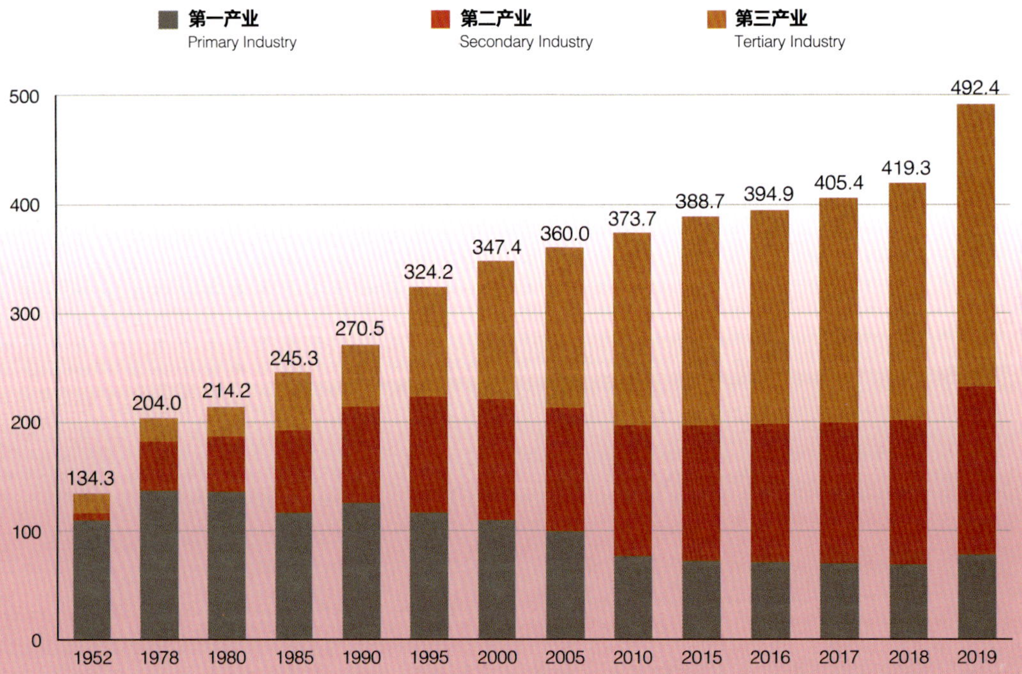

在岗职工平均工资（元）
Average Wage of Staff and Workers (yuan)

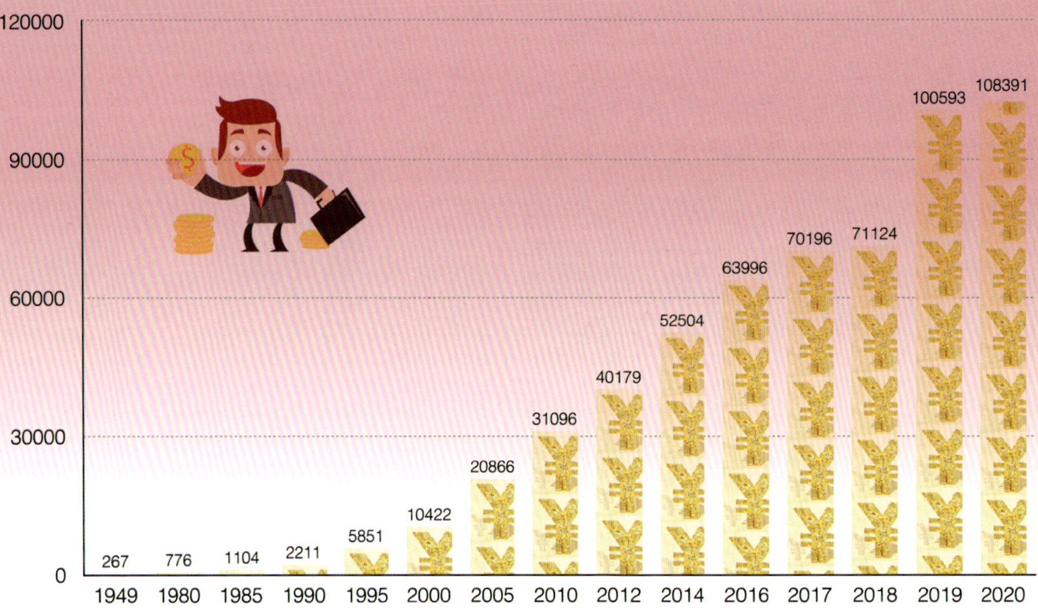

注：1．2006 年以后为法人单位在岗职工口径；2．2019 年以后为城镇非私营单位在岗职工口径。

Notes:1.The data after 2006 are based on the caliber of on-the-job employees of legal entities.
2.The data after 2019 are based on the caliber of on-post staff in urban non private entities.

财政 金融
Government Finance Financial

一般公共预算收入支出（亿元）
General Public Budget Revenue and Expenditure (100 million yuan)

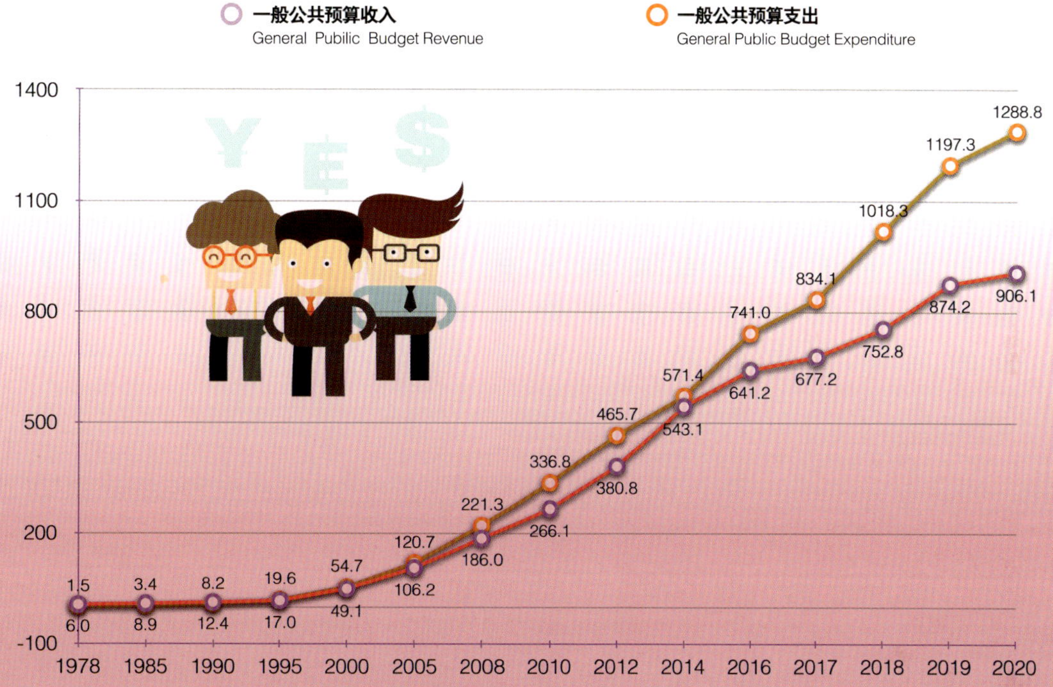

金融机构人民币存、贷款余额（亿元）
The Ending Balance of all Deposits and Loans in RMB of Financial Institutions (100 million yuan)

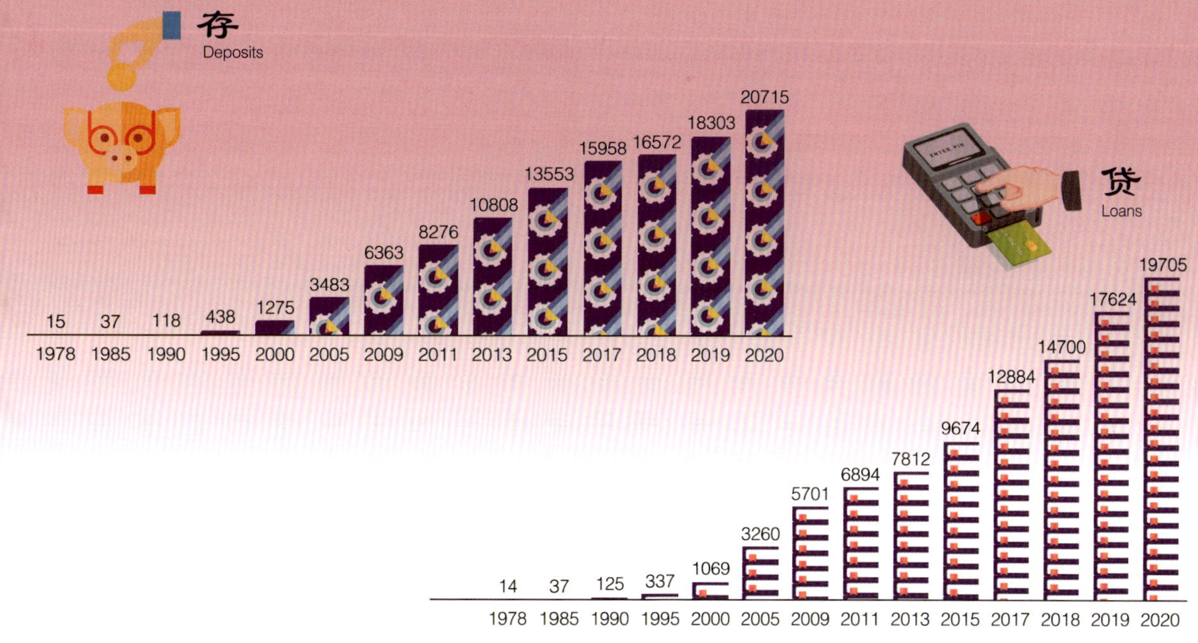

人民生活
People's Livelihood

城乡居民人均可支配收入（元）
Per Capita Disposable Income of Urban and Rural Inhabitant（yuan）

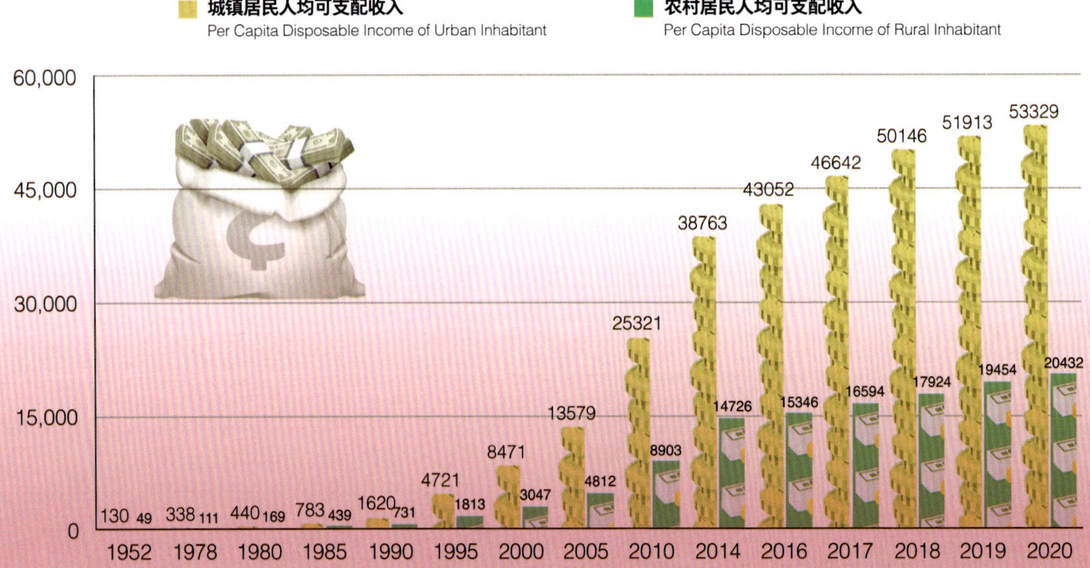

注 城乡一体化改革，2015年起为城镇居民人均支配收入和农村居民人均可支配收入口径 之前年份为城市居民人均可支配收入和农民人均纯收入口径。
Notes:The urban-rural integration reform has been based on the caliber of per capita disposable income of urban and rural residents since 2015; the urban-rural integration reform in previous years was based on the caliber of per capita disposable income of urban residents and the per capita net income of farmers.

城乡居民人均生活消费支出（元）
Per Capita Consumer Expenditure of Urban and Rural Inhabitant（yuan）

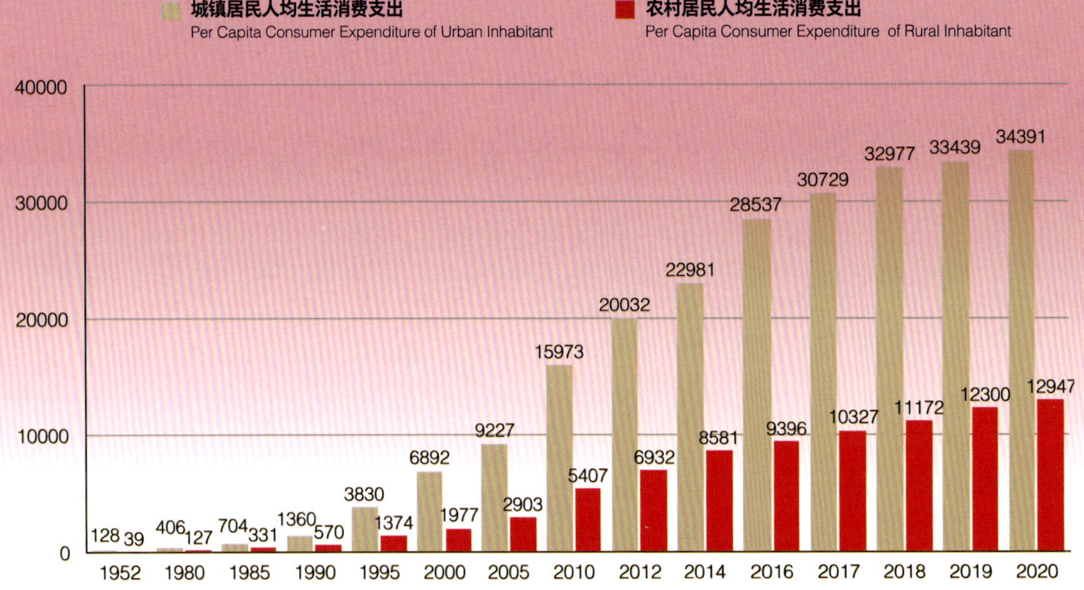

注：从2015年年开始，本市居民收支调查指标采用新口径。“农村居民人均生活消费支出”2014年以前为农民人均生活费支出口径。
Notes: Starting from 2015, the city's residents' income and expenditure survey indicators adopt a new caliber. "Per capita consumption expenditure of Rural Residents" was the “per capita living expenses of farmers” before 2014.

城乡居民恩格尔系数（%）
Engel's Coefficient of Urban and Rural Inhabitant (%)

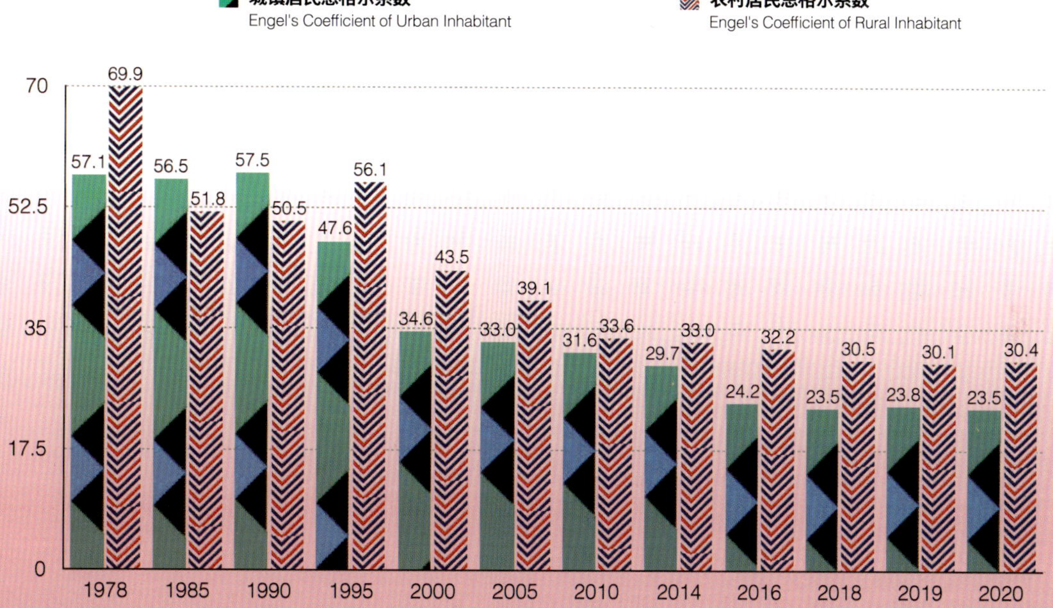

人民币住户存款余额（亿元）
The Balance RMB Household Deposits（100 millon yuan）

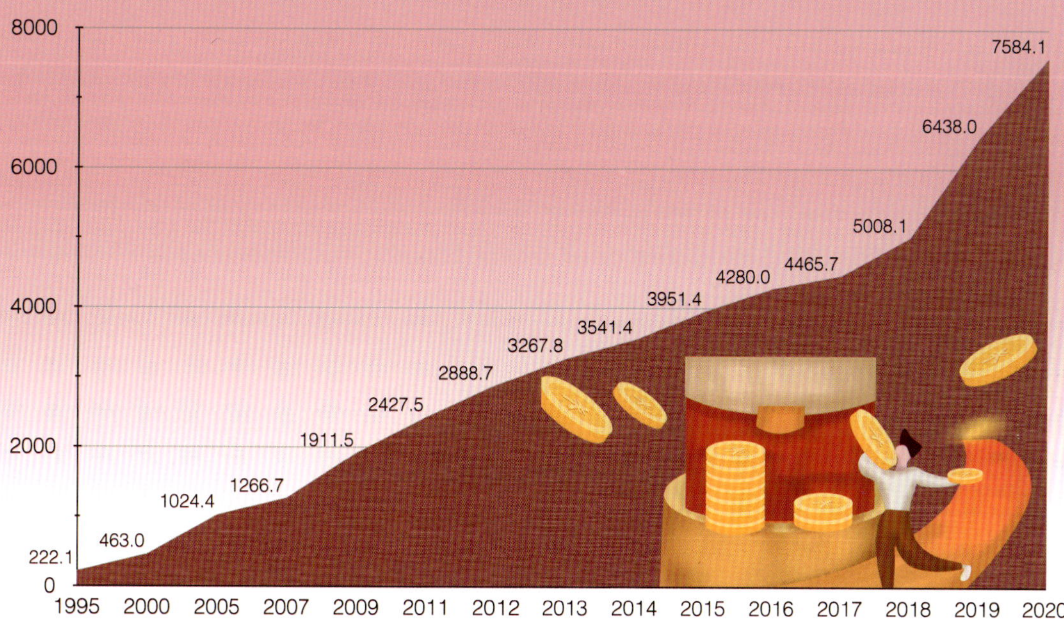

注：2015 年之前为城乡居民人民币储蓄存款余额口径，2015 年调整为住户存款余额口径。
Notes: Before 2015, the caliber was the balance of saving deposit (RMB) of urban and rural residents, and has been adjusted to balance held on deposit of households since 2015.

物价
Prices

居民消费价格指数与商品零售价格指数（以上年为 100）
Consumer Price Index and Retail Price Index (Preceding Last Year=100)

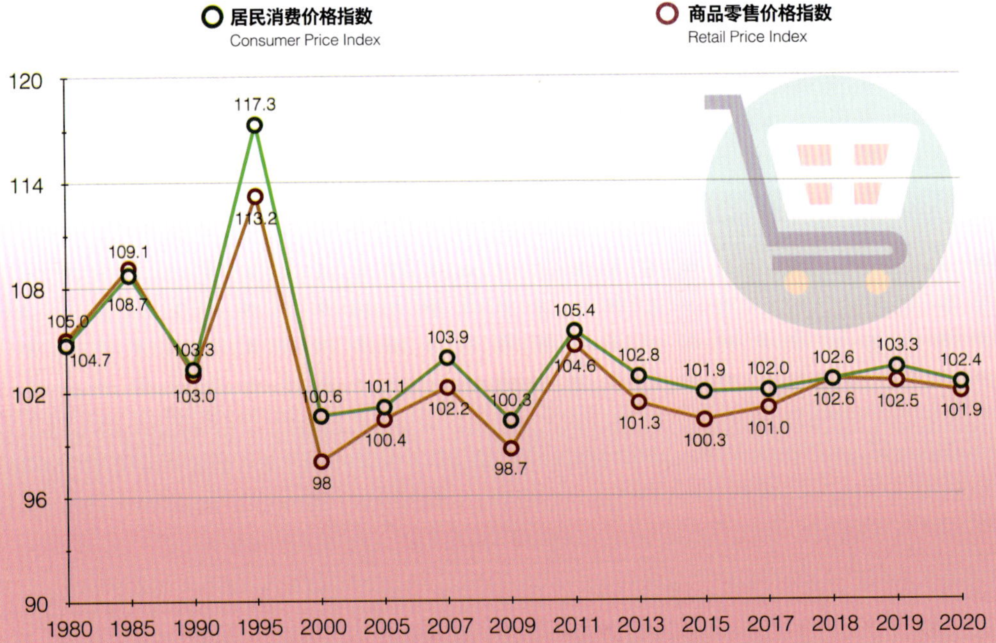

工业生产者出厂价格指数与工业生产者购进价格指数（以上年为 100）
Producer Price Index and Purchasing Price Index for Industrial Products (Preceding Last Year=100)

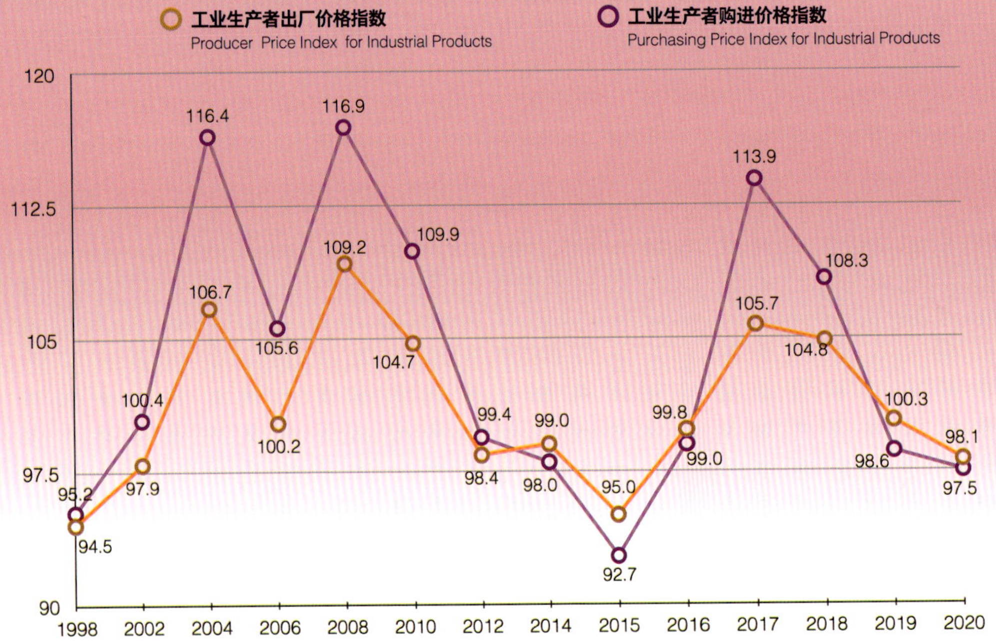

注：2020 年，“工业生产者出厂价格指数”与“工业生产者购进价格指数”指标为全省数据。
Note: In 2020, the “Producer Price Index ” and “Producer Purchasing Price Index ” are province-wide data.

外经外贸
Foreign Trade

实际使用外资金额（万美元）
Actual Use of Foreign Capital (10 000 USD)

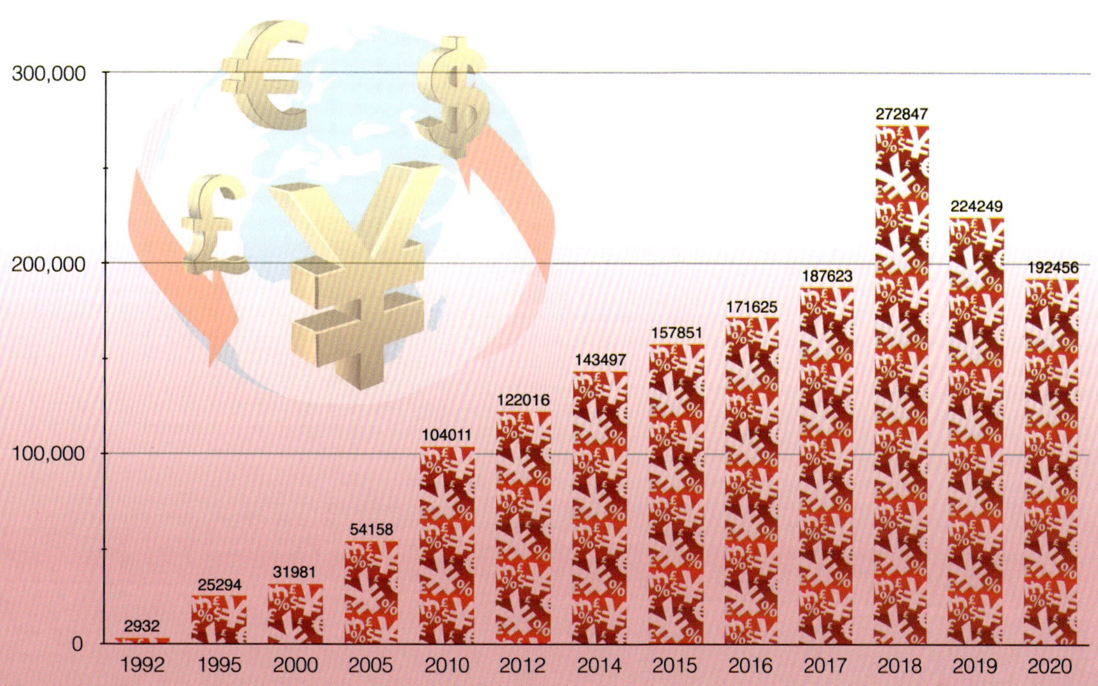

海关进出口总额（万美元）
Total Value of Imports and Exports (10 000 USD)

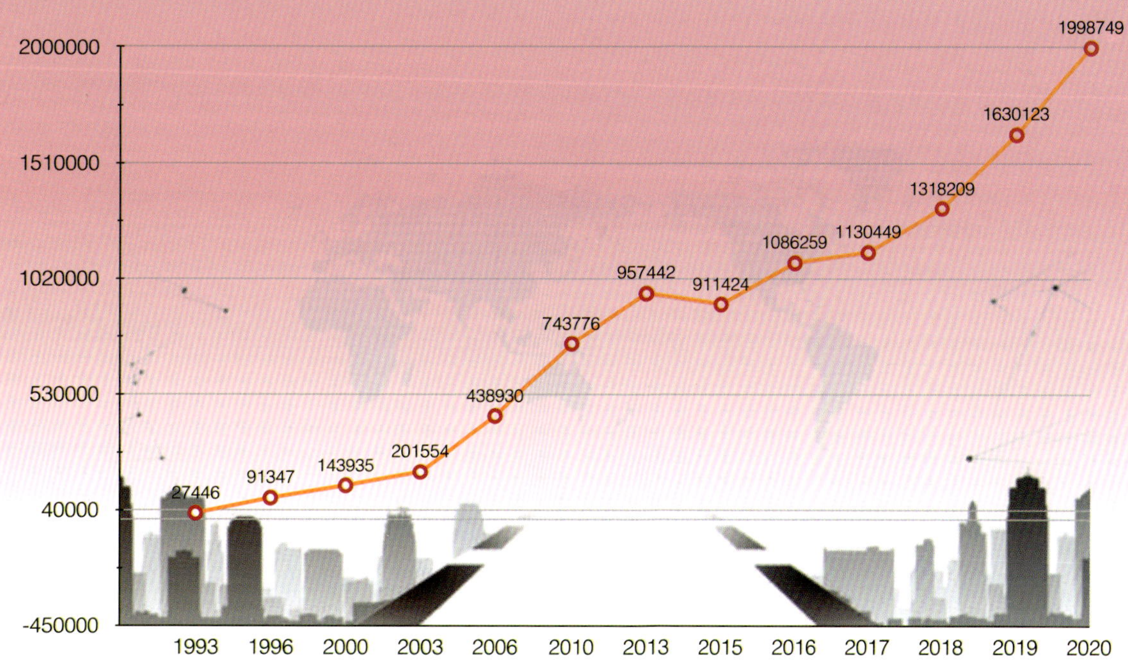

工 业
Industry

规模以上工业营业收入（亿元）
Business Revenue of Industrial Enterprises Above Designated Size (100 million yuan)

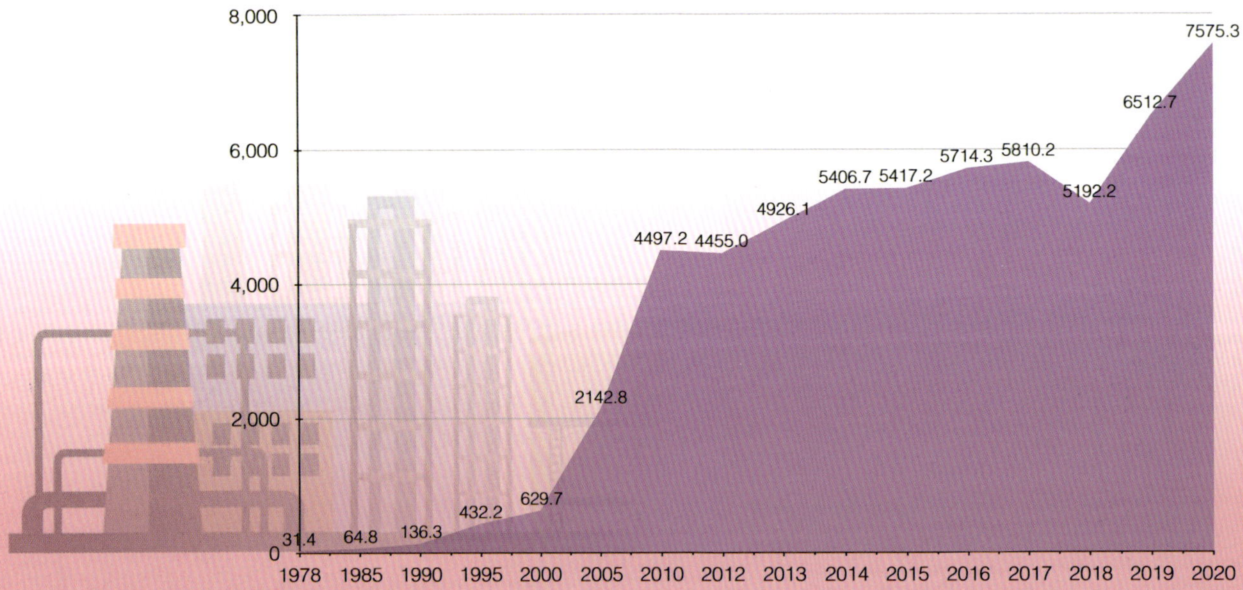

注：2018 年以前为主营业务收入口径。
Notes: Before 2018, the caliber was revenue from principal business.Revenue from principal business.

规模以上工业利税总额（亿元）
Total Profits and Taxes of Industrial Enterprises Above Designated Size (100 million yuan)

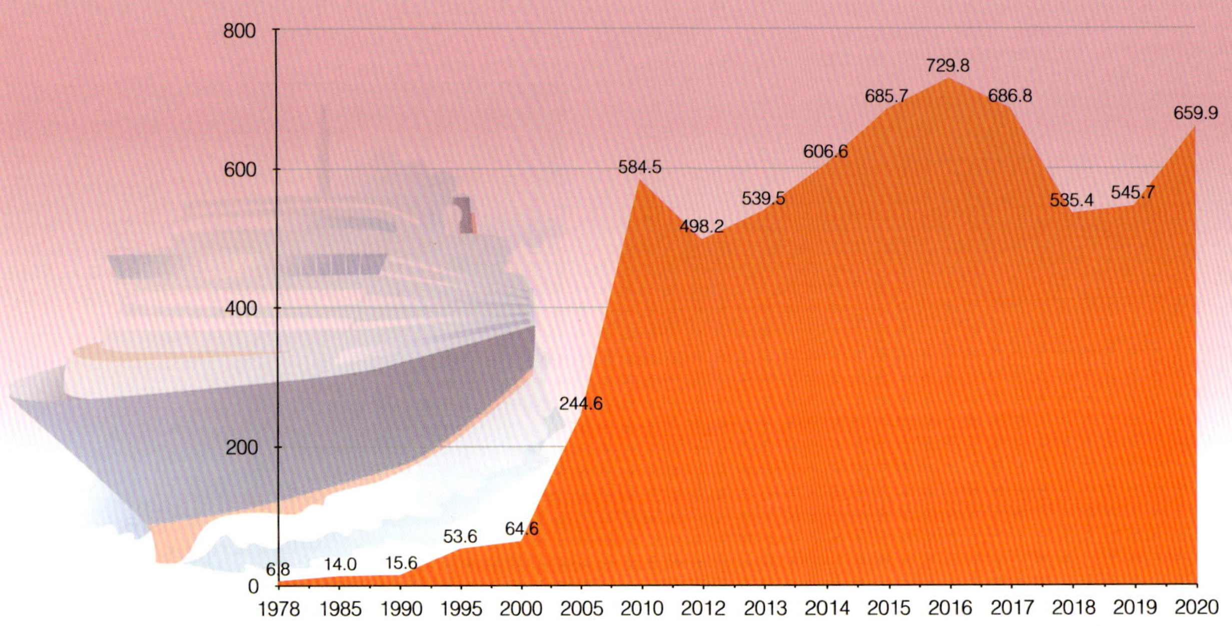

规模以上工业利润总额（亿元）

Total Profits of Industrial Enterprises Above Designated Size (100 million yuan)

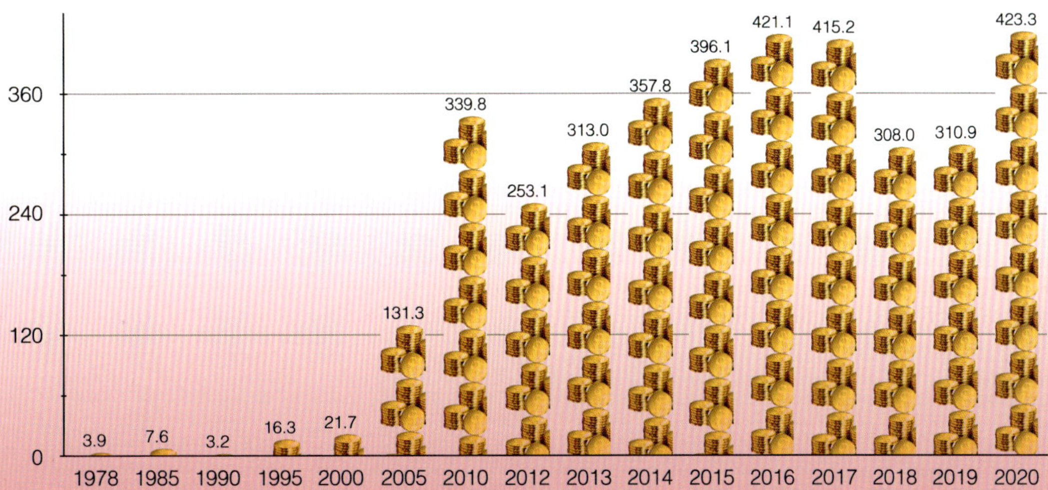

主要工业产品产量

Output of Major Industrial Products

发电量（亿千瓦时）

Power Generating Capacity (100 million kwh)

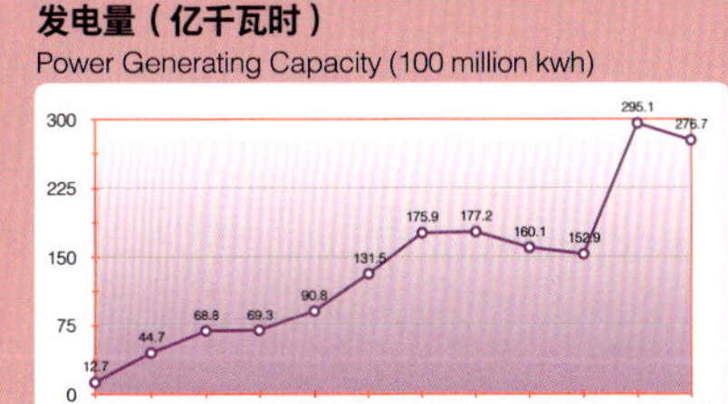

服务器（万台）

Servers (10 000 unit)

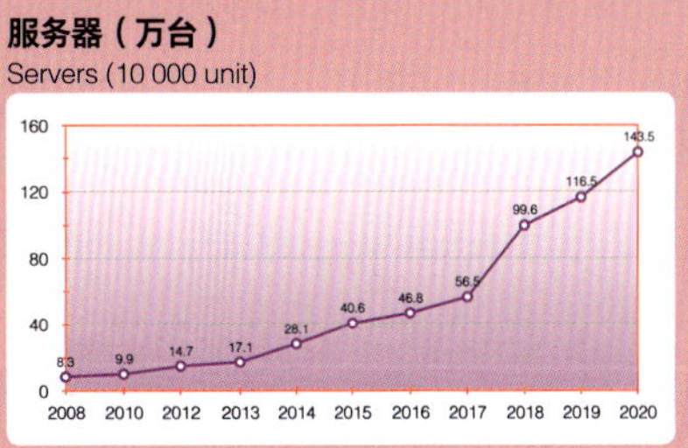

原油加工量（万吨）

Crude Processing Volume (10 000 tons)

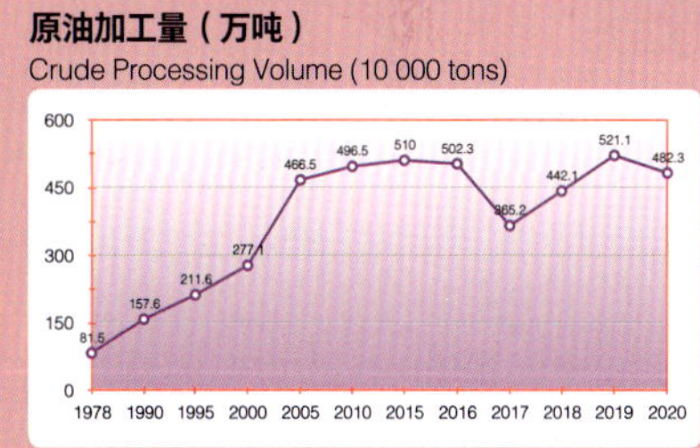

化肥（万吨）

Chemical Fertilizer (10 000 tons)

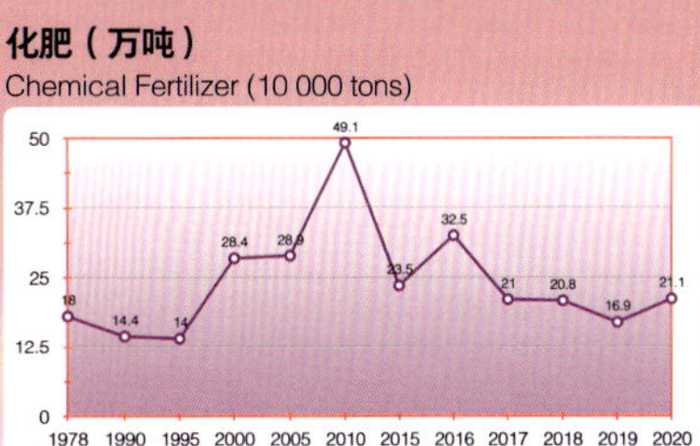

水泥（万吨）

Cement (10 000 tons)

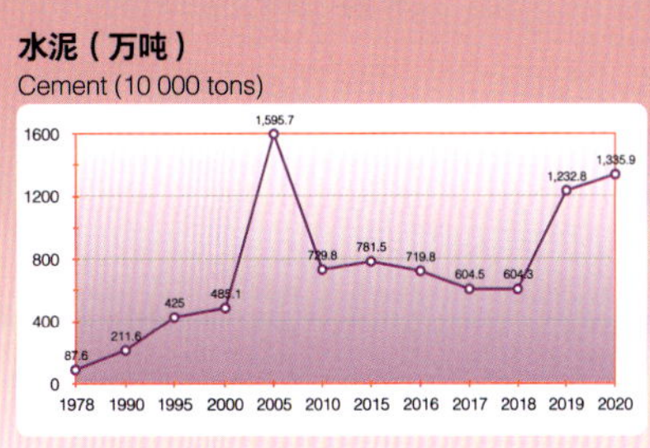

啤酒（万千升）

Beer (10 000 kiloliter)

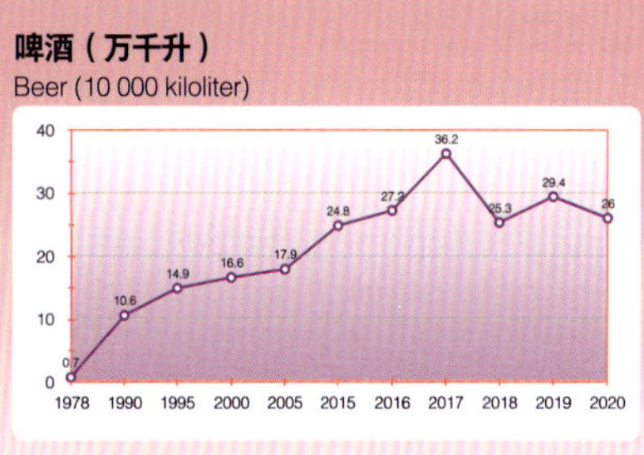

汽车（辆）

Motor Vehicles (unit)

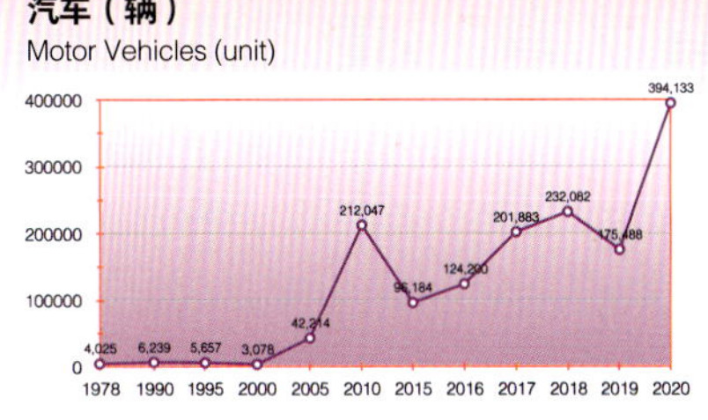

钢（万吨）

Steel (10 000 tons)

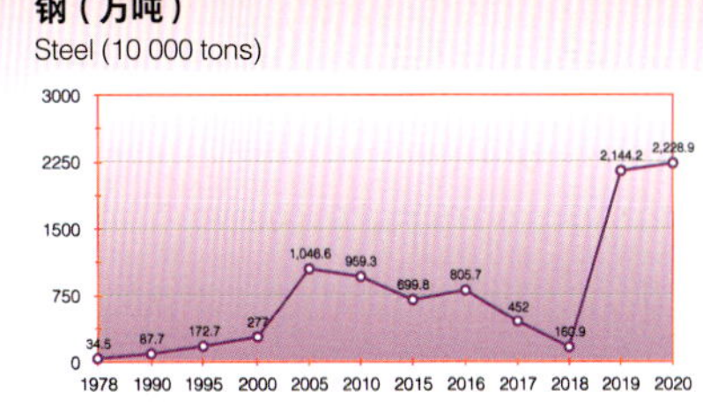

初级形态塑料（万吨）

Primary Plastic (10 000 tons)

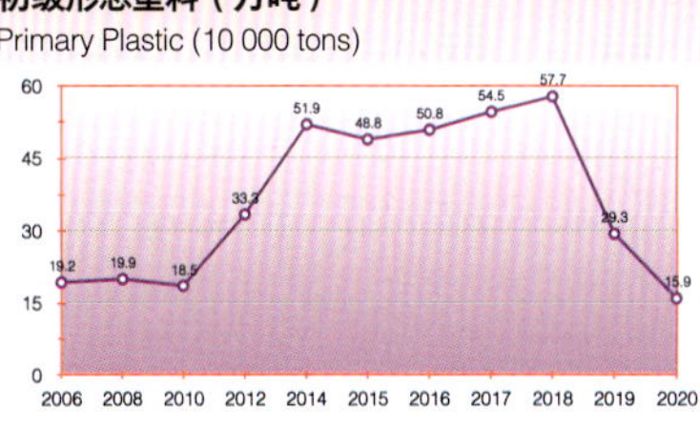

国内贸易 投资
Domestic Trade Investment

社会消费品零售总额及构成（亿元）
Total Retail Sales of Consumer Goods and Composition (100 million yuan)

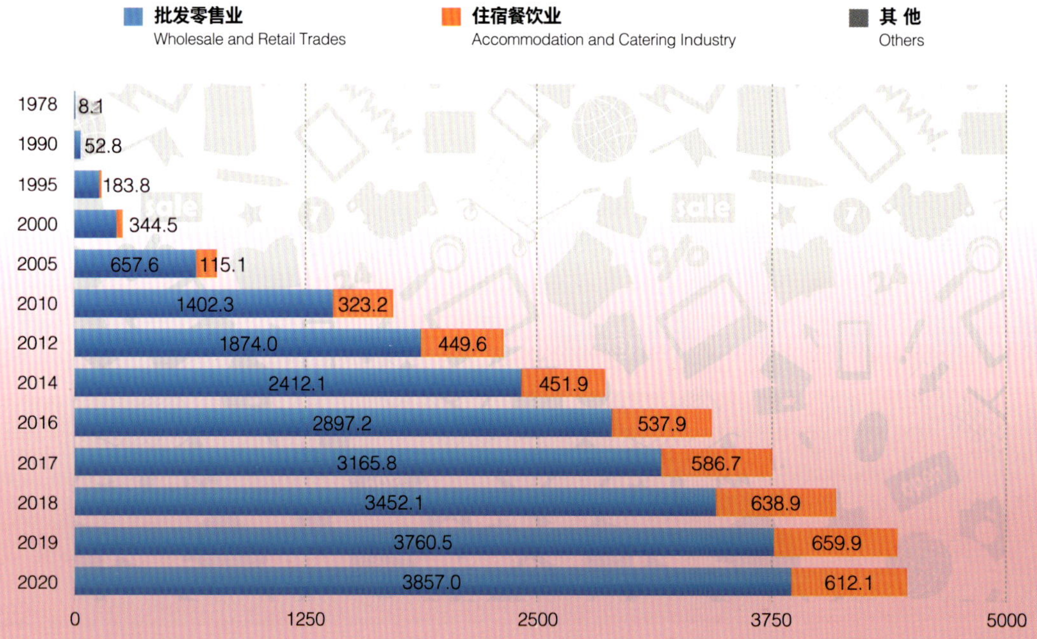

固定资产投资及构成（亿元）
Total Investment in Fixed Assets and Composition (100 million yuan)

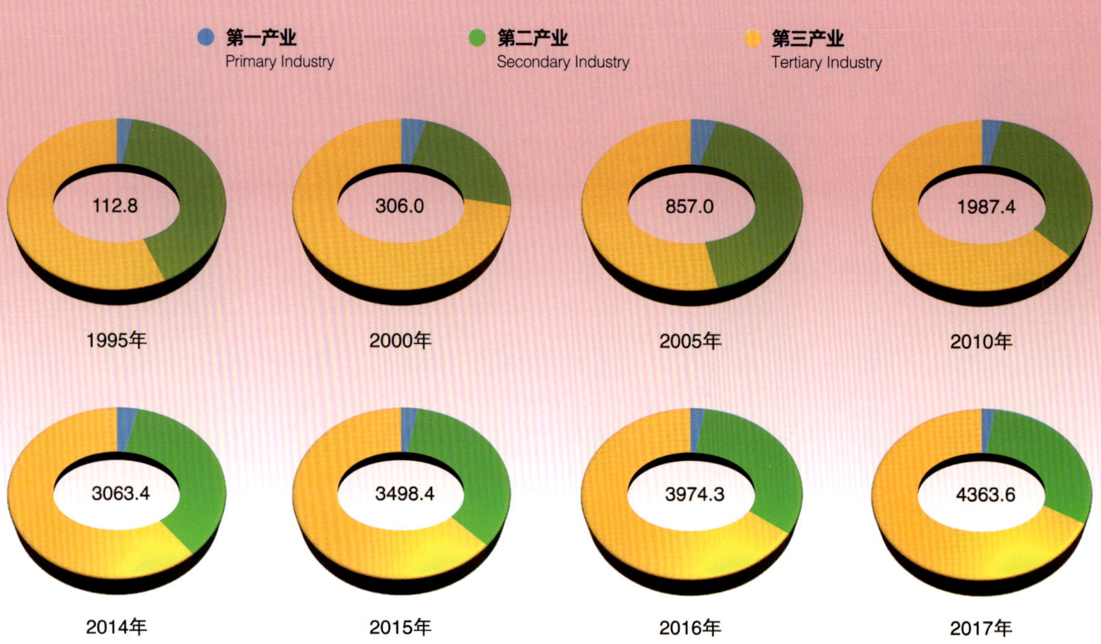

农业
Agriculture

农林牧渔业增加值（亿元）
Added Value of Agriculture, Forestry, Animal Husbandry and Fishery (100 million yuan)

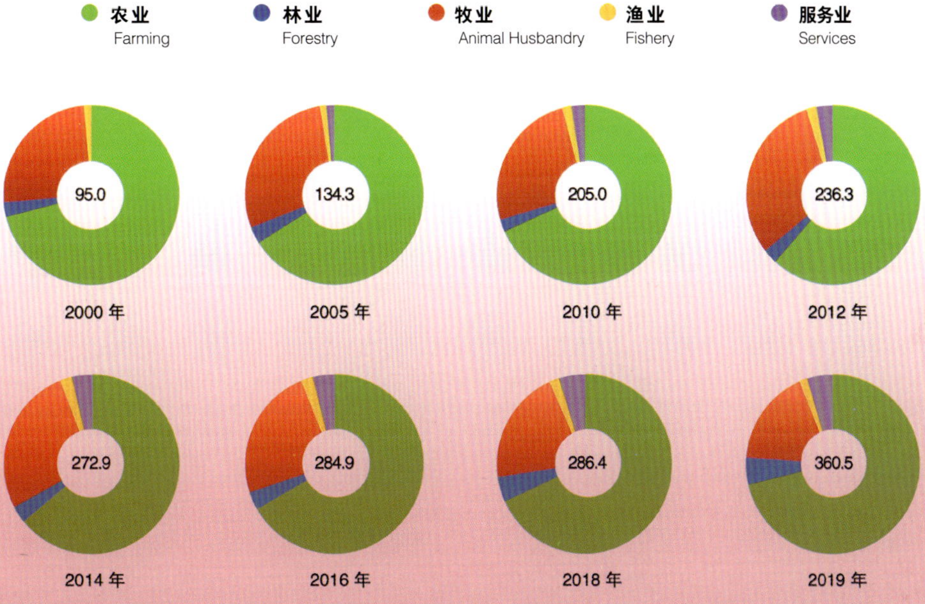

主要农产品产量（万吨）
Output of Main Agricultural Products (10 000 tons)

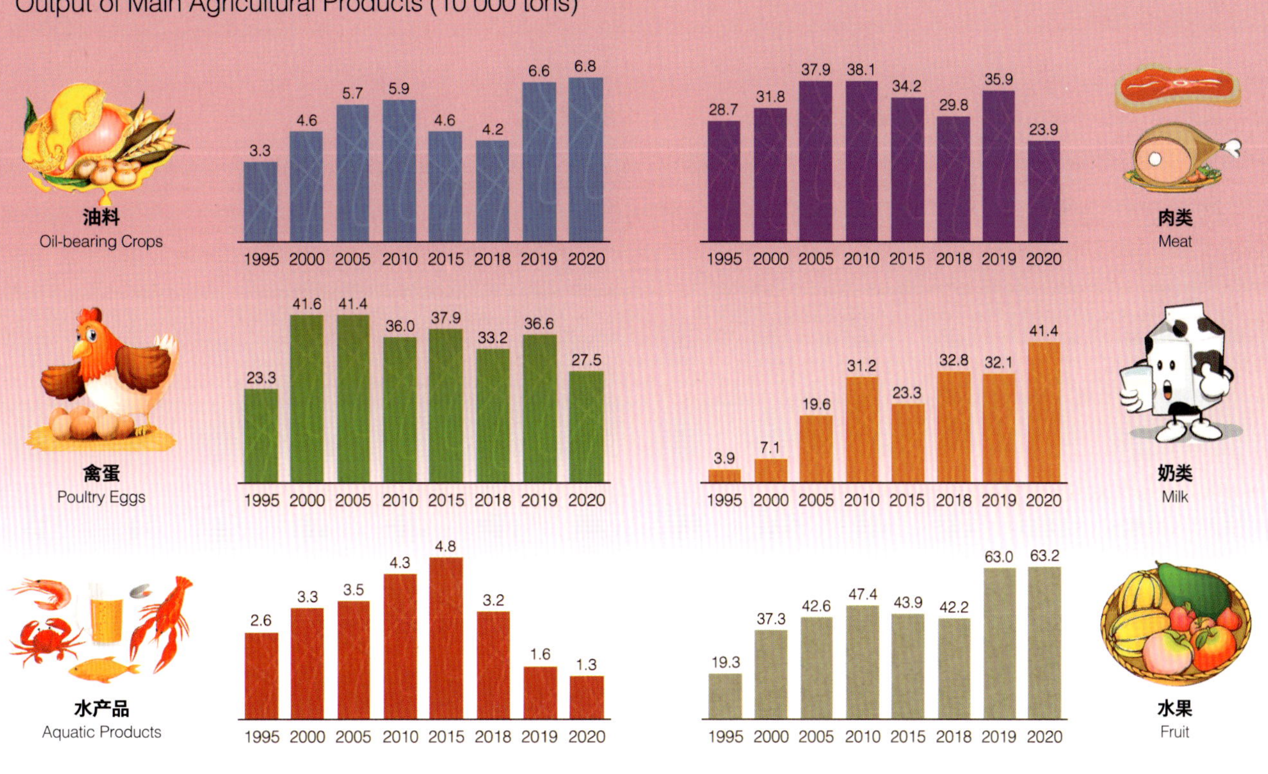

城市建设
Urban Public

供热面积（万平方米）
Area of Central Heating (10 000 sq.m)

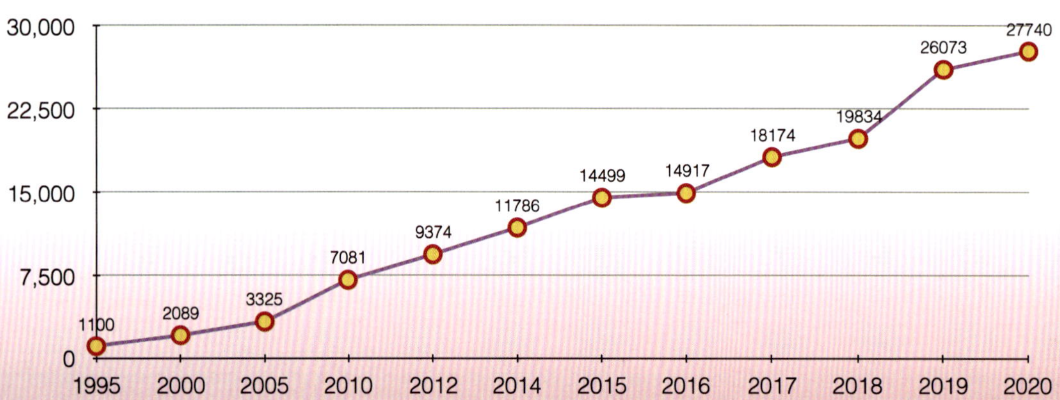

公共交通客运量（万人次）
Public Transportation of Passenger Traffic (10 000 person-times)

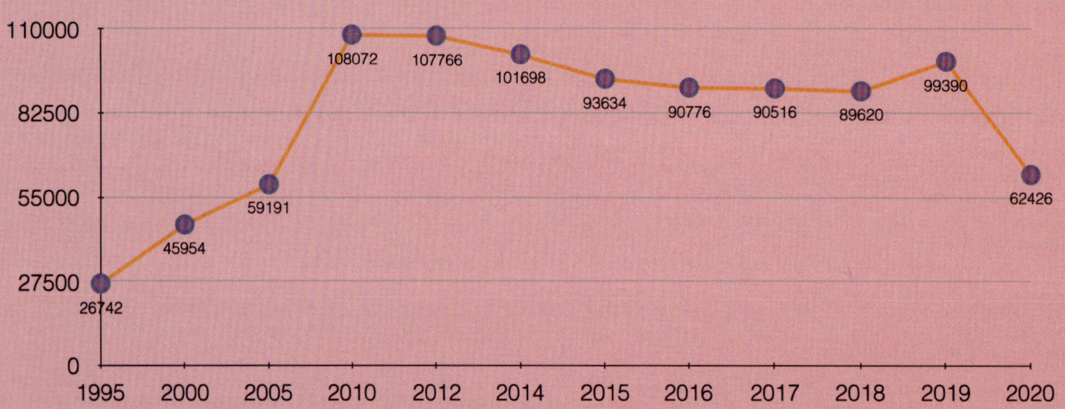

人均公园绿地面积（平方米/人）
Per Capita Public Green Area (sq.m/person)

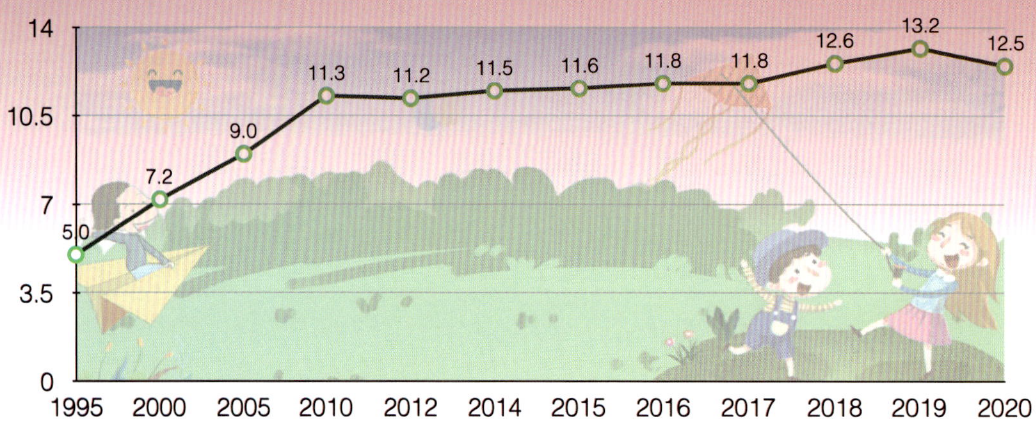

全社会用电量（万千瓦时）
Electricity Consumption (10 000 kwh)

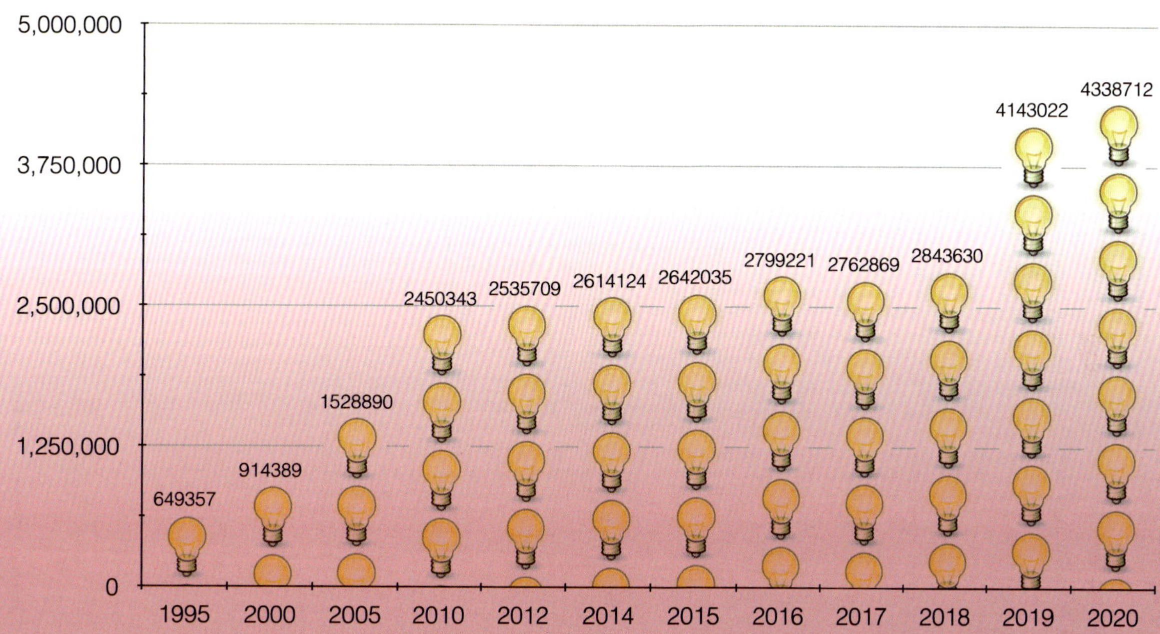

全社会供气量
Total Social Gas Supply

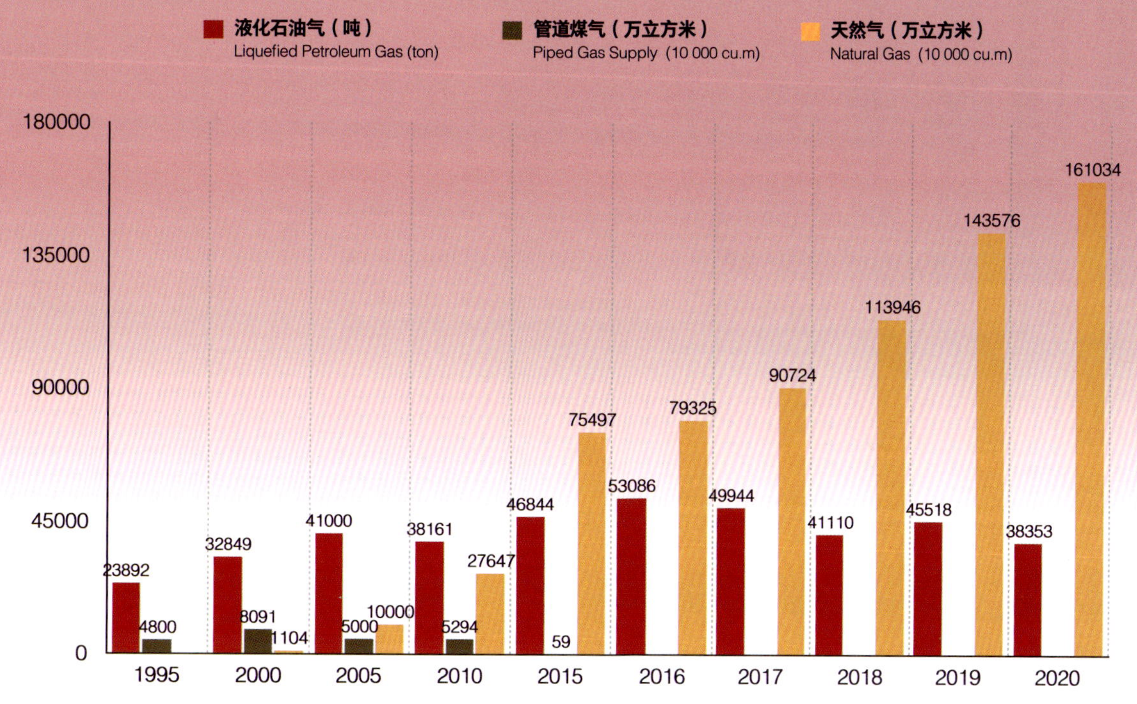

邮电 交通
Transportation Post and Telecommunication

移动电话用户、 宽带互联网接入用户数（万户）
Number of Mobile Telephone Subscribers, Subscribers of Broad Band Internet(10 000 subscribers)

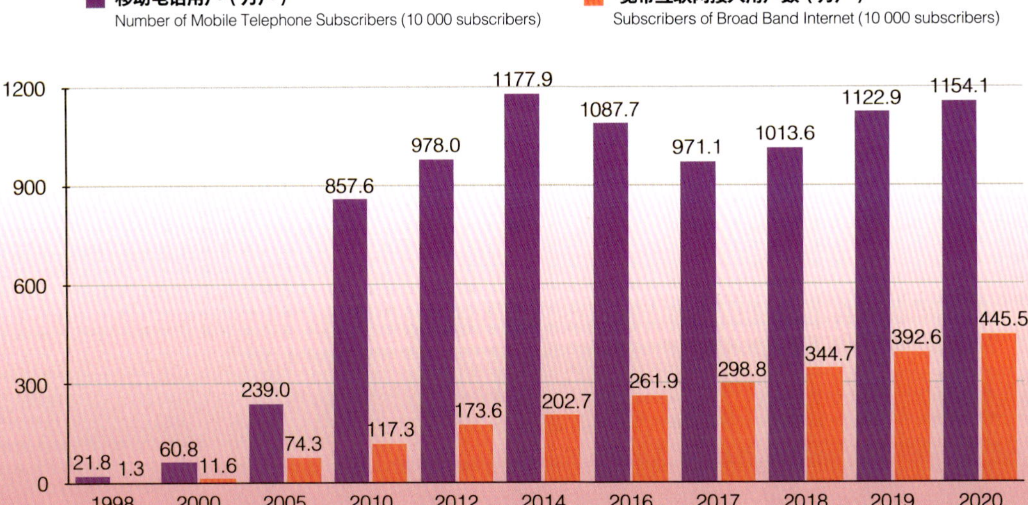

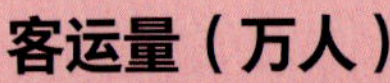

客运量（万人）
Passenger Traffic(10 000 persons)

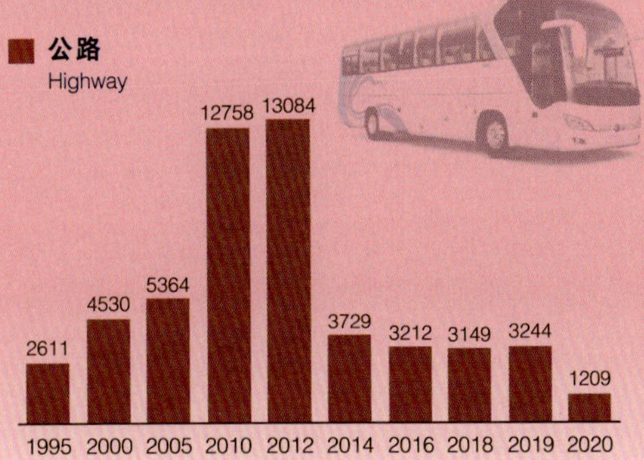

货运量（万吨）
Freight Traffic(10 000 tons)

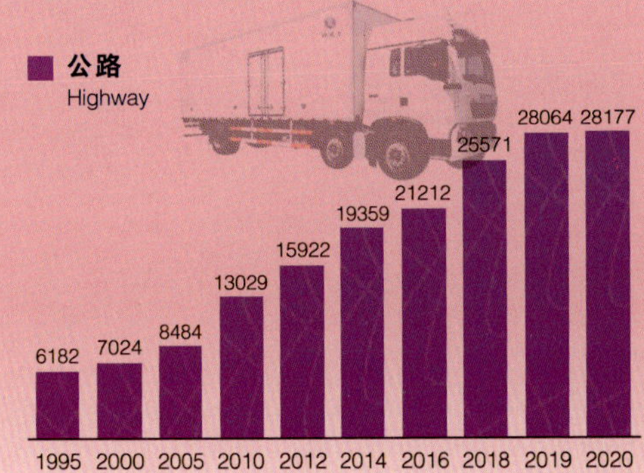

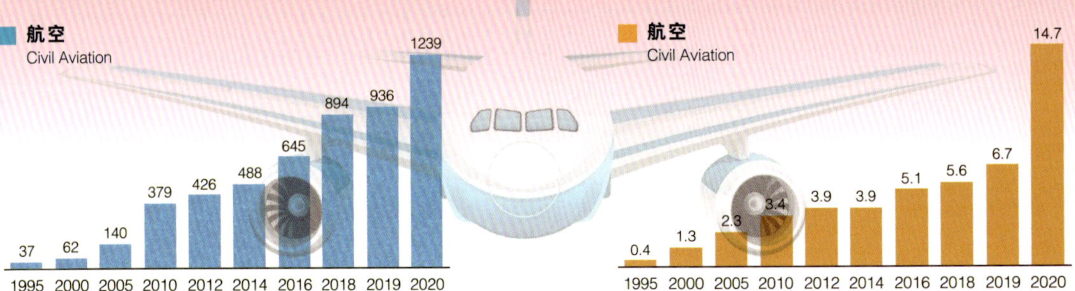

教育 卫生
Education Public Health

各类学校专任教师（人）
Full-time Teachers (person)

各类学校在校学生（万人）
Total Enrollment (10 000 persons)

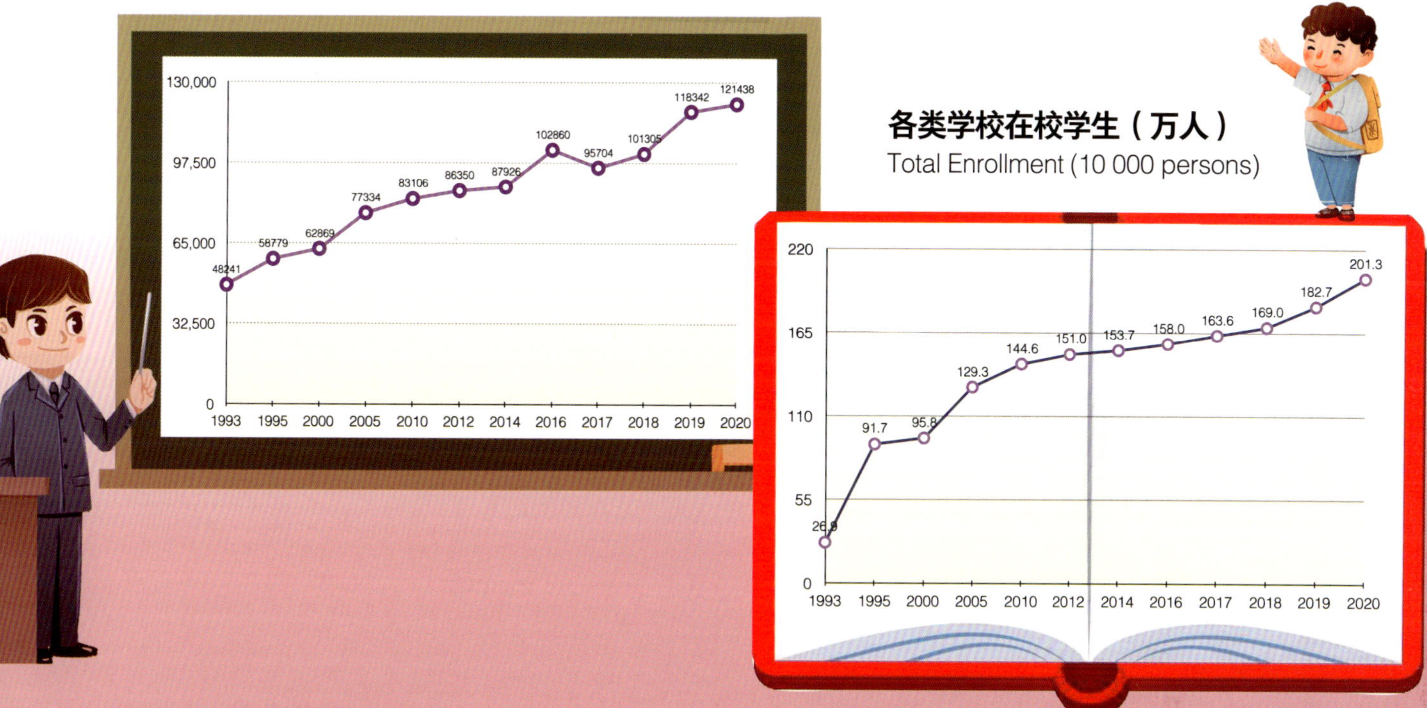

每万人拥有医院床位数（张）
Number of Hospitals Beds per 10000 Population (set)

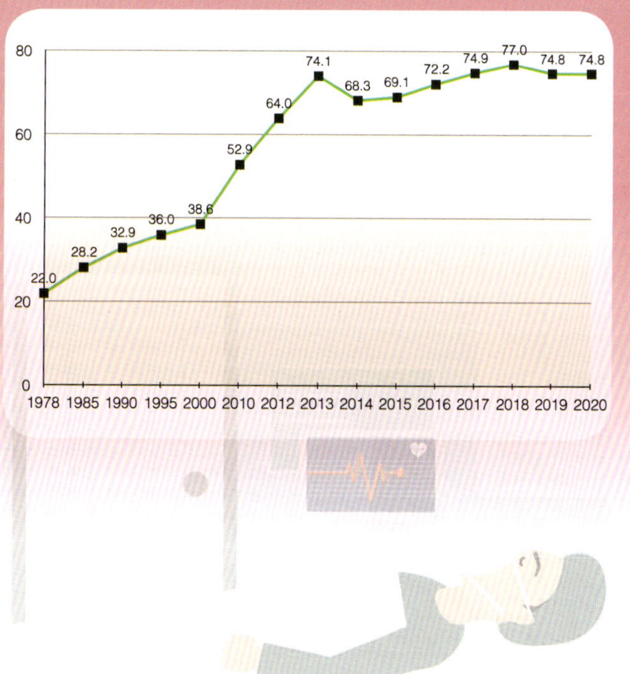

每万人拥有医生数（人）
Number of Doctors per 10000 Population (person)

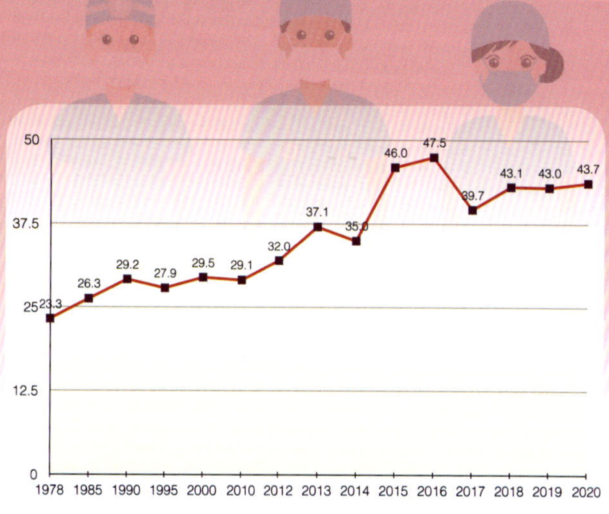

新时代 · 新黄河
New Era·New Yellow River Civilization

黄河的故事灿若繁星
黄河的文化源远流长
黄河的精神振奋人心

Grand Stories of Yellow River as a Multitude of Stars
Profound Cultures of Yellow River with a Long History
Impressive Spirits of Yellow River with Inspiring Enthusiasm

1

行政区划

DIVISIONS OF ADMINISTRATIVE AREAS

1-1 行政区划
Divisions of Administrative Areas

单位：个 (unit)

年份地区	Year and Region	乡 Townships	镇 Towns	街道 Street Communities	村 Village	居委会 Neighborhood Committee	土地面积（平方公里）Land Area (sq.km)
全市主要年份							
1989		57	54	53	4710	702	8227
1990		57	54	48	4752	669	8227
1991		57	54	48	4752	670	8227
1992		57	54	48	4759	670	8227
1993		56	55	48	4756	670	8227
1994		55	56	48	4759	670	8227
1995		48	63	49	4723	721	8227
1996		42	68	49	4704	685	8154
1997		42	68	50	4696	616	8154
1998		42	69	50	4711	505	8154
1999		42	69	50	4714	468	8154
2000		42	69	50	4702	416	8154
2001		28	64	54	4677	417	8177
2002		27	65	54	4657	487	8177
2003		27	61	58	4657	487	8177
2004		27	61	58	4657	487	8177
2005		12	53	64	4628	400	8177
2006		11	53	64	4604	487	8177
2007		11	50	73	4563	500	8177
2008		11	50	73	4551	521	8177
2009		11	50	75	4553	522	8177
2010		6	49	86	4552	532	8177
2011		4	51	86	4538	556	8177
2012		4	51	86	4532	586	8177
2013		2	51	90	4548	597	7998
2014		2	51	90	4547	627	7998
2015		2	46	95	4546	641	7998
2016			39	104	4547	669	7998
2017			29	112	4548	711	7998
2018			29	112	4546	740	7998
2019			40	121	5551	847	10244
2020			29	132	5530	861	10244
2020 年分地区							
市区	Districts unber City		12	129	4246	823	8367
历下区	Li xia			14	13	118	101
市中区	Shi zhong			17	77	117	281
槐荫区	Huai yin			16	92	107	152
天桥区	Tian qiao			15	48	148	259
历城区	Li cheng			21	266	81	1301
长清区	Chang qing		2	8	580	59	1209
章丘区	Zhang qiu		1	17	890	35	1719
济阳区	Ji yang		2	8	566	42	1099
莱芜区	Lai wu		7	8	738	33	1740
钢城区	Gang cheng			5	211	24	506
济南高新区	Ji'nan Gao xin				152	40	
莱芜高新区	Laiwu Gao xin				56	14	
济南先行区	JN Pioneer Area				303	5	
南部山区	Nan shan				254		
平阴县	Ping yin		6	2	336	24	715
商河县	Shang he		11	1	948	14	1162

注：1. 指标“土地面积”2013 年起为第二次全市土地调查数据。
2. 本表内数据由相关主管部门提供。

Note: 1.Indicator "land area" is the city land survey data for the second time as of 2013.
2.The data in this table are provided by the relevant authority departments.

1-2 县区所辖镇、街道办事处(2020年末)

Town and Street Communities Under the Jurisdiction(End of 2020)

县区	Region	镇、街道办事处数量(个) Number of Towns and Street Communities (unit)	镇、街道办事处名称 Name of Towns and Street Communities
历下区	Li xia	14	大明湖街道 千佛山街道 燕山街道 泉城路街道 趵突泉街道 东关街道 解放路街道 建筑新村街道 文化东路街道 甸柳新村街道 姚家街道 智远街道 龙洞街道 舜华路街道
市中区	Shi zhong	17	泺源街道 杆石桥街道 魏家庄街道 大观园街道 四里村街道 六里山街道 七里山街道 二七新村街道 舜玉路街道 舜耕街道 王官庄街道 七贤街道 白马山街道 十六里河街道 兴隆街道 党家街道 陡沟街道
槐荫区	Huai yin	16	西市场街道 五里沟街道 道德街街道 营市街街道 青年公园街道 中大槐树街道 振兴街街道 南辛庄街道 段店北路街道 匡山街道 张庄路街道 美里湖街道 兴福街道 玉清湖街道 腊山街道 吴家堡街道
天桥区	Tian qiao	15	无影山街道 堤口路街道 宝华街街道 工人新村南村街道 工人新村北村街道 官扎营街道 北坦街道 天桥东街街道 纬北路街道 制锦市街道 北园街道 泺口街道 药山街道 桑梓店街道 大桥街道
历城区	Li cheng	21	洪家楼街道 山大路街道 东风街道 全福街道 华山街道 荷花路街道 王舍人街道 鲍山街道 郭店街道 唐冶街道 港沟街道 董家街道 彩石街道 唐王街道 孙村街道 巨野河街 临港街道 遥墙街道 仲宫街道 柳埠街道 西营街道
长清区	Chang qing	10	文昌街道 平安街道 崮云湖街道 五峰山街道 归德街道 张夏街道 万德街道 孝里街道 马山镇 双泉镇
章丘区	Zhang qiu	18	明水街道 双山街道 龙山街道 枣园街道 埠村街道 圣井街道 绣惠街道 相公庄街道 文祖街道 普集街道 官庄街道 高官寨街道 白云湖街道 宁家埠街道 曹范街道 刁镇街道 黄河街道 垛庄镇
济阳区	Ji yang	10	济阳街道 济北街道 回河街道 垛石街道 曲堤街道 孙耿街道 太平街道 崔寨街道 仁风镇 新市镇
莱芜区	Lai wu	15	凤城街道 张家洼街道 高庄街道 口镇街道 羊里街道 方下街道 雪野街道 鹏泉街道 寨里镇 杨庄镇 茶叶口镇 和庄镇 牛泉镇 苗山镇 大王庄镇
钢城区	Gang cheng	5	艾山街道 里辛街道 汶源街道 颜庄街道 辛庄街道
平阴县	Ping yin	8	榆山街道 锦水街道 洪范池镇 东阿镇 孔村镇 孝直镇 玫瑰镇 安城镇
商河县	Shang he	12	许商街道 玉皇庙镇 龙桑寺镇 贾庄镇 殷巷镇 郑路镇 怀仁镇 白桥镇 孙集镇 韩庙镇 张坊镇 沙河镇

2

人口

POPULATION

2-1 主要年份总户数、总人口（户籍人口）
Total Household and Population in Major Years(registered population)

年份 Year	年末总户数（万户） Total year-end Households (10 000 households)	年末总人口（万人） Total year-end Population (10 000 persons)	按性别分（万人） Grouped by Sex (10 000 persons)		性别比（女=100） Sex Ratio (Femal=100)	年平均人口（万人） Annual Average Population (10 000 persons)	比上年增长（‰） Growth Rate (‰)	人口密度（人/平方公里） Density of Population (Person/sq.km)
			男性 Male	女性 Femal				
1952	70.19	318.66	157.68	160.98	97.95	315.94	3.30	387
1957	76.44	346.38	170.30	176.09	96.71	343.25	17.40	421
1962	81.45	351.44	174.55	176.89	98.68	350.18	-4.60	427
1965	83.01	373.22	186.08	187.14	99.43	370.24	19.50	454
1970	89.48	407.50	203.16	204.34	99.42	404.17	16.60	495
1975	96.54	437.73	217.82	219.91	99.05	435.15	9.90	532
1976	98.63	442.09	220.89	221.20	99.86	439.91	10.90	537
1977	100.60	445.05	222.46	222.59	99.94	443.57	8.30	541
1978	102.93	450.67	226.31	224.36	100.87	447.86	9.70	548
1979	105.34	456.37	228.57	227.80	100.34	453.52	12.60	555
1980	106.83	458.61	230.47	228.15	101.02	457.49	8.80	557
1981	110.52	467.93	235.35	232.58	101.19	463.27	12.60	569
1982	112.51	474.23	238.99	235.26	101.59	471.08	16.80	576
1983	114.92	479.38	242.02	237.36	101.54	476.81	12.20	583
1984	116.92	483.85	244.32	239.53	102.00	481.62	10.10	588
1985	120.19	488.39	246.86	241.53	102.21	486.12	9.30	594
1986	122.67	494.06	250.09	243.97	102.51	491.23	10.50	601
1987	125.43	501.03	253.95	247.08	102.78	497.55	12.90	609
1988	130.32	507.18	257.22	249.86	102.95	504.11	13.20	616
1989	134.77	513.39	260.79	252.61	103.24	510.29	12.30	624
1990	140.36	523.60	265.91	257.69	103.19	518.50	16.10	636
1991	143.42	527.43	267.78	259.65	103.13	525.52	13.50	641
1992	147.50	530.70	269.46	261.25	103.14	529.07	6.70	645
1993	149.42	533.53	270.77	262.76	103.05	532.12	5.80	649

2-1 续表 continued

年份 Year	年末总户数（万户）Total year-end Households (10 000 households)	年末总人口（万人）Total year-end Population (10 000 persons)	按性别分（万人）Grouped by Sex (10 000 persons)		性别比（女＝100）Sex Ratio (Femal=100)	年平均人口（万人）Annual Average Population (10 000 persons)	比上年增长（‰）Growth Rate (‰)	人口密度（人/平方公里）Density of Population (Person/sq.km)
			男性 Male	女性 Femal				
1994	153.60	537.31	272.76	264.54	103.11	535.42	6.20	653
1995	156.45	542.12	274.98	267.14	102.93	539.72	8.00	656
1996	156.42	543.45	275.59	267.86	102.89	542.79	5.70	666
1997	157.66	549.20	278.30	270.90	102.73	546.33	6.50	674
1998	160.93	553.54	279.91	273.63	102.30	551.37	9.20	679
1999	163.52	557.63	281.71	275.93	102.09	555.59	7.70	684
2000	166.63	562.65	284.19	278.46	102.06	560.14	8.20	690
2001	168.46	569.00	287.39	281.61	102.06	565.83	10.20	696
2002	170.10	575.01	290.58	284.43	102.16	572.00	10.90	703
2003	172.18	582.56	294.04	288.52	101.91	578.78	11.90	712
2004	173.24	590.08	297.25	292.82	101.51	586.32	13.03	722
2005	177.69	597.44	300.42	297.02	101.15	593.76	12.69	731
2006	179.48	603.35	302.72	300.63	100.70	600.39	11.17	738
2007	181.88	604.85	302.87	301.98	100.29	604.10	6.17	740
2008	184.63	603.99	302.00	301.99	100.00	604.42	0.53	739
2009	187.70	603.27	301.26	302.01	99.75	603.63	-1.30	738
2010	190.65	604.08	301.28	302.80	99.50	603.68	0.08	739
2011	193.61	606.64	302.19	304.44	99.26	605.36	2.78	742
2012	195.79	609.21	303.30	305.91	99.15	607.92	4.23	745
2013	199.67	613.25	304.93	308.32	98.90	611.23	5.44	767
2014	201.93	621.61	309.09	312.52	98.90	617.43	15.64	777
2015	203.59	625.73	310.92	314.80	98.77	623.67	10.11	782
2016	205.45	632.83	314.28	318.55	98.66	629.28	9.00	791
2017	208.08	643.62	319.21	324.41	98.40	638.22	14.21	805
2018	216.64	655.90	324.74	331.15	98.06	649.76	19.08	820
2019	270.26	796.74	395.30	401.44	98.47	726.32	21.47	778
2020	276.35	806.72	399.61	407.11	98.16	801.73	12.45	788

2-2 主要年份市区总户数、总人口（户籍人口）
Total Household and Population of Urban in Major Years(registered population)

年份 Year	年末总户数 （万户） Total year-end Households (10 000 households)	年末总人口 （万人） Total year-end Population (10 000 persons)	按性别分（万人） Grouped by Sex (10 000 persons)		年平均人口 （万人） Annual Average Population (10 000 persons)
			男性 Male	女性 Femal	
1952	26.46	124.96	63.95	61.01	123.83
1957	29.13	143.17	72.05	71.13	140.11
1962	32.25	153.35	78.52	74.83	154.18
1965	34.03	162.82	83.20	79.62	161.90
1970	37.21	167.82	85.61	82.21	168.51
1975	40.67	178.78	90.83	87.95	177.74
1976	41.59	180.99	91.83	89.16	179.88
1977	42.34	181.49	91.92	89.57	181.24
1978	43.79	186.43	94.70	91.73	183.96
1979	45.33	189.26	96.22	93.04	187.84
1980	46.12	190.01	97.22	92.79	189.63
1981	48.64	194.05	99.37	94.69	192.03
1982	50.60	201.31	101.44	99.87	197.68
1983	52.32	205.48	103.42	102.07	203.39
1984	54.30	209.55	105.57	103.99	207.52
1985	56.88	213.28	107.96	105.33	211.42
1986	58.65	216.98	111.54	105.43	215.13
1987	60.54	221.49	113.79	107.70	219.23
1988	63.03	225.00	115.51	109.39	223.25
1989	65.29	228.88	117.49	111.39	226.94
1990	81.22	283.66	145.29	138.36	
1991	83.30	286.20	146.55	139.65	284.93
1992	85.87	288.52	145.19	143.33	287.36
1993	88.02	291.24	149.07	142.17	289.88
1994	90.10	294.60	150.75	143.85	292.92
1995	92.04	299.20	152.97	146.23	296.90

2-2 续表 continued

年份 Year	年末总户数（万户）Total year-end Households (10 000 households)	年末总人口（万人）Total year-end Population (10 000 persons)	按性别分（万人）Grouped by Sex (10 000 persons)		年平均人口（万人）Annual Average Population (10 000 persons)
			男性 Male	女性 Femal	
1996	93.12	302.78	154.58	148.20	300.99
1997	93.90	306.98	156.54	150.44	304.88
1998	96.65	309.90	157.58	152.32	308.44
1999	97.74	313.18	159.19	153.99	311.54
2000	99.25	317.20	161.03	156.17	315.19
2001	100.53	322.45	163.73	158.72	319.83
2002	101.62	327.55	166.43	161.12	325.00
2003	102.71	334.80	169.84	164.96	331.18
2004	102.68	341.73	172.91	168.82	338.27
2005	104.87	347.87	175.41	172.45	344.80
2006	106.19	352.29	177.10	175.19	350.08
2007	107.55	352.71	176.70	176.01	352.50
2008	109.26	350.23	175.08	175.15	351.47
2009	111.07	348.24	173.71	174.53	349.24
2010	112.91	348.02	173.19	174.83	348.13
2011	114.75	349.44	173.51	175.93	348.73
2012	116.49	352.17	174.55	177.62	350.81
2013	118.50	355.38	175.86	179.52	353.78
2014	120.33	360.99	178.55	182.44	358.19
2015	121.96	364.54	180.12	184.42	362.77
2016	154.64	473.33	233.74	239.59	418.94
2017	157.42	483.75	238.48	245.27	478.54
2018	182.76	554.13	273.31	280.82	518.94
2019	236.31	695.09	343.90	351.19	689.31
2020	242.04	705.33	348.36	356.97	700.21

注：1990 年以前的数据中不包括长清区。2016 年起数据包括章丘区。2018 年起数据包括济阳区。2019 年起数据包括莱芜区、钢城区。
Note: The data before 1990 excludes Changqing District. The data as of 2016 includes Zhangqiu District The data as of 2018 includes Jiyang District. Data after the year of 2019 involves Laiwu District and Gangcheng District.

2-3 主要年份人口自然变动情况
Natural Changes of Population in Major Years

年份 Year	申报出生人口 （人） Population of Birth (person)	申报出生率 (‰) Birth Rate (‰)	申报死亡人口 （人） Population of Death (person)	申报死亡率 (‰) Death Rate (‰)	人口自然增长 （人） Population of Natural Growth (person)	人口自然增长率 (‰) Natural Growth Rate (‰)
1952	72861	23.06	29949	9.48	42912	13.58
1957	108432	31.59	38082	11.09	70350	20.50
1962	108029	30.85	44464	12.70	63565	18.15
1965	121364	32.78	39355	10.63	82009	22.15
1970	111861	27.68	29965	7.41	81896	20.27
1975	82939	19.06	33837	7.78	49102	11.28
1976	70065	15.93	34693	7.89	35372	8.04
1977	67413	15.20	33723	7.60	33690	7.60
1978	69541	15.53	31343	7.00	38198	8.53
1979	72596	16.01	30205	6.66	42391	9.35
1980	60336	13.19	32004	7.00	28332	6.19
1981	70327	15.18	31671	6.84	38656	8.34
1982	74147	15.74	28679	6.09	45468	9.65
1983	56454	11.84	30080	6.31	26374	5.53
1984	61156	12.70	32277	6.70	28879	6.00
1985	55386	11.39	31678	6.52	23708	4.87
1986	69901	14.23	30790	6.27	39111	7.96
1987	86752	17.44	30007	6.03	56745	11.41
1988	78922	15.66	32850	6.52	46072	9.14
1989	76380	14.97	30721	6.02	45659	8.95
1990	66806	12.88	33916	6.54	32890	6.34
1991	59374	11.30	32675	6.20	26699	5.10
1992	52825	9.98	34969	6.61	17856	3.37
1993	46007	8.65	35317	6.64	10690	2.01
1994	49940	9.30	35308	6.60	14632	2.70
1995	54132	10.03	34107	6.32	20025	3.71

2–3 续表 continued

年份 Year	申报出生人口（人）Population of Birth (person)	申报出生率（‰）Birth Rate (‰)	申报死亡人口（人）Population of Death (person)	申报死亡率（‰）Death Rate (‰)	人口自然增长（人）Population of Natural Growth (person)	人口自然增长率（‰）Natural Growth Rate (‰)
1996	58254	10.73	36452	6.71	21802	4.02
1997	62245	11.39	35768	6.55	26477	4.84
1998	62490	11.33	36497	6.64	25893	4.69
1999	55931	10.07	34956	6.29	20975	3.78
2000	62059	11.08	39499	7.05	22560	4.03
2001	55536	9.82	33816	5.98	21720	3.84
2002	57317	10.02	36234	6.33	21083	3.69
2003	54599	9.43	42539	7.35	12060	2.08
2004	60670	10.35	38158	6.51	22512	3.84
2005	60240	10.15	37782	6.36	22458	3.78
2006	57706	9.61	39040	6.50	18666	3.11
2007	58367	9.66	39752	6.58	18615	3.08
2008	59600	9.86	39887	6.60	19713	3.26
2009	56694	9.39	40911	6.78	15783	2.61
2010	67162	11.13	50380	8.35	16782	2.78
2011	66563	11.00	40310	6.66	26253	4.34
2012	71449	11.75	49148	8.08	22301	3.67
2013	69351	11.35	41713	6.82	27638	4.53
2014	110503	17.90	41887	6.78	68616	11.11
2015	73688	11.82	41999	6.73	31689	5.09
2016	91941	14.61	39460	6.27	52481	8.34
2017	113766	17.83	62958	9.86	50808	7.96
2018	94694	14.57	45374	6.98	49320	7.59
2019	101723	12.86	52396	6.62	49327	6.24
2020	83782	10.45	58568	7.31	25214	3.14

2-4 分地区户数、人口数 (2020 年)(户籍人口)
Household and Population by Region(2020)(registered population)

地区	Region	户数 (户) Households (household)	人口数 (人) Population (person)	按性别分(人) Grouped by Sex (person)	
				男性 Male	女性 Femal
全市	Total City	2763586	8067252	3996179	4071073
市区	Districts unber City	2420430	7053295	3483614	3569681
历下区	Li xia	253086	741945	362529	379416
市中区	Shi zhong	250210	679362	330464	348898
槐荫区	Huai yin	171127	466306	224972	241334
天桥区	Tian qiao	197103	538424	262128	276296
历城区	Li cheng	374112	1107499	544746	562753
长清区	Chang qing	184363	571902	284638	287264
章丘区	Zhang qiu	318533	1055244	521479	533765
济阳区	Ji yang	175505	599125	301210	297915
莱芜区	Lai wu	383927	993969	497888	496081
钢城区	Gang cheng	112464	299519	153560	145959
平阴县	Ping yin	136135	371976	186205	185771
商河县	Shang he	207021	641981	326360	315621

2-5 计划生育情况 (2020 年)
Basic Statistics of Family Planning (2020)

地区	Region	合法生育(人) Legal Childbearing (person)			出生政策符合率(%) Legitimate Fertility (%)	违法生育(人) Illegal Childbearing (person)		
		一孩 First Child	二孩 Second Child	三孩 Third Child		一孩 First Child	二孩 Second Child	三孩 Third Child
总计	**Total**	**24857**	**31385**	**1508**	**93**	**423**	**119**	**3770**
市区	Districts unber City	22295	27130	1211	94	281	83	2731
历下区	Li xia	2194	2249	72	99	2	3	39
市中区	Shi zhong	1820	2164	94	97	8	2	121
槐荫区	Huai yin	1524	1664	59	97	0	1	94
天桥区	Tian qiao	1396	1480	44	97	10	4	80
历城区	Li cheng	3023	2956	124	96	17	7	246
长清区	Chang qing	1858	2308	68	94	37	9	247
章丘区	Zhang qiu	3313	3826	155	95	43	14	324
济阳区	Ji yang	1160	1925	155	87	51	14	413
莱芜区	Lai wu	2526	3639	172	93	45	7	411
钢城区	Gang cheng	677	1085	53	90	9	5	192
济南高新区	Ji'nan Gao xin	1358	1387	53	97	4	1	72
济南先行区	JN Pioneer Area	816	1443	119	85	51	15	351
南部山区	Nan shan	630	1004	43	92	4	1	141
平阴县	Ping yin	1015	1650	71	94	13	11	165
商河县	Shang he	1547	2605	226	81	129	25	874

2-6 分地区人口机械变动情况（2020 年）

Un-Natural Changes of Population by Region (2020)

地区	Region	迁入人口（人）Move Into the Population (person)	迁入率（‰）Move In Rate (‰)	迁出人口（人）Move Out the Population (person)	迁出率（‰）Move Out Rate (‰)	人口机械增长（人）Mechanical Growth of Population (person)	人口机械增长率（‰）Mechanical Growth Rates of Population (‰)
全市	Total	116498	14.53	41476	5.17	75022	9.36
市区	Districts unber City	103455	14.77	25532	3.65	77923	11.13
历下区	Li xia	23034	31.65	4799	6.59	18235	25.06
市中区	Shi zhong	13985	20.81	3179	4.73	10806	16.08
槐荫区	Huai yin	14786	32.22	1944	4.24	12842	27.99
天桥区	Tian qiao	11748	21.95	1982	3.70	9766	18.25
历城区	Li cheng	26782	24.61	3250	2.99	23532	21.62
长清区	Chang qing	3409	5.96	1417	2.48	1992	3.48
章丘区	Zhang qiu	3518	3.33	2267	2.15	1251	1.19
济阳区	Ji yang	3397	5.68	3063	5.12	334	0.56
莱芜区	Lai wu	2061	2.07	2643	2.66	-582	-0.59
钢城区	Gang cheng	735	2.45	988	3.29	-253	-0.84
平阴县	Ping yin	3045	8.17	4419	11.85	-1374	-3.68
商河县	Shang he	9998	15.56	11525	17.94	-1527	-2.38

2-7 分地区人口自然变动情况（2020 年）

Natural Changes of Population by Region (2020)

地区	Region	申报出生人口（人）Population of Birth (person)	申报出生率（‰）Birth Rate (‰)	申报死亡人口（人）Population of Death (person)	申报死亡率（‰）Death Rate (‰)	人口自然增长（人）Population of Natural Growth (person)	人口自然增长率（‰）Natural Growth Rate (‰)
全市	Total	83782	10.45	58568	7.31	25214	3.14
市区	Districts unber City	74443	10.63	49662	7.09	24781	3.54
历下区	Li xia	8986	12.35	3443	4.73	5543	7.62
市中区	Shi zhong	7394	11.00	4021	5.98	3373	5.02
槐荫区	Huai yin	5850	12.75	2664	5.81	3186	6.94
天桥区	Tian qiao	5508	10.29	3723	6.96	1785	3.34
历城区	Li cheng	15011	13.79	6666	6.12	8345	7.67
长清区	Chang qing	5343	9.34	4652	8.13	691	1.21
章丘区	Zhang qiu	9057	8.58	8370	7.93	687	0.65
济阳区	Ji yang	6723	11.24	4991	8.34	1732	2.90
莱芜区	Lai wu	8216	8.26	8695	8.74	-479	-0.48
钢城区	Gang cheng	2355	7.84	2437	8.12	-82	-0.27
平阴县	Ping yin	3199	8.58	3709	9.95	-510	-1.37
商河县	Shang he	6140	9.56	5197	8.09	943	1.47

2-8 结婚情况
Number of Marriages

单位: 对 (couple)

地区	Region	2015 年	2016 年	2017 年	2018 年	2019 年	2020 年
总计	Total	50300	47457	52663	51383	52300	50521
市直	Departments Directiy Under the Municipal Government	88	82	67	90		
历下区	Li xia	6594	5742	5830	5763	5456	5634
市中区	Shi zhong	5975	5364	5973	5699	5092	5074
槐荫区	Huai yin	3772	3445	3728	3863	3452	3434
天桥区	Tian qiao	4953	4447	4563	4874	4287	3869
历城区	Li cheng	7163	7296	7551	7419	6809	6094
长清区	Chang qing	3777	3649	4331	4003	3930	3547
章丘区	Zhang qiu	6119	6135	7613	6840	6000	6016
济阳区	Ji yang	3938	3615	4023	4248	3629	3154
莱芜区	Lai wu					4514	4054
钢城区	Gang cheng					1183	1117
济南高新区	Ji'nan Gao xin	1577	1593	2516	2621	2533	2783
济南先行区	JN Pioneer Area						560
平阴县	Ping yin	2550	2563	2564	2330	1974	1881
商河县	Shang he	3794	3526	3904	3633	3441	3304

2-9 离婚情况
Number of Divorces

单位: 对 (couple)

地区	Region	2015 年	2016 年	2017 年	2018 年	2019 年	2020 年
总计	Total	25399	26915	32491	31611	35932	36515
法院数	Divorce Case Handled	7395	6909	6024	6228	7034	6887
民政数	Divorces Handled through Civil	18004	20006	26467	25383	28898	29628
市直	Departments Directiy Under the Municipal Government	12	17	25	19		
历下区	Li xia	2382	2800	3474	3322	3644	3889
市中区	Shi zhong	2262	2327	3448	3288	3441	3785
槐荫区	Huai yin	1510	1720	2223	2362	2416	2530
天桥区	Tian qiao	2104	2224	2834	2810	3031	2936
历城区	Li cheng	2666	3177	4337	3664	4195	4398
长清区	Chang qing	1301	1422	1549	1801	1864	1953
章丘区	Zhang qiu	2026	2171	3303	2916	2793	2763
济阳区	Ji yang	1344	1434	1733	1783	1745	1587
莱芜区	Lai Wu					1418	1220
钢城区	Gang cheng					502	432
济南高新区	Ji'nan Gao xin	502	557	1097	1127	1322	1495
济南先行区	JN Pioneer Area						269
平阴县	Ping yin	880	938	993	839	968	938
商河县	Shang he	1015	1219	1451	1452	1559	1433

主要统计指标解释

人口统计资料主要有三个来源 人口普查、人口抽样调查和人口经常性登记。

人口普查 是在国家规定的统一时间内，用统一的方法，统一的调查项目，对全国或某一地区的人口进行的一种专门调查。

人口抽样调查 是从所要研究的总人口中，随机抽取部分人口，并根据对这些人口调查所得到的数据来推算该人口总体相应指标的方法。

人口经常性登记 是指对人口出生、死亡、婚姻、迁移等事件进行连续的、持久的、强制的全面登记制度。

人口数 指一定时点、一定地区范围内的有生命的个人的总和。

年度统计的年末人口数 指每年12月31日24时的人口数。

出生率（又称粗出生率） 指在一定时期内（通常为一年）平均每千人所出生的人数的比率，一般用千分率表示。计算公式为：

出生率 = 年出生人数 / 年平均人数 × 1000‰

式中：出生人数指活产婴儿，即胎儿脱离母体时（不管怀孕月数），有过呼吸或其他生命现象。

出生人数 是指活产婴儿，即胎儿脱离母体时（不管怀孕月数），有过呼吸或其他生命现象。

年平均人数 是指年初、年底人口数的平均数，也可用年中人口数代替。

死亡率（又称粗死亡率） 指在一定时期内（通常为一年）一定地区的死亡人数与同期平均人数（或期中人数）之比，一般用千分率表示。计算公式为：

死亡率 = 年死亡人数 / 年平均人数 × 1000‰

人口自然增长率 指在一定时期内（通常为一年）人口自然增加数（出生人数减死亡人数）与该时期内平均人数（或期中人数）之比，一般用千分率表示。计算公式为：

人口自然增长率 = （本年出生人数 - 本年死亡人数）/ 年平均人数 × 1000‰

人口自然增长率 = 人口出生率 - 人口死亡率

机械增长率 是反映迁移变动的一个相对指标。它表明一个地区在一定时间内迁入人口数与迁出人口数相抵后的差额与总人口数的比率，一般用千分率表示。计算公式为：

机械增长率 = 一定时期的迁入迁出人口差额 / 该时期的平均人口 × 100%

人口密度 指一定时点，一定地区的人口数与该时点、该地区的面积之比，即一定时点的单位土地面积上的人口数，通常以每平方公里的居民人数来表示：

$$人口密度 = \frac{该地区人口数}{该地区土地面积} \times 100\%$$

性别比 反映两性人口间比例的指标，指在总人口中或各年龄组人口中，男性人数与女性人数之比。通常以每100个女性人口相对应的男性人口数。计算公式：

$$性别比 = \frac{男性人口}{女生人口} \times 100\%$$

Explanatory Notes on Main Statistical Indicators

Source of Demographic Data population census, sample survey of population and recurrent registration of population.

Population Census refers to an official survey of total population nationwide or in a given region by an official method within a given period of time in China.

Sample Survey of Population refers to the method of calculating corresponding indicators of total population pursuant to the data originated from the survey of partial population randomly extracted from the total population to be researched.

Recurrent registration of population refers to continuous, persistent and enforced registration system for population birth, death, marriage, and migration , etc.

Total Population refers to the total number of people alive at a certain point of time within a given area.

The Annual Statistics on Total Population is taken at midnight, the 31st of December.

Birth Rate (or Crude Birth Rate) refers to the ratio of births per one thousand people during a certain period of time (generally a year), expressed in permillage. The following formula is used:

Birth rate = number of births/annual average population *1,000‰

Wherein: Births refer to liveborn infants, namely those with breath or other vital signs when breaking away from the mother (regardless of number of months of pregnancy).

Births refer to liveborn infants, namely those with breath or other vital signs when breaking away from the mother (regardless of number of months of pregnancy).

Annual Average Population refers to the mean value of the number of people at the beginning and ending of the year, which can be replaced with the number of people in the middle of the year.

Death Rate (or Crude Death Rate) refers to the ratio of the number of deaths to the average population (or mid period population) during a certain period of time (usually a year), expressed in ‰ . The following formula is used:

Death rate = number of deaths/annual average population *1,000‰

Natural Growth Rate of Population refers to the ratio of natural increase in population (number of births minus number of deaths) in a certain period of time (usually a year) to the average population (or mid period population) of the same period, expressed in ‰ . The following formula is used:

Natural Growth Rate of Population=(number of births – number of deaths)/ annual average population * 1,000‰

Natural Growth Rate of Population=Birth Rate–Death Rate

Mechanical Growth Rate is a relative indicator that reflects changes in the population migration. It shows the ratio of the balance (between the people count moving in and out of a given area) to total population during a certain period of time, expressed in permillage. The following formula is used:

Mechanical growth rate = the balance between people count moving in and out of a given area during a certain period of time/average population * 100%

Population Density refers to the ratio of total population in a given area at a certain point of time to the area at this point of time, namely total population per area of land at a certain point of time, expressed in number of residents per square kilometers:

$$\text{Population density} = \frac{\text{Total population in the region}}{\text{Land area in the region}} \times 100\%$$

Sex ratio refers to the ratio of male to female population in total population or age groups, male population to per 100 female populations. The following formula is used:

$$\text{Sex ratio} = \frac{\text{Male n population}}{\text{Female population}} \times 100\%$$

3

综 合

GENERAL SURVEY

3-1 国民经济和社会发展总量指标
Principal Aggregate Indicators on National Economic and Social Development

指标	Indicators	单位 Unit	1978 年
面积	Area		
土地面积	Land Area	平方公里 (sq.km)	
# 市内十区建成区面积	Built-up Area of Ten Districts in the City	平方公里 (sq.km)	85
人口	Population		
年末总户数（户籍人口）	Total year-end Households (registered population)	万户 (10 000 households)	102.93
年末总人口	Total year-end Population	万人 (10 000 persons)	450.67
# 市区	Population	万人 (10 000 persons)	186.43
# 男性	Male	万人 (10 000 persons)	226.31
年末常住总人口	Total Resident Population at the Year-end	万人 (10 000 persons)	
就业	Employment		
全社会从业人员	Employed Persons	万人 (10 000 persons)	204.04
第一产业	Primary Industry	万人 (10 000 persons)	136.30
第二产业	Secondary Industry	万人 (10 000 persons)	46.06
第三产业	Tertiary Industry	万人 (10 000 persons)	21.68
职工平均工资	Average Wage of Staff and Workers	元 (yuan)	578
城镇非私营单位就业人员平均工资	Average Wage of Employed Persons in Urban Non Private Entities	元 (yuan)	
城镇非私营单位在岗职工平均工资	Average Wage of Staff and Workers in Urban Non Private Entities	元 (yuan)	
城镇私营单位就业人员平均工资	Average Wage of Employed Persons in Urban Private Entities	元 (yuan)	
城镇登记失业人员数	Registered Urban Unemployed Persons	万人 (10 000 persons)	
城镇登记失业率	Registered Urban Unemployment Rate	%	
国民经济核算	National Accounting		
地区生产总值	Gross Domestic Product	亿元 (100 million yuan)	23.60
# 非公有制经济	Non-ppublic Economy	亿元 (100 million yuan)	
第一产业	Primary Industry	亿元 (100 million yuan)	4.16
第二产业	Secondary Industry	亿元 (100 million yuan)	13.32
第三产业	Tertiary Industry	亿元 (100 million yuan)	6.12
人均地区生产总值	Per Capita GDP	元 (yuan)	527
固定资产投资	Investment in Fixed Assets		
固定资产投资	Investment in Fixed Assets	亿元 (100 million yuan)	3.19
第一产业	Primary Industry	亿元 (100 million yuan)	0.55
第二产业	Secondary Industry	亿元 (100 million yuan)	1.15
# 工业	Industry	亿元 (100 million yuan)	0.75
第三产业	Tertiary Industry	亿元 (100 million yuan)	1.29
# 房地产投资	Real Estate Investment	亿元 (100 million yuan)	0.00
财政税收	Fiscal Tax Revenue		
一般公共预算收入	General Pubilic Budget Revenue	亿元 (100 million yuan)	5.90
一般公共预算支出	General Pubilic Budget Expenditure	亿元 (100 million yuan)	1.50
地域税收收入	Regional Tax Revenue	亿元 (100 million yuan)	
国税税收收入	National Tax Revenue	亿元 (100 million yuan)	
地税税收收入	Land Tax Revenue	亿元 (100 million yuan)	

1990 年	1995 年	2000 年	2005 年	2010 年	2015 年	2017 年	2018 年	2019 年	2020 年
8227	8227	8154	8177	8177	7998	7998	7998	10244	10244
103	114	120	295	347	393	464	524	716	794
140.36	156.45	166.63	177.69	190.65	203.59	208.08	216.64	270.26	276.35
523.60	542.12	562.65	597.44	604.08	625.73	643.62	655.90	796.74	806.72
232.30	247.57	317.20	347.87	348.02	458.16	483.75	554.13	695.09	705.33
265.91	274.98	284.19	300.42	301.28	310.92	319.21	324.74	395.30	399.61
				681.80	713.20	732.12	746.04	890.87	920.24
270.54	324.22	347.37	360.00	373.70	388.70	405.38	419.27	492.36	–
125.73	116.13	109.98	99.10	76.66	71.80	69.50	68.80	77.42	–
87.75	106.68	110.81	114.20	120.20	124.70	129.35	132.17	154.27	–
57.06	101.41	126.58	146.70	176.84	192.20	206.53	218.30	260.67	–
2211	5851	10422	20866	31096	58578	70196	71142	–	–
								97482	104990
								100593	108391
								51530	60348
	2.45	3.90	5.75	5.97	3.20	3.23	3.49	3.53	–
	2.30	3.70	3.86	3.84	2.04	2.08	2.06	2.01	2.03
138.24	473.52	944.13	1846.28	3910.53	6100.23	7201.96	7856.56	9443.37	10140.91
		238.32	768.50	1664.43	2599.60	3075.08	3237.50		
23.93	67.64	96.02	134.34	215.17	305.39	317.40	272.42	343.06	361.66
67.36	220.37	414.74	847.47	1637.45	2307.00	2569.22	2829.31	3265.22	3530.67
46.95	185.51	433.38	864.47	2057.90	3487.84	4315.34	4754.83	5835.09	6248.58
2666	8773	16855	28900	57947	85919	98967	106302	106416	110199
30.60	112.76	305.95	857.00	1987.44	3498.42	4363.58	–	–	–
0.52	3.24	13.57	38.28	68.08	102.52	97.54	–	–	–
14.62	46.26	73.14	362.05	677.28	1217.39	1441.82	–	–	–
2.05	45.35	67.72	352.27	667.35	1147.87	1317.64	–	–	–
13.94	63.27	219.24	456.67	1242.08	2178.51	2824.22	–	–	–
2.18	16.46	50.53	121.09	484.50	1014.14	1232.57	1369.35	1576.93	1707.63
12.40	16.99	49.05	106.15	266.13	614.32	677.21	752.82	874.19	906.08
8.20	19.63	54.72	120.66	336.80	658.20	834.06	1018.32	1197.32	1288.80
	53.49	112.35	231.34	527.70	959.33	1134.93	1240.20	1419.58	1369.16
	39.55	72.54	144.20	309.87	494.43	745.63	755.63	–	–
	13.94	39.80	87.14	217.82	464.90	389.30	484.58	–	–

3-1 续表 1 continued 1

指标	Indicators	单位 Unit	1978 年
金融保险	Finance and Insurance		
金融机构人民币存款余额	RMB Deposits Balance of Financial Institutions	亿元 (100 million yuan)	15.43
# 住户存款	Deposits of Households	亿元 (100 million yuan)	1.14
金融机构人民币贷款余额	RMB Loans Balance of Financial Institutions	亿元 (100 million yuan)	14.08
# 短期贷款	Short-term Loans	亿元 (100 million yuan)	–
保险金额	Insured Amount	亿元 (100 million yuan)	
保费收入	Premium Income	万元 (10 000 yuan)	
赔付支出	Claim Payment	万元 (10 000 yuan)	
农业	Agriculture		
农林牧渔业总产值	Gross Output Value of Farming Forestry,Animal Husbandry and Fishery	亿元 (100 million yuan)	6.57
农用机械总动力	total power of agricultural machinery	万千瓦 (10 000kw)	69.70
年末实有耕地面积	Actural cultivated Area at Year-end	千公顷 (1000 ha)	373.19
粮食总产量	Total Output of Grain	万吨 (10 000 tons)	115.38
蔬菜总产量	Total Output of Vegetable	万吨 (10 000 tons)	49.19
肉类总产量	Total Output of meat	万吨 (10 000 tons)	2.50
奶类总产量	Total Output of Milk	万吨 (10 000 tons)	0.40
棉花总产量	Total Output of Cotton	万吨 (10 000 tons)	0.51
规模以上工业	Industry Enterprises above Designated Size		
单位数	Number of Enterprises	个 (unit)	1319
工业总产值	Gross Industrial Output Value	亿元 (100 million yuan)	37.67
营业收入	Revenue from Principal Business	亿元 (100 million yuan)	31.39
利税总额	Total Profits and Taxes	亿元 (100 million yuan)	6.80
利润总额	Total Profits	亿元 (100 million yuan)	3.88
资产总计	Total Assets	亿元 (100 million yuan)	25.68
所有者权益	Owner's Equities	亿元 (100 million yuan)	7.47
建筑业	Construction		
资质以上企业个数	Number of Qualification Enterprises	个 (unit)	10
建筑业总产值	Gross Output Value of Construction Enterprises	亿元 (100 million yuan)	0.68
施工面积	Floor Space under Construction	万平方米 (10 000 sq.m)	
竣工面积	Floor Space of Completed	万平方米 (10 000 sq.m)	49
其中：住宅	Residential	万平方米 (10 000 sq.m)	
交通运输	Transport		
货运量	Freight Traffic		
铁路	Railways	万吨 (10 000 tons)	2191
公路	Highways	万吨 (10 000 tons)	1670
航空	Airways	万吨 (10 000 tons)	

1990 年	1995 年	2000 年	2005 年	2010 年	2015 年	2017 年	2018 年	2019 年	2020 年
117.95	438.01	1274.96	3483.34	7510.44	14174.72	15957.74	16571.87	18303.20	20714.97
51.08	222.06	463.04	1024.42	2187.68	3951.42	4465.73	5008.08	6438.09	7584.12
124.76	337.26	1069.31	3259.86	6319.09	11356.78	12883.66	14700.07	17624.21	19704.88
98.50	239.31	527.31	1240.49	1898.61	2692.81	2929.73	2865.97	3400.21	3829.14
						162712	256399	438422	927748
						3810660	4155535	5322643	6280398
						886699	1033980	1219250	1603108
36.92	114.07	154.30	230.46	361.24	493.04	505.08	514.90	637.30	671.66
183.40	241.20	349.47	426.76	509.68	584.98	442.90	454.62	543.48	543.48
347.56	339.30	333.72	366.99	362.30	358.57	355.66	353.65	353.65	426.04
181.47	252.48	240.27	260.11	289.43	264.55	255.57	251.42	285.46	290.81
126.09	253.54	405.95	529.37	572.05	626.23	591.63	527.22	671.24	673.73
11.38	28.68	31.82	37.93	31.79	34.18	32.50	29.82	35.86	23.92
1.87	3.48	7.09	19.61	31.20	23.27	26.36	32.84	32.13	41.43
5.00	2.91	2.73	3.55	2.94	0.74	0.20	0.29	0.54	0.42
2008	2648	1038	1670	2021	2021	2051	1889	2153	2215
174.89	526.48	680.04	2237.51	4485.61	5339.97	5770.91	4992.28	5839.18	6765.08
136.29	432.17	629.72	2142.84	4497.17	5417.16	5810.16	5192.15	6512.66	7575.34
15.57	53.59	64.62	244.61	584.53	685.71	686.80	535.39	545.70	659.87
3.23	16.30	21.69	131.30	339.76	396.13	415.23	307.98	310.86	423.31
125.25	578.55	958.10	1868.06	3904.42	4987.76	6319.64	5892.64	6663.13	7724.85
36.82	180.86	363.37	630.06	1481.75	2159.78	2268.27	2386.75	2743.28	2967.31
46	141	569	737	739	463	504	507	895	1033
12.56	58.78	141.92	462.65	894.30	1663.83	2218.93	2823.47	3513.98	3748.12
269	1030	1611	3298	4655	10189	11363	12984	14955	17090
170	306	701	1400	1306	2039	2280	2366	3418	3323
77	141	396	884	773	1178	1258	1502	2170	1916
3416	3877	5168	7211	9913	15794	17865	18728	20870	23189
3970	6182	7024	8484	13029	20419	24058	25571	28064	28177
	0.4	1.3	2.0	3.4	4.2	5.0	5.6	6.7	14.7

3-1 续表 2 continued 2

指标	Indicators	单位 Unit	1978 年
客运量	Passenger Traffic		
铁路	Railways	万人 (10 000 persons)	1302
公路	Highways	万人 (10 000 persons)	505
航空	Airways	万人 (10 000 persons)	
民用汽车拥有量	Possession of Private Vehicles	辆 (unit)	1684
# 载客	Passenger Vehicles	辆 (unit)	1353
# 载货	Trucks	辆 (unit)	224
邮电通信	**Post and Telecommunication Services**		
固定电话	Fixed Telephone	万户 (10 000 households)	2.68
# 城市	Urban	万户 (10 000 households)	2.27
移动电话	Mobile Telephone	万户 (10 000 households)	
互联网用户	Internet Broad Band	万户 (10 000 households)	
国内贸易	**Domestic Trade**		
社会消费品零售总额	Total Retail Sales of Consumer Goods	亿元 (100 million yuan)	8.13
# 批发零售业	Wholesale and Retail Trade	亿元 (100 million yuan)	7.07
# 餐饮业	Catering Services	亿元 (100 million yuan)	0.29
对外经济和国际旅游	**Foreign Economy and Trade,Tourism**		
全年货物进出口总额（海关）	Total Value of Imports and Exports（Customs）	万美元 (10 000 USD)	
进口	Imports	万美元 (10 000 USD)	
出口	Exports	万美元 (10 000 USD)	
全年货物进出口总额	Total Value of Imports and Exports	亿元 (100 million yuan)	
进口	Imports	亿元 (100 million yuan)	
出口	Exports	亿元 (100 million yuan)	
全年实际使用外资	Total Amount of Foreign Capital Actually Utilized	万美元 (10 000 USD)	
全年实现合同外资	Total Amount of Contracted Foreign Capital	万美元 (10 000 USD)	
入境游客人数	International Tourists	人 (person)	
外国人	Foreigners	人 (person)	
港澳台同胞	Compatriots from Hong Kong Macao and Taiwan	人 (person)	
国际旅游（外汇）收入	Foreign Exchange Earnings	亿美元 (100 million USD)	
教育	**Education**		
普通高等学校在校生	Total Enrollment of Regular Institutions of Higher Education	万人 (10 000 persons)	1.09
普通高等学校专任教师	Full-time Teachers of Regular Institutions of Higher Education	人 (person)	2947
中等专业学校在校生	Total Enrollment of Secondary Professional Schools	万人 (10 000 persons)	0.68
中等专业学校专任教师	Full-time Teachers of Secondary Professional Schools	人 (person)	1020
普通中学在校生	Total Enrollment of Regular Senior Secondary Schools	万人 (10 000 persons)	30.61
普通中学专任教师	Full-time Teachers of Regular Senior Secondary Schools	人 (person)	19275
小学在校生	Total Enrollment of Regular Primary Schools	万人 (10 000 persons)	60.91
小学专任教师	Full-time Teachers of Regular Primary Schools	人 (person)	24926
文化	**Culture**		
图书馆藏书量	Number of Books in Library	万册 (10 000 copies)	341.0
图书出版种数	Number of Publication	种 (kind)	389
图书量	Books	万册 (10 000 copies)	20166
报纸量	Newspapers	万册 (10 000 copies)	25055
杂志量	Magazines	万份 (10 000 copies)	2209

1990 年	1995 年	2000 年	2005 年	2010 年	2015 年	2017 年	2018 年	2019 年	2020 年
1438	1519	1693	1924	3327	10681	13412	14548	15745	9797
1801	2611	4530	5364	12758	3663	3192	3149	3244	1209
2.6	37.0	62.0	140.0	379.2	533.1	785.6	894.1	936.1	1238.5
39748	86766	129204	347687	807378	1541045	1949707	2160748	2584278	2794278
26032	33968	68625	196415	627849	1400588	1783848	1978951	2370437	2556622
12141	47790	56627	71588	117994	123801	151141	166277	194957	224713
9.87	39.18	106.34	258.90	213.30	165.30	153.10	135.27	148.82	144.78
9.12	36.48	83.08	206.30	177.40	141.00	132.55	118.70	136.30	127.65
	2.3	60.8	239.0	857.6	1090.4	971.1	1013.7	1122.9	1154.1
		11.57	74.34	117.30	231.66	298.75	344.70	392.62	445.48
52.82	183.76	344.45	772.65	1725.46	3141.04	3752.52	4091.08	4420.41	4469.13
38.20	134.53	228.75	657.55	1402.27	2648.44	3165.82	3452.14	3760.47	3857.01
2.56	13.35	37.76	108.44	308.11	473.23	563.82	614.10	632.37	586.62
	66587	143935	376213	743776	911424	1130449	1318209	1630123	1998749
	29812	143935	198370	338888	311763	379887	463119	695064	909323
	36775	143935	177843	404888	599661	750562	855090	935059	1089426
						708.1	825.0	1103.3	1382.7
						257.1	305.7	480.8	627.6
						451.0	519.3	622.5	755.0
	25294	31981	54158	104011	157851	187623	272847	224249	192456
	47449	44074	112072	120903	303100	218692	556119	683441	585244
20583	54468	103990	120164	230985	332942	375469	398721	456585	108524
12705	30011	40990	69762	153327	205477	232260	247086	285071	90926
7878	24457	63000	50402	77658	127465	143209	151635	171514	17700
0.15	0.19	0.32	0.42	1.14	1.84	2.08	2.23	2.75	0.33
3.73	5.66	9.30	38.04	50.53	53.62	54.44	79.63	76.20	89.85
7245	7500	8267	18434	26870	30873	32559	37539	40627	42202
2.51	4.79	5.75	4.79	2.12	1.57	1.28	5.16	5.68	6.28
2890	2890	2916	1578	1334	763	716	3711	4058	3642
22.45	27.15	33.82	30.91	30.18	30.16	30.56	31.18	39.35	39.84
16065	17621	20585	21915	21943	23643	25676	26588	34177	34796
47.57	49.23	41.40	37.88	38.40	41.44	44.66	46.66	54.14	57.01
26922	27417	27417	25201	24801	25795	29109	30605	36067	37219
476.0	524.6	591.7	725.1	941.2	1195.0	1363.3	1442.3	–	–
2001	2603	3851	5389	6586	10234	12364	–	–	–
31685	39025	38471	27919	26603	43860	45501	–	–	–
46930	54460	109199	113751	184706	136480	99089	–	–	–
3321	4579	11177	7195	6995	8572	7809	–	–	–

3-1 续表 3 continued 3

指标	Indicators	单位 Unit	1978 年
卫生	Public Health		
卫生机构数	Number of Health Institutions	个 (unit)	1017
# 医院及卫生院	Hospitals and Township Hospitals	个 (unit)	148
卫生机构床位数	Number of Beds	张 (bed)	11496
# 医院及卫生院	Hospitals and Township Hospitals	张 (bed)	9856
卫生工作人员	Medical Personnel	人 (person)	24949
# 卫生技术人员	Medical Technical Personnel	人 (person)	19198
人民生活	People's Livelihood		
城镇居民人均可支配收入	Per Capita Disposable Income of Urban Residents	元 (yuan)	337.8
城镇居民人均生活消费支出	Per Capita Life Consumption Expenditure of Urban Residents	元 (yuan)	317.9
# 食品	Food	元 (yuan)	181.6
农村居民人均可支配收入	Per Capita Disposable Income of Rural Residents	元 (yuan)	110.5
农村居民人均生活消费支出	Per Capita Life Consumption Expenditure of Rural Residents	元 (yuan)	83.2
# 食品	Food	元 (yuan)	58.2
农民人均住宅居住面积	Rural Residential Area Per Capita	平方米 (sq.m)	9.6
社会治安	Public security		
交通事故起数	Number of Traffic Accidents	起 (case)	
交通事故死伤人数	Deaths and Injuries from Traffic Accidents	人 (person)	
交通事故损失折款	Property Losses from Traffic Accidents	万元 (10 000 yuan)	
火灾事故起数	Number of Fire Accidents	起 (case)	
火灾事故死伤人数	Deaths and Injuries from Fire Accidents	人 (person)	
火灾事故损失折款	Property Losses from Fire Accidents	万元 (10 000 yuan)	

注：1.“职工平均工资”2006 年以前为在岗职工口径，2006 年及以后为法人单位在岗职工口径。
2.“市内十区建成区面积”，2018 年为市内八区口径，2017 年以前为市内七区口径，2015 年以前为市内六区口径。
3. 工业统计指标 1997 年及以前统计口径为乡及乡以上工业企业，1998 年及以后为全部国有及年销售收入 500 万元以上工业企业，2011 年及以后为年主营业务收入 2000 万元及以上工业法人单位。
4. 货运量、客运量中的“铁路”指标，2013 年 3 月铁路系统改革，铁路系统统计数据按新口径执行；“公路指标”自 2014 年起交通部门执行新的公路运输量统计方案，调查范围较老口径有所缩小，2014 年及 2013 年数据均为新口径下交通部反馈数据。
5. 从 2015 年起，全市居民收支调查指标采用新口径。“农村居民人均可支配收入”2014 年以前为农民人均纯收入口径；“农村居民人均生活消费支出”2014 年以前为农民人均生活费支出口径。
6. 规模以上工业“营业收入”，2018 年以前为“主营业务收入”口径。
7.“年末常住总人口”2020 年为第七次全国人口普查数据，调查时点为 2020 年 11 月 1 日零时。以下各表同。

1990 年	1995 年	2000 年	2005 年	2010 年	2015 年	2017 年	2018 年	2019 年	2020 年
1300	1185	1414	2138	5086	5947	5770	6030	7487	7514
178	216	231	246	277	269	289	293	351	343
18214	20747	21698	24695	31947	49311	54855	57460	66623	68831
17216	19534	20830	23524	29844	45195	50142	51207	59697	62072
41444	43648	45166	41499	54711	89117	97663	104347	122370	126681
31130	32848	35669	34129	39366	71778	76273	82834	97532	102172
1619.5	4720.6	8471.3	13578.5	25321.1	39888.7	46642.4	50146.5	51912.6	53328.6
1360.1	3830.4	6891.8	9226.6	15973.3	26318.7	30728.6	32977.1	33438.7	34390.8
781.6	1823.6	2387.1	3046.9	5051.2	6415.0	7229.3	7758.0	7956.3	8071.9
731.1	1812.7	3046.8	4812.3	8903.3	14231.8	16593.8	17924.4	19454.2	20432.1
569.8	1373.6	1976.8	2902.8	5406.6	8597.2	10327.3	11172.3	12300.3	12946.9
287.7	770.8	860.0	1134.8	1818.3	2775.5	3253.2	3409.0	3702.6	3931.3
22.5	24.7	28.6	33.8	40.2	52.6	55.2	54.3	51.1	50.3
509	1231	1306	911	774	2946	3075	3071	3334	3313
518	1345	1364	1186	1121	3885	3219	3618	3925	3747
64	369	357	316	189	840	1020	947	905	1006
309	110	1281	1071	791	2609	1752	1539	4577	4319
67	87	26	3	9	12	11	12	12	16
166	925	471	76	462	1571	599	827	1529	2153

Note: 1. The average salary of employees is the caliber data of employees in the post before 2006, and the caliber data of employees in the legal entity in 2006 and later.

2. "The area of the built-up area in the eight districts of the city", before 2017 adopts the statistical scale of the seven districts in the city, six districts in the city before 2015, and eight districts in the city in 2018.

3. Industrial statistical indicators In 1997 and before, the statistical caliber was industrial enterprises at or above the township level. In 1998 and after, they were all state-owned and with an annual sales income of more than 5 million yuan. In 2011 and beyond, the annual main business income was 20 million yuan and above industrial enterprises legal entities.

4. The "railway" indicator in freight volume and passenger volume, the railway system reform in March 2013, the railway system statistics are implemented according to the new caliber; the "road indicators" since 2014, the transportation department has implemented a new road traffic statistics program. The scope of the survey has been narrower than that of the old one. The data for 2014 and 2013 are the feedback data of the Ministry of Communications under the new caliber.

5. Starting from 2015, the city's residents' income and expenditure survey indicators adopt a new caliber. "per capita disposable income of Rural Residents" was the "per capita net income of Rural Residents" before 2014; "Per capita consumption expenditure of Rural Residents"was the "per capita living expenses of farmers" before 2014.

6."Main operating revenue" of industrial enterprises above designated size adopts the statistical scale of "main operating revenue" before 2018.

7. "Total resident population at the end of year 2020" is subject to the data from the 7th National Population Census as at 0:00, November 1, 2020. (the same below) .

3-2 国民经济和社会发展比例和效益指标
Indicators on Proportions and Efficiency in National Economic and Social Development

指标	Indicators	单位 Unit	1978 年	1985 年
人口	Population			
申报出生率	Birth Rate	‰	15.53	11.39
申报死亡率	Death Rate	‰	7.00	6.52
自然增长率	Natural Growth Rate	‰	8.53	4.87
就业	Employment			
就业者负担人口	Dependency of Employed Population	人 (person)	2.21	1.99
三次产业从业者比例	Composition of Employed Population			
第一产业	Primary Industry	%	66.8	47.5
第二产业	Secondary Industry	%	22.6	31.0
第三产业	Tertiary Industry	%	10.6	21.5
城镇登记失业率	Registered Unemployment Rate in Urban Areas	%		
国民经济核算	National Accounting			
三次产业增加值比例	Composition of Gross Domestic Product			
第一产业	Primary Industry	%		21.1
第二产业	Secondary Industry	%		51.8
第三产业	Tertiary Industry	%		27.1
人均生产总值	Per Capita GDP	元 (yuan)		1263
资本形成率（投资率）	Capital Formation Rate	%		
最终消费率（消费率）	Final Consumption Rate	%		
固定资产投资	Investment in Fixed Assets			
固定资产投资占生产总值比重	Proportion of Fixed Assets Investment in GDP	%		23.7
财政	Finance			
一般公共预算收入占生产总值比重	Proportion of General Public Budget Revenue in GDP	%	25.2	14.5
一般公共预算支出占生产总值比重	Proportion of General Public Budget Expenditure in GDP	%	6.3	5.6
农业	Agriculture			
人均耕地面积	Per Cultivated Area	亩 (mu)	1.24	1.10
每公顷耕地化肥施用量（折纯）	Consumption of Chemical Fertilizers per Hectare	千克 (kg)		225
每公顷播种面积粮食产量	Grain Yield Per Hectare of Sown Area	千克 (kg)	2475	3864
机耕率	Machine-cultivated Rate	%		

1990 年	1995 年	2000 年	2010 年	2015 年	2017 年	2018 年	2019 年	2020 年
12.88	10.03	11.08	11.13	11.82	17.83	14.57	12.86	10.45
6.54	6.32	7.05	8.35	6.73	9.86	6.98	6.62	7.31
6.34	3.71	4.03	2.78	5.09	7.96	7.59	6.24	3.14
1.94	1.67	1.62	1.62	1.61	1.34	1.4	1.5	1.3
46.5	35.8	31.7	20.5	18.5	17.1	16.4	15.7	
32.4	32.9	31.9	32.2	32.1	31.9	31.5	31.3	
21.1	31.3	36.4	47.3	49.4	51.0	52.1	52.9	
	2.45	3.70	3.84	2.04	2.08	2.06	2.01	2.03
17.3	14.3	10.0	5.5	5.0	4.4	3.5	3.6	3.6
48.7	46.5	43.9	41.9	37.8	35.7	36.0	34.6	34.8
34.0	39.2	46.1	52.6	57.2	59.9	60.5	61.8	61.6
2666	8773	16999	57966	85919	98967	106302	106416	110199
39.1	39.5	40.2	52.6	63.0	66.8	–	–	–
37.8	41.9	56.9	46.9	52.3	52.5	–	–	–
22.1	23.8	32.1	50.8	57.3	60.6	–	–	–
9.0	3.6	5.2	15.2	10.1	9.4	9.6	9.3	8.9
5.9	4.1	5.8	16.9	10.8	11.6	13.0	12.7	12.7
1.00	0.94	0.88	0.90	0.87	0.83	0.82		
330	569	641	646	626	589	564		
4273	5512	5354	6192	6117	5660	5659	5956	6053
					87.3	96.7	92.0	

3-2 续表 continued

指标	Indicators	单位 Unit	1978 年	1985 年
规模以上工业	**Industry Enterprises above Designated Size**			
产品销售率	Product Sales Rate	%		
总资产贡献率	Total Asset Contribution Rate	%		
流动资产周转次数	Turnover of Current Asset	次 (times)		
邮电通讯业	**Post and Telecommunication Services**			
每百人拥有电话机	Number of phones Per 100 Population	部 (unit)	0.60	1.26
国内商业	**Domestic Commerce**			
人均消费品零售总额	Total Sales of Consumption Good Per Capita	元 (yuan)	182	500
教育	**Education**			
学龄儿童入学率	School-age Children Enrollment Rate	%		99.44
学校教师负担人数	Teacher-student Ratio	人 (person)	21.28	16.75
高等教育	Higher Education	人 (person)	2.47	6.55
中等教育	Secondary Education	人 (person)	16.65	14.46
小学	Primary Schools	人 (person)	34.99	20.33
卫生	**Public Health**			
每万人拥有医院卫生院数	Number of Health Institutes per 10000 Population	个 (unit)	0.33	0.34
每万人拥有医生数	Number of Doctors per 10000 Population	人 (person)	23.3	26.3
每万人拥有医院床位数	Number of Hospitals Beds per 10000 Population	张 (bed)	22.0	28.2
市政建设	**City Construction**			
城市人口用水普及率	Coverage Rate of Water Supply	%	99.0	100.0
城市用气普及率	Coverage Rate of Natural Gas Supply	%	17.8	26.3
建成区绿化覆盖率	Coverage Rate of Urban Green Areas	%	12.0	23.0
生活	**Life**			
城镇居民恩格尔系数	Engel's Coefficient of Urban Residents	%	57.1	56.5
农村居民恩格尔系数	Engel's Coefficient of Rural Residents	%	69.9	51.8

注：1. “一般公共预算收入占生产总值比重”2012 年 (含) 以前为“地方财政收入”口径；“一般公共预算支出占生产总值比重”2012 年 (含) 以前为“地方财政支出”口径。
2. 由于第三次全国土地调查数据未反馈，“人均耕地面积”“每公顷耕地化肥施用量”相关数据空缺。

1990 年	1995 年	2000 年	2010 年	2015 年	2017 年	2018 年	2019 年	2020 年
	97.12	98.24	98.71	98.23	98.40	97.50	96.80	–
	12.25	8.45	15.98	13.37	17.63	9.93	8.90	9.11
	1.69	1.52	2.11	1.82	1.62	1.38	1.65	1.61
1.89	7.23	18.98	35.31	26.48	23.99	20.82	18.81	18.06
1009	3389	6149	27343	50369	58797	62963	55882	55744
99.03	99.40	99.93	100.00	100.00	100.00	100.00	100.00	100.00
14.20	15.60	15.24	17.40	17.37	17.09	16.68	15.44	16.58
5.15	7.55	11.25	21.76	22.53	23.79	21.21	18.76	21.29
12.99	15.30	16.78	14.72	13.33	12.04	12.87	12.71	11.00
17.67	18.20	15.10	15.48	16.07	15.35	15.25	15.01	15.32
0.34	0.40	0.41	0.46	0.43	0.45	0.45	0.44	0.43
29.2	27.9	29.5	29.1	46.0	39.7	43.1	43.0	43.7
32.9	36.0	38.6	52.9	69.1	74.9	77.0	74.8	74.8
100.0	100.0	100.0	100.0	99.00	99.64	99.78	100.00	100.00
45.7	72.2	90.7	95.5	97.73	99.85	99.87	99.97	100.00
30.0	30.5	36.1	36.9	39.94	40.57	40.52	41.18	40.68
57.5	47.6	34.6	31.6	24.4	23.5	23.5	23.8	23.5
50.5	56.1	43.5	33.6	32.3	31.5	30.5	30.1	30.4

Notes:1. "The proportion of general public budget revenue in total output value" was the caliber of "local financial revenue" before 2012 (inclusive); "The proportion of general public budget expenditure in total output value" was the caliber of "local financial expenditure"

2. Because the third national land survery data have not been released, the data of "arable land per capita" and "fertilizers per hectare of cultivated land" are blank.

3-3 平均每天主要社会经济活动
Selected Indicators on Average Daily Social and Economic Activities

指标	Indicators	单位 Unit	1978 年	1985 年
每天创造的财富				
地区生产总值（当年价）	Gross Domestic Product	万元 (10 000 yuan)	646	1682
第一产业	Primary Industry	万元 (10 000 yuan)	114	354
第二产业	Secondary Industry	万元 (10 000 yuan)	365	872
第三产业	Tertiary Industry	万元 (10 000 yuan)	167	456
一般公共预算收入	General Pubilic Budget Revenue	万元 (10 000 yuan)	163	244
一般公共预算支出	General Pubilic Budget Expenditure	万元 (10 000 yuan)	41	94
固定资产投资	Investment in Fixed Assets	万元 (10 000 yuan)		399
每天生产主要工、农业产品	**Production of Major Industrial Product and Agricultural Products on Average Daily**			
粮食	Grain	吨 (ton)	3161	4479
棉花	Cotton	吨 (ton)	14	136.2
蔬菜	Vegetables	吨 (ton)	1348	2304
猪肉	Pork	吨 (ton)	67	138
奶类	Milk	吨 (ton)	11	23
钢材	Steel	吨 (ton)	689	1197
发电量	Electric Energy Capacity	万千瓦时 (10 000 kwh)	347	724
水泥	Cement	吨 (ton)	2399	3699
化肥	Chemical Fertilizer	吨 (ton)	494	313
金切机床	Metal-cutting Machine Tools	台 (unit)	10	18
汽车	Motor Vehicles	辆 (unit)	12	31
服务器	Server	台 (unit)	-	-
布	Cloth	万米 (10 000 m)	38	50

1990 年	1995 年	2000 年	2010 年	2015 年	2017 年	2018 年	2019 年	2020 年
3787	12973	26087	107138	167130	197314	215248	258722	277074
656	1853	2603	5895	8367	8696	7464	9399	9881
1845	6257	11469	44862	63205	70390	77515	89458	96466
1286	5082	12015	56381	95557	118228	130269	159865	170726
339	465	1344	7291	16831	18554	20625	23950	24757
224	537	1499	9227	18032	22851	27899	32803	35213
838	3089	8382	54450	95847	119550			
4972	6917	6583	7930	7248	7002	6888	7820	7946
137	79.7	74.7	81	20.2	5.5	8	15	12
3455	6946	14733	16478	17157	16209	14444	18390	18408
215	390	478	597	508	460	425	467	350
51	95	194	855	638	722	900	880	1132
1576	2856	6507	26857	19852	11226	6118	61793	63839
1225	1884	1898	3601	4818	4387	4189	8086	7560
5796	11644	13291	19994	21411	16561	16557	35283	36290
396	384	778	1345	644	575	569	463	577
14	11	8	6	10	16	16	20	29
17	16	8	581	263	553	636	481	1077
–	–	–	271	1112	1547	2729	3192	3921
55	41	45	22	44	45	11	11	3

3-3 续表 continued

指标	Indicators	单位 Unit	1978 年	1985 年
每天其他经济活动	**Other Economic Activity on Average Daily**			
最终消费量	Final Consumption	万元 (10 000 yuan)		780
居民消费	Households Expense	万元 (10 000 yuan)		638
农业居民	Rural Households	万元 (10 000 yuan)		367
城镇居民	Urban Households	万元 (10 000 yuan)		271
政府消费	Government Expense	万元 (10 000 yuan)		142
社会消费品零售总额	Total Sales of Consumption Good Per Capita	万元 (10 000 yuan)	261	640
公路货运量	Highways Freight Traffic	万吨 (10 000 tons)	3.2	6.9
公路客运量	Highways Passenger Traffic	万人 (10 000 persons)	1.4	3.1
自来水供水量	Water Supply	万吨 (10 000 tons)	36.9	40
用电量	Electricity Consumption	万千瓦时 (10 000 kwh)	754	747
市内公共车辆乘客人数	Number of City Bus Passengers	万人次 (10 000 person-times)	34.0	62.2
实际使用外资额	Total Amount of Foreign Capital Actually Utilized	万美元 (10 000 USD)		
港澳台及外国来济旅游人数	Compatriots from Hong Kong Macao and Taiwan	人 (person)		27
每天人口变动和婚姻	**Daily Population Changes and Marriages**			
出生	Birth	人 (person)	191	152
死亡	Death	人 (person)	86	87
结婚	Marriages	对 (couple)		
离婚	Divorces	对 (couple)		

注：1. “一般公共预算收入” 指标 1978 年到 1995 年为 “地方财政收入” 口径，“一般公共预算支出” 指标 1978 年到 1995 年为 “地方财政支出” 口径。
2. 按照国家统计局经济普查年度数据使用规定，部分涉及国民经济核算的指标数据空缺。

1990 年	1995 年	2000 年	2010 年	2015 年	2017 年	2018 年	2019 年	2020 年
1580	5524	14833	50253	87412	103538	–	–	–
1274	4567	11098	39460	55221	76801	–	–	–
624	1938	3596	5142	7120	9878	–	–	–
650	2629	7502	34317	48101	66923	–	–	–
306	957	3735	10794	32192	26737	–	–	–
1447	5151	9718	49382	93433	113593	120670	121107	122107
10.9	16.9	19.2	35.7	55.9	65.9	70.1	76.7	76.5
4.9	7.2	12.4	35.0	10.0	8.7	8.6	8.9	3.3
45.3	57.5	76.7	64.5	87.2	98.3	107.5	121.8	123.0
1255	1779	2505	6713.3	7238.5	7569.5	7790.8	11350.8	11855.2
73.3	73.3	125.9	296.1	256.5	248.0	245.5	232.1	144.8
8.5	69.3	87.6	285.0	432.5	514.0	747.5	614.4	524.6
56	149	285	633	912.2	1029	1092.0	1251.0	298.0
183	148	170	184	202	312	259	279	229
93	94	108	138	115	172	124	144	160
103	137	120	153	138	144	141	143	138
	17	20	50	70	89	87	98	100

Notes: 1. The indicator–"general public budget revenue" was the caliber of "local financial revenue" from 1978 to 1995 and the indicator–"general public budget expenditure" was the caliber of "local fiscal expenditure" from 1978 to 1995.

2. Part of index data regarding national economic accounting is missing according to economic census year data use provisions of National Bureau of Statistics.

3-4 国民经济人均指标
Per Indicators of National Economic

指标	Indicator	单位 Unit	1978 年	1985 年
地区生产总值	**Gross Domestic Product**	元 (yuan)	527	1263
主要农产品产量	**Output of Major Agricultural Products**			
粮食	Grain	千克 (kg)	258	336
棉花	Cotton	千克 (kg)	1.14	10.22
猪肉	Pork	千克 (kg)	5.44	10.33
水果	Fruits	千克 (kg)	12.65	14.70
禽蛋	Eggs	千克 (kg)		
蔬菜	Vagatables	千克 (kg)	109.84	173.02
牛奶	Milk	千克 (kg)	0.88	1.76
水产品	Aquatic Products	千克 (kg)	0.29	0.41
主要工业产品产量	**Output of Major Industrial Products**			
钢材	Steel	千克 (kg)	48.1	69.6
发电量	Electric Energy Capacity	千瓦小时 (kwh)	282.5	543.9
水泥	Cement	千克 (kg)	195.5	277.9
化肥	Chemical Fertilizer	千克 (kg)	29.5	18.7
服务器	Server	台 (unit)	–	–
布	Cloth	米 (m)	30.8	37.2
其他经济活动	**Other Economic Activity**			
社会消费品零售总额	Total Sales of Consumption Good Per Capita	元 (yuan)	182	500
一般公共预算收入	General Pubilic Budget Revenue	元 (yuan)	133	183
一般公共预算支出	General Pubilic Budget Expenditure	元 (yuan)	33	70
城乡居民人民币储蓄存款余额	RMB Deposits Balance of Urban and Rural Residents	元 (yuan)	33	236
城镇居民人均可支配收入	Per Capita Disposable Income of Urban Residents	元 (yuan)	338	732
城镇居民人均生活消费支出	Per Capita Life Consumption Expenditure of Urban Residents	元 (yuan)	318	704
农村居民人均可支配收入	Per Capita Disposable Income of Rural Residents	元 (yuan)	111	439
农村居民人均生活消费支出	Per Capita Life Consumption Expenditure of Rural Residents	元 (yuan)	83	330

注：1.“一般公共预算收入”指标 1978 年到 1995 年为“地方财政收入”口径。“一般公共预算支出”指标 1978 年到 1995 年为“地方财政支出”口径。
2. 从 2015 年起，全市发布城乡住户调查一体化改革新口径数据，居民收支调查指标与 2014 年前分别实施的城镇和农村住户调查的调查范围、方法、指标口径、名称有所不同。

1990 年	1995 年	2000 年	2010 年	2015 年	2017 年	2018 年	2019 年	2020 年
2666	8773	16999	57966	85919	98967	106302	106416	110199
350	468	429	479	424	400	340	322	321
9.64	5.38	4.87	4.87	2.36	1.49	0.39	0.61	0.47
15.13	26.33	31.15	36.10	36.46	32.13	20.97	19.22	14.14
12.88	35.81	66.56	78.58	61.89	59.29	57.08	70.93	69.79
18.27	41.29	74.29	59.68	56.86	51.83	44.96	41.22	30.33
243.10	469.77	960.06	996.29	1041.79	962.34	713.35	756.41	743.99
3.46	6.44	12.65	51.68	46.75	48.03	44.43	36.21	45.75
1.80	4.72	5.87	7.06	7.63	6.47	4.32	1.82	1.47
169.1	195.7	424.0	1623.8	1161.8	642.0	302.1	2541.7	2580.2
862.3	1237.0	1231.5	2177.5	2819.9	2508.9	2068.8	3326.0	3055.6
408.0	728.4	866.1	1208.9	1253.1	947.2	817.7	1451.2	1466.7
23.6	23.0	46.5	80.3	37.7	32.9	28.1	19.1	23.3
–	–	–	0.016	0.065	0.088	0.1	0.1	0.2
38.9	19.9	29.5	13.6	25.7	25.7	5.5	4.6	1.2
1009	3468	6332	25577	44243	51566	55353	49812	49352
239	315	876	4409	9850	10611	10186	9851	10006
158	363	977	5579	10553	13069	13778	13492	14232
985	4115	8266	36239	63358	70889	67761	72550	83750
1620	4721	8471	25321	39889	46642	50146	51913	53329
1369	3830	6892	15973	26319	30729	32977	33439	34391
731	1813	3047	8903	14232	16594	17924	19454	20432
570	1374	1977	5407	8597	10327	11172	12300	12947

Notes: 1. The indicator–"general public budget revenue" was the caliber of "local financial revenue" from 1978 to 1995 and the indicator–"general public budget expenditure" was the caliber of "local fiscal expenditure" from 1978 to 1995.

2. From 2015, new caliber data about urban and rural household survey integration reform was published by the city and the survey index of residents' income and expenditure was different from survey scope, method, indicator caliber and name of urban and rural residents implemented before 2014.

3-5 国民经济主要指标及占全国、全省比重（2020年）

Main Indicators of National Economy and Their Proportion in China and Shandong Province(2020)

指标	Indicator	单位 Unit	全国 Country
区划面积	Area	万平方公里 (10 000 sq.km)	960
年末总人口	Total year-end Population	万人 (10 000 persons)	141178
生产总值（当年价）	Gross Domestic Product	亿元 (100 million yuan)	1015986.0
第一产业	Primary Industry	亿元 (100 million yuan)	77754.0
第二产业	Secondary Industry	亿元 (100 million yuan)	384255.0
第三产业	Tertiary Industry	亿元 (100 million yuan)	553977.0
规模以上工业营业收入	Revenue from Business of Industrial Enterprises above Designated Size	亿元 (100 million yuan)	1061400.0
规模以上工业利润总额	Total Profits of Industrial Enterprises above Designated Size	亿元 (100 million yuan)	64516.1
粮食总产量	Total Output of Grain	万吨 (10 000 tons)	66949.0
棉花总产量	Total Output of Cotton	万吨 (10 000 tons)	591.0
固定资产投资额	Investment in Fixed Assets	亿元 (100 million yuan)	527270.0
公路货物周转量	Highways Freight Turnover	亿吨公里 (100 million ton-km)	196618
社会消费品零售总额	Total Sales of Consumption Good Per Capita	亿元 (100 million yuan)	391981.0
实际使用外资	Total Amount of Foreign Capital Actually Utilized	亿美元 (100 million USD)	1444.0
一般公共预算收入	General Pubilic Budget Revenue	亿元 (100 million yuan)	182895.0
一般公共预算支出	General Pubilic Budget Expenditure	亿元 (100 million yuan)	245588
普通本专科在校学生	Enrollment of Regular Institutions of Higher Educatio	万人 (10 000persons)	3285.3
中等职业教育在校学生	Enrollment of Secondary Professional Schools	万人 (10 000persons)	1663
卫生机构数	Number of Health Institutions	个 (unit)	1023000.0
卫生技术人员	Medical Technical Personnel	万人 (10 000persons)	1066.0
# 执业（助理）医师	Licensed Doctors	万人 (10 000persons)	408
城镇居民人均可支配收入	Per Capita Life Consumption Expenditure of Urban Residents	元 (yuan)	43834
农村居民人均可支配收入	Per Capita Disposable Income of Rural Residents	元 (yuan)	17131

全省 Province	济南 Ji'nan	济南占全国比重 (%) Ji'nan Account for Proportion of Country(%)	济南占全省比重 (%) Ji'nan Account for Proportion of Province(%)
15.8	1.0244	0.11	6.49
10152.7	920.2	0.65	9.06
73129.0	10140.91	1.00	13.87
5363.8	361.66	0.47	6.74
28612.2	3530.67	0.92	12.34
39153.1	6248.58	1.13	15.96
84270.4	7387.8	0.70	8.77
4282.9	407.3	0.63	9.51
5446.8	290.80	0.43	5.34
18.3	0.4	0.07	2.19
6784.40	562.40	0.29	8.29
29248.0	4469.1	1.14	15.28
176.5	19.2	1.33	10.88
6560.0	906.1	0.50	13.81
11231.2	1288.8	0.52	11.48
229.2	89.9	2.73	39.20
78	6.3	0.38	8.08
84885.0	7514.0	0.73	8.85
81.4	10.2	0.96	12.53
32.90	4.00	0.98	12.16
43726	53329		
18753	20432		

主要统计指标解释

几点说明：

1. 生产总值及一、二、三次产业增加值，历史数据有所调整，以本年鉴所列数据为准。

2. 生产总值及一、二、三次产业增加值，全部工业增加值，农业总产值等指标的增长速度均以可比价格计算。

3. 由于国家在1994 年开始财税体制改革，1994 年及以后各年的财政收支与以前年份不可比。另外，2000 年财政收入统计口径也有微调。

4. 工业统计口径调整。1998年以前工业统计范围为乡及乡以上独立核算工业企业，1998年，统计范围调整为规模以上工业，即全部国有及年销售收入500万元以上的非国有工业单位，2011年，调整为年主营业务收入2000万元以上。

5. 建筑业统计范围变化。建筑业统计范围1994-1995 年为县及县以上单位，1996-1997年为资质等级四级及以上独立核算建筑业企业，1998 年起为资质等级五级及以上独立核算建筑业企业。

企业（单位）登记注册类型 是以在工商行政管理机关登记注册的具有法人资格的各类企业为划分对象。行政机关、事业单位和社会团体及其他经济组织参照执行。

本项以工商行政管理部门对企业（单位）登记注册的类型为依据，将企业（单位）登记注册类型分为以下几种：

（1）国有企业是指企业全部资产归国家所有，并按《中华人民共和国企业法人登记管理条例》规定登记注册的非公司制的经济组织。不包括有限责任公司中的国有独资公司。

（2）集体企业是指企业资产归集体所有，并按《中华人民共和国企业法人登记管理条例》规定登记注册的经济组织。

（3）股份合作企业是指以合作制为基础，由企业职工共同出资入股，吸收一定比例的社会资产投资组建，实行自主经营，自负盈亏，共同劳动，民主管理，按劳分配与按股分红相结合的一种集体经济组织。

（4）联营企业是指两个及两个以上相同或不同所有制性质的企业法人或事业单位法人，按自愿、平等、互利的原则，共同投资组成的经济组织。

联营企业包括国有联营企业、集体联营企业、国有与集体联营企业和其他联营企业。

（5）有限责任公司是指根据《中华人民共和国登记管理条例》规定登记注册，由两个以上，五十个以下的股东共同出资，每个股东以其所认缴的出资额对公司承担有限责任，公司以其全部资产对其债务承担责任的经济组织。

有限责任公司包括国有独资公司以及其他有限责任公司。

①国有独资公司是指国家授权的投资机构或者国家授权的部门单独投资设立的有限责任公司。

②其他有限责任公司是指国有独资公司以外的其他有限责任公司。

（6）股份有限公司是指根据《中华人民共和国登记管理条例》规定登记注册，其全部注册资本由等额股份构成并通过发行股票筹集资本，股东以其认购的股份对公司承担有限责任，公司以其全部资产对其债务承担责任的经济组织。

（7）私营企业是指由自然人投资设立或由自然人控股，以雇佣劳动为基础的营利性经济组织。包括按照《公司法》、《合伙企业法》、《私营企业暂行条件》规定登记注册的私营有限责任公司、私营股份有限公司、私营合伙企业和私营独资企业。

①私营独资企业是指按《私营企业暂行条例》的规定，由一名自然人投资经营，以雇佣劳动为基础，投资者对企业债务承担无限责任的企业。

②私营合伙企业是指按《合伙企业法》或《私营企业暂行条例》的规定，由两个以上自然人按照协议共同投资、共同经营、共负盈亏，以雇佣劳动为基础，对债务承担无限责任的企业。

③私营有限责任公司是指按《公司法》、《私营企业暂行条例》的规定，由两个以上自然人投资或由单个自然人控股的有限责任公司。

④私营股份有限公司是指按《公司法》的规定，由五个以上自然人投资，或由单个自然人控股的有限公司。

（8）其他内资企业是指上述第（1）条至第（7）条之外的其他内资经济组织。

（9）与港澳台商合资经营企业是指港澳台地区投资者与内地的企业依照《中华人民共和国中外合资经营企业法》及有关法律的规定，按合同规定的比例投资设立、分享利润和分担风险的企业。

（10）与港澳台商合作经营企业是指港澳台地区投资者与内地企业依照《中华人民共和国中外合作经营企业法》及有关法律的规定，依照合作合同的约定进行投资或提供条件设立、分配利润和分担风险的企业。

（11）港澳台商独资经营企业是指依照《中华人民共和国外资企业法》及有关法律的规定，在内地由港澳台地区投资者全额投资设立的企业。

（12）港澳台商投资股份有限公司是指根据国家有关规定，经外经贸部依法批准设立，其中港、澳、台商的股本占公司注册资本的比例达25%以上的股份有限公司。凡其中港、澳、台商的股本占公司注册资本的比例小于25%的，属于内资企业中的股份有限公司。

（13）中外合资经营企业是指外国企业或外国人与中国内地企业依照《中华人民共和国中外合资经营企业法》及有关法律的规定，按合同规定的比例投资设立、分享利润和分担风险的企业。

（14）中外合作经营企业是指外国企业或外国人与中国内地企业依照《中华人民共和国中外合作经营企业法》及有关法律的规定，依照合作合同的约定进行投资或提供条件设立、分配利润和分担风险的企业。

（15）外资企业是指依照《中华人民共和国外资企业法》

及有关法律的规定，在中国内地由外国投资者全额投资设立的企业。

（16）外商投资股份有限公司是指根据国家有关规定，经外经贸部依法批准设立，其中外资的股本占公司注册资本的比例达 25% 以上的股份有限公司。凡其中外资股本占公司注册资本的比例小于 25% 的，属于内资企业中的股份有限公司。

机关、事业单位和社会团体参照《企业登记注册类型与代码》，主要按其经费来源和管理方式划分。具体规定如下：

（1）机关包括国家机关和政党机关，原则上均列为“国有”。但有特殊规定的，如供销社等，则列为“集体”。

（2）事业单位包括经国家机构编制部门和有关业务主管部门批准成立的各类事业单位，不包括实行企业化管理的事业单位。事业单位的划分办法如下：

①由国家财政预算拨款或列入财政预算外资金管理以及经费主要来源于国有主管部门或国有上级单位的事业单位，列为“国有”。

②经费主要来源于集体单位的事业单位，列为“集体”。

③公民个人（或个人合伙）开办的事业单位，列为“私营”。

④上述以外的其他事业单位，如果其经费来源不明确，按管理方式进行归类。

（3）社会团体包括经民政部门批准成立以及未纳入社会团体管理条例范围的工会、妇联等各类社会团体。社会团体的划分办法如下：

①未纳入民政部社会团体管理条例范围的工会、妇联、共青团、青联、工商联、科协、侨联等社会团体，国家拨款设立的基金会或基金管理组织以及经费主要来源于国有业务主管部门或国有上级单位的社会团体，列为“国有”。

②经费主要来源于集体单位的社会团体，列为“集体”。

③公民个人（或个人合伙）开办的社会团体，划为“私营”。

④上述以外的其他社会团体，如果其经费来源不明确，改按管理方式进行归类。

平均增长速度 我国计算平均增长速度有两种方法：一种是习惯上经常使用的“水平法”，又称几何平均法，是以间隔期最后一年的水平同基期水平对比来计算平均每年增长（或下降）速度；另一种是“累计法”，又称代数平均法或方程法，是以间隔期内各年水平的总和同基期水平对比来计算平均每年增长（或下降）速度。在一般正常情况下，两种方法计算的平均每年增长速度比较接近；但在经济发展不平衡、出现大起大落时，两种方法计算的结果差别较大。

本《年鉴》内所列的平均增长速度，除固定资产投资用“累计法”计算外，其余均用“水平法”计算。从某年到某年平均增长速度的年份，均不包括基期年在内。如建国四十三年的平均增长速度是以 1949 年为基期计算的，则写为 1950-1992 年平均增长速度，其余类推。

Explanatory Notes on Main Statistical Indicators

Some explanations:

1. Historical data regarding total output value and value added of the primary industry, the secondary industry and the tertiary industry is adjusted and the data listed in the yearbooks shall prevail.

2. The growth rate of such indicators as total output value, value added of the primary industry, the secondary industry and the tertiary industry, total industrial added value and total value of agricultural output is calculated as per comparable price.

3. Because China started reform of fiscal and tax system from 1994, financial revenue and expenditure in 1994 and later are incomparable to those of previous years. Furthermore, fiscal revenue statistical caliber in 2000 was slightly adjusted.

4. Adjustment of industrial statistical caliber. Industrial statistical range before 1998 covered independent accounting industrial enterprises of township and above. The statistical range was adjusted to industrial enterprises above designated size in 1998, namely all state-owned industrial units and non-state-owned industrial units with annual sales revenue of above RMB 5 million and those with annual main business income of above RMB 20 million in 2011.

5. Change in statistical range in the construction industry. The statistical range in the construction industry covered county and above units from 1994 to 1995, construction enterprises with independent accounting whose qualification level was Level IV and above from 1996 to 1997 or construction enterprises with independent accounting whose qualification level was Level V and above from 1998.

Registration Status of Enterprises (Units) Enterprises are classified according to the registration status of an enterprise with the qualifications of legal person in industrial and commercial administration agencies. Government agencies, institutions, social organizations and other economic organizations shall follow the above classification.

Enterprises (units) are classified into the following categories according to the registration status of an enterprise in industrial and commercial administration agencies:

(1) State-owned Enterprises refer to non-corporation economic units that registered in accordance with the regulations of the people's republic of china for controlling the registration of enterprises as legal persons, where the entire assets are owned by the state. Excluded from this category are solely state-owned companies in the limited liability corporations.

(2) Collective-owned Enterprises refer to economic units where the enterprise assets are owned collectively and which have registered in accordance with the regulations of the people's republic of china for controlling the registration of enterprises as legal persons.

(3) Cooperative Enterprises refer to a form of collective economic units (enterprises) where capitals come mainly from employees as their shares, with certain proportion of capital from the outside, where production is organized on the basis of independent operation, independent accounting for profits and losses, joint work, democratic management, and a distribution system that integrates remuneration according to work with dividend according to capital share.

(4) Joint Ownership Enterprises refer to economic units established by two or more corporate enterprises or corporate institutions of the same or different ownership, through joint investment on the basis of equality, voluntary participation and mutual benefits. They include state joint ownership enterprises, collective joint ownership enterprises, joint state-collective enterprises, other joint ownership enterprises.

They include state joint ownership enterprise, collective joint ownership, joint state-collective enterprises and other joint operation enterprises.

(5) Limited Liability Corporations refer to economic units established with investment from 2-50 investors and registered in accordance with the Regulation of the People' s Republic of China on the Management of Registration of Corporations, each investor bearing limited liability to the corporation depending on its share of investment, and the corporation bearing liability to its debt to the maximum of its total assets.

Limited Liability Corporations include exclusive state funded limited liability corporations and other limited liability corporations.

① State-owned Exclusive Corporations refer to limited liability corporations established with sole investment by the investment organizations or departments authorized by the State.

② Other Limited Liability Corporations refer to other limited liability corporations other than the state-owned exclusive corporations .

(6) Share-holding Corporations Ltd. refer to economic units registered in accordance with the Regulation of the People' s Republic of China on the Management of Registration of Corporations, with total registered capitals divided into equal shares and raised through issuing stocks. Each investor bears limited liability to the corporation depending on the holding of shares, and the corporation bears liability to its debt to the maximum of its total assets.

(7) Private Enterprises refer to profit-making economic units invested and established by natural persons, or controlled by natural persons using employed labour. Included in this category are private limited liability corporations, private share-holding corporations Ltd., private partnership enterprises and private-funded enterprises registered in accordance with the Corporation Law, Partnership Enterprises Law and Interim Regulations on Private Enterprises.

① Private Exclusive Enterprises refer to enterprises invested and operated by one person using employed labour in accordance with Interim Regulations on Private Enterprises , where the investor bears unlimited liability for enterprise debts.

② Private Cooperative Enterprises refer to enterprises jointly invested and managed by more than two natural persons in accordance with Partnership Enterprises Law or Interim Regulations on Private Enterprises using employed labour, where sharing of investment, operation, profits and debts is stipulated under contract. They bear unlimited liabilities for the enterprise debts.

③ Private Limited Liability Corporations refer to the limited liability corporations invested by more than two natural persons or controlled by one natural person according to the stipulations of the Corporations Law and Interim Regulations on Private Enterprises.

④ Private Stock Corporations Ltd. refer to the limited corporations invested by more than five natural persons, or controlled by one natural person in accordance with Corporations Law.

(8) Other Domestic-funded Enterprises refer to other domestic-funded economic organizations other than those specified from Article (1) to Article (7).

(9) Joint Venture Enterprises with Funds from Hong Kong, Macau and Taiwan established by investors from Hong Kong, Macau and Taiwan with enterprises in the mainland of China in accordance with the Law of the People' s Republic of China on Sino-foreign Cooperative Enterprises and other relevant laws, where the establishment of investment and the sharing of profits and risks are stipulated under the joint venture contracts.

(10) Cooperative Enterprises with Funds from Hong Kong, Macau and Taiwan established by investors from Hong Kong, Macau and Taiwan with enterprises in the mainland of China in accordance with the Law of the People' s Republic of China on Sino-foreign Cooperative Enterprises and other relevant laws, where the investment or provision of facilities, and the sharing of profits and risks are stipulated in the cooperative contracts.

(11) Enterprises with Sole (exclusive) Investment from Hong Kong, Macau and Taiwan refer to enterprises established in the mainland of China with exclusive investment from investors from Hong Kong, Macau and Taiwan in accordance with the Law of the People's Republic of China on Wholly Foreign-owned Enterprises and other relevant laws.

(12) Share-holding Corporations Ltd. with Investment from Hong Kong, Macau and Taiwan refer to share-holding corporations Ltd. established with the approved from the Ministry of Foreign Trade and Economic Cooperation in line with relevant State regulations, where the share of investment from Hong Kong, Macau and Taiwan exceeds 25% of the total registered capital of the corporation. In case the share of foreign investment is less than 25% of the total registered capital, the enterprise is to be classified as domestic-funded share-holding corporation Ltd..

(13) Joint Venture Enterprises with Foreign Investment refer to enterprises jointly established by foreign enterprises or foreigners with enterprises in the mainland of China in accordance with the Law of the People's Republic of China on Sino-Foreign Equity Joint Ventures and other relevant laws, where the sharing of investment, profits and risks is stipulated under contract.

(14) Cooperative Enterprises with Foreign Investment refer to enterprises jointly established by foreign enterprises or foreigners with enterprises in the mainland of China in accordance with the Law of the People's Republic of China on Sino-Foreign Contractual Joint Ventures and other relevant laws, where the investment or provision of facilities and the sharing of profits and risks are stipulated under cooperative contracts.

(15) Enterprises with Sole (exclusive) Foreign Investment refer to enterprises established in the mainland of China with exclusive investment from foreign investors in accordance with the Law of the People's Republic of China on Wholly Foreign-owned Enterprises and other relevant laws.

(16) Share-holding Corporations Ltd. with Foreign Investment refer to share-holding corporations Ltd. established with the approval from the Ministry of Foreign Trade and Economic Cooperation in line with relevant State regulations, where the share of investment from foreign investors exceeds 25% of the total registered capital of the corporation. In case the share of foreign investment is less than 25% of the total registered capital, the enterprise is to be classified as domestic-funded share-holding corporation Ltd.

Government Agencies, Institutions and Social Organizations are classified into the following categories by source of funds and manner of management taking reference of the registration status and code of enterprises:

(1) Government agencies: include State and party agencies, classified in principle as State-owned. There are exceptions, such as supply and marketing cooperatives which are classified as collective-owned.

(2) Institutions: include institutions of various types established with the approval by organization and staffing departments of the government, but exclude institutions where enterprise management system is introduced. Institutions are further classified as follows:

① Institutions for which their main budgets are from government budget appropriations or extra-budget funds, or allocated from the budget of their competent government agencies. Such institutions are classified as state-owned.

② Institutions for which their budget mainly come from collective units are classified as collective-owned.

③ Social institutions established by individual or a group of citizens, which are classified as private.

④ Institutions other than those mentioned above for which their sources of budget are not clear are classified by the manner of management.

(3) Social organizations: include social organizations established with the approved from the Ministry of Civil Affairs and organizations that are not covered by social organization management regulations such as trade unions, women' s federations etc. Such organizations are further classified as follows:

① Social organizations that are not covered by social organization management regulations of the Ministry of Civil Affairs such as labor union, women federations, communist youth leagues, youth federation, industrial and commerce associations, scientist associations, overseas Chinese associations,etc., foundations and fund management organizations established with funds from the state, and social organizations whose funds mainly come from the budget of their competent government agencies. Such institutions are classified as State–owned.

② Social organizations for which their budget mainly come from collective units are classified as collective–owned.

③ Social organizations established by individual or a group of citizens are classified as private.

④ Social organizations other than those mentioned above for which their sources of budget are not clear are classified by the manner of management.

Average speed of growth The average speed of growth in China is calculated based on two methods: Customarily, one method –– "level method" (also called as geometric method) is often used to calculate average annual growth (or decline) speed by comparing the level of the final year of the interval with the level during the base period; The other method is "cumulative method" (also called as method of algebraic or equation method) which is used to calculate average annual growth (decline) speed by comparing total level of all years within the interval with the level during the base period. In normal circumstances, average annual growth rates calculated based on these two method are relatively close; However, in case of unbalanced economic development and changing radically, big difference happens to results calculated based on these two methods.

Average speed of growth listed in the Yearbooks of fixed investments is calculated as per "cumulative method" and the rest is calculated pursuant to "level method". Years of average speed of growth from one year to one year are not included into the base period. For example, the average speed of growth in the 43 years after founding of China is calculated based on base period in 1949; average speed of growth from 1950 to 1992 is written down and the rest is analogized.

国民经济核算

NATIONAL ACCOUNTS

4-1 各时期生产总值（按当年价格计算）
Gross Domestic Product in Each Period(Calculated at Current Prices)

年份 Year	地区生产总值（万元）Gross Domestic Product (10 000 yuan)	其中 of which				人均生产总值（元）Per Capita GDP (yuan)
		第一产业 Primary Industry	第二产业 Secondary Industry	第三产业 Tertiary Industry	# 工业 Industry	
1952	38282	14464	11300	12518	10907	121
1957	66616	19282	22378	24956	21840	194
1962	62056	10271	24346	27439	23610	177
1965	96827	18837	44395	33595	43388	262
1970	136085	21582	76949	37554	75571	337
1975	162427	28985	86500	46942	84614	373
“五五”时期						
1976	181751	33447	99797	48507	97215	413
1977	199814	35831	112347	51636	109811	450
1978	235993	41633	133172	61188	128910	527
1979	265619	50144	147679	67796	141048	586
1980	288001	59580	158591	69830	142369	630
“六五”时期						
1981	315623	65646	176516	73461	151131	681
1982	360552	88026	185548	86978	157894	765
1983	420075	116162	204758	99155	179572	881
1984	479948	103502	254684	121762	201017	997
1985	613741	129221	318193	166327	275447	1263
“七五”时期						
1986	712831	148165	344782	219884	286895	1451
1987	845431	175195	402857	267379	328783	1699
1988	1142249	222330	570722	349197	474895	2266
1989	1258319	237692	615209	405418	546591	2466
1990	1382350	239283	673593	469474	604274	2666
“八五”时期						
1991	1633920	253797	765582	614541	677340	3109
1992	2078386	277408	983638	817340	868539	3928
1993	2707637	326614	1331453	1049570	1153600	5088
1994	3718760	494413	1768214	1456133	1544940	6946
1995	4735176	676399	2203700	1855077	1941631	8773

4-1 续表 continued

年份 Year	地区生产总值 （万元） Gross Domestic Product (10 000 yuan)	其中 of which				
		第一产业 Primary Industry	第二产业 Secondary Industry	第三产业 Tertiary Industry	# 工业 Industry	人均生产总值 （元） Per Capita GDP (yuan)
"九五" 时期						
1996	5808366	742400	2749300	2316666	2383100	10701
1997	7099490	825200	3279700	2994590	2788668	12995
1998	8021619	902000	3664300	3455319	2984090	14549
1999	8813156	925171	3998006	3889979	3188000	15863
2000（调整前）	9521798	950125	4186077	4385596	3366075	16999
2000	9441315	960185	4147355	4333775	3319701	16855
"十五" 时期						
2001	10579155	983242	4380564	5215349	3507175	18697
2002	11901167	1000514	5016352	5884300	4023830	20807
2003	13521540	1048068	5886754	6586718	4822007	23362
2004	16002700	1205800	7219300	7577600	6034000	27293
2005	18462792	1343400	8474679	8644713	7158669	28900
"十一五" 时期						
2006	21615316	1451210	9971161	10192945	8441795	33480
2007	25001427	1502995	11287598	12210834	9548644	38301
2008	30067703	1750100	13130913	15186690	11152190	45563
2009	33409059	1870700	14335100	17203259	11913600	50219
2010	39105271	2151700	16374544	20579027	13524244	57947
"十二五" 时期						
2011	44062889	2378573	18289700	23394616	15078800	64310
2012	48036696	2529161	19381399	26126136	16030799	69444
2013	52301948	2847088	20532400	28922460	16906300	74994
2013（新行业）	52301948	2769911	20950832	28581205	16906300	74994
2014	57705966	2902894	22616579	32186493	18221072	82052
2015	61002320	3053916	23070000	34878404	18443700	85919
"十三五" 时期						
2016	65361165	3173113	23689000	38499052	18788300	90999
2017	72019553	3173969	25692200	43153384	20031000	98967
2018	78565600	2724200	28293100	47548300	21450700	106302
2019	94433700	3430600	32652200	58350900	21678700	106416
2020	101409100	3616600	35306700	62485800	23604800	110199

注：1. 2013 年始使用新口径、新行业分类标准（GB-2011）。新行业中：第一产业不再包括农林牧渔服务业；第二产业不再包括开采辅助活动，金属制品、机械和设备修理业；农林牧渔服务业，开采辅助活动，金属制品、机械和设备修理业归入第三产业。后同。
2. 2013 年（新行业）、2014 年为普查口径数据，后同。
3. 2005 年后人均生产总值为常住人口口径，后同。
4. 经济普查年度，2018 年相关指标为快报数据。

Note: 1.New caliber and industry classification standard started to be used from 2013 (GB-2011). In the new industries: The primary industry doesn't include agriculture,forestry, animal husbandry and fishery service industry any longer; The secondary industry doesn't include mining auxiliary activities, metalware and machinery and equipment repair industry; Agriculture, forestry, animal husbandry and fishery service industry, mining auxiliary activities, metalware and machinery and equipment repair industry fall into the tertiary industry. Similarly hereinafter.
2.Economic census survey caliber data in 2013 (new industry) and 2014 arises (the same below).
3.After 2005, the per capita gross domestic product (GDP) of the permanent population caliber(the same below).
4.In the economic census year, related indicator in 2018 is the express data.

4-2 各时期生产总值环比指数(以上年为100)
Circle Indices of Gross Domestic Product (Preceding Last Year=100)

年份 Year	地区生产总值 Gross Domestic Product	其中 of which				
		第一产业 Primary Industry	第二产 Secondary Industry	第三产业 Tertiary Industry	工业 Industry	人均生产总值 Per Capita GDP
1952	123.9	119.1	153.2	132.7	126.2	118.0
1957	97.5	91.7	89.0	112.7	92.3	95.7
1962	105.6	116.7	82.7	121.9	81.3	105.9
1965	120.8	120.4	138.8	105.3	132.9	120.7
1970	113.7	95.9	131.9	100.5	130.8	108.7
1975	139.0	121.5	160.4	117.6	167.8	133.9
"五五" 时期						
1976	104.9	93.2	114.6	104.5	113.1	104.6
1977	106.8	95.0	112.3	106.3	113.9	104.7
1978	113.0	99.3	114.2	119.0	111.9	109.1
1979	112.1	120.0	110.5	110.4	109.0	110.8
1980	113.6	124.5	112.5	107.9	105.7	112.6
"六五" 时期						
1981	109.5	110.1	111.2	105.1	106.1	108.0
1982	116.0	136.2	106.7	120.2	106.1	114.1
1983	117.0	132.5	110.8	114.5	114.2	115.6
1984	118.4	92.3	128.9	127.3	116.0	117.3
1985	105.4	102.9	103.0	112.6	112.9	104.4
"七五" 时期						
1986	110.8	109.4	103.4	126.1	99.4	109.6
1987	112.2	111.9	110.5	115.0	108.4	110.8
1988	119.0	111.8	124.8	115.0	127.2	117.5
1989	103.2	100.1	101.0	108.8	107.8	101.9
1990	108.3	99.2	107.9	114.2	109.0	106.6
"八五" 时期						
1991	112.8	101.2	108.5	124.9	107.0	111.3
1992	122.8	105.5	124.0	128.4	123.8	122.0
1993	121.4	109.7	126.1	119.7	123.8	120.7
1994	118.9	131.0	115.0	120.1	115.9	118.2
1995	113.3	121.7	110.9	112.3	111.8	112.4

4-2 续表 continued

年份 Year	地区生产总值 Gross Domestic Product	其中 of which				
		第一产业 Primary Industry	第二产 Secondary Industry	第三产业 Tertiary Industry	工业 Industry	人均生产总值 Per Capita GDP
"九五"时期						
1996	114.9	102.8	116.9	117.0	115.0	114.3
1997	119.6	108.8	116.7	126.3	114.5	118.8
1998	113.8	110.1	112.6	116.3	107.8	112.8
1999	113.1	109.5	111.8	115.4	110.6	112.2
2000	112.1	106.1	110.8	114.9	112.2	111.2
"十五"时期						
2001	112.1	104.0	109.8	115.9	111.0	110.9
2002	113.2	102.6	114.8	113.9	115.2	112.0
2003	114.5	104.6	118.2	113.0	121.9	113.2
2004	115.6	107.8	119.8	113.0	121.9	114.1
2005	115.6	106.0	117.4	115.4	119.8	114.2
"十一五"时期						
2006	115.7	106.0	117.2	115.6	119.3	114.4
2007	115.8	100.0	115.3	118.5	116.0	114.5
2008	113.0	105.0	110.0	116.8	110.7	111.8
2009	112.2	105.1	112.1	113.1	110.5	111.3
2010	112.7	104.9	111.0	114.9	110.7	111.1
"十二五"时期						
2011	110.6	104.4	111.7	110.3	112.2	108.9
2012	109.5	104.7	109.2	110.1	109.7	108.4
2013	109.6	103.9	110.1	109.7	110.6	108.7
2013(新行业)	109.6	103.7	110.1	109.7	110.6	108.7
2014	108.8	103.9	108.8	109.1	108.9	107.9
2015	108.1	104.1	107.4	108.9	107.1	107.0
"十三五"时期						
2016	107.8	104.1	106.9	108.7	106.9	106.5
2017	108.0	103.3	108.4	108.2	108.9	106.6
2018	107.4	102.5	107.8	107.5	107.0	105.7
2019	107.0	101.3	107.8	107.0	104.1	105.7
2020	104.9	102.2	107.0	103.7	108.2	101.1

4-3 资本形成总额(按当年价格计算)
Gross Capital Formation(Calculated at Current Prices)

单位：万元 (10 000 yuan)

指标	Indicator	2012 年	2013 年	2014 年	2015 年	2016 年	2017 年
资本形成总额	Gross Capital Formation	24140144	30182535	34417750	38457600	40333673	48134888
一、固定资本形成总额	Gross fixed Capitai Formation	21390653	27194510	31268206	33457249	37051965	44000633
1. 住宅	Residential	4209797	6274201	6617872	7438000	9945598	11719804
2. 非住宅建筑物	Non-residential Buildings	9748694	13011712	15557997	14780097	15626960	17892869
3. 机器和设备	Machinery and Equipment	3984376	4499778	5067899	6450000	5880359	6674207
4. 土地改良支出	Land Improvement Expenditure	44788	62574		136928	83868	51369
5. 矿藏勘探费	Mineral Exploration Expenditure	4730	5198	6049	6979	6899	6821
6. 计算机软件	Computer Software	2130000	2276970	2590812	2970366	3407010	3815852
7. 其他	Others	1268268	1064077	1335012	1674879	2101270	2636211
二、存货增加	Changes in Inventories	2749492	2988025	3149544	5000351	3281707	4134254
1. 农林牧渔业	Agriculture, Forestry, Animal Husbandry and Fishery	161773	163227	-1100	-16200	-31854	-13992
2. 工业	Industry	248136	670461	685047	733000	8376	3468105
3. 建筑业	Construction	188246	-532	-603	514751	399574	976845
4. 交通运输、仓储和邮政业	Transport, Storage and Postal Services	1791	2508	2115	-17600	116139	-5000
5. 批发和零售业	Wholesale and Retail Trade	175842	31828	110839	-79000	-104495	869398
6. 住宿和餐饮业	Accommodations and Catering Services	157	-1866	-523	-26000	-21754	-23786
7. 房地产业	Real Estate	1973546	2122399	2347812	4010000	2090306	-1226316
8. 其他服务业	Other Services			5957	-118600	825415	89000

4-4 最终消费支出（按当年价格计算）
Final Consumption Expenditure(Calculated at Current Prices)

单位：亿元 (100 million yuan)

指标	Indicator	2012年	2013年	2014年	2015年	2016年	2017年
最终消费支出	**Final Consumption Expenditures**	**2448.32**	**2728.45**	**2936.20**	**3190.55**	**3466.81**	**3779.14**
居民消费支出	Expenseon Consumption of All Households	1574.06	1747.52	1856.00	2015.55	2227.92	2396.54
农村居民	Rural Households	206.67	226.28	243.72	259.87	282.02	299.67
食品类支出	Food	60.81	64.14	67.29	68.50	74.73	80.26
衣着类支出	Clothing	10.16	10.98	12.95	11.73	12.78	13.48
居住类支出	Residence	30.13	33.68	31.54	38.73	43.34	48.89
家庭设备、用品及服务类支出	Supplies and Services	10.88	13.45	15.99	13.94	15.32	16.17
医疗保健类支出	Health care	23.83	20.54	19.78	17.73	18.81	18.37
交通和通信类支出	Transport and Communications	24.73	30.40	36.10	36.83	39.26	40.44
文教娱乐用品及服务类支出	Recreation,Education and Cultural	10.75	14.17	16.18	21.61	23.93	24.50
金融中介服务虚拟支出	Flinancial Intermediary Services Virtual Expenditure	1.92	2.14	2.33	2.54	2.88	3.12
保险服务消费支出	Insurance Services Expenditure	7.74	8.03	9.42	11.05	11.56	12.68
自有住房服务虚拟支出	Private Housing Service Virtual Expenditure	24.03	26.68	28.02	29.42	30.89	32.43
其他商品和服务类支出	Other Goods and Services Expenditure	1.69	2.06	4.12	7.78	8.52	9.33
城镇居民	Urban Households	1367.39	1521.23	1612.27	1755.68	1945.90	2096.86
食品类支出	Food	336.42	367.27	377.92	415.71	447.72	468.76
衣着类支出	Clothing	138.84	152.42	152.72	155.01	136.57	138.61
居住类支出	Residence	123.43	138.63	172.32	181.63	232.57	266.76
家庭设备、用品及服务类支出	Supplies and Services	96.57	105.23	111.02	126.11	130.78	134.26
医疗保健类支出	Health care	100.39	110.48	110.26	125.36	144.54	155.09
交通和通信类支出	Transport and Communications	220.64	253.86	261.73	288.43	345.54	356.59
文教娱乐用品及服务类支出	Recreation,Education and Cultural	143.21	155.17	170.23	197.80	199.58	211.76
金融中介服务虚拟支出	Flinancial Intermediary Services Virtual Expenditure	38.25	47.12	51.26	55.78	68.43	79.89
保险服务消费支出	Insurance Services Expenditure	14.61	15.17	17.79	20.87	36.04	42.70
自有住房服务虚拟支出	Private Housing Service Virtual Expenditure	98.38	114.15	119.85	125.85	142.71	174.78
实物消费支出	Reality Consumption	5.71	6.18	6.56	9.67	14.28	22.75
其他商品和服务类支出	Other Goods and Services Expenditure	50.94	55.56	60.62	53.46	47.14	44.90
政府消费支出	Government Consumption Expenditure	874.26	980.93	1080.20	1175.00	1238.89	1382.60

4-5 实际最终消费（按当年价格计算）
Final Real Consumption(Calculated at Current Prices)

单位：亿元 (100 million yuan)

指标	Indicator	2012 年	2013 年	2014 年	2015 年	2016 年	2017 年
最终消费	Final Consumption	2448.32	2728.45	2936.20	3190.55	3466.81	3779.14
居民消费	Expense on Consumption of All Households	1907.56	2066.16	2189.96	2378.21	2610.94	2803.24
农村居民	Rural Households	245.83	272.82	292.65	312.03	342.28	360.56
食品类消费	Food	61.32	65.67	68.89	70.13	76.51	82.17
衣着类消费	Clothing	10.24	11.24	13.26	12.01	13.08	13.80
居住类消费	Residence	30.24	34.32	32.14	39.46	44.16	49.81
家庭设备、用品及服务类消费	Supplies and Services	10.97	13.76	16.36	14.26	15.67	16.54
医疗保健类消费	Health care	42.55	40.63	39.13	35.07	37.21	36.34
交通和通信类消费	Transport and Communications	24.95	31.14	36.99	37.73	40.22	41.43
文教娱乐用品及服务类消费	Recreation,Education and Cultural	29.90	37.62	42.95	57.39	63.53	65.06
金融中介服务虚拟消费	FIinancial Intermediary Services Virtual Expenditure	1.94	2.14	2.33	2.53	2.88	3.11
保险服务消费支出	Insurance Services Expenditure	7.80	8.03	9.42	11.05	11.56	12.68
自有住房服务虚拟消费	Private Housing Service Virtual Expenditure	24.21	26.68	28.01	29.41	30.89	32.43
其他商品和服务类消费	Other Goods and Services Expenditure	1.71	1.59	3.18	6.01	6.58	7.21
城镇居民	Urban Households	1661.73	1793.34	1897.31	2066.06	2268.66	2442.68
食品类消费	Food	339.16	364.59	375.17	412.68	444.46	465.35
衣着类消费	Clothing	139.75	151.07	151.37	153.64	135.36	137.39
居住类消费	Residence	124.48	137.67	171.13	180.37	209.96	240.82
家庭设备、用品及服务类消费	Supplies and Services	97.28	104.39	110.13	125.10	129.73	133.19
医疗保健类消费	Health care	230.37	251.57	251.07	285.46	329.14	353.16
交通和通信类消费	Transport and Communications	222.24	251.79	259.60	286.08	322.30	332.62
文教娱乐用品及服务类消费	Recreation,Education and Cultural	298.85	318.87	349.80	406.47	410.13	435.15
金融中介服务虚拟消费	FIinancial Intermediary Services Virtual Expenditure	38.54	47.12	51.27	55.78	68.43	79.89
保险服务消费支出	Insurance Services Expenditure	14.73	15.17	17.79	20.87	36.05	42.71
自有住房服务虚拟消费	Private Housing Service Virtual Expenditure	99.33	114.15	119.86	125.85	142.71	174.79
实物消费消费	Reality Consumption	5.76	6.18	6.56	9.68	14.28	22.75
其他商品和服务类消费	Other Goods and Services Expenditure	51.24	30.77	33.57	29.60	26.11	24.87
政府消费	Government Consumption	540.76	662.28	746.25	811.74	855.87	975.90

4-6 生产总值分布
Distribution of Gross Domestic Product

单位：亿元 (100 million yuan)

年份 Year	政府最终消费 Government Final Consumption	居民最终消费 Household Final Consumption	国内总投资 Total Domestic Investment	国内储蓄总额 Gross Domestic Savings	资金差额 Funding Gap
GDP分布					
1990	14.63	52.28	54.12	71.36	17.24
"八五"时期					
1991	16.43	60.70	56.35	86.26	29.91
1992	20.06	71.02	80.23	116.76	36.53
1993	22.75	90.63	122.66	157.38	34.71
1994	25.57	122.10	152.31	224.21	71.90
1995	34.93	197.61	190.05	240.98	50.93
"九五"时期					
1996	50.21	240.49	236.98	290.14	53.16
1997	98.69	291.30	246.44	319.96	73.52
1998	100.52	347.78	285.39	353.86	68.47
1999	126.27	362.71	347.37	392.34	44.97
2000	132.05	332.70	398.13	479.38	81.25
"十五"时期					
2001	146.90	357.84	418.38	553.18	134.79
2002	161.84	401.23	500.89	627.04	126.16
2003	184.97	430.62	562.41	736.57	174.15
2004	206.80	457.71	760.12	935.75	175.63
2005	223.46	522.10	1017.39	1100.72	83.33
"十一五"时期					
2006	285.51	621.65	1126.39	1254.37	127.98
2007	350.33	820.82	1286.16	1328.99	42.83
2008	431.26	940.61	1577.87	1634.90	57.03
2009	495.31	1022.07	1749.05	1823.53	74.48
2010	636.91	1197.34	2055.73	2076.28	20.55
"十二五"时期					
2011	747.23	1391.82	2360.99	2267.24	−93.75
2012	874.26	1574.06	2414.01	2355.35	−58.66
2013	980.93	1747.52	3018.25	3042.14	23.88
2014	1080.20	1856.00	3441.78	2834.40	−561.73
2015	1175.00	2015.55	3845.76	2909.68	−936.08
"十三五"时期					
2016	1238.89	2227.92	4033.37	3069.31	−964.06
2017	1382.60	2396.54	4813.49	3422.82	−1390.67

4-7 生产总值(2009年—2013年)(分行业、按当年价格计算)

Value of Gross Domestic Product(2009—2013)(Sub Industry, Calculated at Current Prices)

单位：亿元 (100 million yuan)

指标	Indicator	2009年	2010年	2011年	2012年	2013年
地区生产总值	Gross Domestic Product	3340.91	3910.53	4406.29	4803.67	5230.19
第一产业	Primary Industry	187.07	215.17	237.86	252.92	284.71
农林牧渔业	Agriculture, Forestry, Animal Husbandry and Fishery	187.07	215.17	237.86	252.92	284.71
农业	Farming	120.34	149.43	152.55	160.77	186.98
林业	Forestry	8.34	4.73	5.69	6.68	7.89
畜牧业	Animal Husbandry	51.22	53.08	70.61	75.28	78.08
渔业	Fishery	2.88	3.02	3.35	3.54	4.04
农林牧渔服务业	Services of Agriculture,Forestry,Animal Husbandry and Fishing	4.29	4.91	5.66	6.65	7.72
第二产业	Secondary Industry	1433.51	1637.45	1828.97	1938.14	2053.24
工业	Industry	1191.36	1352.42	1507.88	1603.08	1690.63
采矿业	Mining	26.60	31.64	34.11	33.21	56.03
制造业	Manufacture	1073.42	1194.23	1299.80	1490.91	1539.44
电力、燃气及水的生产和供应业	Production and Supply of Electric, Gas and Water	91.34	126.56	173.98	78.96	95.16
建筑业	Construction	242.15	285.03	321.09	335.06	362.61
房屋和土木工程建筑业	Building Construction	193.94	233.87	265.87	279.09	280.86
建筑安装业	Construction Installment	36.02	38.26	38.41	40.22	59.54
建筑装饰业	Construction Decoration	7.51	7.78	11.77	13.03	19.00
其他建筑业	Others	4.69	5.12	5.04	2.72	3.21
第三产业	Tertiary Industry	1720.33	2057.90	2339.46	2612.61	2892.24
交通运输、仓储和邮政业	Transport, Storage and Postal Services	200.27	236.81	296.61	320.41	332.97
铁路运输业	Railway Transport	52.01	56.18	60.70	65.55	63.12
道路运输业	Road Transport	96.68	118.25	152.71	170.27	172.42
城市公共交通业	Public Transportation by City	13.62	14.71	17.08	18.99	18.28
水上运输业	Waterway Transport	0.60	0.73	0.94	1.05	1.18
航空运输业	Air Transport	17.01	24.76	33.73	27.71	31.87
管道运输业	Pipeline Transport	1.20	1.36	1.37	1.40	1.65
装卸搬运和其他运输服务业	Loading and Unloading and Other Transport Services	11.84	13.55	21.59	21.64	26.47

4-7 续表 1 continued 1

指标	Indicator	2009 年	2010 年	2011 年	2012 年	2013 年
仓储业	Storage	5.79	6.09	7.18	10.97	15.00
邮政业	Postal Services	1.52	1.19	1.30	2.83	2.98
信息传输、计算机服务和软件业	**Information Transmission, Computer Services and Software**	**66.24**	**116.38**	**136.70**	**152.10**	**162.58**
电信和其他信息传输服务业	Telecommunications, Radio and Television and Satellite Transmission Services	30.95	31.15	29.93	28.80	33.11
计算机服务业	Internet and related Services	17.95	25.14	31.67	37.99	44.56
软件业	Software and Information Technology Services	17.33	60.09	75.10	85.31	84.90
批发和零售业	**Wholesale and Retail Trade**	**416.50**	**476.43**	**522.96**	**588.50**	**671.63**
批发业	Wholesale	234.13	288.90	335.52	381.87	437.59
零售业	Retail Trade	182.37	187.53	187.44	206.64	234.04
住宿和餐饮业	**Accommodations and Catering Services**	**125.55**	**142.81**	**143.73**	**149.52**	**168.18**
住宿业	Accommodations	12.43	16.44	16.77	17.68	20.76
餐饮业	Catering Services	113.12	126.37	126.96	131.84	147.42
金融业	**Financial Intermediation**	**240.21**	**288.33**	**330.14**	**411.34**	**461.00**
银行业	Banking Sector	164.58	226.00	278.34	357.71	387.31
证券业	Securities Industry	60.51	47.28	32.05	26.87	33.74
保险业	Insurance	10.02	5.37	6.43	6.99	8.16
其他金融活动	Others	5.10	9.68	13.32	19.77	31.80
房地产业	**Real Estate**	**172.63**	**220.79**	**254.98**	**273.94**	**320.56**
房地产开发经营业	Real Estate Development and Management	62.40	83.08	99.19	100.31	124.98
物业管理业	Property Management	18.69	28.65	31.55	32.35	38.34
房地产中介服务业	Real Estate Intermediary Services	10.13	15.53	17.11	17.62	17.62
其他房地产活动	Other Real Estate Activity	7.21	11.05	12.20	13.03	22.87
居民自有住房服务业	Private Housing Service	74.20	82.48	94.94	110.62	116.74
租赁和商务服务业	**Leasing and Business Services**	**88.71**	**107.32**	**131.18**	**145.29**	**153.19**
租赁业	Leasing Services	4.92	7.01	8.39	12.30	15.05
商务服务业	Business Services	83.78	100.31	122.79	132.99	138.14
科学研究、技术服务和地质勘查业	**Scientific Research,Technical Services and Geeological Prospecting Industry**	**57.79**	**63.63**	**69.22**	**69.36**	**75.62**

4-7 续表 2 continued 2

指标	Indicator	2009 年	2010 年	2011 年	2012 年	2013 年
研究与试验发展	Research and Experimental Development	19.95	18.95	22.14	22.85	27.12
专业技术服务业	Special Technical Services	27.36	32.94	33.95	33.78	32.72
科技交流和推广服务业	Science and Technology Promotion and Application Services	6.74	7.16	7.87	7.46	9.79
地质勘查业	Geeological Prospecting Industry	3.74	4.58	5.27	5.27	5.98
水利、环境和公共设施管理业	**Management of Water Conservancy, Environment and Public Facilities**	**12.18**	**13.84**	**13.62**	**14.05**	**17.26**
水利管理业	Management of Water Conservancy	5.06	6.06	5.91	6.21	9.06
环境管理业	Environmental Management	2.46	2.90	2.54	0.07	0.09
公共设施管理业	Management of Public Facilities	4.67	4.87	5.17	7.77	8.11
居民服务和其他服务业	**Services to Households and Other Services**	**32.95**	**40.75**	**46.88**	**52.01**	**57.49**
居民服务业	Services to Households	18.41	22.77	26.18	29.03	30.26
其他服务业	Other Services	14.53	17.98	20.70	22.98	27.24
教育	**Education**	**109.66**	**116.49**	**123.09**	**128.09**	**140.75**
卫生、社会保障和社会福利业	**Health,Social Security and Social Welfare**	**64.87**	**87.30**	**105.00**	**127.60**	**134.11**
卫生	Public Health	56.31	74.52	95.70	117.78	124.11
社会保障业	Social Security	6.37	9.46	7.11	7.48	7.60
社会福利业	Social Welfare	2.19	3.32	2.19	2.34	2.40
文化、体育和娱乐业	**Culture, Sports and Recreation**	**23.60**	**28.01**	**28.40**	**32.21**	**36.29**
新闻出版业	News and Publication	9.99	10.94	11.82	11.59	12.35
广播、电视、电影和音像业	Radio, Television, Film and Video	5.27	6.65	6.97	10.52	11.24
文化艺术业	Culture and Arts	4.26	5.84	4.46	4.19	5.04
体育	Sports	2.08	2.21	2.47	2.55	4.01
娱乐业	Recreation	2.01	2.37	2.68	3.37	3.65
公共管理和社会组织	**Public Management and Social Organizations**	**109.18**	**119.01**	**136.93**	**148.19**	**160.61**

注：旧行业分组（GB-2002）。
Note: Grouping of old industries (GB-2002)

4-8 生产总值(2013年—2017年)(分行业，按当年价格计算)

Value of Gross Domestic Product(2013–2017)(Sub Industry, Calculated at Current Prices)

单位：亿元 (100 million yuan)

指标	Indicator	2013年	2014年	2015年	2016年	2017年
地区生产总值	Gross Domestic Product	5230.19	5770.60	6100.23	6536.12	7201.96
农、林、牧、渔业	Agriculture, Forestry, Animal Husbandry and Fishery	284.71	299.11	314.99	328.24	330.24
农业	Farming	186.98	199.53	210.14	215.11	215.11
林业	Forestry	7.89	8.85	9.96	11.19	11.19
畜牧业	Animal Husbandry	78.08	77.57	80.82	86.47	86.47
渔业	Fishery	4.04	4.33	4.47	4.55	4.63
农、林、牧、渔服务业	Services of Agriculture,Forestry,Animal Husbandry and Fishing	7.72	8.82	9.60	10.93	12.84
工业	Industry	1690.63	1822.11	1844.37	1878.83	2003.10
采矿业	Mining	27.95	30.13	36.89	45.80	49.88
#开采辅助活动	Mining Support Activities	0.03	0.03	0.03	0.03	0.03
制造业	Manufacture	1471.81	1586.27	1715.26	1749.57	1877.08
#金属制品、机械和设备修理业	Metal Products, Machinery and Equipment Repair Industry	3.08	3.32	3.40	3.46	3.60
电力、燃气及水的生产和供应业	Production and Supply of Electric, Gas and Water	190.87	205.71	92.22	83.46	76.14
建筑业	Construction	407.56	442.90	466.06	493.56	569.75
房屋建筑业	Building Construction	236.10	252.57	241.65	279.93	316.15
土木工程建筑业	Civil Engineering Construction	107.82	121.17	178.83	172.85	215.22
建筑安装业	Construction Installment	25.22	27.40	21.12	13.47	15.97
建筑装饰业和其他建筑业	Construction Decoration and Others	38.43	41.76	24.47	27.32	22.41
批发和零售业	Wholesale and Retail Trade	626.68	691.65	715.54	760.76	976.87
批发业	Wholesale	397.64	441.38	453.30	482.02	620.82
零售业	Retail Trade	229.04	250.27	262.24	278.74	356.05
交通运输、仓储和邮政业	Transport, Storage and Post	332.97	364.29	371.63	392.18	415.61
铁路运输业	Railway Transport	63.12	69.06	68.40	72.50	72.40
道路运输业	Road Transport	166.88	181.18	186.88	191.92	198.29

4-8 续表 1 continued 1

指标	Indicator	2013 年	2014 年	2015 年	2016 年	2017 年
水上运输业	Waterway Transport	1.18	1.29	1.32	1.50	1.42
航空运输业	Air Transport	31.87	34.87	35.57	41.51	44.62
管道运输业	Pipeline Transport	21.47	23.49	23.96	24.35	29.71
装卸搬运和运输代理业	Loading, Unloading and Forwarding Agency	26.47	28.96	29.54	27.33	28.63
仓储业	Storage	15.00	16.41	16.74	21.68	27.20
邮政业	Postal Services	6.98	9.04	9.22	11.38	13.33
住宿和餐饮业	**Accommodations and Catering Services**	**168.18**	**180.96**	**188.45**	**202.85**	**218.71**
住宿业	Accommodations	20.76	22.45	22.68	23.99	25.21
餐饮业	Catering Services	147.42	158.51	165.77	178.86	193.50
信息传输、软件和信息技术服务业	**Information Transmission, Software and Information Technology**	**162.58**	**190.17**	**201.95**	**232.78**	**276.11**
电信、广播电视和卫星传输服务	Telecommunications, Radio and Television and Satellite Transmission Services	101.79	119.07	126.45	125.49	164.15
互联网和相关服务	Internet and related Services	4.35	5.09	5.40	18.21	20.24
软件和信息技术服务业	Software and Information Technology Services	56.44	66.02	70.11	89.08	91.72
金融业	**Financial Intermediation**	**461.00**	**541.88**	**641.86**	**719.98**	**776.01**
货币金融服务	Monetary and Financial Services	387.31	437.25	517.93	589.41	657.35
资本市场服务	Capital Market Services	33.74	48.65	57.63	36.42	41.05
保险业	Insurance	8.16	9.59	11.36	23.06	26.76
其他金融业	Others	31.80	46.38	54.94	71.10	50.85
房地产业	**Real Estate**	**320.56**	**369.23**	**415.00**	**463.21**	**500.05**
房地产开发经营业	Real Estate Development and Management	136.61	169.38	190.37	218.55	220.66
物业管理业	Property Management	26.72	25.46	28.62	33.66	35.55
房地产中介服务业	Real Estate Intermediary Services	17.62	17.44	19.60	25.72	29.89
自有房地产经营活动	Own Real Estate Operating Activities	116.74	132.83	134.73	140.19	160.01
其他房地产业	Other Real Estate Industry	22.87	24.13	41.68	45.09	53.94
租赁和商务服务业	**Leasing and Business Services**	**153.19**	**172.19**	**182.86**	**214.29**	**192.31**
租赁业	Leasing Services	15.05	16.92	17.97	25.15	28.46
商务服务业	Business Services	138.14	155.27	164.90	189.14	163.85

4–8 续表 2 continued 2

指标	Indicator	2013 年	2014 年	2015 年	2016 年	2017 年
科学研究和技术服务业	**Scientific Research and Technical Services**	75.62	82.35	90.00	103.15	136.89
研究和试验发展	Research and Experimental Development	6.39	6.96	7.60	10.15	14.42
专业技术服务业	Special Technical Services	50.38	54.86	59.96	68.00	94.49
科技推广和应用服务业	Science and Technology Promotion and Application Services	18.85	20.53	22.43	25.00	27.98
水利、环境和公共设施管理业	**Management of Water Conservancy, Environment and Public Facilities**	17.26	18.80	20.54	24.95	28.81
水利管理业	Management of Water Conservancy	1.88	2.05	2.24	2.50	2.70
生态保护和环境治理业	Ecological Protection and Environmental Management	0.61	0.74	0.80	1.45	2.07
公共设施管理业	Management of Public Facilities	14.77	16.01	17.50	21.00	24.04
居民服务、修理和其他服务业	**Services to Households, Repair and Other Services**	57.49	64.63	68.63	80.79	78.46
居民服务业	Services to Households	30.26	32.21	34.21	39.47	36.39
机动车、电子产品和日用产品修理业	Repair of Motor Vehicle, Electronics and Household Products	9.12	10.25	10.89	13.07	13.44
其他服务业	Other Services	18.11	22.16	23.53	28.25	28.62
教育	**Education**	140.75	153.27	167.51	196.78	232.09
卫生和社会工作	**Health,Social Security and Social Welfare**	134.11	146.04	159.60	176.10	179.89
卫生	Public Health	124.11	135.15	147.70	161.56	164.89
社会工作	Social Work	10.00	10.89	11.90	14.53	15.00
文化、体育和娱乐业	**Culture, Sports and Recreation**	36.29	40.79	43.32	48.60	52.29
新闻和出版业	Journalism and Publishing Activities	12.35	13.88	14.74	17.30	20.63
广播、电视、电影和影视录音	Radio, Television, Motion Picture and Videotape Programme	11.24	14.43	15.33	15.50	15.47
文化艺术业	Culture and Arts	5.04	4.37	4.64	5.69	6.11
体育	Sports	4.01	4.51	4.79	5.55	5.74
娱乐业	Recreation	3.65	3.60	3.83	4.57	4.34
公共管理、社会保障和社会组织	**Public Management, Social Security and Social Organization**	160.61	190.24	207.91	219.08	234.78
第一产业	**Primary Industry**	276.99	290.29	305.39	317.31	317.40
第二产业	**Secondary Industry**	2095.08	2261.66	2307.00	2368.90	2569.22
第三产业	**Tertiary Industry**	2858.12	3218.65	3487.84	3849.91	4315.34

注：新行业分组 (GB–2011)。
Note: Grouping of new industries (GB–2011).

4-9 生产总值贡献率(2009年—2013年)(分行业、按不变价格计算)

Distribution Rate of Gross Domestic Product(Calculated at Fixed Prices)(2009—2013)(Sub Industry, Calculated at Constant Prices)

单位：% (%)

指标	Indicator	2009年	2010年	2011年	2012年	2013年
地区生产总值贡献率	Gross Domestic Product	100.0	100.0	100.0	100.0	100.0
第一产业	Primary Industry	2.3	1.9	2.3	2.6	2.0
农林牧渔业	Agriculture, Forestry, Animal Husbandry and Fishery	2.3	1.9	2.3	2.6	2.0
农业	Farming	1.3	2.3	-1.3	1.4	1.1
林业	Forestry	0.0	-0.6	0.2	0.2	0.2
畜牧业	Animal Husbandry	1.0	0.2	3.3	0.8	0.5
渔业	Fishery	0.0	0.0		0.0	0.0
农林牧渔服务业	Services of Agriculture,Forestry,Animal Husbandry and Fishing	0.0	0.1	0.1	0.2	0.2
第二产业	Secondary Industry	44.6	39.1	46.2	41.2	44.5
工业	Industry	33.8	32.6	39.9	36.0	38.8
采矿业	Mining	3.9	1.1	0.6	0.0	5.9
制造业	Manufacture	15.0	23.3	27.5	58.7	30.6
电力、燃气及水的生产和供应业	Production and Supply of Electric, Gas and Water	14.8	8.2	11.7	-22.7	2.4
建筑业	Construction	10.8	6.5	6.3	5.2	5.6
房屋和土木工程建筑业	Building Construction	11.5	6.3	5.8	4.7	-6.3
建筑安装业	Construction Installment	0.6	0.1	-0.2	0.6	10.5
建筑装饰业	Construction Decoration	-0.9	0.0	0.9	0.4	1.3
其他建筑业	Others	-0.4	0.0	-0.1	-0.5	0.1
第三产业	Tertiary Industry	53.1	59.0	51.5	56.2	53.5
交通运输、仓储和邮政业	Transport, Storage and Postal Services	12.4	6.4	13.0	5.4	2.9
铁路运输业	Railway Transport	1.2	1.1	0.8	1.1	-0.4
道路运输业	Road Transport	9.7	3.1	7.6	4.1	0.9
城市公共交通业	Public Transportation by City	0.1	0.2	0.5	0.4	-0.1
水上运输业	Waterway Transport	0.1	0.2		0.0	0.0
航空运输业	Air Transport	0.9	1.2	2.0	-1.5	0.8

4–9 续表 1 continued 1

指标	Indicator	2009 年	2010 年	2011 年	2012 年	2013 年
管道运输业	Pipeline Transport	0.1	0.0		0.0	0.1
装卸搬运和其他运输服务业	Loading and Unloading and Other Transport Services	0.5	0.4	1.8	0.0	0.8
仓储业	Storage	–0.1	0.1	0.2	0.9	0.7
邮政业	Postal Services	0.0	0.1		0.4	0.0
信息传输、计算机服务和软件业	**Information Transmission, Computer Services and Software**	**2.9**	**7.7**	**4.7**	**3.5**	**2.3**
电信和其他信息传输服务业	Telecommunications, Radio and Television and Satellite Transmission Services	–0.3	0.1	–0.3	–0.3	0.9
计算机服务业	Internet and related Services	2.9	2.6	1.5	1.5	1.4
软件业	Software and Information Technology Services	0.3	5.1	3.5	2.3	–0.1
批发和零售业	**Wholesale and Retail Trade**	**10.5**	**12.4**	**7.6**	**13.5**	**15.7**
批发业	Wholesale	10.6	11.8	9.5	9.4	11.2
零售业	Retail Trade	–0.1	0.6	–1.8	4.1	4.5
住宿和餐饮业	**Accommodations and Catering Services**	**2.0**	**3.4**	**–0.6**	**1.0**	**2.5**
住宿业	Accommodations	–0.1	1.1	0.1	0.2	0.3
餐饮业	Catering Services	2.1	2.4	–0.7	0.8	2.1
金融业	**Financial Intermediation**	**8.7**	**8.8**	**7.0**	**17.5**	**13.9**
银行业	Banking Sector	9.4	11.9	10.0	17.3	9.1
证券业	Securities Industry	0.1	–3.0	–4.0	–1.3	1.7
保险业	Insurance	–0.4	–1.0	0.2	0.1	0.3
其他金融活动	Others	–0.4	0.9	0.8	1.4	2.8
房地产业	**Real Estate**	**5.3**	**8.3**	**4.9**	**3.5**	**8.3**
房地产开发经营业	Real Estate Development and Management	0.7	3.6	3.1	0.0	4.4
物业管理业	Property Management	1.3	2.1	0.4	0.1	1.0
房地产中介服务业	Real Estate Intermediary Services	0.7	1.2	0.2	0.1	–0.1
其他房地产活动	Other Real Estate Activity	0.4	0.7	0.2	0.2	1.9
居民自有住房服务业	Private Housing Service	2.1	0.6	10.0	3.1	1.1
租赁和商务服务业	**Leasing and Business Services**	**5.4**	**3.6**	**5.2**	**2.6**	**0.8**

4-9 续表 2 continued 2

指标	Indicator	2009 年	2010 年	2011 年	2012 年	2013 年
租赁业	Leasing Services	0.4	0.3	0.3	0.9	0.5
商务服务业	Business Services	5.1	3.2	4.9	1.7	0.3
科学研究、技术服务和地质勘查业	**Scientific Research,Technical Services and Geeological Prospecting Industry**	**1.0**	**0.5**	**1.0**	**−0.4**	**0.9**
研究与试验发展	Research and Experimental Development	0.4	−0.6	0.7	0.0	0.7
专业技术服务业	Special Technical Services	0.1	1.0	0.1	−0.3	−0.4
科技交流和推广服务业	Science and Technology Promotion and Application Services	0.4	0.1	0.1	−0.1	0.4
地质勘查业	Geeological Prospecting Industry	0.0	0.0	0.1	0.0	0.1
水利、环境和公共设施管理业	**Management of Water Conservancy, Environment and Public Facilities**	**−0.3**	**−0.2**	**−0.1**	**0.0**	**0.6**
水利管理业	Management of Water Conservancy	0.1	−0.1	−0.1	0.0	0.6
环境管理业	Environmental Management	0.1	0.0	−0.1	−0.6	0.0
公共设施管理业	Management of Public Facilities	−0.5	−0.1		0.6	0.0
居民服务和其他服务业	**Services to Households and Other Services**	**0.7**	**1.8**	**1.3**	**0.9**	**0.9**
居民服务业	Services to Households	0.4	1.0	0.7	0.5	0.1
其他服务业	Other Services	0.3	0.8	0.6	0.4	0.8
教育	**Education**	**2.8**	**1.1**	**1.0**	**0.5**	**1.9**
卫生、社会保障和社会福利业	**Health,Social Security and Social Welfare**	**0.9**	**3.5**	**3.8**	**4.7**	**0.6**
卫生	Public Health	0.6	2.6	4.7	4.7	0.6
社会保障业	Social Security	0.3	0.6	−0.6	0.0	0.0
社会福利业	Social Welfare	0.1	0.2	−0.3	0.0	0.0
文化、体育和娱乐业	**Culture, Sports and Recreation**	**0.7**	**1.1**		**0.7**	**0.7**
新闻出版业	News and Publication	0.3	0.2	0.2	−0.1	0.1
广播、电视、电影和音像业	Radio, Television, Film and Video	0.1	0.3		0.8	0.1
文化艺术业	Culture and Arts	0.1	0.4	−0.4	−0.1	0.2
体育	Sports	0.2	0.0	0.1	0.0	0.3
娱乐业	Recreation	0.0	0.1	0.1	0.1	0.0
公共管理和社会组织	**Public Management and Social Organizations**	**0.1**	**0.7**	**2.6**	**2.8**	**1.7**

注：旧行业分组 (GB−2002)。
Note: Grouping of old industries (GB−2002).

4-10 生产总值贡献率(2013年—2017年)(分行业，按不变价格计算)
Contribution Rate of Gross Domestic Product(2013–2017)(Sub Industry, Calculated at Constant Prices)

单位：%　　(%)

指标	Indicator	2013年	2014年	2015年	2016年	2017年
地区生产总值贡献率	Contribution Rate of Gross Domestic Product	100.00	100.00	100.00	100.00	100.00
农、林、牧、渔业	Agriculture, Forestry, Animal Husbandry and Fishery	2.03	2.26	2.37	2.89	2.28
农业	Farming	1.13	3.36	3.51	1.85	0.94
林业	Forestry	0.20	0.09	0.09	0.29	0.31
畜牧业	Animal Husbandry	0.49	−1.36	−1.43	0.48	0.69
渔业	Fishery	0.03	0.05	0.05	0.03	0.03
农、林、牧、渔服务业	Services of Agriculture,Forestry,Animal Husbandry and Fishing	0.17	0.12	0.16	0.24	0.30
工业	Industry	38.69	36.05	31.40	26.92	33.80
采矿业	Mining	2.91	0.60	−0.36	2.41	1.00
#开采辅助活动	Mining Support Activities	0.00	0.00	0.00	0.00	0.00
制造业	Manufacture	31.06	26.58	26.89	25.49	33.95
#金属制品、机械和设备修理业	Metal Products, Machinery and Equipment Repair Industry	0.06	0.07	0.06	0.05	0.06
电力、燃气及水的生产和供应业	Production and Supply of Electric, Gas and Water	4.73	8.88	4.86	−0.98	−1.15
建筑业	Construction	6.70	7.52	8.58	6.75	5.77
房屋建筑业	Building Construction	4.31	−1.08	4.04	8.60	2.08
土木工程建筑业	Civil Engineering Construction	−3.32	7.07	9.30	−0.92	4.73
建筑安装业	Construction Installment	3.42	0.47	−1.20	−1.59	0.23
建筑装饰业和其他建筑业	Construction Decoration and Others	2.29	1.06	−3.56	0.66	−1.27
批发和零售业	Wholesale and Retail Trade	15.34	10.65	6.58	11.42	17.71
批发业	Wholesale	10.89	7.51	3.55	7.35	13.68
零售业	Retail Trade	4.44	3.13	3.03	4.07	4.02
交通运输、仓储和邮政业	Transport, Storage and Post	2.87	3.58	2.33	3.54	6.29
铁路运输业	Railway Transport	−0.35	−0.78	1.34	0.73	0.31
道路运输业	Road Transport	0.72	2.00	−0.55	0.67	2.11
水上运输业	Waterway Transport	0.03	0.02	−0.01	0.04	−0.01
航空运输业	Air Transport	0.76	0.72	1.00	1.17	0.79

4-10 续表 1 continued 1

指标	Indicator	2013 年	2014 年	2015 年	2016 年	2017 年
管道运输业	Pipeline Transport	0.57	0.16	0.11	0.03	1.13
装卸搬运和运输代理业	Loading, Unloading and Forwarding Agency	0.59	0.47	0.14	–0.52	0.38
仓储业	Storage	0.47	0.35	0.11	1.00	1.15
邮政业	Postal Services	0.10	0.65	0.21	0.43	0.42
住宿和餐饮业	**Accommodations and Catering Services**	**2.45**	**2.28**	**1.16**	**2.04**	**2.05**
住宿业	Accommodations	0.35	0.21	0.22	0.22	0.34
餐饮业	Catering Services	2.10	2.06	0.95	1.82	1.71
信息传输、软件和信息技术服务业	**Information Transmission, Software and Information Technology**	**2.27**	**3.82**	**1.92**	**5.69**	**13.79**
电信、广播电视和卫星传输服务	Telecommunications, Radio and Television and Satellite Transmission Services	2.19	3.39	1.76	–0.65	10.70
互联网和相关服务	Internet and related Services	0.14	0.10	–0.01	2.64	0.79
软件和信息技术服务业	Software and Information Technology Services	–0.06	0.33	0.18	3.69	2.30
金融业	**Financial Intermediation**	**13.84**	**16.01**	**22.21**	**15.56**	**6.25**
货币金融服务	Monetary and Financial Services	9.10	7.35	13.63	14.35	9.08
资本市场服务	Capital Market Services	1.68	4.13	5.86	–4.52	0.64
保险业	Insurance	0.30	0.30	0.59	2.44	0.54
其他金融业	Others	2.74	4.23	2.13	3.29	–4.01
房地产业	**Real Estate**	**8.28**	**6.70**	**10.89**	**7.55**	**–2.19**
房地产开发经营业	Real Estate Development and Management	4.79	5.87	8.17	3.97	–3.86
物业管理业	Property Management	0.71	–0.37	0.67	0.76	–0.34
房地产中介服务业	Real Estate Intermediary Services	–0.11	–0.12	0.44	1.06	0.17
自有房地产经营活动	Own Real Estate Operating Activities	1.10	1.15	1.21	1.42	1.32
其他房地产业	Other Real Estate Industry	1.80	0.17	0.41	0.34	0.52
租赁和商务服务业	**Leasing and Business Services**	**0.77**	**2.49**	**1.67**	**5.85**	**1.67**
租赁业	Leasing Services	0.49	–0.10	0.37	1.43	1.45
商务服务业	Business Services	0.28	2.58	1.30	4.43	0.22

4-10 续表 2 continued 2

指标	Indicator	2013 年	2014 年	2015 年	2016 年	2017 年
科学研究和技术服务业	**Scientific Research and Technical Services**	0.89	0.81	1.40	1.75	3.77
研究和试验发展	Research and Experimental Development	0.18	0.24	0.24	0.44	0.54
专业技术服务业	Special Technical Services	-0.13	-0.36	0.74	1.02	3.22
科技推广和应用服务业	Science and Technology Promotion and Application Services	0.84	0.92	0.41	0.29	0.02
水利、环境和公共设施管理业	**Management of Water Conservancy, Environment and Public Facilities**	0.19	0.18	0.32	0.68	0.52
水利管理业	Management of Water Conservancy	0.11	0.02	0.01	0.03	0.02
生态保护和环境治理业	Ecological Protection and Environmental Management	0.03	0.04	0.01	0.12	0.10
公共设施管理业	Management of Public Facilities	0.05	0.12	0.29	0.53	0.40
居民服务、修理和其他服务业	**Services to Households, Repair and Other Services**	0.85	0.93	0.63	2.28	1.90
居民服务业	Services to Households	0.10	-0.22	0.51	0.97	0.51
机动车、电子产品和日用产品修理业	Repair of Motor Vehicle, Electronics and Household Products	0.33	0.10	-0.01	0.41	0.47
其他服务业	Other Services	0.42	1.05	0.12	0.90	0.92
教育	**Education**	1.85	1.51	2.60	4.23	3.51
卫生和社会工作	**Health,Social Security and Social Welfare**	0.62	1.42	2.48	1.49	-0.59
卫生	Public Health	0.64	1.05	2.38	1.08	-0.55
社会工作	Social Work	-0.02	0.37	0.10	0.41	-0.04
文化、体育和娱乐业	**Culture, Sports and Recreation**	0.67	0.59	0.40	0.94	2.23
新闻和出版业	Journalism and Publishing Activities	0.09	-0.10	-0.06	0.48	1.22
广播、电视、电影和影视录音	Radio, Television, Motion Picture and Videotape Programme	0.09	0.92	-0.01	-0.02	0.46
文化艺术业	Culture and Arts	0.15	-0.21	0.22	0.20	0.26
体育	Sports	0.29	0.03	0.13	0.14	0.21
娱乐业	Recreation	0.04	-0.05	0.12	0.14	0.09
公共管理、社会保障和社会组织	**Public Management, Social Security and Social Organization**	1.69	3.21	3.08	0.40	1.24
第一产业	**Primary Industry**	1.86	2.14	2.21	2.65	1.97
第二产业	**Secondary Industry**	45.33	43.50	39.92	33.63	39.52
第三产业	**Tertiary Industry**	52.81	54.36	57.88	63.72	58.51

注：新行业分组 (GB-2011)。
Note: Grouping of new industries (GB-2011).

4-11 生产总值行业比重(2009年—2013年)(按当年价格计算)
Ratio of Gross Domestic Product by Sector(2009—2013)(Calculated at Current Prices)

单位：% (%)

指标	Indicator	2009年	2010年	2011年	2012年	2013年
生产总值比重	Ratio of Gross Domestic Product	100.0	100.0	100.0	100.0	100.0
第一产业	Primary Industry	5.6	5.5	5.4	5.3	5.4
农林牧渔业	Agriculture, Forestry, Animal Husbandry and Fishery	5.6	5.5	5.4	5.3	5.4
农业	Farming	3.6	3.8	3.5	3.4	3.6
林业	Forestry	0.2	0.1	0.1	0.1	0.2
畜牧业	Animal Husbandry	1.5	1.4	1.6	1.6	1.5
渔业	Fishery	0.1	0.1	0.1	0.1	0.1
农林牧渔服务业	Services of Agriculture,Forestry,Animal Husbandry and Fishing	0.1	0.1	0.1	0.1	0.1
第二产业	Secondary Industry	42.9	41.9	41.5	40.3	39.3
工业	Industry	35.7	34.6	34.2	33.3	32.3
采矿业	Mining	0.8	0.8	0.8	0.7	1.1
制造业	Manufacture	32.1	30.5	29.5	31.0	29.4
电力、燃气及水的生产和供应业	Production and Supply of Electric, Gas and Water	2.7	3.2	3.9	1.6	1.8
建筑业	Construction	7.2	7.3	7.3	7.0	6.9
房屋和土木工程建筑业	Building Construction	5.8	6.0	6.0	5.8	5.4
建筑安装业	Construction Installment	1.1	1.0	0.9	0.8	1.1
建筑装饰业	Construction Decoration	0.2	0.2	0.3	0.3	0.4
其他建筑业	Others	0.1	0.1	0.1	0.1	0.1
第三产业	Tertiary Industry	51.5	52.6	53.1	54.4	55.3
交通运输、仓储和邮政业	Transport, Storage and Postal Services	6.0	6.1	6.7	6.7	6.4
铁路运输业	Railway Transport	1.6	1.4	1.4	1.4	1.2
道路运输业	Road Transport	2.9	3.0	3.5	3.5	3.3
城市公共交通业	Public Transportation by City	0.4	0.4	0.4	0.4	0.3
水上运输业	Waterway Transport	0.0	0.0	0.0	0.0	0.0
航空运输业	Air Transport	0.5	0.6	0.8	0.6	0.6

4-11 续表 1 continued 1

指标	Indicator	2009 年	2010 年	2011 年	2012 年	2013 年
管道运输业	Pipeline Transport	0.0	0.0	0.0	0.0	0.0
装卸搬运和其他运输服务业	Loading and Unloading and Other Transport Services	0.4	0.3	0.5	0.5	0.5
仓储业	Storage	0.2	0.2	0.2	0.2	0.3
邮政业	Postal Services	0.0	0.0	0.0	0.1	0.1
信息传输、计算机服务和软件业	**Information Transmission, Computer Services and Software**	**2.0**	**3.0**	**3.1**	**3.2**	**3.1**
电信和其他信息传输服务业	Telecommunications, Radio and Television and Satellite Transmission Services	0.9	0.8	0.7	0.6	0.6
计算机服务业	Internet and related Services	0.5	0.6	0.7	0.8	0.9
软件业	Software and Information Technology Services	0.5	1.5	1.7	1.8	1.6
批发和零售业	**Wholesale and Retail Trade**	**12.5**	**12.2**	**11.9**	**12.2**	**12.8**
批发业	Wholesale	7.0	7.4	7.6	7.9	8.4
零售业	Retail Trade	5.5	4.8	4.3	4.3	4.5
住宿和餐饮业	**Accommodations and Catering Services**	**3.8**	**3.7**	**3.3**	**3.1**	**3.2**
住宿业	Accommodations	0.4	0.4	0.4	0.4	0.4
餐饮业	Catering Services	3.4	3.2	2.9	2.7	2.8
金融业	**Financial Intermediation**	**7.2**	**7.4**	**7.5**	**8.5**	**8.8**
银行业	Banking Sector	4.9	5.8	6.3	7.4	7.4
证券业	Securities Industry	1.8	1.2	0.7	0.6	0.6
保险业	Insurance	0.3	0.1	0.1	0.1	0.2
其他金融活动	Others	0.2	0.2	0.3	0.4	0.6
房地产业	**Real Estate**	**5.2**	**5.6**	**5.8**	**5.7**	**6.1**
房地产开发经营业	Real Estate Development and Management	1.9	2.1	2.3	2.1	2.4
物业管理业	Property Management	0.6	0.7	0.7	0.7	0.7
房地产中介服务业	Real Estate Intermediary Services	0.3	0.4	0.4	0.4	0.3
其他房地产活动	Other Real Estate Activity	0.2	0.3	0.3	0.3	0.4
居民自有住房服务业	Private Housing Service	2.2	2.1	2.2	2.2	2.2
租赁和商务服务业	**Leasing and Business Services**	**2.7**	**2.7**	**3.0**	**3.0**	**2.9**

4-11 续表 2 continued 2

指标	Indicator	2009 年	2010 年	2011 年	2012 年	2013 年
租赁业	Leasing Services	0.1	0.2	0.2	0.3	0.3
商务服务业	Business Services	2.5	2.6	2.8	2.7	2.6
科学研究、技术服务和地质勘查业	**Scientific Research,Technical Services and Geeological Prospecting Industry**	**1.7**	**1.6**	**1.6**	**1.4**	**1.4**
研究与试验发展	Research and Experimental Development	0.6	0.5	0.5	0.5	0.5
专业技术服务业	Special Technical Services	0.8	0.8	0.8	0.6	0.6
科技交流和推广服务业	Science and Technology Promotion and Application Services	0.2	0.2	0.2	0.2	0.2
地质勘查业	Geeological Prospecting Industry	0.1	0.1	0.1	0.1	0.1
水利、环境和公共设施管理业	**Management of Water Conservancy, Environment and Public Facilities**	**0.4**	**0.4**	**0.3**	**0.3**	**0.3**
水利管理业	Management of Water Conservancy	0.2	0.2	0.1	0.1	0.2
环境管理业	Environmental Management	0.1	0.1	0.1	0.0	0.0
公共设施管理业	Management of Public Facilities	0.1	0.1	0.1	0.2	0.2
居民服务和其他服务业	**Services to Households and Other Services**	**1.0**	**1.0**	**1.1**	**1.1**	**1.1**
居民服务业	Services to Households	0.6	0.6	0.6	0.6	0.6
其他服务业	Other Services	0.4	0.5	0.5	0.5	0.5
教育	**Education**	**3.3**	**3.0**	**2.8**	**2.7**	**2.7**
卫生、社会保障和社会福利业	**Health,Social Security and Social Welfare**	**1.9**	**2.2**	**2.4**	**2.7**	**2.6**
卫生	Public Health	1.7	1.9	2.2	2.5	2.4
社会保障业	Social Security	0.2	0.2	0.2	0.2	0.1
社会福利业	Social Welfare	0.1	0.1	0.0	0.0	0.0
文化、体育和娱乐业	**Culture, Sports and Recreation**	**0.7**	**0.7**	**0.6**	**0.7**	**0.7**
新闻出版业	News and Publication	0.3	0.3	0.3	0.2	0.2
广播、电视、电影和音像业	Radio, Television, Film and Video	0.2	0.2	0.2	0.2	0.2
文化艺术业	Culture and Arts	0.1	0.1	0.1	0.1	0.1
体育	Sports	0.1	0.1	0.1	0.1	0.1
娱乐业	Recreation	0.1	0.1	0.1	0.1	0.1
公共管理和社会组织	**Public Management and Social Organizations**	**3.3**	**3.0**	**3.1**	**3.1**	**3.1**

注：旧行业分组 (GB-2002)。
Note: Grouping of old industries (GB-2002).

4-12 生产总值行业比重(2013年—2017年)(按当年价格计算)
Ratio of Gross Domestic Product by Sector(2013—2017)(Calculated at Current Prices)

单位：%　　(%)

指标	Indicator	2013年	2014年	2015年	2016年	2017年
地区生产总值比重	Ratio of Gross Domestic Product	100.00	100.00	100.00	100.00	100.00
农、林、牧、渔业	Agriculture, Forestry, Animal Husbandry and Fishery	5.44	5.18	5.16	5.02	4.59
农业	Farming	3.57	3.46	3.44	3.29	2.99
林业	Forestry	0.15	0.15	0.16	0.17	0.16
畜牧业	Animal Husbandry	1.49	1.34	1.32	1.32	1.20
渔业	Fishery	0.08	0.08	0.07	0.07	0.06
农、林、牧、渔服务业	Services of Agriculture,Forestry,Animal Husbandry and Fishing	0.15	0.15	0.16	0.17	0.18
工业	Industry	32.32	31.58	30.23	28.75	27.81
采矿业	Mining	0.53	0.52	0.60	0.70	0.69
#开采辅助活动	Mining Support Activities	0.00	0.00	0.00	0.00	0.00
制造业	Manufacture	28.14	27.49	28.12	26.77	26.06
#金属制品、机械和设备修理业	Metal Products, Machinery and Equipment Repair Industry	0.06	0.06	0.06	0.05	0.05
电力、燃气及水的生产和供应业	Production and Supply of Electric, Gas and Water	3.65	3.56	1.51	1.28	1.06
建筑业	Construction	7.79	7.68	7.64	7.55	7.91
房屋建筑业	Building Construction	4.51	4.38	3.96	4.28	4.39
土木工程建筑业	Civil Engineering Construction	2.06	2.10	2.93	2.64	2.99
建筑安装业	Construction Installment	0.48	0.47	0.35	0.21	0.22
建筑装饰业和其他建筑业	Construction Decoration and Others	0.73	0.72	0.40	0.42	0.31
批发和零售业	Wholesale and Retail Trade	11.98	11.99	11.73	11.64	13.56
批发业	Wholesale	7.60	7.65	7.43	7.37	8.62
零售业	Retail Trade	4.38	4.34	4.30	4.26	4.94
交通运输、仓储和邮政业	Transport, Storage and Post	6.37	6.31	6.09	6.00	5.77
铁路运输业	Railway Transport	1.21	1.20	1.12	1.11	1.01
道路运输业	Road Transport	3.19	3.14	3.06	2.94	2.75

4-12 续表 1 continued 1

指标	Indicator	2013 年	2014 年	2015 年	2016 年	2017 年
水上运输业	Waterway Transport	0.02	0.02	0.02	0.02	0.02
航空运输业	Air Transport	0.61	0.60	0.58	0.64	0.62
管道运输业	Pipeline Transport	0.41	0.41	0.39	0.37	0.41
装卸搬运和运输代理业	Loading, Unloading and Forwarding Agency	0.51	0.50	0.48	0.42	0.40
仓储业	Storage	0.29	0.28	0.27	0.33	0.38
邮政业	Postal Services	0.13	0.16	0.15	0.17	0.19
住宿和餐饮业	**Accommodations and Catering Services**	**3.22**	**3.14**	**3.09**	**3.10**	**3.04**
住宿业	Accommodations	0.40	0.39	0.37	0.37	0.35
餐饮业	Catering Services	2.82	2.75	2.72	2.74	2.69
信息传输、软件和信息技术服务业	**Information Transmission, Software and Information Technology**	**3.11**	**3.30**	**3.31**	**3.56**	**3.83**
电信、广播电视和卫星传输服务	Telecommunications, Radio and Television and Satellite Transmission Services	1.95	2.06	2.07	1.92	2.28
互联网和相关服务	Internet and related Services	0.08	0.09	0.09	0.28	0.28
软件和信息技术服务业	Software and Information Technology Services	1.08	1.14	1.15	1.36	1.27
金融业	**Financial Intermediation**	**8.81**	**9.39**	**10.52**	**11.02**	**10.77**
货币金融服务	Monetary and Financial Services	7.41	7.58	8.49	9.02	9.13
资本市场服务	Capital Market Services	0.65	0.84	0.94	0.56	0.57
保险业	Insurance	0.16	0.17	0.19	0.35	0.37
其他金融业	Others	0.61	0.80	0.90	1.09	0.71
房地产业	**Real Estate**	**6.13**	**6.40**	**6.80**	**7.09**	**6.94**
房地产开发经营业	Real Estate Development and Management	2.61	2.94	3.12	3.34	3.06
物业管理业	Property Management	0.51	0.44	0.47	0.51	0.49
房地产中介服务业	Real Estate Intermediary Services	0.34	0.30	0.32	0.39	0.42
自有房地产经营活动	Own Real Estate Operating Activities	2.23	2.30	2.21	2.14	2.22
其他房地产业	Other Real Estate Industry	0.44	0.42	0.68	0.69	0.75
租赁和商务服务业	**Leasing and Business Services**	**2.93**	**2.98**	**3.00**	**3.28**	**2.67**
租赁业	Leasing Services	0.29	0.29	0.29	0.38	0.40
商务服务业	Business Services	2.64	2.69	2.70	2.89	2.28

4–12 续表 2 continued 2

指标	Indicator	2013 年	2014 年	2015 年	2016 年	2017 年
科学研究和技术服务业	Scientific Research and Technical Services	1.45	1.43	1.48	1.58	1.90
研究和试验发展	Research and Experimental Development	0.12	0.12	0.12	0.16	0.20
专业技术服务业	Special Technical Services	0.96	0.95	0.98	1.04	1.31
科技推广和应用服务业	Science and Technology Promotion and Application Services	0.36	0.36	0.37	0.38	0.39
水利、环境和公共设施管理业	Management of Water Conservancy, Environment and Public Facilities	0.33	0.33	0.34	0.38	0.40
水利管理业	Management of Water Conservancy	0.04	0.04	0.04	0.04	0.04
生态保护和环境治理业	Ecological Protection and Environmental Management	0.01	0.01	0.01	0.02	0.03
公共设施管理业	Management of Public Facilities	0.28	0.28	0.29	0.32	0.33
居民服务、修理和其他服务业	Services to Households, Repair and Other Services	1.10	1.12	1.13	1.24	1.09
居民服务业	Services to Households	0.58	0.56	0.56	0.60	0.51
机动车、电子产品和日用产品修理业	Repair of Motor Vehicle, Electronics and Household Products	0.17	0.18	0.18	0.20	0.19
其他服务业	Other Services	0.35	0.38	0.39	0.43	0.40
教育	Education	2.69	2.66	2.75	3.01	3.22
卫生和社会工作	Health,Social Security and Social Welfare	2.56	2.53	2.62	2.69	2.50
卫生	Public Health	2.37	2.34	2.42	2.47	2.29
社会工作	Social Work	0.19	0.19	0.20	0.22	0.21
文化、体育和娱乐业	Culture, Sports and Recreation	0.69	0.71	0.71	0.74	0.73
新闻和出版业	Journalism and Publishing Activities	0.24	0.24	0.24	0.26	0.29
广播、电视、电影和影视录音	Radio, Television, Motion Picture and Videotape Programme	0.21	0.25	0.25	0.24	0.21
文化艺术业	Culture and Arts	0.10	0.08	0.08	0.09	0.08
体育	Sports	0.08	0.08	0.08	0.08	0.08
娱乐业	Recreation	0.07	0.06	0.06	0.07	0.06
公共管理、社会保障和社会组织	Public Management, Social Security and Social Organization	3.07	3.30	3.41	3.35	3.26
第一产业	Primary Industry	5.30	5.03	5.01	4.85	4.41
第二产业	Secondary Industry	40.06	39.19	37.82	36.24	35.67
第三产业	Tertiary Industry	54.65	55.78	57.18	58.90	59.92

注：新行业分组 (GB–2011)。
Note: Grouping of new industries (GB–2011).

4-13 分地区生产总值(2020年)
Value of Gross Domestic Product by Region(2020)

单位：亿元 (100 million yuan)

指标	Indicator	济南市 Total City	历下区 Li xia	市中区 Shi zhong	槐荫区 Huai yin	天桥区 Tian qiao	历城区 Li cheng	长清区 Chang qing	章丘区 Zhang qiu	济阳区 Ji yang
地区生产总值	Gross Domestic Product	10140.9	1910.4	1059.6	624.3	564.6	1017.0	338.8	1002.5	205.5
第一产业	Primary Industry	361.7	0.0	1.6	2.1	1.3	21.2	33.9	82.1	33.1
第二产业	Secondary Industry	3530.7	432.9	214.8	182.4	199.7	266.9	162.1	523.9	97.6
第三产业	Tertiary Industry	6248.6	1477.5	843.2	439.7	363.6	729.0	142.7	396.4	74.7

4-13 续表 continued

指标	Indicator	莱芜区 Lai wu	钢城区 Gang cheng	济南高新区 Ji'nan Gao xin	莱芜高新区 Lai wu Gao xin	济南先行区 JN Pioneer Area	南部山区 Nan shan	平阴县 Ping yin	商河县 Shang he
地区生产总值	Gross Domestic Product	641.6	300.2	1291.5	165.7	53.0	63.1	233.3	179.9
第一产业	Primary Industry	59.5	10.5	3.7	1.7	12.8	15.6	34.2	48.1
第二产业	Secondary Industry	277.3	198.9	620.7	42.0	23.5	11.1	130.4	51.9
第三产业	Tertiary Industry	304.7	90.7	667.1	122.1	16.7	36.4	68.7	80.0

4-14 生产总值(2020年)(分行业，按当年价格计算)
Value of Gross Domestic Product(2020)(Sub Industry，Calculated at Current Prices)

单位：亿元 (100 million yuan)

指标	Indicator	2020年
地区生产总值	**Gross Domestic Product**	**10140.91**
农、林、牧、渔业	**Agriculture, Forestry, Animal Husbandry and Fishery**	**380.30**
农、林、牧、渔服务业	Services of Agriculture,Forestry,Animal Husbandry and Fishing	18.64
工业	**Industry**	**2360.48**
#开采辅助活动	Mining Support Activities	0.02
#金属制品、机械和设备修理业	Metal Products, Machinery and Equipment Repair Industry	11.59
建筑业	**Construction**	**1181.80**
批发和零售业	**Wholesale and Retail Trade**	**1345.00**
批发业	Wholesale	727.47
零售业	Retail Trade	617.53
交通运输、仓储和邮政业	**Transport, Storage and Post**	**494.57**
住宿和餐饮业	**Accommodations and Catering Services**	**140.69**
住宿业	Accommodations	17.53
餐饮业	Catering Services	123.16
金融业	**Financial Intermediation**	**968.52**
房地产业	**Real Estate**	**797.80**
房地产业(K门类)	Real estate industry(K category)	578.19
自有房地产经营活动	Own Real Estate Operating Activities	219.61
其他服务业	**Other Services**	**2471.75**
营利性服务业	Profit service industry	1440.37
非营利性服务业	Non-Profit service industry	1031.38
第一产业	**Primary Industry**	**361.66**
第二产业	**Secondary Industry**	**3530.67**
第三产业	**Tertiary Industry**	**6248.58**

4-15 规模以上服务业企业分行业主要经济指标（2020年）
Main Economic Indicators of Service Enterpriese Above Designated Size by Sector(2020)

单位：万元

指标	Indicator	单位数（个）Number of Enterprises (unit)	固定资产原价 Original Value of Fixed Assets	本年折旧 Depreciation in the Year
合计	Total	1917	53111607	2391300
交通运输、仓储和邮政业	Transport, Storage and Postal Services	355	42482072	1682327
信息传输、软件和信息技术服务业	Information Transmission, Software and Information Technology	258	6427708	435813
房地产业	Real Estate	222	1074431	59821
租赁和商务服务业	Leasing and Business Services	452	1202651	77074
科学研究和技术服务业	Scientific Research,Technical Services	364	739791	64097
水利、环境和公共设施管理业	Management of Water Conservancy, Environment and Public Facilities	33	506288	33007
居民服务、修理和其他服务业	services to Households, Repair and Other Services	68	77091	4786
教育	Education	42	152779	8023
卫生和社会工作	Health and Social Work	56	154041	12259
文化、体育和娱乐业	Culture, Sports and Recreation	67	294755	14093

(10 000 yuan)

折旧率 (%) Depreciation Rate(%)	营业收入 Business Revenue	税金及附加 Taxes and Other Surcharges	营业利润 Profits from Business	利润总额 Total Profits	应付职工薪酬（本年贷方累计发生额） Total Wages Payable	从业人员平均人数（人） Average Number of Employees (person)	人均工资（元） Per Capita Wages (yuan)	应交增值税 Value Added Tax Payable
4.5	27160101	133227	1867809	1937392	6079791	508665	119524	696321
4.0	12291774	31631	–259069	–260175	2784078	177696	156676	277336
6.8	5335589	22967	33146	47361	1189639	97059	122569	172998
5.6	1187805	21874	83023	91016	327258	59342	55148	37010
6.4	2724990	25942	1298283	1302496	576128	67248	85672	71843
8.7	3744862	20018	448425	458069	802106	54506	147159	112968
6.5	444981	3454	71537	76568	66083	14612	45225	6036
6.2	219395	793	14739	15748	60012	14656	40947	4189
5.3	253540	430	20447	24692	84293	7804	108013	1601
8.0	363026	172	28728	26647	97660	9779	99867	684
4.8	594140	5946	128550	154970	92534	5963	155181	11655

主要统计指标解释

国内生产总值（GDP） 指一个国家（或地区）所有常住单位在一定时期内生产活动的最终成果。国内生产总值有三种表现形态，即价值形态、收入形态和产品形态。从价值形态看，它是所有常住单位在一定时期内生产的全部货物和服务价值超过同期中间投入的全部非固定资产货物和服务价值的差额，即所有常住单位的增加值之和；从收入形态看，它是所有常住单位在一定时期内创造并分配给常住单位和非常住单位的初次收入分配之和；从产品形态看，它是所有常住单位在一定时期内最终使用的货物和服务价值与货物和服务净出口价值之和。在实际核算中，国内生产总值有三种计算方法，即生产法、收入法和支出法。三种方法分别从不同的方面反映国内生产总值及其构成。国统字〔2004〕4号文规定：地区GDP的中文名称改为“地区生产总值”。

生产法 生产法是从生产过程中生产的货物和服务总产品价值入手，剔除生产过程中投入的中间产品的价值，得到增加价值的一种方法。计算公式为：

增加值=总产出-中间投入

将国民经济各行业的增加值相加，得到国内生产总值。

总产出、中间投入和增加值具有相同的生产范围，即常住生产单位货物和服务的生产。它不仅包括常住生产单位为其他单位提供的货物和服务的生产，而且包括为本单位使用的货物和服务的生产，但是，住户为自己最终消费生产的服务，只计算自有住房服务和付酬家庭雇员提供的服务，不包括住户成员为本住户最终消费而生产的自给性家庭服务。

收入法 收入法也称为分配法。按收入法计算生产总值是从生产过程创造收入的角度，对常住单位的生产活动成果进行核算。按照这种计算方法，增加值由劳动者报酬、生产税净额、固定资产折旧和营业盈余四个部分组成。计算公式为：

增加值=劳动者报酬+生产税净额+固定资产折旧+营业盈余

国民经济各部门的增加值之和等于生产总值。

在计算劳动者报酬时，需要注意作为劳动者报酬的实物性收入与中间消耗的界限。如果生产单位为其从事生产活动的劳动者提供的货物或服务，可以由劳动者在自己闲暇的时间里满足他们的需要，并且可以改善和提高他们的实际生活水平，同时，其他普通消费者也可以在市场上购买到这些货物和服务，那么就属于劳动者的实物收入。生产单位为了生产能正常进行，为劳动者购买的货物和提供的服务，如因特殊工作需要提供的服装或鞋，因公出差提供的运输和旅馆服务费用等，属于中间投入。

支出法 支出法是从最终使用的角度反映国内生产总值最终使用去向的一种方法。最终使用包括货物和服务的最终消费支出、资本形成总额、货物和服务净出口三部分，计算公式为：

国内生产总值=最终消费支出+资本形成总额+货物和服务净出口

按支出法计算的生产总值，在计算最终消费支出，包括居民消费支出和政府消费支出时，是从支出的最终承担者的角度计算的，而不是从最终实际消费者的角度计算的；在计算资本形成总额时，固定资本形成总额只包括通过生产活动生产出来的固定资产，不包括自然资产，存货增加不包括由于价格因素影响产生的持有收益。

按三种方法计算的国内生产总值反映的是同一经济总体在同一时期的生产活动成果，因此，从理论上讲，三种计算方法所得到的结果应该是一致的。但是，在实践中，由于受资料来源的口径限制和计算方法的影响，要保证这三种计算方法所得到的结果完全相等几乎是不可能的。在国内生产总值的三种计算方法中，生产法和收入法都是对各产业部门的增加值进行核算，为了就每一产业部门取得一致的增加值数据，根据资料来源状况，我国在核算实践中，有的产业部门，如农业、工业的增加值，确定以生产法的计算结果为准，有的产业部门，如部分服务业增加值，确定以收入法的计算结果为准，因此，我国的生产法国内生产总值等于收入法国内生产总值。但是，支出法国内生产总值与生产法和收入法国内生产总值之间存在统计误差，有的年份支出法国内生产总值大于生产法和收入法国内生产总值，有的年份结果相反。我国通常以生产法和收入法国内生产总值数据为准，将上述统计误差控制在一定范围。各种公开发表的国内生产总值总量和增长速度数据均是生产法和收入法的计算结果。按三种方法计算的国内生产总值数据之间具有如下关系：

国内生产总值=生产法国内生产总值

=收入法国内生产总值

=支出法国内生产总值+统计误差

可比价格 指计算各种总量指标所采用的扣除了价格变动因素的价格，可进行不同时期总量指标的对比。按可比价格计算总量指标有两种方法：一种是直接用产品产量乘某一年的不变价格计算；另一种是用价格指数进行缩减。

不变价格 指以同类产品某年的平均价格作为固定价格，用于计算各年的产品价值。按不变价格计算的产品价值消除了价格变动因素，不同时期对比可以反映生产的发展速度。新中国成立后，随着工农业产品价格水平的变化，国家统计局先后九次制定了全国统一的工业产品不变价格和农业产品不变价格。从1952 年到1957 年使用1952 年工（农）业产品不变价格，从1957 年到1970 年使用1957 年不变价格，从1971 年到1980 年使用1970 年不变价格，从1981 年到1990 年使用1980 年不变价格，从1991 年到2000年使用1990年不变价格，从2001年到2005年使用2000年不变价格，从2006年到2010年使用2005年不变价格，从2011年到2015年使用2010年不变价格，从2016年开始使用2015年不变价格。

三次产业 根据社会生产活动历史发展的顺序对产业结构的划分，产品直接取自自然界的部门称为第一产业，对初级产品进行再加工的部门称为第二产业。为生产和消费提供各种服

务的部门称为第三产业。它是世界上通用的产业结构分类，但各国的划分不尽一致。我国的三次产业划分是:

第一产业是指农、林、牧、渔业(不含农、林、牧、渔服务业)。

第二产业是指采矿业（不含开采辅助活动），制造业（不含金属制品、机械和设备修理业），电力、热力、燃气及水生产和供应业，建筑业。

第三产业即服务业，是指除第一产业、第二产业以外的其他行业。第三产业包括: 批发和零售业，交通运输、仓储和邮政业，住宿和餐饮业，信息传输、软件和信息技术服务业，金融业，房地产业，租赁和商务服务业，科学研究和技术服务业，水利、环境和公共设施管理业，居民服务、修理和其他服务业，教育，卫生和社会工作，文化、体育和娱乐业，公共管理、社会保障和社会组织，国际组织，以及农、林、牧、渔业中的农、林、牧、渔服务业，采矿业中的开采辅助活动，制造业中的金属制品、机械和设备修理业。

国内支出总额　指一个国家（或地区）所有常住单位在一定时期内用于最终消费和投资，以及净出口的货物和服务支出总额，它反映本期生产的国内生产总值的使用构成。这一总量就是支出法测算的国内生产总值，具体包括最终消费支出、资本形成总额、货物和服务净出口。

最终消费　指常住单位在一定时期内的货物和服务的全部最终消费。总消费分为居民消费和政府消费。

居民实际最终消费　指常住住户获得的所有消费品和消费服务的价值。包括以下二类 (1) 居民自身通过支出所得到的个人货物和服务，其价值即居民在个人消费品和消费服务上承担的支出，包括虚拟支出。(2) 作为为居民服务的非营利机构和政府的实物转移得到的个人货物和服务。其价值即为居民非营利机构和政府在个人消费品和服务上的支出。包括虚拟支出。

资本形成总额　指常住单位在一定时期内获得减去处置的固定资产和存货的净额，包括固定资本形成总额和存货增加。

居民消费支出　居民消费支出包括居民实际最终消费中第 (1) 项内容。所以居民实际最终消费大于居民消费支出。

政府实际最终消费　指政府向社会或社会中某些部门提供的公共消费服务的价值。其价值即政府在公共服务上的支出。

政府消费支出　指(1)政府在个人消费品和消费服务。(2)在公共消费服务上承担的支出，包括虚拟支出。

总投资　指常住单位在一定时期内对固定资产和库存的投资支出合计，分为固定资产形成和库存增加两项。

（1）固定资本形成总额　指从常住单位在一定时期内购置、转入和自产自用的固定资产中，扣除已有固定资产的销售和转出后的价值。固定资产形成包括在一定时期内完成的建筑工程、安装工程和设备器具购置价值，以及新增役、种、奶、毛、娱乐用牲畜和新增经济林价值等。

（2）库存增加　指常住单位一定时期内库存实物量变动的市场价值。期初与期末差额为正值表示库存增加，负值表示库存减少。具体包括本期购买的原材料、燃料和储备物资等商品库存；本期生产的产成品、半成品和在制品等产品库存。

货物和服务净出口　指货物和服务出口减货物和服务进口的差额。出口包括常住单位向非常住单位出售或无偿转让的各种货物和服务的价值；进口包括常住单位从非常住单位购买或无偿得到的各种货物和服务的价值。由于服务活动的提供与使用同时发生，因此服务的进出口业务并不发生出入境现象，一般把常住单位从国外得到的服务作为进口，非常住单位从本国得到的服务作为出口。货物的出口和进口都按离岸价格计算。

来自国外的净要素收入　指一定国家（或地区）来自国外（地区外）的生产税及进口税（扣除生产及进口补贴）、劳动者报酬和财产收入，减去支付给国外（地区外）的生产税及进口税（扣除生产及进口补贴）、劳动者报酬和财产收入的差额。国内生产总值加上来自国外的净要素收入等于国民生产总值。

总产出　总产出是指一定时期内一个国家（或地区）常住单位生产的所有货物和服务的价值，即包括新增价值，也包括转移价值。它反映常住单位生产活动的总规模。总产出按生产者价格计算。

中间投入　中间投入是指常住单位在生产或提供货物与服务过程中，消耗和使用的所有非固定资产货物和服务的价值，中间投入也称为中间消耗。一般按购买者价格计算。

增加值　增加值是指常住单位生产过程创造的新增价值和固定资产的转移价值。它可以按生产法计算，也可以按收入法计算，按生产法计算，它等于总产出减去中间投入；按收入法计算，它等于劳动者报酬、生产税净额、固定资产折旧和营业盈余之和。

固定资产折旧　指一定时期内为弥补固定资产损耗而应提取的补偿价值，它反映了全部固定资产在本期生产中的资产转移价值。各类企业的固定资产折旧是指从成本费用中提取的折旧费。对不计提折旧的单位，如政府机关、事业单位、学校医院、部队和居民住房则应进行虚拟折旧。

劳动者报酬　指劳动者为常住单位提供劳务而获得的各种报酬，它反映劳动者参与增加值创造而获得的原始收入。具体包括从各种来源开支的货币工资和实物工资，即单位以工资、福利、社会保险等形式，从成本、费用和利润中为劳动者支付的各种开支，以及个体和其他劳动者通过参加社会生产活动所获得的各种劳动报酬。

生产税净额　指生产税与补贴之差，它反映政府从本期创造的增加值中所得到的原始收入份额。生产税是指政府对生产单位的生产经营活动所征收的各种税、附加和规费，具体包括销售（营业）税金及附加、增值税、管理费开支的税、应交纳的养路费、排污费和水电附加等，以及烟酒专卖上缴政府的专项收入。补贴与生产税相反，是政府对生产单位的单方面收入转移，因此视为负税处理，包括政策亏损补贴、粮食系统价格补贴、外贸企业出口退税收入等。

营业盈余　指常住单位创造的增加值扣除固定资产折旧价值、支付劳动者报酬和上缴政府生产税净额后的余额，它反映企业参与增加值创造而应得到的原始收入份额。该指标相当于企业的营业利润，但要扣除利税后项目中支付的工资、福利及公益金等。

非金融企业部门　非金融企业部门是指由以营利为目的、

从事非金融经济活动的所有常住非金融企业组成的集合。包括农业企业、工业、建筑业企业、流通企业、服务企业、执行企业会计制度的事业单位；行政事业单位下属的独立核算单位（即企业化管理的事业单位）亦划入本部门。

金融机构部门 金融机构部门是指由从事金融活动的所有常住独立核算单位组成的集合。在我国的新国民经济核算体系中，将其分为三大类：银行机构、保险机构和非银行金融机构。

银行机构为中央银行（中国人民银行）、政策性银行（国家开发银行、农业开发银行、进出口银行）和商业银行（中国工商银行、中国农业银行、中国银行、中国建设银行、交通银行、中信实业银行、中国投资银行、光大银行、城市合作银行等），以及若干区域性银行或私营银行（如华夏银行、民生银行等）。

政府部门 政府部门是指由行使国家管理职能的行政单位和为社会提供非市场化服务的事业单位（即所谓非盈利性机构单位）组成的集合。包括国家机关、政党机关、社会团体及执行预算会计制度的事业单位等。军事单位及所属的非独立核算单位也包括在本部门中。由于目前在我国非盈利机构主要是由国家拨款资助的事业单位，因此我国将为政府和为居民服务的非盈利机构统一归进政府部门。

我国的政府部门由行政单位和非盈利的事业单位组成。其中“财政”作为一个特殊的部门归列于政府部门。

住户部门 住户部门是指由所有常住居民户组成的集体。包括城镇常住居民户、农村常住居民户和城乡个体经营单位。由于个体经营单位的资产负债及财务收支还不能完全独立于所属住户，因此把个体经营单位也划入住户部门。

住户内的成员共同享用其生活设施、共同消费一些货物和服务，其收入和财产的部门或全部被集中起来，因此他们也有权利参与或影响整个住户的经济活动。

国外部门 国外部门指与我国常住机构单位发生经济往来的所有非常住机构单位组成的集合，增列国外部门并不要求编制其整个资产负债表，而只限于记录常住机构单位与非常住机构单位之间所进行的交易及往来活动的累计存量，即仅仅是为了反映我国经济总体与国外进行经济往来活动及结果的总规模和结构关系。

非金融资产 根据我国新国民经济核算体系中有关资产负债项目的基本定义和联合国1993 年SNA 的定义，“非金融资产”是指机构单位单独或共同对其执行所有权或处置权，并通过在核算期内持有或使用它们可从中获得经济利益的，除金融资产以外的经济资产。

非金融资产按是否具有物质形态划分为有形资产和无形资产，按产生的方式或过程可划分为生产资产和非生产资产。在非金融资产中，“生产资产”由固定资产、存货和珍贵物品组成。“非生产资产”可大致分为两类，一类是资源资产，即有形非生产资产，由土地资产、水资源资产、地下资产和非培育生物资产组成；另一类是无形非生产资产，如专利权、租约和其他可转让合同、购买的商誉等。

由于我国目前在资产负债核算中所面临的资料来源和技术条件的限制，我们仅将非金融资产简单地划分为固定资产、存货和其他非金融资产三类。

贡献率 各产业的贡献率是分析经济效益的一个指标，它是指第一、二、三产业增量与生产总值增量之比。

规模以上服务业法人单位 包括：交通运输、仓储和邮政业，信息传输、软件和信息技术服务业，租赁和商务服务业，科学研究和技术服务业，水利、环境和公共设施管理业，居民服务业、修理和其他服务业，教育，卫生和社会工作，文化、体育和娱乐业；以及物业管理、房地产中介服务等行业。

Explanatory Notes on Main Statistical Indicators

GDP refers to the final products at market prices produced by all residents in a country (or a region) during a certain period of time. Gross domestic product is expressed in three different forms, i.e., value, income, and products respectively. GDP in its value form refers to the total value of all goods and services produced by all resident units during a certain period of time, minus the total value of input of goods of non-fixed assets and services; in other term, it is the sum of the value-added of all resident units. GDP in the form of income includes the income created by all resident units and distributed to resident and non-resident units. GDP in the form of products refers to the value of all goods and services for final consumption by all resident units minus the net exports of goods and services during a given period of time. In the practice of national accounting, gross domestic product is calculated with three approaches, i.e., production approach, income approach and expenditure approach, which reflect gross domestic product and its composition from different aspects. In the actual calculation, GDP is based on three calculation methods-production approach, income approach and expenditure approach. These three methods reflect GDP and its composition from different aspects. GTZi (2004) No. 4 document prescribes: Chinese name of regional GDP is "regional gross domestic product".

Production Approach focuses on the total value of goods and services produced in production activities. GDP by Production Approach equals the value of total output minus that of input consumed in production process. The calculation formula is:

GDP by Production Approach= gross output– intermediate input

The sum of value added made by different industries is GDP.

Gross output, intermediate input and value added have the same production scope, i.e., production of goods and services by resident units. It not only includes the production of goods and services by resident units for other units, but that used for the unit. However, services finally consumed and produced by households only include own housing services and services provided by paid family employees (excluding self-supporting family services produced by the household member for final consumption of the household).

Income Approach (also known as distribution approach): refers to the method measuring the final results of production activities from the perspective of income made by all residents. GDP of income approach includes laborers' remuneration, net taxes on production, depreciation of fixed assets and operating surplus. The calculation formula is:

GDP by income approach= laborers' remuneration + net taxes on production + depreciation of fixed assets+ operating surplus

The sum of value added made by different industries is GDP.

In the calculation of labourers' remunerations, it's necessary to define the limit between material incomes and intermediate consumption among labourers' remunerations. If goods or units provided by production units for its labourers engaging in production activity can be met by such labourers in their spare time, improve and raise their actual living level, and other ordinary consumers can purchase such goods and services in the market, these goods and services are classified into material incomes of labourers. Goods purchased by production units for labourers and relevant services for the purpose of successful production, such as clothes or shoes provided due to special work need and transportation and hotel service charges in the business trip, are classified into intermediate input.

Expenditure Approach refers to the method measuring the final results of production activities of a country during a given period from the perspective of final use. It includes final consumption expenditure, total capital formation and net export of goods and services.

GDP by expenditure approach = final consumption expenditure+ gross capital formation+ net export of goods and services

For GDP by expenditure approach, the final consumption expenditure, including household consumption expenditure and government consumption expenditure, is calculated from the perspective of final bearer of expenditure, not from the perspective of final consumers; in the calculation of gross capital formation, gross fixed capital formation only includes fixed assets produced by production activities, excluding natural assets, where increases in inventories do not include holding gains.

GDP by three approaches reflects the results of production activities of the same economic entity during the same period, so theoretically results from three calculation approaches shall be consistent. However, in practice, it's almost impossible to ensure results from these three approaches are completely equal due to the caliber limit of data source and the influence of calculation approaches. Among three calculation approaches of GDP, production approach and income approach are used for business accounting of the value added of each industry sector. For the purpose of consistent data regarding value added of each industrial sector, the value added of some industrial sectors (such as agriculture and industry) is subject to the calculation result of the production approach and the value added of some industry sectors (such as some service industries) is subject to the calculation result of the income approach in the accounting practice in China according to data source, thus China's GDP by production approach is equal to that by income approach. However, statistical error exists between GDP by expenditure approach and that by production approach and income approach. GDP by expenditure approach is more than that by production approach and income approach in some years and it turns out just the opposite in some other years. GDP by production approach and income approach prevail in China generally and the above statistical error shall be controlled to a certain range. Various data regarding total volume and growth rate of GDP published is the calculation result based on production approach and income approach.

The following relationships between data regarding GDP calculated based on above–mentioned three methods are as follows:

GDP= GDP by production approach

= GDP by income approach

= GDP by expenditure approach+ statistical error

Constant Price refers to the price without the effect of price change. By using constant price, total amount of indices of different periods can be compared. There are two methods in which total amount indices are obtained, one using current price of some year to multiply the physical volume of certain products and the other using price index.

Fixed Price refers to the average price of similar products in a given period, with which the product value of different period can be calculated. The product value calculated at fixed price can show the growth rate of production in different periods. Since 1949, NBS has framed the united industrial and agricultural fixed price 8 times, including the fixed price of 1952 used from 1952 to 1957, the fixed price of 1957 used from 1957 to 1970, the fixed price of 1970 used from 1971 to 1980, the fixed price of 1980 used from 1981 to 1990, the fixed price of 1990 used from 1991 to 2000, the fixed price of 2000 used from 2001 to 2005, the fixed price of 2005 used from 2006 to 2010, the fixed price of 2010 used from 2011 to 2015, and the fixed price of 2015 used from 2016.

Three Industries Classification of economic activities into three branches of industries is based on the development of production. Primary industry refers to the production activities that obtain products from nature. Secondary industry refers to the production activities that process primary goods. Tertiary industry refers to the production activities that provide primary and secondary industries with services. Classification of economic activities into three branches of industries is a common practice in the world, although the grouping varies to some extent from country to country.

Economic activities of China are categorized into following industries:

Primary industry refers to agriculture, forestry, animal husbandry and fishery (not contain agriculture, forestry, animal husbandry and fishery service industry).

Secondary industry refers to mining industry (not contain mining auxiliary activities), manufacturing industry (not contain metal products, machinery and equipment repair industry), electricity, heat, gas and water production and supply industry and construction industry.

The tertiary industry is the service industry, refers to all other economic activities not included in primary or secondary industry. According to the economic condition in China, tertiary industry includes Wholesale and Retail Trades, Transport, Storage and Post, Information Transmission, Computer Services and Software, Hotels and Catering Services, Financial Intermediation, Real Estate, Leasing and Business Services, Scientific Research, Technical Services and Geologic Prospecting, Management of Water Conservancy, Environment and Public Facilities, Services to Households and Other Services, Education, Health and Social Security and Social Welfare, Culture, Sports and Entertainment, Public Management and Social Organization, and International Organizations, as well as agriculture, forestry, animal husbandry and fishery services in the agriculture, forestry, animal husbandry and fishery, mining auxiliary activities in the mining industry, metalware, machinery and equipment repair industry in the manufacturing industry.

Gross Domestic Expenditure refers to total expenditures on goods and services of all resident units used for final consumption and investment and net export in a certain period of time in a country (or region) and reflects usage composition of GDP produced in the current period. The gross domestic expenditure is GDP by expenditure approach, including final consumption expenditure, gross capital formation and net export value of such goods and services.

Final Consumption refers to the final consumption of all goods and services of the resident unit within a certain period of time. Total consumption is classified into household consumption and government consumption.

Final Consumption of Households refers to the value of all consumer goods and consumption services obtained by permanent households, including two categories below (1) personal goods and services obtained by the resident based on expenditure whose value is the expenditure regarding individual consumer's goods and consumption services borne by the resident, including virtual expenditure and (2) personal goods and services obtained by physical transfer of non–profit organization and government serving the resident whose value is the expenditure regarding individual consumer's goods and consumption service borne by non–profit organization and government serving the resident, including virtual expenditure.

Total Capital Formation refers to the fixed assets acquired minus those disposed of and the net value of inventory, including the total fixed capital formation and the increase in inventory.

Household Consumption Expenditure includes Item (1) content in the residents' actual final consumption, so the residents' actual final consumption is more than household consumption expenditure.

Actual Final Consumption of Government refers to the value of public consumption services provided by the government to the society or some departments in the society whose value is the public service expenditure of the government.

Government Consumption Expenditure refers to the expenditure regarding (1) individual consumer's goods and consumption services and (2) public consumption services borne by the government, including virtual expenditure.

Total Investment refers to total investment expenditures of resident unit relating to fixed assets and inventories within a certain period of time, divided into formation of fixed assets and increase in inventories.

(1) Gross fixed capital formation refers to the value arising after deduction of sales and roll–out of existing fixed assets from fixed assets of the resident unit purchased, transferred in and produced independently

within a certain period of time. Gross fixed capital formation includes the value of constructional engineering and installation project and equipment purchase completed within a certain period of time and the value of new livestock for service, breeding, milk, wool and recreation and economic forest.

(2) Increase in Inventory refers to the market value of the change in physical quantity of inventory of resident units within a certain period of time. In case that the difference between the beginning and the end is positive, it means an increase in inventories; in case that the difference between the beginning and the end is negative, it means decrease in inventories, including inventory of commodities such as raw material, fuel and restock purchased in the current period and inventory of such products as finished products, semi–finished products and products in process produced in the current period.

Net Export of Goods and Services refers to the difference of the exports of goods and services minus imports of goods and services. The exports include the value of various goods and services sold or gratuitously transferred by the resident units to the non– resident units; The imports include the value of various goods and services purchased or gratuitously obtained by the resident units from the non– resident units; Because the provision of services and the use of them happen simultaneously, the acquisition of services by the resident units from abroad is usually treated as import while the acquisition of services by non–resident units in this country is usually treated as export. The export and import of goods are calculated at FOB.

Net Factor Income from Abroad refers to the difference of net production tax and import tax (deducting production and import subsidies), labourers' remunerations and property income of a country (or region) from abroad minus production and import duties (deducting production and import subsidies), remuneration for labourers and property income paid to foreign country (region). The result after GDP plus foreign net factor income equals to GNP.

Gross Output Gross output refers to the value of all goods and services produced by resident units in a country (or region) within a certain period of time, including newly–increased value and transfer value which reflects the total scale of production activities of resident units. Gross output is calculated in line with producer's price.

Intermediate Input Intermediate input refers to the value of all non–permanent asset goods and services consumed and used in the process of resident units producing or providing goods and services, which is also called as intermediate consumption and is generally calculated pursuant to purchaser price.

Value Added refers to the newly–increased value created by the resident unit in the production process and transfer value of fixed assets which can be calculated based on production approach or income approach. The added value equals to the result after grass output is deducted by intermediate input in case of being calculated based on production approach or the sum of remuneration for labourers, net production tax, depreciation of fixed assets and operating surplus in case of being calculated based on income approach.

Depreciation of Fixed Assets refers to the compensated value extracted to make up for losses of fixed assets within a certain period of time which reflects the asset transfer value of all fixed assets in the production in the current period. Depreciation of fixed assets of various enterprises refers to the depreciation cost extracted from the cost. Units of no calculation of depreciation (such as government agency, public institution, school and hospital, troops and residents' housing) shall be subject to virtual depreciation.

Remuneration for Labourers refers to various remunerations because the worker provides the resident unit with labor service which reflects original income obtained by the worker due to participate in creation of value added, including monetary wages and wages in kind from various sources (namely various expenditures paid by the unit to the worker based on costs, expenses and profits in the form of salary, welfare and social insurance as well as various remunerations of labor obtained by individual and other labourers by participating in social production activity.

Net Production Tax refers to the balance between production tax and subsidy which reflects the original income share obtained by the government from the added value which is created in the current period. Net production tax refers to various taxes additional taxes and levies and charges levied against production and operation activities of production units by the government, including sales (business) taxes and surcharges, added–value tax, tax on overhead expenses, road toll, sewage charge and utility surcharge which shall be paid and special revenue of the government paid for a state monopoly of sales of tobacco and alcoholic drinks. The subsidy is contrary to the net production tax. The former is unilateral transfer of income of the government to the production unit, thus it's deemed negative tax, including policy loss subsidies, food system price subsidies, export tax rebate income of foreign trade enterprises.

Operating Surplus refers to the balance after the value added which is created by resident units is deducted by value of depreciation of fixed assets and used for payment of remuneration for labourers and net production tax of the government which reflects the original income share to be obtained after the enterprise participates in creating the value added. The indicator is equivalent to operating profit of the enterprise but deduction of salary, welfare and welfare fund paid in the after–tax project.

Non–Financial Institutions Sector refer to all resident non–financial businesses for a lucrative purpose which engage in non–financial economic activities, including agricultural enterprises, industrial enterprises, construction enterprises, circulation enterprises, service enterprises and public institutions implementing the enterprise accounting system; Independent accounting units (namely public institutions based on enterprise–style management) subordinate to the administrative institution are included into non–financial corporate sectors.

Financial Institutions Sector refer to all resident independent accounting units engaging in financial activities. In the new national economic accounting system in China, financial institutions sector are divided into three categories: banking institution, insurance institute and non-bank financial institution.

Banking institutions include central bank (The People's Bank of China), policy banks (China Development Bank, Agricultural Development Bank of China and The Export-Import Bank of China), commercial banks (ICBC, ABC, Bank of China, CCB, Bank of Communications, China CITIC Bank, China Investment Bank, China Everbright Bank and Urban Partnership Bank) as well as several regional banks and private banks (such as Huaxia Bank and China Minsheng Bank).

Government Departments Government departments refer to administrative units exercising state administration functions and public institutions providing the society with non-market service (namely so-called non-profit organization), including state organs, Party organs, social organization and public institution implementing the budget accounting system. The military unit and non-independent accounting unit subordinate to the military unit are also included into government departments. Non-profit organizations in China are mainly public institution subsidized by state appropriation, so China uniformly classy non-profit organizations serving the government and residents into government departments.

Government departments in China are composed by administrative units and non-profit public institutions. "Financial department" (special department) is classified as government department.

Household Sector refers to the collective constituted by all resident households, including permanent urban households, permanent rural households and urban and rural self-employed units. Because assets and liabilities and financial revenues of individual business unit fail to be completely independent from corresponding household, the individual business unit is included into household sector.

Members in the household share domestic installation as well as consume some goods and services together whose income and property departments may be collected, so they also have the right to participate in or affect economic activities of the whole household.

Foreign Departments Foreign departments refer to all non-resident institutional units with economic exchanges with resident institutional units in China. In case of increasing foreign departments, preparation of the whole balance sheet isn't required, but it's necessary to record the cumulative stock of transactions and exchanges between resident institutional unit and non-resident institutional unit, namely only reflecting economic exchange between China's economic entity and foreign entity and total scale and structural relationship of corresponding results.

Non-financial Assets "Non-financial assets" refer to economic assets against which the institutional unit executes the ownership or disposal right independently or together with an economic interest obtained by holding or usage within the accounting period except for financial assets according to basic definition about assets and liabilities in the new national economic accounting system in China and definition regarding SNA of UN in 1993.

Non-financial assets can be classified into tangible assets and intangible assets based on whether physical form exists or productive assets and non-productive assets based on production way or process. In the non-financial assets, "productive assets" are constituted by fixed assets, inventories and valuables. "Non-productive assets" can be roughly divided into two categories, including resource assets (namely tangible non-productive assets, consisting of land assets, water resource assets, underground assets and non-breeding biological assets) and intangible non-productive assets (such as patent right, rental agreement and other transferrable contract and goodwill purchased).

Due to the restriction of data source and technical conditions in the assets and liabilities, accounting in China now, we only simply divide non-financial assets into three categories-fixed assets, inventories and other non-financial assets.

Rate of Contribution Rate of contribution of each industry is an indicator for analyzing economic benefit which refers to the ratio between the increment of primary, secondary and tertiary industries and increment of total output value.

Above State Designated Scale Service Industry Legal Entities include: transportation, warehousing and postal services, information transmission, software, and information technology service industry, leasing and business service, scientific research and technological services, water conservancy, environment and public facility management, resident service, repair and other service industries, education, health and social work, culture, sports and entertainment as well as property management, real estate agency service.

5

劳动就业

LABOR AND EMPLOYMENT

5-1 按三次产业分从业人员及构成
Number of Employed Persons and Structure by Type of Industry

年份 Year	从业人员（万人） Total Employed Persons(10 000 persons)				构成（合计＝100） Composition in Percentage(Total=100)		
	合计 Total	第一产业 Primary Industry	第二产业 Secondary Industry	第三产业 Tertiary Industry	第一产业 Primary Industry	第二产业 Secondary Industry	第三产业 Tertiary Industry
1952	134.26	109.87	5.86	18.53	81.8	4.4	13.8
1957	144.29	118.65	13.12	12.52	82.2	9.1	8.7
1962	137.58	106.50	16.45	14.63	77.4	12.0	10.6
1965	143.67	107.68	20.96	15.03	74.9	14.6	10.5
1970	161.18	118.15	30.32	12.71	73.3	18.8	7.9
1975	192.59	135.95	41.56	15.08	70.6	21.6	7.8
1978	204.04	136.30	46.06	21.68	66.8	22.6	10.6
1980	214.21	135.16	51.30	27.75	63.1	23.9	13.0
1985	245.32	116.59	76.08	52.65	47.5	31.0	21.5
1990	270.54	125.73	87.75	57.06	46.5	32.4	21.1
1991	276.18	130.36	87.99	57.83	47.2	31.9	20.9
1992	280.19	127.09	85.59	67.51	45.4	30.5	24.1
1993	285.69	124.25	89.91	71.53	43.5	31.5	25.0
1994	303.46	122.62	91.64	89.20	40.4	30.2	29.4
1995	324.22	116.13	106.68	101.41	35.8	32.9	31.3
1996	332.33	107.70	113.91	110.72	32.4	34.3	33.3
1997	337.43	108.17	113.93	115.33	32.0	33.8	34.2
1998	341.63	109.32	113.38	118.93	31.9	33.2	34.9
1999	344.48	109.56	112.98	121.94	31.8	32.8	35.4
2000	347.37	109.98	110.81	126.58	31.7	31.9	36.4
2001	350.10	109.99	109.24	130.87	31.4	31.2	37.4
2002	352.70	108.01	109.14	135.55	30.6	30.9	38.5
2003	355.30	104.90	110.60	139.80	29.5	31.1	39.4
2004	358.50	99.30	113.30	145.90	27.7	31.6	40.7
2005	360.00	99.10	114.20	146.70	27.5	31.7	40.8
2006	361.80	99.00	115.20	147.60	27.4	31.8	40.8
2007	364.30	98.80	116.30	149.20	27.1	31.9	41.0
2008	367.36	98.01	116.95	152.40	26.7	31.8	41.5
2009	372.25	97.80	119.15	155.30	26.3	32.0	41.7
2010	373.70	76.66	120.20	176.84	20.5	32.2	47.3
2011	375.50	74.95	120.70	179.85	20.0	32.1	47.9
2012	379.30	74.30	123.10	181.90	19.6	32.5	47.9
2013	382.30	73.40	122.19	186.71	19.20	32.00	48.80
2014	385.70	72.50	123.30	189.90	18.80	31.97	49.24
2015	388.70	71.80	124.70	192.20	18.47	32.08	49.45
2016	394.93	70.90	126.90	197.13	17.95	32.13	49.92
2017	405.38	69.50	129.35	206.53	17.14	31.91	50.95
2018	419.27	68.80	132.17	218.30	16.41	31.52	52.07
2019	492.36	77.42	154.27	260.67	15.72	31.33	52.94

5-2 主要年份职工工资
Wage of Staff and Workers in Major Years

年份 Year	职工工资总额（万元）Total Wages of Staff and Workers(10 000yuan)				职工平均工资（元）Average Wage of Staff and Workers(yuan)			
	合计 Total	国有经济 State-owned Units	城镇集体经济 Urban Collective-owned Units	其他经济 Others	合计 Total	国有经济 State-owned Units	城镇集体经济 Urban Collective-owned Units	其他经济 Others
1952	4881	4587	294	–	442	453	324	–
1957	14553	11654	2899	–	586	621	480	–
1962	19412	16409	3003	–	577	607	451	–
1965	20367	16821	3546	–	617	664	461	–
1970	21226	17314	3912	–	549	578	449	–
1975	29239	22662	6577	–	557	615	420	–
1978	37840	28733	9107	–	578	626	465	–
1980	55900	41809	14091	–	776	821	668	–
1985	92092	67756	24330	6	1104	1169	954	894
1986	111934	84269	27643	22	1298	1384	1092	882
1987	126263	96322	29673	268	1422	1515	1185	1603
1988	166206	130287	35515	404	1806	1946	1427	2304
1989	190106	150899	38654	553	2037	2199	1577	2614
1990	210618	166250	43003	1365	2211	2370	1751	2460
1991	229540	181185	46091	2264	2368	2535	1872	2658
1992	267295	214311	49565	3419	2710	2938	2020	2919
1993	327226	264252	54442	8532	3323	3547	2524	3553
1994	465966	371403	67351	27212	4736	5209	2975	4922
1995	581432	465311	79932	36189	5851	6561	3623	5663
1996	700636	562645	89126	48865	7031	7839	4290	6875
1997	792368	636694	67999	57675	7896	8761	4954	7303
1998	717927	578788	68455	70684	8326	9022	5459	7410
1999	756696	608052	67273	81371	9083	9929	5766	7818
2000	857337	639312	59468	158557	10422	11761	6211	8651
2001	950851	713222	60818	176811	11980	13462	7061	9945
2002	1120837	846978	74672	199187	14395	16362	8188	11729
2003	1256160	930392	69554	256214	16027	18197	9331	12942
2004	1420491	1049033	73150	298308	18029	20759	10587	13974
2005	1966782	1126918	77722	762142	20866	24626	11890	18164
2006	2459044	1326412	140974	991658	21808	26550	12332	19305
2007	3086928	1680494	166960	1239474	26085	31910	15763	22500
2008	3735956	2049453	202995	1483509	30798	37191	19296	26645
2009	4241838	2227992	177020	1836825	34544	41239	21365	30368
2010	4695402	2462874	179365	2053164	36833	43339	22593	32740
2011	5569118	2647111	169476	2752531	41959	49342	26646	37851
2012	6458632	2811390	161513	3485729	45924	52845	32180	42294
2013	7927677	2766005	170176	4991497	53650	58842	37264	51891
2014	8464904	2912941	148424	5403539	59534	66810	40170	56945
2015	8885256	3282169	143078	5460009	67112	78733	47013	62283
2016	10068893	3715397	162695	6190800	74834	88887	51370	69107
2017	10694345	3776127	124702	6793516	82192	98770	54790	75814
2018	11496722	3869498	98327	7528898	89168	109052	62941	81935
2019	14170697	4846897	87776	9236024	97482	123249	66047	88204
2020	16196772				104990			

注：1. 本表中 1998 年及以后年份数据均为在岗职工口径，国有、集体、其他分组按 1998 年新标准。2006 年及以后年份数据为非私营单位从业人员口径。
2.2020 年，国家统计局修订劳动工资统计制度，省统计局未反馈国有经济、城镇集体经济、其他经济相关分类数据。

Note: 1.In this table, the data for 1998 and subsequent years are the caliber of on-the-job workers, and the data of state-owned, collective and other groups base the new standard in 1998. Data for 2006 and subsequent years are the caliber of employees in non-private units.
2.In 2020, the State Statistics Bureau revised the labor wages statistics data, while the categorical data of the state-owned business, town collective economics and other haven' t been released by the provincial bureau.

5-3 城镇非私营单位就业人员人数（2020 年）
Number of Employed Persons in Urban Non Private Entities(2020)

单位：人 (person)

指标	Indicator	就业人员 Employed Persons	# 在岗职工 Staff and Workers
合计	Total	1549779	1454132
按国民经济行业分组	Grouped by Sector		
农、林、牧、渔业	Agriculture,Forestry,Animal Husbandry and Fishing	1470	1470
采矿业	Mining	14627	14377
制造业	Manufacturing	252351	244613
电力、热力、燃气及水生产和供应业	Production and Distribution of Electricity, Heating Power, Gas and Water	19193	19039
建筑业	Construction	296273	263436
批发和零售业	Wholesale and Retail Trade	81253	79810
交通运输、仓储和邮政业	Traffic,Transport,Storage and Post	76633	74771
住宿和餐饮业	Hotels and Catering Services	23128	20035
信息传输、软件和信息技术服务业	Information Transfer, Software and Information Technology Services	90053	89927
金融业	Financial Intermediation	92769	58436
房地产业	Real Estate	63530	62128
租赁和商务服务业	Leasing and Business Services	48262	48019
科学研究和技术服务业	Scientific Research and Development,Technical Services	67345	65254
水利、环境和公共设施管理业	Management of Water Conservancy, Environment and Public Facilities	18888	18033
居民服务、修理和其他服务业	Services to Households, Repair and Other Services	8450	8294
教育	Education	154491	150662
卫生和社会工作	Health and Social Work	92568	89915
文化、体育和娱乐业	Culture,Sports and Entertainment	18466	17762
公共管理、社会保障和社会组织	Public Administration, Social Security and Social Organizations	130029	128151

5-4 城镇非私营单位就业人员工资总额(2020年)

Total Wage of Employed Persons in Urban Non Private Entities(2020)

单位：万元 (10 000 yuan)

指标	Indicator	就业人员工资总额 Wage Bill of Employed Persons	#在岗职工工资总额 Total Wage of Staff and Workers
合计	Total	16196772	15671255
按国民经济行业分组	Grouped by Sector		
农、林、牧、渔业	Agriculture,Forestry,Animal Husbandry and Fishing	15275	15275
采矿业	Mining	128679	126702
制造业	Manufacturing	2314398	2282237
电力、热力、燃气及水生产和供应业	Production and Distribution of Electricity, Heating Power, Gas and Water	204001	203415
建筑业	Construction	2746829	2516474
批发和零售业	Wholesale and Retail Trade	639835	631676
交通运输、仓储和邮政业	Traffic,Transport,Storage and Post	804039	796080
住宿和餐饮业	Hotels and Catering Services	106549	102809
信息传输、软件和信息技术服务业	Information Transfer, Software and Information Technology Services	909368	908730
金融业	Financial Intermediation	1260857	1095001
房地产业	Real Estate	455702	449644
租赁和商务服务业	Leasing and Business Services	432459	430579
科学研究和技术服务业	Scientific Research and Development,Technical Services	828365	809157
水利、环境和公共设施管理业	Management of Water Conservancy, Environment and Public Facilities	147399	145736
居民服务、修理和其他服务业	Services to Households, Repair and Other Services	42298	41584
教育	Education	1840784	1820504
卫生和社会工作	Health and Social Work	1355650	1339946
文化、体育和娱乐业	Culture,Sports and Entertainment	232554	229679
公共管理、社会保障和社会组织	Public Administration, Social Security and Social Organizations	1731754	1726028

5-5 城镇非私营单位就业人员平均工资 (2020 年)
Average Wage of Employed Persons in Urban Non Private Entities(2020)

单位：元 (yuan)

指标	Indicator	就业人员平均工资 Average Wage of Employed Persons	# 在岗职工平均工资 Average Wage of Total Wage of Staff
合计	Total	104990	108391
按国民经济行业分组	Grouped by Sector		
农、林、牧、渔业	Agriculture,Forestry,Animal Husbandry and Fishing	110352	110352
采矿业	Mining	88095	88399
制造业	Manufacturing	93771	94664
电力、热力、燃气及水生产和供应业	Production and Distribution of Electricity, Heating Power, Gas and Water	108170	108752
建筑业	Construction	93258	96548
批发和零售业	Wholesale and Retail Trade	78308	78700
交通运输、仓储和邮政业	Traffic,Transport,Storage and Post	103707	105233
住宿和餐饮业	Hotels and Catering Services	46800	52242
信息传输、软件和信息技术服务业	Information Transfer, Software and Information Technology Services	101684	101745
金融业	Financial Intermediation	130997	185886
房地产业	Real Estate	72138	72820
租赁和商务服务业	Leasing and Business Services	90334	90406
科学研究和技术服务业	Scientific Research and Development,Technical Services	127001	127695
水利、环境和公共设施管理业	Management of Water Conservancy, Environment and Public Facilities	79847	82013
居民服务、修理和其他服务业	Services to Households, Repair and Other Services	51283	51410
教育	Education	120494	122018
卫生和社会工作	Health and Social Work	147794	150114
文化、体育和娱乐业	Culture,Sports and Entertainment	126905	130232
公共管理、社会保障和社会组织	Public Administration, Social Security and Social Organizations	130200	131623

5-6 社会保障基本情况
Basic Conditions of Social Sewrity

单位：万人 (10 000 persons)

指标	Indicator	2015年	2016年	2017年	2018年	2019年	2020年
职工基本养老保险参保人数	Urban Basic Pension Insurance	266.14	284.28	304.63	331.66	408.33	437.30
#企业	Enterpris	241.07	259.26	279.65	306.59	378.63	345.26
事业机关	Institution and Government Agency	25.08	25.02	24.98	25.06	29.70	18.99
职工基本医疗保险参保人数	Medcial Care Insurance	208.09	214.48	228.68	241.54	288.04	313.52
参加失业保险人数	Unemployment Insurance	130.08	135.78	147.19	158.29	189.70	213.60
工伤保险参保人数	Work Injury Insurance	144.46	161.22	187.51	220.47	262.56	278.60
生育保险参保人数	Maternity Insurance	136.43	142.17	152.73	163.97	201.24	213.10

注：1. “职工基本养老保险参保人数” “企业”及“事业机关”包含离退休人员。
2.2019年职工基本养老保险参保人数中事业机关数据修订为29.7万人。

Note: 1.The caliber "number of employees with basic endowment insurance", " enterprise" and "business organ" contains the retired after.
2.In 2019, the number of employees from the state-owned organization among the insured of the basic endowment insurance is revised to 297,000.

主要统计指标解释

从业人员 指在本单位工作，并取得工资或其他形式劳动报酬的人员。

城镇登记失业人员 是指具有本地城镇户口，有劳动能力，目前无业，有求职愿望并在街道（乡镇）劳动保障部门办理了求职登记的人员。

城镇登记失业率 指报告期末，登记失业人员期末实有人数占期末从业人员总数与登记失业人员期末实有人数之和的比重。

在岗职工 指在本单位工作且与本单位签订劳动合同，并由单位支付各项工资和社会保险、住房公积金的人员，以及上述人员中由于学习、病伤、产假等原因暂未工作仍由单位支付工资的人员。

在岗职工工资总额 指本单位在报告期内直接支付给本单位全部在岗职工的劳动报酬总额。

在岗职工平均工资 指本单位在岗职工在报告期内平均每人所得的工资额。

Explanatory Notes on Main Statistical Indicators

Employees refer to persons who work in the unit and receive remuneration payment or other forms of payment.

Registered Urban Unemployed Persons refer to persons with local urban registration and labor capacity who are unemployed currently, have the job-hunting desire and handle registering at an employment agency at the street (town) labor security department.

Registered Urban Unemployment Rate refers to the ratio of the actual number of unemployed people registered at the end of the reporting period to the sum of the total number of employees at the end of the reporting period and the sum of the actual number of unemployed people registered at the end of the reporting period.

Fully Employed staff and Workers refer to persons who work in the unit and sign a labor contract with working units for whom working units pays various wages, social insurances and housing provident fund, and persons who have their work posts, but are temporarily absent from work for reasons of study or on sick, injury or maternal leave and still receive wages from their working units.

Total Wages Bill refers to the total remuneration payment to staff and workers in working units during the reporting period.

Average Wage refers to average wage per person within the reporting period for staff and workers in working units.

6

固定资产投资

INVESTMENT IN FIXED ASSETS

6-1 固定资产投资
Total Investment in Fixed Assets

单位：万元 (10 000 yuan)

指标	Indicator	2011 年	2012 年	2013 年	2014 年	2015 年	2016 年	2017 年
固定资产投资额	Investment in Fixed Assets	19343389	21860756	26383337	30634425	34984158	39743278	43635821
按管理渠道分	By Management Channels							
城镇集体以上投资	Above Urban Collective Investment	13059328	14005706	18189147	20297503	23817574	27091510	30334660
房地产开发投资	Real Estate Development Investment	5271575	6633153	7211744	9173706	10141433	11639381	12325712
农村投资	Rural Investment	1012486	1221898	982446	1163216	1025151	1012387	975449
按经济类型分	Registration Status							
国有经济	State-owned	7334983	6595774	8770551	6421555	8236033	7175934	8700130
集体经济	Collective-owned	1802483	1920132	2165782	2309282	1809902	1298005	1458316
联营经济	Joint Ownership Units		195897	100213	17820	30882	1808	
股份制经济	Share-holding	5682038	1234405	1448535	5814573	7403146	10826143	12722943
外商投资经济	Fund from Overseas	408736	466383	336618	384940	284944	771449	410019
港澳台投资经济	Fund from Hong Kong,Macao and Taiwan	586347	634574	546675	177167	270022	961601	1129955
个体经济	Self-employed	2956158	3318099	30342	4423319	4447149	6788160	39804
其他经济	Others	572644	1169661	2044857	1912063	2360647	1683680	1002734
按投资用途分	By Investment Purpose							
第一产业	Primary Industry	486482	624114	982446	1163216.064	1025151	1012387	975449
第二产业	Secondary Industry	6073178	7337047	9078831	10985385.51	12173905	13019930	14418169
#工 业	Industry	5767374	7018465	8060463	10410562.18	11478708	12373806	13176351
第三产业	Tertiary Industry	12783729	13899596	16322060	18485823.43	21785102	25710961	28242203
投资资金来源	Fund of Different Sources							
国家资金	State Appropriations	1317777	1693582	1302138	1240862	691574	1360695	1353707
国内贷款	Domestic Loans	1579846	517431	2173131	341374	73212	3656032	3343213
债券	Bond							40902
利用外资	Overseas Funds	68300	226374	262823	32757	44835	327727	250555
自筹资金	Self-raised Fund	14843051	16405182	19166006	19058000	23594834	28216931	28042143
其他资金	Others	3469710	4139026	5741361	454265	342083	10839004	10267805

注：自 2011 年起固定资产投资统计口径由 50 万元调整为 500 万元。
Note: Statistical caliber of fixed-asset investment as of 2011 was adjusted to RMB 5 million from 0.5 million.

6-2 固定资产投资分类(2020年)
Classification of Fixed Assets Investment(2020)

指标	Indicator	固定资产投资额比上年增长(%) Growth Rate of Investment in Fixed Assets(%)
本年完成投资	Investment Completed This Year	4.0
按构成分	Investment by Structure	
建筑安装工程	Construction and Installation	-2.8
设备工器具购置	Purchase of Equipment and Instruments	10.4
#购置旧设备	Purchase of Second-hand Equipment	16.6
其他费用	Others	26.5
按产业分	Grouped by Three Strata of Industry	
第一产业	Primary Industry	-15.2
第二产业	Secondary Industry	27.3
第三产业	Tertiary Industry	0.6
按单位登记注册类型分	Registration Status	
内资	Domestically-invested	4.8
国有	State-owned	-15.0
集体	Collective-owned	46.9
股份合作	Joint-equity Cooperative	22.2
私营个体	Private Enterprises	11.4
港澳台投资	Fund from Hong Kong,Macao and Taiwan	-9.9
#港澳台股份有限公司	Share-holding	200.3
外商投资	Fund from Overseas	-12.0
#外商合资经营	Joint Venture	107.0
#外商独资	Foreign Funded	-35.4
其他	Others	-3.9
按建设性质分	Investment by Type of Construction	
新建	New Construction	8.6
扩建	Expansion	-17.4
改建和技术改造	Reconstruction and Technical Transformation	13.1
其他	Others	1.9
按国民经济行业分	Investments in Fixed Assets by Sector	

6-2 续表 continued

指标	Indicator	固定资产投资额比上年增长 (%) Growth Rate of Investment in Fixed Assets(%)
农、林、牧、渔业	Farming, Forestry, Animal Husbandry and Fishery	-11.5
采矿业	Mining	-9.1
制造业	Manufacture	18.6
电力、热力、燃气及水生产和供应业	Production and Supply of Electric, Heat, Gas and Water	82.5
建筑业	Construction	
批发和零售业	Wholesale and Retail Trade	0.8
交通运输、仓储和邮政业	Transport, Storage and Postal Services	-8.7
住宿和餐饮业	Accommodations and Catering Services	-42.7
信息传输、软件和信息技术服务业	Information Transmission, Computer Services and Software	-8.3
金融业	Finance	-92.5
房地产业	Real Estate	0.5
租赁和商务服务业	Leasing and Business Services	-0.7
科学研究和技术服务业	Scientific Research and Technical Services	13.0
水利、环境和公共设施管理业	Management of Water Conservancy,Environment and Public Facilities	79.3
居民服务、修理和其他服务业	Households services, Repair and Other Service	-35.9
教育	Education	-18.6
卫生和社会工作	Health and Social Work	59.6
文化、体育和娱乐业	Culture, Sports and Recreation	-30.1
公共管理、社会保障和社会组织	Public Management,Social Security and Social Organizations	20.8
新增固定资产（万元）	Newly Increased Fixed Assets(10 000 yuan)	12412572
施工项目个数（个）	Number of Project under Construction(unit)	2612
# 新开工	Started This Year	1419
竣工项目个数（个）	Number of Buildings Completed(unit)	823
施工房屋面积（万平方米）	Project under Construction(10 000 sq.m)	10353.0
# 住 宅	Residential Buildings	6700.9
竣工房屋面积（万平方米）	Project Completed and Put into Use(10 000 sq.m)	1273.0
# 住宅	Residential Buildings	913.6

6-3 房地产开发投资分类(2020年)
Classification of Estate Development Investment(2020)

指标	Indicator	房地产开发投资 Estate Development Investment
本年完成投资额(万元)	**Investment Completed This Year(10 000 yuan)**	**17076304**
按构成分	**Investment by Structure**	
建筑工程	Construction	10195398
安装工程	Installation	1172528
设备、工器具购置	Purchase of Equipment and Instruments	265076
其他费用	Others	5443302
按单位登记注册类型分	**Registration Status**	
内资	**Domestic Fund**	**15873939**
国有	State-owned	228209
集体	Collective-owned	
股份合作	Cooperative	52262
联营	Joint Ownership Units	
国有联营	State-owned Joint	
集体联营	Collective-owned Joint	
其他联营企业	Other Joint Ownership Units	
有限责任公司	Limited Liability	11261111
国有独资公司	Solely State-owned Company	1729759
其他有限责任公司	Other Limited Liability Company	9531352
股份有限公司	Share-holding Corporations Ltd.	334054
私营	Private	3805633
其它内资	Other Domestic Fund	192670
港澳台投资	**Fund from Hong Kong,Macao and Taiwan**	**1118503**
港澳台商合资经营	Joint Venture	724395
港澳台商合作经营	Collaborative Operation	
港澳台商独资	Solely Foreign-owned	394108
港澳台股份有限公司	Share-holding	
外商投资	**Fund from Overseas**	**83862**
外商合资经营	Joint Venture	65675
外商合作经营	Collaborative Operation	
外商独资	Foreign Funded	2076
外商股份有限公司	Share-holding	3400
其他外商投资企业	Other Fund from Overseas	12711
个体经营	**Self-employed**	
新增固定资产(万元)	**Newly Increased Fixed Assets (10 000 yuan)**	**5297407**
施工项目个数(个)	**Number of Project under Construction(unit)**	**817**
#新开工	Started This Year	
竣工项目个数(个)	**Number of Buildings Completed(unit)**	
施工房屋面积(万平方米)	**Project under Construction(10 000 sq.m)**	**10353.04**
#住宅	Residential Buildings	6700.92
竣工房屋面积(万平方米)	**Project Completed and Put into Use(10 000 sq.m)**	**1272.97**
#住宅	Residential Buildings	913.57

6-4 固定资产投资资金来源 (2020 年)
Investment by Source of Funds (2020)

指标	Indicator	固定资产投资额比上年增长 (%) Growth Rate of Investment in Fixed Assets (%)	房地产开发投资 (万元) Estate Development Investment (10 000 yuan)
本年资金来源合计	Total Funds of All Sources	3.1	32649106
上年末结余资金	Fund Left from Last Year	-7.9	7586350
本年资金来源小计	Fund of All Sources in Currrent Year	5.4	25062756
国家预算资金	State Budgetary Funds	125.3	
国内贷款	Domestic Loans	8.9	5878343
债券	Bond	-28.4	
利用外资	Foreign Investment	66.9	72400
其中：外商直接投资	Foreign Direct Investment		
自筹资金	Self-Raising Funds	-7.6	7176418
其中：企、事业单位自有资金	Enterprise and Intitutions Own Funds		
其他资金来源	Others Capital Source	8.3	11935595

6-5 新增主要生产能力和效益 (2020 年)
Newly Increased Production Capacity and Administrative(2020)

项目 Item	单位 Unit	新增生产能力 Newly Increased This Year
年产 5 万辆新能源商用车项目	辆 / 年 (unit/year)	20000
专用汽车智能焊接机器人生产线	辆 / 年 (unit/year)	4999
济南到泰安高速公路（济南段）	公里 (km)	25
G220 东深线长清陈庄至长清平阴界段改建工程	公里 (km)	19.8
国道一零五京澳线平阴绕城段改建工程	公里 (km)	12.4
110 千伏时东输变电工程	公里 (km)	12
国电投商河一期 100MW 风电场项目	万千瓦 (10 000kw)	10
G220 至济青高速公路王舍人互通立交连接线工程	公里 (km)	1.7

6-6 历年房地产开发建设情况
Basic Situations of Real Estate Development in Major Years

指标	Indicator	单位 Unit	2015 年	2016 年	2017 年	2018 年	2019 年	2020 年
计划总投资	Intended Investment	万元 (10 000 yuan)	55571721	65080572	75662272	90392774	111989855	120132064
本年完成投资	Investment Completed in Current Year	万元 (10 000 yuan)	10141433	11639381	12325712	13693456	15769302	17076304
按构成分	Grouped by Use of Funds							
建筑工程	Construction	万元 (10 000 yuan)	6083337	7329570	8643701	7920264	9183871	10195398
安装工程	Installation	万元 (10 000 yuan)	1126053	1614742	1446801	1409538	1606223	1172528
设备、工器具购置	Purchase of Equipment and Instruments	万元 (10 000 yuan)	78310	152443	172327	178895	406018	265076
其他费用	Others	万元 (10 000 yuan)	2853733	2542621	2062883	4184759	4573190	5443302
#旧建筑物购置费	Purchase of Used Building	万元 (10 000 yuan)	1892	35444	4742	196	9701	6041
土地购置	Purchase of Land	万元 (10 000 yuan)	2545842	2241602	1683185	3780143	4231601	5040479
按工程用途分	Grouped by Use of Buildings							
住宅	Residential Buildings	万元 (10 000 yuan)	7254184	8055689	8227871	9285419	11356997	12043120
办公楼	Office Buildings	万元 (10 000 yuan)	1379919	1112954	1058113	1047097	1312853	1693130
商业营业用房	Buildings for Business	万元 (10 000 yuan)	833683	1665634	1907938	1879155	1662057	1693638
其他	Others	万元 (10 000 yuan)	673647	805104	1131790	1481785	1437395	1646416
本年新增固定资产	Newly Increased Fixed Assets	万元 (10 000 yuan)	1815666	3770747	3061175	4698943	3988646	5297407
待开发土地面积	Space of Land to be Developed	万平方米 (10 000 sq.m)	291.87	225.80	138.80	302.35	455.30	278.98
本年购置土地面积	Space of Land Purchased in Current Year	万平方米 (10 000 sq.m)	274.45	170.34	144.77	265.91	280.40	106.04
房屋施工面积	Floor Space Under Construction	万平方米 (10 000 sq.m)	6625.90	7912.30	8006.85	9112.05	9979.96	10353.04
房屋竣工面积	Floor Space Completed	万平方米 (10 000 sq.m)	579.05	1134.10	631.29	1203.81	1070.03	1272.97
竣工房屋价值	Value of Buildings Completed	万元 (10 000 yuan)	1389148	2639414	1615213	3172322	2844724	3321996
竣工住宅	Residential Buildings Completed	套 (unit)	27877	68682	45775	70120	60422	77790

6-7 历年房地产开发公司经营情况
Real Estate Development and Managment in Major Years

指标	Indicator	单位 Unit	2015年	2016年	2017年	2018年	2019年	2020年
开发公司家数	Number of Real Estate Enterprises	家 (unit)	570	622	646	706	710	704
企业资本金	Enterprises Funds	万元 (10 000 yuan)	7612830	9270991	10505186	12994960	14920358	15884470
资产与负债	Property debt							
资产总计	Assets	万元 (10 000 yuan)	57218796	72602423	85586496	113393735	128868654	136819137
负债总计	Liabilities	万元 (10 000 yuan)	46478285	58406976	68738188	93511277	106654306	113236782
所有者权益	Owners' Equity	万元 (10 000 yuan)	10740511	14195447	16848309	19882458	22214348	23582355
损益情况	Net Income or Loss							
经营收入	Revenues from Business	万元 (10 000 yuan)	7076463	11913217	11218828	12495191	14411472	14853884
土地转让收入	Revenues from Land Transfer	万元 (10 000 yuan)	14820	2409	1501	952885	150739	344311
商品房销售收入	Revenues from Commercial Housing Sale	万元 (10 000 yuan)	6265506	11227539	10803498	11087179	11656310	11934688
房屋出租收入	Housing Rental Income	万元 (10 000 yuan)	79458	106425	109982	90017	99996	109568
其他收入	Others	万元 (10 000 yuan)	716679	576844	302963	126592	134461	472363
经营成本	Business Cost	万元 (10 000 yuan)	5515583	968896	8352620	8570149	10131040	11087743
经营税金及附加	Business Tax and Extra Charges	万元 (10 000 yuan)	573637	706161	658995	951196	1036931	977022
利润总额	Total Profits	万元 (10 000 yuan)	401995	606344	875949	2177983	2287980	1719277
房屋销售与出租	House for Sales and Rent							
本年实际销售房屋面积	Floor Space of Buildings to Sales	平方米 (sq.m)	11911661	14242514	12152665	12346236	12464708	13357486
#住宅	Residential Buildings	平方米 (sq.m)	9234805	12316804	9737162	9636143	10206808	11452394
本年房屋实际销售额	Total Sales of Buildings	万元 (10 000 yuan)	9159131	11750932	11725660	14737908	13807789	15719460
#住宅	Residential Buildings	万元 (10 000 yuan)	6954738	10357228	9462791	11728181	11738543	14065259
待售房屋面积	Floor Space of Waiting For Sale	平方米 (sq.m)	1694588	1720232	1398451	980301	1064915	1474183
#住宅	Residential Buildings	平方米 (sq.m)	864938	931437	740636	542047	635088	906322
出租房屋面积	Floor Space of Buildings to Lease	平方米 (sq.m)	229415	182137	66089	1794	39132	2385

6-8 房地产开发公司经营情况 (2020 年)
Real Estate Development and Management(2020)

单位：万元　(10 000 yuan)

指标	Indicator	合计 Total	内资企业 Domestic Enterprise 小计 Total	# 国有 State-owned	外资企业 Foreign-owned Enterprise 小计 Total	# 港澳台商 Hong kong,Macao and Taiwan Investment
开发公司家数（家）	Number of Real Estate Enterprises(unit)	704	671	19	33	25
按资质分	by Qualification Criteria					
# 一级资质	First Grade	24	24	2		
二级资质	Second Grade	51	48	3	3	3
三级资质	Third Grade	86	83	6	3	1
四级资质	Forth Grade	10	8	1	2	2
企业资本金	Enterprises Funds	15884470	13741567	66785	2142903	1999735
资产与负债	Property debt					
资产总计	Assets	136819137	130305835	1575306	6513302	5766216
负债总计	Liabilities	113236782	109161859	1431930	4074923	3583056
所有者权益	Owners' Equity	23582355	21143976	143376	2438379	2183160
损益情况	Net Income or Loss					
经营收入	Revenues from Business	14853884	14587469	64952	266415	236847
土地转让收入	Revenues from Land Transfer	344311	344311			
商品房销售收入	Revenues from Commercial Housing Sale	11934688	11749441	58887	185246	155948
房屋出租收入	Housing Rental Income	109568	42042	2985	67527	67527
其他收入	Others	472363	462319	379	10044	10035
经营成本	Business Cost	11087743	10887646	40018	200097	163311
经营税金及附加	Business Tax and Extra Charges	977022	956356	12609	20666	20210
利润总额	Total Profits	1719277	1748732	-2819	-29456	-5045

主要统计指标解释

固定资产投资额 指以货币形式表现的在一定时期内建造和购置固定资产的工作量以及与此有关的费用的总称。

房地产开发投资 指各种登记注册类型的房地产开发法人单位统一开发的住宅、厂房、仓库、饭店、宾馆、度假村、写字楼、办公楼等房屋建筑物，配套的服务设施，土地开发工程（如道路、给水、排水、供电、供热、通讯、平整场地等基础设施工程）和土地购置的投资；不包括单纯的土地开发和交易活动。

固定资产投资的资金来源 根据固定资产投资的资金来源不同，分为国家预算内资金、国内贷款、债券、利用外资、自筹资金和其他资金来源。

（1）国家预算内资金：指各级政府用于固定资产投资的财政资金，包括中央预算资金和地方预算资金。

（2）国内贷款：指报告期固定资产投资项目单位向银行及非银行金融机构借入用于固定资产投资的各种国内借款，包括银行利用自有资金及吸收存款发放的贷款、上级拨入的国内贷款、国家专项贷款，地方财政专项资金安排的贷款、国内储备贷款、周转贷款等。

（3）债券：指企业或金融机构为筹集用于固定资产投资的资金向投资者出具的承诺按一定发行条件还本付息的债务凭证，包括金融债券和企业债券。

（4）利用外资：指报告期收到的境外（包括外国及港澳台地区）资金（包括设备、材料、技术在内）。包括对外借款（外国政府贷款、国际金融组织贷款、出口信贷、外国银行商业贷款、对外发行债券和股票）、外商直接投资、外商其他投资（包括补偿贸易、加工装配由外商提供的设备价款、国际租赁，外商投资收益的再投资资金）。不包括我国自有外汇资金（国家外汇、地方外汇、留成外汇、调济外汇和中国境内银行自有资金发放的外汇贷款等）。各类外资按报告期的外汇牌价（中间价）折成人民币计算。

（5）自筹资金：指在报告期内筹集的用于项目建设和购置的资金。包括自有资金、股东投入资金和借入资金，但不包括各类财政性资金、从各类金融机构借入资金和国外资金。

（6）其他资金来源：指在报告期收到的除以上各种资金之外的用于固定资产投资的资金。包括社会集资、个人资金、无偿捐赠的资金及其他单位拨入的资金等。

固定资产投资按建设性质分 建设项目的性质一般分为新建、扩建、改建和技术改造、单纯建造生活设施、迁建、恢复、单纯购置。

（1）新建：指从无到有“平地起家”开始建设的项目。现有企业、事业、行政单位投资的项目一般不属于新建。但如有的单位原有基础很小，经过建设后新增的固定资产价值超过该企业、事业、行政单位原有固定资产价值（原值）三倍以上的，也应作为新建。

（2）扩建：指为扩大原有产品的生产能力（或效益）或增加新的产品生产能力，而增建的生产车间（或主要工程）、分厂、独立的生产线等项目。行政、事业单位在原单位增建业务性用房（如学校增建教学用房、医院增建门诊部、病房等）也作为扩建。

（3）改建和技术改造：指对原有设施进行技术改造或更新（包括相应配套的辅助性生产、生活福利设施）的建设项目。

（4）单纯建造生活设施：指在不扩建、改建生产性工程和业务用房的情况下，单纯建造职工住宅、托儿所、子弟学校、医务室、浴室、食堂等生活设施的项目。

（5）迁建：指为改变生产能力布局或由于城市环境保护和安全生产的需要等原因而搬迁到另地建设的项目。在搬迁另地的建设过程中，不论是维持原来规模还是扩大规模都按迁建来统计。

（6）恢复：指因自然灾害、战争等原因，使原有固定资产全部或部分报废，以后又投资恢复建设的项目。不论是按原规模恢复还是在恢复的同时进行扩建的都按恢复项目统计。尚未建成投产的建设项目因自然灾害而损坏重建的，仍按原有建设性质划分。

（7）单纯购置：指单纯购置不需要安装的设备、工具、器具而不进行工程建设的项目。有些调查单位当年虽然只从事一些购置活动，但其设计中规定有建筑安装活动，应根据设计文件的内容来确定建设性质，不得作为单纯购置统计。

固定资产投资按构成分 固定资产投资活动按其工作内容和实现方式分为建筑工程、安装工程、设备工器具购置、其他费用三个部分。

（1）建筑工程：指各种房屋、建筑物的建造工程，又称建筑工作量。这部分投资额必须兴工动料，通过施工活动才能实现，是固定资产投资额的重要组成部分。

（2）安装工程：指各种设备、装置的安装工程，又称安装工作量。

（3）设备工器具购置：指报告期内购置或自制的，达到固定资产标准的设备、工具、器具的价值。

（4）其他费用：指在固定资产建造和购置过程中发生的，除建筑安装工程和设备、工器具购置投资完成额以外的应当分摊计入固定资产投资项目的费用，不指经营中财务上的其他费用。

新增生产能力（或工程效益）名称 指建成投产项目或工程新增生产能力（或工程效益）的名称。

建设规模 指建设项目或工程设计文件中规定的全部设计能力（或工程效益）。包括已经建成投产和尚未建成投产的工程的生产能力（或工程效益）。它是以实物形态表示固定资产投资规模的指标，反映建设项目或工程全部建成投产（或交付使用）后，能够为社会提供多少设计能力（或工程效益）。

房屋施工面积 指报告期内施工的全部房屋建筑面积。

房屋竣工面积 指报告期内房屋建筑按照设计要求已全部完工，达到住人和使用条件，经验收鉴定合格或达到竣工验收标准，可正式移交使用的各栋房屋建筑面积的总和。

本年新增固定资产 指在报告期已经完成建造和购置过程，并已交付生产或使用单位的固定资产的价值，包括已经建成投入生产或交付使用的工程投资和达到固定资产标准的设备、工具、器具的投资及有关应摊入的费用。属于增加固定资产价值的其他建设费用，应随同交付使用的工程一并计入新增固定资产。

房地产开发本年完成投资 指各种登记注册类型的房地产开发法人单位本年内统一开发的住宅、厂房、仓库、饭店、宾馆、度假村、写字楼、办公楼等房屋建筑物，配套的服务设施，土地开发工程（如道路、给水、排水、供电、供热、通讯、平整场地等基础设施工程）和土地购置的投资；不包括单纯的土地开发和交易活动。

土地购置和开发情况

（1）待开发土地面积：指经有关部门批准，通过各种方式获得土地使用权，但尚未开工建设的土地面积。

（2）本年土地购置面积：指在本年内通过各种方式获得土地使用权的土地面积。

商品房屋销售与出租情况

（1）商品房销售面积：指报告期内出售商品房屋的合同总面积（即双方签署的正式买卖合同中所确定的建筑面积）。商品房销售面积由现房销售面积和期房销售面积两部分组成。

①现房销售面积：指在报告期内正式签订买卖合同、已经竣工达到入住条件的商品房屋建筑面积。包括以一次性付款方式和分期付款方式销售的现房建筑面积。

②期房销售面积：指在报告期内正式签订买卖合同、正在建设尚未竣工交付使用的商品房屋建筑面积。包括以一次性付款方式和分期付款方式销售的商品房屋建筑面积。期房销售建筑面积竣工后不再结转为现房销售建筑面积。

（2）待售面积：指报告期末已竣工的可供销售或出租的商品房屋建筑面积中，尚未销售或出租的商品房屋建筑面积，包括以前年度竣工和本期竣工的房屋面积，但不包括报告期已竣工的拆迁还建、统建代建、公共配套建筑、房地产公司自用及周转房等不可销售或出租的房屋面积。按照商品房待售时间的长短可以划分为待售一年以下、待售一到三年（含一年）和待售三年以上（含三年）。

（3）房屋出租面积：指在报告期末房屋开发单位出租的商品房屋的全部面积。

（4）商品房销售额：指报告期内出售商品房屋的合同总价款（即双方签署的正式买卖合同中所确定的合同总价）。该指标与商品房销售面积同口径，由现房销售额和期房销售额两部分组成。

①现房销售额：指报告期内销售的已竣工商品房屋的合同总价款。包括现房销售前期预收的定金、预收款、首付款及全部按揭贷款的本金等款项。该指标与现房销售面积同口径。

②期房销售额：指报告期内销售的正在建设尚未竣工的商品房屋的合同总价款。包括预售房屋前期预收的定金、预收款、首付款及全部按揭贷款的本金等项。该指标与期房销售面积同口径。

Explanatory Notes on Main Statistical Indicators

Total Investment in Fixed Assets refers to the volume of activities in construction and purchases of fixed assets and related fees during a certain period of time, expressed in monetary terms.

Investment in Real Estate Development refers to the investment by real estate development units of various types of ownership in buildings and structures (such as residence, factory, warehouse, restaurant, hotel, resort, office building and administration building), supporting service facilities and land development engineering (including infrastructure projects such as road, water supply, drainage, power supply, heat supply, communication and land grading) excluding activities in pure land transactions.

Source of Funds for Investment in Fixed Assets include national budgetary funds, domestic loans, foreign investment, self–raised funds, and others depending on the source of investment.

(1) National budgetary funds refers to financial funds used by governments at all levels for fixed–asset investment, including central budget funds and local budget funds.

(2) Domestic loans refer to loans of various forms borrowed by investing units from banks and non–bank financial institutions during the reference period for the purpose of investment in fixed assets, including the loan issued by the bank by self–owned funds and deposit taking, domestic loans appropriated by superior, national special loan, loan arranged by special funds for local finance, domestic reserve loan and revolving credit.

(3) Bonds: refer to the certificate of indebtedness issued by the enterprise or the financial institution to the investor for raising the capital of fixed–asset investment with capital and interest promised to be repaid as per certain issue terms, including financial bond and enterprise bond.

(4) Foreign investment: refer to overseas (including foreign countries, Hong Kong, Macau and Taiwan) funds (including equipment, materials and technology) received in the reporting period, including foreign borrowings (loans from foreign governments and international financial organizations, export credit, commercial loans from foreign banks and issue of bonds and stocks overseas), foreign direct investment and other foreign investments (including compensation trade, the price of processing and assembling the equipment provided by foreign business, international leasing, funds from foreign direct investment income that are reinvested in fixed assets domestically). Excluded from this category is capital in foreign exchanges owned by China (foreign exchanges owned by the central and local governments, foreign exchanges retained by enterprises, foreign exchanges by enterprises through the regulating mechanism, loans in foreign exchanges issued by the Bank of China with its own fund, etc.). In calculating the utilization of foreign capital, foreign currencies are converted into CNY applying the exchange rate (central parity rate) at the end of the reference period. .

(5) Self–raised funds: refer to the fund raised in the reporting period and used for construction and purchase of the project, including self–owned funds, capital invested by shareholders and borrowed funds other than various financial funds, capital borrowed from various financing institutions and offshore funds.

(6) Other refer to funds for investment in fixed assets received in the reporting period, except for the above–mentioned various capitals, including funds raised in society, personal money, voluntary donations and capital from other units.

Investment in Fixed Assets by Type of Construction The construction projects in general can be classified, by the type of construction, into new construction, expansion, reconstruction and technical transformation, simple construction of living facilities, relocation, recovery and simple purchase.

(1) New construction: refers to the project that started construction from scratch. Projects invested by the existing enterprises, institutions or agencies is not considered as new construction. In case the assets of the existing unit are quite small, and the value of newly added fixed assets exceeds the original value of assets by three times, the expansion will be considered as new construction.

(2) Expansion: refers to construction of new production workshops (or major projects), branch factories or independent production lines, for the purpose of increasing the production capacity (or improving efficiency) of the original products. Newly constructed houses for the operation of institutions and administrative organizations (such as the newly constructed buildings for teaching in schools, buildings for clinics or wards in hospitals, etc.) are also classified as expansion.

(3) Reconstruction and technical transformation: refer to the construction project for technical transformation or renewal for original facilities (including corresponding supporting auxiliary production and living welfare facilities).

(4) Simple construction of living facilities: refers to the project of simply constructing living facilities such as staff houses, nurseries, schools for children of employees, medical rooms, shower rooms and canteens, etc. without expanding or reconstructing productive engineering and business housing.

(5) Relocation: refer to the project moved to other place for construction for the purpose of changing production capacity layout or urban environment protection and safety production requirements. In the process of being moved to other places for construction, whether it is to maintain the original scale or augment the scale, it will be counted as relocation.

(6) Recovery: refers to the project with original fixed assets scrapped in whole or in part due to natural disaster or war which is invested to recover construction later. Regardless of recovery as per

original size or expansion at the time of recovery, it will be counted as recovery. If the construction project which has not been completed and gone into operation is reconstructed due to being damaged by natural disaster, it is still classified according to the original type of construction.

(7) Simple purchase: refers to the project of simply purchasing equipment, tools and appliances which do not need to be installed without engineering construction. Although some investigating units only engaged in some purchase activities in that year, construction and installation activities were specified in their design, so it is necessary to confirm the type of construction in line with the content of the design document, and should not be counted as simple purchase.

Investment in fixed assets by Structure Fixed-asset investment activities are divided into construction engineering, installation engineering, purchase of equipment & tools and other expenses in terms of working content and implementation model.

(1) Construction engineering: refers to the construction of various houses and buildings, also called as construction workload. Such investment volume must be implemented through construction activities based on utilization of materials, which is an important part of fixed investments.

(2) Installation engineering: refers to installation of various equipment and devices, also called as installation workload.

(3) Purchase of equipment and tools: refers to the value of purchased or home-made equipment, tools and appliances within the reporting period, which reach to fixed-asset standards.

(4) Other expenses: refer to expenses incurred in the construction and purchase process of fixed assets which shall be allocated and included into the fixed-asset investment project, except for the expenses of construction and installation engineering and purchase of equipment & tools, and not refer to other financial expenses in the operation.

Newly Increased Production Capacity (or Project Efficiency) refers to the name of new production capacity (or project benefit) of the project or the engineering completed and put into operation.

Scale of Construction refers to all design ability (or project benefit) specified in the design document for construction project or engineering, including production capacity (or project benefit) completed and put into production and not yet be completed and put into production. It is an indicator showing the scale of investment in fixed assets in the matter form and reflects the design capability (or project benefit) provided for the society after the construction project or engineering is completed and put into production (or delivered for use).

Construction area of the house refers to building area of all houses constructed in the reporting period.

Housing completion area refers to total building areas of all houses which have been completed in accordance with design requirements in the reporting period, reach to living and using conditions, pass acceptance and verification or reach to the completion acceptance standards and can be formally handed over for use.

New fixed assets in this year refer to the value of fixed assets having been delivered to the production or use unit with construction and purchase process completed in the reporting period, including investment in projects completed and put into production or delivered for use and investment in equipment, tools and appliances reaching to fixed-asset standards and related expenses which shall be included. Other construction costs falling into the added fixed-asset value shall be included into new fixed assets together with the project delivered for use.

Investment completed in current year in real estate development refers to buildings and structures (such as residence, factory, warehouse, restaurant, hotel, resort, office building and administration building), supporting service facilities and land development engineering (including infrastructure projects such as road, water supply, drainage, power supply, heat supply, communication and land grading) and investment in land purchase uniformly developed by real estate development legal entity in the current year based on all kinds of businesses; excluding simple land development and trading activities.

Land purchase and development

(1) Land area to be developed: refers to the area of the land approved by related department with land use right obtained by all means but not yet under construction.

(2) Land acquisition area in the current year: refers to the area of the land with land use right obtained by all means in the current year.

Sales and rental of the residential property

(1) Sales area of residential property: refers to the total area in the contract of residential properties sold within the reporting period (namely the building area set forth in the sales contract formally signed by both parties). Sales area of the residential property is composed by two parts -- sales area of completed houses and sales area of the property under construction.

① Sales area of completed houses: refers to the building area of the residential property which has been completed and reached to living conditions with the sales contract formally signed within the reporting period, including the building area of completed houses sold by one-off payment and installment payment.

② Sales area of property under construction: refer to the building area of residential properties under construction which has not yet been delivered for use with the sales contract formally signed within the reporting period, including the building area of residential properties sold by one-off payment and installment payment. The sales building area of the property under construction will not be transfered to the sales building area of the competed house after being completed.

(2) Area to be sold: refers to the building area of residential properties not sold or rented in the building area of residential properties available for sale or renting which has been completed at the end of the reporting period, including the area of houses completed before and in the current period, and other than the area of housings not available for sale or renting such as the housing built due to demolition, the housing uniformly

built by the government, public matching buildings, the housing used by the real estate company and the relocation housing in the reporting period. As per the waiting time for sales of the residential property, the housings can be divided into the one waiting for sales for less than one year, the one waiting for sales for more than one year (one year included) but less than three years and the one waiting for sales for more than three years (three years included).

(3) Area of rental housing: refers to all areas of the residential property rented out by the house development unit at the end of the reporting period.

(4) Sales amount of residential property: refers to the total price in the contract of residential properties sold within the reporting period (namely the total contract price set forth in the sales contract formally signed by both parties). The indicator shares the same caliber with the sales area of the residential property, and it consists two parts -- sales amount of completed houses and sales amount of the property under construction.

① Sales amount of completed houses: refer to total contract price of residential properties completed and sold within the reporting period, including deposits, prepayments and down payment as well as all principal of all mortgage loans. The indicator shares the same caliber with the sales area of the completed houses.

② Sales amount of property under construction: refer to total contract price of residential properties under construction sold within the reporting period, including deposits, prepayments and down payment as well as all principal of all mortgage loans. The indicator shares the same caliber with the sales area of the property under construction.

7

城市公用事业和环境保护

URBAN PUBLIC UTILITIES
AND ENVIRONMENTAL
PROTECTION

7-1 城市道路与公共交通
Basic Statistics on Muncipal Engineering and Public Transportation

指标	Indicator	2015 年	2016 年	2017 年	2018 年	2019 年	2020 年
城市道路	City Roads						
道路长度（公里）	Length of Roads (km)	5350	5422	5663	5788	6987	7301
道路面积（万平方米）	Area of Roads(10 000 sq.m)	9523	9724	10224	10529	12653	13138
城市桥梁（座）	Number of Bridges(unit)	845	927	935	1021	1136	978
#立交桥（座）	Interchange(unit)	77	82	82	85	95	79
路灯（盏）	Number of Streetlights(unit)	167462	170314	188598	195014	213259	185188
人均拥有道路面积（平方米）	Per Capita Road Arae(sq.m)	26.10	26.20	22.96	23.03	20.30	19.70
公共交通	Public Transportation						
年末营运车辆（辆）	Number of Operating Vehicles(unit)	15236	15539	16850	16644	19676	18915
公共汽车	Buses	5537	5846	7157	6951	8383	8188
#无轨电车	Trolley Buses	140	121	121	106	109	126
出租汽车	Number of Taxis	9699	9693	9693	9693	11293	10727
客运总量（万人次）	Total Passenger Traffic(10 000 person-times)	93634	90776.1	90515.6	89619.7	99389.9	62425.9
轨道交通	Rail Traffic						
配属车辆数（辆）	Number of Vehicles(unit)					204	204
运营里程（公里）	Length in Operatio(km)					47.7	47.7
客运总量（万人次）	Total Passenger Traffic(10 000 person-times)					573.5	867.6

注：2020 年，“城市桥梁”使用新统计口径。
Notes: In 2020, “Urban bridges” adopt new statistical caliber.

7-2 水、电、气、热供应情况
Basic Statistics on Water, Electricity, Gas and Heating in Cities

指标	Indicator	单位 Unit	2015年	2016年	2017年	2018年	2019年	2020年
自来水	**Water**							
年末水厂生产能力	Production Capacity of Water Supply	万吨/日 (10 000 tons/day)	201.74	211.47	215.57	220.27	241.00	243.00
年末管线长度	Length of Water Supply Pioelines	公里 (km)	4325.56	4241.04	4779.01	5277.13	5703.60	6033.59
全年供水量	Volume of Water Supply	万吨 (10 000 tons)	31826.63	33191.11	35865.07	39226.16	44452.30	45182.90
人均日生活用水	Per Capita Daily Water Consumption	升 (litre)	138.95	142.78	139.58	140.37	134.79	125.47
城市人口用水普及率	Coverage Rate of Water Supply	%	99	99.57	99.64	99.78	100.00	100.00
用电量	**Electricity Consumption**							
全社会用电量	Electricity Consumption	万千瓦时 (10 000 kwh)	2642035	2799221	2762869	2843630	4143022	4338712
工业	Industrial Electricity Consumption	万千瓦时 (10 000 kwh)	1420304	1470794	1319975	1215034	2215281	2395876
城乡居民生活用电	Household Electricity Consumption	万千瓦时 (10 000 kwh)	522513	554853	598578	667505	776162	796871
液化石油气和管道煤气	**Liquefied Petroleum Gas and Piped Gas**							
液化石油气全年供气量	Total Liquefied Petroleum Gas Supply	吨 (ton)	46844.2	53086.2	49944.0	41110.0	45518.0	38353.0
生活用	Residential Use	吨 (ton)	21866	19771	23462	20458	25935	22119
居民用气人口	Population Uses Gas	万人 (10 000 persons)	87.1	77.39	55.93	46.81	59.90	52.59
天然气供气量	Total Natural Gas Supply	万立方米 (10 000 cu.m)	75496.75	79325.47	90724.36	113945.56	143576.00	161034.00
生产用	Production Use	万立方米 (10 000 cu.m)	58196.06	60994.42	69361.61	88821.02	96706.80	113916.82
生活用	Residential Use	万立方米 (10 000 cu.m)	17300.69	18331.05	21362.75	25124.54	46869.20	47117.18
居民用气人口	Population Uses Gas	万人 (10 000 persons)	269.44	291.56	388.63	409.70	560.90	614.20
管道煤气供气量	Piped Gas Supply	万立方米 (10 000 cu.m)	59	–	–	–	–	–
生产用	Production Use	万立方米 (10 000 cu.m)	59	–	–	–	–	–
生活用	Residential Use	万立方米 (10 000 cu.m)	0	–	–	–	–	–
居民用气人口	Population Uses Gas	万人 (10 000 persons)	0	–	–	–	–	–
用气普及率	Coverage Rate of Gas Supply	%	97.73	99.42	99.85	99.87	99.97	100.00
集中供热	**Central Heating**							
管道长度	Pipe Length	公里 (km)	3277	2742	6104	7010	8893	10426
供热面积	Heating Area	万平方米 (10 000 sq.m)	14499	14917	18174	19834	26073	27740

注：本表指标为“–”的，是指济南市已不再使用“管道煤气”。
Notes: The indicator"–",in this table refers Jinan no Longer Use Piped Gas.

7-3 环境状况及污染治理情况
Basic Statistics on Environment and Treatment of Pollution

指标	Indicator	单位 Unit	2015年	2016年	2017年	2018年	2019年	2020年
环境质量状况	**Environment Condition**							
环境空气细颗粒物（$PM_{2.5}$）浓度年均值	Annual Average Concentration of $PM_{2.5}$	mg/m^3	0.087	0.073	0.063	0.052	0.053	0.047
环境空气二氧化硫浓度年均值	Annual Average Concentration of SO_2	mg/m^3	0.050	0.038	0.025	0.017	0.015	0.012
环境空气二氧化氮浓度年均值	Annual Average Concentration of NO_2	mg/m^3	0.048	0.045	0.046	0.045	0.041	0.035
环境空气可吸入颗粒物 (PM_{10}) 浓度年均值	Annual Average Concentration of PM_{10}	mg/m^3	0.157	0.141	0.130	0.112	0.103	0.086
集中式饮用水源地水质达标率	Standard rate of concentrate Water Source Area	% (%)	100.00	100.00	100.00	100.00	100.00	100.00
区域环境噪声昼间平均等效声级	Area Whole-day Average Noise Value	分贝 (db)	53.7	53.1	53.7	53.3	54.9	54.4
道路交通噪声平均等效声级	Traffic Average Noise Value	分贝 (db)	70.0	69.8	69.7	69.5	69.6	69.1
污染物排放情况	**Discharge of Major Pollutants**							
废水排放总量	Volume of Waste Water Discharged	万吨 (10 000 tons)	39454	34530	34693	34693		
# 工业废水排放量	Volume of Industrial Waste Water Discharged	万吨 (10 000 tons)	7415	5993	5949	5949		
化学需氧量排放量	Volume of COD Emission	吨 (ton)	107743	30202	28701	28701		
# 工业化学需氧量排放量	Volume of Industrial COD Emission	吨 (ton)	5515	2777	2594	2594		
氨氮排放量	Volume of Ammonia Nitrogen	吨 (ton)	9050	4306	4255	4255		
# 工业氨氮排放量	Volume of Industrial Ammonia Nitrogen	吨 (ton)	360	186	197	197		
二氧化硫排放量	Volume of Sulphur Dioxide Discharged	吨 (ton)	99653	44403	32502	32502		
# 工业二氧化硫排放量	Volume of Industrial Sulphur Dioxide Discharged	吨 (ton)	70327	28458	16545	16545		
氮氧化物排放量	Volume of Nitrogen Oxides Discharged	吨 (ton)	91614	61075	23316	23316		
# 工业氮氧化物排放量	Volume of Industrial Nitrogen Oxides Discharged	吨 (ton)	63781	34502	21254	21254		
机动车氮氧化物排放量	Volume of Vehicle Nitrogen Oxides	吨 (ton)	24080	24472				
烟（粉）尘排放量	Volume of Soot and Dust Discharged	吨 (ton)	108643	64253	32794	32794		
# 工业烟（粉）尘排放量	Volume of Industrial Soot and Dust Discharged	吨 (ton)	92900	54677	25060	25060		

注：1. 从2014年工业烟（粉）统计口径增加钢铁、水泥等行业无组织排放量。
2. "机动车氮氧化物排放量"指标，自2017年起，国家只核定到省级数据。
3. 污染物排放情况数据，根据生态环境部统一工作安排，暂时使用2017年已公布数据，2018年数据待第二次全国污染源普查完成后统一发布。
4. 根据国家统一安排部署，对2016-2019年环统数据进行更新，目前最终数据国家尚未反馈；2020年环境统计工作正在开展，还未形成汇总数据。

Notes: 1. Industry unorganized emission (including steel and cement, etc.) was added to the statistical caliber of industrial smoke (powder) from 2014.
2. The indicator-"nitrogen oxide emission from motor vehicles" was only verified to provincial data by the state from 2017.
3. As for data on yearbook pollutant discharge, the data published in 2017 is temporarily used as per the unified arrangement of Ministry of Ecology and Environment and the data in 2018 will be uniformly published after completion of the 2nd national census of pollution sources.
4. Based on the unified arrangement and deployment, the data of 2016 to 2019 is updated, while the final data has not been provided by the state; the environmental statistical works is undergoing, and the summarized data has not been released.

7-4 城市园林绿化、环境卫生及其他
Basic Statistics on Parks, Gardens, Green Areas and Urban Sanitation in Cities

指标	Indicator	单位 Unit	2015 年	2016 年	2017 年	2018 年	2019 年	2020 年
园林绿化	Parks Gardens and Green Areas							
年末园林绿地面积	Garden Green Area at Year-end	公顷 (ha)	17561	18162.9	19528.6	20701.0	28199.3	31087.8
# 公园面积	Area of Parks	万平方米 (10 000 sq.m)	3190	3190	3414	3930	3688	3754
人均公园绿地面积	Per Capita Public Green Areas	平方米 / 人 (sq.m/person)	11.6	11.8	11.8	12.6	13.2	12.5
建成区绿化覆盖率	Coverage of Green Area	%	39.94	40.12	40.57	40.52	41.18	40.69
城市卫生	Urban Health							
污水集中处理率	Centralized Sewage Treatment Rate	%	95.85	96.33	95.98	96.59	97.73	98.17
清运垃圾	Garbage Clearance	万吨 (10 000 tons)	158	179.68	192.22	202.64	278.75	278.03
清运粪便	Garbage Disposal	万吨 (10 000 tons)	48.2	10.5	–	–	–	–
公共厕所	Public Lavatory	座 (unit)	1060	1077	1075	1086	1122	1203
城市维护费收支	Expenditure and Earning for City Maintenance							
维护费收入	Earning for City Maintenance	万元 (10 000 yuan)	1693759	1843784	–	–	–	–
维护费支出	Expenditure for City Maintenance	万元 (10 000 yuan)	1681108	1571443	–	–	–	–

注：本表指标为“–”的，部门相关统计制度中已经不在进行统计。
Notes: The indicator “–” in this table means statistics are no longer in the relevant statistical system of the department.

主要统计指标解释

年末自来水生产能力 指年底城建部门管理的自来水厂和自备水源的社会单位取水、净化、送水、出厂输水干管等环节的实际生产能力。

年末供水管道长度 指从送水泵到用户水表之间所有管道的长度。

全年供水总量 指公用自来水厂和自备水源的社会单位全年的供水总量，包括有效供水量及损失水量。

生活用水量 指居民日常生活与公共福利设施的用水量，包括居民、饮食店、旅馆、医院、理发店、浴池、洗衣店、游泳池、商店、学校、机关、部队等单位的用水量。

城市人口用水普及率 指城市用水的非农业人口数（不包括临时人口和流动人口）与城市非农业人口总数之比。计算公式为：

用水普及率＝城市用水的非农业人口数／城市非农业人口数 ×100%

城市用气普及率 指使用煤气（包括人工煤气、液化石油气、天然气）的城市非农业人口数（不包括临时人口和流动口）与城市非农业人口总数之比。计算公式为：

城市用气普及率＝城市用气的非农业人口数／城市非农业人口总数 ×100%

年底实有铺装道路长度 指除土路外，路面经过铺装宽度在 3.5 米以上的道路，包括高级、次高级道路和普通道路。

城市桥梁 指城市范围内，修建在河道上的桥梁和道路与道路立交、道路跨越铁路的立交桥及人行天桥。包括永久性桥和半永久性桥，不包括临时性桥、铁路桥、涵洞。

城市污水日处理能力 指污水处理厂每昼夜处理污水量的设计能力。

年末实有公共汽（电）车 指年底可参加营运的全部车辆数，包括营运车辆数和库存查封未参加营运的车辆。不包括非营运车辆，如架线车、油罐车、工程车、货车及其他专用车辆和借入的客运车辆。

绿地面积 指报告期末用作园林和绿化的各种绿地面积。包括公园绿地、生产绿地、防护绿地、附属绿地和其他绿地的面积。

公园绿地 城市中向公众开放的、以游憩为主要功能，有一定的游憩设施和服务设施，同时兼有健全生态、美化景观、防灾减灾等综合作用的绿化用地。它是城市建设用地、城市绿地系统和城市市政公用设施的重要组成部分。

工业废水排放量 指报告期内经过企业厂区所有排放口排到企业外部的工业废水量。包括生产废水、外排的直接冷却水、废气治理设施废水、超标排放的矿井地下水和与工业废水混排的厂区生活污水，不包括独立外排的间接冷却水（清浊不分流的间接冷却水应计算在内）。

化学需氧量（COD） 测量有机和无机物质化学分解所消耗氧的质量浓度的水污染指数。废气排放总量 指燃料燃烧和生产工艺过程中排放的各种废气总量，以标准状态下每年万标立方米表示。

二氧化硫排放量 指报告期内企业在燃料燃烧和生产工艺过程中排入大气的二氧化硫总质量。工业中二氧化硫主要来源于化石燃料（煤、石油等）的燃烧，还包括含硫矿石的冶炼或含硫酸、磷肥等生产的工业废气排放。

氮氧化物排放量 指报告期内企业在燃料燃烧和生产工艺过程中排入大气的氮氧化物总质量。

烟（粉）尘排放量 指报告期内企业在燃料燃烧和生产工艺过程中排入大气的烟尘及工业粉尘的总质量之和。烟尘或工业粉尘排放量可以通过除尘系统的排风量和除尘设备出口烟尘浓度相乘求得。

工业粉尘排放量 指企业在生产工艺过程中排放的颗粒物重量。如钢铁企业的耐火材料粉尘、焦化企业的筛焦系统粉尘、烧结机的粉尘、石灰窑的粉尘、建材企业的水泥粉尘等。不包括电厂排放大气的烟尘。

Explanatory Notes on Main Statistical Indicators

Year-end Tap Water Production Capacity refers to actual capacity of such links as water intaking, purification, water carriage and leaving factory water main pipe of the waterworks managed by urban construction department and social unit water source prepared at the end of the year.

Length of Water Supply Pipelines at the Year-end refers to the total length of all the pipelines between the water pumps and the user water meters.

Annual Volume of water supply refers to annual total water supply of public waterworks and social unit with water source prepared, including both the effective water supply and loss during the water supply.

Consumption of Water for Residential Use refers to water consumption in the daily life of residents and by public amenities and facilities, including water consumption by residents, eateries, hotels, hospitals, barber shops, common bathing pools, laundries, swimming pools, shops, schools, organs and troops, etc..

Urban Population Water Penetration Rate refers to the ratio between non-agricultural population of municipal water (excluding temporary and floating population) and total urban non-agricultural population. The calculation formula is:

Water penetration rate = non-agricultural population of municipal water / urban non-agricultural population * 100%

Urban Gas Popularizing Rate refers to the ratio between urban non-agricultural population (excluding temporary population and migrant population) using the coal gas (including manufactured gas, liquefied petroleum gas and natural gas) and total urban non-agricultural population. The calculation formula is:

Urban gas popularizing rate = non-agricultural population of municipal gas / total urban non-agricultural population * 100%

Year-end Actual Length of Paved Road refers to roads whose pavement width exceeds 3.5 m except for unsurfaced road (including senior, sub-senior and ordinary roads).

Urban Bridges refer to bridge and road built above the river, interchange between roads, highway interchange based on road spanning railway and pedestrian overpass, both permanent and semi-permanent bridges are included, other than temporary bridge, railway bridge and culvert in the scope of the city.

Daily Urban Sewage Treatment Capacity refers to the design capability of the sewage quantity treated by sewage treatment works every day and night.

Year-end Existing Buses (Public Trolleys) refer to all vehicles which can be put into operation at the end of the year, including number of vehicles put into operation and vehicles with inventory sealed up which are not put into operation other than non-operating vehicles, such as overhead line vehicle, oil tank truck, engineering vehicle, truck, other special vehicle and borrowed passenger service vehicle.

Green Area refers to a green area for gardening and greening. Including parks, green spaces, protective green, the accessory Greenbelt and other green areas at the end of referenced period.

Park Green Land refers to the green land which is open to the public for relaxation and has services facilities and is used for ecological protection, landscaping and disaster reduction. It is an important part of construction land, urban green space and municipal public facilities. public facilities.

Industrial Waste Water Discharged refers to the volume of industrial waste water discharged through all of the drainage system to the outside of factory complex by enterprises during the report period. It includes discharged waste water from production, direct cooling water, waste gas treatment facilities, mine groundwater beyond the standard and domestic sewage mixed with industrial waste water, does not include independently discharged indirect cooling water (voicing split-less indirect cooling water should be taken into account).

Chemical Oxygen Demand (COD) refers to index of water pollution measuring the mass concentration of oxygen consumed by the chemical breakdown of organic and inorganic matter. Total exhaust emission refers to total quantity of various exhaust gases discharged in the process of fuel burning and production which is expressed with 10,000 standard cubic meters each year under the standard state.

SO_2 Emission refers to total volume of SO2 discharged into air during the process of fuel combustion and industrial production in enterprises in a given time, and is mainly caused by the combustion of fossil fuel, ore smelting and the discharge of industrial waste gas during the production of sulfuric acid and phosphate fertilizers.

Nitrogen Oxides Emission refers to total volume of nitrogen oxides discharged into air during the process of fuel combustion and industrial production.

Industrial Soot and Dust Emission refers to volume of soot and dust in smoke emitted in process of fuel burning and industrial production in premises of enterprises in the report period. It is calculated by multiplying exhaust volume of dust removal system by dust concentration.

Emission Load of Industrial Dust refers to the weight of particulate matters discharged in the process of production (such as fireproofing dust of the iron and steel enterprise, coke screening system dust of the coke making enterprise, dust of the sintering machine, dust of the lime kiln and cement dust of the building material industry), excluding smoke discharged by the power plant in to the atmosphere.

8

财政和金融保险

GOVERNMENT FINANCE AND FINANCIAL INSURANCE

8-1 各时期地方财政收支及指数
Expenditures and Indices of Major Years

年份 Year	一般公共预算收入 (万元) General Pubilic Budget Revenue (10 000yuan)	一般公共预算支出 (万元) General Pubilic Budget Expenditure (10 000yuan)	指数(%)(以上年为100) Indices(%)(Preceding Year=100)	
			一般公共预算收入 General Pubilic Budget Revenue	一般公共预算支出 General Pubilic Budget Expenditure
1999	460690	497667	119.9	110.8
2000	490485	547210	110.5	110.4
"十五"时期				
2001	596061	703720	121.5	128.6
2002	662511	775046	115.4	110.2
2003	761064	884597	119.6	114.3
2004	890364	1016953	120.9	115.0
2005	1061547	1206643	120.7	118.7
"十一五"时期				
2006	1284388	1469762	121.0	121.8
2007	1570192	1799787	122.3	122.5
2008	1860155	2213190	118.5	123.1
2009	2101923	2599178	113.0	117.4
2010	2661314	3368037	126.6	129.6
"十二五"时期				
2011	3249315	3968831	122.1	117.8
2012	3808218	4656731	117.0	117.3
2013	4820722	5193190	113.9	111.5
2014	5431278	5714138	112.7	110.0
2015	6143172	6581813	113.1	115.2
"十三五"时期				
2016	6412167	7412641	104.4	112.6
2017	6772100	8340600	105.6	112.5
2018	7528162	10183179	111.2	122.1
2019	8741898	11973158	107.2	107.0
2020	9060751	12887953	103.6	107.6

注：2013 年财政部门对一般公共预算收入口径进行调整，2013 年一般公共预算收入指数为可比口径。2018 年及之前数据不包括原莱芜市数据。

Note: In 2013, the financial department adjusted the caliber of general public budget revenue. In 2013, the index of general public budget income index was comparable caliber.

8-2 地方财政收入 (2020 年)
Local Financial Revenue(2020)

单位：万元 (10 000yuan)

指标	Indicator	全市合计 Total	市本级 Cities					县区级 Counties
			小计 Total	市直 Departments Directiy Under the Municipal Government	莱芜高新区 Lai wu Gao xin	济南先行区 JN Pioneer Area	南部山区 Nan shan	
一般公共预算收入	**General Pubilic Budget Revenue**	9060751	973820	812737	105241	39096	16746	8086931
增值税	Value-added Tax	2554506	54631		33378	12957	8296	2499875
企业所得税	Enterprise Income Tax	1243482	18791		13127	5041	623	1224691
个人所得税	Personal Income Tax	343709	4032		2761	582		339677
资源税	Resource Tax	58522	652		539	74	39	57870
城市维护建设税	Tax on City Maintenance and Construction	426461	11452	1776		2169	1354	415009
房产税	Tax on Real Estates	244428	3832		2667	841	324	240596
印花税	Stamp Tax	135566	2873		1541	1187	145	132693
城镇土地使用税	Holding tax on urban and county land	269840	7108		6015	701	392	262732
土地增值税	Land Value Added Tax	814536	12666		8265	3487	914	801870
车船税	Tax on vehicles and Their Registration	114972	3635		3632	1	2	111337
耕地占用税	Farmland Occupation Tax	87359	4642		746	3896		82717
契税	Contract tax	656853	16366		14038	2300	28	640487
环境保护税	Environmental Protection Tax	13907	91		80	6	5	13816
专项收入	Specific Revenue	711040	382051	373138	5871	1659	1383	328989
行政事业性收费收入	Income from Administrative Fees	408179	161893	155960	5137	793	3	246286
罚没收入	Penalty and Confiscatory Income	143659	74766	74346	206	148	66	68893
国有资本经营收入	Profits of State-owned Enterprises	48265						48265
国有资源（资产）有偿使用收入	Revenue of Compensable Use of State-owned Resources (Assets)	663431	114426	107823	866	3254	2483	549005
捐赠收入	Donation Income	9696	186	179	7			9510
政府住房基金收入	Government Housing Fund Income	104486	99236	99236				5250
其他收入	Others	5748	344	279	65			5404
政府性基金收入	**Government Funds Income**	8182380	5721005	5423081	122912	174875	137	2461375
#城市基础设施配套收入	Urban Infrastructure Supporting Income	644104	371691	333328	19875	18351	137	272413

8-3 各区财政收入 (2020 年)
Financial Revenue by District(2020)

单位：万元

指标	Indicator	合计 Total	历下区 Li xia	市中区 Shi zhong
一般公共预算收入	**General Pubilic Budget Revenue**	**7693798**	**1515651**	**1003256**
增值税	Value-added Tax	2393613	476961	254109
企业所得税	Enterprise Income Tax	1192957	250540	186175
个人所得税	Person al Income Tax	326311	84927	57277
资源税	Resource Tax	49985	1458	7923
城市维护建设税	Tax on City Maintenance and Construction	403484	92182	38020
房产税	Tax on Real Estates	233245	64190	30634
印花	Stamp Tax	128848	30734	14464
城镇土地使用税	Holding tax on urban and county land	244283	14418	12071
土地增值税	Land Value Added Tax	783314	257580	110623
车船税	Tax on vehicles and Their Registration	64018	20204	8683
耕地占用税	Farmland Occupation Tax	77162	2178	4720
契税	Contract tax	616606	95475	96541
环境保护税	Environmental Protection Tax	12629	392	308
专项收入	Specific Revenue	313889	72587	25963
行政事业性收费收入	Income from Administrative Fees	227886	5443	19398
罚没收入	Penalty and Confiscatory Income	60388	3911	4780
国有资本经营收入	Profits of State-owned Enterprises	45672		
国有资源（资产）有偿使用收入	Revenue of Compensable Use of State-owned Resources (Assets)	499037	41237	131266
捐赠收入	Donation Income	7954		117
政府住房基金收入	Government Housing Fund Income	5222	774	
其他收入	Others	5299		
政府性基金收入	**Government Funds Income**	**2055009**		
# 城市基础设施配套收入	Urban Infrastructure Supporting Income	222183		

(10 000yuan)

槐荫区 Huai yin	天桥区 Tian qiao	历城区 Li cheng	长清区 Chang qing	章丘区 Zhang qiu	济阳区 Ji yang	莱芜区 Lai wu	钢城区 Gang cheng	济南高新区 Ji'nan Gao xin
528374	441191	1112812	266216	700470	277431	334265	212629	1301503
150530	118701	311875	93542	223577	78482	132870	104111	448855
41557	59205	248285	20784	88909	27176	27133	11578	231615
29962	17620	30440	5994	13706	3823	6835	4319	71408
304	648	1787	3621	6941	970	13893	7914	4526
22597	17645	47821	13003	34067	12064	20632	15256	90197
18128	14880	19228	7222	14129	4702	7683	8055	44394
7159	7387	12109	3450	11945	2914	6350	3520	28816
12911	11282	47623	14268	52313	17256	19934	17221	24986
83624	48836	130326	19616	41328	20334	6380	585	64082
2271	1322	6367	1985	3485	13871	4225	1248	357
2575	2419	11729	7128	9106	4938	5767	5281	21321
67492	44796	118058	13943	66646	25036	14372	2042	72205
94	156	622	129	1333	167	4373	4896	159
15105	11676	37275	11799	28498	10271	18047	13302	69366
8934	3008	53540	34721	55292	5909	31984	2966	6691
1943	2041	4573	3408	7614	24329	1635	3889	2265
44900							772	
17092	79522	25854	9689	37148	24770	11151	5331	115977
16	39	4673	1908	40	419	742		
				408				4040
1321				3978				
	8381		24587	1475737	351957	75228	22461	96658
	8381		24126	71767	14161	8979	550	94219

8-4 各县财政收入(2020年)
Financial Revenue by County(2020)

单位：万元　　(10 000yuan)

指标	Indicator	合计 Totl	平阴县 Ping yin	商河县 Shang he
一般公共预算收入	General Pubilic Budget Revenue	393133	242946	150187
增值税	Value-added Tax	106262	68562	37700
企业所得税	Enterprise Income Tax	31734	25613	6121
个人所得税	Personal Income Tax	13366	9134	4232
资源税	Resource Tax	7885	7331	554
城市维护建设税	Tax on City Maintenance and Construction	11525	7295	4230
房产税	Tax on Real Estates	7351	4744	2607
印花税	Stamp Tax	3845	2379	1466
城镇土地使用税	Holding tax on urban and county land	18449	7520	10929
土地增值税	Land Value Added Tax	18556	9148	9408
车船税	Tax on vehicles and Their Registration	47319	19783	27536
耕地占用税	Farmland Occupation Tax	5555	1036	4519
契税	Contract tax	23881	9182	14699
环境保护税	Environmental Protection Tax	1187	1113	74
专项收入	Specific Revenue	15100	8728	6372
行政事业性收费收入	Income from Administrative Fees	18400	13062	5338
罚没收入	Penalty and Confiscatory Income	8505	5581	2924
国有资本经营收入	Profits of State-owned Enterprises	2593	2567	26
国有资源（资产）有偿使用收入	Revenue of Compensable Use of State-owned Resources (Assets)	49968	39158	10810
捐赠收入	Donation Income	1556	1019	537
政府住房基金收入	Government Housing Fund Income	28	28	0
其他收入	Others	105	0	105
政府性基金收入	Government Funds Income	406366	160530	245836
#城市基础设施配套收入	Urban Infrastructure Supporting Income	50230	11668	38562

8-5 地方财政支出 (2020 年)
Local Financial Expenditures(2020)

单位：万元 (10 000yuan)

指标	Indicator	全市合计 Total	市本级 Cities					县区级 Counties
			小计 Total	市直 Departments Directiy Under the Municipal Government	莱芜高新区 Lai wu Gao xin	济南先行区 JN Pioneer Area	南部山区 Nan shan	
一般公共预算支出	**General Pubilic Budget Expenditure**	**12887953**	**4995029**	**4418894**	**105649**	**295359**	**175127**	**7892924**
一般公共服务支出	General Public Service	1381988	342406	289682	11431	18955	22338	1039582
国防支出	Defence Expenditure	30734	16753	16703			50	13981
公共安全支出	Public Security	670792	465435	463434	654	166	1181	205357
教育支出	Education	2110114	462406	394256	23826	2024	42300	1647708
科学技术	Science andTechnology	396473	165028	146712	7855	10371	90	231445
文化旅游体育与传媒支出	Culture、Tourism、Sports and Media	129142	80215	78620	32	398	1165	48927
社会保障和就业支出	Social Security and Employment	1740439	735054	687387	3520	16558	27589	1005385
卫生健康支出	Health	987187	459965	432368	6438	10042	11117	527222
节能环保支出	Energy-saving and Environment Protection	376265	126555	112485	6480	1776	5814	249710
城乡社区支出	Urban and Rural Community Affairs	2838242	1355687	1137705	19051	180527	18404	1482555
农林水支出	Farming、Forestry and Irrigation Affairs	886919	220601	166362	2925	13394	37920	666318
交通运输支出	Transport	214453	134660	123387	30	9273	1970	79793
资源勘探信息等支出	Exploration and Information Affairs	191327	35382	18220	16616	454	92	155945
商业服务业等支出	Commerce and Services Affairs	125487	18270	17869	96	15	290	107217
金融支出	Financial Supervision Affairs	31540	2003	1627	376			29537
援助其他地区支出	Aid to Other Area	32554	15579	154 43	136			16975
自然资源海洋气象等支出	Natural Resources Marine Meteorological	175873	102592	100968	397	50	1177	73281
住房保障支出	Housing Security Affairs	395695	192584	155668	2326	31355	3235	203111
粮油物资储备支出	Grain and Oil Reserves	18627	7954	7754	100		100	10673
债务付息支出	Pay Principle and Interest for Public Debt	85556	29863	28818	1045			55693
其他支出	Other Expenditure	16189	3252	1265	1987			12937
政府性基金支出	**Government Funds Expenditure**	**12099945**	**5711386**	**4971789**	**199079**	**523313**	**17205**	**6388559**
#城乡社区支出	Urban and Rural Community Affairs	2838242	1355687	1137705	19051	180527	18404	1482555

8-6 各区地方财政支出（2020年）
Local Financial Expenditures by District(2020)

单位：万元

指标	Indicator	合计 Total	历下区 Li xia	市中区 Shi zhong
一般公共预算支出	General Pubilic Budget Expenditure	7018115	779234	680641
一般公共服务支出	General Public Service	943897	158624	120722
国防支出	Defence Expenditure	13318	8905	1087
公共安全支出	Public Security	168932	25359	22912
教育支出	Education	1458375	214212	187140
科学技术	Science andTechnology	228571	12331	5012
文化旅游体育与传媒支出	Culture、Tourism、Sports and Media	43307	3288	2415
社会保障和就业支出	Social Security and Employment	895061	101993	90965
卫生健康支出	Health	470927	51052	47112
节能环保支出	Energy-saving and Environment Protection	209987	6260	26642
城乡社区支出	Urban and Rural Community Affairs	1348095	132647	110154
农林水支出	Farming、Forestry and Irrigation Affairs	539842	11524	18485
交通运输支出	Transport	60238	32	971
资源勘探信息等支出	Exploration and Information Affairs	149550	5190	6189
商业服务业等支出	Commerce and Services Affairs	102936	5033	922
金融支出	Financial Supervision Affairs	28148	15512	992
援助其他地区支出	Aid to Other Area	16612	3010	2407
国土海洋气象等支出	Land and Weather Affairs	65589	2949	11157
住房保障支出	Housing Security Affairs	178806	14503	19820
粮油物资储备支出	Grain and Oil Reserves	9825	372	650
国债还本付息支出	Pay Principle and Interest for Public Debt	47349		1282
其他支出	Other Expenditure	12937	124	
政府性基金支出	Government Funds Expenditure	5668581	299004	394973
# 城乡社区支出	Urban and Rural Community Affairs	1348095	132647	110154

(10 000yuan)

槐荫区 Huai yin	天桥区 Tian qiao	历城区 Li cheng	长清区 Chang qing	章丘区 Zhang qiu	济阳区 Ji yang	莱芜区 Lai wu	钢城区 Gang cheng	济南高新区 Ji'nan Gao xin
458616	385603	876195	536612	822179	478705	626016	242312	1132002
58682	62061	126524	74951	98279	48681	65420	20237	109716
186	624	275	851	806	45	261	278	
19011	13129	15843	11466	15069	13023	10770	5656	16694
90062	100797	167118	115860	225079	88499	134087	45353	90168
3872	5813	37893	2044	7596	7860	3574	1810	140766
2195	1753	6046	7849	10713	4388	3373	1213	74
93421	82687	88090	83891	114778	83163	93126	27253	35694
45053	40748	42881	39978	72323	37655	56893	17253	19979
14431	16189	23915	21296	23163	5701	43993	16763	11634
73000	36272	196000	33626	84333	88609	40377	47668	505409
25132	7884	80049	101146	87457	60939	78021	22485	46720
811	416	10948	5497	11910	7874	10342	4823	6614
5570	2758	4887	3770	11183	2598	38200	4247	64958
2673	762	30928	976	5149	943	1358	293	53899
81		45	120	408	6	330	32	10622
737	649	2268		5052	267	375	230	1617
1521	1101	6490	13376	8756	6135	7558	3959	2587
17422	6356	31748	14235	28824	16699	15739	6929	6531
270	550	2601	919	1940	776	484	183	1080
2087	3195	731	830	5755	3890	16644	8554	4381
			3038	1041		3386	5348	
256830	346342	516597	279704	1827814	508499	426845	125298	686675
73000	36272	196000	33626	84333	88609	40377	47668	505409

8-7 各县地方财政支出 (2020 年)
Local Financial Expenditures by County(2020)

单位：万元 (10 000yuan)

指标	Indicator	合计 Total	平阴县 Ping yin	商河县 Shang he
一般公共预算支出	General Pubilic Budget Expenditure	874809	368858	505951
一般公共服务支出	General Public Service	95685	42048	53637
国防支出	Defence Expenditure	663	384	279
公共安全支出	Public Security	36425	17445	18980
教育支出	Education	189333	73575	115758
科学技术	Science andTechnology	2874	1324	1550
文化旅游体育与传媒支出	Culture、Tourism、Sports and Media	5620	3363	2257
社会保障和就业支出	Social Security and Employment	110324	48977	61347
卫生健康支出	Health	56295	21366	34929
节能环保支出	Energy-saving and Environment Protection	39723	9131	30592
城乡社区支出	Urban and Rural Community Affairs	134460	71300	63160
农林水支出	Farming、Forestry and Irrigation Affairs	126476	35326	91150
交通运输支出	Transport	19555	9661	9894
资源勘探信息等支出	Exploration and Information Affairs	6395	3184	3211
商业服务业等支出	Commerce and Services Affairs	4281	3198	1083
金融支出	Financial Supervision Affairs	1389	1055	334
援助其他地区支出	Aid to Other Area	363	231	132
自然资源海洋气象等支出	Natural Resources Marine Meteorological	7692	4589	3103
住房保障支出	Housing Security Affairs	24305	15110	9195
粮油物资储备支出	Grain and Oil Reserves	848	559	289
国债还本付息支出	Pay Principle and Interest for Public Debt	8344	5060	3284
其他支出	Other Expenditure			
政府性基金支出	Government Funds Expenditure	719978	283926	436052
# 城乡社区支出	Urban and Rural Community Affairs	134460	71300	63160

8-8 金融机构本外币各项存、贷款期末余额

The Ending Balance of all Deposits and Loans in RMB and Foreign Currencies of Financial Institutions

单位：万元 (10 000yuan)

指标	Indicator	2016 年	2017 年	2018 年	2019 年	2020 年
金融机构本外币各项存款余额	The Balance of RMB and Foreign Currencies Deposits in Financial Institutions	155374463	165605979	170601377	186460860	210649849
#住户存款	Household Deposits	43448420	45241390	50672701	64970029	76475384
非金融企业存款	Non-financial Corporate Deposits	69796525	73973987	72213088	77067935	87238924
广义政府存款	General Government Deposits	30738367	35586733	36530329	35087861	36351481
非银行业金融机构存款	Non-bank Financial Intermediary Deposits	8457783	7083306	6729522	7629436	9239886
金融机构本外币各项贷款余额	The Balance of RMB and Foreign Currencies Loans in Financial Institutions	130961411	143502995	160599213	187687420	207202433
#住户贷款	Household Loans	24694440	31418600	37617608	47041192	54682406
非金融企业及机关团体贷款	Non-financial Corporate and Institution Loans	90455320	98004377	109865593	129406853	142485017
短期贷款	Short-term Loans	27912544	30184576	29398790	34665784	38736145
中长期贷款	Medium and Long-term Loans	51574175	61606175	72421049	82655910	91489364
票据融资	Bill Financing	9670794	3896507	4995957	8682607	8566014
融资租赁	Finance Lease	1129383	2181289	2870478	3240815	3592611
各项垫款	Bill Financing	168425	135831	179319	161737	100884
非银行业金融机构贷款	Non-bank Financial Intermediary Loans	73	50000	0	200000	0

8-9 金融机构人民币各项存、贷款期末余额

The Ending Balance of all Deposits and Loans in RMB of Financial Institutions

单位：万元 (10 000yuan)

指标	Indicator	2016 年	2017 年	2018 年	2019 年	2020 年
金融机构人民币各项存款余额	The Balance of RMB Deposits in Financial Institutions	150327948	159577448	165718671	183032033	207149738
#住户存款	Household Deposits	42799454	44657303	50080833	64380943	75841225
非金融企业存款	Non-financial Corporate Deposits	68394947	72288512	70776618	75805636	85613093
广义政府存款	General Government Deposits	30735405	35426387	36493478	34923450	36297466
非银行业金融机构存款	Non-bank Financial Intermediary Deposits	8232449	6942272	6630358	7571079	9193889
金融机构人民币各项贷款余额	The Balance of RMB Loans in Financial Institutions	113701787	128836570	147000678	176242063	197048849
#住户贷款	Household Loans	24693431	31417225	37616195	47038338	54680859
非金融企业及机关团体贷款	Non-financial Corporate and Institution Loans	88019574	96407415	108452714	128277535	141659442
短期贷款	Short-term Loans	27188058	29297325	28659735	34002100	38291441
中长期贷款	Medium and Long-term Loans	49896069	60896806	71747225	82190276	91128303
票据融资	Bill Financing	9670794	3896507	4995957	8682607	8566014
融资租赁	Finance Lease	1129383	2181289	2870478	3240815	3592611
各项垫款	Bill Financing	135271	135488	179319	161737	81074
非银行业金融机构贷款	Non-bank Financial Intermediary Loans	0	50000	-	200000	0

8-10 保险业务情况
Insurance Business

指标	Indicator	2017 年	2018 年	2019 年	2020 年
保险金额（亿元）	Amount Insured (100 million yuan)	162712	256399	438422	927748
保费收入（万元）	Premium Income(10 000 yuan)	3810660	4155535	5322643	6280398
财产险	Property Insurance	758326	843871	1174143	1255657
人身险	Life Insurance	3052334	3311664	4148500	5024741
赔付支出（万元）	Claim Payment(10 000 yuan)	886699	1033980	1219250	1603108
财产险	Property Insurance	366337	421493	562261	683340
人身险	Life Insurance	520363	612471	656989	919768

注：2018 年以前为区划调整前数据。
Note: Data before the year of 2018 are the data of administrative division before the adjustment.

8-11 证券机构及证券交易情况
Institution and Trading Summary for Stocks

单位：亿元 (100 million yuan)

指标	Indicator	2015 年	2016 年	2017 年	2018 年	2019 年	2020 年
注册地在济南证券公司数（个）	Stocks Institutions in Ji'nan(Unit)	1	1	1	1	1	1
证券营业部（个）	Securities Business Department(Unit)	78	83	92	87	92	91
证券交易额	Trading Volume of Securities Business Department	54575	34687	30975	28482	36453	47753
股票	Stock	38091	19183	15987	12126	18621	28606
基金	Fund	4568	1449	2361	2111	2197	3528
债券	Bond	11899	14045	12602	14119	15536	15444
其他	Others	17	10	25	126	99	174

注：1. 数据由金融办提供。
2.2018 年以前为区划调整前数据。
Note: 1.Data are provided by the Municipal financial office.
2. Data before the year of 2018 are the data of administrative division before the adjustment.

主要统计指标解释

一般公共预算收入 指国家财政参与社会产品分配所取得的收入，是实现国家职能的财力保证。主要包括：（1）各项税收：包括国内增值税、国内消费税、进口货物增值税和消费税、出口货物退增值税和消费税、营业税、企业所得税、个人所得税、资源税、城市维护建设税、房产税、印花税、城镇土地使用税、土地增值税、车船税、船舶吨税、车辆购置税、关税、耕地占用税、契税、烟叶税等。（2）非税收入：包括专项收入、行政事业性收费、罚没收入和其他收入。财政收入按现行分税制财政体制划分为中央本级收入和地方本级收入。

一般公共预算支出 指国家财政将筹集起来的资金进行分配使用，以满足经济建设和各项事业的需要。主要包括：一般公共服务、外交、国防、公共安全、教育、科学技术、文化体育与传媒、社会保障和就业、医疗卫生与计划生育、节能环保、城乡社区、农林水、交通运输、资源勘探信息等、商业服务业等、金融、援助其他地区、国土海洋气象等、住房保障、粮油物资储备、政府债务付息等方面的支出。财政支出根据政府在经济和社会活动中的不同职权，划分为中央财政支出和地方财政支出。

存款 指企业、机关、团体或居民根据资金必须收回的原则，把货币资金存入银行或其他信贷机构保管并取得一定利息的一种信用活动形式。根据存款对象或性质的不同可划分为企业存款、财政存款、机关团体存款、基本建设存款、储蓄存款、农村存款、委托存款、其他存款等科目。它是银行信贷资金的主要来源。

贷款 指银行或其他信贷机构根据资金必须归还的原则，按一定利率，为企业、个人等提供资金的一种信用活动形式。我国银行贷款分为短期贷款、中期流动资金贷款、中长期贷款、信托贷款、融资租赁、委托贷款、票据融资、各项垫款等。

保险金额 指保险人承担赔偿或者给付保险金责任的最高限额。

Explanatory Notes on Main Statistical Indicators

General Public Budget Revenue refers to the revenue of the government finance by means of participating in the distribution of the social products, which is the financial resources for ensuring the government to function. The contents of government revenue have been changed several times. Now it includes the following main items : (1) Various tax revenues: Include domestic value-added tax, domestic excise duty, value-added tax and consumption tax on imported goods, VAT refund and consumption tax on exports, business tax, corporate income tax, individual income tax, resource tax, urban maintenance and construction tax, building taxes, stamp duty, city and town land use tax, land value increment tax, vehicle and vessel tax, tonnage tax, vehicle purchase tax, tariff, farmland conversion tax, deed tax and tobacco taxes. (2) Non-tax revenues: Included in this category are special revenue, revenue from administrative and institutional fees, confiscated income and other income. Fiscal revenues are divided into revenue at the central level and local income pursuant to the current tax-sharing financial system.

General Public Budget Expenditure refers to the distribution and use of the funds the government finances has raised, so as to meet the needs of economic construction and various causes. It includes the following main items: expenditures regarding general public service, diplomacy, national defense, public security, education, science and technology, culture, sports and media, social security and employment, health care and family planning, energy conservation and environment protection, urban and rural communities, agroforestry water, transportation, resource exploration information, commercial service industry, finance, assistance to other areas, territorial marine meteorology, housing security, reserves of grain, oil and materials and payment of government debt interest, etc. Fiscal expenditure is divided into central fiscal expenditure and local fiscal expenditure in accordance with different function and power of government in economic and social activities.

Deposit is a form of credit by which enterprises, institutions, organizations or households can put money into banks and other credit institutions for safekeeping and interest earning under the principle of free withdrawal. According to different depositors, deposits are divided into enterprise deposits, treasury deposits, deposits of government agencies and organizations, capital construction deposits, savings deposits, rural saving deposits, entrusted deposits and other deposits. Deposits are major sources of the credit funds of banks.

Loan is a form of credit by which banks and other credit institutions provide funds at certain interest rate to enterprises and individuals in the light of the principle of unconditional repayment. Loans from Chinese Banks include circulating capital loans, fixed assets loans, loans to urban and rural individuals engaged in industrial and commercial business and agricultural loans.

Amount Insured refers to the maximum that the insurant will get for the claim of the case insured.

物价

PRICE

9-1 主要年份物价指数(以上年价格为100)
Price Indices of Major Years(Preceding Last Year=100)

年份 Year	居民消费价格指数 Consumer Price Index	#食品 Food	#服务项目 Services	零售物价指数 Retail Price Index
1951	108.5	105.3	98.7	109.8
1952	101.5	103.9	101.0	101.2
1955	101.6	101.3	103.4	101.4
1956	100.5	100.7	100.6	100.5
1965	107.3	111.5	97.5	108.0
1970	98.4	99.0	100.0	98.3
1971	100.0	100.5	100.0	100.0
1972	100.1	100.3	100.0	100.1
1973	99.5	99.6	97.9	99.7
1974	99.4	99.1	99.9	99.5
1975	100.2	100.0	100.0	100.2
1976	100.4	100.0	100.0	100.4
1977	99.2	99.9	91.2	100.0
1978	100.3	100.3	100.0	100.3
1979	101.1	101.7	100.5	101.1
1980	104.7	107.9	100.0	105.0
1981	101.9	102.2	100.1	102.0
1982	101.1	101.6	100.3	101.2
1983	100.1	100.3	100.9	100.1
1984	101.9	101.1	109.8	101.3
1985	108.7	112.2	103.3	109.1
1986	106.2	107.6	104.9	106.3
1987	109.5	111.9	104.9	109.8
1988	122.4	128.0	108.8	123.4
1989	116.2	111.2	113.5	116.4
1990	103.3	102.6	108.0	103.0
1991	106.7	107.6	106.9	106.7
1992	110.4	108.7	122.2	109.3
1993	114.7	109.8	138.0	112.1
1994	124.8	133.9	114.5	122.7
1995	117.3	123.0	115.1	113.2
1996	109.1	109.7	116.2	106.3
1997	102.9	101.8	107.8	101.5
1998	100.9	99.4	119.0	98.9
1999	99.1	97.3	127.6	96.9
2000	100.6	97.9	129.0	98.0
2001	100.3	100.8	106.1	98.8
2002	98.8	100.2	101.3	97.8
2003	99.9	103.6	100.3	98.0
2004	102.5	107.4	101.2	100.6
2005	101.1	102.7	101.2	100.4
2006	100.9	102.4	100.9	100.3
2007	103.9	111.6	101.8	102.2
2008	105.7	115.5	101.8	104.5
2009	100.3	102.7	102.4	98.7
2010	102.1	107.3	100.6	101.3
2011	105.4	111.3	104.4	104.6
2012	102.4	103.6	102.2	101.8
2013	102.8	104.9	102.7	101.3
2014	102.2	103.2	102.9	101.2
2015	101.9	101.4	101.6	100.3
2016	102.7	103.9	103.5	100.8
2017	102.0	98.5	104.2	101.0
2018	102.6	102.8	102.1	102.6
2019	103.3	112.0	101.4	102.5
2020	102.4	112.3	99.0	101.9

9-2 主要年份物价指数（以 1950 年价格为 100）
Price Indices of Major Years(Preceding 1950=100)

年份 Year	居民消费价格指数 Consumer Price Index	# 食品 Food	# 服务项目 Services	零售物价指数 Retail Price Index
1951	108.5	105.3	98.7	109.8
1952	110.1	109.4	103.7	111.1
1955	117.2	123.7	108.2	118.4
1956	117.8	124.6	108.8	119.0
1965	127.7	141.5	116.9	130.7
1970	123.0	141.6	110.1	126.0
1971	123.0	142.3	110.1	126.0
1972	123.1	142.7	110.1	126.1
1973	122.5	142.1	107.8	125.8
1974	121.8	140.9	107.7	125.1
1975	122.0	140.9	107.7	125.4
1976	122.5	140.9	107.7	125.9
1977	121.5	140.7	98.2	125.9
1978	121.9	141.1	98.2	126.3
1979	123.2	143.5	98.6	127.6
1980	129.0	154.9	98.6	134.0
1981	131.5	158.3	98.7	136.7
1982	132.9	160.8	99.0	138.3
1983	133.0	161.3	99.9	138.5
1984	135.6	163.1	109.7	140.3
1985	147.4	183.0	113.3	153.0
1986	156.5	195.8	118.9	162.7
1987	171.4	219.1	124.7	178.6
1988	209.8	280.4	135.7	220.4
1989	234.8	311.8	154.0	256.5
1990	251.8	319.9	166.3	264.2
1991	268.7	344.2	177.8	281.9

9-2 续表 continued

年份 Year	居民消费价格指数 Consumer Price Index	# 食品 Food	# 服务项目 Services	零售物价指数 Retail Price Index
1992	296.6	376.2	217.3	308.1
1993	340.2	413.1	299.8	345.4
1994	424.6	570.4	343.3	423.8
1995	498.1	709.7	395.1	479.7
1996	543.4	797.7	459.1	509.9
1997	559.2	782.5	494.9	551.6
1998	564.2	777.8	588.9	545.5
1999	559.1	756.8	751.4	528.6
2000	562.4	740.9	969.3	518.0
2001	564.1	746.8	1028.4	511.8
2002	557.3	748.3	1041.8	500.5
2003	556.7	775.2	1044.9	490.5
2004	570.6	832.6	1057.4	493.4
2005	576.9	855.1	1070.1	495.4
2006	582.1	875.6	1079.7	496.9
2007	604.8	977.2	1099.1	507.8
2008	639.3	1128.7	1118.9	530.7
2009	641.2	1159.2	1145.8	523.8
2010	654.7	1243.8	1152.7	530.6
2011	690.2	1384.7	1203.1	555.1
2012	706.8	1434.5	1229.5	565.1
2013	726.6	1504.8	1262.7	572.4
2014	742.6	1553.0	1299.3	579.3
2015	756.7	1574.7	1320.1	581.0
2016	777.1	1636.1	1366.3	585.6
2017	792.6	1611.6	1423.7	591.5
2018	813.3	1656.7	1453.6	606.8
2019	840.1	1855.5	1473.9	622.0
2020	860.3	2083.7	1459.2	633.8

9-3 分月居民消费价格指数(2020年，以上年同期价格为100)
Consumer Price Indices by Month(2020，Preceding Last Year=100)

指标	Indicator	全年 Total	一月 January	二月 February
居民消费价格总指数	Consumer Price Index	102.4	106.1	104.7
非食品烟酒价格指数	Non-food,tobacco and alcohol Price Index	99.2	100.7	100.0
服务价格指数	Services Price Index	99.0	100.5	99.6
工业品价格指数	Industrial Products Price Index	99.3	100.8	100.6
消费品价格指数	Consumer Goods Price Index	104.5	109.6	107.8
扣除食品和能源价格指数	Excluding Food and Energy Price Index	100.4	101.3	101.0
一、食品烟酒	Food,Tobacco and Liquor	109.9	119.2	115.5
1. 食品	Food	112.3	126.3	120.3
(1) 粮食	Grain	101.7	102.8	101.4
(2) 薯类	Tuber	101.7	108.9	112.0
(3) 豆类	Beans	102.2	100.9	101.5
(4) 食用油	Edible Oil	98.1	99.1	95.1
食用植物油	Edible Vegetable Oil	96.4	96.2	92.1
(5) 菜	Vegetables	105.4	123.3	96.7
鲜菜	Fresh Vegetables	105.9	125.2	96.6
(6) 畜肉类	Livestock Meat	142.0	195.5	191.2
猪肉	Pork	155.2	245.6	238.2
(7) 禽肉类	Poultry	105.6	112.5	115.9
(8) 水产品	Aquatic Products	105.0	104.7	104.6
(9) 蛋类	Eggs	95.7	103.9	106.3
鸡蛋	Hen's Eggs	93.8	103.3	106.0
(10) 奶类	Milk	98.0	101.5	101.9
(11) 干鲜瓜果类	Dried and Fresh Melons and Fruits	91.8	94.6	90.9
鲜瓜果	Fresh Melons and Fruits	91.0	93.5	89.9
(12) 糖果糕点类	Candy and Cakes	98.1	101.1	101.9
(13) 调味品	Condiment	102.1	99.8	98.2
(14) 其他食品类	Other Foods	99.4	98.6	99.8
2. 茶及饮料	Tea and Beverages	99.6	99.8	99.6
3. 烟酒	Tobacco and Liquor	101.9	104.1	104.4
(1) 烟草	Tobacco	100.0	100.0	100.0
(2) 酒类	Liquor	103.9	108.4	109.2
4. 在外餐饮	Outside Catering	107.3	108.1	108.0
二、衣着	Clothing	99.9	101.1	101.5
1. 服装	Garments	101.3	101.9	102.4
(1) 男式服装	Men's Clothing	100.8	101.0	101.8
(2) 女式服装	Women's Clothing	102.1	103.3	103.5
(3) 儿童服装	Children's Clothing	98.8	98.2	99.3
2. 服装材料	Clothing Material	96.5	100.0	100.0
3. 其他衣着及配件	Other Clothing and Accessories	98.9	97.7	97.7
4. 衣着加工服务费	Clothing processing service fee	102.4	102.0	102.0

三月 March	四月 April	五月 May	六月 June	七月 July	八月 August	九月 September	十月 October	十一月 November	十二月 December
103.9	103.3	103.0	102.6	102.8	103.0	101.9	100.0	98.4	99.3
99.5	99.3	99.5	98.9	98.6	98.8	98.8	98.7	98.5	98.5
99.3	99.6	99.8	99.1	98.5	98.3	98.5	98.6	98.2	98.2
99.7	98.9	99.2	98.8	98.7	99.3	99.2	98.9	98.9	98.9
106.8	105.7	105.1	104.9	105.5	105.9	104.1	100.8	98.6	99.9
100.8	100.8	101.1	100.5	100.2	100.2	100.1	99.9	99.4	99.3
114.4	113.0	111.5	111.5	112.9	112.9	109.1	102.7	98.3	100.9
118.8	116.7	114.5	114.4	116.0	116.3	110.9	101.9	96.4	100.4
103.6	104.0	103.5	103.5	101.8	101.4	101.8	100.4	97.2	99.0
118.0	115.5	108.5	99.8	92.5	88.0	95.1	92.2	94.6	93.1
102.0	102.5	105.0	106.4	102.0	102.4	101.6	101.0	100.8	100.3
94.6	95.4	98.0	96.6	98.8	98.4	99.3	99.5	101.2	101.5
92.0	93.2	96.2	94.7	96.7	96.5	98.0	98.3	101.4	101.5
102.0	95.4	94.5	108.1	102.8	109.9	116.2	115.0	104.3	100.9
102.2	95.3	94.1	108.9	103.1	110.7	117.8	116.2	104.5	100.9
174.8	174.3	169.6	166.2	171.9	155.8	125.2	101.2	89.5	98.9
207.2	208.2	201.8	193.4	200.8	173.8	131.1	97.8	85.5	97.0
118.6	111.5	109.0	111.6	115.6	108.8	99.3	90.6	88.0	94.4
103.8	104.8	106.4	105.1	106.4	108.3	107.6	106.8	103.1	98.7
111.1	104.7	99.9	92.6	92.6	91.8	87.8	86.8	84.3	92.7
112.2	104.0	98.1	89.0	89.6	89.1	84.6	83.7	82.0	91.8
100.3	99.2	98.2	97.0	97.6	97.5	97.4	96.7	94.6	94.2
91.1	87.4	79.8	72.7	70.3	86.7	107.6	106.9	114.8	119.1
89.6	84.9	76.8	66.5	62.3	82.0	112.3	114.6	125.2	128.3
99.5	98.5	102.9	97.7	94.2	96.1	95.0	94.8	96.6	99.5
102.3	103.0	103.5	102.0	102.5	104.3	101.8	101.8	101.6	104.1
99.8	98.4	102.3	103.9	104.1	98.6	98.5	96.8	97.3	95.1
99.2	99.3	98.8	99.3	100.4	100.0	99.4	98.1	100.5	100.6
103.7	103.6	104.1	103.4	101.8	100.2	99.8	99.6	99.7	99.0
100.0	100.0	100.0	100.0	100.0	100.0	100.0	100.0	100.0	100.0
107.7	107.5	108.4	107.1	103.6	100.5	99.7	99.2	99.4	98.1
107.8	107.9	107.5	108.0	110.0	109.7	108.4	106.8	103.2	102.8
100.6	99.4	100.3	99.2	98.5	98.8	100.0	99.4	100.2	100.6
101.4	100.3	101.2	100.4	100.1	100.5	101.9	101.0	101.8	102.3
100.4	99.1	100.1	100.0	99.4	99.6	102.1	101.2	101.8	102.9
102.9	101.8	102.3	101.4	101.2	101.7	102.0	101.3	102.2	102.1
97.7	97.4	99.7	97.6	96.7	97.4	100.4	99.3	100.3	101.3
100.0	100.0	100.0	100.0	93.0	93.0	93.0	93.0	93.0	93.0
98.7	98.7	99.4	99.7	99.7	99.9	98.7	98.9	98.9	99.1
102.0	102.0	101.3	101.3	103.7	103.7	103.7	102.3	102.3	102.3

9-3 续表 1 continued 1

指标	Indicator	全年 Total	一月 January	二月 February
5. 鞋类	Footwear	95.7	99.0	99.2
(1) 鞋	Shoes	95.6	99.0	99.1
(2) 鞋类加工服务	Footwear Processing Services	101.4	102.3	102.3
三、居住	Residence	98.5	100.2	100.5
1. 租赁房房租	Rental Housing Rent	104.5	114.8	114.4
2. 住房保养维修及管理	Housing Maintenance	101.7	101.4	101.4
(1) 住房装潢材料	Housing Decoration Materials	101.5	100.3	100.3
(2) 物业管理费	Property Management Fee	100.0	100.0	100.0
(3) 住房装潢维修	Housing Decoration Maintenance	102.8	103.3	103.3
3. 水电燃料	Water, Electricity and Fuels	99.8	100.3	100.3
(1) 水	Water	100.0	100.0	100.0
(2) 电	Electricity	100.0	100.0	100.0
(3) 燃气	Gas	100.9	100.0	100.0
(4) 取暖费	Heating Fee	100.0	100.0	100.0
(5) 其他燃料	Other Fuel	94.5	104.7	104.0
4. 自有住房	Self-owned House	96.5	98.2	98.8
四、生活用品及服务	**Daily Necessities and Services**	**99.4**	**99.1**	**99.4**
1. 家具及室内装饰品	Furniture and Interior Decorations	101.6	100.5	100.8
(1) 家具	Furniture and Interior Decorations	102.0	100.7	100.7
(2) 室内装饰品	Interior Decorations	100.3	99.8	101.3
2. 家用器具	Household Appliances	98.5	96.7	96.6
(1) 大型家用器具	Large Household Appliances	98.6	97.1	97.1
(2) 小家电	Small Household Appliances	98.1	94.7	94.7
3. 家用纺织品	Home Textiles	94.5	90.3	91.0
(1) 床上用品	Bedding Article	93.9	88.8	89.5
(2) 窗帘门帘	Curtain	102.3	102.1	102.1
(3) 其他家用纺织品	Other Household Textiles	92.8	95.7	96.5
4. 家庭日用杂品	The Family Daily Sundry Goods	100.3	100.9	101.6
(1) 洗涤卫生用品	Washing Sanitary Articles	101.9	101.9	103.8
(2) 厨具餐具茶具	Kitchenware, Tableware, Tea Set	98.7	98.7	98.9
(3) 家用手工工具	Home Hand Tools	100.1	100.0	100.0
(4) 其他家庭日用杂品	Other Household Articles For Daily Use	96.6	99.9	97.2
5. 个人护理用品	Personal Care Products	98.7	102.3	102.5
(1) 化妆品	Cosmetics	96.8	103.3	103.3
(2) 其他护理用品类	Other Nursing Products	100.6	101.2	101.7
6. 家庭服务	Family Services	100.8	101.9	101.9
五、交通和通信	**Transport and Communication**	**95.7**	**99.3**	**96.5**
1. 交通	Transport	94.1	101.9	97.5
(1) 交通工具	Transport Tools	98.1	100.3	100.4
(2) 交通工具用燃料	Transport Fuels	85.8	107.4	97.4

三月 March	四月 April	五月 May	六月 June	七月 July	八月 August	九月 September	十月 October	十一月 November	十二月 December
98.1	96.3	97.3	94.6	92.8	92.8	93.9	94.2	95.0	95.1
98.0	96.2	97.2	94.5	92.6	92.7	93.8	94.1	94.9	95.0
102.3	102.3	102.3	102.3	102.3	101.1	100.0	100.0	100.0	100.0
99.1	99.4	98.8	97.9	97.3	97.4	97.7	97.9	97.9	98.0
112.2	113.1	111.5	107.5	97.5	96.9	98.0	98.6	97.8	97.9
101.4	101.5	101.9	101.9	102.0	102.4	102.4	102.0	101.3	100.7
100.3	100.6	101.4	101.5	101.7	102.6	102.7	102.7	102.7	100.9
100.0	100.0	100.0	100.0	100.0	100.0	100.0	100.0	100.0	100.0
103.3	103.3	103.3	103.3	103.3	103.3	103.3	102.2	100.3	100.8
99.8	99.5	99.3	99.3	99.5	99.5	99.5	99.9	100.4	100.4
100.0	100.0	100.0	100.0	100.0	100.0	100.0	100.0	100.0	100.0
100.0	100.0	100.0	100.0	100.0	100.0	100.0	100.0	100.0	100.0
100.0	101.2	101.2	101.2	101.2	101.2	101.2	101.2	101.2	101.2
100.0	100.0	100.0	100.0	100.0	100.0	100.0	100.0	100.0	100.0
96.3	89.1	85.8	86.0	88.9	88.5	88.6	95.9	103.6	103.6
96.8	97.3	96.4	95.3	95.3	95.6	96.0	96.1	96.1	96.4
99.8	**100.2**	**100.4**	**100.0**	**99.6**	**98.7**	**99.2**	**98.8**	**98.6**	**98.8**
101.3	100.6	101.2	101.1	101.1	102.5	102.9	102.7	102.0	102.8
101.4	101.4	101.4	101.4	101.4	103.2	103.7	102.9	102.9	103.0
100.9	98.0	100.8	100.1	100.1	100.1	100.1	102.0	98.8	102.0
98.0	97.2	97.6	98.0	98.5	98.9	99.9	99.7	102.1	99.3
98.7	97.5	97.7	98.0	98.6	98.9	99.5	99.3	102.1	98.8
94.7	95.6	97.0	97.5	98.2	99.2	101.9	101.5	102.4	101.2
96.1	98.8	99.1	105.0	100.4	92.4	93.7	89.3	87.2	92.6
95.3	98.6	99.6	107.2	100.9	91.5	92.9	87.7	85.1	91.8
102.1	102.1	102.1	102.1	102.1	102.1	103.8	103.8	103.8	100.0
98.0	98.0	88.1	83.2	91.9	91.9	90.9	93.0	93.0	93.0
100.7	102.2	101.6	101.2	101.2	99.2	99.0	98.7	97.2	99.8
102.2	104.0	103.8	103.4	103.7	101.2	100.5	99.6	97.1	101.4
99.5	100.3	99.1	99.8	99.0	97.9	97.1	97.6	98.0	97.9
100.0	100.0	100.0	100.0	100.0	100.0	100.0	100.5	100.5	100.5
97.2	98.5	97.6	95.4	95.8	93.3	95.7	96.2	95.8	96.0
101.2	101.9	101.6	97.0	96.1	95.9	96.3	97.3	97.5	94.6
101.2	102.8	102.6	93.2	92.5	91.5	92.9	94.6	94.6	89.8
101.2	100.9	100.5	101.1	100.0	100.6	99.9	100.1	100.6	99.6
100.9	100.9	101.6	100.9	100.4	100.4	100.4	100.4	99.9	99.9
94.5	**93.4**	**94.8**	**95.1**	**95.8**	**96.8**	**96.3**	**95.9**	**94.9**	**95.3**
93.5	91.7	92.5	93.2	93.9	94.8	93.7	93.0	91.5	92.4
100.1	99.9	99.3	98.2	97.5	98.5	97.8	97.5	94.2	93.8
85.2	79.1	77.4	80.3	83.8	85.7	84.8	82.4	82.0	85.2

9–3 续表 2 continued 2

指标	Indicator	全年 Total	一月 January	二月 February
(3) 交通工具使用和维修	Vehicle Use and Maintenance	99.4	100.6	93.9
(4) 交通费	Travelling Expenses	94.5	97.2	91.1
2. 通信	Signal Communication	98.5	94.9	94.8
(1) 通信工具	Communication Tools	100.5	93.0	92.5
(2) 通信服务	Communication Services	98.8	96.4	96.4
(3) 邮递服务	Mailing Service	89.1	81.1	81.1
六、教育文化和娱乐	**Education Culture and Recreation**	**99.6**	**102.0**	**99.3**
1. 教育	Education	101.3	102.5	102.5
(1) 教育用品	Educational Supplies	108.6	112.7	112.7
(2) 教育服务	Education Services	101.0	102.1	102.1
2. 文化娱乐	Culture and Entertainment	97.9	101.5	96.3
(1) 文娱耐用消费品	Recreational Consumer Durables	96.4	96.4	96.3
(2) 其他文娱用品	Other Entertainment Products	99.4	99.6	99.7
(3) 文化娱乐服务	Cultural and Recreational Services	96.6	104.1	99.8
(4) 旅游	Tourism	98.5	102.8	94.2
七、医疗保健	**Health Care**	**100.0**	**99.8**	**100.5**
1. 药品及医疗器具	Drugs and Medical Devices	99.4	98.9	100.4
(1) 中药	Traditional Chinese Medicine	101.1	103.1	103.1
(2) 西药	West Medicine	99.5	99.7	99.2
(3) 滋补保健品	Western Medicine	96.3	92.9	100.3
(4) 医疗卫生器具	Medical and Health Equipment	102.7	101.5	101.5
(5) 保健器具	Healthcare Apparatus	99.7	100.0	100.0
2. 医疗服务	Medical Services	100.6	100.7	100.7
(1) 综合医疗类	Comprehensive Health Care	103.5	103.8	103.8
(2) 诊断类	Diagnostic	98.8	98.7	98.7
(3) 治疗类	Therapeutic	100.5	100.6	100.6
(4) 康复类	Rehabilitation	100.0	100.0	100.0
(5) 中医医疗服务类	Chinese Medicine Services	100.0	100.0	100.0
(6) 其他医疗服务	Other Medical Services	100.0	100.0	100.0
八、其他用品和服务	**Other Supplies and Services**	**108.6**	**106.9**	**107.5**
1. 其他用品类	Other Products	113.0	110.4	111.9
(1) 首饰手表	Jewelry Watches	115.8	112.7	114.7
(2) 其他杂项用品	Other Miscellaneous Supplies	104.4	103.4	103.4
2. 其他服务类	Other Services	104.2	103.7	103.4
(1) 旅馆住宿	Hotel Accommodation	105.9	109.2	103.4
(2) 美容美发洗浴	Hairdressing Bath	108.6	106.0	106.3
(3) 养老服务	Pension Services	101.3	100.0	100.0
(4) 金融保险	Finance and Insurance	101.6	101.2	101.9
(5) 其他服务类	Other Service	102.6	105.4	105.4

三月 March	四月 April	五月 May	六月 June	七月 July	八月 August	九月 September	十月 October	十一月 November	十二月 December
95.3	95.5	100.0	101.5	101.3	101.3	101.3	101.3	101.3	99.8
88.4	88.4	98.1	98.4	97.7	97.1	92.7	94.2	94.7	97.6
96.2	96.4	98.9	98.4	99.2	100.3	101.1	101.1	101.2	100.6
100.2	101.5	100.6	97.8	96.3	102.4	106.9	106.1	106.7	103.5
96.4	96.4	100.0	100.0	100.0	100.0	100.0	100.0	100.0	100.0
81.1	81.1	81.1	81.1	97.8	97.8	97.8	100.0	99.8	99.8
100.7	**101.6**	**101.0**	**100.2**	**99.4**	**98.6**	**98.7**	**98.1**	**97.9**	**97.3**
102.5	102.5	102.3	101.6	101.3	101.4	100.0	99.5	99.5	99.5
112.6	112.9	112.9	112.6	113.2	113.2	104.4	99.6	100.1	100.1
102.1	102.1	101.9	101.1	100.9	100.9	99.8	99.5	99.5	99.5
98.9	100.7	99.7	98.9	97.6	96.0	97.4	96.8	96.2	95.0
94.6	95.5	96.0	96.6	95.7	96.5	97.5	96.9	98.7	96.2
98.3	100.0	99.6	98.5	99.7	99.5	98.6	99.5	98.9	100.7
100.1	99.4	99.4	99.6	100.5	93.8	89.3	90.6	91.7	91.3
100.0	103.0	100.9	99.4	96.7	95.7	100.2	98.3	96.4	94.5
100.3	**99.6**	**100.5**	**99.9**	**99.8**	**99.6**	**99.5**	**100.1**	**100.2**	**99.9**
99.9	98.6	100.3	99.1	99.0	98.6	98.4	99.5	99.8	99.9
103.1	102.9	102.9	99.8	99.8	99.8	99.8	99.8	99.8	99.6
98.9	99.0	99.1	99.1	99.9	100.1	100.1	99.7	99.7	99.2
98.9	92.9	100.3	96.4	94.3	92.3	91.5	98.3	98.3	99.6
101.5	101.5	101.5	104.0	104.0	104.0	104.0	101.0	104.0	104.0
100.0	100.0	100.0	99.4	99.4	99.4	97.9	99.4	99.4	102.2
100.7	100.7	100.7	100.7	100.7	100.7	100.7	100.7	100.7	100.0
103.8	103.8	103.8	103.8	103.8	103.8	103.8	103.8	103.8	100.0
98.7	98.7	98.7	98.7	98.7	98.7	98.7	98.7	98.7	100.0
100.6	100.6	100.6	100.6	100.6	100.6	100.6	100.6	100.6	100.0
100.0	100.0	100.0	100.0	100.0	100.0	100.0	100.0	100.0	100.0
100.0	100.0	100.0	100.0	100.0	100.0	100.0	100.0	100.0	100.0
100.0	100.0	100.0	100.0	100.0	100.0	100.0	100.0	100.0	100.0
109.4	**108.0**	**109.2**	**109.1**	**109.3**	**111.6**	**108.1**	**109.0**	**107.7**	**107.6**
114.7	113.7	115.0	114.6	114.8	118.8	112.2	109.9	111.0	109.8
119.2	117.3	119.0	117.4	117.9	123.0	114.1	111.1	112.9	111.3
101.5	103.0	103.1	106.0	105.5	104.9	106.1	106.1	104.7	104.8
104.3	102.4	103.5	103.7	103.8	104.1	103.7	107.9	104.3	105.3
102.7	90.7	96.1	98.3	101.4	104.1	95.9	138.7	115.4	117.8
109.6	107.8	108.9	108.9	108.9	108.9	108.9	108.9	108.9	111.5
100.0	101.7	101.7	101.7	101.7	101.7	101.7	101.7	101.7	101.7
101.9	101.9	101.9	101.9	101.9	101.9	103.3	101.7	99.7	99.7
105.4	105.4	105.4	105.4	100.0	100.0	100.0	100.0	100.0	100.0

9-4 分月商品零售价格指数 (2020 年，以上年同期价格为 100)
Retail Price Indices by Month(2020，Preceding Last Year=100)

指 标	Indicator	全年 Total	一月 January	二月 February
商品零售价格指数	Retail Price Indices	101.9	105.5	104.2
一、食品	Food	111.3	122.6	117.7
二、饮料、烟酒	Beverages, Tobacco and Liquor	101.3	102.8	103.0
三、服装、鞋帽	Garments, Shoes and Hats	100.0	101.1	101.5
四、纺织品	Textiles	94.3	90.5	91.1
五、家用电器及音像器材	Household Appliances, Music and Video Equipment	96.7	95.7	95.8
六、文化办公用品	Cultural and Office Appliances	99.7	98.7	99.2
七、日用品	Articles for Daily Use	99.0	99.3	99.8
八、体育娱乐用品	Sports and Recreation Articles	99.5	99.9	99.8
九、交通、通信用品	Transportation and Communication Appliances	100.3	99.7	100.1
十、家具	Furniture	102.0	100.7	100.7
十一、化妆品	Cosmetics	98.8	103.3	103.3
十二、金银饰品	Gold and Silver Ornaments	119.7	115.4	118.0
十三、中西药品及医疗保健用品	Traditional Chinese and Western Medicines and Health Care Articles	99.3	98.8	100.3
十四、书报杂志及电子出版物	Books, Newspapers, Magazines and Electronic Publications	104.3	106.0	106.0
十五、燃料	Fuels	89.0	105.7	97.9
十六、建筑材料及五金电料	Building Materials and Hardware	101.1	100.2	100.1

三月 March	四月 April	五月 May	六月 June	七月 July	八月 August	九月 September	十月 October	十一月 November	十二月 December
103.2	102.4	102.1	101.9	102.3	102.7	101.6	99.5	98.2	99.0
116.5	114.8	113.1	113.3	114.9	115.0	110.5	102.9	97.7	100.8
102.4	102.4	102.6	102.3	101.4	100.2	99.7	99.3	99.9	99.4
100.6	99.4	100.2	99.1	98.4	98.7	100.0	99.5	100.3	100.7
96.1	98.8	99.7	105.9	99.6	91.7	92.9	88.5	86.4	92.0
96.1	95.9	95.9	96.4	96.2	96.5	97.6	97.3	99.5	97.3
98.6	99.8	100.4	100.5	99.8	99.6	99.4	99.9	99.7	100.9
99.3	100.2	99.3	99.0	99.1	99.0	98.1	98.1	97.9	99.5
98.3	99.5	100.0	98.6	100.2	99.7	98.6	98.7	100.1	100.1
101.4	101.9	101.5	100.1	99.3	100.7	101.3	100.8	98.7	97.7
101.4	101.4	101.4	101.4	101.4	103.2	103.7	102.9	102.9	103.0
102.0	103.1	102.0	96.8	96.0	95.6	95.7	97.0	96.9	94.3
123.5	121.1	123.2	122.2	122.7	128.5	117.8	114.2	116.6	114.5
99.8	98.4	100.2	99.0	98.9	98.5	98.3	99.5	99.8	99.8
106.0	106.1	106.1	106.1	106.3	106.3	101.8	100.4	100.7	100.7
88.3	83.8	82.4	84.8	87.6	89.1	88.4	86.6	86.2	88.7
100.1	100.6	101.2	101.0	101.3	102.0	102.1	102.2	102.0	100.6

9-5 主要年份零售商品和服务项目年平均价格
Per Retail and Services Price of Major Years

商品名称	Name	规格等级牌号 Grade	单位 Unit	1978 年	1980 年	1985 年
面粉	Flour	特一	元 / 千克 (yuan/kg)	0.50	0.50	0.50
粳米	Japonica	标一	元 / 千克 (yuan/kg)	0.34	0.34	0.40
小米	Millet	一等	元 / 千克 (yuan/kg)	0.27	0.27	0.44
土豆	Potato		元 / 千克 (yuan/kg)	0.19	0.22	0.30
豆腐	Doufu	水豆腐	元 / 千克 (yuan/kg)	0.16	0.18	0.26
猪肉	Pork	净肉	元 / 千克 (yuan/kg)	1.72	1.95	2.65
牛肉	Beef	净肉	元 / 千克 (yuan/kg)	1.26	1.76	2.91
羊肉	Mutton	净肉	元 / 千克 (yuan/kg)	1.38	1.88	2.80
鸡蛋	Hen's Egg	新鲜完整	元 / 千克 (yuan/kg)	1.58	2.20	2.60
海带	Kelp	盐干一级	元 / 千克 (yuan/kg)	1.18	1.26	1.32
大白菜	Chinese Cabbage	一等	元 / 千克 (yuan/kg)	0.11	0.07	0.09
菠菜	Spinage	一等	元 / 千克 (yuan/kg)	0.08	0.09	0.28
油菜	Oilseed rape	一等	元 / 千克 (yuan/kg)	0.05	0.07	0.26
芹菜	Celery	一等	元 / 千克 (yuan/kg)	1.13	0.11	0.39
韭菜	Chinese Chives	一等	元 / 千克 (yuan/kg)	0.15	0.16	0.54
黄瓜	Cucumber	一等	元 / 千克 (yuan/kg)	0.19	0.18	0.47
西红柿	Tomato	一等	元 / 千克 (yuan/kg)	0.15	0.18	0.53
茄子	Eggplant	一等	元 / 千克 (yuan/kg)	0.14	0.11	0.27
青椒	Green Pepper	一等	元 / 千克 (yuan/kg)	0.23	0.20	0.47
大葱	Allium Fistulosum	一等	元 / 千克 (yuan/kg)	0.11	0.12	0.28
黑木耳	Black Fungus	甲级	元 / 千克 (yuan/kg)	30.00	32.00	34.86
精盐	Salt	再制盐	元 /500 克 (yuan/500g)	0.16	0.16	0.14
酱油	Soy Sauce	二级	元 / 千克 (yuan/kg)	0.22	0.22	0.34
味精	Aginomoto	含麸酸钠 80% 以上	元 / 千克 (yuan/kg)	10.80	9.68	12.60
绵白糖	Soft Sugar	国产机制一级	元 / 千克 (yuan/kg)	1.60	1.70	1.70
红糖	Brown Sugar	一级	元 / 千克 (yuan/kg)	1.30	1.30	1.30
啤酒	Beer	熟 12 度瓶装	元 / 瓶 (yuan/unit)	0.58	0.58	0.73
苹果	Apple	一级	元 / 千克 (yuan/kg)	0.82	0.90	1.19
桔子	Orange	一级	元 / 千克 (yuan/kg)	1.30	1.52	2.35
西瓜	watermelon	一级	元 / 千克 (yuan/kg)	0.24	0.28	0.32
香蕉	Banana	一级	元 / 千克 (yuan/kg)	1.46	1.65	1.82
自来水	Tap Water	生活用水	元 / 吨 (yuan/ton)	0.08	0.08	0.09
照明用电	Lighting Electricity	民用 220V	元 / 度 (yuan/kwh)	0.18	0.18	0.18
平信	Ordinary Mail	外埠	元 / 封 (yuan/unit)	0.08	0.08	0.08
注射费	Injection Fees	肌肉注射	元 / 次 (yuan/unit)	0.10	0.10	0.10
住院费	Hospitalization Fees	普通床位	元 / 天 (yuan/day)			
学杂费	Tuition and Fees	高中学生	元 / 学期 (yuan/semester)	2.50	2.50	2.50
公园门票	Park Tickets	大明湖	元 / 张 (yuan/unit)	0.03	0.03	0.03
理发	Haircut	男理一级全活	元 / 次 (yuan/unit)	0.30	0.30	0.45
洗澡	Bath		元 / 次 (yuan/unit)	0.24	0.24	0.30
课本	Textbook	高中语文一年级	元 / 本 (yuan/unit)			
银花	Silver	一等	元 / 千克 (yuan/kg)	6.65	8.00	18.00

注：1. 大明湖景区 2017 年开始免费入园。
2. 由于居民消费价格是指数比较，所以理发和洗澡所选的规格品与上年不一致，绝对价格无可比性。
3. 因消费升级，商品和服务规格变化较大，零售商品和服务项目年平均价格自 2019 年起停止更新。

1990 年	1995 年	2000 年	2005 年	2010 年	2013 年	2014 年	2015 年	2016 年	2017 年	2018 年
0.50	2.24	1.78	2.86	4.14	5.07	5.41	5.43	5.46	5.64	8.54
1.04	3.33	2.03	3.08	4.76	5.91	5.91	6.04	6.05	6.00	6.06
1.32	2.66	2.07	3.26	6.99	8.58	14.10	14.63	10.51	11.49	10.87
0.36	1.48	1.48	1.92	4.53	3.61	3.72	3.80	3.84	3.53	3.84
0.70	1.43	1.55	2.14	4.31	5.21	5.99	6.24	5.97	5.88	6.11
5.52	12.91	12.87	14.90	25.18	33.04	30.57	32.37	35.78	35.49	32.88
5.43	12.06	10.99	16.34	36.47	64.52	65.00	66.58	69.02	69.46	69.25
5.91	15.49	15.04	22.07	44.80	75.33	79.23	76.29	76.85	69.67	79.86
4.96	5.99	3.99	5.72	7.48	8.52	10.87	9.25	8.41	8.18	9.75
3.60	5.35	5.36	8.76	19.29	30.35	33.43	32.50	28.87	27.15	25.51
0.13	0.72	0.91	1.64	3.23	2.77	2.29	2.84	2.80	2.41	2.93
0.50	0.90	1.57	2.21	6.69	7.61	6.53	7.91	8.53	7.41	8.81
0.63	1.11	1.26	1.83	5.05	5.84	5.17	6.43	7.14	6.08	7.46
0.60	1.22	1.25	2.28	4.99	5.46	4.07	5.62	5.06	5.13	5.68
1.01	1.80	1.98	2.99	6.55	7.05	6.47	7.42	5.33	4.97	5.59
0.99	2.45	2.53	3.16	5.67	6.26	5.36	5.96	6.03	5.67	7.53
1.02	2.66	2.07	2.90	6.01	6.60	6.37	7.02	6.97	7.24	7.69
0.89	2.67	2.51	3.07	6.05	6.34	5.60	6.14	6.66	6.14	7.48
1.34	4.13	3.15	4.10	6.45	7.48	6.38	8.07	7.61	7.00	9.03
0.54	1.46	1.31	2.51	6.16	6.95	5.94	6.56	9.59	6.44	6.19
48.95	59.16	68.57	65.13	86.80	121.45	128.14	122.59	118.11	122.67	128.34
0.31	0.70	1.10	2.02	1.50	3.83	3.84	4.28	5.17	5.97	6.18
0.68	1.83	2.40	4.53	6.74	7.04	6.75	6.61	7.14	7.05	8.69
16.50	22.81	14.26	15.67	19.33	21.02	21.34	22.19	21.94	22.56	22.92
2.60	6.89	6.12	5.43	9.75	15.15	15.89	16.08	14.38	14.25	15.39
2.21	6.32	5.90	5.54	9.80	15.62	15.54	14.70	15.68	18.29	21.07
1.41	2.13	2.30	2.42	2.61	2.68	2.77	2.76	2.72	2.49	2.62
2.48	3.86	2.72	3.19	8.93	12.04	14.96	15.11	10.86	11.86	11.85
2.27	3.37	2.35	3.30	7.45	10.29	11.97	9.06	10.72	13.86	11.96
0.58	3.20	2.70	3.06	4.72	5.56	5.88	5.57	5.16	5.60	5.26
2.93	4.78	4.05	4.02	6.39	7.28	9.70	7.01	7.04	6.63	8.24
0.19	0.51	1.60	2.78	3.15	3.15	3.15	4.00	4.21	4.21	4.21
0.18	0.29	0.43	0.53	0.55	0.55	0.56	0.56	0.56	0.56	0.56
0.13	0.20	0.80	0.80	1.20	1.20	1.20	1.20	1.20	1.20	1.20
0.20	0.25	1.67	2.00	2.00	2.00	2.00	2.00	2.00	2.00	2.00
2.50	4.00	7.67	15.00	26.67	26.67	23.33	23.33	33.89	36.67	36.67
12.00	49.00	600.00	800.00	800.00	800.00	800.00	800.00	800.00	800.00	800.00
0.30	4.33	13.48	15.63	30.00	30.00	30.00	30.00	30.00		
1.30	5.63	10.00	17.50	20.50	25.00	25.21	25.21	32.38	25.10	27.70
0.58	5.00	8.00	12.00	30.00	38.00	53.00	58.00	58.00	68.00	68.00
2.00	2.55	6.41	4.60	6.47	6.47	6.47	6.47	6.47	6.44	6.39
28.00	70.00	93.00	87.22	325.00	314.10	361.17	352.71	325.00	324.39	403.83

Note: 1. Daming Lake Scenic spot has been free since 2017.

2. Because the consumer price of residents is an index comparison, the standard products selected for haircut and bath are inconsistent with the previous year, and the absolute price is incomparable."

3. Because of consumption upgrading and large exchanges in commodity and service specifications, the annual average price of retail commodity and service items has not been updated since 2019.

9-6 住宅销售价格指数(2020年，以上月价格为100)

Sales Price of Residential Buildings(2020,Preceding Last Month=100)

指标	Indicator	1月 January	2月 February	3月 March	4月 April	5月 May	6月 June
新建住宅	New Residential Buildings	99.5	99.8	99.6	100.0	100.5	100.3
新建商品住宅	New Commercial Residential Buildings	99.5	99.8	99.6	100.0	100.5	100.3
90平方米及以下	Buildings below 90sq.m	99.9	99.1	100.3	99.1	100.4	101.1
90-144平方米	Buildings 90-144 sq.m	99.3	100.1	99.5	99.9	100.5	100.3
144平方米以上	Buildings above 144sq.m	100.1	99.1	99.8	100.6	100.7	100.0
二手住宅	Second-hand House	99.8	99.6	100.0	99.9	100.0	99.9
90平方米及以下	Buildings below 90sq.m	99.5	100.1	100.1	99.6	99.6	100.5
90-144平方米	Buildings 90-144 sq.m	99.9	99.3	99.8	100.1	100.6	99.2
144平方米以上	Buildings above 144sq.m	100.6	99.1	99.9	100.1	100.0	100.2

9-6 续表 continued

指标	Indicator	7月 July	8月 August	9月 September	10月 October	11月 November	12月 December
新建住宅	New Residential Buildings	100.1	99.6	100.0	99.8	99.7	99.9
新建商品住宅	New Commercial Residential Buildings	100.1	99.6	100.0	99.8	99.7	99.9
90平方米及以下	Buildings below 90sq.m	99.5	99.7	100.5	100.2	99.2	99.7
90-144平方米	Buildings 90-144 sq.m	100.2	99.8	100.1	99.8	99.8	100.0
144平方米以上	Buildings above 144sq.m	100.4	99.1	99.6	99.9	99.6	99.7
二手住宅	Second-hand House	100.1	99.5	99.6	99.7	99.6	99.5
90平方米及以下	Buildings below 90sq.m	100.1	99.4	99.7	99.5	99.9	99.4
90-144平方米	Buildings 90-144 sq.m	100.2	99.7	99.5	99.9	99.4	99.5
144平方米以上	Buildings above 144sq.m	100.1	99.4	99.3	99.7	99.0	99.7

9-7 住宅销售价格指数(2020 年，以上年同期价格为 100)

Sales Price of Residential Buildings (2020,Preceding Last Year=100)

指 标	Indicator	1 月 January	2 月 February	3 月 March	4 月 April	5 月 May	6 月 June
新建住宅	New Residential Buildings	99.7	99.0	97.8	96.8	96.9	96.9
新建商品住宅	New Commercial Residential Buildings	99.7	99.0	97.8	96.8	96.9	96.9
90 平方米及以下	Buildings below 90sq.m	101.6	100.8	100.6	99.2	99.1	100.2
90-144 平方米	Buildings 90-144 sq.m	98.7	98.2	96.9	95.7	95.7	95.7
144 平方米以上	Buildings above 144sq.m	102.0	100.5	99.5	99.3	99.8	99.4
二手住宅	Second-hand House	97.2	96.4	95.9	96.1	96.4	96.4
90 平方米及以下	Buildings below 90sq.m	96.9	96.6	96.1	95.9	95.3	95.7
90-144 平方米	Buildings 90-144 sq.m	96.8	95.7	95.3	95.9	97.0	96.4
144 平方米以上	Buildings above 144sq.m	99.2	97.9	97.5	97.6	97.7	98.9

9-7 续表 continued

指 标	Indicator	7 月 July	8 月 August	9 月 September	10 月 October	11 月 November	12 月 December
新建住宅	New Residential Buildings	96.8	96.7	97.1	97.9	98.3	99.0
新建商品住宅	New Commercial Residential Buildings	96.8	96.7	97.1	97.9	98.3	99.0
90 平方米及以下	Buildings below 90sq.m	99.3	98.6	99.1	100.1	99.2	98.5
90-144 平方米	Buildings 90-144 sq.m	95.6	95.8	96.4	97.3	98.1	99.1
144 平方米以上	Buildings above 144sq.m	99.4	98.6	98.2	98.6	98.3	98.7
二手住宅	Second-hand House	96.7	97.1	96.9	97.3	97.5	97.2
90 平方米及以下	Buildings below 90sq.m	95.7	96.6	97.0	97.0	97.4	97.3
90-144 平方米	Buildings 90-144 sq.m	96.9	97.1	96.5	97.3	97.5	97.1
144 平方米以上	Buildings above 144sq.m	99.1	98.7	97.7	97.8	97.4	97.4

9-8 主要年份工业生产者出厂、购进价格指数（以上年价格为100）

Purchasing Price Index for Industrial Producers and Producer Price Index for Manufactured Goods in Main Years (Preceding last year=100)

年份 Year	工业生产者出厂价格指数 Producer Price Indices for Industrial Products	工业生产者购进价格指数 Industrial Producer Purchasing Price Indices
1998	94.5	95.2
1999	98.9	97.6
2000	104.8	114.5
2001	99.8	101.4
2002	97.9	100.4
2003	103.2	111.2
2004	106.7	116.4
2005	102.3	111.3
2006	100.2	105.6
2007	103.9	105.0
2008	109.2	116.9
2009	96.2	94.3
2010	104.7	109.9
2011	105.3	108.2
2012	98.4	99.4
2013	98.8	97.8
2014	99.0	98.0
2015	95.0	92.7
2016	99.8	99.0
2017	105.7	113.9
2018	104.8	108.3
2019	100.3	98.6
2020	98.1	97.5

注：2020年，“工业生产者出厂价格指数”与“工业生产者购进价格指数”指标为全省数据。
Note: In 2020, the “Producer Price Index ” and “Producer Purchasing Price Index ” are province-wide data.

主要统计指标解释

居民消费价格 是指城乡居民购买并用于日常生活消费的商品和服务项目的价格。

居民消费价格指数 反映一定时期内居民所消费商品及服务项目的价格水平变动趋势和变动程度的相对数。居民消费价格水平的变动率在一定程度上反映了通货膨胀（或紧缩）的程度。编制居民消费价格指数的目的，是了解全国各地价格变动的基本情况，分析研究价格变动对社会经济和居民生活的影响，满足各级政府制定政策和计划、进行宏观调控的需要，以及为国民经济核算提供参考依据。

调查内容是城乡居民购买并用于日常生活消费的商品和服务项目的价格。调查内容根据全国城乡居民家庭消费支出调查资料以及居民消费结构和消费习惯确定，按用途划分为8个大类，262个基本分类，包括食品烟酒、衣着、居住、生活用品及服务、交通和通信、教育文化和娱乐、医疗保健、其他用品和服务。

商品零售价格 是商品在流通过程中最后一个环节的价格，是工业、商业、餐饮业和其他零售企业向城乡居民、机关团体出售生活消费品和办公用品的价格。

商品零售价格指数 反映市场商品零售价格的变动趋势和变动程度。其目的在于掌握商品价格的变动趋势，为国家宏观调控和国民经济核算提供参考依据。

调查内容是工业、商业、餐饮业和其他行业的零售商品以及农民对非农业居民出售商品的价格。包括食品、饮料烟酒、服装鞋帽、纺织品、家用电器及音像器材、文化办公用品、日用品、体育娱乐用品、交通通信用品、家具、化妆品、金银饰品、中西药品及医疗保健用品、书报杂志及电子出版物、燃料、建筑材料及五金电料等16个大类，197个基本分类的商品零售价格。

工业生产者价格 工业生产者价格包括工业企业产品第一次出售时的出厂价格和企业作为中间投入的原材料、燃料、动力购进价格（简称工业生产者购进价格）。工业生产者价格调查的目的在于及时、准确、科学地反映各工业行业产品价格水平及其变动趋势和幅度，为国民经济核算、计算工业发展速度、宏观经济分析和调控、理顺价格体系等提供科学、准确的依据。

工业生产者价格指数 是由工业生产者出厂价格指数和工业生产者购进价格指数两部分组成。

工业生产者出厂价格指数 是反映一定时期内全部工业产品第一次出售时的出厂价格总水平的变动趋势和变动幅度的相对数。

工业生产者购进价格指数 是反映作为中间投入的原材料、燃料、动力购进价格总水平的变动趋势和变动幅度的相对数。

住宅销售价格 指房产所有权转移时买卖双方实际成交的价格（合同价格）。房产买卖时，买房人购买的是房产的所有权，卖房人将房产所有权出让，同时要获得房产所有权出让的价格补偿。它主要包括新建住宅销售和二手住宅销售两部分。

住宅销售价格指数 是综合反映住宅商品价格总体变化趋势和变化幅度的相对数。各市住宅销售价格指数是由新建住宅销售价格指数和二手住宅销售价格指数组成。

Explanatory Notes on Main Statistical Indicators

Consumer Price refers to the price of goods and services purchased and used for daily life consumption by urban and rural residents.

Consumer Price index reflects the price changing trend of commodities and services consumed by residents in a certain period, and the relative number of the changing degree. The change rate of Consumer Price Index may reflect the degree of inflation (deflation) to a certain extent. The purpose for preparing Consumer Price Index is to get a basic known about the price variation across the country, analyze the influence of price variation upon social economy and residential livings, satisfy the requirements of government at all levels for preparing policies and plans, and carrying out macroeconomic regulation, and provide a reference basis for national economic accounting.

The investigation content is the price of goods and services purchased and used for daily life consumption by urban and rural residents. The investigation content is confirmed pursuant to survey data regarding national urban and rural residents' household consumption expenditure and resident consumption structure as well as consumption habit which is divided into 8 categories (262 basic types) as per purpose, including food, alcohol and tobacco, clothing, housing, daily necessities and services, transportation and communication, education, culture and entertainment, health care and other goods and services.

Retail Price refers to the prices in the last link of the production circulation process. It is the prices that industrial, commercial, catering and other retail enterprises sell daily consumer goods and products for office use to urban and rural residents and institutions and social organizations.

Retail Price Indices reflects the changing trend and degree of the retail prices of commodities in the market to master the changing trend of commodity retail prices and provide a reference basis for state macro-control and national economic accounting.

The research content involves the prices of retail goods in industry, business, catering and other industries as well as the prices of goods sold by the farmer to the non-agricultural residents, including the commodities of 16 categories (including 197 basic types) -- food, beverage alcohol & tobacco, clothing & shoes, textile, household appliances and audio & video equipment, cultural & office goods, daily necessities, sports & entertainment goods, transportation & communication supplies, furniture, cosmetics, gold & silver accessories, traditional Chinese and western medicines & healthcare supplies, newspapers & magazines and electronic publications, fuel, building materials & hardware.

Industrial Producer Price covers the ex-factory price when products of industrial enterprises are sold for the first time and the purchase price (called as industrial producer purchase price for short) of raw materials, fuels and power which are intermediate inputs of the enterprise. The investigation of industrial producer price is aimed at timely, accurately and scientifically reflecting the price level of products and the corresponding trend and range of changing in various industries, and providing scientific and accurate basis for national economic accounting, computing industry development speed, macroeconomic analysis and regulation and straightening out the price system, etc.

Industrial Producer Price Index is constituted by Producer Price Indices for Industrial Products and Purchasing Price Indices for Industrial Producers.

Producer Price Indices for Industrial Products reflect the trend and degree of changes in general ex-factory prices of all manufactured goods for first sale during a given period.

Purchasing Price Indices for Industrial Producers reflect changes in the level and degree of purchasing prices such as intermediate input such as raw materials, fuels and power.

The Sales Price of Residential refers to the actual price (contract price) of the transaction between the buyer and the seller when the house ownership is transferred. When the house property is sold, the house buyer purchases the ownership of the house property and the house seller transfers the ownership of the house property with price compensation for house property ownership transfer obtained at the same time. Housing sales mainly include sales of newly built house and sales of second-hand house.

Price Index for Residential reflects the trend and degree of changes in prices of real estate. The price index for real estate is constituted by the price index for the new houses and the price index for the second-hand house.

10

人民生活

PEOPLE´ S LIVELIHOOD

10-1 人民物质文化生活提高情况
Improvement in People´s Material and Cultural Life

指　标	Indicator	单位 (unit)	1978 年	1990 年
就业	Employment			
每一农村劳动力负担人数	Average Dependents Per Labor Force	人 (person)	1.70	1.61
每一城镇就业者负担人数	Dependents Per Urban Employee	人 (person)	1.89	1.72
城镇登记失业率	Registered Urban Unemployment Rate	% (%)		
收入与支出	Income and Expenditure			
农村居民人均可支配收入	Per Capita Disposable Income of Rural Inhabitant	元 (yuan)	111	731
农村居民人均生活消费支出	Per Capita Consumer Expenditure of Rural Inhabitant	元 (yuan)	83	570
农村居民恩格尔系数	Engel's Coefficient of Rural Inhabitant	% (%)	69.9	50.5
城镇居民人均可支配收入	Per Capita Disposable Income of Urban Inhabitant	元 (yuan)	338	1620
城镇居民人均生活消费支出	Per Capita Consumer Expenditure of Urban Inhabitant	元 (yuan)	318	1360
城镇居民恩格尔系数	Engel's Coefficient of Urban Inhabitant	% (%)	57.1	57.5
居民储蓄	Household Savings			
城乡居民年末储蓄存款余额	Deposits of Urban and Rural Residents	亿元 (100 million yuan)	1.3	51.1
人均储蓄存款余额	Per Capita Savings Balance	元 (yuan)	28.5	975.5
住房面积	Area of Building			
农村人均住房建筑面积	Rural Per Capita Living Space	平方米 (sq.m)	9.6	22.5
城镇人均住房建筑面积	Urban Per Capita Living Space	平方米 (sq.m)	4.1	7.5
交通通讯	Traffic and Communication			
农村每百户拥有摩托车	Number of Motorcycles Owned by Per 100 Rural Households	辆 (unit)		4.0
城市每百户拥有摩托车	Number of Motorcycles Owned by Per 100 Urban Households	辆 (unit)		7.7
城市公用事业	Urban Utilities			
城市人口用水普及率	Urban water Penetration Rate	% (%)	99	100
每万人拥有公园绿地面积	Green Area of Park Per 10000 Population	公顷 (ha)	1.6	4
文化生活	Culture Life			
城市每百户拥有彩色电视机	Number of Color TV Sets Owned by Per 100 Rural Households	台 (set)	–	61.3
农村每百户拥有彩色电视机	Number of Color TV Sets Owned by Per 100 Urban Households	台 (set)	–	70.0
教育卫生	Education and Public Health			
每万人口中在校大学生数	Number of College Students Per 10 000 Population	人 (person)	22	71
每万人拥有卫生技术人员	Number of Health Technical Personnel Per 1oooo Population	人 (person)	10.98	59.45
每万人拥有医院病床	Number of Beds of Hospitals and Health Centers Per 1oooo Population	张 (unit)	22.01	32.88

注：1. “城镇居民人均生活消费支出” 1990 年以前为 “生活费支出” 。
2. “人均住宅建筑面积”，2009 年以前(不含)为 “使用面积” 口径，2002 年以前(不含)为 “居住面积” 口径。
3. 从 2015 年起，全市发布城乡住户调查一体化改革新口径数据，居民收支调查指标与 2014 年前分别实施的城镇和农村住户调查的调查范围、方法、指标口径、名称有所不同。(以下相关表同)。
4. “农村居民人均可支配收入” 2014 年以前为 “农民人均纯收入” 口径。

2000 年	2010 年	2015 年	2016 年	2017 年	2018 年	2019 年	2020 年
1.40	1.35	1.38	1.42	1.31	1.4	1.4	1.4
1.71	1.67	1.80	1.87	1.35	1.4	1.5	1.3
3.70	3.84	2.04	2.17	2.08	2.06	2.01	2.03
3047	8903	14232	15346	16594	17924	19454	20432
1977	5407	8597	9396	10327	11172	12300	12947
43.5	33.6	32.3	32.2	31.5	30.5	30.1	30.4
8471	25321	39889	43052	46642	50146	51913	53329
6892	15973	26319	28537	30729	32977	33439	34391
34.6	31.6	24.4	24.2	23.5	23.5	23.8	23.5
463.0	2187.7	3951.4	4279.9	4465.7	5008.1	6438.1	7584.1
8229.6	36239.0	63358.0	68012.6	69971.2	77076.2	81389.8	94596.7
28.6	40.2	52.6	53.8	55.2	54.3	51.1	50.3
10.5	29.7	44.9	45.5	47.8	46.5	39.0	39.3
61.0	84.9	79.1	75.8	76.3	51.7	58.5	57.7
34.3	13.3	15.1	13.5	16.1	11.6	12.9	13.1
100	100	99.00	99.57	99.64	99.78	100.00	100.00
7.2	11.3	11.55	11.81	11.79	12.59	13.20	12.45
132.3	115.5	110.5	110.6	111.1	106.0	105.1	105.9
125.0	122.2	114.0	118.3	118.4	114.1	113.0	110.0
165	1064	1141	1154	1241	1226	1040	1121
63.40	65.2	100.6	105.6	104.2	111.0	109.5	112.8
38.57	52.9	69.1	72.2	74.9	77.0	74.8	74.8

Note: 1. "Per capita living expenditure of urban residents" was "cost of living expenses" before 1990.
2. "Per capita housing area" was the caliber of "usable area" before 2009 (excluding) and was the caliber of "living area" before 2002 .
3. Since 2015, the city has released new caliber data for the integrated reform of urban and rural household surveys. The survey indicator of residents' income and expenditure was different from the survey scope, method, index caliber and name of urban and rural households carried out before 2014. (The same below).
4. "Per capita disposable income of rural residents" was the caliber of "rural per capita net income" before 2014.

10-2 各时期城镇居民生活情况
Basic Conditions of Urban Households in Each Period

年 份 Year	人均可支配收入 (元) Per Capita Annual Disposable Income (yuan)	人均生活消费支出(元) Per Capita Consumer Expenditure(yuan)		就业者负担人数 (人) Average Dependents Per Employee (person)	人均住宅建筑面积 (平方米) Per Capita Floor Space (sq.m)
		小 计 Total	#人均食品支出 Per Capita Food Expenditure		
1949	64.53	61.30	37.39		4.09
1952	130.00	127.84	77.98		4.11
1957	206.50	194.15	117.69		3.64
1962	201.74	209.84	131.42		3.48
1965	219.51	212.82	131.59		3.31
1970					3.51
1975					3.66
1978	337.80	317.88	181.56	1.89	4.06
1980	440.09	405.53	230.11	1.67	4.22
"六五"时期					
1981	487.19	452.77	256.67	1.73	4.40
1982	502.97	468.03	275.30	1.70	4.57
1983	552.37	484.87	293.32	1.66	4.93
1984	671.89	537.27	326.97	1.69	5.10
1985	783.00	703.82	397.33	1.68	5.21
"七五"时期					
1986	946.46	836.50	474.62	1.70	7.40
1987	1057.48	943.58	534.12	1.73	7.30
1988	1272.83	1150.44	635.11	1.70	7.50
1989	1487.91	1355.64	745.32	1.71	7.50
1990	1619.50	1360.08	781.58	1.72	7.50
"八五"时期					
1991	1854.33	1569.26	896.62	1.71	7.60
1992	2148.49	1781.21	979.03	1.73	7.65
1993	2873.94	2394.03	1146.02	1.74	7.80
1994	3951.94	3224.73	1566.59	1.72	7.90
1995	4720.55	3830.38	1823.64	1.80	8.00
"九五"时期					
1996	5681.49	4422.91	2161.00	1.71	8.00

10–2 续表 continued

年 份 Year	人均可支配收入（元） Per Capita Annual Disposable Income (yuan)	人均生活消费支出（元） Per Capita Consumer Expenditure(yuan)		就业者负担人数（人） Average Dependents Per Employee (person)	人均住宅建筑面积（平方米） Per Capita Floor Space (sq.m)
		小 计 Total	# 人均食品支出 Per Capita Food Expenditure		
1997	6261.21	5210.40	2185.11	1.62	8.10
1998	6757.12	5440.10	2179.99	1.61	9.89
1999	7162.48	6415.39	2204.76	1.66	10.00
2000	8471.32	6891.75	2387.06	1.71	10.50
"十五" 时期					
2001	9564.99	7465.04	2386.84	1.74	10.70
2002	10094.13	7818.33	2575.21	1.72	17.83
2003	11012.86	8395.36	2610.75	1.68	18.85
2004	12005.06	8580.54	2784.87	1.65	19.50
2005	13578.46	9226.61	3046.93	1.73	19.55
"十一五" 时期					
2006	15340.17	10713.13	3335.31	1.74	20.1
2007	18005.10	12389.69	3900.91	1.72	21.0
2008	20802.17	13904.59	4466.18	1.87	21.5
2009	22721.65	14764.28	4836.78	1.86	29.4
2010	25321.06	15973.32	5051.18	1.67	29.7
"十二五" 时期					
2011	28891.97	18045.58	5722.65	1.71	30.3
2012	32569.75	20031.67	6162.16	1.72	–
2013	35647.59	21666.94	6624.32	–	–
2014	38762.77	22980.67	6814.14	2.04	–
2015	39888.71	26318.72	6415.00	1.80	44.9
"十三五" 时期					
2016	43052.16	28536.93	6908.01	1.87	45.5
2017	46642.40	30728.60	7229.30	1.35	47.8
2018	50146	32977	7758	1.4	46.5
2019	51913	33439	7956	1.4	39.0
2020	53329	34391	8072	1.3	39.3

注：1. 可支配收入 1983 年以前为生活费收入，消费性支出 1992 年以前为生活费支出。
2. "人均住宅建筑面积"，2009 年以前（不含）为"使用面积"口径，2002 年以前（不含）为"居住面积"口径。

Note: 1. The disposable income was living expenditure income before 1983, and the consumption expenditure was previously the cost–of–living expenditure before 1992.
2. "Per capita housing area", was the caliber of "usable area" before 2009 (excluding) and was the caliber of "living area"before 2002.

10-3 主要年份农村居民生活情况
Basic Conditions of Rural Households in Major Years

年份 Year	人均可支配收入（元）Per Capita Annual Disposable Income (yuan)	人均生活消费支出（元）Per Capita Consumer Expenditure(yuan)		每一劳动力负担人数（人）Average Dependents Per Labor Force (person)	人均住宅建筑面积（平方米）Per Capita Floor Space (sq.m)
		小计 Total	# 人均食品支出 Per Capita Food Expenditure		
1952	49.4	39.2	29.2	1.8	7.5
1957	63.6	57.9	34.8	1.8	7.8
1962	67.7	59.9	36.3	1.8	8.0
1965	92.6	69.7	46.1	1.8	8.2
1970	82.7	67.2	42.2	1.7	8.5
1975	79.1	59.5	40.8	1.7	9.0
1978	110.5	83.2	58.2	1.7	9.6
1980	168.9	127.1	85.8	1.6	10.5
1985	439.2	330.5	171.1	1.6	16.9
1990	731.1	569.8	287.7	1.6	22.5
1991	810.1	610.6	303.7	1.6	23.7
1992	865.3	660.5	335.1	1.6	21.1
1993	1031.4	724.8	371.4	1.6	22.9
1994	1401.0	942.5	511.0	1.6	24.1
1995	1812.7	1373.6	770.8	1.4	24.7
1996	2328.1	1728.1	926.2	1.4	26.9
1997	2600.0	1799.7	922.0	1.4	27.1
1998	2826.4	1872.5	935.9	1.4	27.4
1999	2943.7	1841.2	876.7	1.4	28.3
2000	3046.8	1976.8	860.0	1.4	28.6
2001	3215.7	2057.8	852.5	1.5	29.9
2002	3355.8	2133.9	849.5	1.4	30.6
2003	3619.3	2316.2	900.7	1.4	32.5
2004	4198.7	2543.1	1040.4	1.4	32.9
2005	4812.3	2902.8	1134.8	1.4	33.8
2006	5480.0	3415.3	1199.8	1.4	35.3
2007	6300.1	3789.8	1423.0	1.4	37.3
2008	7180.2	4385.4	1628.2	1.4	38.7
2009	7804.8	4733.1	1686.3	1.4	39.4
2010	8903.3	5406.6	1818.3	1.4	40.2
2011	10411.8	5905.1	2147.3	1.4	41.2
2012	11786.2	6932.2	2465.4	1.4	42.9
2013	13247.6	7798.7	2640.8	1.4	43.9
2014	14726.0	8581.4	2831.4	1.4	-
2015	14231.8	8597.2	2775.5	1.4	52.6
2016	15345.6	9396.3	3028.0	1.4	53.8
2017	16593.8	10327.3	3253.2	1.3	55.2
2018	17924	11172	3409	1.4	54.3
2019	19454	12300	3703	1.4	51.1
2020	20432	12947	3931	1.4	50.3

注：1. “人均可支配收入” 2014 年以前为 “农民人均纯收入” 口径。
2. “人均住宅建筑面积”，2009 年以前（不含）为 “使用面积” 口径，2002 年以前（不含）为 “居住面积” 口径。

Note: 1. "Per capita disposable income" was the caliber of "rural per capita net income" before 2014.
2. "Per capita housing area" was the caliber of "usable area" before 2009 (excluding) and was the caliber of "living area" before 2002 (excluding).

10-4 每百户城镇居民家庭主要耐用消费品拥有量
Number of Durable Consumer Goods Owned Per 100 Urban Households in Major Years

商品名称	Indicator	单位 Unit	1995 年	2000 年	2005 年	2010 年	2015 年	2018 年	2019 年	2020 年
摩托车	Motorcycles	辆 (Unit)	13.0	34.3	30.1	13.3	15.1	11.6	12.9	13.1
助力车	Moped	辆 (Unit)			18.1	40.2	72.0	80.8	78.5	
家用汽车	Automobiles	辆 (Unit)			5.4	22.7	47.6	53.7	54.0	58.5
洗衣机	Washing Machines	台 (set)	91.5	100.0	97.0	93.2	98.5	99.3	98.6	98.4
电冰箱	Refrigerators	台 (set)	92.0	99.3	97.0	96.7	101.8	103.2	104.0	104.0
彩色电视机	Color TV Sets	台 (set)	95.0	132.3	126.8	115.5	110.5	106.0	105.1	105.9
家用电脑	Computers	台 (set)		20.0	54.2	81.0	90.8	80.6	81.8	83.2
组合音响	Music Center	台 (set)	10.5	29.0	26.8	16.2	–	0.0	0.0	
摄像机	Pickup Cameras	台 (set)		2.3	4.0	10.8	16.9	0.0	0.0	
照相机	Cameras	台 (set)	40.5	76.0	59.2	54.0	56.1	36.4	32.9	33.8
其它中高档乐器	High-grade Instruments	件 (Unit)	6.5	12.3	6.4	3.5	5.7	13.1	16.3	15.0
微波炉	Microwave Oven	台 (set)		32.3	53.2	55.8	58.7	61.0	59.2	
空调器	Air Conditioner	台 (set)	16.0	65.0	104.4	121.5	146.3	172.8	166.6	166.4
淋浴热水器	Water Heaters	台 (set)	36.5	81.3	79.3	82.0	100.3	101.1	99.0	100.6
消毒碗柜	Sterilized Cupboard	台 (set)			5.4	6.5	6.2	0.0	0.0	
洗碗机	Dish-washing Machine	台 (set)			1.0	0.3	2.1	2.6	3.1	
健身器材	Fitness Equipment	台 (set)		4.7	6.4	4.3	10.2	7.8	8.2	
住宅电话	Fixed-line Phones	台 (set)	38.0	86.7	88.6	46.3	54.7	26.5	20.8	19.2
移动电话	Mobile Phones	台 (set)		28.7	145.2	179.7	213.5	219.5	222.9	225.7

10-5 农村每百户居民家庭主要耐用消费品拥有量
Number of Major Durable Consumer Goods Owend Per 100 Rural Households

商品名称	Indicator	单位 Unit	2012 年	2013 年	2015 年	2016 年	2017 年	2018 年	2019 年	2020 年
洗衣机	Washing Machines	台 (set)	86	88	86	90	90	95	93	91
电冰箱	Refrigerators	台 (set)	91	92	91	97	97	97	99	98
摩托车	Motorcycles	辆 (unit)	62	65	79	76	76	52	58	58
家用汽车	Automobiles	辆 (unit)					44	42	39	37
彩色电视机	Color TV Sets	台 (set)	118	119	114	118	118	114	113	110
照相机	Cameras	台 (set)	14	16	8	9	9	6	6	3
抽油烟机	Range Hoods	台 (set)	28	34	28	36	38	45	56	
空调器	Air Conditioner	台 (set)	39	46	56	67	74	87	93	90
热水器	Water Heaters	台 (set)	69	69	74	79	82	87	82	86
电话机	Phones	部 (set)	58	55	47	48	46	26	21	20
移动电话	Mobile Phones	部 (set)	186	195	214	224	231	245	232	229
家用计算机	Computers	台 (set)	39	43	40	43	43	41	39	43

10-6 居民人均可支配收入和消费支出 (2020 年)
Per Capital Annual Income and Per Capital Annual Expenditure(2020)

单位：元 (yuan)

指标名称	Item	全体居民 All Households	城镇居民 Urban Households	农村居民 Rural Households
可支配收入	Disposable Income	43056	53329	20432
工资性收入	Income of Wages and Salaries	24866	31071	11198
经营净收入	Net Business Income	4329	2875	7532
财产净收入	Income from Properties	6396	9099	443
转移净收入	Income from Transfer	7466	10284	1259
消费支出	Consumption Expenditure	27695	34391	12947
食品烟酒	Food,Tobacco and liquor	6779	8072	3931
衣着	Clothing	1597	2033	637
居住	Residence	8272	10697	2931
生活用品及服务	Household Appliances and Services	1949	2459	825
交通通信	Transport and Communications	3622	4391	1928
教育文化娱乐	Recreation,Education and Cultural Services	2903	3651	1256
医疗保健	Health care and Medical Services	2018	2368	1247
其他用品和服务	Miscellaneous Goods and Services	555	720	192

主要统计指标解释

可支配收入 指调查户在调查期内获得的、可用于最终消费支出和储蓄的总和，即调查户可以用来自由支配的收入。可支配收入既包括现金，也包括实物收入。按照收入的来源，可支配收入包含四项，分别为：工资性收入、经营净收入、财产净收入、转移净收入。计算公式为：

可支配收入 = 工资性收入+经营净收入+财产净收入+转移净收入

其中：经营净收入 = 经营收入-经营费用-生产性固定资产折旧-生产税

财产净收入 = 财产性收入 - 财产性支出

转移净收入 = 转移性收入 - 转移性支出

工资性收入 指就业人员通过各种途径得到的全部劳动报酬和各种福利，包括受雇于单位或个人、从事各种自由职业、兼职和零星劳动得到的全部劳动报酬和福利。

经营净收入 指住户或住户成员从事生产经营活动所获得的净收入，是全部经营收入中扣除经营费用、生产性固定资产折旧和生产税之后得到的净收入。

财产净收入 指住户或住户成员将其所拥有的金融资产、住房等非金融资产和自然资源交由其他机构单位、住户或个人支配而获得的回报并扣除相关的费用之后得到的净收入。财产净收入包括利息净收入、红利收入、储蓄性保险净收益、转让承包土地经营权租金净收入、出租房屋净收入、出租其他资产净收入和自有住房折算净租金等。

转移性收入 指国家、单位、社会团体对住户的各种经常性转移支付和住户之间的经常性收入转移。包括养老金或退休金、社会救济和补助、政策性生产补贴、政策性生活补贴、救灾款、经常性捐赠和赔偿、报销医疗费、住户之间的赡养收入，本住户非常住成员寄回带回的收入等。转移性收入不包括住户之间的实物馈赠。

转移性支出 指调查户对国家、单位、住户或个人的经常性或义务性转移支付。包括缴纳的税款、各项社会保障支出、赡养支出、经常性捐赠和赔偿支出以及其他经常转移支出等。

消费支出 指住户用于满足家庭日常生活消费需要的全部支出，包括用于消费品的支出和用于服务性消费的支出。根据用途不同，消费支出可划分为食品烟酒、衣着、居住、生活用品及服务、交通通信、教育文化娱乐、医疗保健、其他用品及服务八大类。根据来源不同，消费支出可划分为现金消费支出、实物消费支出（含自产自用、来自单位、来自政府和其他社会组织）。

食品烟酒 指用于各种食品和烟草、酒类的支出，包括食品和烟酒两个中类。

衣着 指与居民穿着有关的支出，包括服装、服装材料、鞋类、其他衣类及配件、衣着相关加工服务的支出。

居住 指与居住有关的支出，包括房租、水、电、燃料、物业管理等方面的支出，也包括自有住房折算租金。

生活用品及服务 指家庭及个人的各类生活品及家庭服务。包括家具及室内装饰品、家用器具、家用纺织品、家庭日用杂品、个人用品和家庭服务。

交通通信 指用于交通和通信工具及相关的各种服务费、维修费和车辆保险等支出。

教育文化和娱乐 指用于教育和文化娱乐方面的支出。

医疗保健 指用于医疗和保健的药品、用品和服务的总费用。包括医疗器具及药品，以及医疗服务。

其他用品及服务 指无法直接归入上述各类支出的其他用品与服务支出。

就业者负担人数 指家庭人口与就业人口之比。

城镇家庭可支配收入（老口径） 指家庭成员得到可用于最终消费支出和其它非义务性支出以及储蓄的总和，即居民家庭可以用来自由支配的收入。它是家庭总收入扣除交纳的所得税、个人交纳的社会保障支出以及记账补贴后的收入。计算公式为：

可支配收入=家庭总收入-交纳所得税-个人交纳的社会保障支出-记帐补贴

农村居民纯收入（老口径） 指农村住户当年从各个来源得到的总收入相应地扣除所发生的费用后的收入总和。计算方法：

纯收入=总收入-家庭经营费用支出-税费支出-生产性固定资产折旧

纯收入主要用于再生产投入和当年生活消费支出，也可用于储蓄和各种非义务性支出。“农民人均纯收入”按人口平均的纯收入水平，反映的是一个地区或一个农户农村居民的平均收入水平。

农村居民人均可支配收入与改革前的农民纯收入指标的主要区别是：可支配收入扣除了赠送农村以外亲友支出、农村居民用于购买住房、汽车等生活性贷款的利息支出，以及个人交纳的养老、医疗等社会保障支出，纯收入则不扣。同时，计算农村居民人均收入的分母调整为农村常住人口，调整了外出农民工寄带回收入的归类。

Explanatory Notes on Main Statistical Indicators

Disposable Income refers to the sum of households income that can be used for final consumption expenditure and savings during the period of investigation. Disposable income includes cash and real income. According to sources of income, disposable income includes the wage income, net operating income, net property income, and net transfer income. The formula for computing:

Disposable income = the wage income + net operating income + net property income + net transfer income

Net operating income = Income – operating costs – depreciation of productive fixed assets – production tax

Net property income = income from property – property expenditure

The transfer of net income = income from transfer – transfer expenditure

Wage Income refers to income and all kinds of welfare obtained by labors employed by different establishments, working independently or part–time.

Net Operating Income refers to the net income from operation run by the members of households, and it equals to total income minus operating costs and depreciation of productive fixed assets and taxes on production.

Net Property Income refers to the net income obtained from the financial assets, non–financial assets such as housing and natural resources provided by its owners to other establishments, households or individuals. It includes net interest income, bonus, net income from saving insurance, net income from the transfer of the right to land contractual management, income from house renting, income from renting of other assets and net rental income of home ownership.

Income from Transfer refers to the regular transfer received from governments, institutions, social organizations to households and between households. It includes old–age and retirement pension, disaster relief funds, regular donation and compensation, reimbursement of medical fees, supporting income between households, income from non–resident members of households, etc. Income from transfer do not include gifts in kinds between households.

Transfer Expenditure refers to the regular or obligatory expenditure provided by the households to governments, institutions, other households or residents. It includes taxes, social security expenditure, supporting expenditure, regular donation and compensation expenditure, etc.

Expenditure refers to the consumption of all expenditures needs to meet the family daily life, including the expenditures on consumer goods and services. According to different purposes, consumption can be divided into tobacco & food, clothing, housing, daily necessities & services, transportation & communication, education & culture & entertainment, health care, and other goods & services. According to different sources, consumption expenditures can be divided into cash consumption and physical consumption expenditures (including self–occupied, from the unit, from the government and other social organizations).

Tobacco & Food refers to all kinds of expenditure on foods, tobaccos and beverages, including food and tobacco.

Clothing refers to the expenditure on clothes, clothing materials, shoes, accessories and charges for clothing production process.

Housing refers to the expenditure related to residing, including the expenditure on rent, water, fuel, power and real estate management and net rental income of home ownership.

Daily Necessities & Services refer to the expenditure on daily necessities and home service, including the expenditure on furniture, decoration, appliance, textile, personal items and home service.

Transportation & Communication refer to the expenditure on transportation, communication, related service, maintenance, and vehicle insurance.

Education & Culture & Entertainment refer to the expenditure on education, culture and entertainment.

Health Care refers to the sum of the expenditure on health care, medicine, related products and service, including the medical devices, drug as well as medical services.

Other Services refer to the expenditure on the goods and services that cannot be included in the categories mentioned above.

Number of Dependents per Employee refers to the ratio between number of persons in households and the number of employers in the household.

Urban Households Disposable Income (in previous cope) refers to the sum of households' income used for final consumption expenditure and savings during the period of investigation, meaning the income that is disposable for households. Disposable income is the general income of households minus income tax, social security expenditure and subsidy for account–keeping. The formula for computing:

Disposable Income of Households = General income – income tax – personal social security expenditure – subsidy for account keeping

Rural Households Net Income (in previous cope) refers to the total income of rural households from all sources minus all corresponding expenses. The formula for calculation is as follows:

Net income = total income – household operation expenses – taxes and fees – depreciation of fixed assets for production

Net income is mainly used as input for reproduction and as consumption expenditure of the year, and also used for savings and non–compulsory expenses of various forms. "Per capita net income of farmers" is the level of net income averaged by population which reflects the average income level of rural households in a given area.

The main difference between rural household disposable income and rural household net income is that the disposable income does not include the expenditure of donations to urban relatives, the expenditure on houses and vehicles purchasing, interest expenditure on consumer loans, and expenditure on pension and health care, but the net income includes all the expenditure mentioned above. When calculating the average income of rural household, the denominator is changed to permanent rural residents, and the classification of income brought back by migrant workers is also changed.

农 业

AGRICULTURE

11-1 各时期农业主要经济指标
Major Economic Indicators of Agriculture in Each Period

年份 Year	农村劳动力 （万人） Rural Labor (10 000 persons)	农林牧渔业总产值 （亿元） Gross Output Value of Farming,Forestry, Animal Husbandry and Fishery (100 million yuan)	农业机械总动力 （万千瓦） Total Power of Agricultural Machinery (10 000 kw)	年末实有耕地面积 （千公顷） Actual Cultivated Area (1000 ha)	粮食总产量 （万吨） Output of Grain (10 000 tons)	蔬菜总产量 （万吨） Output of Vegetables (10 000 tons)	肉类总产量 （万吨） Output of Meat (10 000 tons)	粮食单产 （千克/公顷） Output Per Hectare of Grain (kg/ha)
1949	106.51	1.50	–	469.85	51.63	10.72	0.24	825
1952	112.35	1.91	–	481.17	62.75	8.61	0.40	960
1957	121.09	2.79	0.32	479.58	67.92	15.86	0.66	1065
1962	108.44	1.33	2.98	412.34	39.74	27.67	0.72	765
1965	111.74	2.61	4.84	410.02	73.80	29.12	1.12	1350
1970	123.91	2.75	14.32	396.49	75.47	31.81	1.21	1470
1975	141.00	4.07	48.04	382.05	100.46	42.00	2.07	2025
1978	140.05	6.57	69.70	373.19	115.38	49.19	2.50	2475
1979	141.60	7.48	80.63	372.45	122.56	49.42	2.92	2610
1980	143.19	7.79	88.45	370.87	116.54	58.13	3.69	2565
"六五"时期								
1981	146.52	11.73	94.47	369.80	121.27	49.85	3.99	2865
1982	149.07	14.47	106.60	369.22	121.13	63.45	4.31	3060
1983	152.39	18.07	112.19	368.45	147.41	65.66	4.66	3570
1984	158.23	19.00	123.92	367.35	160.60	86.91	5.03	3915
1985	162.51	18.36	130.41	357.41	163.50	84.11	5.43	3915
"七五"时期								
1986	165.86	20.91	147.36	353.96	168.16	118.86	6.44	3855
1987	168.56	24.65	156.23	352.18	167.25	101.52	7.13	3945
1988	171.44	34.24	172.89	350.56	167.95	122.83	8.68	4080
1989	173.38	35.14	182.40	349.59	162.45	117.99	9.70	3945
1990	176.83	36.92	183.40	347.56	181.47	126.09	11.38	4273
"八五"时期								
1991	180.09	40.13	191.00	344.76	207.55	146.87	13.50	4779
1992	182.51	45.14	191.50	343.29	198.29	170.61	15.36	4655
1993	183.78	57.81	194.40	341.54	232.21	205.62	19.12	4963
1994	183.42	85.37	207.40	339.97	237.66	226.39	26.14	5237
1995	183.55	114.07	241.20	339.30	252.48	253.54	28.68	5512

注：1. 自 2005 年始年末实有耕地面积有国土资源局提供，暂无 2009 年数据。
2. 依据 2006 年农业普查数据，对 1997 年至 2007 年蔬菜面积、产量做了相应调整。
3. 粮食作物产量、播种面积自 2012 年开始由山东调查总队反馈。
4. 按照国务院农普办要求，由国家统计局山东调查总队根据第三次农业普查数据，对 2016-2017 年市县（区）粮食播种面积 . 单产和总产量等数据进行了修订。
5. 依据 2016 年农业普查数据，对 2007 年至 2017 年农林牧渔业总产值做了相应调整。
6. 依据 2016 年农业普查数据，对 2008 年至 2017 年蔬菜总产量、肉类总产量做了相应调整。
7. 2019 年农业数据为区划调整后的数据，以下各表同。
8. 由于第三次全国国土调查数据未反馈，"年末实有耕地面积"2019 年相关数据延用 2018 年数据。
9. 由于第三次全国国土调查数据未反馈，"年末实有耕地面积"2020 年相关数据延用 2018 年数据；2020 年数据为区划调整后数据。
10. 由于市农业农村局未提供农业机械类指标数据，延用 2019 年数据。以下相关各表同。

11-1 续表 continued

年份 Year	农村劳动力（万人）Rural Labor (10 000 persons)	农林牧渔业总产值（亿元）Gross Output Value of Farming,Forestry, Animal Husbandry and Fishery (100 million yuan)	农业机械总动力（万千瓦）Total Power of Agricultural Machinery (10 000 kw)	年末实有耕地面积（千公顷）Actual Cultivated Area (1000 ha)	粮食总产量（万吨）Output of Grain (10 000 tons)	蔬菜总产量（万吨）Output of Vegetables (10 000 tons)	肉类总产量（万吨）Output of Meat (10 000 tons)	粮食单产（千克/公顷）Output Per Hectare of Grain (kg/ha)
"九五"时期								
1996	184.68	117.65	247.07	337.25	267.08	350.36	30.43	5602
1997	186.68	131.69	258.50	335.90	240.34	328.64	24.75	5064
1998	186.54	141.45	273.30	334.83	273.10	344.67	27.38	5634
1999	188.27	148.61	297.55	333.72	279.01	366.78	29.89	5752
2000	189.15	154.30	349.47	333.72	240.27	405.95	31.82	5354
"十五"时期								
2001	189.87	162.27	409.07	331.75	239.08	435.20	33.23	5480
2002	190.98	167.99	410.17	329.35	189.86	478.34	31.87	4440
2003	192.71	180.30	417.43	325.18	220.56	504.81	33.29	5448
2004	191.31	204.39	418.54	324.89	242.74	515.26	35.35	5807
2005	190.21	230.46	426.76	366.99	260.11	529.37	37.93	5932
"十一五"时期								
2006	190.80	247.70	429.62	361.74	267.91	536.28	38.74	6042
2007	191.16	262.51	446.60	358.80	268.01	522.24	31.85	6064
2008	190.45	302.00	466.00	361.33	281.50	520.25	30.22	6230
2009	195.56	318.06	486.00		289.47	560.83	31.39	6246
2010	196.85	361.24	509.68	362.30	289.43	572.05	31.79	6192
"十二五"时期								
2011	197.38	399.90	527.39	361.25	295.84	590.02	32.43	6315
2012	198.74	422.75	538.66	360.28	286.03	606.11	33.22	6285
2013	199.80	470.55	552.06	361.01	266.60	629.54	33.59	5997
2014	199.73	479.50	567.02	360.24	271.19	638.22	34.10	6109
2015	200.45	493.04	584.98	358.57	264.55	626.23	34.18	6117
"十三五"时期								
2016	200.46	501.72	447.83	357.60	275.43	611.25	31.72	5778
2017	198.91	505.08	442.90	355.66	255.57	591.63	32.50	5660
2018	189.10	514.90	454.62	353.65	251.42	527.22	29.82	5659
2019	239.03	637.30	543.48	353.65	285.46	671.24	35.86	5956
2020	222.13	671.66	543.48	426.04	290.81	673.73	23.92	6053

Note: 1. Since 2005, the actual cultivated area has been provided by Land Resources Bureau. No data for 2009.

2. According to the data of the agricultural census in 2006, the area and yield of the vegetables from 1997 to 2007 were adjusted accordingly.

3. Grain crop yield and sown area have been reported by Shandong Survey Team since 2012.

4. According to the requirements of Agricultural Census Office of the State Council, Shandong Survey Team of National Bureau of Statistics revised the grain sown area, yield per unit and total yield of each city and country (district) from 2016–2017 based on the data from the third agricultural census.

5. According to the data of the agricultural census in 2016, the total output value of agriculture, forestry, animal husbandry and fishery in the period from 2007 to 2017 was adjusted accordingly.

6. According to the data of the agricultural census in 2016, the total output value of vegetable and meat in the period from 2008 to 2017 was adjusted accordingly.

7. The data of agriculture in 2019 is the adjusted data by the administrative division (the same below).

8. "Actual cultivated area at the end of year " in 2019 uses the data in the year of 2018 because no data of the third national land survey has been reflected.

9. As the data of the Third National Territorial Survey has not been provided, the "existing agricultural acreage to year end" of 2020 adopts the data of 2018; the data of 2020 is collected after administrative division adjusting.

10. Due to the municipal bureau of agriculture and rural affairs didn' t provide data on agricultural machines index, thus the data of 2019 is adopted. The same for the following tables.

11–2 农村基层组织和农业基本情况
Basic Conditions of Rural Grassroots Units and Agriculture

指标	Indicator	单位 Unit	2015 年	2016 年	2017 年	2018 年	2019 年	2020 年
乡镇数量	Number of Towns	个 (Unit)	48	39	29	29	40	29
#镇	Towns	个 (Unit)	46	39	29	29	40	29
村民委员会	Village Committee	个 (Unit)	4546	4547	4548	4546	5551	5530
乡村户数	Rural Households	万户 (10 000 households)	101.96	103.14	102.31	101.96	139.19	133.69
乡村人口	Rural Numbers	万人 (10 000 persons)	360.29	362.55	359.18	355.74	456.10	430.65
家庭从业人员	FamilyPractitioner	万人 (10 000 persons)	200.45	200.46	198.91	189.10	239.03	222.13
男	Male	万人 (10 000 persons)	106.07	106.06	105.38	99.96	127.55	119.06
女	Female	万人 (10 000 persons)	94.38	94.40	93.52	89.15	111.48	103.07
地类面积	Land Category Area	公顷 (ha)	799841	799841	799841	799841	799841	1024445
耕地	Cultivated Land	公顷 (ha)	358568	357601	355659	353652	353652	426036
其中水浇地	Irrigated Land	公顷 (ha)	264016	263310	261894	263885	263885	299089
园地	Garden Land	公顷 (ha)	26054	25957	25801	25675	25675	41361
林地	Forest Land	公顷 (ha)	84676	84484	84175	83947	83947	121243
草地	Grazing and Pasture Land	公顷 (ha)	57250	57151	57018	56879	56879	88864
城镇村及工矿用地	Land for Urban Village, Mining and Manufacturing	公顷 (ha)	142969	144219	146819	149020	149020	183415
交通运输用地	Land for Transport Facilities	公顷 (ha)	29135	29319	29617	30216	30216	37537
水域及水利设施用地	Land for Water Conservancy Facilities	公顷 (ha)	50962	50875	50696	50531	50531	61157
其它土地	Other Land	公顷 (ha)	50227	50236	50055	49921	49921	64833
年末耕地总资源	Total Cultivated Area	公顷 (ha)	396365	395292	393224	391040	391040	479990
农业机械总动力	total power of agricultural machinery	万千瓦 (10 000 kw)	584.98	447.83	442.90	454.62	543.48	543.48
农用大中型拖拉机	Large and Medium-sized Tractors	台 (set)	24328	25574	24329	20208	23553	23553
农用小型拖拉机	Small Tractors	台 (set)	36964	35492	27179	30152	49911	49911
谷物联合收割机	Combine Harvester	台 (set)	12933	14365	13948	14380	15746	15746
柴油机	Diesel Engine	台 (set)	85775	84583	82173			
割晒机	Cutter-Rower	台 (set)	3357	3103	2935			
脱粒机	Thresher	台 (set)	20178	20450	19917	19660	27007	27007
农村用电量	Electricity Consumption in Rural Area	亿千瓦时 (100 million kwh)	26.51	25.66	24.40	23.58	32.87	32.70
农作物总播种面积	Total Sown Area of Farm Crops	千公顷 (1000 ha)	562.4	598.9	566.1	549.0	615.6	614.3

注：1. 按照国务院农普办要求，由国家统计局山东调查总队根据第三次农业普查数据，对 2016–2017 年市、县（区）粮食播种面积数据进行了修订
2. 由于第三次全国国土调查数据未反馈，“地类面积”2019 年相关数据延用 2018 年数据，以下相关各表同。
3. 由于第三次全国国土调查数据未反馈，“地类面积”2020 年相关数据延用 2018 年数据；2020 年数据为区划调整后数据。以下相关各表同。

Note:1. According to the requirements of Agricultural Census Office of the State Council, Shandong Survey Team of National Bureau of Statistics revised the grain sown area, of each city and country (district) from 2016–2017 based on the data from the third agricultural census.
2. "Land Category Area" data in 2019 uses the data of year 2018 because no data of the third national land survey has been reflected (the same below).
3.As the data of the Third National Territorial Survey has not been provided, the land data of 2020 adopts the data of 2018; the data of 2020 is collected after administrative division adjusting. The same for the following related tables.

11-3 分地区农村基层组织和农业基本情况 (2020 年)

Basic Conditions of Rural Grassroots Units and Agriculture by Region(2020)

指标	Indicator	单位 Unit	济南市 Ji'nan	历下区 Li xia
乡镇数量	Number of Towns	个 (Unit)	29	
#镇	Towns	个 (Unit)	29	
村民委员会	Village Committee	个 (Unit)	5530	13
乡村户数	Rural Households	万户 (10 000 households)	133.69	
乡村总人口	Rural Numbers	万人 (10 000 persons)	430.65	
乡村劳动力	FamilyPractitioner	万人 (10 000 persons)	257.70	
男	Male	万人 (10 000 persons)	138.85	
女	Female	万人 (10 000 persons)	118.84	
地类面积	Land Category Area	公顷 (ha)	1024445	10118
耕地	Cultivated Land	公顷 (ha)	426036	276
其中水浇地	Irrigated Land	公顷 (ha)	299089	78
园地	Garden Land	公顷 (ha)	41361	25
林地	Forest Land	公顷 (ha)	121243	1901
草地	Grazing and Pasture Land	公顷 (ha)	88864	436
城镇村及工矿用地	Land for Urban Village, Mining and Manufacturing	公顷 (ha)	183415	7262
交通运输用地	Land for Transport Facilities	公顷 (ha)	37537	59
水域及水利设施用地	Land for Water Conservancy Facilities	公顷 (ha)	61157	38
其它土地	Other Land	公顷 (ha)	64833	120
年末耕地总资源	Total Cultivated Area	公顷 (ha)	479990	276
农业机械总动力	total power of agricultural machinery	万千瓦 (10 000 kw)	543	3.31
农用大中型拖拉机	Large and Medium-sized Tractors	台 (set)	23553	55
农用小型拖拉机	Small Tractors	台 (set)	49911	565
谷物联合收割机	Combine Harvester	台 (set)	15746	31
脱粒机	Thresher	台 (set)	27007	20
农村用电量	Electricity Consumption in Rural Area	亿千瓦小时 (100 million kwh)	32.70	
农作物总播种面积	Total Sown Area of Farm Crops	千公顷 (1000 ha)	614.30	

市中区 Shi zhong	槐荫区 Huai yin	天桥区 Tian qiao	历城区 Li cheng	长清区 Chang qing	章丘区 Zhang qiu	济阳区 Ji yang	莱芜区 Lai wu	钢城区 Gang cheng	平阴县 Ping yin	商河县 Shang he
				2	1	2	7		6	11
				2	1	2	7		6	11
77	92	120	672	580	890	797	794	211	336	948
4.76	1.38	2.33	16.74	13.69	24.56	12.40	28.44	6.15	8.83	14.42
15.85	5.23	9.69	52.45	45.73	81.91	45.10	73.90	16.60	30.05	54.15
8.87	3.09	7.89	29.65	25.38	51.22	27.32	44.85	10.41	16.86	32.15
4.67	1.65	4.10	15.56	13.78	27.17	16.23	23.89	5.74	8.88	17.20
4.21	1.44	3.79	14.09	11.60	24.05	11.09	20.96	4.67	7.99	14.95
28149	15161	25897	130121	120859	171909	109881	173961	50642	71506	116240
5401	3263	9477	31801	46147	78263	70253	57932	14451	33201	75570
1436	1416	8940	17390	20489	52301	67022	31626	3577	19745	75067
1104	40	88	13632	4392	3782	377	10710	4975	1949	286
3698	431	1767	23091	20691	14624	4391	29004	8292	10398	2954
4149	118	130	15628	15154	16428	494	25498	6487	3997	345
10163	7783	9066	29872	14746	28793	15852	25148	9247	9747	15736
867	723	1337	5033	3772	6205	4130	5877	1444	2806	5284
358	2625	3773	4600	4911	8011	11563	8680	1946	3207	11446
2411	179	258	6465	11046	15802	2820	11112	3800	6200	4619
6659	3549	10716	39401	52628	90141	73396	69648	19302	37036	77238
12.71	4	16.26	50.42	49.18	93.40	99.37	63.61	18.58	43.42	89.00
364	266	542	1645	2876	3371	4693	2070	458	1678	5535
386	333	2261	5368	3489	2243	3299	16060	4525	5013	6369
114	158	344	1235	1339	3739	2601	825	153	731	4476
121	2634	1158	1227	886	2193	6053	6320	1291	705	4399
2.00	0.56	0.62	2.88	2.93	8.82	2.14	7.27	0.59	2.43	2.46
4.10	2.41	12.85	25.53	56.18	139.27	116.00	60.07	10.60	50.01	137.33

11-4 各时期农林牧渔业增加值(按当年价格计算)

Added Value of Agriculture, Forestry, Animal Husbandry and Fishery in Each Period(Calculated at Current Prices)

单位:亿元 (100 million yuan)

年份 Year	合计 Total	其中 of which 农业 Farming	林业 Forestry	牧业 Animal Husbandry	渔业 Fishery	农林牧渔服务业 Services of Agriculture,Forestry,Animal Husbandry and Fishing
1957	1.89	1.42	–	0.47	–	–
1962	1.01	0.76	–	0.25	–	–
1965	1.85	1.39	–	0.46	–	–
1970	2.11	1.58	–	0.53	–	–
1975	2.84	2.13	–	0.71	–	–
1978	4.08	2.94	0.19	0.89	0.06	–
1980	5.84	4.21	0.27	1.28	0.08	–
1985	12.16	8.75	0.57	2.66	0.18	–
"七五"时期						
1986	13.94	10.03	0.65	3.05	0.21	–
1987	16.21	11.66	0.76	3.55	0.24	–
1988	22.05	15.87	1.03	4.83	0.32	–
1989	22.74	16.37	1.06	4.98	0.33	–
1990	22.70	16.34	1.06	4.97	0.33	–
"八五"时期						
1991	24.68	18.00	0.95	5.31	0.42	–
1992	27.74	19.52	1.31	6.38	0.53	–
1993	35.66	23.83	1.45	9.72	0.66	–
1994	49.44	33.39	2.02	13.48	0.55	–
1995	67.24	49.59	1.97	14.95	0.75	–
"九五"时期						
1996	72.74	55.35	2.68	13.49	1.22	–
1997	81.07	62.25	2.95	14.66	1.21	–
1998	88.06	67.07	2.67	16.92	1.40	–
1999	92.52	67.30	2.21	21.33	1.68	–
2000	95.01	67.57	2.51	23.56	1.37	–

11–4 续表 continued

年份 Year	合计 Total	其中 of which 农业 Farming	林业 Forestry	牧业 Animal Husbandry	渔业 Fishery	农林牧渔服务业 Services of Agriculture,Forestry,Animal Husbandry and Fishing
"十五"时期						
2001	97.17	68.96	2.25	24.49	1.47	–
2002	98.74	68.88	2.44	25.99	1.43	–
2003	104.90	70.71	2.87	28.51	1.22	1.60
2004	120.47	80.17	3.15	33.86	1.50	1.77
2005	134.34	88.66	4.05	38.14	1.59	1.90
"十一五"时期						
2006	145.12	95.80	4.54	40.32	1.77	2.69
2007	148.53	95.54	5.26	42.19	1.98	3.56
2008	171.05	105.38	7.58	51.14	3.11	3.83
2009	180.67	114.54	8.12	50.27	3.24	4.50
2010	205.01	139.90	4.57	51.77	3.53	5.24
"十二五"时期						
2011	224.58	140.49	5.45	68.43	4.08	6.14
2012	236.29	145.64	6.34	72.50	4.48	7.33
2013	262.72	166.61	7.42	74.73	5.30	8.65
2014	272.90	174.90	8.25	73.78	5.93	10.05
2015	284.25	181.19	9.20	76.39	6.36	11.11
"十三五"时期						
2016	284.92	189.87	9.28	68.36	6.16	11.26
2017	279.91	185.71	10.72	66.27	4.86	12.36
2018	286.44	195.16	12.86	59.27	5.13	14.02
2019	360.51	256.98	17.49	63.16	5.44	17.45

注：依据2016年农业普查数据，对2007年至2017年农林牧渔业增加值做了相应调整。
Note: According to the data of the agricultural census in 2016, the value added of agriculture, forestry, animal husbandry and fishery in the period from 2007 to 2017 was adjusted accordingly.

11-5 各时期农林牧渔业总产值（按当年价格计算）
Gross Output Value of Agriculture, Forestry, Animal Husbandry and Fishery in Each Period(Calculated at Current Prices)

单位：亿元 (100 million yuan)

年份 Year	合计 Total	其中 of which 农业 Farming	林业 Forestry	牧业 Animal Husbandry	渔业 Fishery	农林牧渔服务业 Services of Agriculture,Forestry,Animal Husbandry and Fishing
1952	1.91	1.67	0.04	0.18	0.02	-
1957	2.79	2.41	0.09	0.28	0.01	-
1962	1.33	1.18	0.03	0.12	-	-
1965	2.61	2.25	0.07	0.28	0.01	-
1970	2.75	2.32	0.10	0.32	0.01	-
1975	4.07	3.48	0.13	0.44	0.02	-
1978	6.57	5.63	0.20	0.72	0.02	-
1980	7.78	6.66	0.18	0.93	0.01	-
1985	18.36	14.63	0.75	2.93	0.05	-
“七五”时期						
1986	20.91	16.81	0.79	3.23	0.08	-
1987	24.65	19.50	0.99	4.05	0.11	-
1988	34.24	24.83	1.42	7.67	0.32	-
1989	35.14	25.04	1.24	8.47	0.39	-
1990	36.92	24.70	1.41	10.36	0.45	-
“八五”时期						
1991	40.13	26.44	1.47	11.64	0.58	-
1992	45.14	29.01	1.70	13.71	0.72	-
1993	57.81	36.00	1.98	18.86	0.97	-
1994	85.37	52.36	2.80	29.38	0.83	-
1995	114.07	71.48	2.71	38.69	1.19	-
“九五”时期						
1996	117.65	77.16	3.35	35.25	1.89	-
1997	131.69	87.91	3.86	38.04	1.88	-
1998	141.45	93.56	3.55	42.17	2.17	-
1999	148.61	96.81	3.12	46.27	2.41	-
2000	154.30	100.18	3.64	48.34	2.14	-
“十五”时期						
2001	162.27	105.54	3.27	51.16	2.30	-
2002	167.99	106.27	3.51	55.84	2.37	-
2003	180.30	109.41	4.11	60.90	2.05	3.83
2004	204.39	121.28	4.49	71.87	2.50	4.25
2005	230.46	137.01	5.56	80.56	2.69	4.64

11-5 续表 continued

年份 Year	合计 Total	其中 of which 农业 Farming	林业 Forestry	牧业 Animal Husbandry	渔业 Fishery	农林牧渔服务业 Services of Agriculture,Forestry,Animal Husbandry and Fishing
"十一五"时期						
2006	247.72	147.98	6.44	84.86	2.89	5.55
2007	262.51	154.32	7.28	91.33	3.18	6.41
2008	302.00	173.32	10.63	104.53	4.54	8.97
2009	318.06	192.96	11.16	98.96	4.79	10.18
2010	361.24	231.08	6.87	106.40	5.31	11.58
"十二五"时期						
2011	399.90	240.80	7.98	131.55	6.05	13.51
2012	422.75	251.57	9.00	139.90	6.88	15.39
2013	470.55	284.66	10.34	149.46	8.01	18.07
2014	479.50	291.94	11.19	147.57	8.76	20.03
2015	493.04	296.93	12.15	153.12	9.32	21.52
"十三五"时期						
2016	501.72	298.63	13.20	156.28	9.88	23.74
2017	505.08	296.75	15.25	159.23	7.80	26.06
2018	514.90	318.55	17.72	141.48	7.28	29.88
2019	637.30	424.04	24.99	144.53	6.79	36.96
2020	671.66	447.15	29.82	149.14	6.10	39.46
2020 年分地区 Region						
历下区 Li xia						
市中区 Shi zhong	3.01	0.80	0.36	1.67	0.00	0.17
槐荫区 Huai yin	3.81	2.60	0.58	0.24	0.27	0.11
天桥区 Tian qiao	6.46	3.83	0.35	1.90	0.16	0.22
历城区 Li cheng	76.77	59.37	6.99	5.04	0.30	5.07
长清区 Chang qing	61.98	42.40	2.73	14.23	0.21	2.41
章丘区 Zhang qiu	154.31	101.17	4.92	36.57	1.03	10.62
济阳区 Ji yang	79.18	55.54	3.01	15.60	1.45	3.58
莱芜区 Lai Wu	109.71	76.49	3.16	25.53	1.18	3.36
钢城区 Gang Cheng	19.38	9.83	1.70	6.91	0.07	0.87
平阴县 Ping yin	65.28	42.94	2.34	13.95	0.32	5.72
商河县 Shang he	91.79	52.17	3.69	27.49	1.11	7.33

注：依据 2016 年农业普查数据，对 2007 年至 2017 年农林牧渔业总产值做了相应调整。

Note: According to the data of the agricultural census in 2016, the total output value of agriculture, forestry, animal husbandry and fishery in the period from 2007 to 2017 was adjusted accordingly.

11-6 各时期农林牧渔业总产值定基指数(以1952年为100)

Gross Output Value and Indices of Farming, Forestry, Animal Husbandry in Each Period(1952=100)

年份 Year	合计 Total	其中 of which			
		农业 Farming	林业 Forestry	牧业 Animal Husbandry	渔业 Fishery
1952	100.00	100.00	100.00	100.00	100.00
1957	116.18	114.55	170.35	119.90	109.96
1962	73.32	74.42	69.10	69.25	20.68
1965	123.31	121.76	147.34	141.38	28.95
1970	151.35	146.28	254.82	184.02	58.65
1975	201.09	196.80	317.61	226.74	78.38
"五五"时期					
1976	198.67	185.64	340.19	269.52	118.70
1977	197.95	190.19	373.20	218.87	56.26
1978	208.10	203.90	304.32	239.93	57.89
1979	233.93	224.05	316.47	293.89	53.70
1980	264.53	259.07	286.30	330.80	43.98
"六五"时期					
1981	279.36	279.29	281.28	377.56	55.36
1982	312.68	308.75	346.83	460.13	51.95
1983	402.03	369.18	434.91	460.59	57.98
1984	493.28	436.59	572.67	651.29	69.52
1985	505.48	460.68	992.56	841.94	161.47
"七五"时期					
1986	531.29	488.47	964.62	857.25	229.32
1987	560.14	506.85	1075.00	960.76	291.92
1988	585.14	510.86	992.11	1191.92	383.08
1989	571.95	483.32	886.96	1320.55	495.30
1990	607.77	449.63	1126.99	1931.15	695.49
"八五"时期					
1991	670.19	488.17	1189.04	2204.93	830.45
1992	712.62	491.78	1298.34	2574.55	1007.33
1993	844.31	566.55	1420.51	3221.58	1209.21
1994	945.74	603.90	1671.10	2864.71	1064.29
1995	1093.57	657.49	1508.72	4905.57	1945.11

11-6 续表 continued

年份 Year	合计 Total	其中 of which			
		农业 Farming	林业 Forestry	牧业 Animal Husbandry	渔业 Fishery
"九五"时期					
1996	1197.20	727.03	1818.36	5258.95	2224.25
1997	1273.56	820.27	2002.99	5116.96	2202.07
1998	1426.28	914.05	1858.14	5907.41	2516.54
1999	1486.09	934.64	2110.21	6277.65	2639.47
2000	1569.90	991.58	2255.81	6620.62	2441.73
"十五"时期					
2001	1599.32	1005.16	1700.16	6905.18	2646.43
2002	1638.09	997.16	1826.57	7349.57	2712.97
2003	1711.88	1072.24	1977.78	7726.93	2324.25
2004	1804.32	1132.29	1979.76	8121.00	2803.05
2005	1930.62	1188.90	2237.13	8770.68	2802.30
"十一五"时期					
2006	2046.15	1249.31	2454.25	9245.35	3003.10
2007	2046.15	1334.26	2610.83	9006.43	3540.65
2008	2148.45	1422.32	2783.14	9231.59	3204.85
2009	2260.17	1524.73	2964.04	9342.35	3323.43
2010	2367.76	1584.02	1815.08	10311.68	3416.48
"十二五"时期					
2011	2471.94	1658.47	2016.56	10600.40	3508.72
2012	2588.12	1724.80	2216.20	11151.62	3768.36
2013	2689.05	1762.74	2491.01	11809.56	3877.64
2014	2801.99	1845.58	2724.66	12116.60	3916.41
2015	2919.67	1924.93	2986.23	12540.68	4033.90
"十三五"时期					
2016	3045.21	2007.70	3317.70	12967.06	4187.19
2017	3157.88	2126.15	3689.28	13278.26	4203.93
2018	3095.96	2215.44	4105.56	12733.85	4330.04
2019	3123.82	2290.76	5037.52	11587.80	3814.77
2020	3205.04	2361.77	5979.54	11460.33	3715.59

11-7 主要农作物播种面积及产量
Sown Areas and Output of Main Farm Crops

指标	Indicator	2015年	2016年	2017年	2018年	2019年	2020年
农作物总播种面积（万公顷）	Total Sown Area of Crops(10 000 ha)	56.24	59.89	56.61	54.90	61.56	61.43
粮食作物	Grain Crops	43.25	47.67	45.15	44.43	47.93	48.04
谷物	Cereals	41.65	46.05	43.79	43.25	46.33	46.38
小麦	Wheat	20.99	22.00	21.58	21.38	21.89	21.73
稻谷	Rice	0.21	0.20	0.18	0.14	0.14	0.06
玉米	Corn	19.82	22.93	21.07	20.84	23.18	23.53
谷子	Millet	0.54	0.86	0.91	0.86	1.09	1.03
高粱	Chinese Sorghum	0.09	0.05	0.05	0.02	0.01	0.01
其他	Others	0.01	0.01	0.00	0.01	0.01	0.01
豆类	Beans	0.71	0.85	0.70	0.62	0.77	0.77
薯类	Tubers	0.88	0.77	0.66	0.56	0.83	0.90
油料作物	Oil-bearing Crops	1.30	1.00	1.00	1.02	1.92	1.81
#花生	Peanuts	1.13	0.88	0.87	0.90	1.81	1.67
棉花	Cotton	0.71	0.62	0.20	0.28	0.38	0.35
蔬菜	Vegetable	9.42	9.13	8.86	7.89	10.03	9.86
果用瓜	Melon	1.28	1.20	1.16	1.07	0.98	0.96
其他作物	Other Farm Crops	0.28	0.26	0.25	0.21	0.32	0.40
果园种植面积（万公顷）	Orchard Area(10 000 ha)	3.35	3.20	3.16	3.09	3.89	3.95
#苹果	Apple	1.29	1.18	1.18	1.13	1.24	1.20
梨	Pear	0.16	0.14	0.14	0.16	0.18	0.19
葡萄	Grape	0.10	0.10	0.10	0.11	0.11	0.11
桃	Peach	0.47	0.49	0.49	0.72	1.00	1.03
农作物总产量（万吨）	Total Output of Farm Crops(10 000 tons)						
粮食作物	Grain Crops	264.55	275.43	255.57	251.42	285.46	290.81
谷物	Cereals	257.65	268.30	249.47	246.12	276.48	280.74
小麦	Wheat	129.75	127.31	123.79	121.78	135.31	137.37
稻谷	Rice	1.52	1.55	1.36	1.18	1.21	0.52
玉米	Corn	124.39	136.65	121.25	119.82	136.11	139.16
谷子	Millet	1.74	2.64	2.97	3.27	3.80	3.64
高粱	Chinese Sorghum	0.22	0.11	0.11	0.04	0.03	0.02
其他	Other Cereals	0.03	0.04	0.00	0.03	0.03	0.03
豆类	Beans	1.92	2.25	1.82	1.67	2.12	2.13
薯类	Tubers	4.99	4.87	4.28	3.63	6.86	7.93
油料作物	Oil-bearing Crops	4.59	3.53	3.59	4.15	6.57	6.82
#花生	Peanuts	4.23	3.25	3.31	3.87	6.31	6.48

11-7 续表 continued

指标	Indicator	2015 年	2016 年	2017 年	2018 年	2019 年	2020 年
棉花	Cotton	0.74	0.69	0.20	0.29	0.54	0.42
蔬菜	Vegetable	626.23	611.25	591.63	527.22	671.24	673.73
果用瓜	Melon	77.00	70.74	67.51	59.65	48.02	49.49
水果总产量（万吨）	**Output of Fruits(10 000 tons)**	**43.94**	**41.08**	**43.15**	**42.19**	**62.95**	**63.20**
# 苹果	Apple	20.62	18.33	18.59	16.00	20.22	18.92
梨	Pear	4.83	4.26	3.98	3.40	4.19	3.80
葡萄	Grape	3.16	2.86	3.00	3.00	3.13	3.21
桃	Peach	10.71	11.08	13.10	11.86	21.40	21.87
杏	Apricot	0.83	0.78	0.75	3.02	4.11	4.01
枣（鲜）	Jujube	1.00	1.02	1.02	0.89	1.21	1.01
柿子（鲜）	Persimmon	0.24	0.23	0.23	1.24	2.29	2.51
山楂	Hawthorn	0.54	0.55	0.55	0.63	2.19	2.80
樱桃	Cherry	1.59	1.49	1.45	1.51	2.78	3.82
其他	Others	0.50	0.48	0.47	0.64	1.19	0.98
农作物单位面积产量（公斤 / 公顷）	**Output per Hectare of Farm Crops (kg/ha)**						
粮食作物	Grain Crops	6117	5778	5660	5659	5956	6053
谷物	Cereals	6186	5826	5697	5690	5968	6053
小麦	Wheat	6182	5787	5736	5696	6181	6321
稻谷	Rice	7259	7698	7645	8288	8334	8250
玉米	Corn	6276	5960	5754	5748	5872	5914
谷子	Millet	3220	3071	3252	3809	3490	3522
高粱	Chinese Sorghum	2497	2097	2228	2074	1941	1958
其他	Others	3000	2716	0	3062	2750	2813
豆类	Beans	2683	2659	2614	2716	2747	2784
薯类	Tubers	5673	6371	6462	6462	8248	8835
油料作物	Oil-bearing Crops	3545	3531	3609	4083	3418	3761
# 花生	Peanuts	3747	3713	3795	4327	3495	3878
棉花	Cotton	1040	1106	1037	1029	1410	1193
蔬菜	Vegetable	66460	66918	66798	66852	66895	68337
果用瓜	Melon	60263	46939	58724	55628	48797	51472

注：1. 依据 2006 年农业普查数据，对 1997 年至 2007 年蔬菜面积、产量做了相应调整。
2. 按照国务院农普办要求，由国家统计局山东调查总队根据第三次农业普查数据，对 2016–2017 年市、县（区）粮食播种面积、单产和总产量等数据进行修订。
3. 依据 2016 年农业普查数据，对 2008 年至 2017 年种植业相关品种面积、产量做了相应调整。

Note: 1. According to the data of the agricultural census in 2006, the area and yield of the vegetables from 1997 to 2007 were adjusted.
2. According to the requirements of Agricultural Census Office of the State Council, Shandong Survey Team of National Bureau of Statistics revised the grain sown area, yield per unit and total yield of each city and country (district) from 2016–2017 based on the data from the third agricultural census.
3. According to the agricultural census data in 2016, the area and yield of planting related varieties from 2008 to 2017 were adjusted.

11-8 林、牧、渔业生产情况
Basic Statistics on Forestry，Animal Husbandry and Fishery

指标	Indicator	单位 Unit	2015 年	2016 年	2017 年	2018 年	2019 年	2020 年
林业生产	Production of Forestry							
造林面积	Forested Area	公顷 (ha)	12013	3504	3809	4902	10758	10939
四旁植树	Surrounding Tree Planting	万株 (10000 trees)	1311	1312	1301	1306	1576	1527
育苗面积	Area of Nursery Garden	公顷 (ha)	14439	11773	10645	10174	11579	10750
果品产量	Output of Fruits	吨 (ton)	573064	539475	596994	555042	686868	653290
木材采伐量	Timber Cut	立方米 (cu.m)	132014	157238	214946	283354	355596	298532
牧业生产	Production of Animal Husbandry							
大牲畜存栏	Stocked Large Livestock	万头 (10 000 heads)	28.11	28.97	31.63	26.30	24.42	15.26
# 役畜	Draught Animal	万头 (10 000 heads)	0.26	0.19	0.02	0.02		
# 牛	Cattle	万头 (10 000 heads)	27.86	28.69	31.36	26.17	24.27	15.20
猪存栏	Stocked Pigs	万头 (10 000 heads)	128.51	116.73	120.13	102.95	129.26	122.86
羊存栏	Stocked Sheep	万只 (10 000 heads)	89.71	93.27	96.60	87.61	100.13	66.01
家禽存栏	Stocked Poultry	万只 (10 000 heads)	2784.87	2743.90	2467.54	2300.42	3440.94	2523.33
猪出栏数	Slaughtered Pigs	万头 (10 000 heads)	214.97	194.15	198.43	185.59	217.66	157.03
羊出栏数	Slaughtered Sheep and Goats	万只 (10 000 heads)	132.07	149.03	153.23	143.84	164.26	86.91
肉类总产量	Output of Meat	吨 (ton)	341829	317201	325036	298180	358655	239186
# 猪牛羊肉	Meat	吨 (ton)	259954	235990	246561	223735	236601	164537

11-8 续表 continued

指标	Indicator	单位 Unit	2015 年	2016 年	2017 年	2018 年	2019 年	2020 年
猪肉	Pork	吨 (ton)	185546	162114	168054	155005	170584	128052
牛肉	Beef	吨 (ton)	55852	53203	57206	46438	40698	21020
羊肉	Mutton	吨 (ton)	18557	20673	21301	22292	25319	15465
禽肉	Poultry Meat	吨 (ton)	81113	80447	77809	74164	120194	73887
奶类	Milk	吨 (ton)	232705	214620	263642	328412	321323	414297
# 牛奶	Cow Milk	吨 (ton)	232702	214617	263638	328410	321321	414297
禽蛋	Poultry Eggs	吨 (ton)	378577	386440	394001	332303	365810	274673
# 鸡蛋	Hen's Eggs	吨 (ton)	362017	368636	375517	313234	343650	–
渔业生产	Aquatic Products							
水产品产量	Total Aquatic Products	吨 (ton)	47565	46709	41279	31911	16167	13294
捕捞	Fishing	吨 (ton)	650	465	186	289	3513	3291
养殖	Cultured	吨 (ton)	46915	46244	41093	31622	12654	10003
养殖面积	Breeding Area of Aquatic Products	公顷 (ha)	7285	7079	6673	5228	4380	4304
养殖单产	Aquaculture Yield	公斤 / 公顷 (kg/ha)	6440	6533	6158	6049	2889	2324

注：依据 2016 年农业普查数据，对 2008 年至 2017 年牧业生产有关指标做了相应调整。
Note: According to the data of agricultural census in 2016, the relevant indicators of animal husbandry production from 2008 to 2017 were adjusted accordingly.

11-9 分地区主要农作物播种面积及产量(2020年)
Sown Areas and Output of Main Farm Crops by Region(2020)

指标	Indicator	济南市 Total City	历下区 Li xia	市中区 Shi zhong
农作物播种总面积(公顷)	Total Sown Area of Crops(ha)	614352		4095
粮食	Grain	480439		3986
谷物	Cereals	463800		3944
小麦	Wheat	217307		1418
稻谷	Rice	627		
玉米	Corn	235292		2364
谷子	Millet	10341		161
高粱	Chinese Sorghum	127		
其他	Others	107		
豆类	Beans	7665		35
薯类	Tubers	8974		8
油料作物	Oil-bearing Crops	18122		6
#花生	Peanuts	16717		5
棉花	Cotton	3540		9
蔬菜	Vegetable	98590		85
果用瓜	Melon	9616		9
其他作物	Other Farm Crops	4046		1
果园种植面积(公顷)	Orchard Area(ha)	39490		242
#苹果	Apple	11982		48
梨	Pear	1870		1
葡萄	Grape	1106		13
桃	Peach	10290		118
农作物产量(吨)	Total Output of Farm Crops(ton)			
粮食作物	Grain Crops	2908066		18961
谷物	Cereals	2807445		18833
小麦	Wheat	1373685		8286
稻谷	Rice	5170		
玉米	Corn	1391620		10227
谷子	Millet	36423		320
高粱	Chinese Sorghum	248		
其他	Other Cereals	300		
豆类	Beans	21338		64
薯类	Tubers	79283		64

槐荫区 Huai yin	天桥区 Tian qiao	历城区 Li cheng	长清区 Chang qing	章丘区 Zhang qiu	济阳区 Ji yang	莱芜区 Lai wu	钢城区 Gang cheng	平阴县 Ping yin	商河县 Shang he
2408	12853	25530	56180	139274	115997	60072	10599	50014	137329
2140	12288	19726	44088	107147	99302	31400	4308	35140	120912
2085	12219	19104	41378	102318	98293	29302	3874	30514	120770
872	5769	5779	16692	51933	53007	5851	532	16679	58774
198	15		24	50	340				
1015	6435	11939	20968	47785	44946	22417	3175	12253	61996
		1384	3586	2436		1033	166	1574	
		1	3	115				8	
		1	106						
55	69	281	1092	2674	971	232	35	2113	107
		340	1619	2154	38	1867	400	2514	35
45	31	314	3950	1854	352	5639	3628	2297	6
1	31	311	3667	1636	341	5530	3628	1561	6
	63	22	178	707	219	528	238	1016	561
219	392	3665	7851	24620	14318	22128	2369	8665	14278
4	15	1770	113	4946	1253	185	56	1014	252
1	65	33			551	192		1882	1320
	216	11198	3092	6319	823	6150	3234	7736	480
	29	2876	108	2649	115	719	330	5024	84
	64	821	54	275	73	179	274	59	71
	4	40	14	384	46	233	20	296	56
	107	4526	876	864	485	960	2004	207	144
13087	69378	104105	263639	622849	612962	193434	24154	194277	791221
12962	69194	100448	243568	596212	609857	174163	20715	170990	790504
5242	34038	34385	97410	325962	339470	36922	3163	92312	396496
1584	112		201	419	2853				
6136	35043	61570	128193	263496	267534	134905	17098	73409	394008
		4487	17461	6113		2336	454	5253	
		2	7	222				17	
		4	296						
125	184	824	2975	8048	2787	566	94	5303	369
		2834	17096	18589	318	18705	3345	17984	348

11-9 续表 continued

指标	Indicator	济南市 Total City	历下区 Li xia	市中区 Shi zhong
油料作物	Oil-bearing Crops	68153		11
#花生	Peanuts	64835		11
棉花	Cotton	4223		9
蔬菜	Vegetable	6737316		4062
果用瓜	Melon	494931		391
水果总产量(吨)	**Output of Fruits(ton)**	**632006**		**3530**
#苹果	Apple	189205		1257
梨	Pear	38033		17
葡萄	Grape	32070		533
桃	Peach	218666		1169
杏	Apricot	40090		392
枣(鲜)	Jujube	10111		25
柿子(鲜)	Persimmon	25069		13
山楂	Hawthorn	27989		48
樱桃	Cherry	38153		70
其他	Others	9771		1
农作物单位面积产量(公斤/公顷)	**Output per Hectare of Farm Crops(kg/ha)**			
粮食作物	Grain Crops	6053		4757
谷物	Cereals	6053		4775
小麦	Wheat	6321		5842
稻谷	Rice	8250		
玉米	Corn	5914		4326
谷子	Millet	3522		1981
高粱	Chinese Sorghum	1958		
其他	Others	2813		
豆类	Beans	2784		1825
薯类	Tubers	8835		8449
油料作物	Oil-bearing Crops	3761		1933
#花生	Peanuts	3878		1959
棉花	Cotton	1193		1057
蔬菜	Vegetable	68337		47898
果用瓜	Melon	51472		41914

注：粮食作物产量、播种面积自2012年开始由山东调查总队反馈。
Note: Grain crop yield and sown area have been reported by Shandong Survey Team since 2012.

槐荫区 Huai yin	天桥区 Tian qiao	历城区 Li cheng	长清区 Chang qing	章丘区 Zhang qiu	济阳区 Ji yang	莱芜区 Lai wu	钢城区 Gang cheng	平阴县 Ping yin	商河县 Shang he
221	92	1502	17866	5956	1817	21781	9550	9324	32
10	92	1496	17162	5543	1782	21508	9550	7651	32
	103	30	243	762	294	667	304	1098	713
9540	16035	207431	518642	1815187	1223875	1122944	193836	655890	969874
160	616	80513	4616	247056	72956	6936	3067	67378	11243
	6793	143245	56754	73179	22963	101317	105600	100950	17674
	877	22226	2553	38545	3483	19009	17546	80939	2770
	2311	17289	1791	2735	2537	4181	1261	1747	4163
	92	1934	557	10782	1102	4324	678	7682	4386
	3173	76387	12478	11256	12777	18400	75575	3542	3908
	116	9426	15322	501	520	11520	1087	266	939
	110	243	250	5547	756	1565	274	409	932
	24	1727	6800	138	784	12829	2120	418	216
		10294	113	581	122	12683	3152	685	309
		1781	16797	2858	65	13601	2101	879	
	89	1808	11	57	817	980	1600	4356	51
6114	5646	5278	5980	5813	6173	6160	5606	5529	6544
6217	5663	5258	5886	5827	6204	5944	5347	5604	6546
6008	5900	5950	5836	6277	6404	6310	5940	5535	6746
8004	7482		8467	8466	8380				
6048	5446	5157	6114	5514	5952	6018	5385	5991	6355
		3242	4869	2510		2261	2730	3338	
		2285	2638	1933				2054	
		4052	2801						
2247	2652	2927	2725	3009	2871	2442	2698	2510	3456
		8328	10563	8629	8295	10019	8369	7154	10063
4962	3000	4785	4523	3213	5157	3862	2632	4060	5025
11875	3000	4816	4680	3388	5222	3889	2632	4902	5025
	1650	1351	1365	1077	1339	1264	1280	1080	1272
43656	40884	56596	66065	73727	85478	50748	81822	75695	67926
45410	40688	45495	40894	49955	58209	37559	54643	66474	44661

11-10 分地区林、牧、渔业生产情况 (2020 年)

Basic Statistics on Forestry, Animal Husbandry and Fishery by Region(2020)

指标	Indicator	单位 Unit	济南市 Total City	历下区 Li xia
林业生产	Production of Forestry			
造林面积	Forested Area	公顷 (ha)	10939	
四旁植树	Surrounding Tree Planting	万株 (10000 trees)	1527	132
育苗面积	Area of Nursery Garden	公顷 (ha)	10750	
果品产量	Output of Fruits	吨 (ton)	653290	
木材采伐量	Timber Cut	立方米 (cu.m)	298532	
牧业生产	Production of Animal Husbandry			
大牲畜存栏	Stocked Large Livestock	万头 (10 000 heads)	15.26	
# 役畜	Draught Animal	万头 (10 000 heads)		
# 牛	Cattle	万头 (10 000 heads)	15.20	
猪存栏	Stocked Pigs	万头 (10 000 heads)	122.86	
羊存栏	Stocked Sheep	万只 (10 000 heads)	66.01	
家禽存栏	Stocked Poultry	万只 (10 000 heads)	2523.33	
猪出栏数	Slaughtered Pigs	万头 (10 000 heads)	157.03	
羊出栏数	Slaughtered Sheep and Goats	万只 (10 000 heads)	86.91	
肉类总产量	Output of Meat	吨 (ton)	239186	
# 猪牛羊肉	Meat	吨 (ton)	164537	
猪肉	Pork	吨 (ton)	128052	
牛肉	Beef	吨 (ton)	21020	
羊肉	Mutton	吨 (ton)	15465	
禽肉	Poultry Meat	吨 (ton)	73887	
奶类	Milk	吨 (ton)	414297	
# 牛奶	Cow Milk	吨 (ton)	414297	
禽蛋	Poultry Eggs	吨 (ton)	274673	
渔业生产	Aquatic Products			
水产品产量	Total Aquatic Products	吨 (ton)	13294	
捕捞	Fishing	吨 (ton)	3291	
养殖	Cultured	吨 (ton)	10003	
养殖面积	Breeding Area of Aquatic Products	公顷 (ha)	4304	
养殖单产	Aquaculture Yield	公斤 / 公顷 (kg/ha)	2324	

市中区 Shi zhong	槐荫区 Huai yin	天桥区 Tian qiao	历城区 Li cheng	长清区 Chang qing	章丘区 Zhang qiu	济阳区 Ji yang	莱芜区 Lai wu	钢城区 Gang cheng	平阴县 Ping yin	商河县 Shang he
566	27	111	2317	709	1734	512	2409	993	509	1052
151	89	115	245	102	190	105	178	60	61	99
24	33		3612	3470	767	641	528	39	123	1513
8362		481	347203	50045	23178	14030	90009	55605	43609	20768
	1337	9432	10047	59041	42472	54684	37398	13000	22021	49100
0.10	0.01	0.06	0.65	2.04	0.53	1.36	1.25	0.14	2.84	6.28
0.10	0.01	0.05	0.64	2.03	0.53	1.34	1.25	0.14	2.84	6.28
0.71	0.05	1.01	3.34	9.14	22.24	6.27	27.42	14.04	14.04	24.60
2.28	0.21	2.88	2.64	5.92	8.06	5.63	15.22	6.24	4.07	12.87
15.10	3.69	40.20	116.03	190.73	636.68	129.99	508.44	144.29	352.32	385.86
1.04	0.07	1.38	4.52	14.44	35.83	9.42	30.77	17.61	6.45	35.51
2.90	0.26	3.22	3.36	6.29	11.71	7.27	18.03	7.34	5.50	21.04
2323	149	3365	10029	18114	56040	14930	52602	20015	15739	45880
2001	132	2002	6281	14209	35008	11099	31345	17068	7373	38020
895	72	1235	3703	11476	29944	7359	25250	14045	4885	29188
657	13	217	1746	1685	3177	2346	3000	1672	1497	5009
449	47	550	831	1048	1887	1394	3095	1351	990	3823
322	17	1361	3734	3892	21001	3786	20672	2947	8294	7861
812	2	452	9380	53851	11684	36216	8051	3291	99342	191217
812	2	452	9380	53851	11684	36216	8051	3291	99342	191217
4200	472	2137	16543	34406	53984	10446	56300	16687	39517	39981
	1200	252	346	850	1500	3164	3480	196	712	1594
				103		28	3150			10
	1200	252	346	747	1500	3136	330	196	712	1584
	120	16	30	345	360	711	1710	270	446	296
	10000	15750	11533	2165	4166	4411	192	725	1596	5351

11-11 农业“四化”情况（2020 年）

Basic Statistics on Four Modernization of Agriculture(2020)

指标 Indicator	机耕面积（千公顷） Machine-Cultivated Area (1000 hectares)	有效灌溉面积（千公顷） Effective Irrigated Area (1000 hectares)	农用化肥施用量（吨折纯） Consumption of Chemical Fertilizer (tons convert to pure volume)	每公顷耕地化肥施用量（公斤折纯） Consumption of Chemical Fertilizers Per Hectare (kg convert to pure volume)	农药施用量（吨） Pesticides Mption (tons)	每公顷耕地农药施用量（公斤） Consumption of Pesticides Per Hectare (kg)
全市 Total City		294.0	205007		3231.4	
历下区 Li xia						
市中区 Shi zhong		2.7	713		29.7	
槐荫区 Huai yi		2.1	196		4.5	
天桥区 Tian qiao		8.5	2917		24.2	
历城区 Li cheng		25.0	13453		346.9	
长清区 Chang qing		25.1	12033		326.8	
章丘区 Zhang qiu		57.5	46292		402.3	
济阳区 Ji yang		53.0	27290		636.7	
莱芜区 Lai Wu		32.9	27873		712.0	
钢城区 Gang Cheng		4.6	3696		226.1	
平阴县 Ping yin		18.7	14236		133.8	
商河县 Shang he		63.9	56307		388.5	

注：由于第三次全国国土调查数据未反馈，“每公顷耕地化肥施用量”“每公顷耕地农药施用量”相关数据空缺。
Note: Relevant data to "the amount of chemical fertilizers applied per hectare of cultivated land" and "the amount of pesticide applications per hectare of cultivated land" are null due to no data reflections of 3rd National Land Survey.

11-12 主要农副产品产量与上年和历史最高年份比较

Output of Major Agricultral Products in Comparision with Last Year and Maximum Year

指标	Indicator	2020 年	2019 年	历史最高年 Maximum Year		2020 年为历史最高年的% 2020 Account for Historic High	2020 年为 2019 年的% 2020 Account for 2019
				年份 Year	产量 Output		
农产品产量（万吨）	Total Output of Farm Crops(10 000 tons)						
粮食总产量	Output of Grain Crops	290.81	285.46	2011	295.84	98.3	101.9
# 小麦	Wheat	137.37	135.31	2020	137.37	100.0	101.5
稻谷	Rice	0.52	1.21	2000	9.89	5.3	43.0
玉米	Corn	139.16	136.11	2011	143.96	96.7	102.2
薯类	Tubers	7.93	6.86	1995	23.10	34.3	115.6
经济作物（万吨）	Commercial Crop(10 000 tons)						
# 棉花	Cotton	0.42	0.54	1999	5.00	8.4	78.0
油料花生	Peanuts	6.48	6.31	2020	6.48	100.0	102.8
蔬菜总产量	Output of Vegetables	673.73	671.24	2020	673.73	100.0	100.4
水果总产量	Output of Fruits	49.49	62.95	2019	62.95	78.6	78.6
水产品总产量（万吨）	Total Aquatic Products(10 000 tons)	1.3	1.6	2015	4.80	27.1	82.2

主要统计指标解释

农林牧渔业总产值 是以货币表现的农、林、牧、渔业全部产品的总量，它反映一定时期内农林牧渔业生产的总规模和总成果。

农、林、牧、渔四业的统计范围是辖区内各种经济组织类型、各个系统的全部农林牧渔业生产单位和非农行业单位附属的农林牧渔业生产活动单位。不包括农业科学试验机构进行的农业生产。

农林牧渔业总产值的核算范围是本辖区内在一定时期内生产的农业、林业、牧业、渔业产品的价值和对农林牧渔业生产活动进行的各种支持性服务活动的价值总和，执行日历年度。

（1）农业产值，包括谷物和其他作物产值：蔬菜，园艺作物产值：水果，坚果，饮料和香料产值；中药材产值。其中谷物和其他作物产值包括谷物、薯类、豆类、棉花、油料，糖料，麻类、烟叶和其他农作物的产值。其他农作物包括青饲料，绿肥、牧草、桑叶及采集的野生植物。

（2）林业，包括林木的培育和种植（不包括茶园、桑园和果园的栽培，管理和收获等活动）。林产品的采集和竹木采伐。

（3）牧业，包括除渔业养殖以外的一切动物饲养和放牧以及捕猎野兽野禽产值。

（4）渔业，包括水生动物和海藻类植物的养殖和捕捞。

（5）农林牧渔服务业，包括灌溉，农产品初加工。农机服务，病虫害防治、森林防火、兽医服务、鱼苗及鱼种场等对农林牧渔业生产活动进行的各种支持性服务活动。但不包括各种科学技术和专业技术服务活动。农林牧渔业总产值核算采用“产品法”进行计算，即用产品产量乘以价格以求出各种产品产值，然后加总求得各业产值，最后各业相加求得农林牧渔业总产值。

1957 年以前的农业总产值中包括了厩肥和农民自给性手工业（如农民自制衣服、鞋、袜，自己从事粮食初步加工等）。1958 年及以后的农业总产值，林业中增加了村及村以下竹木采伐产值；牧业中取消了厩肥产值；副业中取消了农民自给性手工业产值，增加了村及村以下办的工业产值；渔业中增加了海洋捕捞水产品产值。1980 年及以后的农业总产值，在副业中增加了农民家庭兼营工业商品性部分的产值。从 1984 年起村及村以下办工业产值划归工业。从 1993 年起取消副业，将采集野生植物产值和农民家庭兼营商品性工业产值划归农业产值，捕猎野兽、野禽产值划入牧业产值。2003 年根据新的国民经济行业分类，农林牧渔服务业划归第一产业。原农业产值中的农民家庭兼营商品性工业产值划归工业产值；林业中竹木采伐产值统计范围由村及村以下改为全社会。

农林牧渔业增加值 是指农、林、牧、渔及农林牧渔服务业生产货物或提供服务活动而增加的价值，为农林牧渔业现价总产值扣除农林渔业现价中间投入后的余额。

农林牧渔业增加值的核算范围同农林牧渔业总产值的核算范围相同。

农林牧渔业增加值的计算方法：采用生产法和分配法（收入法）两种。

1. 生产法计算公式：

农林牧渔业增加值 = 农林牧渔业总产值 - 农林牧渔业中间消耗

2. 分配法计算公式：

农林牧渔业增加值 = 固定资产折旧 + 劳动者报酬 + 生产税净额 + 营业盈余

其中：生产税净额 = 生产税收 - 生产补贴

粮食产量 指日历年度内生产的全部粮食数量。按收获季节包括夏收粮食、早稻和秋收粮食，按作物品种包括谷物、薯类和豆类。其产量计算方法：谷物按脱粒后的原粮计算，豆类按去豆荚后的干豆计算；薯类（包括甘薯和马铃薯，不包括芋头和木薯）1964 年以前按每 4 公斤鲜薯折 1 公斤粮食计算，从 1964 年开始改为按 5 公斤鲜薯折 1 公斤粮食计算；城市郊区作为蔬菜的薯类（如马铃薯等）按鲜品计算，并且不作粮食统计。1989 年以前全国粮食产量数据主要靠全面报表取得，1989 年开始使用抽样调查数据。

油料产量 指全部油料作物的生产量。包括花生、油菜籽、芝麻、向日葵籽、胡麻籽（亚麻籽）和其他油料。不包括大豆、木本油料和野生油料。花生以带壳干花生计算。

水产品产量 指人工养殖的水产品和天然生长的水产的捕捞量。包括海水的鱼类、虾蟹类、贝类和藻类以及淡水的鱼类、虾蟹类和贝类，不包括淡水水生植物。

猪、牛、羊肉产量 指当年出栏并已屠宰的猪、牛、羊的肉产量。即屠宰后除去头蹄下水后带骨肉（即胴体重）的重量。

耕地面积 指年初可以用来种植农作物、经常进行耕锄的田地，包括熟地、当年新开荒地、连续撂荒未满三年的耕地和当年的休闲地（轮歇地），还包括以种植农作物为主并附带种植桑树、茶树、果树和其他林木的土地，以及沿海、沿湖地区已围垦利用的“海涂”、“湖田”等面积。

不包括属于专业性的桑园、茶园、果园、果木苗圃、林地、芦苇地、天然或人工草地面积。

农作物播种面积 指实际播种或移植有农作物的面积。凡是实际种植有农作物的面积，不论种植在耕地上还是种植在非耕地上，均包括在农作物播种面积中。在播种季节基本结束后，因遭灾而重新改种和补种的农作物面积，也包括在内。

灌溉面积 有效灌溉面积，指具有一定的水源，地块比较平整，灌溉工程或设备已经配套，在一般年景下半年能够进行正常灌溉的耕地面积。

农用化肥施用量 指本年内实际用于农业生产的化肥数量，包括氮肥、磷肥、钾肥和复合肥。化肥施用量要求按折纯量计算数量。折纯量是指把氮肥、磷肥、钾肥分别按含氮、含五氧化二磷、含氧化钾的百分之一百成份进行折算后的数量。复合肥按其所含主要成分折算。

农业机械总动力 指主要用于农、林、牧、渔业的各种动力机械的动力总和。包括耕作机械、排灌机械、收获机械、农产品加工机械、运输机械、植物保护机械、牧业机械、林业机械、渔业机械和其他农业机械（内燃机按引擎马力折成瓦（特）计算），电动机按功率折成瓦特计算。不包括专门用于乡办工业、基本建设、非农业运输、科学试验和教学等非农业生产方面用的动力机械与作业机械。

Explanatory Notes on Main Statistical Indicators

Gross Output Value of Farming, Forestry, Animal Husbandry and Fishery refers to the total volume of products of farming, forestry, animal husbandry and fishery in monetary expression, which reflects the total scale and the total result of farming, forestry, animal husbandry and fishery production during a given period.

The scope of statistics of farming, forestry, animal husbandry and fishing covers various economic organizations in the area under administration as well as agriculture, forestry, animal husbandry and fishery production activity units which all agriculture, forestry, animal husbandry and fishing production units and units in non-agricultural industries of all systems are subordinate to, excluding agricultural production by agricultural science experiment organization.

The scope of accounting of the gross output value of farming, forestry, animal husbandry and fishery is the sum of the value of agriculture, forestry, animal husbandry and fishery products produced in the area under administration within a certain period and the value of various supportive service activities in agriculture, forestry, animal husbandry and fishery production activities based on a calendar year.

(1) The value of agricultural production includes the output value of cereal and other crop: output value of vegetables and horticultural plants: output value of fruits, nuts, beverages and spices; output value of traditional Chinese medicinal materials. Output value of cereal and other crops includes that of cereal, potato, bean, cotton, oil plants, sugar, bast fiber plants, tobacco and other crops. Other crops include green feed, green manure, pasture, folium mori and collected wild plants.

(2) Forestry includes cultivation and plantation of the forest (excluding cultivation, management and harvesting of tea plantation, mulberry plantation and orchard). Acquisition of forest products and bamboo and wood cutting.

(3) Animal husbandry includes output value of animal feeding and grazing and hunting wild animals and wildfowls except for fishery breeding.

(4) Fishery includes breeding and fishing of aquatic animals and seaweed plants.

(5) Farming, forestry, animal husbandry and fishery service industry include irrigation and primary processing of agricultural products. Various supportive service activities (such as agricultural machinery service, pest control, forest fire prevention, veterinary service and fry and seed farm) for agriculture, forestry, animal husbandry and fishery production activities, excluding various service activities of scientific technology and professional technology. The gross output value of farming, forestry, animal husbandry and fishery is calculated by "product approach", which means the gross output value of agriculture, forestry, animal husbandry and fishery is obtained after adding the output value of all industries obtained by adding the output value of various products originating from the production output multiplying by the price.

Gross output value of farming before 1957 includes animal manure and peasant self-catering handicraft industry (including homemade clothes, shoes and socks of farmers as well as preliminary processing of grain by farmers). As for the gross output value of agriculture in 1958 and later, the output value of bamboo and wood cutting of the village and below is added in the forestry; output value of animal manure is cancelled in the animal husbandry; output value of peasant self-catering handicraft industry is cancelled and output value of the industry of the village and below is added in the sideline; output value of aquatic products based on marine fishing is added in the fishery. As for gross output value of agriculture in 1980 and later, output value of industrial commodities concurrently operated by the peasant family is added in the sideline. Output value of the industry of the village and below from 1984 was incorporated into value of industrial output. The sideline was cancelled from 1993. The output value of wild plants acquired and output of commercial industry concurrently operated by peasant family are classified into value of agricultural production and output of wild animals and wild birds hunted is included into output of animal husbandry. Agriculture, forestry, animal husbandry and fishery service industry was classified into the primary industry in 2003 pursuant to the new classification of national economy industries. Output value of the commercial industry concurrently operated by the peasant family in the original value of agricultural production is included into value of industrial output; the scope of statistics of the output value of bamboo and wood cutting in the forestry is changed to the whole society.

Value added of agriculture, forestry, animal husbandry and fishery refers to the value added due to production of goods or provision of service in agriculture, forestry, animal husbandry and fishing and agriculture, it is the balance of the total output value at the current price of agriculture, forestry, animal husbandry and fishery minus by intermediate input at the current price of agriculture, fishing and forestry.

The scope of accounting of the value added of agriculture, forestry, animal husbandry and fishery is the same to the gross output value of farming, forestry, animal husbandry and fishery.

The method for computing the value added of farming, forestry, animal husbandry and fishery: Production approach and distribution approach (income approach) are adopted:

1. Calculation formula of production approach:

Value added of agriculture, forestry, animal husbandry and fishery = gross output value of agriculture, forestry, animal husbandry and fishery − intermediate consumption of agriculture, forestry, animal husbandry and fishery

2. Calculation formula of distribution approach:

Value added of agriculture, forestry, animal husbandry and fishery

= depreciation of fixed assets + remuneration for workers + net production tax + operating surplus

Wherein: Net production tax = production tax – production subsidy

Grain output refers to the total output of grains produced within a calendar year. It includes summer crops, early rice and autumn crops by harvest seasons; and covers cereals, tubers and beans by type of crops. Output of cereals cover husked grain only. Output of beans refers to dry beans without pods. The output of tubers (sweet potatoes and potatoes, not including taros and cassava) are converted with the ratio of 4:1, i.e. 4 kilograms of fresh tubers were equivalent to 1 kilogram of grain before 1964. Since 1964 the ratio has been changed to 5:1. Tubers consumed as vegetables (such as potatoes) in cities and suburbs are calculated as fresh vegetables and their output is not included in the output of grain. Data on grain production before 1989 were obtained through the comprehensive statistical reporting system. Since 1989, data from sample surveys are used.

Output of Oil–bearing Crops refers to the total production of oil bearing crops of various kinds, including peanuts, sesame, sunflower seeds, flax seeds, and other oil bearing crops. Soybeans, oil bearing woody plants, and wild oil–bearing crops are not included. Only shelled dry peanuts are included.

Output of Aquatic Products refers to catches of both artificially cultured and naturally grown aquatic products, including fish, shrimps, crabs, shellfish and algae in sea and fish, shrimps, crabs and shellfish in fresh water. Freshwater plants are not included.

Output of Pork, Beef, and Mutton refers to the output of meat of slaughtered hogs, cattle, sheep and goats with head, feet, and offal taken away.

Cultivated Area refers to area of the farmland used to plant crops at the beginning of the year which is often plowed, including cultivated land, new cultivated land that very year, arable land abandoned for less than three years consecutively, fallow land (rotation land) that very year, the land mainly planting crops complemented by plantation of white mulberry, tea tree, fruit tree and other forest as well as "shoal" and "shoaly land" having been subject to reclamation and utilization in coastal and lake–side areas.

Excluded from this category are professional mulberry field, tea garden, orchard, nurseries of young plants, woods, reeds, natural or artificial grass area.

Sown Area of Crops refers to area of land sown or transplanted with crops regardless of being in cultivated area or non–cultivated area. Area of land re–sown due to natural disasters is also included.

Irrigation effective irrigation area refers to cultivated area with some water sources, which is smooth, provided with irrigation engineering or equipment and capable of normal irrigation in the latter half of general year.

Consumption of Chemical Fertilizers in Agriculture refers to the quantity of chemical fertilizers applied in agriculture in the year, including nitrogenous fertilizer, phosphate fertilizer, potash fertilizer, and compound fertilizer. The consumption of chemical fertilizers is required in calculation to convert the gross weight into weight containing 100% effective component (e.g. 100% nitrogen content in nitrogenous fertilizer, 100% phosphorous pent oxide contents in phosphate fertilizer, 100% potassium oxide contents in potash fertilizer). Compound fertilizer is converted with its major component.

Total Power of Farm Machinery refers to total mechanical power of machinery used in farming, forestry, animal husbandry, and fishery, including ploughing, irrigation and drainage, harvesting, transport, plant protection, stock breeding, forestry and fishery. The power of internal combustion engines is required to convert horsepower into watts and the power of electric motors is required to be converted into watts. Machinery employed for non– agricultural purposes, such as the machines used in township run and village run industry, construction, non–agricultural transport, scientific experiments and teaching, is excluded.

工 业

INDUSTRY

12-1 各时期全部工业基本情况
Basic Statistics on Total Industry in Each Period

年份 Year	全部工业单位数（个）Number of Industial Enterprises (Unit)		工业总产值（亿元）Gross Industrial Output Value (100 million yuan)		工业增加值（亿元）Value Added of Industry Enterprises (100 million yuan)		国有独立核算工业（万元）State-owned Independent Accounting Industrial (10 000 yuan)	
	合计 Total	#国有单位 State-owned	合计 Total	#国有单位 State-owned	合计 Total	#国有单位 State-owned	利润总额 Total Profits	利税总额 Total Profits and Taxes
1949	52	–	1.20	0.52	0.40	0.15	190	541
1952	92	–	2.97	1.65	1.09	0.52	1616	2761
1957	399	–	6.90	6.13	2.18	1.84	5742	10065
1962	847	286	6.67	5.61	2.36	1.80	3293	8242
1965	724	247	11.99	10.09	4.34	3.39	16246	22906
1970	828	285	23.12	17.93	7.56	5.64	19347	31834
1975	1041	326	26.41	18.87	8.46	5.50	11555	27846
1978	1319	398	39.06	25.87	12.89	7.11	28852	53031
1979	1353	359	42.95	28.90	14.10	8.01	31875	57532
1980	1535	356	45.31	30.37	14.24	8.85	32909	59572
"六五"时期								
1981	1538	350	47.61	31.72	15.11	9.47	35077	62657
1982	1619	357	51.98	33.91	15.79	10.01	32062	64673
1983	1674	369	59.06	36.99	17.96	11.49	35870	60308
1984	1981	325	66.96	39.78	20.10	13.17	45869	83520
1985	2584	477	74.41	44.66	27.54	16.97	61274	112154
"七五"时期								
1986	3005	369	86.93	48.71	28.69	17.53	54804	115006
1987	3957	361	107.63	56.16	32.88	19.40	58715	125775
1988	5252	372	138.05	68.58	47.49	25.09	80173	156056
1989	7655	380	158.53	76.19	54.66	30.51	76571	170703
1990	11020	394	222.63	116.92	60.43	37.11	25084	125522
"八五"时期								
1991	12211	376	245.73	131.35	67.73	43.35	36715	151718
1992	15374	373	303.33	162.35	86.85	48.97	55463	193000
1993	19392	376	448.25	230.93	115.36	69.65	57984	223445
1994	22009	366	614.08	236.40	154.49	69.64	60393	240473
1995	24621	495	752.23	279.16	194.16	83.12	65335	316289

12-1 续表 continued

年份 Year	全部工业单位数（个）Number of Industial Enterprises (Unit)		工业总产值（亿元）Gross Industrial Output Value (100 million yuan)		工业增加值（亿元）Value Added of Industry Enterprises (100 million yuan)		国有独立核算工业（万元）State-owned Independent Accounting Industrial (10 000 yuan)	
	合计 Total	#国有单位 State-owned	合计 Total	#国有单位 State-owned	合计 Total	#国有单位 State-owned	利润总额 Total Profits	利税总额 Total Profits and Taxes
“九五”时期								
1996	32902	425	834.45	260.16	238.31	91.30	79615	337807
1997	33000	325	897.59	263.34	278.87	92.99	95267	343426
1998	32793	227	966.62	234.03	298.41	94.28	42152	292991
1999	29319	211	981.78	212.95	318.80	79.51	-2340	254619
2000	30899	195	994.00	237.14	336.61	81.00	34824	292198
“十五”时期								
2001	34135	169	1090.70	140.44	356.72	64.69	49222	226242
2002	30064	155	1302.00	144.78	410.98	49.16	28011	234986
2003	30258	126	1544.50	167.30	494.55	68.80	53363	302975
2004	31163	115	1981.80	150.70	620.14	37.21	-3943	72684
2005	31370	102	2447.51	177.00	786.11	66.49	268573	354111
“十一五”时期								
2006	35370	86	2806.94	193.10	861.48	73.95	315323	458191
2007	36112	76	3389.09	283.32	985.78	103.65	364790	751182
2008	36416	80	4829.16	338.24	1140.14	136.55	418265	853091
2009	37656	77	5096.98	345.44	1191.36	166.36	422898	885006
2010	37521	66	5800.39	404.38	1352.42	284.75	643216	1162785
“十二五”时期								
2011	36750	54	5544.60	478.10	1507.88		561683	1217350
2012	35917	52	5535.25	491.20	1603.08		646193	1401892
2013	38443	30	5711.48	280.63	1690.63		551967	665206
2014	38753	25	5861.98	246.26	1822.11		507491	611865
2015	38793	24	5877.28	204.79	1844.37		517575	571354
“十三五”时期								
2016	34310	16	6059.16	157.83	1878.83		540739	622714
2017	33725	12	6395.21	147.27	2003.10		583734	589999
2018	31270	13	5641.61	15.50	2145.10			5014
2019					2167.87			
2020					2360.48			

注：1. 工业增加值、工业总产值按当年价格计算。
2. 1985、1995 年因工业普查对教育局校办工厂统计方法的规定，故国有单位较多。
3. 2001 年后炼油、浪潮、将军等原国有企业陆续改制，故国有数字较以前年份有所减小。
4. 2004 年第一次经济普查后，统计年鉴包含济南供电公司年报数据。
5. 非经济普查年度，除“工业增加值”外，其它指标空缺。

Note: 1. Industrial value added and total industrial output value are calculated according to the current year’s prices.
2. There were many state-owned units in 1985 and 1995 due to the provisions regarding statistical approach for school-run factories of Education Bureau from industrial census.
3. Original state-owned enterprises such as Oil Refining, Inspur and General were subject to restructuring in succession after 2001, so the quantity of state-owned enterprises decreased in comparison to that of previous years.
4. After the economic census for the first time in 2004, statistical yearbook includes annual report data of Ji’nan Power Supply Company.
5.In years other than the year of economic census, indicators are blank, excluding "Value Added of Industrial Enterprises".

12-2 各时期规模以上工业基本情况
Basic Statistics of Industrial Enterprises Above Designated Size in Each Period

单位：亿元 (100 million yuan)

年份 Year	单位数 (个) Number of Industial Enterprises (unit)	工业总产值 Gross Industrial Output Value	工业增加值 Value Added of Industry Enterprises	营业收入 Revenue from Principal Business	利税总额 Total Profits and Taxes	利润总额 Total Profits	资产总计 Total Assets	所有者权益 Owner's Equities
1949	52	1.06	0.40	0.91	0.07	0.03	0.58	0.17
1952	92	2.83	1.02	2.40	0.32	0.18	1.89	0.55
1957	399	6.04	2.08	5.85	1.04	0.60	2.85	0.83
1962	847	6.65	2.15	6.87	0.92	0.39	5.66	1.65
1965	724	11.89	4.07	9.49	2.47	1.73	5.93	1.73
1970	828	22.94	7.29	19.30	3.66	2.22	10.67	3.10
1975	1041	26.16	7.94	19.70	3.47	1.55	17.21	5.01
1978	1319	37.67	9.94	31.39	6.80	3.88	25.68	7.47
1979	1353	38.79	11.18	35.51	7.21	4.13	27.19	7.91
1980	1535	43.60	12.15	36.90	7.51	4.26	29.22	8.50
"六五" 时期								
1981	1538	42.26	12.77	39.84	7.98	4.37	31.49	9.20
1982	1619	45.58	13.63	42.94	8.13	4.18	34.52	10.08
1983	1674	49.64	14.86	46.38	8.84	4.74	38.09	11.12
1984	1981	55.95	17.91	52.16	10.46	5.82	41.66	12.16
1985	1915	66.98	23.10	64.76	13.98	7.62	47.09	13.75
"七五" 时期								
1986	2036	75.67	24.54	73.98	14.38	7.07	56.79	16.70
1987	2004	88.17	27.24	86.19	15.88	7.52	64.21	18.88
1988	1984	107.76	35.39	113.84	19.65	10.37	81.67	24.01
1989	1993	118.88	43.20	131.86	20.88	9.73	104.34	30.68
1990	2008	174.89	41.63	136.29	15.57	3.23	125.25	36.82
"八五" 时期								
1991	1985	194.29	44.84	160.58	18.46	4.97	138.34	40.81
1992	1941	236.37	60.16	200.54	23.48	7.84	167.44	49.39
1993	2156	319.49	104.43	309.91	31.88	10.26	338.15	99.61
1994	2202	414.81	113.71	346.13	41.69	13.61	462.34	136.14
1995	2648	526.48	130.88	432.17	53.59	16.30	578.55	180.86

注：1. 工业增加值、工业总产值按当年价格计算。
2. 1997 年及以前统计口径为乡及乡以上工业企业，1998 年及以后为全部国有及年销售收入 500 万元以上工业企业，2011 年及以后为年主营业务收入 2000 万元以上工业企业。
3. 1991 年及以前"工业增加值"指标为"工业净产值"指标。
4. 2018 年及以前"营业收入""营业成本""税金及附加"指标为"主营业务收入""主营业务成本"及"主营业务税金及附加"指标。以下相关各表同。
5. 自 2019 年起，不再包含省直单位相关数据。以下相关各表同。
6. 自 2019 年起，数据为济南市、莱芜市区划调整后合并数据，之前年度数据为原济南市数据。以下相关各表同。
7. 表中的合计数和部分计算数据因小数取舍而产生的误差，均未作机械调整。以下相关各表同。

12-2 续表 continued

年份 Year	单位数 （个） Number of Industial Enterprises (unit)	工业总产值 Gross Industrial Output Value	工业增加值 Value Added of Industry Enterprises	营业收入 Revenue from Principal Business	利税总额 Total Profits and Taxes	利润总额 Total Profits	资产总计 Total Assets	所有者权益 Owner's Equities
"九五"时期								
1996	2301	549.40	175.21	494.99	66.82	27.83	705.50	225.53
1997	1843	603.30	194.42	605.81	70.12	26.99	882.36	286.59
1998	1060	593.83	189.88	539.29	58.56	18.62	882.38	297.81
1999	1064	628.59	201.38	579.64	59.17	15.97	931.22	302.21
2000	1038	680.04	219.19	629.72	64.62	21.69	958.10	363.37
"十五"时期								
2001	1015	786.70	252.61	746.92	77.79	28.45	984.71	369.40
2002	1125	1009.04	325.98	917.31	92.71	32.13	1120.60	407.36
2003	1319	1318.54	426.30	1223.76	132.84	54.71	1312.97	440.85
2004	1512	1781.78	560.15	1677.93	175.98	83.68	1473.90	507.63
2005	1670	2237.51	722.11	2142.84	244.61	131.30	1868.06	630.06
"十一五"时期								
2006	1752	2591.65	797.70	2490.94	289.78	153.74	2000.62	702.78
2007	1820	3189.09	926.58	3086.85	358.87	199.73	2337.09	903.87
2008	2016	3862.64	1052.48	3766.93	425.72	220.79	2899.47	1123.03
2009	2156	3950.77	1154.01	3868.70	500.63	275.85	3478.94	1572.11
2010	2021	4485.61	1313.00	4497.17	584.53	339.76	3904.42	1481.75
"十二五"时期								
2011	1417	4028.49	–	4165.19	453.47	242.63	3932.90	1407.89
2012	1647	4248.29	–	4454.97	498.24	253.06	4109.29	1582.77
2013	1901	4777.47	–	4926.11	539.49	312.95	4249.79	1671.91
2014	1984	5253.05	–	5406.67	606.60	357.82	4564.86	1846.32
2015	2021	5339.97	–	5417.16	685.71	396.13	4987.76	2159.78
"十三五"时期								
2016	1962	5486.56	–	5714.29	729.75	421.11	5501.88	2301.94
2017	2051	5770.91	–	5810.16	686.80	415.23	6319.64	2268.27
2018	1889	4992.28	–	5192.15	535.39	307.98	5892.64	2386.75
2019	2153	5839.18	–	6512.66	545.70	310.86	6663.13	2743.28
2020	2215	6765.08	–	7575.34	659.87	423.31	7724.85	2967.31

Note: 1. The value added and total output of industrial enterprises are calculated as per the price of the years.

2. The statistic scale of year 1997 and before involves industrial enterprises in rural areas and above level, that of year 1998 and onwards involves all state-owned industrial enterprises and industrial enterprises with the annual sales revenue of RMB 5 million, and that of year 2011 and onwards involves industrial enterprises with the annual main operating income of RMB 20 million.

3. "Value added of industrial enterprises" in year 1991 and before refers to the indicator of "net value of industiral output".

4. "Operating income", "operating cost" and "taxes and surcharges" indicators in year 2019 and before refer to "main operating income", "main operating cost" and "main operating taxes and surcharges" (the same below).

5. Since 2019, statistics does not include data of units directly under provincial jurisdiction (the same below).

6. Since 2019, the data used refer to the combined data after the adjustment of administrative division between Jinan City and Laiwu City, and the data before 2019 are data of original Jinan City (the same below).

7.Errors in totals and part of calculations in the table are produced by decimal trade-offs, not mechanically adjusted (the same below).

12-3 各时期主要工业产品产量
Output of Major Industrial Products in Each Period

年份 Year	钢 (万吨) Steel (10 000 tons)	发电量 (亿千瓦小时) Electric Energy Production (100 million kwh)	水泥 (万吨) Cement (10 000 tons)	化肥 (万吨) Chemical Fertilizer (10 000 tons)	金切机床 (台) Metal-cutting Machine Tools(unit)	汽车 (辆) Motor Vehicles (unit)	服务器 (万台) Servers (10 000 unit)	布 (万米) Cloth (10 000 m)
1949	–	0.29	0.15	–	40	–	–	2682
1952	–	0.55	1.08	1.62	565	–	–	5104
1957	0.03	1.07	1.29	0.48	2312	–	–	5573
1962	0.57	4.20	4.85	0.81	1140	12	–	2160
1965	0.54	5.65	19.24	3.79	2061	335	–	4853
1970	7.01	11.28	38.06	4.87	4718	1775	–	11665
1975	22.81	11.07	58.48	9.06	3994	3507	–	12547
1978	34.54	12.65	87.55	18.02	3610	4025	–	13806
1979	33.19	11.92	93.77	11.07	3771	4515	–	14300
1980	36.34	11.95	98.86	12.78	4414	5641	–	15236
"六五"时期								
1981	34.23	11.12	96.50	11.62	3336	5099		16290
1982	34.96	11.15	104.64	13.23	4262	5993	–	17657
1983	41.24	13.01	112.38	15.37	4816	7249	–	17963
1984	43.80	23.49	117.17	14.53	5533	7947	–	16522
1985	52.64	26.44	135.10	11.44	6686	9400	–	18082
"七五"时期								
1986	57.24	27.01	154.51	12.31	7472	7600		12346
1987	64.09	28.83	158.92	13.00	7007	5225	–	20137
1988	75.23	42.97	182.80	13.69	7280	6741	–	19374
1989	81.58	43.98	198.95	14.48	6806	7701	–	21744
1990	87.68	44.71	211.56	14.44	5121	6239	–	20155
"八五"时期								
1991	105.42	56.43	248.33	14.90	5330	7096		20119
1992	113.34	61.46	335.61	14.64	7443	8544	–	14896
1993	139.35	69.00	340.35	14.47	6724	10132	–	13205
1994	166.19	66.87	384.00	15.62	3297	9380	–	16062
1995	172.72	68.75	425.02	14.03	4109	5657	–	15046

12-3 续表 continued

年份 Year	钢 (万吨) Steel (10 000 tons)	发电量 (亿千瓦小时) Electric Energy Production (100 million kwh)	水泥 (万吨) Cement (10 000 tons)	化肥 (万吨) Chemical Fertilizer (10 000 tons)	金切机床 (台) Metal-cutting Machine Tools(unit)	汽车 (辆) Motor Vehicles (unit)	服务器 (万台) Servers (10 000 unit)	布 (万米) Cloth (10 000 m)
"九五"时期								
1996	205.49	63.50	379.32	13.73	3855	7125	–	13710
1997	237.70	59.14	392.23	13.89	2526	5656	–	14213
1998	267.33	60.06	379.40	17.29	1508	3615	–	11286
1999	265.29	64.24	474.47	22.91	1955	3738	–	14782
2000	277.04	69.29	485.12	28.41	2908	3078	–	16493
"十五"时期								
2001	293.83	69.81	572.28	28.71	3528	7395	–	14107
2002	394.41	69.12	867.71	28.29	4522	12152		16027
2003	507.70	77.60	925.20	28.50	6751	19989	–	17040
2004	688.30	74.70	1343.90	40.30	8904	29648	–	16336
2005	1046.60	90.80	1595.70	28.90	7166	42214	–	14018
"十一五"时期								
2006	1131.26	100.14	1960.64	31.44	10057	59242	–	22852
2007	1214.90	130.37	733.98	40.31	9473	100133	–	27469
2008	1123.20	124.25	734.58	48.52	5110	109107	8.3	11786
2009	1051.67	128.76	761.72	57.77	2400	129900	9.7	7500
2010	959.33	131.45	729.79	49.09	2165	212047	9.9	8191
"十二五"时期								
2011	835.80	154.48	824.70	44.20	2024	170717	13.0	11461
2012	694.50	156.60	776.00	55.20	4237	141269	14.7	14908
2013	711.14	162.55	782.20	33.29	4297	165963	17.1	14574
2014	746.20	178.47	832.40	28.60	4902	139751	28.1	14070
2015	699.80	175.87	781.50	23.50	3807	96184	40.6	15539
"十三五"时期								
2016	805.70	177.20	719.80	32.50	4679	124200	46.8	15585
2017	452.03	160.12	604.48	21.00	6013	201883	56.5	16407
2018	160.92	152.90	604.32	20.77	5964	232082	99.6	4032
2019	2144.18	295.10	1287.82	16.91	7237	175488	116.5	4095
2020	2228.91	276.70	1335.88	21.09	8998	394133	143.5	1144

注：按经济普查规定汽车产量不含底盘。
Note: The automotive output excludes chassis in line with the provisions of economic census.

12-4 规模以上工业主要经济指标(2020年)

Main Economic Indicators of Industrial Enterprises Above Designated Size(2020)

指标	Indicator	企业单位数(个) Number of Industial Enterprises (unit)	亏损企业数(个) Loss Enterpriss (unit)	工业总产值(现价)(亿元) Gross Indutrial Output Value (Current Prices) (100 million yuan)	平均用工人数(万人) Average of Employed Persons (10 000 persons)
总计	Total	2215	391	6765.08	40.03
按登记注册类型分组	by Status of Registration				
内资企业	Domestic Funded Enterprises	2073	376	5558.49	34.12
国有企业	State-owned Enterprises	29	7	99.00	0.60
中央企业	Central Enterprises	5		10.11	0.02
地方企业	Local Enterprises	24	7	88.89	0.58
集体企业	Collective-owned Enterprises	7	2	6.87	0.13
股份合作企业	Cooperative Enterprises	4		1.86	0.06
联营企业	Joint Ownership Enterprises	1		0.90	0.02
国有联营企业	State Joint Ownership Enterprises				
集体联营企业	Collective Joint Ownership Enterprises	1		0.90	0.02
国有与集体联营企业	Joint State-collective Enterprises				
其他联营企业	Other Joint Ownership Enterprises				
有限责任公司	Limited Liability Corporations	551	133	1969.10	14.60
国有独资公司	State Sole Funded Corporations	40	12	167.91	1.98
其他有限责任公司	Other Limited Liability Corporations	511	121	1801.19	12.62
股份有限公司	Share-holding Corporations Ltd.	89	20	1856.79	5.25
私营企业	Private Enterprises	1391	214	1623.42	13.46
私营独资企业	Private-funded Enterprises	39	3	14.44	0.17
私营合伙企业	Private Partnership Enterprises	1	1	0.26	0.01
私营有限责任公司	Private Limited Liability Corporations	1280	201	1475.39	12.33
私营股份有限公司	Private Share-holding Corporations Ltd.	71	9	133.33	0.95
其他企业	Other Enterprises	1		0.54	0.01
港、澳、台商投资企业	Enterprises with Funds from Hong Kong,Macao and Taiwan	60	3	888.69	3.64
合资经营企业(港或澳、台资)	Joint-venture Enterprises	31	2	280.53	1.69
合作经营企业(港或澳、台资)	Cooperative Enterprises	1		12.81	0.12
港澳台商独资经营企业	Enterprises with Sole Investment	28	1	595.35	1.83
港澳台商投资股份有限公司	Share-holding Corporations Ltd.				
其他港澳台商投资企业	Other Enterprises with Funds from Hong Kong,Macao and Taiwan				

12-4 续表 1 continued 1

指标	Indicator	企业单位数（个）Number of Industial Enterprises (unit)	亏损企业数（个）Loss Enterpriss (unit)	工业总产值（现价）(亿元) Gross Indutrial Output Value (Current Prices) (100 million yuan)	平均用工人数（万人）Average of Employed Persons (10 000 persons)
外商投资企业	Foreign Funded Enterprises	82	12	317.90	2.26
中外合资经营企业	Joint-venture Enterprises	34	7	96.24	1.00
中外合作经营企业	Cooperation Enterprises	2		2.32	0.02
外资企业	Enterprises with Sole Fund	42	5	136.72	1.09
外商投资股份有限公司	Share-holding Corporations Ltd. with Foreign Investment	4		82.62	0.15
其他外商投资企业	Other Foreign Funded Enterprises				
按轻重工业分	**by Light & Heavy Industry**				
轻工业	Light Industry	580	117	1010.79	10.70
重工业	Heavy Industry	1635	274	5754.29	29.32
按企业规模分	**by Enterprise Size**				
大型企业	Large-sized Enterprises	60	8	3863.16	15.31
中型企业	Medium-sized Enterprises	172	26	1160.13	8.65
小型企业	Small-sized Enterprises	1770	320	1628.42	15.40
微型企业	Micro-sized Enterprises	213	37	113.36	0.66
按工业行业分	**by Sector**				
煤炭开采和洗选业	Mining and Washing of Coal	3	2	5.66	0.28
石油和天然气开采业	Extraction of Petroleum and Natural Gas	3	1	5.64	0.04
黑色金属矿采选业	Mining and Processing of Ferrous Metal Ores	9	2	56.27	0.84
有色金属矿采选业	Mining and Processing of Non-Ferrous Metal Ores				
非金属矿采选业	Mining and Processing of Non-metal Ores	10	2	12.84	0.10
开采专业及辅助性活动	Professional and Support Activities for Mining				
其他采矿业	Mining of Other Ores				
农副食品加工业	Processing of Food from Agricultural Products	85	24	132.58	0.82
食品制造业	Manufacture of Foods	67	13	129.06	1.70
酒、饮料和精制茶制造业	Manufacture of Liquor, Beverages and Refined Tea	17	3	52.49	0.50
烟草制品业	Manufacture of Tobacco	1		1.19	0.02
纺织业	Manufacture of Textile	47	9	42.84	0.58
纺织服装、服饰业	Manufacture of Textile, Wearing Apparel and Accessories	22	7	11.00	0.60
皮革、毛皮、羽毛及其制品和制鞋业	Manufacture of Leather, Fur, Feather and Related Products and Footwear	4		2.52	0.03
木材加工和木、竹、藤、棕、草制品业	Processing of Timber, Manufacture of Wood, Bamboo, Rattan,Palm and Straw Products	11		6.27	0.06

12–4 续表 2 continued 2

指标	Indicator	企业单位数（个）Number of Industial Enterprises (unit)	亏损企业数（个）Loss Enterpriss (unit)	工业总产值（现价）(亿元) Gross Indutrial Output Value (Current Prices) (100 million yuan)	平均用工人数（万人）Average of Employed Persons (10 000 persons)
家具制造业	Manufacture of Furniture	14	4	8.69	0.18
造纸和纸制品业	Manufacture of Paper and Paper Products	39	5	39.59	0.41
印刷和记录媒介复制业	Printing and Reproduction of Recording Media	40	11	39.28	0.64
文教、工美、体育和娱乐用品制造业	Manufacture of Articles for Culture, Education Arts and Crafts,Sport and Entertainment Activities	22	8	12.78	0.27
石油、煤炭及其他燃料加工业	Processing of Petroleum, Coal and Other Fuels	15	2	258.97	0.33
化学原料和化学制品制造业	Manufacture of Raw Chemical Materials and Chemical Products	105	8	277.27	1.78
医药制造业	Manufacture of Medicines	68	6	298.56	2.68
化学纤维制造业	Manufacture of Chemical Fibres	10	3	13.11	0.11
橡胶和塑料制品业	Manufacture of Rubber and Plastics Products	58	5	31.94	0.42
非金属矿物制品业	Manufacture of Non–metallic Mineral Products	282	40	412.31	3.39
黑色金属冶炼和压延加工业	Smelting and Pressing of Ferrous Metals	36	14	1200.60	3.57
有色金属冶炼和压延加工业	Smelting and Pressing of Non–ferrous Metals	25	4	21.14	0.18
金属制品业	Manufacture of Metal Products	241	39	337.58	3.02
通用设备制造业	Manufacture of General Purpose Machinery	252	39	305.94	3.92
专用设备制造业	Manufacture of Special Purpose Machinery	205	41	237.19	2.45
汽车制造业	Manufacture of Automobiles	120	13	1407.06	4.21
铁路、船舶、航空航天和其他运输设备制造业	Manufacture of Railway, Ship, Aerospace and Other Transport Equipments	28	5	66.63	0.75
电气机械和器材制造业	Manufacture of Electrical Machinery and Apparatus	137	29	358.83	1.90
计算机、通信和其他电子设备制造业	Manufacture of Computers, Communication and Other Electronic Equipment	62	18	635.42	1.32
仪器仪表制造业	Manufacture of Measuring Instruments and Machinery	72	7	77.30	0.88
其他制造业	Other Manufacture	4		3.10	0.02
废弃资源综合利用业	Utilization of Waste Resources	8	3	13.14	0.06
金属制品、机械和设备修理业	Repair Service of Metal Products, Machinery and Equipment	5	1	10.28	0.20
电力、热力生产和供应业	Production and Supply of Electric Power and Heat Power	49	15	156.24	1.10
燃气生产和供应业	Production and Supply of Gas	21	2	57.99	0.32
水的生产和供应业	Production and Supply of Water	18	6	25.80	0.34

注：2019 年年报起，取消“工业销售产值”指标。后续各表同。
Note: From 2019 onwards, "Sales Output of Industrial Enterprises" is cancelled (the same below).

12-5 规模以上国有及国有控股工业主要经济指标(2020年)

Main Economic Indicators of State-Owned and State-Controlled Industrial Enterprises Above Designated Size(2020)

指标	Indicator	企业单位数(个) Number of Industial Enterprises (unit)	亏损企业数(个) Loss Enterpriss (unit)	工业总产值(现价)(亿元) Gross Indutrial Output Value (Current Prices) (100 million yuan)	平均用工人数(万人) Average of Employed Persons (10 000 persons)
总计	Total	211	50	2901.90	10.37
按登记注册类型分组	by Status of Registration				
内资企业	Domestic Funded Enterprises	198	50	2691.21	9.52
国有企业	State-owned Enterprises	29	7	99.00	0.60
中央企业	Central Enterprises	5		10.11	0.02
地方企业	Local Enterprises	24	7	88.89	0.58
集体企业	Collective-owned Enterprises				
股份合作企业	Cooperative Enterprises				
联营企业	Joint Ownership Enterprises				
有限责任公司	Limited Liability Corporations	149	37	943.85	5.68
国有独资公司	State Sole Funded Corporations	40	12	167.91	1.98
其他有限责任公司	Other Limited Liability Corporations	109	25	775.94	3.70
股份有限公司	Share-holding Corporations Ltd.	20	6	1648.37	3.23
私营企业	Private Enterprises				
其他企业	Other Enterprises				
港、澳、台商投资企业	Enterprises with Funds from Hong Kong,Macao and Taiwan	7		171.78	0.60
合资经营企业(港或澳、台资)	Joint-venture Enterprises	6		158.97	0.48
合作经营企业(港或澳、台资)	Cooperative Enterprises	1		12.81	0.12
港澳台商独资经营企业	Enterprises with Sole Investment				
港澳台商投资股份有限公司	Share-holding Corporations Ltd.				
其他港澳台商投资企业	Other Enterprises with Funds from Hong Kong,Macao and Taiwan				
外商投资企业	Foreign Funded Enterprises	6		38.91	0.25
中外合资经营企业	Joint-venture Enterprises	5		36.88	0.24
中外合作经营企业	Cooperation Enterprises	1		2.02	0.02
外资企业	Enterprises with Sole Fund				
外商投资股份有限公司	Share-holding Corporations Ltd. with Foreign Investment				
其他外商投资企业	Other Foreign Funded Enterprises				
按轻重工业分	by Light & Heavy Industry				

12-5 续表 1 continued 1

指标	Indicator	企业单位数（个）Number of Industial Enterprises (unit)	亏损企业数（个）Loss Enterpriss (unit)	工业总产值（现价）(亿元) Gross Indutrial Output Value (Current Prices) (100 million yuan)	平均用工人数（万人）Average of Employed Persons (10 000 persons)
轻工业	Light Industry	39	14	75.97	1.08
重工业	Heavy Industry	172	36	2825.93	9.29
按企业规模分	by Enterprise Size				
大型企业	Large-sized Enterprises	22	5	2311.11	6.42
中型企业	Medium-sized Enterprises	48	9	345.59	2.44
小型企业	Small-sized Enterprises	123	31	236.76	1.46
微型企业	Micro-sized Enterprises	18	5	8.44	0.05
按工业行业分	by Sector				
煤炭开采和洗选业	Mining and Washing of Coal				
石油和天然气开采业	Extraction of Petroleum and Natural Gas	2	1	4.57	0.03
黑色金属矿采选业	Mining and Processing of Ferrous Metal Ores	2	1	21.04	0.44
有色金属矿采选业	Mining and Processing of Non-Ferrous Metal Ores				
非金属矿采选业	Mining and Processing of Non-metal Ores	3		3.45	0.05
开采专业及辅助性活动	Professional and Support Activities for Mining				
其他采矿业	Mining of Other Ores				
农副食品加工业	Processing of Food from Agricultural Products	3	1	0.97	0.02
食品制造业	Manufacture of Foods	5	2	10.11	0.15
酒、饮料和精制茶制造业	Manufacture of Liquor, Beverages and Refined Tea	3		21.48	0.21
烟草制品业	Manufacture of Tobacco	1		1.19	0.02
纺织业	Manufacture of Textile	3	2	2.20	0.06
纺织服装、服饰业	Manufacture of Textile, Wearing Apparel and Accessories	3	3	2.54	0.14
皮革、毛皮、羽毛及其制品和制鞋业	Manufacture of Leather, Fur, Feather and Related Products and Footwear				
木材加工和木、竹、藤、棕、草制品业	Processing of Timber, Manufacture of Wood, Bamboo, Rattan,Palm and Straw Products				
家具制造业	Manufacture of Furniture				
造纸和纸制品业	Manufacture of Paper and Paper Products	2		3.94	0.02
印刷和记录媒介复制业	Printing and Reproduction of Recording Media	7	2	6.58	0.16

12-5 续表 2 continued 2

指标	Indicator	企业单位数（个）Number of Industial Enterprises (unit)	亏损企业数（个）Loss Enterprise (unit)	工业总产值（现价）(亿元) Gross Indutrial Output Value (Current Prices) (100 million yuan)	平均用工人数（万人）Average of Employed Persons (10 000 persons)
文教、工美、体育和娱乐用品制造业	Manufacture of Articles for Culture, Education, Arts and Crafts,Sport and Entertainment Activities				
石油、煤炭及其他燃料加工业	Processing of Petroleum, Coal and Other Fuels	1		208.59	0.15
化学原料和化学制品制造业	Manufacture of Raw Chemical Materials and Chemical Products	8	1	37.52	0.27
医药制造业	Manufacture of Medicines	2		6.84	0.09
化学纤维制造业	Manufacture of Chemical Fibres	2		3.74	0.04
橡胶和塑料制品业	Manufacture of Rubber and Plastics Products				
非金属矿物制品业	Manufacture of Non-metallic Mineral Products	17	1	47.40	0.36
黑色金属冶炼和压延加工业	Smelting and Pressing of Ferrous Metals	6	3	643.94	1.92
有色金属冶炼和压延加工业	Smelting and Pressing of Non-ferrous Metals	1		6.48	0.02
金属制品业	Manufacture of Metal Products	12	5	43.82	0.27
通用设备制造业	Manufacture of General Purpose Machinery	11		62.49	0.98
专用设备制造业	Manufacture of Special Purpose Machinery	12	3	33.94	0.30
汽车制造业	Manufacture of Automobiles	12	1	749.96	1.50
铁路、船舶、航空航天和其他运输设备制造业	Manufacture of Railway, Ship, Aerospace and Other Transport Equipments	9		43.13	0.40
电气机械和器材制造业	Manufacture of Electrical Machinery and Apparatus	23	8	140.50	0.53
计算机、通信和其他电子设备制造业	Manufacture of Computers, Communication and Other Electronic Equipment	7	2	580.75	0.58
仪器仪表制造业	Manufacture of Measuring Instruments and Machinery	7		23.15	0.21
其他制造业	Other Manufacture	1		2.17	0.01
废弃资源综合利用业	Utilization of Waste Resources				
金属制品、机械和设备修理业	Repair Service of Metal Products, Machinery and Equipment	1		1.31	0.02
电力、热力生产和供应业	Production and Supply of Electric Power and Heat Power	25	7	135.97	0.93
燃气生产和供应业	Production and Supply of Gas	8	1	34.33	0.22
水的生产和供应业	Production and Supply of Water	12	6	17.81	0.29

12-6 规模以上私营工业企业主要经济指标(2020年)
Main Economic Indicators of Private Industrial Enterprises Above Designated Size(2020)

指标	Indicator	企业单位数(个) Number of Industial Enterprises (unit)	亏损企业数(个) Loss Enterpriss (unit)	工业总产值(现价)(亿元) Gross Indutrial Output Value (Current Prices) (100 million yuan)	平均用工人数(万人) Average of Employed Persons (10 000 persons)
总计	Total	1391	214	1623.42	13.46
按登记注册类型分组	by Status of Registration				
内资企业	Domestic Funded Enterprises	1391	214	1623.42	13.46
私营企业	Private Enterprises	1391	214	1623.42	13.46
私营独资企业	Private-funded Enterprises	39	3	14.44	0.17
私营合伙企业	Private Partnership Enterprises	1	1	0.26	0.01
私营有限责任公司	Private Limited Liability Corporations	1280	201	1475.39	12.33
私营股份有限公司	Private Share-holding Corporations Ltd.	71	9	133.33	0.95
其他企业	Other Enterprises				
按轻重工业分	by Light & Heavy Industry				
轻工业	Light Industry	356	68	278.34	3.54
重工业	Heavy Industry	1035	146	1345.08	9.92
按企业规模分	by Enterprise Size				
大型企业	Large-sized Enterprises	7	1	287.10	1.69
中型企业	Medium-sized Enterprises	45	5	338.05	2.10
小型企业	Small-sized Enterprises	1183	187	906.85	9.16
微型企业	Micro-sized Enterprises	156	21	91.43	0.50
按工业行业分	by Sector				
煤炭开采和洗选业	Mining and Washing of Coal	1	1	0.69	
石油和天然气开采业	Extraction of Petroleum and Natural Gas				

12-6 续表 1 continued 1

指标	Indicator	企业单位数（个）Number of Industial Enterprises (unit)	亏损企业数（个）Loss Enterpriss (unit)	工业总产值（现价）(亿元) Gross Indutrial Output Value (Current Prices) (100 million yuan)	平均用工人数（万人）Average of Employed Persons (10 000 persons)
黑色金属矿采选业	Mining and Processing of Ferrous Metal Ores	1		6.71	0.02
有色金属矿采选业	Mining and Processing of Non-Ferrous Metal Ores				
非金属矿采选业	Mining and Processing of Non-metal Ores	7	2	9.39	0.05
开采专业及辅助性活动	Professional and Support Activities for Mining				
其他采矿业	Mining of Other Ores				
农副食品加工业	Processing of Food from Agricultural Products	57	13	83.00	0.54
食品制造业	Manufacture of Foods	38	9	39.85	0.70
酒、饮料和精制茶制造业	Manufacture of Liquor, Beverages and Refined Tea	3		1.98	0.02
烟草制品业	Manufacture of Tobacco				
纺织业	Manufacture of Textile	32	6	18.91	0.31
纺织服装、服饰业	Manufacture of Textile, Wearing Apparel and Accessories	14	3	4.34	0.15
皮革、毛皮、羽毛及其制品和制鞋业	Manufacture of Leather, Fur, Feather and Related Products and Footwear	3		1.59	0.01
木材加工和木、竹、藤、棕、草制品业	Processing of Timber, Manufacture of Wood, Bamboo, Rattan,Palm and Straw Products	11		6.27	0.06
家具制造业	Manufacture of Furniture	12	3	7.62	0.17
造纸和纸制品业	Manufacture of Paper and Paper Products	31	4	20.91	0.27
印刷和记录媒介复制业	Printing and Reproduction of Recording Media	22	5	14.98	0.25
文教、工美、体育和娱乐用品制造业	Manufacture of Articles for Culture, Education, Arts and Crafts,Sport and Entertainment Activities	17	6	10.76	0.22
石油、煤炭及其他燃料加工业	Processing of Petroleum, Coal and Other Fuels	10	2	29.52	0.12
化学原料和化学制品制造业	Manufacture of Raw Chemical Materials and Chemical Products	65	6	125.27	0.62
医药制造业	Manufacture of Medicines	33	5	21.45	0.27

12-6 续表 2 continued 2

指标	Indicator	企业单位数（个）Number of Industial Enterprises (unit)	亏损企业数（个）Loss Enterpriss (unit)	工业总产值（现价）(亿元) Gross Indutrial Output Value (Current Prices) (100 million yuan)	平均用工人数（万人）Average of Employed Persons (10 000 persons)
化学纤维制造业	Manufacture of Chemical Fibres	5	2	1.66	0.03
橡胶和塑料制品业	Manufacture of Rubber and Plastics Products	44	3	23.89	0.26
非金属矿物制品业	Manufacture of Non-metallic Mineral Products	200	29	227.15	1.73
黑色金属冶炼和压延加工业	Smelting and Pressing of Ferrous Metals	22	6	325.35	0.89
有色金属冶炼和压延加工业	Smelting and Pressing of Non-ferrous Metals	20	2	10.44	0.11
金属制品业	Manufacture of Metal Products	175	29	159.12	1.43
通用设备制造业	Manufacture of General Purpose Machinery	175	25	110.45	1.47
专用设备制造业	Manufacture of Special Purpose Machinery	137	20	150.48	1.45
汽车制造业	Manufacture of Automobiles	75	6	63.25	0.87
铁路、船舶、航空航天和其他运输设备制造业	Manufacture of Railway, Ship, Aerospace and Other Transport Equipments	6	1	11.69	0.14
电气机械和器材制造业	Manufacture of Electrical Machinery and Apparatus	74	12	62.57	0.42
计算机、通信和其他电子设备制造业	Manufacture of Computers, Communication and Other Electronic Equipment	31	7	23.70	0.33
仪器仪表制造业	Manufacture of Measuring Instruments and Machinery	48	3	30.65	0.42
其他制造业	Other Manufacture	3		0.93	0.02
废弃资源综合利用业	Utilization of Waste Resources	7	2	9.99	0.05
金属制品、机械和设备修理业	Repair Service of Metal Products, Machinery and Equipment	2	1	0.45	
电力、热力生产和供应业	Production and Supply of Electric Power and Heat Power	3	1	2.01	0.03
燃气生产和供应业	Production and Supply of Gas	5		4.99	0.02
水的生产和供应业	Production and Supply of Water	2		1.40	0.01

12-7 规模以上工业资产实力(2020 年)

Capital Power of Industrial Enterprises Above Designated Size(2020)

单位：亿元

指标	Indicator	流动资产合计 Total Current Assets	其中 of which 应收账款 Receivable	存货 Inventory
总计	Total	4708.38	1292.24	956.99
按登记注册类型分组	by Status of Registration			
内资企业	Domestic Funded Enterprises	3906.17	1175.64	812.02
国有企业	State-owned Enterprises	83.79	21.43	17.52
中央企业	Central Enterprises	9.97	3.84	1.29
地方企业	Local Enterprises	73.83	17.58	16.23
集体企业	Collective-owned Enterprises	3.71	1.60	1.03
股份合作企业	Cooperative Enterprises	2.03	0.50	0.43
联营企业	Joint Ownership Enterprises	0.27	0.20	0.02
国有联营企业	State Joint Ownership Enterprises			
集体联营企业	Collective Joint Ownership Enterprises	0.27	0.20	0.02
国有与集体联营企业	Joint State-collective Enterprises			
其他联营企业	Other Joint Ownership Enterprises			
有限责任公司	Limited Liability Corporations	1604.66	384.99	294.87
国有独资公司	State Sole Funded Corporations	291.20	64.84	50.59
其他有限责任公司	Other Limited Liability Corporations	1313.46	320.15	244.28
股份有限公司	Share-holding Corporations Ltd.	1008.09	206.42	271.33
私营企业	Private Enterprises	1202.51	560.34	226.71
私营独资企业	Private-funded Enterprises	5.40	2.82	0.99
私营合伙企业	Private Partnership Enterprises	0.21	0.07	0.05
私营有限责任公司	Private Limited Liability Corporations	1098.88	528.11	204.88
私营股份有限公司	Private Share-holding Corporations Ltd.	98.02	29.35	20.79
其他企业	Other Enterprises	1.12	0.17	0.12
港、澳、台商投资企业	Enterprises with Funds from Hong Kong,Macao and Taiwan	593.60	69.53	95.96
合资经营企业(港或澳、台资)	Joint-venture Enterprises	236.32	36.38	30.02
合作经营企业(港或澳、台资)	Cooperative Enterprises	5.14	0.39	1.23
港澳台商独资经营企业	Enterprises with Sole Investment	352.14	32.76	64.71
港澳台商投资股份有限公司	Share-holding Corporations Ltd.			
其他港澳台商投资企业	Other Enterprises with Funds from Hong Kong,Macao and Taiwan			
外商投资企业	Foreign Funded Enterprises	208.61	47.07	49.00
中外合资经营企业	Joint-venture Enterprises	70.35	21.10	19.40
中外合作经营企业	Cooperation Enterprises	2.48	0.32	0.88
外资企业	Enterprises with Sole Fund	84.73	21.74	19.60
外商投资股份有限公司	Share-holding Corporations Ltd. with Foreign Investment	51.04	3.91	9.12
其他外商投资企业	Other Foreign Funded Enterprises			
按轻重工业分	by Light & Heavy Industry			
轻工业	Light Industry	812.53	173.99	149.08
重工业	Heavy Industry	3895.85	1118.25	807.91
按企业规模分	by Enterprise Size			
大型企业	Large-sized Enterprises	2213.88	385.61	482.55
中型企业	Medium-sized Enterprises	1013.19	367.11	199.42
小型企业	Small-sized Enterprises	1351.94	475.15	261.33
微型企业	Micro-sized Enterprises	129.38	64.38	13.70

(100 million yuan)

固定资产净额 Net Fixed Assets	固定资产原价 Original Value of Fixed Assets	流动负债合计 Current Liabilities Total	非流动负债合计 Non-Current Liabilities Total	所有者权益合计 Total Owner's Equities	其中 of which: 实收资本 Paid- up Capital	其中 of which: 国家资本 Official Capital
1648.60	**3085.85**	**4101.63**	**636.60**	**2967.31**	**1362.55**	**345.15**
1463.09	2692.57	3545.38	557.09	2354.05	1064.36	333.81
39.05	65.38	90.82	30.47	29.35	18.14	8.97
15.05	15.98	9.88	10.71	8.18	6.48	2.61
24.01	49.40	80.94	19.75	21.17	11.66	6.37
2.60	4.93	2.26	1.19	3.00	0.42	
0.45	0.86	1.06	0.06	1.70	0.16	
0.40	0.91	0.28	0.08	0.37	0.02	
0.40	0.91	0.28	0.08	0.37	0.02	
942.44	1589.92	1585.91	328.14	1204.66	582.78	221.03
181.56	286.00	277.48	97.89	230.33	98.76	55.72
760.88	1303.92	1308.43	230.25	974.33	484.02	165.31
238.67	537.81	784.77	78.18	626.31	192.62	99.74
239.32	492.53	1080.19	118.96	487.03	269.74	4.07
1.55	3.69	5.55	0.31	2.02	1.49	
0.11	0.28	0.20	0.11	0.05	0.04	
218.16	452.14	1012.98	106.66	399.74	236.49	3.95
19.50	36.43	61.46	11.88	85.21	31.72	0.12
0.16	0.21	0.10		1.63	0.48	
112.38	252.12	430.51	54.63	418.00	193.41	8.26
53.14	112.20	136.55	29.54	187.16	75.50	7.95
3.79	6.37	5.36	0.32	3.77	0.40	0.30
55.45	133.55	288.60	24.77	227.07	117.51	
73.13	141.17	125.74	24.89	195.26	104.78	3.08
22.00	51.87	55.29	3.83	45.01	44.27	2.44
0.62	1.67	0.88	0.01	2.29	1.08	0.64
41.68	72.92	43.10	16.29	95.74	47.57	
8.83	14.72	26.47	4.76	52.22	11.86	
242.56	452.04	550.04	53.21	705.86	258.99	10.23
1406.04	2633.81	3551.59	583.39	2261.45	1103.56	334.92
903.83	1683.78	2024.39	304.83	1463.66	548.53	194.30
323.47	612.75	839.74	107.43	643.74	245.09	81.35
372.31	691.69	1154.59	144.23	805.86	533.11	64.04
48.99	97.63	82.90	80.10	54.06	35.82	5.45

12-7 续表 continued

指标	Indicator	流动资产合计 Total Current Assets	其中 of which	
			应收账款 Receivable	存货 Inventory
按工业行业分	by Sector			
煤炭开采和洗选业	Mining and Washing of Coal	5.62	0.86	0.39
石油和天然气开采业	Extraction of Petroleum and Natural Gas	31.35	31.21	0.14
黑色金属矿采选业	Mining and Processing of Ferrous Metal Ores	40.01	2.80	3.20
有色金属矿采选业	Mining and Processing of Non-Ferrous Metal Ores			
非金属矿采选业	Mining and Processing of Non-metal Ores	10.10	1.44	2.34
开采专业及辅助性活动	Professional and Support Activities for Mining			
其他采矿业	Mining of Other Ores			
农副食品加工业	Processing of Food from Agricultural Products	50.37	17.22	14.27
食品制造业	Manufacture of Foods	51.23	5.41	13.87
酒、饮料和精制茶制造业	Manufacture of Liquor, Beverages and Refined Tea	48.54	3.18	8.49
烟草制品业	Manufacture of Tobacco	3.08	0.25	0.10
纺织业	Manufacture of Textile	27.23	6.63	7.97
纺织服装、服饰业	Manufacture of Textile, Wearing Apparel and Accessories	12.80	2.36	3.67
皮革、毛皮、羽毛及其制品和制鞋业	Manufacture of Leather, Fur, Feather and Related Products and Footwear	2.28	0.26	0.59
木材加工和木、竹、藤、棕、草制品业	Processing of Timber, Manufacture of Wood, Bamboo, Rattan,Palm and Straw Products	2.53	1.06	0.71
家具制造业	Manufacture of Furniture	5.46	1.58	1.34
造纸和纸制品业	Manufacture of Paper and Paper Products	23.92	6.55	8.55
印刷和记录媒介复制业	Printing and Reproduction of Recording Media	32.52	7.43	5.55
文教、工美、体育和娱乐用品制造业	Manufacture of Articles for Culture, Education, Arts and Crafts,Sport and Entertainment Activities	12.52	2.08	7.07
石油、煤炭及其他燃料加工业	Processing of Petroleum, Coal and Other Fuels	103.71	64.14	11.12
化学原料和化学制品制造业	Manufacture of Raw Chemical Materials and Chemical Products	200.65	32.46	30.74
医药制造业	Manufacture of Medicines	366.41	81.46	45.59
化学纤维制造业	Manufacture of Chemical Fibres	9.87	1.81	2.87
橡胶和塑料制品业	Manufacture of Rubber and Plastics Products	23.55	9.39	4.46
非金属矿物制品业	Manufacture of Non-metallic Mineral Products	373.05	181.74	45.59
黑色金属冶炼和压延加工业	Smelting and Pressing of Ferrous Metals	433.43	176.26	101.40
有色金属冶炼和压延加工业	Smelting and Pressing of Non-ferrous Metals	21.01	4.97	5.73
金属制品业	Manufacture of Metal Products	247.47	67.48	54.22
通用设备制造业	Manufacture of General Purpose Machinery	312.91	86.91	74.53
专用设备制造业	Manufacture of Special Purpose Machinery	262.30	74.24	64.82
汽车制造业	Manufacture of Automobiles	825.54	113.66	206.23
铁路、船舶、航空航天和其他运输设备制造业	Manufacture of Railway, Ship, Aerospace and Other Transport Equipments	65.04	20.57	9.65
电气机械和器材制造业	Manufacture of Electrical Machinery and Apparatus	344.05	113.38	79.65
计算机、通信和其他电子设备制造业	Manufacture of Computers, Communication and Other Electronic Equipment	401.94	104.44	108.81
仪器仪表制造业	Manufacture of Measuring Instruments and Machinery	76.31	24.98	14.64
其他制造业	Other Manufacture	2.68	1.92	0.46
废弃资源综合利用业	Utilization of Waste Resources	2.64	0.57	0.12
金属制品、机械和设备修理业	Repair Service of Metal Products, Machinery and Equipment	7.89	3.52	2.65
电力、热力生产和供应业	Production and Supply of Electric Power and Heat Power	171.63	21.47	9.77
燃气生产和供应业	Production and Supply of Gas	51.04	9.32	4.43
水的生产和供应业	Production and Supply of Water	45.67	7.23	1.27

固定资产净额 Net Fixed Assets	固定资产原价 Original Value of Fixed Assets	流动负债合计 Current Liabilities Total	非流动负债合计 Non-Current Liabilities Total	所有者权益合计 Total Owner's Equities	其中 of which 实收资本 Paid- up Capital	其中 of which 国家资本 Official Capital
3.14	7.14	17.47	0.02	-7.47	1.42	0.30
5.03	30.47	1.83	2.44	34.87	5.18	
33.51	66.97	47.99	9.59	40.39	30.86	2.40
6.44	7.92	14.68	1.19	7.53	5.43	0.64
10.43	18.43	50.04	8.49	12.64	10.51	0.41
49.01	81.41	42.57	4.19	67.86	35.30	0.37
21.81	50.88	33.57	2.28	55.77	45.82	0.37
0.99	1.47	1.24		2.89	0.95	0.95
11.34	20.37	29.11	2.84	13.57	6.84	0.69
7.66	13.15	11.47	1.82	12.15	4.65	
0.27	0.50	2.16		0.45	0.28	
1.34	2.11	3.76		0.83	0.51	
1.71	2.54	5.05	0.14	2.95	2.21	
6.83	19.75	22.15	4.53	12.87	8.68	1.44
17.60	36.35	25.25	2.42	32.68	17.70	1.55
3.99	5.74	12.30	0.30	5.97	4.07	
41.25	105.30	109.89	11.54	35.67	33.39	27.49
96.35	159.62	203.48	80.51	128.52	53.83	11.93
77.30	138.17	207.52	20.14	320.81	71.34	2.05
5.93	10.03	6.02	2.68	13.01	11.75	0.14
6.51	14.15	14.35	1.19	16.81	11.46	
87.41	171.34	298.70	27.57	179.40	61.86	7.95
398.50	783.97	586.23	40.67	292.87	178.73	118.89
3.61	7.58	19.05	0.21	8.94	3.26	0.88
63.33	116.28	214.38	16.23	145.75	59.63	2.74
88.77	152.64	201.30	15.61	230.37	109.32	8.17
37.53	62.28	188.07	62.69	142.22	56.90	2.97
81.83	200.05	721.98	19.20	330.81	143.07	17.06
11.55	32.33	47.22	22.08	48.41	31.85	2.40
65.50	114.40	294.42	15.28	212.86	112.28	38.90
27.09	45.91	246.99	18.66	221.29	51.66	9.25
10.24	19.89	43.56	1.43	51.36	29.81	4.64
0.60	0.74	1.90		1.43	1.09	
1.43	1.71	3.56	1.35	1.85	1.27	
2.79	6.27	4.66	0.09	6.83	2.37	1.22
288.16	469.95	256.61	156.61	188.75	111.14	65.65
31.18	44.93	50.59	15.53	56.76	18.90	1.79
40.61	63.14	60.52	67.10	36.65	27.26	11.91

12-8 规模以上国有及国有控股工业资产实力(2020年)
Capital Power of State-Owned and State-Controlled Industrial Enterprises Above Designated Size(2020)

单位：亿元

指标	Indicator	流动资产合计 Total Current Assets	其中 of which	
			应收账款 Receivable	存货 Inventory
总计	Total	1692.53	342.20	403.43
按登记注册类型分组	by Status of Registration			
内资企业	Domestic Funded Enterprises	1543.16	329.86	383.35
国有企业	State-owned Enterprises	83.79	21.43	17.52
中央企业	Central Enterprises	9.97	3.84	1.29
地方企业	Local Enterprises	73.83	17.58	16.23
集体企业	Collective-owned Enterprises			
股份合作企业	Cooperative Enterprises			
联营企业	Joint Ownership Enterprises			
有限责任公司	Limited Liability Corporations	706.95	173.92	135.58
国有独资公司	State Sole Funded Corporations	291.20	64.84	50.59
其他有限责任公司	Other Limited Liability Corporations	415.74	109.08	84.99
股份有限公司	Share-holding Corporations Ltd.	752.42	134.52	230.25
私营企业	Private Enterprises			
其他企业	Other Enterprises			
港、澳、台商投资企业	Enterprises with Funds from Hong Kong,Macao and Taiwan	123.01	5.98	12.77
合资经营企业(港或澳、台资)	Joint-venture Enterprises	117.86	5.59	11.54
合作经营企业(港或澳、台资)	Cooperative Enterprises	5.14	0.39	1.23
港澳台商独资经营企业	Enterprises with Sole Investment			
港澳台商投资股份有限公司	Share-holding Corporations Ltd.			
其他港澳台商投资企业	Other Enterprises with Funds from Hong Kong,Macao and Taiwan			
外商投资企业	Foreign Funded Enterprises	26.36	6.36	7.31
中外合资经营企业	Joint-venture Enterprises	24.16	6.10	6.51
中外合作经营企业	Cooperation Enterprises	2.20	0.26	0.79
外资企业	Enterprises with Sole Fund			
外商投资股份有限公司	Share-holding Corporations Ltd. with Foreign Investment			
其他外商投资企业	Other Foreign Funded Enterprises			
按轻重工业分	by Light & Heavy Industry			
轻工业	Light Industry	71.81	9.48	17.47
重工业	Heavy Industry	1620.72	332.72	385.96
按企业规模分	by Enterprise Size			
大型企业	Large-sized Enterprises	1115.45	154.31	275.89
中型企业	Medium-sized Enterprises	322.94	91.56	82.03
小型企业	Small-sized Enterprises	238.84	92.28	44.53
微型企业	Micro-sized Enterprises	15.31	4.05	0.98
按工业行业分	by Sector			
煤炭开采和洗选业	Mining and Washing of Coal			
石油和天然气开采业	Extraction of Petroleum and Natural Gas	28.23	28.10	0.14
黑色金属矿采选业	Mining and Processing of Ferrous Metal Ores	16.59	0.84	0.99

(100 million yuan)

固定资产净额 Net Fixed Assets	固定资产原价 Original Value of Fixed Assets	流动负债合计 Current Liabilities Total	非流动负债合计 Non-Current Liabilities Total	所有者权益合计 Total Owner's Equities	其中 of which 实收资本 Paid- up Capital	其中 of which 国家资本 Official Capital
854.14	1587.73	1701.30	347.42	1016.31	526.04	320.52
818.49	1519.30	1587.79	323.97	921.14	487.95	310.68
39.05	65.38	90.82	30.47	29.35	18.14	8.97
15.05	15.98	9.88	10.71	8.18	6.48	2.61
24.01	49.40	80.94	19.75	21.17	11.66	6.37
615.08	1034.38	850.01	246.16	532.39	352.53	205.84
181.56	286.00	277.48	97.89	230.33	98.76	55.72
433.52	748.38	572.53	148.27	302.05	253.77	150.12
164.35	419.54	646.96	47.35	359.40	117.28	95.88
29.46	53.81	91.25	20.85	81.15	30.04	7.18
25.67	47.44	85.89	20.53	77.37	29.63	6.88
3.79	6.37	5.36	0.32	3.77	0.40	0.30
6.20	14.62	22.26	2.60	14.02	8.05	2.66
5.61	13.05	21.41	2.60	12.02	7.04	2.02
0.58	1.57	0.85		2.00	1.02	0.64
26.26	50.82	53.60	15.22	51.82	27.29	9.53
827.88	1536.91	1647.70	332.21	964.49	498.75	310.99
584.56	1100.91	1141.80	201.65	661.89	304.99	190.98
167.94	288.66	350.79	77.14	174.17	117.60	74.43
77.65	161.47	184.67	47.36	173.75	94.13	51.30
23.98	36.68	24.05	21.27	6.49	9.32	3.81
4.40	28.44	1.76	1.78	30.75	4.48	
10.68	29.85	18.81	8.87	18.45	24.82	0.14

12-8 续表 continued

指标	Indicator	流动资产合计 Total Current Assets	其中 of which	
			应收账款 Receivable	存货 Inventory
有色金属矿采选业	Mining and Processing of Non-Ferrous Metal Ores			
非金属矿采选业	Mining and Processing of Non-metal Ores	2.66	0.13	0.09
开采专业及辅助性活动	Professional and Support Activities for Mining			
其他采矿业	Mining of Other Ores			
农副食品加工业	Processing of Food from Agricultural Products	4.04	0.11	1.73
食品制造业	Manufacture of Foods	5.05	0.79	1.34
酒、饮料和精制茶制造业	Manufacture of Liquor, Beverages and Refined Tea	12.20	0.93	2.75
烟草制品业	Manufacture of Tobacco	3.08	0.25	0.10
纺织业	Manufacture of Textile	1.81	0.55	0.62
纺织服装、服饰业	Manufacture of Textile, Wearing Apparel and Accessories	6.75	0.48	1.61
皮革、毛皮、羽毛及其制品和制鞋业	Manufacture of Leather, Fur, Feather and Related Products and Footwear			
木材加工和木、竹、藤、棕、草制品业	Processing of Timber, Manufacture of Wood, Bamboo, Rattan,Palm and Straw Products			
家具制造业	Manufacture of Furniture			
造纸和纸制品业	Manufacture of Paper and Paper Products	4.22	0.44	1.04
印刷和记录媒介复制业	Printing and Reproduction of Recording Media	6.51	1.56	1.07
文教、工美、体育和娱乐用品制造业	Manufacture of Articles for Culture, Education, Arts and Crafts,Sport and Entertainment Activities			
石油、煤炭及其他燃料加工业	Processing of Petroleum, Coal and Other Fuels	27.00	4.61	6.24
化学原料和化学制品制造业	Manufacture of Raw Chemical Materials and Chemical Products	24.79	2.74	5.11
医药制造业	Manufacture of Medicines	14.70	1.54	0.84
化学纤维制造业	Manufacture of Chemical Fibres	2.99	0.10	1.70
橡胶和塑料制品业	Manufacture of Rubber and Plastics Products			
非金属矿物制品业	Manufacture of Non-metallic Mineral Products	38.29	20.57	5.20
黑色金属冶炼和压延加工业	Smelting and Pressing of Ferrous Metals	116.19	1.09	30.25
有色金属冶炼和压延加工业	Smelting and Pressing of Non-ferrous Metals	8.73	2.22	1.75
金属制品业	Manufacture of Metal Products	26.88	3.73	11.04
通用设备制造业	Manufacture of General Purpose Machinery	114.32	27.49	20.86
专用设备制造业	Manufacture of Special Purpose Machinery	62.69	15.95	18.21
汽车制造业	Manufacture of Automobiles	438.81	52.31	131.55
铁路、船舶、航空航天和其他运输设备制造业	Manufacture of Railway, Ship, Aerospace and Other Transport Equipments	43.77	7.78	5.48
电气机械和器材制造业	Manufacture of Electrical Machinery and Apparatus	142.85	53.25	45.18
计算机、通信和其他电子设备制造业	Manufacture of Computers, Communication and Other Electronic Equipment	333.35	85.17	93.86
仪器仪表制造业	Manufacture of Measuring Instruments and Machinery	20.92	6.99	5.13
其他制造业	Other Manufacture	1.96	1.63	0.14
废弃资源综合利用业	Utilization of Waste Resources			
金属制品、机械和设备修理业	Repair Service of Metal Products, Machinery and Equipment	1.59	0.76	0.48
电力、热力生产和供应业	Production and Supply of Electric Power and Heat Power	112.42	11.28	5.89
燃气生产和供应业	Production and Supply of Gas	31.49	3.11	2.11
水的生产和供应业	Production and Supply of Water	37.65	5.69	0.93

固定资产净额 Net Fixed Assets	固定资产原价 Original Value of Fixed Assets	流动负债合计 Current Liabilities Total	非流动负债合计 Non-Current Liabilities Total	所有者权益合计 Total Owner's Equities	其中 of which	
					实收资本 Paid- up Capital	其中 of which 国家资本 Official Capital
4.08	4.33	7.15	1.07	4.76	3.85	0.64
0.48	0.83	0.82	4.08	-0.15	0.50	0.41
2.98	6.16	2.69	0.08	5.64	0.94	0.32
6.46	13.10	8.13	0.78	10.88	6.13	0.37
0.99	1.47	1.24		2.89	0.95	0.95
2.22	3.21	3.53	0.12	1.53	0.74	0.69
1.12	3.62	7.25	0.24	4.14	0.55	
1.16	2.18	3.27		2.83	1.82	1.44
3.72	9.82	4.43	0.40	6.57	5.35	1.06
33.83	88.94	36.07	5.78	27.97	27.49	27.49
25.39	43.01	30.27	37.60	-6.10	5.77	3.66
3.18	4.79	9.17	7.11	8.29	2.70	2.00
2.54	3.13	2.00	2.32	5.27	5.20	0.14
14.54	28.03	38.20	3.91	20.79	7.16	3.26
292.84	558.99	290.29	29.58	148.25	119.65	118.89
1.20	2.65	7.59		3.13	0.88	0.88
8.73	15.07	28.98	3.81	8.23	5.71	2.63
36.77	61.38	56.39	3.88	96.54	38.71	5.26
9.16	14.67	62.73	5.58	15.79	11.97	2.23
23.15	63.02	375.93	8.52	122.12	29.93	17.04
9.08	20.40	38.30	5.39	35.35	26.18	2.40
33.00	59.15	152.55	7.13	73.62	50.72	38.47
6.59	12.27	213.83	14.25	146.86	23.51	9.07
3.86	6.52	14.18	0.04	12.37	6.12	4.64
0.59	0.70	1.33		1.25	1.00	
0.34	0.73	0.82		1.15	0.20	0.16
250.89	410.01	198.06	124.94	144.88	85.93	63.72
21.32	30.55	32.48	14.85	41.29	13.08	0.67
38.87	60.69	53.08	55.32	20.97	13.99	11.91

12-9 规模以上工业损益及分配(2020年)

Profit，Loss and Distribution of Industrial Enterprises Above Designated Size(2020)

单位：亿元

指标	Indicator	营业收入 Business Revenue	营业成本 Business Cost	税金及附加 Taxes and Other Charges
总计	Total	7575.34	6401.83	101.20
按登记注册类型分组	by Status of Registration			
内资企业	Domestic Funded Enterprises	6368.32	5461.73	94.57
国有企业	State-owned Enterprises	101.72	86.37	1.05
中央企业	Central Enterprises	9.84	7.94	0.03
地方企业	Local Enterprises	91.89	78.44	1.01
集体企业	Collective-owned Enterprises	6.87	5.93	0.04
股份合作企业	Cooperative Enterprises	1.87	1.19	0.02
联营企业	Joint Ownership Enterprises	0.90	0.43	0.03
国有联营企业	State Joint Ownership Enterprises			
集体联营企业	Collective Joint Ownership Enterprises	0.90	0.43	0.03
国有与集体联营企业	Joint State-collective Enterprises			
其他联营企业	Other Joint Ownership Enterprises			
有限责任公司	Limited Liability Corporations	2291.69	1904.11	16.87
国有独资公司	State Sole Funded Corporations	215.88	194.15	1.89
其他有限责任公司	Other Limited Liability Corporations	2075.81	1709.96	14.99
股份有限公司	Share-holding Corporations Ltd.	2045.06	1789.54	69.09
私营企业	Private Enterprises	1919.64	1673.96	7.46
私营独资企业	Private-funded Enterprises	14.19	12.93	0.06
私营合伙企业	Private Partnership Enterprises	0.19	0.15	0.01
私营有限责任公司	Private Limited Liability Corporations	1777.23	1566.94	6.74
私营股份有限公司	Private Share-holding Corporations Ltd.	128.03	93.94	0.65
其他企业	Other Enterprises	0.57	0.20	0.01
港、澳、台商投资企业	Enterprises with Funds from Hong Kong,Macao and Taiwan	891.56	700.61	4.58
合资经营企业(港或澳、台资)	Joint-venture Enterprises	296.27	223.29	1.66
合作经营企业(港或澳、台资)	Cooperative Enterprises	16.58	11.80	0.11
港澳台商独资经营企业	Enterprises with Sole Investment	578.71	465.52	2.80
港澳台商投资股份有限公司	Share-holding Corporations Ltd.			
其他港澳台商投资企业	Other Enterprises with Funds from Hong Kong,Macao and Taiwan			
外商投资企业	Foreign Funded Enterprises	315.45	239.49	2.05
中外合资经营企业	Joint-venture Enterprises	98.13	78.13	0.65
中外合作经营企业	Cooperation Enterprises	2.65	1.89	0.02
外资企业	Enterprises with Sole Fund	134.68	100.63	0.96
外商投资股份有限公司	Share-holding Corporations Ltd. with Foreign Investment	79.99	58.85	0.42
其他外商投资企业	Other Foreign Funded Enterprises			
按轻重工业分	by Light & Heavy Industry			
轻工业	Light Industry	1020.61	710.84	7.88
重工业	Heavy Industry	6554.73	5691.00	93.31
按企业规模分	by Enterprise Size			
大型企业	Large-sized Enterprises	4446.53	3783.55	80.86
中型企业	Medium-sized Enterprises	1265.50	1044.16	8.85
小型企业	Small-sized Enterprises	1736.16	1463.24	10.77
微型企业	Micro-sized Enterprises	127.14	110.89	0.71

(100 million yuan)

销售费用 Selling Expenses	管理费用 Administrative Expenses	利息费用 Interest Expenses	利润总额 Total Profits	所得税费用 Income Tax Payable	亏损企业亏损总额 Total Loss of Loss Enterprises	利税总额 Total Profits and Taxes	应交增值税 Value-added Tax Payable
260.65	230.01	54.25	423.31	68.38	45.98	659.87	135.37
212.01	194.18	49.95	260.39	40.42	45.10	462.74	107.78
1.54	4.88	0.68	7.01	1.82	1.22	9.58	1.52
0.15	0.19	0.38	1.70	0.22		1.86	0.13
1.39	4.69	0.30	5.32	1.60	1.22	7.71	1.38
0.04	0.59	0.01	0.23	0.04	0.03	0.45	0.18
0.27	0.27	0.01	0.12	0.02		0.23	0.09
	0.07	0.01	0.36	0.09		0.47	0.08
	0.07	0.01	0.36	0.09		0.47	0.08
103.00	76.77	30.32	132.05	20.01	18.63	196.25	47.32
6.68	11.13	2.74	3.76	-1.97	4.27	7.93	2.28
96.32	65.64	27.58	128.29	21.98	14.36	188.32	45.04
51.11	44.42	9.13	52.24	9.16	14.66	146.77	25.44
55.98	67.12	9.79	68.23	9.27	10.55	108.79	33.10
0.44	0.39	0.03	0.25	0.04	0.03	0.61	0.29
0.02	0.03		-0.02		0.02	-0.01	
48.09	61.96	8.25	52.68	7.30	9.83	88.37	28.94
7.42	4.74	1.51	15.32	1.94	0.67	19.82	3.86
0.09	0.06		0.15	0.02		0.21	0.05
31.72	20.49	2.78	117.01	20.86	0.25	142.21	20.62
10.07	10.38	0.56	46.32	10.06	0.23	55.65	7.66
3.94	0.06		0.65	0.16		1.16	0.40
17.71	10.05	2.22	70.04	10.64	0.02	85.41	12.56
16.92	15.35	1.52	45.90	7.10	0.63	54.92	6.97
4.98	5.12	0.39	6.67	1.21	0.39	9.49	2.18
0.02	0.33		0.27	0.04		0.33	0.04
4.62	8.53	0.76	21.56	4.27	0.24	25.80	3.28
7.29	1.37	0.37	17.40	1.59		19.29	1.47
108.25	44.73	5.43	125.28	18.16	3.98	160.47	27.30
152.39	185.29	48.82	298.02	50.22	42.00	499.40	108.06
139.03	98.87	25.21	258.82	41.80	13.32	408.87	69.19
54.51	47.18	14.16	81.03	14.00	12.11	116.30	26.42
64.46	78.98	13.50	78.81	12.25	17.81	126.94	37.36
2.65	4.98	1.37	4.65	0.33	2.75	7.77	2.40

12-9 续表 continued

指标	Indicator	营业收入 Business Revenue	营业成本 Business Cost	税金及附加 Taxes and Other Charges
按工业行业分	by Sector			
煤炭开采和洗选业	Mining and Washing of Coal	5.67	4.60	0.26
石油和天然气开采业	Extraction of Petroleum and Natural Gas	5.64	4.91	0.47
黑色金属矿采选业	Mining and Processing of Ferrous Metal Ores	57.56	36.21	1.65
有色金属矿采选业	Mining and Processing of Non-Ferrous Metal Ores			
非金属矿采选业	Mining and Processing of Non-metal Ores	10.00	6.58	0.49
开采专业及辅助性活动	Professional and Support Activities for Mining			
其他采矿业	Mining of Other Ores			
农副食品加工业	Processing of Food from Agricultural Products	142.07	132.61	0.27
食品制造业	Manufacture of Foods	130.04	102.19	0.91
酒、饮料和精制茶制造业	Manufacture of Liquor, Beverages and Refined Tea	55.37	42.95	1.83
烟草制品业	Manufacture of Tobacco	1.23	0.66	0.01
纺织业	Manufacture of Textile	44.51	37.62	0.23
纺织服装、服饰业	Manufacture of Textile, Wearing Apparel and Accessories	13.64	10.96	0.18
皮革、毛皮、羽毛及其制品和制鞋业	Manufacture of Leather, Fur, Feather and Related Products and Footwear	2.54	2.33	0.01
木材加工和木、竹、藤、棕、草制品业	Processing of Timber, Manufacture of Wood, Bamboo, Rattan,Palm and Straw Products	6.97	6.24	0.02
家具制造业	Manufacture of Furniture	8.73	7.67	0.05
造纸和纸制品业	Manufacture of Paper and Paper Products	42.57	35.26	0.21
印刷和记录媒介复制业	Printing and Reproduction of Recording Media	40.42	33.18	0.30
文教、工美、体育和娱乐用品制造业	Manufacture of Articles for Culture, Education, Arts and Crafts,Sport and Entertainment Activities	13.68	11.21	0.11
石油、煤炭及其他燃料加工业	Processing of Petroleum, Coal and Other Fuels	305.49	226.78	64.38
化学原料和化学制品制造业	Manufacture of Raw Chemical Materials and Chemical Products	301.45	241.03	1.85
医药制造业	Manufacture of Medicines	294.47	120.09	2.61
化学纤维制造业	Manufacture of Chemical Fibres	13.19	10.01	0.12
橡胶和塑料制品业	Manufacture of Rubber and Plastics Products	31.36	26.81	0.16
非金属矿物制品业	Manufacture of Non-metallic Mineral Products	421.92	353.80	2.93
黑色金属冶炼和压延加工业	Smelting and Pressing of Ferrous Metals	1686.06	1618.04	4.68
有色金属冶炼和压延加工业	Smelting and Pressing of Non-ferrous Metals	27.09	24.89	0.07
金属制品业	Manufacture of Metal Products	413.03	354.91	1.90
通用设备制造业	Manufacture of General Purpose Machinery	318.06	248.15	2.13
专用设备制造业	Manufacture of Special Purpose Machinery	261.31	194.73	1.35
汽车制造业	Manufacture of Automobiles	1443.11	1239.44	4.79
铁路、船舶、航空航天和其他运输设备制造业	Manufacture of Railway, Ship, Aerospace and Other Transport Equipments	64.35	53.16	0.51
电气机械和器材制造业	Manufacture of Electrical Machinery and Apparatus	389.22	330.61	1.85
计算机、通信和其他电子设备制造业	Manufacture of Computers, Communication and Other Electronic Equipment	656.15	582.75	0.93
仪器仪表制造业	Manufacture of Measuring Instruments and Machinery	77.46	52.44	0.50
其他制造业	Other Manufacture	2.97	2.50	
废弃资源综合利用业	Utilization of Waste Resources	13.50	13.02	0.13
金属制品、机械和设备修理业	Repair Service of Metal Products, Machinery and Equipment	9.44	6.79	0.12
电力、热力生产和供应业	Production and Supply of Electric Power and Heat Power	168.59	147.32	1.81
燃气生产和供应业	Production and Supply of Gas	65.91	54.32	0.13
水的生产和供应业	Production and Supply of Water	30.58	25.04	1.26

销售费用 Selling Expenses	管理费用 Administrative Expenses	利息费用 Interest Expenses	利润总额 Total Profits	所得税费用 Income Tax Payable	亏损企业亏损总额 Total Loss of Loss Enterprises	利税总额 Total Profits and Taxes	应交增值税 Value-added Tax Payable
0.07	0.81	0.09	-0.20		0.22	0.34	0.29
	0.35	0.03	-0.12	-0.09	0.41	0.77	0.42
0.26	9.25	1.12	5.43	1.90	1.33	10.77	3.69
0.45	0.93	0.03	1.22	0.32	0.03	2.05	0.33
3.68	2.37	0.50	1.33	0.26	0.57	3.13	1.53
7.42	5.36	0.37	13.56	2.83	0.37	17.60	3.14
4.88	1.72	0.68	3.64	0.99	0.46	7.13	1.67
	0.18		1.08	0.16		1.20	0.11
1.11	1.47	0.44	2.52	0.24	0.23	3.37	0.62
1.31	1.17	0.10	0.03	0.04	0.17	0.38	0.17
0.01	0.07		0.07			0.12	0.04
0.25	0.11	0.10	0.11			0.21	0.07
0.45	0.40	0.02	0.12	0.03	0.08	0.36	0.19
1.69	1.94	0.37	2.10	0.41	0.12	3.03	0.72
1.52	2.38	0.23	3.66	0.34	0.25	4.98	1.02
1.05	0.73	0.28	0.19	0.04	0.11	0.58	0.28
0.71	6.31	0.90	5.64	1.38	1.41	81.93	11.91
13.37	9.62	6.83	22.96	3.25	1.91	31.31	6.50
64.65	17.50	1.79	71.85	10.09	0.26	86.55	12.08
0.27	0.57	0.08	1.01	0.15	0.28	1.04	-0.08
1.18	1.34	0.25	1.05	0.11	0.18	1.90	0.69
17.75	18.28	3.27	23.06	4.15	1.74	38.31	12.32
7.32	21.39	10.28	11.92	1.89	6.08	32.55	15.95
0.30	1.37	0.11	0.40	0.10	0.19	0.73	0.25
9.85	10.51	3.90	23.40	3.58	3.55	33.42	8.12
18.44	20.69	1.58	24.11	1.59	4.49	34.77	8.54
15.36	14.30	2.37	21.83	2.68	2.60	28.52	5.34
42.01	23.89	4.33	115.25	20.87	1.12	140.85	20.81
1.80	5.17	0.12	4.59	0.72	0.31	6.18	1.08
17.90	13.76	2.54	21.30	2.20	3.44	28.76	5.61
14.36	17.32	2.17	12.21	2.24	8.03	16.77	3.63
6.13	5.20	0.19	9.09	1.14	0.11	12.01	2.42
0.04	0.11		0.24	0.04		0.28	0.03
0.03	0.21	0.01	0.39	0.06	0.13	1.56	1.03
0.08	1.79	0.08	0.44	0.07		0.91	0.34
1.08	6.80	7.38	7.99	2.71	5.22	13.16	3.36
2.52	2.15	0.27	7.56	1.45	0.05	7.92	0.22
1.32	2.47	1.42	2.28	0.43	0.53	4.44	0.90

12-10 规模以上国有及国有控股工业损益及分配（2020 年）
Profit, Loss and Distribution of State-Owned and State-Controlled Industrial Enterprises Above Designated Size(2020)

单位：亿元

指标	Indicator	营业收入 Business Revenue	营业成本 Business Cost	税金及附加 Taxes and Other Charges
总计	Total	3177.24	2796.92	78.60
按登记注册类型分组	by Status of Registration			
内资企业	Domestic Funded Enterprises	2962.02	2628.21	77.65
国有企业	State-owned Enterprises	101.72	86.37	1.05
中央企业	Central Enterprises	9.84	7.94	0.03
地方企业	Local Enterprises	91.89	78.44	1.01
集体企业	Collective-owned Enterprises			
股份合作企业	Cooperative Enterprises			
联营企业	Joint Ownership Enterprises			
有限责任公司	Limited Liability Corporations	1033.52	903.32	9.25
国有独资公司	State Sole Funded Corporations	215.88	194.15	1.89
其他有限责任公司	Other Limited Liability Corporations	817.64	709.16	7.36
股份有限公司	Share-holding Corporations Ltd.	1826.78	1638.52	67.35
私营企业	Private Enterprises			
其他企业	Other Enterprises			
港、澳、台商投资企业	Enterprises with Funds from Hong Kong,Macao and Taiwan	175.34	135.75	0.70
合资经营企业（港或澳、台资）	Joint-venture Enterprises	158.75	123.95	0.59
合作经营企业（港或澳、台资）	Cooperative Enterprises	16.58	11.80	0.11
港澳台商独资经营企业	Enterprises with Sole Investment			
港澳台商投资股份有限公司	Share-holding Corporations Ltd.			
其他港澳台商投资企业	Other Enterprises with Funds from Hong Kong,Macao and Taiwan			
外商投资企业	Foreign Funded Enterprises	39.88	32.95	0.26
中外合资经营企业	Joint-venture Enterprises	37.53	31.27	0.24
中外合作经营企业	Cooperation Enterprises	2.35	1.69	0.02
外资企业	Enterprises with Sole Fund			
外商投资股份有限公司	Share-holding Corporations Ltd. with Foreign Investment			
其他外商投资企业	Other Foreign Funded Enterprises			
按轻重工业分	by Light & Heavy Industry			
轻工业	Light Industry	80.15	57.68	1.56
重工业	Heavy Industry	3097.09	2739.23	77.05
按企业规模分	by Enterprise Size			
大型企业	Large-sized Enterprises	2536.55	2260.08	71.94
中型企业	Medium-sized Enterprises	368.86	301.18	3.92
小型企业	Small-sized Enterprises	258.07	223.12	2.65
微型企业	Micro-sized Enterprises	13.76	12.54	0.08
按工业行业分	by Sector			
煤炭开采和洗选业	Mining and Washing of Coal			
石油和天然气开采业	Extraction of Petroleum and Natural Gas	4.58	4.13	0.36
黑色金属矿采选业	Mining and Processing of Ferrous Metal Ores	21.50	11.88	0.77

(100 million yuan)

销售 费用 Selling Expenses	管理 费用 Administrative Expenses	利息 费用 Interest Expenses	利润 总额 Total Profits	所得税 费用 Income Tax Payable	亏损企业 亏损总额 Total Loss of Loss Enterprises	利税 总额 Total Profits and Taxes	应交 增值税 Value-added Tax Payable
70.64	69.99	27.48	102.26	18.51	17.16	227.27	46.40
59.49	64.81	27.16	76.56	12.05	17.16	196.10	41.89
1.54	4.88	0.68	7.01	1.82	1.22	9.58	1.52
0.15	0.19	0.38	1.70	0.22		1.86	0.13
1.39	4.69	0.30	5.32	1.60	1.22	7.71	1.38
26.77	36.57	19.50	34.58	4.06	10.82	64.82	20.99
6.68	11.13	2.74	3.76	−1.97	4.27	7.93	2.28
20.10	25.44	16.76	30.82	6.04	6.56	56.90	18.71
31.18	23.36	6.98	34.96	6.16	5.11	121.70	19.39
9.66	2.87	0.27	23.19	5.91		27.53	3.64
5.72	2.80	0.27	22.54	5.75		26.37	3.24
3.94	0.06		0.65	0.16		1.16	0.40
1.49	2.31	0.05	2.51	0.56		3.63	0.86
1.48	2.03	0.05	2.27	0.52		3.34	0.83
0.02	0.28		0.24	0.03		0.29	0.03
12.16	3.90	0.54	4.94	0.76	0.74	8.48	1.98
58.49	66.09	26.93	97.32	17.75	16.42	218.79	44.42
45.68	45.19	16.76	73.02	12.62	10.36	177.70	32.74
18.15	12.77	7.72	18.20	3.87	2.00	30.54	8.42
6.71	11.34	2.49	11.09	1.87	3.63	18.83	5.09
0.10	0.68	0.51	−0.05	0.16	1.17	0.20	0.16
	0.29	0.03	−0.23	−0.10	0.41	0.48	0.35
0.08	6.40	0.39	−1.31	0.21	1.32	1.11	1.66

12-10 续表 continued

指标	Indicator	营业收入 Business Revenue	营业成本 Business Cost	税金及附加 Taxes and Other Charges
有色金属矿采选业	Mining and Processing of Non-Ferrous Metal Ores			
非金属矿采选业	Mining and Processing of Non-metal Ores	3.11	1.48	0.27
开采专业及辅助性活动	Professional and Support Activities for Mining			
其他采矿业	Mining of Other Ores			
农副食品加工业	Processing of Food from Agricultural Products	1.54	1.31	0.01
食品制造业	Manufacture of Foods	9.47	7.69	0.06
酒、饮料和精制茶制造业	Manufacture of Liquor, Beverages and Refined Tea	25.58	18.29	1.09
烟草制品业	Manufacture of Tobacco	1.23	0.66	0.01
纺织业	Manufacture of Textile	2.30	2.18	0.02
纺织服装、服饰业	Manufacture of Textile, Wearing Apparel and Accessories	2.73	2.22	0.03
皮革、毛皮、羽毛及其制品和制鞋业	Manufacture of Leather, Fur, Feather and Related Products and Footwear			
木材加工和木、竹、藤、棕、草制品业	Processing of Timber, Manufacture of Wood, Bamboo, Rattan,Palm and Straw Products			
家具制造业	Manufacture of Furniture			
造纸和纸制品业	Manufacture of Paper and Paper Products	4.26	3.47	0.02
印刷和记录媒介复制业	Printing and Reproduction of Recording Media	6.69	5.27	0.09
文教、工美、体育和娱乐用品制造业	Manufacture of Articles for Culture, Education, Arts and Crafts,Sport and Entertainment Activities			
石油、煤炭及其他燃料加工业	Processing of Petroleum, Coal and Other Fuels	205.61	131.12	64.03
化学原料和化学制品制造业	Manufacture of Raw Chemical Materials and Chemical Products	35.58	26.28	0.40
医药制造业	Manufacture of Medicines	6.89	3.25	0.11
化学纤维制造业	Manufacture of Chemical Fibres	3.97	3.63	0.04
橡胶和塑料制品业	Manufacture of Rubber and Plastics Products			
非金属矿物制品业	Manufacture of Non-metallic Mineral Products	52.05	41.79	0.58
黑色金属冶炼和压延加工业	Smelting and Pressing of Ferrous Metals	764.58	734.55	2.89
有色金属冶炼和压延加工业	Smelting and Pressing of Non-ferrous Metals	12.53	11.56	0.03
金属制品业	Manufacture of Metal Products	53.26	47.98	0.26
通用设备制造业	Manufacture of General Purpose Machinery	69.65	54.63	0.62
专用设备制造业	Manufacture of Special Purpose Machinery	35.52	29.28	0.20
汽车制造业	Manufacture of Automobiles	812.36	727.41	1.93
铁路、船舶、航空航天和其他运输设备制造业	Manufacture of Railway, Ship, Aerospace and Other Transport Equipments	44.57	36.55	0.39
电气机械和器材制造业	Manufacture of Electrical Machinery and Apparatus	164.66	148.33	0.83
计算机、通信和其他电子设备制造业	Manufacture of Computers, Communication and Other Electronic Equipment	601.63	542.95	0.59
仪器仪表制造业	Manufacture of Measuring Instruments and Machinery	22.89	16.70	0.15
其他制造业	Other Manufacture	2.17	1.81	
废弃资源综合利用业	Utilization of Waste Resources			
金属制品、机械和设备修理业	Repair Service of Metal Products, Machinery and Equipment	1.31	0.99	0.01
电力、热力生产和供应业	Production and Supply of Electric Power and Heat Power	145.37	128.99	1.65
燃气生产和供应业	Production and Supply of Gas	37.72	30.99	0.06
水的生产和供应业	Production and Supply of Water	21.91	19.55	1.10

销售费用 Selling Expenses	管理费用 Administrative Expenses	利息费用 Interest Expenses	利润总额 Total Profits	所得税费用 Income Tax Payable	亏损企业亏损总额 Total Loss of Loss Enterprises	利税总额 Total Profits and Taxes	应交增值税 Value-added Tax Payable
0.02	0.42	0.02	0.64	0.15		1.03	0.12
0.13	0.15	0.02	-0.04	0.01	0.06		0.03
0.61	0.36	0.01	0.54	0.01	0.10	0.67	0.07
4.25	0.50	0.07	1.43	0.36		3.34	0.82
	0.18		1.08	0.16		1.20	0.11
0.03	0.11	0.01	-0.04		0.04	0.01	0.03
0.13	0.44	0.01	-0.07		0.07	-0.18	-0.14
0.08	0.34		0.25	0.03		0.31	0.03
0.33	0.64	0.02	0.49	0.10	0.10	0.86	0.28
0.20	5.01	0.40	4.90	1.15		79.09	10.16
4.26	1.72	3.03	-0.89	0.15	1.77	0.52	1.01
2.57	0.58	0.39	0.88	0.04		1.42	0.43
0.05	0.08		0.07	-0.01		-0.02	-0.13
2.55	2.51	0.42	4.86	0.86	0.14	7.33	1.89
4.38	7.79	8.60	1.18	-0.29	4.75	12.94	8.87
0.05	0.90		0.04	0.01		0.10	0.03
1.03	1.11	0.79	0.56	0.17	0.64	1.50	0.67
3.56	4.40	0.18	5.17	-2.25		8.16	2.37
1.12	1.78	1.49	0.41	0.13	0.73	0.83	0.22
23.16	8.62	1.93	47.99	11.21	0.02	57.42	7.50
1.43	3.70	0.06	3.97	0.54		5.14	0.78
4.86	4.98	1.09	1.44	0.26	1.97	4.37	2.10
10.61	6.88	1.61	16.00	1.90	0.20	19.03	2.45
1.36	1.11	0.03	2.62	0.30		3.43	0.65
0.01	0.07		0.21	0.04		0.24	0.03
0.01	0.07	0.02	0.12	0.01		0.21	0.07
0.35	5.39	5.68	5.91	2.36	4.30	10.75	3.18
2.09	1.39	0.19	4.08	0.91	0.02	4.19	0.04
1.32	2.06	0.99	-0.02	0.10	0.53	1.82	0.73

12-11 分地区规模以上工业主要经济指标(2020年)

Main Economic Indicators of Industrial Enterprises Above Designated Size by Region(2020)

单位：亿元

指标	Indicator	全市 Total	历下区 Li xia	市中区 Shi zhong	槐荫区 Huai yin	天桥区 Tian qiao
企业单位数（个）	Number of Industial Enterprises(unit)	2215	44	52	70	109
工业总产值	Gross Industrial Output Value	6765.08	289.94	535.99	182.29	129.28
资产与负债	Assets and Liabilities					
资产总计	Total Assets	7724.85	366.03	513.87	294.60	266.11
流动资产合计	Total Fixed Assets	4708.38	152.86	393.76	208.02	126.07
存货	Inventory	956.99	19.81	117.11	34.89	21.06
应收账款	Receivable	1292.24	31.54	92.81	42.43	34.04
固定资产净额	Net Value of Fixed Assets	1648.60	113.13	39.59	29.69	84.94
流动负债合计	Current Liabilities Total	4101.63	183.76	328.86	123.91	138.69
非流动负债合计	Non-Current Liabilities Total	636.60	51.59	49.44	11.97	65.79
所有者权益合计	Total Owner's Equities	2967.31	130.67	135.57	158.73	61.63
实收资本	Paid- up Capital	1362.55	61.60	39.29	47.01	44.52
国家资本	Official Capital	345.15	42.00	23.38	6.07	13.83
损益及分配	Profit,Loss and Distribution					
营业收入	Business Revenue	7575.34	290.70	632.46	182.82	134.12
营业成本	Business Cost	6401.83	203.33	575.46	151.10	115.21
税金及附加	Taxes and Other Charges	101.20	64.53	1.76	0.92	0.79
管理费用	Cost of Management	230.01	10.62	9.44	15.00	8.49
利润总额	Total Profits	423.31	8.55	21.53	9.02	1.34
应交所得税	Income Tax Payable	68.38	2.13	4.07	1.74	0.77
亏损企业亏损总额	Total Loss of Loss Enterprises	45.98	3.37	0.07	6.78	4.19
利税总额	Total Profits and Taxes	659.87	83.52	27.28	13.12	4.60
本年应交增值税	Value-added Tax Payable	135.37	10.44	3.99	3.18	2.47

(100million yuan)

历城区 Li cheng	长清区 Chang qing	章丘区 Zhang qiu	济阳区 Ji yang	莱芜区 Lai wu	钢城区 Gang cheng	平阴县 Ping yin	商河县 Shang he	济南高新区 Ji nan gao xin	济南先行区 JN Pioneer Area	南部山区 Nan shan
146	181	509	119	270	109	118	138	303	32	15
273.21	249.31	1363.62	152.03	926.09	799.70	283.19	132.97	1393.92	43.14	10.41
471.68	339.91	1370.31	211.13	1084.73	666.67	364.06	155.29	1560.11	39.90	20.46
301.89	218.99	827.95	133.33	672.34	221.72	218.68	93.41	1105.79	19.38	14.19
43.89	47.87	160.63	24.42	123.48	60.01	41.54	21.49	233.24	3.01	4.52
101.47	73.39	160.49	48.73	310.58	23.91	44.60	29.74	284.26	11.00	3.25
74.44	76.16	255.00	47.66	286.48	345.69	83.58	40.68	162.20	7.48	1.88
243.93	163.54	731.37	77.31	697.28	398.78	128.66	80.90	772.71	17.76	14.17
39.45	34.94	90.93	18.39	90.46	34.54	22.96	14.27	106.52	4.21	1.16
176.52	141.43	545.58	114.71	296.98	233.35	212.45	60.13	676.49	17.93	5.13
103.02	80.31	260.59	46.35	215.58	157.92	52.50	36.39	204.54	11.00	1.92
8.14	8.46	29.99	3.87	29.00	129.79	6.10	2.36	42.14	0.02	
294.84	273.40	1396.02	148.48	1414.19	932.33	279.84	133.48	1407.44	44.47	10.74
229.20	225.78	1132.91	116.72	1308.07	874.49	217.35	116.33	1092.46	35.24	8.17
1.83	1.60	8.58	1.34	5.67	4.18	2.13	0.78	6.30	0.33	0.43
15.24	12.71	36.43	8.90	33.23	13.53	10.99	5.07	47.88	1.71	0.79
26.28	16.84	126.37	13.35	27.46	15.64	30.00	4.26	117.74	4.50	0.43
4.14	–0.25	18.92	2.91	6.49	1.73	4.96	0.39	19.36	0.94	0.07
2.33	1.52	3.09	0.96	8.77	5.83	1.08	1.15	6.65	0.06	0.13
36.11	25.16	166.92	18.39	51.60	32.55	40.40	6.91	146.04	6.18	1.09
8.00	6.71	31.97	3.70	18.47	12.72	8.27	1.86	22.00	1.34	0.24

12-12 规模以上大中型工业企业经营情况(2020年)
Main Indicators of Large and Medium-Sized Enterprises(2020)

单位：亿元

指标	Indicator	企业单位数（个）Number of Industial Enterprises (unit)	亏损企业（个）Loss Nterprises (unit)	工业总产值（现价）Gross Industrial Output Value (Current Prices)
总计	Total	232	34	5023.29
按登记注册类型分组	by Status of Registration			
内资企业	Domestic Funded Enterprises	185	31	3949.91
国有企业	State-owned Enterprises	4		71.62
中央企业	Central Enterprises			
地方企业	Local Enterprises	4		71.62
集体企业	Collective-owned Enterprises			
股份合作企业	Cooperative Enterprises	1		0.76
联营企业	Joint Ownership Enterprises			
有限责任公司	Limited Liability Corporations	98	20	1481.61
国有独资公司	State Sole Funded Corporations	13	5	115.58
其他有限责任公司	Other Limited Liability Corporations	85	15	1366.03
股份有限公司	Share-holding Corporations Ltd.	30	5	1770.77
私营企业	Private Enterprises	52	6	625.14
私营独资企业	Private-funded Enterprises			
私营合伙企业	Private Partnership Enterprises			
私营有限责任公司	Private Limited Liability Corporations	48	6	557.86
私营股份有限公司	Private Share-holding Corporations Ltd.	4		67.29
其他企业	Other Enterprises			
港、澳、台商投资企业	Enterprises with Funds from Hong Kong,Macao and Taiwan	22		831.93
合资经营企业（港或澳、台资）	Joint-venture Enterprises	12		250.68
合作经营企业（港或澳、台资）	Cooperative Enterprises	1		12.81
港澳台商独资经营企业	Enterprises with Sole Investment	9		568.44
港澳台商投资股份有限公司	Share-holding Corporations Ltd.			
其他港澳台商投资企业	Other Enterprises with Funds from Hong Kong,Macao and Taiwan			
外商投资企业	Foreign Funded Enterprises	25	3	241.45
中外合资经营企业	Joint-venture Enterprises	11	1	71.21
中外合作经营企业	Cooperation Enterprises			
外资企业	Enterprises with Sole Fund	12	2	88.39
外商投资股份有限公司	Share-holding Corporations Ltd. with Foreign Investment	2		81.85
其他外商投资企业	Other Foreign Funded Enterprises			
按轻重工业分	by Light & Heavy Industry			
轻工业	Light Industry	67	8	614.95
重工业	Heavy Industry	165	26	4408.34
按企业规模分	by Enterprise Size			
大型企业	Large-sized Enterprises	60	8	3863.16
中型企业	Medium-sized Enterprises	172	26	1160.13
小型企业	Small-sized Enterprises			
微型企业	Micro-sized Enterprises			
按工业行业分	by Sector			
煤炭开采和洗选业	Mining and Washing of Coal	2	1	4.97

(100 million yuan)

资产总计 Total Assets	负债合计 Total Liabilities	营业收入 Business Revenue	利润总额 Total Profits	利税总额 Total Profits and Taxes	平均用工人数（万人）Average of Employed Persons (10 000 persons)
5383.79	**3276.40**	**5712.04**	**339.84**	**525.17**	**23.97**
4335.99	2735.12	4655.34	194.47	350.69	19.11
54.44	43.64	65.41	5.96	7.76	0.33
54.44	43.64	65.41	5.96	7.76	0.33
1.72	0.73	0.83	0.01	0.07	0.03
2311.25	1438.15	1784.73	109.31	158.09	10.42
514.14	319.95	159.81	1.04	3.89	1.70
1797.11	1118.19	1624.91	108.27	154.20	8.72
1321.61	778.64	1951.74	44.03	136.05	4.53
646.98	473.96	852.64	35.15	48.72	3.79
580.30	444.28	789.17	23.93	35.15	3.56
66.68	29.67	63.47	11.22	13.57	0.23
799.51	438.10	817.94	108.33	131.02	3.26
310.80	145.11	251.07	42.54	50.12	1.50
9.45	5.68	16.58	0.65	1.16	0.12
479.26	287.31	550.28	65.14	79.74	1.63
248.29	103.17	238.76	37.05	43.46	1.60
72.07	43.31	72.87	4.42	6.39	0.72
94.28	29.10	86.78	15.48	18.07	0.74
81.93	30.76	79.10	17.15	19.00	0.14
864.71	364.29	619.29	103.03	127.36	6.24
4519.08	2912.11	5092.75	236.81	397.81	17.73
3792.88	2329.22	4446.53	258.82	408.87	15.31
1590.91	947.17	1265.50	81.03	116.30	8.65
9.71	17.30	4.98	-0.20	0.33	0.28

12-12 续表 continued

指标	Indicator	企业单位数（个）Number of Industial Enterprises (unit)	亏损企业（个）Loss Nterprises (unit)	工业总产值（现价）Gross Industrial Output Value (Current Prices)
石油和天然气开采业	Extraction of Petroleum and Natural Gas			
黑色金属矿采选业	Mining and Processing of Ferrous Metal Ores	4	1	43.48
有色金属矿采选业	Mining and Processing of Non-Ferrous Metal Ores			
非金属矿采选业	Mining and Processing of Non-metal Ores	1		1.74
开采专业及辅助性活动	Professional and Support Activities for Mining			
其他采矿业	Mining of Other Ores			
农副食品加工业	Processing of Food from Agricultural Products	6	2	35.57
食品制造业	Manufacture of Foods	10		90.30
酒、饮料和精制茶制造业	Manufacture of Liquor, Beverages and Refined Tea	6	1	39.58
烟草制品业	Manufacture of Tobacco			
纺织业	Manufacture of Textile	3		11.67
纺织服装、服饰业	Manufacture of Textile, Wearing Apparel and Accessories	5	3	6.14
皮革、毛皮、羽毛及其制品和制鞋业	Manufacture of Leather, Fur, Feather and Related Products and Footwear			
木材加工和木、竹、藤、棕、草制品业	Processing of Timber, Manufacture of Wood, Bamboo, Rattan,Palm and Straw Products			
家具制造业	Manufacture of Furniture	2	1	4.37
造纸和纸制品业	Manufacture of Paper and Paper Products	3		11.52
印刷和记录媒介复制业	Printing and Reproduction of Recording Media	3		8.36
文教、工美、体育和娱乐用品制造业	Manufacture of Articles for Culture, Education, Arts and Crafts,Sport and Entertainment Activities	1		1.71
石油、煤炭及其他燃料加工业	Processing of Petroleum, Coal and Other Fuels	3	1	244.33
化学原料和化学制品制造业	Manufacture of Raw Chemical Materials and Chemical Products	8	1	143.35
医药制造业	Manufacture of Medicines	16		259.04
化学纤维制造业	Manufacture of Chemical Fibres			
橡胶和塑料制品业	Manufacture of Rubber and Plastics Products	1	1	1.75
非金属矿物制品业	Manufacture of Non-metallic Mineral Products	24	1	178.40
黑色金属冶炼和压延加工业	Smelting and Pressing of Ferrous Metals	9	3	1176.96
有色金属冶炼和压延加工业	Smelting and Pressing of Non-ferrous Metals	1		3.62
金属制品业	Manufacture of Metal Products	14	2	121.69
通用设备制造业	Manufacture of General Purpose Machinery	20	4	167.70
专用设备制造业	Manufacture of Special Purpose Machinery	16	3	111.80
汽车制造业	Manufacture of Automobiles	20	1	1304.14
铁路、船舶、航空航天和其他运输设备制造业	Manufacture of Railway, Ship, Aerospace and Other Transport Equipments	6		47.23
电气机械和器材制造业	Manufacture of Electrical Machinery and Apparatus	21	3	226.23
计算机、通信和其他电子设备制造业	Manufacture of Computers, Communication and Other Electronic Equipment	10	2	592.40
仪器仪表制造业	Manufacture of Measuring Instruments and Machinery	4		16.06
其他制造业	Other Manufacture			
废弃资源综合利用业	Utilization of Waste Resources			
金属制品、机械和设备修理业	Repair Service of Metal Products, Machinery and Equipment	1		6.84
电力、热力生产和供应业	Production and Supply of Electric Power and Heat Power	7	3	125.29
燃气生产和供应业	Production and Supply of Gas	3		27.09
水的生产和供应业	Production and Supply of Water	2		9.96

资产总计 Total Assets	负债合计 Total Liabilities	营业收入 Business Revenue	利润总额 Total Profits	利税总额 Total Profits and Taxes	平均用工人数（万人） Average of Employed Persons (10 000 persons)
86.51	49.63	44.77	4.57	9.41	0.77
10.73	7.28	1.79	0.54	0.73	0.04
18.21	16.54	41.84	0.17	0.54	0.28
73.39	23.70	90.73	11.92	14.94	1.13
36.27	19.11	40.96	2.66	5.49	0.39
13.38	9.06	14.67	0.05	0.40	0.16
18.72	10.68	8.59		0.19	0.44
3.90	3.11	4.50	0.05	0.18	0.09
13.39	9.20	13.85	1.33	1.79	0.12
9.97	5.22	8.50	0.74	0.88	0.16
6.28	5.54	1.61	0.03	0.13	0.05
142.80	112.53	289.58	4.48	79.85	0.24
266.06	201.06	156.15	13.83	18.99	0.92
496.19	203.68	255.20	66.26	78.50	2.22
6.72	4.23	1.86	−0.15	0.01	0.05
220.28	107.33	186.94	18.03	24.75	1.62
898.19	611.72	1657.35	12.17	32.60	3.44
8.03	4.82	3.42	0.08	0.13	0.05
173.15	58.62	120.22	20.60	25.82	1.26
286.23	123.62	180.55	16.28	22.53	2.00
213.46	157.47	127.28	11.14	13.93	0.97
961.73	666.14	1342.67	111.08	133.16	3.24
72.90	38.22	48.72	2.68	3.74	0.48
326.42	187.97	253.27	19.44	24.15	1.15
421.55	233.64	614.09	10.08	13.39	0.80
20.33	9.95	15.89	2.63	3.19	0.23
7.79	2.74	6.18	0.29	0.63	0.17
381.51	253.33	133.75	5.13	9.87	0.83
86.76	44.64	29.09	3.92	3.97	0.22
93.23	78.31	13.04	0.01	0.94	0.17

12-13 规模以上大中型工业企业一览表 (2020 年)

Summary of Large and Medium-Sized Enterprises(2020)

企业名称 Number of Industial Enterprises	登记注册类型 Status of Registration	企业规模 Enterprise Size	所属行业 Sector
浪潮电子信息产业股份有限公司	股份有限公司	大型	计算机整机制造
中国重汽集团济南卡车股份有限公司	股份有限公司	大型	汽柴油车整车制造
山东钢铁股份有限公司	股份有限公司	大型	钢压延加工
山东泰山钢铁集团有限公司	其他有限责任公司	大型	钢压延加工
山东富伦钢铁有限公司	私营有限责任公司	大型	钢压延加工
中国重汽集团济南商用车有限公司	港澳台商独资	大型	汽柴油车整车制造
莱芜钢铁集团银山型钢有限公司	其他有限责任公司	大型	钢压延加工
中国石油化工股份有限公司济南分公司	股份有限公司	大型	原油加工及石油制品制造
中国重汽集团济南动力有限公司	港澳台商独资	大型	汽车零部件及配件制造
济南市九羊福利钢铁有限公司	私营有限责任公司	中型	炼铁
中国重汽集团济南桥箱有限公司	与港澳台商合资经营	大型	汽车零部件及配件制造
齐鲁制药有限公司	其他有限责任公司	大型	化学药品制剂制造
山东闽源钢铁有限公司	其他有限责任公司	大型	钢压延加工
中国重汽集团济南橡塑件有限公司	其他有限责任公司	大型	汽车车身、挂车制造
山东圣泉新材料股份有限公司	私营有限股份公司	大型	初级形态塑料及合成树脂制造
九阳股份有限公司	外商投资股份有限公司	中型	家用厨房电器具制造
临工集团济南重机有限公司	私营有限责任公司	大型	矿山机械制造
山东泰山轧钢有限公司	私营有限责任公司	中型	钢压延加工
山东宝鼎煤焦化有限公司	私营有限责任公司	中型	煤制液体燃料生产
山东电力设备有限公司	国有独资公司	中型	变压器、整流器和电感器制造
玫德集团有限公司	其他有限责任公司	大型	建筑装饰及水暖管道零件制造
华能莱芜发电有限公司	其他有限责任公司	中型	火力发电
重汽（济南）汽车部件有限公司	国有	大型	汽车零部件及配件制造
重汽（济南）轻卡有限公司	其他有限责任公司	大型	汽柴油车整车制造
山东泰山焦化有限公司	其他有限责任公司	中型	炼焦
山东中车风电有限公司	其他有限责任公司	中型	发电机及发电机组制造
大汉科技股份有限公司	其他有限责任公司	大型	生产专用起重机制造
伊莱特能源装备股份有限公司	外商投资股份有限公司	大型	锻件及粉末冶金制品制造
济南圣泉集团股份有限公司	股份有限公司	大型	初级形态塑料及合成树脂制造
齐鲁安替制药有限公司	与港澳台商合资经营	大型	化学药品原料药制造
山东鲁碧建材有限公司	其他有限责任公司	大型	水泥制造
华能济南黄台发电有限公司	其他有限责任公司	大型	火力发电
济南二机床集团有限公司	国有独资公司	大型	金属成形机床制造
济南伊利乳业有限责任公司	其他有限责任公司	大型	液体乳制造
山东晋煤明水化工集团有限公司	其他有限责任公司	大型	有机化学原料制造
济南热电有限公司	国有独资公司	大型	热力生产和供应
费斯托气动有限公司	外资企业	大型	气压动力机械及元件制造
济南澳海炭素有限公司	其他有限责任公司	中型	石墨及碳素制品制造
山东国舜建设集团有限公司	私营有限责任公司	大型	环境保护专用设备制造
中国石油集团济柴动力有限公司	国有独资公司	大型	内燃机及配件制造
济南轻骑铃木摩托车有限公司	中外合资经营	大型	摩托车整车制造
山东省万兴食品有限公司	其他有限责任公司	中型	蔬菜加工
华电章丘发电有限公司	其他有限责任公司	中型	热电联产
山东安信制药有限公司	与港澳台商合资经营	大型	化学药品原料药制造
山东旺旺食品有限公司	外资企业	大型	液体乳制造
济南热力集团有限公司	国有独资公司	大型	热力生产和供应
济南万瑞炭素有限责任公司	私营有限责任公司	中型	石墨及碳素制品制造

12-13 续表 1 continued 1

企业名称 Number of Industial Enterprises	登记注册类型 Status of Registration	企业规模 Enterprise Size	所属行业 Sector
中国重汽集团济南特种车有限公司	国有	中型	汽柴油车整车制造
鲁中矿业有限公司	其他有限责任公司	大型	铁矿采选
济南达利食品有限公司	私营有限责任公司	大型	饼干及其他焙烤食品制造
中粮可口可乐饮料(济南)有限公司	与港澳台商合作经营	大型	果菜汁及果菜汁饮料制造
福士汽车零部件（济南）有限公司	外资企业	大型	汽车零部件及配件制造
华熙生物科技股份有限公司	其他有限责任公司	中型	生物药品制造
齐鲁动物保健品有限公司	其他有限责任公司	大型	兽用药品制造
莱芜钢铁集团泰东实业有限公司	其他有限责任公司	大型	耐火陶瓷制品及其他耐火材料制造
卧龙电气章丘海尔电机有限公司	与港澳台商合资经营	大型	微特电机及组件制造
浪潮商用机器有限公司	与港澳台商合资经营	中型	计算机整机制造
山东明泉新材料科技有限公司	其他有限责任公司	中型	其他基础化学原料制造
金雷科技股份公司	股份有限公司	中型	发电机及发电机组制造
积成电子股份有限公司	股份有限公司	大型	配电开关控制设备制造
济南裕兴化工有限责任公司	其他有限责任公司	大型	专项化学用品制造
山东正泰电缆有限公司	其他有限责任公司	中型	电线、电缆制造
济南港华燃气有限公司	与港澳台商合资经营	大型	天然气生产和供应业
济南邦德激光股份有限公司	股份有限公司	大型	其他金属加工机械制造
中车山东机车车辆有限公司	其他有限责任公司	大型	铁路机车车辆制造
中国重汽集团济南专用车有限公司	其他有限责任公司	中型	改装汽车制造
平阴山水水泥有限公司	与港澳台商合资经营	中型	水泥制造
山东山水水泥集团有限公司	港澳台商独资	大型	水泥制造
山东济华燃气有限公司	与港澳台商合资经营	中型	天然气生产和供应业
莱钢集团矿山建设有限公司	其他有限责任公司	中型	铁矿采选
山东省章丘鼓风机股份有限公司	股份有限公司	大型	风机、风扇制造
莱芜钢铁集团莱芜矿业有限公司	其他有限责任公司	大型	铁矿采选
华润双鹤利民药业（济南）有限公司	其他有限责任公司	中型	化学药品制剂制造
山东齐发药业有限公司	其他有限责任公司	中型	化学药品原料药制造
山东晋煤日月化工有限公司	其他有限责任公司	中型	有机化学原料制造
济南泰山阳光冶金有限公司	其他有限责任公司	中型	炼铁
济南迈克管道科技股份有限公司	港澳台商独资	中型	金属结构制造
山东电工电气日立高压开关有限公司	中外合资经营	中型	配电开关控制设备制造
济南水务集团有限公司	国有独资公司	大型	自来水生产和供应
济南佳宝乳业有限公司	其他有限责任公司	大型	液体乳制造
山东水泥厂有限公司	其他有限责任公司	中型	水泥制造
维达纸业（山东）有限公司	港澳台商独资	中型	机制纸及纸板制造
科兴生物制药股份有限公司	股份有限公司	大型	基因工程药物和疫苗制造
济南西门子变压器有限公司	中外合资经营	中型	变压器、整流器和电感器制造
济南龙山炭素有限公司	私营有限责任公司	中型	石墨及碳素制品制造
博世汽车转向系统（济南）有限公司	外资企业	中型	液压动力机械及元件制造
泰富特钢悬架（济南）有限公司	其他有限责任公司	中型	弹簧制造
济南统一企业有限公司	与港澳台商合资经营	中型	茶饮料及其他饮料制造
山东宏业纺织股份有限公司	股份有限公司	中型	棉纺纱加工
济南重工股份有限公司	股份有限公司	中型	矿山机械制造
济南森峰科技有限公司	其他有限责任公司	中型	其他专用仪器制造
济南金威刻科技发展有限公司	其他有限责任公司	中型	其他非金属加工专用设备制造
山东鲁银新材料科技有限公司	其他有限责任公司	中型	锻件及粉末冶金制品制造
莱芜泰禾生化有限公司	其他有限责任公司	中型	食品及饲料添加剂制造
西电济南变压器股份有限公司	股份有限公司	中型	变压器、整流器和电感器制造

12–13 续表 2 continued 2

企业名称 Number of Industial Enterprises	登记注册类型 Status of Registration	企业规模 Enterprise Size	所属行业 Sector
济南锅炉集团有限公司	私营有限责任公司	大型	锅炉及辅助设备制造
济南鲁冠混凝土有限责任公司	私营有限责任公司	中型	水泥制品制造
济南黄河特钢有限责任公司	其他有限责任公司	中型	钢压延加工
济南中海炭素有限公司	其他有限责任公司	中型	石墨及碳素制品制造
山东奥太电气有限公司	其他有限责任公司	中型	金属切割及焊接设备制造
济南金麒麟刹车系统有限公司	私营有限责任公司	大型	汽车零部件及配件制造
山东力诺瑞特新能源有限公司	中外合资经营	中型	太阳能器具制造
莱芜新希望六和食品有限公司	私营有限责任公司	中型	禽类屠宰
济南海川投资集团有限公司	私营有限责任公司	中型	石墨及碳素制品制造
山东福瑞达生物工程有限公司	其他有限责任公司	中型	化妆品制造
山东力诺特种玻璃股份有限公司	股份有限公司	中型	日用玻璃制品制造
山东博士伦福瑞达制药有限公司	与港澳台商合资经营	中型	化学药品制剂制造
山东宏济堂制药集团股份有限公司	股份有限公司	大型	中成药生产
济南新峨嵋实业有限公司	私营有限责任公司	中型	锻件及粉末冶金制品制造
山东太古飞机工程有限公司	与港澳台商合资经营	大型	航空航天器修理
青岛啤酒（济南）有限公司	其他有限责任公司	中型	啤酒制造
山东华凌电缆有限公司	私营有限责任公司	中型	电线、电缆制造
山东温岭精锻科技有限公司	私营有限责任公司	中型	锻件及粉末冶金制品制造
山东银鹭食品有限公司	港澳台商独资	中型	含乳饮料和植物蛋白饮料制造
山东福牌阿胶股份有限公司	股份有限公司	中型	中成药生产
山东朗进科技股份有限公司	股份有限公司	中型	制冷、空调设备制造
济南轻骑标致摩托车有限公司	中外合资经营	中型	摩托车整车制造
山东能源重装集团莱芜装备制造有限公司	其他有限责任公司	中型	矿山机械制造
济南沃德汽车零部件有限公司	中外合资经营	大型	汽车零部件及配件制造
济南重工集团有限公司	其他有限责任公司	中型	隧道施工专用机械制造
山东鲁中啤酒原料有限公司	私营有限责任公司	中型	其他未列明农副食品加工
山东桑乐集团有限公司	其他有限责任公司	中型	太阳能器具制造
山推建友机械股份有限公司	股份有限公司	中型	建筑材料生产专用机械制造
济南宇飞食品有限公司	私营有限责任公司	中型	禽类屠宰
济南市城建材料开发服务中心	国有	中型	水泥制品制造
莱芜莱新铁矿有限责任公司	其他有限责任公司	中型	铁矿采选
济南鑫贝西生物技术有限公司	私营有限责任公司	中型	其他医疗设备及器械制造
山东华森建材集团有限公司	其他有限责任公司	中型	水泥制品制造
山东恒瑞德电力设备有限公司	私营有限责任公司	中型	配电开关控制设备制造
山东爱普电气设备有限公司	其他有限责任公司	中型	其他输配电及控制设备制造
山东天岳先进科技股份有限公司	股份有限公司	中型	电子专用材料制造
山东福瑞达医药集团有限公司	其他有限责任公司	中型	生物药品制造
山东晨熙智能科技有限公司	私营有限责任公司	中型	包装装潢及其他印刷
山东济南发电设备厂有限公司	国有独资公司	中型	发电机及发电机组制造
济南迈克阀门科技有限公司	其他有限责任公司	中型	阀门和旋塞制造
山东华熙海御生物医药有限公司	外资企业	中型	生物药品制造
章丘重型锻造有限公司	私营有限责任公司	中型	锻件及粉末冶金制品制造
山东莱芜煤矿机械有限公司	国有独资公司	中型	矿山机械制造
安莉芳（山东）服装有限公司	港澳台商独资	大型	运动休闲针织服装制造
山东山大电力技术股份有限公司	股份有限公司	中型	其他专用仪器制造
山东万祥矿业有限公司	其他有限责任公司	大型	烟煤和无烟煤开采洗选
济南泉华包装制品有限公司	与港澳台商合资经营	中型	纸和纸板容器制造
济南轻骑大韩摩托车有限责任公司	中外合资经营	中型	摩托车整车制造

12-13 续表 3 continued 3

企业名称 Number of Industial Enterprises	登记注册类型 Status of Registration	企业规模 Enterprise Size	所属行业 Sector
济南中维世纪科技有限公司	私营有限责任公司	中型	集成电路制造
济南鲁东耐火材料有限公司	中外合资经营	中型	耐火陶瓷制品及其他耐火材料制造
济南市莱芜燃气热力有限责任公司	其他有限责任公司	中型	天然气生产和供应业
山东博科生物产业有限公司	其他有限责任公司	中型	医疗实验室及医用消毒设备和器具制造
国机铸锻机械有限公司	其他有限责任公司	中型	铸造机械制造
章丘华明水泥有限公司	其他有限责任公司	中型	水泥制造
中集车辆（山东）有限公司	中外合资经营	中型	汽车用发动机制造
山东天鹅棉业机械股份有限公司	股份有限公司	中型	棉花加工机械制造
济南和盛热力有限公司	其他有限责任公司	中型	热力生产和供应
山东上好佳食品工业有限公司	港澳台商独资	中型	饼干及其他焙烤食品制造
齐鲁宏业纺织集团有限公司	私营有限责任公司	中型	棉纺纱加工
山东北辰机电设备股份有限公司	私营有限股份公司	中型	金属压力容器制造
山东福贞金属包装有限公司	外资企业	中型	金属包装容器及材料制造
济南泓泉制水有限公司	其他有限责任公司	中型	自来水生产和供应
济南弘正科技有限公司	港澳台商独资	中型	摩托车零部件及配件制造
济南中燃科技发展有限公司	私营有限责任公司	中型	其他金属加工机械制造
山东中天华泰新材料有限公司	私营有限责任公司	中型	石墨及碳素制品制造
济南市冶金科学研究所有限责任公司	其他有限责任公司	中型	有色金属合金制造
山东大鲁阁织染工业有限公司	外资企业	中型	棉纺纱加工
山东大旺食品有限公司	外资企业	中型	饼干及其他焙烤食品制造
山东汇金股份有限公司	股份有限公司	中型	汽车零部件及配件制造
山东慧达汽车部件有限公司	私营有限责任公司	中型	汽车零部件及配件制造
山东平阴丰源炭素有限责任公司	其他有限责任公司	中型	石墨及碳素制品制造
济南宜和食品有限公司	中外合资经营	中型	酱油、食醋及类似制品制造
山东科源制药股份有限公司	股份有限公司	中型	化学药品原料药制造
山东金钟科技集团股份有限公司	股份有限公司	中型	衡器制造
山东小鸭集团家电有限公司	国有独资公司	中型	其他家用电力器具制造
迈大食品（山东）有限公司	外资企业	中型	饼干及其他焙烤食品制造
济南大阳食品有限公司	私营有限责任公司	中型	禽类屠宰
山东鲁信天一印务有限公司	其他有限责任公司	中型	包装装潢及其他印刷
济南世纪创新水泥有限公司	私营有限责任公司	中型	水泥制造
山东百脉泉酒业有限公司	股份有限公司	中型	白酒制造
济南三星灯饰有限公司	其他有限责任公司	中型	舞台及场地用灯制造
济南黄台煤气炉有限公司	其他有限责任公司	中型	气体、液体分离及纯净设备制造
济南中船设备有限公司	私营有限责任公司	中型	船用配套设备制造
济南冶金化工设备有限公司	其他有限责任公司	中型	冶金专用设备制造
山东欧克家具有限公司	私营有限责任公司	中型	木质家具制造
中国重汽集团济南豪沃客车有限公司	其他有限责任公司	中型	汽柴油车整车制造
济南晶恒电子有限责任公司	国有独资公司	中型	半导体分立器件制造
山东小鸭精工机械有限公司	其他有限责任公司	中型	汽车零部件及配件制造
中孚信息股份有限公司	股份有限公司	中型	信息安全设备制造
济南圣都食品有限公司	私营有限责任公司	中型	肉制品及副产品加工
山东鲁得贝车灯股份有限公司	股份有限公司	中型	汽车零部件及配件制造
济南台有玻璃制品有限公司	其他有限责任公司	中型	日用玻璃制品制造
神思电子技术股份有限公司	股份有限公司	中型	其他计算机制造
山东新升实业发展有限责任公司	国有独资公司	中型	热电联产
山东耀华玻璃有限公司	私营有限责任公司	中型	其他玻璃制造
济南科盛电子有限公司	其他有限责任公司	中型	光电子器件制造

12-13 续表 4 continued 4

企业名称 Number of Industial Enterprises	登记注册类型 Status of Registration	企业规模 Enterprise Size	所属行业 Sector
山东明仁福瑞达制药股份有限公司	股份有限公司	中型	中成药生产
莱芜朝阳电子有限公司	其他有限责任公司	中型	电力电子元器件制造
山东通发实业有限公司	私营有限责任公司	中型	建筑工程用机械制造
济南实达紧固件有限公司	私营有限责任公司	中型	紧固件制造
济南虫洞智能家居设施有限公司	私营有限责任公司	中型	木质家具制造
济南界龙科技有限公司	外资企业	中型	电阻电容电感元件制造
山东地矿慧通特种轮胎有限公司	其他有限责任公司	中型	轮胎制造
山东华氟化工有限责任公司	其他有限责任公司	中型	化学试剂和助剂制造
济南二机床铸造有限公司	国有独资公司	中型	黑色金属铸造
平阴鲁西装备科技有限公司	其他有限责任公司	中型	其他金属加工机械制造
山东九龙新材料有限公司	私营有限责任公司	中型	耐火陶瓷制品及其他耐火材料制造
山东力创科技股份有限公司	私营有限股份公司	中型	电力电子元器件制造
山东济钢环保新材料有限公司	国有	中型	石灰石、石膏开采
山东银鹰炊事机械有限公司	其他有限责任公司	中型	其他金属加工机械制造
济南元首针织股份有限公司	股份有限公司	中型	运动休闲针织服装制造
山东巧夺天工家具有限公司	私营有限责任公司	中型	其他工艺美术及礼仪用品制造
济南方圣混凝土构件有限公司	私营有限责任公司	中型	砼结构构件制造
山东宏达科技集团有限公司	私营有限责任公司	中型	金属压力容器制造
山东越宫钢构件有限公司	其他有限责任公司	中型	其他建筑、安全用金属制品制造
济南金木铸造有限公司	私营有限责任公司	中型	汽车零部件及配件制造
济南趵突泉酿酒有限责任公司	其他有限责任公司	中型	白酒制造
济南莱钢钢结构有限公司	其他有限责任公司	中型	金属结构制造
济南翼菲自动化科技有限公司	私营有限责任公司	中型	工业机器人制造
山东阿尔普尔节能装备有限公司	其他有限责任公司	中型	制冷、空调设备制造
海湾电子（山东）有限公司	中外合资经营	中型	半导体分立器件制造
济南市白象科技发展有限公司	其他有限责任公司	中型	冶金专用设备制造
济南明鑫制药股份有限公司	私营有限股份公司	中型	化学药品原料药制造
济南双凤耐火材料有限公司	私营有限责任公司	中型	隔热和隔音材料制造
金德利餐饮有限公司	其他有限责任公司	中型	米、面制品制造
山东裕兴电工器材有限公司	私营有限责任公司	中型	电子元器件与机电组件设备制造
济南巨鑫机车车辆配件有限公司	私营有限责任公司	中型	锻件及粉末冶金制品制造
济南银鹰食品机械有限公司	其他有限责任公司	中型	农副食品加工专用设备制造
山东新华印务有限 公司	国有独资公司	中型	书、报刊印刷
山东冠世针织有限公司	外资企业	中型	运动休闲针织服装制造
济南市长清计算机应用公司	股份合作	中型	供应用仪器仪表制造
济阳元首针织有限责任公司	其他有限责任公司	中型	其他针织或钩针编织服装制造
济南思迈迩制衣有限公司	私营有限责任公司	中型	运动机织服装制造
山东博特生物资源制品有限公司	私营有限责任公司	中型	其他纸制品制造
山东省莱芜市辛庄煤矿有限公司	其他有限责任公司	中型	烟煤和无烟煤开采洗选
莱芜环球汽车零部件有限公司	外资企业	中型	汽车零部件及配件制造
莱芜科林光电有限公司	其他有限责任公司	中型	光伏设备及元器件制造

12-14 主要工业产品生产量(2020 年)
Output of Major Industrial Products(2020)

主要工业产品名称	Major Industrial Products above Designated Size	单位 Unit	生产量 Proction
铁矿石原矿	Crude Iron ore	万吨 (10 000 tons)	565.9
铁矿石成品矿	Iron ore finished ore	万吨 (10 000 tons)	2359.2
铁精矿	Iron ore concentrate	万吨 (10 000 tons)	2227.8
石灰石	Lime Powder	万吨 (10 000 tons)	130.8
饲料	Feed	万吨 (10 000 tons)	108.8
鲜、冷藏肉	Frozen,Fresh Meat	万吨 (10 000 tons)	15.1
乳制品	Milk Products	万吨 (10 000 tons)	49.0
液体乳	Liquid Milk	万吨 (10 000 tons)	47.9
酱油	Soy Sauce	万吨 (10 000 tons)	11.6
食品添加剂	Food Additives	万吨 (10 000 tons)	14.3
饲料添加剂	Feed Additive	万吨 (10 000 tons)	4.1
饮料酒	Liquor	万千升 (10 000 kiloliter)	26.8
白酒(折 65 度，商品量)	Liquor (65 degree discount, commercial quantity)	万千升 (10 000 kiloliter)	0.8
啤酒	Beer	万千升 (10 000 kiloliter)	26.0
饮料	Drinks	万吨 (10 000 tons)	161.5
碳酸型饮料(汽水)	Carbonated Drinks	万吨 (10 000 tons)	55.9
包装饮用水	Bottled Drinking Water	万吨 (10 000 tons)	22.3
果汁和蔬菜汁类饮料	Juice and Vegetable Juice Beverage	万吨 (10 000 tons)	33.0
布	Cloth	万米 (10 000 m)	1144.4
服装	Garments	万件 (10 000 pieces)	4303.9
家具	Furniture	万件 (10 000 pieces)	33.3
纸制品	Paper Products	万吨 (10 000 tons)	23.7
瓦楞纸箱	Corrugated Box	万吨 (10 000 tons)	13.4
单色印刷品	Monochrome Print	万令 (10 000 ream)	236.3
多色印刷品	Ploychrome Print	万对开色令 (10 000 color folio ream)	958.6
纯苯	Purified Petroleum Benzin(e)	万吨 (10 000 tons)	7.4
精甲醇	Extracted Methanol	万吨 (10 000 tons)	76.8
硅	Silicon	万吨 (10 000 tons)	2.6
合成氨(无水氨)	Synthetic Ammonia	万吨 (10 000 tons)	60.0
农用氮、磷、钾化学肥料(折纯)	Chemical Fertilizer	万吨 (10 000 tons)	21.1
尿素(折含氮 100%)	Urea	万吨 (10 000 tons)	20.8
化学农药原药(折有效成分 100%)	Chemical Pesticide	吨 (ton)	15233.5
涂料	Paint	万吨 (10 000 tons)	2.7
初级形态塑料	Primary Plastic	万吨 (10 000 tons)	15.9
化学试剂	Chemical Reagent	万吨 (10 000 tons)	12.3
表面活性剂	Surface active agent	万吨 (10 000 tons)	3.9
化学药品原药	Chemical Medicine	吨 (ton)	8794.6
中成药	Traditional Chemical Medicine	吨 (ton)	6038.2
兽用药品	Veterinary Drugs	吨 (ton)	17771.8
化学纤维	Chemical Fiber	万吨 (10 000 tons)	6.1
橡胶轮胎外胎	Rubber Tyre Cover	万条 (10 000 tires)	18.6

12-14 续表 1 continued 1

主要工业产品名称	Major Industrial Products above Designated Size	单位 Unit	生产量 Proction
塑料制品	Plastic Articles	万吨 (10 000 tons)	14.1
硅酸盐水泥熟料	Portland Cement Clinker	万吨 (10 000 tons)	570.7
水泥	Cement	万吨 (10 000 tons)	1335.9
石灰	Lime	万吨 (10 000 tons)	56.9
商品混凝土	Concrete	万立方米 (10 000 cu.m)	2516.7
水泥混凝土排水管	Cement and Concrete Drainage Pipes	千米 (km)	147.4
水泥混凝土压力管	Cement and Concrete Pressure Pipes	千米 (km)	343.0
砖	Brick	亿块 (100 million unit)	2.2
钢化玻璃	Stalinite	万平方米 (10 000 sq.m)	91.4
中空玻璃	Hollow Glass	万平方米 (10 000 sq.m)	155.8
耐火材料制品	Refractory Product	万吨 (10 000 tons)	65.9
石墨及碳素制品	Graphite and Carbon Products	万吨 (10 000 tons)	172.7
生铁	Cast Iron	万吨 (10 000 tons)	2116.5
粗钢	Crude Steel	万吨 (10 000 tons)	2228.9
钢材	Steel	万吨 (10 000 tons)	2336.5
钢结构	Steel Structure	万吨 (10 000 tons)	115.6
金属切削工具	Metal Cutting Tool	万件 (10 000 unit)	324.7
锻件	Forge Piece	万吨 (10 000 tons)	113.6
粉末冶金零件	Sintered Metal Products	万吨 (10 000 tons)	1.3
电站锅炉	Utility Boilers	蒸发量吨 (evaporation ton)	4163.0
发动机	Engine	万千瓦 (10 000kw)	6167.1
汽车用发动机	Automotive Engine	万千瓦 (10 000kw)	6083.2
金属切削机床	Metal-cutting Machine Tools	台 (unit)	8998
起重机	Lifting Equipment	万吨 (10 000 tons)	41.0
电梯、自动扶梯及升降机	Elevators, Escalators and Lifts	台 (unit)	7756
液压元件	Hydraulic Components	万件 (10 000 unit)	49.6
气动元件	Pneumatic Components	万件 (10 000 unit)	1464.6
鼓风机	Air Blower	万台 (10 000 unit)	3.0
工商用制冷、空调设备	Commercial Refrigeration Equipment	万台 (10 000 unit)	2.3
金属紧固件	Metal Fastener	万吨 (10 000 tons)	4.8
弹簧	Spring	万吨 (10 000 tons)	9.0
矿山专用设备	Mining Equipment	万吨 (10 000 tons)	6.4
金属冶炼设备	Metal Smelting Equipment	万吨 (10 000 tons)	4.2
炼油、化工生产专用设备	Special Equipment for Oil Refining and Chemical Protection	吨 (ton)	13770.4
农产品初加工机械	Agricultural Primary Processing Machinery	万台 (10 000 unit)	4.3
电子工业专用设备	Special Equipment for Electrionic Industry	万台 (10 000 unit)	7.7
棉花加工机械	Cotton Processing Machinery	台 (unit)	1685
医疗仪器设备及器械	Medical Instruments	万台 (10 000 unit)	6.5
工业机器人	Industrial Robot	套 (unit)	1960
载货汽车	Trucks	万辆 (10 000 unit)	39.4
改装汽车	Modified Cars	万辆 (10 000 unit)	2.1
铁路货车	Railway Freight Wagons	辆 (unit)	3418

12-14 续表 2 continued 2

主要工业产品名称	Major Industrial Products above Designated Size	单 位 Unit	生产量 Proction
摩托车整车	Motorcycles	万辆 (10 000 unit)	38.0
发电机组（发电设备）	Power Generating Equipment	万千瓦 (10 000kw)	493.7
电动机	Electromotor	万千瓦 (10 000kw)	279.1
变压器	Transformer	万千伏安 (10 000 KVA)	13645.4
高压开关设备（11 万伏以上）	High Voltage Switchgear (over 110,000 volts)	万台 (10 000 unit)	1.1
安全、自动化监控设备	Safety and Automatic Monitoring Equipment	台 (套)(unit)	21545
通信及电子网络用电缆	Cable for Communications and Electronic Network	万对千米 (10 000 pairs.km)	3.5
电力电缆	Power Cable	万千米 (10 000 km)	14.6
太阳能热水器	Solar Water Heater	万平方米 (10 000 sq.m)	135.8
灯具及照明装置	Lamps and Lighting Fixtures	万套 (台个)(10 000 unit)	12.6
电子计算机整机	Computers	万台 (10 000 unit)	144.9
服务器	Servers	万台 (10 000 unit)	143.5
半导体分立器件	Discrete Semiconductor Devices	亿只 (100 million unit)	113.0
传感器	Transducer	万只 (10 000 unit)	749.0
集成电路	Integrated Circuit	万块 (10 000 unit)	889.2
电子元件	Eletronic Components	亿只 (100 million unit)	23.6
电声器件	Electroacoustic Device	万只 (10 000 unit)	847.0
印制电路板	Print-circuit Board	万平方米 (10 000 sq.m)	128.8
工业自动调节仪表与控制系统	Industrial Automatic Instrument and Control System	台 (套)(unit)	19749
电工仪器仪表	Electrical Instrument	万台 (10 000 unit)	632.4
汽车仪器仪表	Automobile Instrument	万台 (10 000 unit)	145.2
钟	Clock	万只 (10 000 unit)	63.9
自来水生产量	Tap Water Production	亿立方米 (100 million cu.m)	6.7
原油加工量	Crude Processing Volume	万吨 (10 000 tons)	482.3
汽油	Gasoline	万吨 (10 000 tons)	169.4
柴油	Diesel Oil	万吨 (10 000 tons)	128.6
燃料油	Fuel Oil	万吨 (10 000 tons)	1.1
石脑油	Naphtha	万吨 (10 000 tons)	4.4
液化石油气	Liquefied Petroleum	万吨 (10 000 tons)	32.8
石油焦	Petroleum Coke	万吨 (10 000 tons)	16.2
石油沥青	Asphalt	万吨 (10 000 tons)	14.7
发电量	Power Generating Capacity	亿千瓦时 (100 million kwh)	276.7
其中：火力发电量	Thermal Power Generation	亿千瓦时 (100 million kwh)	267.7
风力发电量	Wind Power Generation	亿千瓦时 (100 million kwh)	7.6
垃圾发电量	Garbage Power Generation	亿千瓦时 (100 million kwh)	6.9
煤气生产量	Gas Power Generation	亿立方米 (100 million cu.m)	235.2

12-15 工业企业能源购进、消费及库存(2020年)

Purchases, Consumption and Invetory of Main Energy Source in Industrial Enterprises(2020)

能源名称	Energy	计量单位 Unit	年初库存量 Beginning Stock	本年购进量 Purchases This Year	本年工业生产消费 Industrial Consumption of This Year	年末库存量 Year-end Stock
能源合计	Total Energy	吨标准煤 (tons of SCE)	0	0	48458121	0
原煤	Raw Coal	吨 (ton)	958205	16071366	16460245	523295
洗精煤	Cleaned Coal	吨 (ton)	317086	6785726	6859976	233888
其他洗煤	Other Cleaned Coal	吨 (ton)	143941	3501401	3482758	162315
煤制品	Coal Product	吨 (ton)	85380	854810	927861	67462
焦炭	Coke	吨 (ton)	166291	9201453	10266924	202686
天然气	Natural Gas	万立方米 (10 000 cu.m)	0	80391	80154	0
液化天然气	Liquefied Nutural Gas	吨 (ton)	14	14071	14192	30
原油	Crude Oil	吨 (ton)	81997	4837229	4822505	96721
汽油	Gasoline	吨 (ton)	57	4020	4531	38
煤油	Kerosene	吨 (ton)	4	40	52	1
柴油	Diesel Oil	吨 (ton)	1810	45053	38833	1107
燃料油	Fuel Oil	吨 (ton)	337	597	749	185
液化石油气	Liquefied Petroleum	吨 (ton)	46	835	838	0
炼厂干气	Refinery Dry Gas	吨 (ton)	0	110	189865	0
其他石油制品	Other Petroleum Product	吨 (ton)	0	47469	534234	0
热力	Heating	百万千焦 (MkJ)	0	5672710	9266389	0
电力	Electricity	万千瓦时 (10 000 kwh)	0	1730930	2150337	0
其他燃料	Other Fuel	吨标准煤 (tons of SCE)	2	1168	1011	0

注：按照经济普查要求，免填能源合计中，年初库存、购进量、年末库存。

Note: According to requirements of economic census, it's unnecessary to fill in inventory and volume of purchase at the beginning of the year and the inventory at the end of the year in the total energy.

12-16 工业分行业主要能源消费量(2020年)

Consumption of Main Energy Source in Industrial Enterprises by Sector(2020)

指标	Indicator	原煤（吨）Coal (ton)	汽油（吨）Gasoline (ton)	煤油（吨）Kerosene (ton)	柴油（吨）Diesel Oil (ton)	燃料油（吨）Fuel Oil (ton)	热力（百万千焦）Heating (MkJ)	电力（万千瓦时）Electricity (10 000 kwh)
总计	Total	16460245	4531	52	38833	749	9266389	2150337
采矿业	Mining							
煤炭开采和洗选业	Mining and Washing of Coal	34767	6	0	26	0	0	4487
石油和天然气开采业	Extraction of Petroleum and Natural Gas	0	0	0	8	0	0	3987
黑色金属矿采选业	Mining and Processing of Ferrous Metal Ores	27879	50	0	2000	0	130856	55920
非金属矿采选业	Mining and Processing of Non-Ferrous Metal Ores	0	0	0	1988	0	0	2546
制造业	Manufacture							
农副食品加工业	Processing of Food from Agricultural Products	29021	116	0	127	0	50287	12800
食品制造业	Manufacture of Foods	53352	159	0	351	0	335207	29563
酒、饮料和精制茶制造业	Manufacture of Wine, Drinks and Refined Tea	0	64	0	213	0	132481	12958
纺织业	Manufacture of Textile	0	3	0	1	0	131822	29230
纺织服装、服饰业	Manufacture of Textile Wearing Apparel and Finery	0	19	0	7	0	28950	1948
皮革、毛皮、羽毛及其制品和制鞋业	Manufacture of Leather, Fur, Feather and Related Products and Footwear	0	0	0	0	0	0	316
木材加工及木、竹、藤、棕、草制品业	Processing of Timbers, Manufacture of Wood, Bamboo, Rattan, Palm, and Straw Products	0	0	0	0	0	0	6979
家具制造业	Manufacture of Furniture	0	13	0	20	0	0	2003
造纸及纸制品业	Manufacture of Paper and Paper Products	20842	16	0	11	0	318891	16538
印刷和记录媒介复制业	Printing and Reproduction of Recording Media	0	180	0	214	0	71903	12472
文教、工美、体育和娱乐用品制造业	Manufacture of Articles for Culture, Education, Arts and Crafts,Sport and Entertainment Activities	0	17	0	0	0	0	1888
石油、煤炭及其他燃料加工业	Processing of Petroleum, Coal and Other Fuels	0	73	10	225	0	416576	61276
化学原料及化学制品制造业	Manufacture of Chemical Raw Material and Chemical Products	2559591	42	0	1056	0	4364080	266646

12-16 续表 2 continued 2

指标	Indicator	原煤（吨）Coal (ton)	汽油（吨）Gasoline (ton)	煤油（吨）Kerosene (ton)	柴油（吨）Diesel Oil (ton)	燃料油（吨）Fuel Oil (ton)	热力（百万千焦）Heating (MkJ)	电力（万千瓦时）Electricity (10 000 kwh)
医药制造业	Manufacture of Medicines	36130	96	0	15	0	2404913	72103
化学纤维制造业	Manufacture of Chemical Fiber	7481	16	0	15	0	19196	5875
橡胶和塑料制品业	Manufacture of Rubber and Plastic	0	86	0	98	0	26196	15043
非金属矿物制品业	Manufacture of Non-metallic Mineral Products	954499	764	0	16485	0	182540	183839
黑色金属冶炼及压延加工业	Manufacture and Processing of Ferrous Metals	2353455	56	0	7014	0	158339	672641
有色金属冶炼及压延加工业	Manufacture & Processing of Non-ferrous Metals	0	11	0	54	0	12853	5102
金属制品业	Manufacture of Metal Products	10179	255	0	734	0	0	124945
通用设备制造业	Manufacture of General Purpose Machinery	0	652	21	1339	0	20	40631
专用设备制造业	Manufacture of Special Purpose Machinery	0	393	0	219	0	0	26750
汽车制造业	Manufacture of Automotive	0	169	8	3983	0	425163	113819
铁路、船舶、航空航天和其他运输设备制造业	Manufacture of Railroad,Marine,Aerospace and Other Transportation Equipment	0	204	1	153	0	49471	12199
电气机械及器材制造业	Manufacture of Electrical Machinery &Equipment	0	293	12	30	0	0	31218
计算机、通信和其他电子设备制造业	Manufacture of Computer, Communications and Other Electronic Equipment	0	154	0	16	0	1877	15578
仪器仪表制造业	Manufacture of Measuring Instrument	0	364	0	53	0	0	2005
其他制造业	Other Manufacture	0	25	0	0	0	0	788
废弃资源综合利用业	Utilization of Waste Resources	0	0	0	27	0	0	6813
金属制品、机械和设备修理业	Metal Products, Machinery and Equipment Repair Industry	0	0	0	0	0	0	509
电力、热力、燃气及水生产和供应业	**Production and Supply of Electric Power and Heat Power**							
电力、热力生产和供应业	Production and Supply of Electric Power and Heat Power	10373049	23	0	2289	749	4767	267157
燃气生产和供应业	Production and Supply of Gas	0	104	0	24	0	0	1336
水的生产和供应业	Production and Supply of Water	0	106	0	39	0	0	30426

主要统计指标解释

按照国家统计方法制度规定，1998 年独立核算工业统计范围由原乡及乡以上调整为全部国有及年销售收入500 万元以上非国有工业企业，2011 年规模以上工业企业统计范围调整为年主营业务收入2000 万元以上。同时，统计分类中的原经济组织类型分组相应地调整为按企业登记注册类型分组。

工业 指从事自然资源的开采，对采掘品和农产品进行加工和再加工的物质生产部门。具体包括：(1) 对自然资源的开采，如采矿、晒盐等（但不包括禽兽捕猎和水产捕捞）；(2) 对农副产品的加工、再加工，如粮油加工、食品加工、缫丝、纺织、制革等；(3) 对采掘品的加工、再加工，如炼铁、炼钢、化工生产、石油加工、机器制造、木材加工等，以及电力、自来水、煤气的生产和供应等；(4) 对工业品的修理、翻新，如机器设备的修理、交通运输工具（如汽车）的修理等。

工业统计调查单位为独立核算法人工业企业。

独立核算法人工业企业指从事工业生产经营活动的单位。独立核算法人工业企业应同时具备以下条件：①依法成立，有自己的名称、组织机构和场所，能够承担民事责任；②独立拥有和使用资产，承担负债，有权与其他单位签订合同；③独立核算盈亏，并能够编制资产负债表。

本年鉴中涉及的企业登记注册类型：

国有及国有控股企业 指国有企业加上国有控股企业。国有企业（即原全民所有制工业或国营工业）指企业全部资产归国家所有，并按《中华人民共和国企业法人登记管理条例》规定登记注册的非公司制的经济组织。包括国有企业、国有独资公司和国有联营企业。1957 年以前的公私合营和私营工业，后均改造为国营工业，1992 年改为国有工业，这部分工业的资料不单独分列时，均包括在国有企业内。国有控股企业是对混合所有制经济的企业进行的“国有控股”分类。它是指这些企业的全部资产中国有资产（股份）相对其他所有者中的任何一个所有者占资（股）最多的企业。该分组反映了国有经济控股情况。

集体企业 指企业资产归集体所有，并按《中华人民共和国企业法人登记管理条例》规定登记注册的经济组织。

股份合作企业 指以合作制为基础，由企业职工共同出资入股，吸收一定比例的社会资产投资组建，实行自主经营，自负盈亏，共同劳动，民主管理，按劳分配与按股分红相结合的一种集体经济组织。

联营企业 指两个及两个以上相同或不同所有制性质的企业法人或事业单位法人，按自愿、平等、互利的原则，共同投资组成的经济组织。联营企业包括：

国有联营企业指国有企业与国有企业间的联营；

集体联营企业指集体企业与集体企业间的联营；

国有与集体联营企业指国有企业与集体企业间的联营。

有限责任公司　指根据《中华人民共和国公司登记管理条例》规定登记注册，由两个以上，五十个以下的股东共同出资，每个股东以其所认缴的出资额对公司承担有限责任，公司以其全部资产对其债务承担责任的经济组织。

有限责任公司包括国有独资公司以及其他有限责任公司。

股份有限公司 指根据《中华人民共和国企业法人登记管理条例》规定登记注册，其全部注册资本由等额股份构成并通过发行股票筹集资本，股东以其认购的股份对公司承担有限责任，公司以其全部资产对其债务承担责任的经济组织。

私营企业 指由自然人投资设立或由自然人控股，以雇佣劳动为基础的营利性经济组织。包括按照《公司法》、《合伙企业法》、《私营企业暂行条例》规定登记注册的私营有限责任公司、私营股份有限公司、私营合伙企业、私营独资企业和个人独资企业。

港、澳、台商投资企业 指企业注册登记类型中的港、澳、台资合资、合作、独资经营企业和股份有限公司之和。

外商投资企业 指企业注册登记类型中的中外合资、合作经营企业、外资企业和外商投资股份有限公司之和。

“三资”企业系指港、澳、台商投资企业和外资企业的简称。

轻工业 指主要提供生活消费品和制作手工工具的工业。按其所使用的原料不同，可分为两大类：(1) 以农产品为原料的轻工业，是指直接或间接以农产品为基本原料的轻工业。主要包括食品制造、饮料制造、烟草加工、纺织、缝纫、皮革和毛皮制作、造纸以及印刷等工业；(2) 以非农产品为原料的轻工业，是指以工业品为原料的轻工业。主要包括文教体育用品、化学药品制造、合成纤维制造、日用化学制品、日用玻璃制品、日用金属制品、手工工具制造、医疗器械制造、文化和办公用机械制造等工业。

重工业 指为国民经济各部门提供物质技术基础的主要生产资料的工业。按其生产性质和产品用途，可以分为下列三类：(1) 采掘（伐）工业，是指对自然资源的开采，包括石油开采、煤炭开采、金属矿开采、非金属矿开采等工业；(2) 原材料工业，指向国民经济各部门提供基本材料、动力和燃料的工业。包括金属冶炼及加工、炼焦及焦炭、化学、化工原料、水泥、人造板以及电力、石油和煤炭加工等工业；(3) 加工工业，是指对工业原材料进行再加工制造的工业。包括装备国民经济各部门的机械设备制造工业、金属结构、水泥制品等工业，以及为农业提供的生产资料如化肥、农药等工业。

根据上述划分原则，修理业中以重工业产品为修理作业对象的划为重工业，反之划为轻工业。

工业总产值 是以货币表现的工业企业在一定时期内生产的已出售或可供出售工业产品总量，它反映一定时间内工业生产的总规模和总水平。它包括：在本企业内不再进行加工，经检验、包装入库（规定不需包装的产品除外）的成品价值，对外加工费收入，自制半成品、在产品期末初差额价值。工业总产值采用“工厂法”计算，即以工业企业作为一个整体，按企业工业生产活动的最终成果来计算，企业内部不允许重复计算，不能把企业内部各个车间（分厂）生产的成果相加。但在企业之间、行业之间、地区之间存在着重复计算。

轻重工业总产值的划分也是按“工厂法”计算的，即一个工业企业在正常情况下生产的主要产品的性质属于轻工业，则该企业的全部总产值作为轻工业总产值。如生产的主要产品的性质属于重工业，则该企业的全部总产值作为重工业总产值。

工业增加值　是指工业行业在报告期内以货币表现的工业生产活动的最终成果。

实收资本　指企业实际收到的投资人投入的资本。按投资主体可分为国家资本、集体资本、法人资本、个人资本、港澳台资本和外商资本等。

资产总计　指企业拥有或控制的能以货币计量的经济资源。包括各种财产、债权和其他权利。资产按其流动性划分为流动资产、长期投资、固定资产、无形及递延资产和其他资产。

（1）流动资产指企业可以在一年内或者超过一年的一个生产周期内变现或耗用的资产合计。包括现金及各种存款、短期投资、应收及预付款项、存货等。

（2）固定资产指企业固定资产净值、固定资产清理、在建工程、待处理固定资产损失所占用的资金合计。

（3）无形资产指企业长期使用而没有实物形态的资产。包括专利权、非专利技术、商标权、著作权、土地使用权、商誉等。

负债合计　指企业承担的能以货币计量，将以资产或劳务偿付的债务。负债一般按偿还期长短分为流动负债和长期负债、递延税项等。

（1）流动负债指企业在一年内或者超过一年的一个营业周期内需要偿还的债务合计，其中包括短期借款、应付及预收款项、应付工资、应交税金和应交利润等。

（2）长期负债指企业在一年以上或者超过一年的一个营业周期以上需要偿还的债务合计，其中包括长期借款、应付债务、长期应付款项等。

所有者权益　指企业投资人对企业净资产的所有权。企业净资产等于企业全部资产减去全部负债后的余额，其中包括投资者对企业的最初投入，以及资本公积金、盈余公积金和未分配利润，对股份制企业即为股东权益。

固定资产原价　指企业在建造、购置、安装、改建、扩建、技术改造某项固定资产时所支出的全部货币总额。它一般包括买价、包装费、运杂费和安装费等。

营业收入　指企业从事销售商品、提供劳务和让渡资产使用权等生产经营活动形成的经济利益流入。包括“主营业务收入”和“其他业务收入”。

营业成本　指企业从事销售商品、提供劳务和让渡资产使用权等生产经营活动发生的实际成本。包括“主营业务成本”和“其他业务成本”。

税金及附加　指企业因从事生产经营活动按税法规定应缴纳的消费税、城市维护建设税、资源税、环境保护税、教育费附加及房产税、土地使用税、车船使用税、印花税等相关税费。

利润总额　指企业在一定会计期间的经营成果，是生产经营过程中各种收入扣除各种耗费后的盈余，反映企业在报告期内实现的盈亏总额。

平均用工人数　是指报告期平均实际拥有的，参与本企业生产经营活动的人员数。

利税总额　指企业产品销售税金及附加、利润总额和应交增值税之和。

本年应交增值税　指按照税法规定，以销售货物、服务、无形资产、不动产或提供加工、修理修配劳务的增值额和货物进口金额为计税依据而课征的一种流转税。

Explanatory Notes on Main Statistical Indicators

As per provisions of national system of statistical method, the scope of statistics of the independent accounting industry in 1998 was adjusted to all state–owned enterprises and non–state industrial enterprises with above RMB 5 million annual sales revenue from those of village and above and the scope of statistics of above state designated scale industrial enterprises in 2011 was adjusted to above RMB 20 million annual income of main business. Meanwhile, grouping of original economic organizations in the statistical classification is adjusted to grouping based on enterprise registration type accordingly.

Industry refers to the material production sector which is engaged in extraction of natural resources and processing and reprocessing of minerals and agricultural products, including (1) extraction of natural resources, such as mining, salt production (but not including hunting and fishing); (2) processing and reprocessing of farm and sideline produces, such as rice husking, flour milling, wine making, oil pressing, silk reeling, spinning and weaving, and leather making; (3) manufacture of industrial products, such as steel making, iron smelting, chemicals manufacturing, petroleum processing, machine building, timber processing; water and gas production and electricity generation and supply; (4)repairing of industrial products such as the repairing of machinery and means of transport (including cars).

Units of industrial statistics survey corporate are industrial enterprises with independent accounting system.

Corporate industrial enterprises with independent accounting system refer to enterprises engaging in industrial production activities, which meet the following requirements: (1)They are established legally, having their own names, organizations, location, able to take civil liability; (2)They possess and use their assets independently, assume liabilities, and are entitled to sign contracts with other units; (3)They are financially independent and compile their own balance sheets.

Enterprises covered in the industrial statistics in this Yearbook include following categories by their registration:

State–owned and State–holding Enterprises refer to state owned enterprises plus state holding enterprises. State owned enterprises (originally known as state run enterprises with ownership by the whole society) are non–corporate economic entities registered in accordance with the Regulation of the People's Republic of China on the Management of Registration of Legal Enterprises, where all assets are owned by the state. Included in this category are state owned enterprises, state funded corporations and state owned joint operation enterprises. Public–private partnerships industries and private industries, which existed before 1957, were transformed into state run industries since 1957, and into state owned industries after 1992. Statistics on those enterprises are included in the state owned industries instead of grouping them separately. State–holding enterprise is a sub–classification of enterprises with mixed ownership, referring to enterprises where the percentage of state assets (or shares by the state) is larger than any other single shareholder of the same enterprise. This sub–classification illustrates the control of the state over a particular industry.

Collective–owned Enterprises refer to economic entities registered in accordance with the Regulation of the People's Republic of China on the Management of Registration of Legal Enterprises, where assets are owned by collectively.

Share–holding Cooperative Enterprises refer to economic units set up on cooperative basis, with funding partly from members of the enterprise and partly from outside investment, which are collective economic organizations with characteristics of self–employed, self–financing, working together, democratic management, distributing by work and shares.

Joint Operation Enterprises refer to economic units that are established by joint investment by two or more corporate enterprises or institutions of the same or different types of ownership on voluntary, equal and mutual beneficial basis. They include:

State owned joint operation enterprises (joint operation between state owned enterprises);

Collective joint operation enterprises (joint operation between collective enterprises, and

State collective joint operation enterprises (joint operation between state and collective enterprises)

Limited Liability Corporations refer to economic units registered in accordance with the Regulation of the People's Republic of China on the Management of Registration of Corporations, with capitals from 2 to 49 investors, each investor bears limited liability to the corporation depending on his/her holding of shares, and the corporation bears liability to its debt to the maximum of its total assets.

Limited liability corporations cover state–owned exclusive company and other limited liability corporations.

Share–holding Corporations Ltd. refer to economic units registered in accordance with the Regulation of the People's Republic of China on the Management of Registration of Corporate Enterprises, with total registered capitals divided into equal shares and raised through issuing stocks. Each investor bears limited liability to the corporation depending on the holding of shares, and the corporation bears liability to its debt to the maximum of its total assets.

Private Enterprises refer to economic units invested on controlled (by holding the majority of the shares) by natural persons who hire labors for profit making activities. Included in this category are private limited liability corporations, private share–holding corporations Ltd., private partnership enterprises and private sole investment enterprises registered in accordance with the Corporation Law, Partnership Enterprise Law and

Tentative Regulation on Private Enterprises.

Enterprises with Funds from Hong Kong, Macao and Taiwan refers to all industrial enterprises registered as the joint venture, cooperative, sole investment industrial enterprises and limited liability corporations with funds from Hong Kong, Macao and Taiwan.

Foreign Funded Enterprises refers to all industrial enterprises registered as the joint venture, cooperative, foreign companies and foreign investment Co. Ltd..

Enterprise with Hong Kong, Macao, Taiwan and foreign fund refer to all the enterprises with funds from Hong Kong Macao and Taiwan and foreign funded enterprises.

Light industry refers to the industry that produces consumer goods and hand tools. It consists of two categories, depending on the materials used: (1) Industries using farm products as raw materials. These are branches of light industry which directly or indirectly use farm products as basic raw materials, including the manufacture of food and beverages, tobacco processing, textile, clothing, fur and leather manufacturing, paper making, printing, etc.(2) Industries using non-farm products as raw materials. These are branches of light industry which use manufactured goods as raw materials, including the manufacture of cultural, educational articles and sports goods, chemicals, synthetic fiber, chemical products for daily use, glass products for daily use, metal products for daily use, hand tools, medical apparatus and instruments, and the manufacture of cultural and clerical machinery.

Heavy Industry refers to the industry which produces capital goods, and provides various sectors of the national economy with necessary material and technical basis. It consists of the following three branches according to the purpose of production or the use of products: (1) Mining, quarrying and logging industry refers to the industry that extracts natural resources, including extraction of petroleum, coal, metal and non-metal ores. (2) Raw materials industry refers to the industry that provides various sectors of the national economy with raw materials, fuels and power. It includes smelting and processing of metals, coking and coke chemistry, chemical materials, cement, plywood, power, petroleum refining and coal dressing. (3) Manufacturing industry refers to the industry that processes raw materials. It includes machine building industry which equips sectors of the national economy, industries of metal structure and cement products, industries producing means of agricultural production, such as chemical fertilizers and pesticides.

According to the above principle of classification, the repairing trades, which are engaged primarily in repairing products of heavy industry are classified into heavy industry while these engaged in repairing products of light industry are classified into light industry.

Gross Industrial Output Value refers to total industrial products which were sold or are available for sale produced by industrial enterprise within a certain period of time and expressed with currency and reflects total scale and total level of industrial production within a certain period of time. It includes: value of finished product not processed in the enterprise which are put in storage after inspection and packaging (except products specified not to be packaged), external processing fee income and the value of the difference between the end of the period and the beginning of the period of self-made semi-manufactured goods. Gross industrial output value is calculated as per "factory approach", that is to say that gross industrial output value is calculated according to final result of industrial production activities of enterprises based on industrial enterprise as a whole. Repeated calculation in the enterprise and adding production results of all workshops (branch factories) in the enterprise are forbidden. However, the repeated calculation between enterprises, industries and regions exists.

Gross output value of light and heavy industries is also calculated according to "factory approach", that is to say that total output value of the enterprise is used as gross output of the light industry if major products produced by an industrial enterprise under normal circumstances fall into light industry. Gross output value of the enterprise is use as gross output value of heavy industry if major products produced fall into heavy industry.

Value-added of Industry refers to the final results of industrial production of industrial enterprises in currency during the reference period

Paid-up capital refers to the capital actually received by the enterprise and invested by the investor. Paid-up capital can be divided into national capital, collectively owned capital, corporate capital, personal capital, Hong Kong, Macao and Taiwan capital and foreign capital as per investors.

Total Assets refer to all economic resources, in monetary terms, that is owned or controlled by enterprises, including properties, creditors equity and other economic rights of all forms. Classified by the degree of equitability, total assets include circulating assets, long-term investment, fixed assets, intangible assets and deferred assets, and other assets.

(1)Current assets refer to assets that an enterprise can convert into cash or use during one year or one production cycle that may exceeds one year, including cash and savings deposits of various forms, short-term investment, receivable and prepaid money, inventories, etc..

(2) Fixed assets refer to the total amount of net fixed assets of the enterprise, disposal of fixed assets, project under construction and losses on pending fixed assets.

(3) Intangible assets refer to the assets without physical form used by the enterprise for a long time. It consists of patent right, non-patent technology, trademark right, copyright, chartered right, land use right, etc..

Total Liabilities refer to the liabilities borne by the enterprise which can be measured with currency and repaid by assets or labor services. Liabilities are generally divided into current liabilities, long-term liabilities and deferred tax on the basis of repayment period.

(1) Current liabilities (also called quick liabilities or immediate liabilities) refer to enterprises' total debt payable within an operating cycle of one year or over one year, including short term loans, payables and

advance payments, wages payable, taxes payable and profit payable, etc..

(2) Long–term liabilities refers enterprises' total debt payable within an operating cycle of one year or over one year, including long–term loans, payable liabilities, long–term payables, etc..

Owner's Equity refers to the ownership of net assets of enterprise by its investors. The net assets equal the total assets minus total liabilities of the enterprise, including the actual assets invested into the enterprise by investors, accumulation of capitals and operating surplus and non–distributed profits (namely stockholders' equity for corporate enterprise).

Original Value of Fixed Assets refers to the total value, in monetary terms, that an enterprise spent on fixed assets, through construction, purchase, installation, transformation, expansion or technical upgrading. Generally, it covers cost of purchase, packing, transportation and installation, etc..

Business Revenue refers to the inflow of economic benefits gained by enterprises engaged in production and operation activities, such as selling commodities, providing labor services, and transferring asset use rights, including "main business income" and "other business income."

Business Cost refers to the actual cost incurred by enterprises in production and operation activities, such as selling goods, providing labor services, and transferring asset use rights. including "main business cost" and "other business cost". It is filled in the report based on the cumulative number of the current year in "business cost" item of the "profit statement" accounting.

Taxes and Surcharges refers to the consumption tax, urban maintenance and construction tax, resource tax, environmental protection tax, education surcharges, and real estate tax, land use tax, vehicle and vessel use tax, stamp tax and other related taxes and fees due in accordance with the tax law for their production and business activities .

Total Profits refer to the operating result of the enterprise during a certain accounting period, they are the balance of the production and operation process after all incomes are deducted by various costs, reflect the total amount of profit and loss achieved within the reporting period. Total profit is the amount after operating profit plus non–business income and then minus non–business expenditure, which shall be filled in and reported pursuant to the cumulative data in the current year in the item "total profit" in the "profit statement".

Average Number of Workers refers to the average number of personnel actually owned and participating in production and operation activities of the enterprise within the reporting period.

Total Profits and Taxes refer to the sum of sales taxes, charges, revenues and VAT of the products in the enterprise.

VAT payable this year refers to a turnover tax that pursuant to the VAT of goods and services sales, invisible assets, real estate, machining provided, repair services and to the amount of goods import in accordance with the taxes laws.

13

建 筑 业

CONSTRUCTION

13-1 建筑业主要指标
Main Indicators of Construction Enterprises

指标	Indicator	单位 Unit	2015 年	2016 年	2017 年	2018 年	2019 年	2020 年
汇总单位数	Number of Enterprises	个 (unit)	463	460	504	507	895	1033
建筑业增加值	Construction Inscreased	万元 (10 000 yuan)	2826306	2805982	3308084	5136408	5849207	5200503
建筑业总产值	Gross Output Value	万元 (10 000 yuan)	16638332	18647972	22189343	28234734	35139777	37481222
按隶属关系分	by Ownership							
中央属	Central	万元 (10 000 yuan)	7693792	9079591	11379540	14747883	17350365	20148118
地方属	Local	万元 (10 000 yuan)					11793174	10596000
省属	Provincial	万元 (10 000 yuan)	1664077	1853736	2391026	3039149		
市属	Region	万元 (10 000 yuan)	3222554	3676145	5195869	6391344		
县及县以下	County	万元 (10 000 yuan)	1608569	1711315	570463	641220		
其他	Others	万元 (10 000 yuan)	2449340	2327185	2652445	3415138	5996238	6737105
按工程性质分	by Sector							
建筑工程	Building and Civil Engineering Construction	万元 (10 000 yuan)	14422832	16291789	19476820	25182882	31199367	33447869
安装工程	Construction Installation	万元 (10 000 yuan)	1744180	1998465	2051423	2329541	3015885	3288008
其他产值	Others	万元 (10 000 yuan)	471320	357718	661100	722311	924525	745346
竣工产值	Value of Construction Completed	万元 (10 000 yuan)	7613104	7415119	7987351	8691856	12943615	12789160
房屋施工面积	Floor Space Completed	万平方米 (10 000 sq.cm)	10189	10293	11363	12984	14955	17090
#本年新开工	Startde This year	万平方米 (10 000 sq.cm)	2991	3222	3694	4842	4705	5349
房屋竣工面积	Floor Space Completed	万平方米 (10 000 sq.cm)	2039	2298	2280	2366	3418	3323
#住宅	Residential	万平方米 (10 000 sq.cm)	1178	1379	1258	1502	2170	1916
所有者权益	Creditors'Equity	万元 (10 000 yuan)	4015082	4433678	5900444	6269077	8130630	7894051
利润总额	Total Profits	万元 (10 000 yuan)	568473	573258	836297	810897	1051261	1087848
工资总额	Total wages	万元 (10 000 yuan)	1638141	1812042	2185631	3480056	3793574	3295738

注：建筑业增加值 2006 年起采用以企业营业利润为主的收入法计算。
Note: The value added of construction output was calculated as per income method mainly involving enterprise operating profit as of 2006.

13-2 建筑业增加值构成(2020 年)

Value Added of Construction by Structure(2020)

单位：万元 (10 000yuan)

指标（总承包与专业承包）	Indicator	建筑业增加值 Construction Inscreased	本年提取固定资产折旧 Fixed Assets Depreciation in the Year	税金及附加 Taxes and Other Charges	营业利润 Profits from Business	应付职工薪酬（本年贷方累计发生额） Total Wages Payable
总计	Total	5200503	204691	625902	1074172	3295738
其中：国有及国有控股企业	State-owned and State-controlled Enterprises	3370099	129550	359358	853536	2027655
一、按登记注册类型分组	Grouped by Registration Status					
内资企业	Domestic Funded	5198439	204686	625783	1074075	3293896
国有企业	State-owned	379502	3820	60488	53778	261417
集体企业	Collective-owned Enterprises	32611	1067	5615	1322	24606
股份合作企业	Cooperative Enterprises	6162	-80	2865	1020	2357
联营企业	Joint Ownership Enterprises					
其他联营企业	Other Joint Ownership Enterprises					
有限责任公司	Limited Liability Corporations	3404387	137629	372679	817969	2076110
国有独资公司	State Sole Funded Corporations	952377	35389	81516	243785	591687
其他有限责任公司	Other Limited Liability Corporations	2452010	102240	291163	574184	1484423
股份有限公司	Share-holding Corporations Ltd.	290664	16611	32994	51759	189300
私营企业	Private Enterprises	1085114	45638	151143	148228	740106
私营独资企业	Private-funded Enterprises	3607	404	1353	273	1577
私营有限责任公司	Private Limited Liability Corporations	1067605	44451	148310	144593	730251
私营股份有限公司	Private Share-holding Corporations Ltd.	13902	782	1480	3363	8277
其他企业	Other Enterprises					
港、澳、台商投资企业	Enterprises with Funds from Hong Kong,Macao and Taiwan					
外商投资企业	Foreign Funded Enterprises	2063	5	119	96	1843
中外合资经营企业	Joint-venture Enterprises	257	5	25	-263	491
外商投资股份有限公司	Foreign Investment Limited Liability Company	1806		95	359	1352
二、按国民经济行业分组	by Sector					
房屋建筑业	Building Construction	2354676	49020	263281	458671	1583705
土木工程建筑业	Civil Engineering Construction	2333914	125426	285525	505755	1417208
建筑安装业	Construction Installation	273893	16017	39847	43892	174136
建筑装饰和其他建筑业	Construction Decoration and Others	238021	14228	37250	65854	120689
三、按隶属关系分组	by Ownership					
中央	Central	1924482	103912	207900	507677	1104993
地方	Local	1725316	42530	195675	340740	1146371
其他	Others	1550705	58248	222327	225755	1044375
四、按企业资质等级分组	by Qualification Criteria					
施工总承包	Construction Contract	4758310	178046	557587	983372	3039306
特级	Special Grade	2973172	94271	327252	719981	1831668
一级	First Grade	1043185	42028	104281	159194	737681
二级	Second Grade	353668	19476	59273	33503	241417
三级以下	Third Grade and below	388286	22271	66781	70694	228540
专业承包	Professional Contract	442192	26645	68315	90800	256433
一级	First Grade	204149	6704	29359	57041	111045
二级	Second Grade	141546	8799	22773	18008	91966
三级以下	Third Grade and below	96497	11142	16183	15751	53422

13-3 建筑企业资产实力(2020年)
Assets of Construction Enterprises (2020)

单位：万元

指标（总承包与专业承包）	Indicator	流动资产合计 Liquid Assets	#存货 Inventory
总计	Total	30673224	3379916
其中：国有及国有控股企业	State-owned and State-controlled Enterprises	22399389	1849743
一、按登记注册类型分组	Grouped by Registration Status		
内资企业	Domestic Funded	30658963	3372749
国有企业	State-owned	2915050	30577
集体企业	Collective-owned	88681	15064
股份合作企业	Stock-holding Cooperation	147840	116340
联营企业	Joint-owned		
其他联营企业	Others		
有限责任公司	Company with Limited Liabilition	21072182	2280270
国有独资公司	State-owned	5850974	469730
其他有限责任公司	Others	15221209	1810540
股份有限公司	Stock-holding Company limited	1671674	132071
私营企业	Private Enterprises	4763535	798428
私营独资企业	Solely Owned	20404	5314
私营有限责任公司	Private Limited Liability Corporations	4675789	772169
私营股份有限公司	Private Share-holding Corporations Ltd.	67343	20946
其他企业	Others		
港、澳、台商投资企业	Enterprises with Funds from Hong Kong,Macao and Taiwan		
外商投资企业	Foreign Funded Enterprises	14262	7166
中外合资经营企业	Joint-venture Enterprises	4499	1120
外商投资股份有限公司	Foreign Investment Limited Liability Company	9763	6046
二、按国民经济行业分组	by Sector		
房屋建筑业	Building Construction	9751607	1387973
土木工程建筑业	Civil Engineering Construction	18054544	1617989
建筑安装业	Construction Installation	1354652	194132
建筑装饰和其他建筑业	Construction Decoration and Others	1512422	179822
三、按隶属关系分组	by Ownership		
中央	Central	12231822	869603
地方	Local	10981708	1321088
其他	Others	7459695	1189225
四、按企业资质等级分组	by Qualification Criteria		
施工总承包	Construction Contract	28187257	3019397
特级	Special Grade	18366184	1547573
一级	First Grade	5797318	814166
二级	Second Grade	2104547	345873
三级以下	Third Grade and below	1919208	311784
专业承包	Professional Contract	2485967	360519
一级	First Grade	1202468	231565
二级	Second Grade	822022	88474
三级以下	Third Grade and below	461477	40480

（10 000yuan）

固定资产合计 Fixed Assets	固定资产原价 Original Value of Fixed Assets	流动负债合计 Current Liabilities Total	非流动负债合计 Non-Current Liabilities Total	负债合计 Total Liabilitie	所有者权益合计 Total Creditors' Equity
1116738	2353607	27952300	1331599	29454789	7894051
674400	1468972	21457995	1148997	22606993	5234715
1114917	2350245	27934750	1331599	29437239	7884548
33885	102978	3373137	32819	3405956	613525
11494	17281	78166	461	78887	37625
1855	3802	157361		166311	-10796
705634	1474083	19532247	1099694	20725541	4957704
177309	420300	5458437	306809	5765246	1137527
528325	1053783	14073810	792885	14960295	3820178
59937	169303	1172157	88407	1278448	555591
302112	582800	3621683	110218	3782095	1730898
1848	2723	13804		13872	8936
294695	568061	3554393	109840	3714350	1699896
5568	12015	53486	378	53874	22066
1821	3362	17550		17550	9504
44	291	2606		2606	1937
1777	3071	14945		14945	7566
317921	602058	8138051	278327	8448325	2443391
635300	1413816	17641098	968122	18706695	4405553
71286	185450	1051349	19067	1082750	504572
92230	152284	1121802	66084	1217019	540535
365671	952273	12189048	702342	12891391	2867429
357236	639099	9956264	496415	10485890	2493400
393831	762235	5806988	132842	6077508	2533222
961648	2033629	26069597	1259182	27453633	6978109
500149	999112	17846372	1090055	18936427	4285813
197340	533454	4907650	89719	4997369	1381236
127389	258095	1734380	53390	1904944	674397
136770	242969	1581196	26018	1614893	636664
155089	319978	1882702	72417	2001156	915942
50979	117309	985166	10173	1001652	391881
46662	89555	597481	14596	618592	350804
57448	113113	300055	47648	380913	173257

13-4 建筑业施工产值构成(2020年)
Output Value of Construction by Structure(2020)

单位:万元 (10 000 yuan)

指标 (总承包与专业承包)	Indicator	合计 Total	建筑工程 Constructional Engineering	安装工程 Installation Project	其他产值 Other Value	竣工产值 Value of Construction Completed
总计	**Total**	**37481222**	**33447869**	**3288008**	**745346**	**12789160**
其中:国有及国有控股企业	State-owned and State-controlled Enterprises	28429381	26092165	2091710	245505	8059066
一、按登记注册类型分组	**Grouped by Registration Status**					
内资企业	Domestic Funded	37476147	33447869	3282951	745327	12789160
国有企业	State-owned	139794	136429		3365	47378
集体企业	Collective-owned	83475	81461	1920	94	57673
股份合作企业	Stock-holding Cooperation	56912	55250	1662		6310
联营企业	Joint-owned					
其他联营企业	Others					
有限责任公司	Company with Limited Liabilition	30514998	27918209	2252123	344667	9585977
国有独资公司	State-owned	9192055	8123075	1068319	661	3134797
其他有限责任公司	Others	21322943	19795134	1183804	344006	6451180
股份有限公司	Stock-holding Company limited	1902439	1626281	253288	22870	491700
私营企业	Private Enterprises	4778529	3630240	773959	374330	2600123
私营独资企业	Private Sole-proprietorship Enterprises	22277	19704	450	2123	17088
私营有限责任公司	Private Limited Liability Corporations	4630548	3488797	770263	371488	2509952
私营股份有限公司	Private Share-holding Corporations Ltd.	125705	121739	3246	719	73084
港、澳、台商投资企业	Enterprises with Investment from Hong Kong,Macao and Taiwan					
外商投资企业	Foreign Funded	5076		5057	19	
中外合资经营企业	Chinese-foreign Joint Venture	2100		2100		
外商投资股份有限公司	Foreign Investment Limited Liability Company	2976		2957	19	
二、按国民经济行业分组	**by Sector**					
房屋建筑业	Building Construction	16178281	15384521	709809	83951	7680988
土木工程建筑业	Civil Engineering Construction	18187687	16297462	1503021	387205	3681628
建筑安装业	Construction Installation	1427082	417376	927371	82335	622837
建筑装饰和其他建筑业	Construction Decoration and Others	1688172	1348510	147807	191855	803707
三、按隶属关系分组	**by Ownership**					
中央	Central	20148118	18551253	1471471	125394	5598986
地方	Local	10596000	9890847	580897	124255	4109258
其他	Others	6737105	5005769	1235640	495696	3080916
四、按企业资质等级分组	**by Qualification Criteria**					
施工总承包	Construction Contract	34795799	31623683	2597253	574863	11548671
特级	Special Grade	24349424	22947615	1287479	114330	7961226
一级	First Grade	6836995	5970282	802726	63987	1887279
二级	Second Grade	1492164	1151772	232216	108176	896814
三级及以下	Third Grade and below	2117216	1554014	274832	288370	803352
专业承包	Professional Contract	2685424	1824186	690755	170483	1240489
一级	First Grade	1430315	969956	353379	106980	597023
二级	Second Grade	853039	542568	254668	55804	433537
三级及以下	Third Grade and below	402069	311662	82708	7699	209928

13-5 建筑企业损益及分配(2020年)
Output Value of Construction by Structure(2020)

单位：万元 (10 000yuan)

指标（总承包与专业承包）	Indicator	营业收入 Business Revenue	利税总额 Total Profits and Taxes	营业利润 Profits from Business	利润总额 Total Profits	应付职工薪酬（本年贷方累计发生额） Total Wages Payable
总计	Total	36638241	1713750	1074172	1087848	3295738
其中：国有及国有控股企业	State-owned and State-controlled Enterprises	27447046	1219520	853536	860162	2027655
一、按登记注册类型分组	Grouped by Registration Status					
内资企业	Domestic Funded	36628004	1713521	1074075	1087739	3293896
国有企业	State-owned	1898502	114218	53778	53730	261417
集体企业	Collective-owned	78324	6863	1322	1248	24606
股份合作企业	Stock-holding Cooperation	65840	3965	1020	1101	2357
联营企业	Joint-owned					
其他联营企业	Others					
有限责任公司	Company with Limited Liabilition	27066499	1196475	817969	823796	2076110
国有独资公司	State-owned	8499234	327316	243785	245800	591687
其他有限责任公司	Others	18567265	869159	574184	577996	1484423
股份有限公司	Stock-holding Company limited	1775285	89514	51759	56520	189300
私营企业	Private Enterprises	5743555	302486	148228	151343	740106
私营独资企业	Private Sole-proprietorship Enterprises	39769	1624	273	271	1577
私营有限责任公司	Private Limited Liability Corporations	5635744	295542	144593	147233	730251
私营股份有限公司	Private Share-holding Corporations Ltd.	68042	5320	3363	3840	8277
其他企业	Others					
港、澳、台商投资企业	Enterprises with Investment from Hong Kong,Macao and Taiwan					
外商投资企业	Foreign Funded Enterprises	10236	229	96	110	1843
中外合资经营企业	Joint-venture Enterprises	2100	-238	-263	-263	491
外商投资股份有限公司	Foreign Investment Limited Liability Company	8136	467	359	372	1352
二、按国民经济行业分组	by Sector					
房屋建筑业	Building Construction	15634492	725399	458671	462118	1583705
土木工程建筑业	Civil Engineering Construction	17579551	799296	505755	513772	1417208
建筑安装业	Construction Installation	1627100	87114	43892	47267	174136
建筑装饰和其他建筑业	Construction Decoration and Others	1797097	101941	65854	64692	120689
三、按隶属关系分组	by Ownership					
中央	Central	19434863	716199	507677	508299	1104993
地方	Local	8848162	539285	340740	343610	1146371
其他	Others	8355216	458266	225755	235939	1044375
四、按企业资质等级分组	by Qualification Criteria					
施工总承包	Construction Contract	33586737	1554176	983372	996589	3039306
特级	Special Grade	23527531	1049901	719981	722649	1831668
一级	First Grade	5839512	264919	159194	160638	737681
二级	Second Grade	1853771	94828	33503	35556	241417
三级以下	Third Grade and below	2365924	144528	70694	77747	228540
专业承包	Professional Contract	3051504	159574	90800	91259	256433
一级	First Grade	1567152	85607	57041	56248	111045
二级	Second Grade	982208	41997	18008	19224	91966
三级以下	Third Grade and below	502144	31970	15751	15787	53422

13-6 施工工程施工面积(2020年)

Number of Floor Space Under Construction (2020)

单位：万平方米 (10 000sq.m)

指标(总承包与专业承包)	Indicator	房屋建筑施工面积 Floor Space under Construction	#本年新开工面积 Started This Year	房屋建筑竣工面积 Floor Space Completed	#住宅房屋 (Residential)	竣工房屋价值(万元) Value of Construction Completed (10 000 yuan)
总计	Total	17090	5349	3323	1916	7852692
其中：国有及国有控股企业	State-owned and State-controlled Enterprises	11199	3496	1777	917	5183612
一、按登记注册类型分组	Grouped by Registration Status					
内资企业	Domestic Funded	17090	5349	3323	1916	7852692
国有企业	State-owned	96	50	1	1	2000
集体企业	Collective-owned	45	10	17	13	34254
股份合作企业	Stock-holding Cooperation	7	6	4	4	6000
联营企业	Joint-owned					
其他联营企业	Others					
有限责任公司	Company with Limited Liabilition	13838	4202	2429	1409	6353727
国有独资公司	State-owned	3969	851	603	288	1947004
其他有限责任公司	Others	9869	3352	1826	1121	4406723
股份有限公司	Stock-holding Company limited	693	228	126	78	266070
私营企业	Private Enterprises	2412	853	746	411	1190641
私营独资企业	Private Sole-proprietorship Enterprises	0.03		0.03	0.03	243
私营有限责任公司	Private Limited Liability Corporations	2389	843	736	406	1173162
私营股份有限公司	Private Share-holding Corporations Ltd.	23	10	10	5	17237
港、澳、台商投资企业	Enterprises with Investment from Hong Kong,Macao and Taiwan					
外商投资企业	Foreign Funded Enterprises					
二、按国民经济行业分组	by Sector					
房屋建筑业	Building Construction	15429	4644	2935	1778	7210122
土木工程建筑业	Civil Engineering Construction	1385	555	152	46	514176
建筑安装业	Construction Installation	70	37	97	59	65421
建筑装饰和其他建筑业	Construction Decoration and Others	206	113	139	32	62973
三、按隶属关系分组	by Ownership					
中央	Central	8965	2725	1289	625	4258867
省(自治区、直辖市)	Provincial	5502	1589	1250	847	2411867
地区(州、盟、省辖市)及以下、其他	Region	2624	1035	783	444	1181957
四、按企业资质等级分组	by Qualification Criteria					
施工总承包	Construction Contract	16797	5233	3098	1804	7756451
特级	Special Grade	12515	3754	2096	1137	6048459
一级	First Grade	3361	1073	645	476	1176799
二级	Second Grade	483	230	194	94	330887
三级及以下	Third Grade and below	438	175	163	97	200306
专业承包	Professional Contract	293	116	225	112	96241
一级	First Grade	189	74	110	65	60122
二级	Second Grade	96	36	106	40	24073
三级及以下	Third Grade and below	8	6	9	7	12046

13-7 济南市建筑业特级、一级资质企业一览表(2020年)
Summary of Construction Enterprises with Grade Ⅰ Qualification(2020)

企业名称 Name	隶属关系 Ownership	登记注册类型 Status of Registration	所属行业 Sector
中建八局第二建设有限公司	中央	其他有限责任公司	住宅房屋建筑
中铁十四局集团有限公司	中央	其他有限责任公司	铁路工程建筑
中建八局第一建设有限公司	中央	国有独资公司	住宅房屋建筑
济南宏铁建筑装饰工程有限公司	中央	其他有限责任公司	住宅装饰和装修
中铁十四局集团第四工程有限公司	中央	国有独资公司	铁路工程建筑
中铁十四局集团隧道工程有限公司	中央	其他有限责任公司	铁路工程建筑
中铁济南工程技术有限公司	中央	其他有限责任公司	铁路工程建筑
山东送变电工程有限公司	中央	股份有限公司	架线及设备工程建筑
中铁十局集团建筑工程有限公司	中央	其他有限责任公司	住宅房屋建筑
中铁十局集团电务工程有限公司	中央	其他有限责任公司	铁路工程建筑
中铁十局集团第一工程有限公司	中央	其他有限责任公司	公路工程建筑
山东济铁工程建设集团有限公司	中央	其他有限责任公司	铁路工程建筑
中国铁路通信信号集团济南工程有限公司	中央	其他有限责任公司	架线及设备工程建筑
山东黄河顺成水利水电工程有限公司	中央	国有独资公司	管道工程建筑
中国电建集团山东电力建设第一工程有限公司	中央	国有独资公司	架线及设备工程建筑
中国电建集团核电工程有限公司	中央	其他有限责任公司	架线及设备工程建筑
中广核宏达环境科技有限责任公司	中央	其他有限责任公司	环保工程施工
中铁十四局集团第三工程有限公司	中央	其他有限责任公司	铁路工程建筑
中铁十局集团有限公司	中央	国有独资公司	铁路工程建筑
山东省齐鲁装饰设计院	地方	集体企业	公共建筑装饰和装修
山东省装饰集团有限公司	地方	国有独资公司	公共建筑装饰和装修
山东省深基建设工程总公司	地方	国有企业	住宅房屋建筑
中炬装饰工程集团有限公司	地方	其他有限责任公司	公共建筑装饰和装修
济南易通城市建设集团股份有限公司	地方	股份有限公司	市政道路工程建筑
山东省城建工程集团公司	地方	股份合作企业	住宅房屋建筑
济南长城空调公司	地方	股份合作企业	管道和设备安装
山东泉景建设有限公司	地方	其他有限责任公司	住宅房屋建筑
济南普利供水工程有限公司	地方	其他有限责任公司	管道工程建筑
山东省路桥集团有限公司	地方	其他有限责任公司	其他道路、隧道和桥梁工程建筑
山东省机械施工有限公司	地方	其他有限责任公司	场地准备活动
济南二建集团工程有限公司	地方	其他有限责任公司	住宅房屋建筑
山东汇通建设集团有限公司	地方	国有独资公司	市政道路工程建筑
济南城建集团有限公司	地方	国有独资公司	铁路工程建筑
山东汇友市政园林集团有限公司	地方	国有独资公司	其他未列明建筑业
山东建勘集团有限公司	地方	国有独资公司	场地准备活动
济南消防工程有限公司	地方	其他有限责任公司	电气安装
济南四建(集团)有限责任公司	地方	其他有限责任公司	住宅房屋建筑
山东省高速路桥养护有限公司	地方	其他有限责任公司	其他道路、隧道和桥梁工程建筑
济南建设设备安装有限责任公司	地方	其他有限责任公司	管道和设备安装
普利置业集团股份有限公司	地方	股份有限公司	住宅房屋建筑
济南建工总承包集团有限公司	地方	其他有限责任公司	住宅房屋建筑
山东省大通公路工程有限责任公司	地方	其他有限责任公司	公路工程建筑
山东亚特尔集团股份有限公司	地方	股份有限公司	管道和设备安装
中化学交通建设集团有限公司	地方	其他有限责任公司	公路工程建筑
济南能源工程集团有限公司	地方	国有独资公司	管道和设备安装
山东平安建设集团有限公司	地方	其他有限责任公司	住宅房屋建筑

13-7 续表 1 continued 1

企业名称 Name	隶属关系 Ownership	登记注册类型 Status of Registration	所属行业 Sector
济南长兴建设集团有限公司	地方	其他有限责任公司	住宅房屋建筑
章丘市第二建筑安装（集团）有限责任公司	地方	其他有限责任公司	住宅房屋建筑
济南通达公路工程有限公司	地方	国有独资公司	公路工程建筑
山东三箭建设工程管理有限公司	地方	国有独资公司	住宅房屋建筑
山东三箭建设工程股份有限公司	地方	股份有限公司	住宅房屋建筑
中儒科信达建设集团有限公司	地方	其他有限责任公司	住宅房屋建筑
山东飞越钢结构工程有限公司	地方	其他有限责任公司	其他建筑安装
山东欧瑞装饰有限公司	地方	其他有限责任公司	住宅装饰和装修
山东莱芜建设集团有限公司	地方	其他有限责任公司	住宅房屋建筑
山东泰东公路工程有限公司	地方	其他有限责任公司	公路工程建筑
莱芜市庚鑫市政工程有限公司	地方	其他有限责任公司	管道和设备安装
济南铸诚建筑工程集团有限公司	地方	其他有限责任公司	住宅房屋建筑
山东安泰智能工程有限公司	地方	其他有限责任公司	电气安装
济南市市政工程建设集团有限公司	地方	国有独资公司	市政道路工程建筑
山东双利电子工程有限公司	地方	其他有限责任公司	电气安装
山东江森机电工程有限公司	其他	私营有限责任公司	管道和设备安装
济南岩土工程公司	其他	国有企业	其他土木工程建筑施工
山东海威装饰工程有限公司	其他	私营有限责任公司	公共建筑装饰和装修
山东展鸿华商装饰工程有限公司	其他	私营有限责任公司	住宅装饰和装修
鸿鑫工程有限公司	其他	私营有限责任公司	公共建筑装饰和装修
山东天宝建设集团有限公司	其他	其他有限责任公司	住宅房屋建筑
山东万得福装饰工程有限公司	其他	其他有限责任公司	公共建筑装饰和装修
永隆装饰工程有限公司	其他	私营有限责任公司	公共建筑装饰和装修
山东省建设建工（集团）有限责任公司	其他	私营有限责任公司	住宅房屋建筑
山东省建设建工集团装饰装璜有限公司	其他	其他有限责任公司	公共建筑装饰和装修
济南百士岩土工程有限公司	其他	其他有限责任公司	市政道路工程建筑
山东奥深智能工程有限公司	其他	私营有限责任公司	其他未列明建筑业
山东德铭工程建设有限公司	其他	私营有限责任公司	住宅装饰和装修
山东宇宸建设工程有限公司	其他	私营有限责任公司	管道和设备安装
瑞森新建筑有限公司	其他	私营有限责任公司	其他房屋建筑业
山东华森装饰工程有限公司	其他	私营有限责任公司	公共建筑装饰和装修
济南万泰建筑装饰工程有限公司	其他	私营有限责任公司	住宅装饰和装修
山东省邮电工程有限公司	其他	其他有限责任公司	架线及设备工程建筑
山东海瑞林装饰工程有限公司	其他	私营有限责任公司	公共建筑装饰和装修
济南凯诚消防自控设备有限公司	其他	私营有限责任公司	电气安装
山东同大装饰有限公司	其他	私营有限责任公司	公共建筑装饰和装修
山东费尔消防技术工程有限公司	其他	私营有限责任公司	电气安装
山东涌泉安全科技有限公司	其他	私营有限责任公司	其他建筑安装
山东通海装饰工程有限公司	其他	私营有限责任公司	公共建筑装饰和装修
山东恒霖建设工程有限公司	其他	私营有限责任公司	住宅房屋建筑
山东宏雁电子系统工程有限公司	其他	私营有限责任公司	电气安装
山东华森建筑消防项目管理有限公司	其他	私营有限责任公司	电气安装
山东世纪装饰工程股份有限公司	其他	私营股份有限公司	住宅装饰和装修
济南华海建设集团有限公司	其他	私营有限责任公司	住宅房屋建筑
山东顺河路桥工程有限公司	其他	其他有限责任公司	市政道路工程建筑
山东坚瑞建设股份有限公司	其他	股份有限公司	其他未列明建筑业
山东中大净化工程有限公司	其他	私营有限责任公司	其他建筑安装
山东清尚建筑装饰设计工程有限公司	其他	私营有限责任公司	住宅装饰和装修

13-7 续表 2 continued 2

企业名称 Name	隶属关系 Ownership	登记注册类型 Status of Registration	所属行业 Sector
山东三盛防水工程有限公司	其他	私营有限责任公司	环保工程施工
山东深博建筑工程有限公司	其他	私营有限责任公司	管道和设备安装
风派特装饰工程有限公司	其他	私营有限责任公司	建筑幕墙装饰和装修
山东润霖消防工程有限公司	其他	私营有限责任公司	电气安装
济南四建集团智能消防工程有限责任公司	其他	其他有限责任公司	其他建筑安装
山东建科特种建筑工程技术中心	其他	其他有限责任公司	建筑幕墙装饰和装修
山东凯罗福环保节能科技有限公司	其他	私营有限责任公司	住宅装饰和装修
辉瑞（山东）环境科技有限公司	其他	私营有限责任公司	公共建筑装饰和装修
山东福缘来装饰有限公司	其他	私营有限责任公司	住宅装饰和装修
山东福思特建筑装饰有限公司	其他	私营有限责任公司	建筑幕墙装饰和装修
千庭景观建设有限公司	其他	私营有限责任公司	市政道路工程建筑
山东昌舜岩土工程有限公司	其他	私营有限责任公司	场地准备活动
山东中恒建设集团有限公司	其他	私营有限责任公司	住宅房屋建筑
山东盛顺装饰有限公司	其他	私营有限责任公司	住宅装饰和装修
山东群雄建设工程有限公司	其他	私营有限责任公司	公共建筑装饰和装修
济南昊兴市政工程有限公司	其他	私营有限责任公司	管道工程建筑
沃尔德项目管理有限公司	其他	其他有限责任公司	住宅装饰和装修
山东深装总装饰工程工业有限公司	其他	私营有限责任公司	公共建筑装饰和装修
山东鸿图科技有限公司	其他	私营有限责任公司	其他建筑安装
山东彩旺建设有限公司	其他	私营有限责任公司	电气安装
奥斯福集团有限公司	其他	私营有限责任公司	电气安装
济南东元改建加固工程有限公司	其他	私营有限责任公司	其他房屋建筑业
山东志坚建筑工程有限公司	其他	私营有限责任公司	其他房屋建筑业
济南众联深基工程有限公司	其他	私营有限责任公司	场地准备活动
山东泰景楼宇安全技术有限公司	其他	私营有限责任公司	其他未列明建筑业
山东宏岳消防工程有限公司	其他	私营有限责任公司	其他建筑安装
山东亿威市政工程有限公司	其他	其他有限责任公司	市政道路工程建筑
山东昶博建筑工程有限公司	其他	私营有限责任公司	其他房屋建筑业
山东大禹水务建设集团有限公司	其他	其他有限责任公司	水源及供水设施工程建筑
山东港基建设集团有限公司	其他	其他有限责任公司	住宅房屋建筑
山东鑫龙装饰工程有限公司	其他	私营有限责任公司	公共建筑装饰和装修
山东汇富建设集团有限公司	其他	私营有限责任公司	住宅房屋建筑
山东长泰建设集团工程有限公司	其他	私营有限责任公司	住宅房屋建筑
山东润诚机电工程有限公司	其他	私营有限责任公司	电气安装
山东福源设备安装有限公司	其他	私营有限责任公司	管道和设备安装
山东福源建设集团有限公司	其他	私营有限责任公司	管道和设备安装
济南长兴安装工程公司	其他	其他有限责任公司	其他建筑安装
山东科发建设工程有限公司	其他	其他有限责任公司	建筑幕墙装饰和装修
山东泰实建筑工程有限公司	其他	其他有限责任公司	住宅房屋建筑
山东鲁桥建设有限公司	其他	其他有限责任公司	公路工程建筑
山东津单幕墙有限公司	其他	私营有限责任公司	建筑幕墙装饰和装修
远大建设工程有限公司	其他	私营有限责任公司	公共建筑装饰和装修
山东洁昕建筑装饰工程设计有限公司	其他	私营有限责任公司	公共建筑装饰和装修
山东北成环境工程有限公司	其他	私营有限责任公司	环保工程施工
山东洪雨防水工程有限公司	其他	私营有限责任公司	其他未列明建筑业
山东中安消防设施维修有限公司	其他	私营有限责任公司	其他未列明建筑业
山东正顺建设集团有限公司	其他	私营有限责任公司	住宅房屋建筑

13–7 续表 3 continued 3

企业名称 Name	隶属关系 Ownership	登记注册类型 Status of Registration	所属行业 Sector
山东省莱芜市宏强建筑安装工程有限公司	其他	私营有限责任公司	其他房屋建筑业
山东天翼安全技术有限公司	其他	私营有限责任公司	电气安装
山东信达建设工程有限公司	其他	私营有限责任公司	其他房屋建筑业
济南信高工程技术有限公司	其他	私营有限责任公司	电气安装
山东清华康利城市照明研究设计院有限公司	其他	其他有限责任公司	电气安装
山东太平洋环保股份有限公司	其他	私营股份有限公司	其他建筑安装
山东中宝置业有限公司	其他	私营有限责任公司	住宅房屋建筑
优士科技发展有限公司	其他	私营有限责任公司	电气安装
山东鲁光信息工程有限公司	其他	私营有限责任公司	电气安装
山东省鲁美建材装饰有限公司	其他	私营有限责任公司	建筑幕墙装饰和装修
山东宏业发展集团有限公司	其他	私营有限责任公司	架线及设备工程建筑
山东水发鲁润水务科技有限公司	其他	其他有限责任公司	环保工程施工
山东天启智能工程有限公司	其他	私营有限责任公司	其他未列明建筑业
山东华尔泰建筑工程有限公司	其他	私营有限责任公司	电气安装
山东鑫联通信科技有限公司	其他	私营有限责任公司	电气安装
中直科创股份有限公司	其他	股份有限公司	建筑幕墙装饰和装修
山东金岛消防安全工程有限公司	其他	私营有限责任公司	电气安装
济南金宇公路产业发展有限公司	其他	其他有限责任公司	公路工程建筑
雪山集团有限公司	其他	私营有限责任公司	管道和设备安装
山东省建设建工集团消防工程有限公司	其他	私营有限责任公司	电气安装
万旭装饰工程有限公司	其他	私营有限责任公司	住宅装饰和装修
阿郎装饰股份有限公司	其他	私营股份有限公司	公共建筑装饰和装修
山东千业建设工程有限公司	其他	私营有限责任公司	建筑幕墙装饰和装修
山东思达特信息科技有限公司	其他	私营有限责任公司	电气安装
山东华盛特克科技有限公司	其他	私营有限责任公司	电气安装
山东建华土木有限公司	其他	私营有限责任公司	住宅房屋建筑
山东省亘基工程有限公司	其他	私营有限责任公司	其他房屋建筑业
山东万林建设工程有限公司	其他	私营有限责任公司	住宅装饰和装修
山东铁迅建设工程有限公司	其他	私营有限责任公司	电气安装
山东航空港建设工程有限公司	其他	私营有限责任公司	其他土木工程建筑施工
山东省建设集团有限公司	其他	私营有限责任公司	其他房屋建筑业
山东惠诚建筑有限公司	其他	私营有限责任公司	其他房屋建筑业
山东宇顺建筑工程有限公司	其他	私营有限责任公司	住宅房屋建筑
济南佳宸装饰安装有限公司	其他	私营有限责任公司	公共建筑装饰和装修
山东太平洋环保股份有限公司	其他	私营有限责任公司	其他建筑安装
山东水发鲁润水务科技有限公司	其他	其他有限责任公司	环保工程施工
山东安泰智能工程有限公司	地方	其他有限责任公司	电气安装
山东天启智能工程有限公司	其他	私营有限责任公司	其他未列明建筑业
山东博安智能科技股份有限公司	其他	私营股份有限公司	电气安装
济南金宇公路产业发展有限公司	其他	其他有限责任公司	公路工程建筑
山东海威装饰工程有限公司	其他	私营有限责任公司	公共建筑装饰和装修
山东彩旺建设有限公司	其他	私营有限责任公司	电气安装
山东奥斯福市政工程有限公司	其他	私营有限责任公司	电气安装
山东清华康利城市照明研究设计院有限公司	其他	其他有限责任公司	电气安装
济南东元改建加固工程有限公司	其他	私营有限责任公司	其他房屋建筑业

主要统计指标解释

建筑业统计单位 指从事房屋、构筑物建造和设备安装活动的法人企业。建筑业法人企业应同时具备的条件是：①依法成立，有自己的名称、组织机构和场所，能够承担民事责任；②独立拥有和使用资产，承担负债，有权与其他单位签订合同；③独立核算盈亏，能够编制资产负债表。

建筑业总产值（即自行完成施工产值） 是以货币表现的建筑安装企业在一定时期内生产的建筑业产品的总和。建筑业总产值包括：

（1）建筑工程产值：指列入建筑工程预算内的各种工程价值。

（2）设备安装工程产值：指设备安装工程价值，不包括被安装设备本身价值。

（3）房屋、构筑物修理产值：指房屋、构筑物修理所完成的价值，但不包括被修理房屋、构筑物本身的价值和生产设备的修理价值。

（4）非标准设备制造产值：指加工制造没有定型的、非标准的生产设备的加工费和原材料价值，以及附属加工厂为本企业承建工程制作的非标准设备的价值。

建筑业增加值 指建筑业企业在报告期内以货币表现的建筑业生产经营活动的最终成果。目前建筑业增加值采用分配法（收入法）计算，即从收入的角度出发，根据生产要素在生产过程中应得的收入份额计算。具体计算公式为：

建筑业增加值＝本年提取的固定资产折旧＋应付工资＋应付福利费＋管理费用中的劳动待业保险金、税金＋工程结算税金及附加＋工程结算利润

房屋建筑施工面积 指在报告期内施工的全部房屋建筑面积，包括本期新开工的房屋面积、上期施工跨入本期继续施工的房屋面积、上期停缓建在本期恢复施工的房屋面积、本期竣工的房屋面积及本期施工后又停缓建的房屋面积。

房屋建筑竣工面积 指在报告期内房屋建筑按照设计要求全部完工，达到了住人和使用条件，经验收鉴定合格，正式移交使用单位的房屋建筑面积。

营业收入 指企业经营主要业务和其他业务所确认的收入总额。营业收入合计包括“主营业务收入”和“其他业务收入”。根据会计“利润表”中“营业收入”项目的本期总额数填报。

营业利润 指企业从事生产经营活动所取得的利润。执行2006年《企业会计准则》的企业，营业利润为营业收入减去营业成本、营业税金及附加、销售费用、管理费用、财务费用、资产减值损失，再加上公允价值变动收益和损益收益。未执行2006年《企业会计准则》的企业，营业利润为主营业务收入减去主营业务成本、主营业务税金及附加，加上其他业务利润后，再减支销售费用、管理费用、财务费用后的金额。

Explanatory Notes on Main Statistical Indicators

Statistical Unit in Construction refers to corporate enterprise engaged in the construction of buildings, structures and the installation of equipment. A corporate construction enterprise should meet the following requirements: ① being set up in line with relevant legal basis, having its full name, organization and location, and capable of taking civil liabilities; ② independently possessing and using its assets and assuming its liabilities, and entitled to sign contracts with other institutions; ③ making independent accounts of its profits and losses, and capable of compiling its own balance sheet.

Gross Output Value of Construction (i.e. complete construction output value independently) is the sum of construction products produced by construction and installation enterprises embodied with currency within a certain period. It includes:

(1) Output value of construction projects: the value of projects covered by the project budgets;

(2) Value of equipment installation projects: the value of the installation of equipment, (excluding the own value of the equipment to be installed);

(3) Output value of repair of buildings and structures: the value created through the repairs of buildings or structures. It does not include the value of buildings or structures being repaired and the value of the repair of production equipment;

(4) Output value of manufactured non-standard equipment: the value of non-standard production equipment including raw materials and manufacturing cost, made for the construction project. It also includes the output value of equipment manufactured by subsidiary workshops.

Value added of Construction refers to the final result of the activities of production and operation of enterprises of construction industry in monetary terms during the reporting period. Now, the construction value added is calculated in terms of distribution approach (income approach), namely calculation based on earned income of production factors in the production process from the perspective of the income. Specific calculation formula is:

Construction value added= depreciation of fixed assets extracted this year+ wages payable+ welfare payable+ unemployment insurance and taxes in the administration expense + project settlement tax and surcharge + project settlement profits

Floor Space of Buildings under Construction refers to floor space of buildings under construction during the reporting period, including newly started buildings, buildings started earlier and continued during the reporting period, and buildings suspended earlier but restarted during the reporting period, buildings completed during the reporting period, and buildings under construction and then suspended during the reporting period.

Floor Space of Buildings Completed refers to the floor space of buildings that are completed in the reporting period in accordance with the requirements of the design, up to the standard for living in and putting into use, and have been checked and accepted by concerned departments as qualified ones.

Operating Income refers to the total income of main business or other businesses of the enterprise confirmed. Total operating incomes include "main business income" and "other business income" which is filled in pursuant to total amount of "operating income" in the "profit statement" in the current period.

Operating Profit refers to the profit obtained by the enterprise after engaging in production and operation activities. As for enterprises subject to 2006 Accounting Standards for Business Enterprises, the operating profit is the result after the operating income minus operating cost, business tax and surcharge, selling expense, administration expense, financial expense and assets impairment loss and then plus income from fair value changes and income from profit and loss. As for enterprises do not subject to 2006 Accounting Standards for Business Enterprises, the operating profit is the amount after main business income minus main business cost and tax and extra charges of main business and then plus profit from other business and finally minus selling expense, administration expense and financial expense.

14

运输与邮电

TRANSPORTATION POST AND TELECOMMUNICATIONS

14-1 邮电业务量
Postal and Telecommunications Services

指标	Indicator	单位 Unit	2015 年	2016 年	2017 年	2018 年	2019 年	2020 年
国内分类业务量	**Domestic Classified Business Volume**							
固定电话数	Number of Fixed Telephone	万户（10 000 subscribers）	165.30	155.90	153.10	135.27	148.82	144.78
年末市内电话	Urban Fixed Telephone Subscribers at Year-end	万户（10 000 subscribers）	141.00	135.89	132.55	118.70	136.30	127.65
年末农村电话	Rural Telephone Subscribers at Year-end	万户（10 000 subscribers）	24.30	19.07	19.23	16.47	12.20	2.78
年末住宅电话	Number of Fixed Telephone Subscribers at Year-end	万户（10 000 subscribers）	86.40	71.79	79.54	67.64	25.56	14.26
年末移动电话用户	Number of Mobile Telephone Subscribers at Year-end	万户（10 000 subscribers）	1090.40	1087.71	971.10	1013.65	1122.86	1154.06
4G 电话用户数	4G Mobile Phone Subscribers	万户（10 000 subscribers）	306.60	442.10	623.50	725.01	888.81	922.67
宽带互联网接入用户数	Subscribers of Broad Band Internet	户（subscriber）	2316600	2618800	2987500	3447000	3926200	4454800
每百人互联网用户数	Number of Internet User per 100 Population	户/百人 (subscriber/100 person)	37.02	41.38	46.81	53.05	49.63	55.56
邮电局所	Post & Telecommunication offices	处 (place)	204	204	207	207	252	252
国际及港澳分类业务量	**International.Hong kong and Macao Classified Business Volume**							
函件	Letters	万件 (10 000 pieces)	19.49	16.10	27.67	51.95	45.75	13.02
包件	Package	万件 (10 000 pieces)	0.84	1.24	1.35	0.76	0.60	0.60

14-2 交通运输业基本情况
Basic Conditions of Transportation

指标	Indicator	2015年	2016年	2017年	2018年	2019年	2020年
铁路客运量（万人）	Railways Passenger Traffic(10 000 persons)	10681.1	11923.7	13411.8	14547.7	15745.1	9797.4
铁路客运周转量（亿人公里）	Railways Passenger Turnover(100 million passengers-km)	662.5	703.8	754.6	784.6	795.3	431.9
铁路货运量（万吨）	Railways Freight Traffic(10 000 tons)	15793.8	16749.1	17865.2	18728.0	20869.8	23188.8
铁路货运周转量（亿吨公里）	Railways Freight Turnover(100 million ton-km)	1088.0	1153.0	1254.9	1288.4	1460.5	1566.1
公路客运量（万人）	Highways Passenger Traffic(10 000 persons)	3663.0	3212.0	3192.0	3149.0	3244.0	1209.0
公路旅客周转量（亿人公里）	Highways Passenger Turnover(100 million passengers-km)	54.2	52.2	52.7	52.9	54.1	17.1
公路货运量（万吨）	Highways Freight Traffic(10 000 tons)	20419.0	21212.0	24058.0	25571.0	28064.0	28177.0
公路货物周转量（亿吨公里）	Highways Freight Turnover(100 million ton-km)	393.8	419.0	459.5	474.0	561.4	562.4
民航客运量（万人次）	Civil Aviation Passenger Traffic(10 000 person-times)	533.1	645.1	785.6	894.1	936.1	1238.5
民航客运周转量（亿人公里）	Civil Aviation Passenger Turnover(100 million passengers-km)	227.7	272.9	334.3	368.5	376.5	256.3
民航货运量（万吨）	Civil Aviation Freight Turnover(10 000 tons)	4.2	5.1	5.0	5.6	6.7	14.7
公路通车里程（公里）	Length of Highways in Operation(km)						
公路通车里程	Length of Highways in Operation	13104	12730.2	12856.8	12637.7	17770.9	18117.2
#高速公路	Expressway	419	462.2	488.5	488.5	653.6	737.8
有铺装、简易铺装路面	Poved Roads	12906	12603.9	12735.7	12579.4	17290.0	18117.2
未铺装路面	UnPoved Roads	198	126.3	121.1	58.3	480.9	0.0
民用航空	Civil Aviation						
执行航线（条）	Perform Routes(line)	152	125	150	182	198	208
通航城市（个）	Navigable Cities(unit)	55	64	82	96	120	91
起飞架次（架次）	Plane Flights(Sorties)	86158	100152	115529	126828	129994	102375
民用车辆（辆）	Civil Vehicles(unit)						
民用汽车	Civil Vehicles	1541045	1742313	1949707	2160748	2584278	2794278
私人汽车	Private Vehicles	1505308	1573761	1764574	1948815	2332421	2512357
载客汽车	Passenger Vehicles	1400588	1592737	1783848	1978951	2370437	2556622
#大型	Large	11194	12206	13539	14002	15767	15535
载货汽车	Trucks	123801	134741	151141	166277	194957	224713
#重型	Heavy	24653	27303	31632	36720	41904	46148
其它汽车	Others	16656	14835	14718	15520	18884	
专项作业车	Special Operation vehicles						12943
摩托车	Motorcycles	126540	73568	106168	133743	258382	329477
挂车	Wheeler	7497	8191	9102	9851	12538	14842

注：1. 公路通车里程自2006年起调整统计口径，增加了村道公路统计。
2. 因省交通厅公路局统计口径变化，自2012年起，公路通车里程按路面类型分为有铺装路面、简易铺装路面和未铺装路面。
3. 铁路系统统计数据来自中国铁路济南局集团有限公司。
4. 2020年起，因公安部"公安交通管理综合应用平台"调整，修改了机动车报表统计口径，增加"专项作业车"等部分车型的统计，不再提供"其它"类汽车保有量。
5.2019年，交通运输部组织开展道路货物运输量专项调查，对公路货运数据进行重新核算，因此2019年公路货运量和公路货物周转量两项指标统一采用折算后的新数据。
6.2020年起，民航客运量、货运量统计口径调整为出港和进港合计数。

Note: 1. The mileage in highway open to traffic was adjusted to be statistical caliber as of 2006, increasing statistics of village road highway.
2. Due to the change in statistical caliber of provincial communications department and highway administration bureau, the mileage in highway open to traffic was divided into dry pavement, easy pavement and unpaved road in light of pavement type as of 2012.
3. Statistical data of railway system comes from China Railway Jinan Group Co., Ltd.
4. Since 2020, due to the adjustment of the "Public Traffic Management Integrated Application Platform", the statistical caliber of motor vehicles statement is varied, the statistics on "special motor vehicle" is supplemented, while "Population of Other Vehicles" is not listed longer.
5. In 2019, the Ministry of Transport organized ad hoc survey on the road freight volume, and recalculated the volume, thus the two indexes as the highway freight volume and turnover volume of freight traffic of 2019 all adopted new data after conversion.
6. Since 2020, the passenger transport volume of civil aviation, and the statistical caliber of freight traffic volume are adjusted as the total number of departures and arrivals.

14-3 规模以上交通运输、仓储和邮政业企业财务指标(2020 年)
Main Financial Indicators of Transport,Storage and Postal Services above Designated Size(2020)

单位:万元 (10 000 yuan)

指标	Indicator	交通运输、仓储和邮政业 Transport,Storage and Postal Services
单位数	Number	355
年初存货	Inventory at Beginning of year	207546
流动资产合计	Total Liquid Assets	13074229
其中:应收账款	Receivable	1885649
其中:存货	Inventory	287347
固定资产原价	Original Value of Fixed Assets	42482072
本年折旧	Depreciation in the Year	1682327
资产总计	Total Assets	85286410
负债合计	Total Liabilities	40091519
所有者权益合计	Total Creditors'Equity	45194891
营业收入	Business Revenue	12291774
营业成本	Business Cost	12126150
税金及附加	Taxes and Other Surcharges	31631
销售费用	Sales Expenses	154208
管理费用	Management Expenses	522107
研发费用	Research and Development Expenses	13544
财务费用	Financial Expenses	733697
投资收益	Investment Interests	777873
其他收益	Other Revenues	233421
营业利润	Profits from Business	-259069
营业外收入	Profits from Non-Business	59002
营业外支出	Expense from Non-Business	60108
利润总额	Total Profits	-260175
所得税费用	Income Tax Expense	76933
应付职工薪酬(本年贷方累计发生额)	Total Wages Payable	2784078
应交增值税	Value-added Tax Payable	277336
从事服务业活动的从业人员平均人数(人)	Average of Empolyed Persons (person)	177696

14-4 分地区公路交通(2020 年)
Road Transportation by Region(2020)

单位：公里 (km)

指标	Indicator	济南市 Ji'nan	其中 of which		
			市区 Urban	平阴县 Ping yin	商河县 Shang he
公路通车里程	Length of Highways in Operation	18117.2	14410.7	1015.1	2691.4
# 高速公路	Expressway	737.8	644.3	60.8	32.7
有铺装、简易铺装路面	Poved Road	18117.2	14410.7	1015.1	2691.4
未铺装路面	UnPoved Road	0.0	0.0	0.0	0.0

主要统计指标解释

公路里程 指在一定时期内实际达到《公路工程技术标准JTJ01-88》规定的等级公路，并经公路主管部门正式验收交付使用的公路里程数。包括大中城市的郊区公路以及通过小城镇街道部分的公路里程和桥梁、渡口的长度，不包括大中城市的街道、厂矿、林区生产用道和农业生产用道的里程。两条或多条公路共同经由同一路段，只计算一次，不得重复计算里程长度。它是反映公路建设发展规模的重要指标，也是计算运输网密度等指标的基础资料。

民用航空航线里程 指民航运输定期班机飞行的航线长度的总和。航线长度按机场之间的距离计算，通常有两种计算方法：一是将每条航线长度相加称为重复计算航线里程；一是将两线或两条以上航线经过同一区段里程，只计算一次航线长度称为不重复计算航线里程。一般常用的是后者，它能确切反映民航运输网的规模，是表明民航事业为国民经济服务和方便人民生活程度的主要指标。

货（客）运量 指在一定时期内，各种运输工具实际运送的货物（旅客）数量。它是反映运输业为国民经济和人民生活服务的数量指标，也是制定和检查运输生产计划、研究运输发展规模和速度的重要指标。货运按吨计算，客运按人计算。货物不论运输距离长短、货物类别，均按实际重量统计。旅客不论行程远近或票价多少，均按一人一次客运量统计；半价票、小孩票也按一人统计。

货物（旅客）周转量 指在一定时期内，由各种运输工具运送的货物（旅客）数量与其相应运输距离的乘积之总和。它是反映运输业生产总成果的重要指标，也是编制和检查运输生产计划，计算运输效率、劳动生产率以及核算运输单位成本的主要基础资料。计算货物周转量通常按发出站与到达站之间的最短距离，也就是计费距离计算。计算公式为：

货物(旅客)周转量 = Σ(货物(旅客)运输量 × 运输距离)

移动电话用户 指在移动电话营业部门登记，通过移动电话交换机进入移动电话网、占有移动电话号码的电话用户。用户数量以实际办理登记手续进入邮电部门移动电话网的户数进行计算，一部或一台移动电话统计为一户。

电话用户 指接入国家公众固定电话网，并按固定电话业务进行经营管理的电话用户。1997 年以前，电话用户分为市内电话用户和农村电话用户。市内电话用户是指接入县城及县以上城市电话网上的电话用户；农村电话用户是指接入县邮电局农话台及县以下农村电话交换点，以县城为中心(除市话用户外)联通县、乡（镇）、行政村、村民小组的用户。从1997 年起，电话用户数分组调整为以用户所在区域划分为“城市电话用户”和“乡村电话用户”，与过去的按市内电话和农村电话划分方法不同。而电话用户数、电话机部数统计方法不变。

Explanatory Notes on Main Statistical Indicators

Length of Highways refers to the length of highways which are built in conformity with the grades specified in the Technical Standard JTJ01–88 for Highway Engineering within a certain period of time, and have been formally checked and accepted by the departments of highways and put into use. The length of highways includes that of the suburb highways at large and medium sized cities, highways passing through streets at small cities and towns, and also the length of bridges and ferries. It does not include the length of streets in big and medium sized cities and highways built for the production purpose at factories, mines, forest areas and agricultural areas. If two or more highways go to the same section of the way, the length of the section is only calculated for once and no duplication is allowed. The length of highways is an important indicator to show the development of the highway construction and to provide essential information to calculate the transport network density.

Mileage of Civil Aviation Routes refers to the sum of the length of the route of scheduled civil aviation flight. The length of the route is calculated as the distance between airports. There are usually two calculation methods: First, repeated calculation of route mileage is deemed in case of adding the length of each route; Second, no repeated calculation of route mileage is deemed if the length of the route is only calculated once when no less than two routes pass the same zone. The second one is usually used, as it can precisely show the size of the civil aviation network and also is the major indicator of indicating the extent of civil aviation serving the national economy and the people.

Freight (Passenger) Traffic refers to the volume or freight (passenger) transported with various means in a certain period. It provides a quantitative measure to show how the transportation industry serves the national economy and people, and is also an important indicator for planning the transport industry and for studying the development scale and speed of the transport industry. Freight transport is calculated in tons and passenger traffic is calculated in the number of persons. Despite the type of freight and traveling distance, the freight transport is calculated in the actual weight of the goods. And despite the traveling distance and ticket price, the passenger traffic is calculated by the principle that one person can be counted only once in one travel. The passengers who travel with a half–price ticket or a child ticket is also calculated as one person.

Tonnage Mileage (Passenger turnover) refers to the sum of the products of the volume of transported cargos (passengers) multiplying by the transport distance. It is an important indicator to reflect the achievement of transportation industry, to prepare and examine the transport plan and to measure the efficiency, the labor productivity and the unit cost of transport. Normally, the shortest distance between the departure station and the destination station (i.e., the payable distance) is the basis to calculate the Tonnage mileage. The formula is as follows:

Tonnage mileage (passenger turnover) = Σ (freight (passenger) traffic* distance of transportation)

Wireless Subscribers refer to persons who have registered at the mobile phone business department and hence connected with the mobile telephone communication network through the mobile telephone switchboards and occupy mobile telephone numbers. The number of subscribers is calculated in line with the number of users actually handling the registration procedures and entering the mobile telephone network of the post and telecommunications departments. One mobile telephone is deemed as one household.

Telephone Subscribers refer to telephone subscribers entering the national public fixed telephone network and undergoing operating management based on fixed telephone services. Before 1997, telephone subscribers were divided into local telephone subscribers and rural telephone subscribers. Local telephone subscribers refer to telephone subscribers accessing to the urban telephone network of county and above; Rural telephone subscribers refer to telephone subscribers accessing to the agricultural telephone station of the county post and telecommunications office and the rural telephone exchange of those below country, and connecting with county, township (town), administrative village and group of villagers based on the county as the center (except for city telephone users). From 1997, grouping of telephone users is adjusted to "city telephone subscribers" and "rural telephone subscribers" in light of regions where subscribers are, which is different from partition method -- local call and rural call in the past. The statistical approaches for counting telephone subscribers and telephones numbers remain unchanged.

15

国内贸易

DOMESTIC TRADE

15-1 各时期分行业社会消费品零售

Total Retail Sales of Consumer Goods by Section in Each Period

单位：万元 (10 000 yuan)

年份 Year	社会消费品零售总额 Retail Sale of Consumer Goods						
	总计 Total	批发零售业 Wholesale and Retail Trades	住宿业 Hotels Services	餐饮业 Catering Services	制造业 Manufacture	其他 Others	农民对非农业居民 Farmers to Non-agricultural Residents
1949	11426	7312		556	3514	–	44
1952	22248	16985		1223	3592	–	448
1957	34568	29279		1935	2381	3	970
1962	41436	35784		1655	2946	266	785
1965	40795	36470		1829	1856	287	353
1970	42993	39397		1537	1468	321	270
1975	60105	53239		2565	2914	1217	170
1978	81335	70661		2907	5120	2222	425
1979	96036	80703		4000	9060	823	1450
1980	119775	95121		4392	16489	1299	2474
"六五时期"							
1981	135236	103303		5388	21353	2157	3035
1982	152094	116241		8165	21398	2778	3512
1983	167948	127884		9225	23569	2953	4317
1984	200301	150233		11342	29563	4506	4657
1985	243080	181867		14823	32342	5535	8513
"七五时期"							
1986	294102	219730		17880	35565	5456	15471
1987	331504	240192		20305	45386	8963	16658
1988	425984	300090		30808	60463	12300	22323
1989	484392	343978		28634	71653	9729	30398
1990	528221	382047		25599	71505	10886	38184
"八五时期"							
1991	597989	424836		27443	78452	14186	53072
1992	711774	535080		37096	77951		61647
1993	985251	723914		56059	80101		125177
1994	1426472	1037687		86141	99621		203023
1995	1837618	1345321		133501	115105		243691

15-1 续表 continued

年份 Year	社会消费品零售总额 Retail Sale of Consumer Goods						
	总计 Total	批发零售业 Wholesale and Retail Trades	住宿业 Hotels Services	餐饮业 Catering Services	制造业 Manufacture	其他 Others	农民对非农业居民 Farmers to Non-agricultural Residents
“九五时期”							
1996	2234590	1570947		176100	141201		346342
1997	2568584	1744014		216727	177219		430624
1998	2834024	1893486		255616	207595		477327
1999	3092091	2043078		305333	225132		518548
2000	3444527	2287545		377550	233128		546304
“十五时期”							
2001	3857141	2574216		485494	237545		559886
2002	4321225	2935804		613178	231947		540296
2003	5115396	4373831		741565	–		–
2004	6689452	5691288	57973	940191	–		–
2005	7726458	6575543	66490	1084425	–		–
“十一五时期”							
2006	8974064	7571831	78098	1324135	–		–
2007	10526639	8791908	86322	1648409	–		–
2008	12922856	10684195	96391	2142271	–		–
2009	15254265	12710608	105378	2438279	–		–
2010	17254574	14022650	150810	3081114	–		–
“十二五时期”							
2011	20231045	16338362	175067	3717616	–		–
2012	23235965	18740304	187466	4308195	–		–
2013	26338714	22006709	177160	4154845	–		–
2014	28640303	24120903	182090	4337310	–	–	–
2015	31410419	26484428	193710	4732280	–	–	–
“十三五时期”							
2016	34350723	28971634	210316	5168774	–	–	–
2017	37525226	31658152	228909	5638165	–	–	–
2018	40910775	34521369	248418	6140988	–	–	–
2019	44204092	37604716	275686	6323691			
2020	44691335	38570115	255049	5866171	–	–	–

注：1992 年至 2019 年社会消费品零售总额及分组数据根据第四次全国经济普查数据进行了修订。
Note: Total retail volume of social consumption and grouping data from 1992 to 2019 are revised according to the fourth national economic census.

15-2 限额以上批发零售业法人企业商品销售情况（2020 年）

Total Purchase Sales and Inventory by Sector Above Designated Size(2020)

单位：万元 (10 000 yuan)

指标	Indicator	商品销售总额 Total Sale Value		
		合计 Total	批发 Wholesalel	零售 Retail
总计	Total	85676904.4	71324038.4	14352866.0
一、批发业	Wholesale Trade	73480077.0	70815642.5	2664434.5
农、林、牧、渔产品批发	Wholesale of Agricultural, Forestry, Livestock and Fishery Products	686240.4	604455.5	81784.9
食品、饮料及烟草制品批发	Wholesale of Food, Beverages and Tobaccos	4136223.6	3795904.4	340319.2
纺织、服装及家庭用品批发	Wholesale of Textiles, Wearing Apparel and Household Articles	2525700.1	2351180.0	174520.1
文化、体育用品及器材批发	Wholesale of Culture, Sports Appliances and Equipments	2767574.5	2024150.4	743424.1
医药及医疗器材批发	Wholesale of Medicines and Medical Appliances	7944991.0	7905370.4	39620.6
矿产品、建材及化工产品批发	Wholesale of Mineral Products, Building Materials and Chemical Products	46242193.4	45260272.5	981920.9
机械设备、五金产品及电子产品批发	Wholesale of Machinery, Hardware and Electronic Products	8429298.4	8140942.7	288355.7
贸易经纪与代理	Trade Broker and Agency	196983.3	189460.6	7522.7
其他批发业	Other Wholesale not Classified Elsewhere	550872.3	543906.0	6966.3
内资企业	Domestic Invested Enterprises	67434753.8	64770604.7	2664149.1
国有企业	State-owned Enterprises	6462696.5	6460435.8	2260.7
集体企业	Collective-owned Enterprises	3051.6	3051.6	
股份合作企业	Cooperative Enterprises			
联营企业	Joint Ownership Enterprises			
有限责任公司	Limited Liability Corporations	25093055.4	23255159.3	1837896.1
股份有限公司	Share-holding Corporations Ltd.	1778863.0	1580391.4	198471.6
私营企业	Private Enterprises	34093413.8	33468134.3	625279.5
其他企业	Other Enterprises	3673.5	3432.3	241.2
港、澳、台商投资企业	Enterprises with Investment from Hong Kong, Macao and Taiwan	2247296.6	2247011.2	285.4

15-2 续表 continued

指标	Indicator	商品销售总额 Total Sale Value		
		合计 Total	批发 Wholesalel	零售 Retail
外商投资企业	Foreign Invested Enterprises	3798026.6	3798026.6	
二、零售业	Retail Trade	12196827.4	508395.9	11688431.5
综合零售	Integrated Retail	2073445.1	5178.0	2068267.1
食品、饮料及烟草制品专门零售	Special Retail of Food, Beverages and Tobaccos	306222.6	22058.0	284164.6
纺织、服装及日用品专门零售	Special Retail of Textiles, Garments and Daily Consumer Articles	371817.3	13618.3	358199.0
文化、体育用品及器材专门零售	Special Retail of Culture, Sports Appliances and Equipments	385032.1	61444.0	323588.1
医药及医疗器材专门零售	Special Retail of Medicines and Medical Appliances	649297.3	8269.2	641028.1
汽车、摩托车、零配件和燃料及其他动力销售	Retail of Motor Vehicles, Motorcycles, Parts, and Fuel and Other Powers	5911092.1	184596.9	5726495.2
家用电器及电子产品专门零售	Special Retail of Household Electric Appliances and Electronic Products	1390570.0	59862.2	1330707.8
五金、家具及室内装饰材料专门零售	Special Retail of Hardware, Furniture and Interior Decoration Materials	103871.3	4950.6	98920.7
货摊、无店铺及其他零售业	Stalls, Non-shop and Other Retails	1005479.6	148418.7	857060.9
内资企业	Domestic Invested Enterprises	11141324.9	500471.6	10640853.3
国有企业	State-owned Enterprises	373635.6		373635.6
集体企业	Collective-owned Enterprises	19876.6		19876.6
股份合作企业	Cooperative Enterprises	17429.1	371.0	17058.1
联营企业	Joint Ownership Enterprises			
有限责任公司	Limited Liability Corporations	2812223.3	157478.6	2654744.7
股份有限公司	Share-holding Corporations Ltd.	939916.9	20731.3	919185.6
私营企业	Private Enterprises	6978243.4	321890.7	6656352.7
其他企业	Other Enterprises			
港、澳、台商投资企业	Enterprises with Investment from Hong Kong, Macao and Taiwan	553372.5	1856.9	551515.6
外商投资企业	Foreign Invested Enterprises	502130.0	6067.4	496062.6

15-3 限额以上批发零售贸易企业资产实力(2020年)
Capital Power of Wholesales and Retail Sales Trade Above Designated Size(2020)

单位：万元

指标名称	Indicator	法人企业数(个) Number of Corporation Enterprises (unit)	流动资产合计 Total Working Capitals
总计	Total	3754	31220692.9
一、批发业	Wholesale Trade	2844	25478957.8
农、林、牧、渔产品批发	Wholesale of Agricultural, Forestry, Livestock and Fishery Products	53	804269.1
食品、饮料及烟草制品批发	Wholesale of Food, Beverages and Tobaccos	165	1718320.6
纺织、服装及家庭用品批发	Wholesale of Textiles, Wearing Apparel and Household Articles	143	1415334.5
文化、体育用品及器材批发	Wholesale of Culture, Sports Appliances and Equipments	79	1437262.3
医药及医疗器材批发	Wholesale of Medicines and Medical Appliances	292	4557576.5
矿产品、建材及化工产品批发	Wholesale of Mineral Products, Building Materials and Chemical Products	1444	10914045.4
机械设备、五金产品及电子产品批发	Wholesale of Machinery, Hardware and Electronic Products	627	4237462.2
贸易经纪与代理	Trade Broker and Agency	7	101419.2
其他批发业	Other Wholesale not Classified Elsewhere	34	293268.0
内资企业	Domestic Invested Enterprises	2823	23184687.9
国有企业	State-owned Enterprises	28	2263082.9
集体企业	Collective-owned Enterprises	1	999.0
股份合作企业	Cooperative Enterprises		
联营企业	Joint Ownership Enterprises		
有限责任公司	Limited Liability Corporations	341	10040650.2
股份有限公司	Share-holding Corporations Ltd.	26	746357.7
私营企业	Private Enterprises	2425	10131956.6
其他企业	Other Enterprises	2	1641.5
港、澳、台商投资企业	Enterprises with Investment from Hong Kong, Macao and Taiwan	8	1621059.8
外商投资企业	Foreign Invested Enterprises	13	673210.1

(10 000 yuan)

其中 of which	固定资产原价 Original Value of Fixed Assets	累计折旧 Depreciation	其中 of which	资产总计 Total Assets	负债合计 Total Liabilities	所有者权益合计 Total Creditors' Equity	其中 of which
存货 Inventory			本年折旧 Depreciation in the Year				实收资本 Paid-up Capital
4260278.4	3129527.7	1239263.5	182070.3	39768136.4	30042771.7	9725060.3	6460090.0
3287363.2	2023666.9	770438.6	109665.9	32281542.4	24128319.1	8155187.4	4933262.8
120494.8	74009.2	23952.4	3268.7	893667.3	764911.2	128756.1	100100.5
567271.4	315426.3	128284.2	42403.6	2079934.3	1399302.8	680631.5	236150.3
291471.1	131749.1	32172.3	7150.6	1688301.3	1451976.6	236324.7	120380.0
295716.4	275213.3	115306.1	11794.6	2021681.9	1350633.9	672068.7	172262.9
542437.7	284567.1	102849.9	22697.1	5232180.0	4324377.0	907803.0	515479.5
813357.5	668452.1	274019.8	-13252.8	15345428.9	10691385.5	4653610.5	3124156.7
606150.3	249307.7	89612.0	34452.7	4599149.1	3820333.4	780192.0	598885.1
24334.8	1570.3	687.9	63.9	103426.0	73296.3	30129.7	20120.0
26129.2	23371.8	3554.0	1087.5	317773.6	252102.4	65671.2	45727.8
2711437.4	1898546.8	728049.7	99468.2	29746487.7	22187052.0	7561399.8	4558381.2
207799.9	296804.1	106054.5	-38053.1	5011623.7	1631082.6	3380541.1	1714932.7
519.1	48.3			1075.8	634.8	441.0	50.0
1117463.2	920193.8	364710.1	71376.4	11977904.5	10210062.9	1769470.8	1177074.1
47220.5	30983.8	14498.1	1612.8	1213369.2	944955.9	268413.3	139142.8
1338004.9	649171.9	242511.8	64512.6	11539793.3	9399195.1	2140933.1	1526262.2
429.8	1344.9	275.2	19.5	2721.2	1120.7	1600.5	919.4
462575.3	117811.1	38985.2	9035.8	1801300.5	1444039.0	357261.5	252019.2
113350.5	7309.0	3403.7	1161.9	733754.2	497228.1	236526.1	122862.4

15-3 续表 continued

指标名称	Indicator	法人企业数（个）Number of Corporation Enterprises (unit)	流动资产合计 Total Working Capitals
二、零售业	**Retail Trade**	**910**	**5741735.1**
综合零售	Integrated Retail	71	2364708.7
食品、饮料及烟草制品专门零售	Retail of Food, Beverages and Tobaccos	82	143288.4
纺织、服装及日用品专门零售	Special Retail of Textiles, Garments and Daily Consumer Articles	72	209604.4
文化、体育用品及器材专门零售	Retail of Culture, Sports Appliances and Equipments	57	226627.4
医药及医疗器材专门零售	Retail of Medicines and Medical Appliances	62	360099.9
汽车、摩托车、零配件和燃料及其他动力销售	Cars,motorcycles,spare part and fuel and other power sales	339	1579929.4
家用电器及电子产品专门零售	Special Retail of Household Electric Appliances and Electronic Products	133	567804.7
五金、家具及室内装饰材料专门零售	Special Retail of Hardware, Furniture and Decoration Materials	23	35432.1
货摊、无店铺及其他零售业	Non-shop and Other Retails	71	254240.1
内资企业	Domestic Funded Enterprises	890	5492293.8
国有企业	State-owned	13	121622.9
集体企业	Collective-owned	9	7006.0
股份合作企业	Cooperative Enterprises	5	6607.4
联营企业	Joint Ownership Enterprises		
有限责任公司	Limited Liability Corporations	197	980521.1
股份有限公司	Share-holding Corporations Limited	13	1962791.3
私营企业	Private Enterprises	653	2413745.1
其他企业	Other Enterprises		
港、澳、台商投资企业	Enterprises with Funds from Hong Kong, Macao and Taiwan	9	168756.2
外商投资企业	Foreign Funded Enterprises	11	80685.1

其中 of which	固定资产原价 Original Value of Fixed Assets	累计折旧 Depreciation	其中 of which	资产总计 Total Assets	负债合计 Total Liabilities	所有者权益合计 Total Creditors' Equity	其中 of which
存货 Inventory			本年折旧 Depreciation in the Year				实收资本 Paid-up Capital
972915.2	**1105860.8**	**468824.9**	**72404.4**	**7486594.0**	**5914452.6**	**1569872.9**	**1526827.2**
116050.9	562084.3	251384.0	23760.5	3169903.9	2738761.3	431123.2	597857.8
30069.9	48999.4	21257.6	2978.6	185253.5	158606.3	26647.2	32238.2
70470.2	43007.7	10075.0	3380.2	310582.4	247920.1	62390.9	90927.3
92992.2	38009.4	12630.5	2470.7	283274.1	154970.4	127737.2	62983.0
96020.7	24065.5	12623.4	7135.4	435475.5	287475.7	147820.9	63530.3
463947.2	291403.2	129903.8	25757.2	2033658.7	1539258.5	494097.1	484734.6
46075.0	13829.6	5081.6	986.8	651681.3	530556.5	120195.6	90623.4
8474.4	45365.3	10073.8	3667.7	101992.2	61827.2	40165.0	11962.8
48814.7	39096.4	15795.2	2267.3	314772.4	195076.6	119695.8	91969.8
921566.0	941606.9	401440.8	60855.6	6945977.9	5583186.9	1360522.5	1374263.5
23125.4	9882.0	5064.9	1186.5	136837.2	116483.5	20353.7	12335.0
1284.5	4237.7	1570.5	235.5	12527.9	2181.7	10346.2	604.3
3478.8	785.8	428.5	66.7	7468.3	5002.6	2465.7	2410.7
237775.6	291172.4	108901.7	17127.1	1358989.7	919451.2	439538.5	344603.1
65024.6	336702.6	151853.3	10923.5	2571022.9	2196452.5	374570.4	147702.9
590877.1	298826.4	133621.9	31316.3	2859131.9	2343615.4	513248.0	866607.5
26248.2	68411.2	32299.5	3120.3	226794.3	155728.5	71065.8	28110.2
25101.0	95842.7	35084.6	8428.5	313821.8	175537.2	138284.6	124453.5

15-4 限额以上批发零售贸易企业损益及分配(2020年)

Profit Loss and Distribution of Wholesales and Retail Sales Trade Above Designated Size (2020)

单位:万元

指标名称	Indicator	法人企业数(个) Number of Corporation Enterprises (unit)	主营业务收入 Revenue from Principal Business	营业成本 Cost of Business
总计	Total	3754	76376177.9	72403366.8
一、批发业	Wholesale Trade	2844	66053442.7	63307004.3
农、林、牧、渔产品批发	Wholesale of Agricultural, Forestry, Livestock and Fishery Products	53	655795.9	626810.8
食品、饮料及烟草制品批发	Wholesale of Food, Beverages and Tobaccos	165	3754527.9	3287025.9
纺织、服装及家庭用品批发	Wholesale of Textiles, Wearing Apparel and Household Articles	143	2247578.3	2114348.8
文化、体育用品及器材批发	Wholesale of Culture, Sports Appliances and Equipments	79	2618584.6	2299891.7
医药及医疗器材批发	Wholesale of Medicines and Medical Appliances	292	7114605.8	6492278.9
矿产品、建材及化工产品批发	Wholesale of Mineral Products, Building Materials and Chemical Products	1444	41278634.6	40591253.8
机械设备、五金产品及电子产品批发	Wholesale of Machinery, Hardware and Electronic Products	627	7699840.4	7235717.0
贸易经纪与代理	Trade Broker and Agency	7	189487.8	179434.9
其他批发业	Other Wholesale not Classified Elsewhere	34	494387.4	480242.5
内资企业	Domestic Invested Enterprises	2823	60579360.5	58074055.0
国有企业	State-owned Enterprises	28	6122700.9	6099059.3
集体企业	Collective-owned Enterprises	1	2723.1	2629.2
股份合作企业	Cooperative Enterprises			
联营企业	Joint Ownership Enterprises			
有限责任公司	Limited Liability Corporations	341	22304587.3	21171672.7
股份有限公司	Share-holding Corporations Ltd.	26	1540823.7	1466961.0
私营企业	Private Enterprises	2425	30604852.0	29331085.1
其他企业	Other Enterprises	2	3673.5	2647.7
港、澳、台商投资企业	Enterprises with Investment from Hong Kong, Macao and Taiwan	8	2096387.7	1931110.6
外商投资企业	Foreign Invested Enterprises	13	3377694.5	3301838.7

(10 000 yuan)

税金及附加 Taxes and Surcharges	销售费用 Cost of Sales	管理费用 Cost of Management	财务费用 Cost of Finance	营业利润 Profits from Business	利润总额 Total Profits	所得税费用 Income Tax Expense	应付职工薪酬（本年贷方累计发生额） Total Wages Payable	应交增值税 Value-added Tax Payable
258598.4	2254964.8	1134129.8	371638.5	876791.4	930193.5	159841.5	1181897.7	417411.9
224445.6	1274584.7	821823.8	292294.6	824494.9	865102.7	123025.4	728645.9	224047.8
309.8	13526.3	10228.9	29963.2	7684.0	11652.3	464.8	11142.0	565.7
112638.4	116851.4	142889.4	-837.9	147867.3	150730.3	33085.7	90646.2	44019.6
2494.3	75705.4	30483.5	7842.6	13399.0	11870.4	3766.9	38535.8	15597.1
4531.6	106909.5	101067.1	-3204.5	116927.6	118144.8	5068.4	124201.5	5682.7
66761.0	342773.3	158541.1	51541.3	114047.9	115665.7	22349.6	142192.1	111853.7
30362.7	361413.2	241974.1	117823.3	384493.3	396108.5	41020.7	167583.3	621.1
6719.1	240578.5	129491.9	87181.3	38281.3	56852.1	16716.7	147630.5	42527.1
130.7	7188.5	1165.8	435.8	1211.7	1678.8	62.9	2106.6	384.7
498.0	9638.6	5982.0	1549.5	582.8	2399.8	489.7	4607.9	2796.1
220263.5	1186997.6	748863.7	266399.9	750907.2	789925.1	106579.0	676391.5	210171.7
10644.1	24218.2	67144.2	24153.1	286734.5	306378.6	13331.8	37301.4	-86426.7
1.8		21.9	-0.8	71.0	71.0	3.6	16.4	14.5
132783.0	497683.1	274196.7	131779.8	273568.2	296469.1	63768.6	331970.9	145314.3
1442.3	29861.8	12330.8	15041.4	43981.4	31458.6	1187.3	16863.3	4557.7
75389.8	634437.3	395052.1	95426.5	146424.8	155419.6	28287.7	290015.4	146686.3
2.5	797.2	118.0	-0.1	127.3	128.2		224.1	25.6
2026.7	72893.8	62126.6	24358.3	18806.1	19332.0	4399.2	36990.2	7584.2
2155.4	14693.3	10833.5	1536.4	54781.6	55845.6	12047.2	15264.2	6291.9

15-4 续表 continued

指标名称	Indicator	法人企业数（个）Number of Corporation Enterprises (unit)	主营业务收入 Revenue from Principal Business	营业成本 Cost of Business
二、零售业	Retail Trade	910	10322735.2	9096362.5
综合零售	Integrated Retail	71	1551468.2	1310030.7
食品、饮料及烟草制品专门零售	Retail of Food, Beverages and Tobaccos	82	278326.4	230065.0
纺织、服装及日用品专门零售	Special Retail of Textiles, Garments and Daily Consumer Articles	72	391406.5	322112.8
文化、体育用品及器材专门零售	Retail of Culture, Sports Appliances and Equipments	57	341988.3	286228.7
医药及医疗器材专门零售	Retail of Medicines and Medical Appliances	62	592070.3	459512.4
汽车、摩托车、零配件和燃料及其他动力销售	Cars,motorcycles,spare part and fuel and other power sales	339	5294725.5	4911830.1
家用电器及电子产品专门零售	Special Retail of Household Electric Appliances and Electronic Products	133	985097.6	918461.4
五金、家具及室内装饰材料专门零售	Special Retail of Hardware, Furniture and Decoration Materials	23	92887.6	68717.0
货摊、无店铺及其他零售业	Non-shop and Other Retails	71	794764.8	589404.4
内资企业	Domestic Funded Enterprises	890	9381207.1	8311158.9
国有企业	State-owned	13	321916.5	303591.0
集体企业	Collective-owned	9	17857.3	16231.0
股份合作企业	Cooperative Enterprises	5	15429.8	13040.9
联营企业	Joint Ownership Enterprises			
有限责任公司	Limited Liability Corporations	197	2477177.4	2213402.5
股份有限公司	Share-holding Corporations Limited	13	554266.8	442763.1
私营企业	Private Enterprises	653	5994559.3	5322130.4
其他企业	Other Enterprises			
港、澳、台商投资企业	Enterprises with Funds from Hong Kong, Macao and Taiwan	9	495698.8	439753.7
外商投资企业	Foreign Funded Enterprises	11	445829.3	345449.9

税金及附加 Taxes and Surcharges	销售费用 Cost of Sales	管理费用 Cost of Management	财务费用 Cost of Finance	营业利润 Profits from Business	利润总额 Total Profits	所得税费用 Income Tax Expense	应付职工薪酬（本年贷方累计发生额） Total Wages Payable	应交增值税 Value-added Tax Payable
34152.8	980380.1	312306.0	79343.9	52296.5	65090.8	36816.1	453251.8	193364.1
11024.6	253387.7	69740.5	41765.9	28990.3	30018.2	5970.4	124192.6	25176.8
877.9	28744.7	8309.5	796.9	10572.0	13665.6	4433.7	14105.6	3685.1
1367.3	58471.5	21813.4	2110.2	-8636.4	-9271.4	931.6	30343.5	2653.4
3140.7	33880.9	16015.9	2354.9	4222.8	5316.0	756.7	23748.2	3818.6
1746.6	104226.4	24967.2	1251.1	13349.8	14812.6	3873.9	53710.4	11862.1
12079.6	226213.2	110206.8	27017.4	35078.0	39745.8	16660.8	140219.7	125702.6
909.6	57686.6	21952.6	2495.3	-9943.1	-8385.0	787.8	22081.1	5562.6
887.8	11285.7	12268.8	2010.9	-2426.9	-2249.2	117.0	6802.1	1859.1
2118.7	206483.4	27031.3	-458.7	-18910.0	-18561.8	3284.2	38048.6	13043.8
29466.6	857978.9	278547.3	75279.3	40505.5	51938.6	28827.7	414630.4	179466.8
633.4	12388.9	7131.4	5222.1	2989.3	3261.0	598.0	11800.9	63578.0
42.3	862.3	940.6	7.5	-68.1	-44.4	9.6	910.6	186.9
29.5	1701.1	599.5	42.6	81.6	108.8	18.0	647.2	163.4
8317.0	198571.4	77563.1	17030.2	26984.2	30761.6	13066.1	110428.7	39456.2
6065.7	146899.6	37638.8	29457.3	4689.0	4742.2	-728.9	62367.6	13396.6
14378.7	497555.6	154673.9	23519.6	5829.5	13109.4	15864.9	228475.4	62685.7
2947.0	37326.9	3963.6	237.9	20587.5	21235.8	5629.6	11343.2	4887.9
1739.2	85074.3	29795.1	3826.7	-8796.5	-8083.6	2358.8	27278.2	9009.4

15-5 限额以上餐饮业主要经济指标(2020 年)
Main Economic Indicators of Enterprises in Cataring Trades Above Designated Size (2020)

单位：万元

指标名称	Indicator	法人企业数（个）Number of Corporation Enterprises (unit)	资产总计 Total Assests	负债合计 Total Liabilities	所有者权益 Owners' Equity
总计	Total	385	612780.8	559521.0	52931.1
正餐服务	Restaurant	250	491381.1	458772.0	32640.6
快餐服务	Fast Food	117	96603.4	82907.2	13336.0
饮料及冷饮服务	Beverages and Cold Drinks	3	1453.2	755.0	698.2
餐饮配送及外卖送餐服务	Catering Distribution and Delivery Service	10	9242.1	3197.2	6044.9
其他餐饮业	Others	5	14101.0	13889.6	211.4
内资企业	Domestic Invested Enterprises	382	580704.7	515993.9	64382.1
国有企业	State-owned Enterprises	14	63714.3	32014.5	31304.9
集体企业	Collective-owned Enterprises	1	989.4	454.4	535.0
股份合作企业	Cooperative Enterprises	2	1616.0	630.7	985.3
联营企业	Joint Ownership Enterprises				
有限责任公司	Limited Liability Corporations	55	199734.5	209560.4	-10194.3
股份有限公司	Share-holding Corporations Ltd.	2	5674.4	1728.3	3946.1
私营企业	Private Enterprises	306	308605.3	271374.8	37665.1
其他企业	Other Enterprises	2	370.8	230.8	140.0
港、澳、台商投资企业	Enterprises with Investment from Hong Kong, Macao and Taiwan	2	31807.0	43213.9	-11406.9
外商投资企业	Foreign Invested Enterprises	1	269.1	313.2	-44.1

(10 000 yuan)

其中 of which 实收资本 Paid-up Capital	主营业务收入 Revenue from Principal Business	营业成本 Cost of Business	销售费用 Expenses on Business	管理费用 Expenses on Management	财务费用 Expenses on Finance	营业利润 Profits from Business	利润总额 Total Profits	应付职工薪酬（本年贷方累计发生额）Total Wages Payable
92998.1	395383.1	190194.4	144046.5	80535.6	9530.5	-9405.8	-4205.5	106304.1
70962.6	262833.9	122598.3	95459.0	70114.8	8178.0	-9695.5	-5424.5	69552.3
18562.8	105275.9	52550.0	41845.5	7547.8	1308.4	390.6	1080.2	30692.9
100.0	5238.5	1935.6	2303.4	333.9	0.7	664.7	664.2	1210.5
2681.7	12327.0	8360.9	2357.9	1737.0	35.9	4.4	105.5	2358.7
691.0	9707.8	4749.6	2080.7	802.1	7.5	-770.0	-630.9	2489.7
88445.0	358889.4	176305.9	122956.5	78601.8	8408.5	-8553.0	-3680.9	88827.3
6598.1	20065.9	6507.8	8268.6	8736.5	-129.9	-2856.3	-1990.6	9753.1
300.0	629.4	129.1	125.3	338.9	129.2	-93.7	-91.0	119.0
876.8	1403.7	537.3	534.2	401.8	-8.4	-53.2	-3.3	429.1
20764.7	95823.0	47698.0	33264.5	24439.8	3179.2	3874.8	4843.6	23200.4
4185.8	2329.0	940.4	575.1	2091.2	33.7	-1266.9	-205.8	772.3
55719.6	237855.1	120108.6	79867.3	42592.6	5205.7	-8157.7	-6233.8	54472.7
	783.3	384.7	321.5	1.0	-1.0			80.7
4553.1	35735.5	13494.6	20739.5	1876.1	1121.9	-808.8	-480.5	17465.6
	758.2	393.9	350.5	57.7	0.1	-44.0	-44.1	11.2

15-6 限额以上住宿业主要经济指标(2020 年)

Main Economic Indicators of Enterprises in Quartering Trades Above Designated Size(2020)

单位：万元

指标名称	Indicator	法人企业数(个) Number of Corporation Enterprises (unit)	资产总计 Total Assests	负债合计 Total Liabilities	所有者权益 Owners' Equity
总计	Total	176	656358.0	533007.8	122671.4
旅游饭店	Tourist Hotel	52	468569.3	297969.4	169073.6
一般旅馆	General Hotel	111	171888.8	210490.3	-37595.1
民宿服务	Home Lodging Services				
露营地服务	Campground Services				
其他住宿业	Other Accommodation Services	13	15899.9	24548.1	-8807.1
内资企业	Domestic Invested Enterprises	173	642858.1	523226.7	118952.6
国有企业	State-owned Enterprises	12	241695.8	111483.3	128686.2
集体企业	Collective-owned Enterprises	2	8785.9	10022.2	-1236.3
股份合作企业	Cooperative Enterprises	2	14362.8	12486.9	1875.9
联营企业	Joint Ownership Enterprises				
有限责任公司	Limited Liability Corporations	33	130577.7	165402.8	-34825.1
股份有限公司	Share-holding Corporations Ltd.	3	583.7	376.2	207.5
私营企业	Private Enterprises	121	246852.2	223455.3	24244.4
其他企业	Other Enterprises				
港、澳、台商投资企业	Enterprises with Investment from Hong Kong, Macao and Taiwan	2	12690.2	9026.8	3663.4
外商投资企业	Foreign Invested Enterprises	1	809.7	754.3	55.4

(10 000 yuan)

其中 of which 实收资本 Paid-up Capital	主营业务收入 Revenue from Principal Business	营业成本 Cost of Business	销售费用 Expenses on Business	管理费用 Expenses on Management	财务费用 Expenses on Finance	营业利润 Profits from Business	利润总额 Total Profits	应付职工薪酬（本年贷方累计发生额）Total Wages Payable
128720.9	264156.6	94620.4	120232.6	77038.1	6277.5	−23396.5	−19603.7	78028.1
77453.3	155725.2	58414.0	68024.5	46110.4	2117.4	−11249.1	−7204.8	50662.5
48754.4	94991.3	31932.1	45694.8	27689.4	3901.5	−11542.3	−11870.4	24363.2
2513.2	13440.1	4274.3	6513.3	3238.3	258.6	−605.1	−528.5	3002.4
123635.3	259700.2	94148.7	118309.7	74827.8	6302.0	−23331.2	−19389.1	75861.9
45315.2	63026.5	18891.6	33451.6	21956.1	−1987.0	−7339.4	−2933.9	20796.7
1883.4	3176.9	896.9	2958.1	752.3	13.0	−1422.1	−1407.7	1170.5
1416.5	3487.1	1721.6	1091.6	882.0	15.0	−227.4	−85.6	739.4
29715.6	100344.6	32457.4	54105.8	26629.4	1465.0	−9647.5	−10863.1	34938.1
531.0	1191.3	426.0	702.0	325.2	2.8	−272.1	−262.0	494.8
44773.6	88473.8	39755.2	26000.6	24282.8	6793.2	−4422.7	−3836.8	17722.4
4585.6	4039.1	432.9	1642.9	2037.9	−25.4	9.7	−155.3	1984.8
500.0	417.3	38.8	280.0	172.4	0.9	−75.0	−59.3	181.4

15-7 限额以上住宿业和餐饮业法人企业经营情况(2020年)

Main Economic Indicators of Enterprises in Quartering Trades and Catering Trades Above Designated Size(2020)

指标名称	Indicator	法人企业数(个) Number of Corporation Enterprises (unit)	从业人员期末人数(人) Engaged Persons at Year-end (person)	营业额(万元) Business Revenue (10 000yuan)
总计	Total	561	36593	691063.3
一、住宿业	Hotels	176	14002	278889.9
旅游饭店	Tourist Hotel	52	8385	167617.1
一般旅馆	General Hotel	111	4937	97194.9
民宿服务	Home Lodging Services			
露营地服务	Campground Services			
其他住宿业	Other Accommodation Services	13	680	14077.9
内资企业	Domestic Invested Enterprises	173	13765	274185.2
国有企业	State-owned Enterprises	12	3274	60979.8
集体企业	Collective-owned Enterprises	2	214	3306.4
股份合作企业	Cooperative Enterprises	2	189	3552.0
联营企业	Joint Ownership Enterprises			
有限责任公司	Limited Liability Corporations	33	6199	111418.9
股份有限公司	Share-holding Corporations Ltd.	3	109	1208.5
私营企业	Private Enterprises	121	3780	93719.6
其他企业	Other Enterprises			
港、澳、台商投资企业	Enterprises with Investment from Hong Kong, Macao and Taiwan	2	200	4264.0
外商投资企业	Foreign Invested Enterprises	1	37	440.7
二、餐饮业	Catering Services	385	22591	412173.4
正餐服务	Restaurant	250	14801	274989.7
快餐服务	Fast Food	117	6278	108579.6
饮料及冷饮服务	Beverages and Cold Drinks	3	183	5412.9
餐饮配送及外卖送餐服务	Catering Distribution and Delivery Service	10	685	13292.6
其他餐饮业	Others	5	644	9898.6
内资企业	Domestic Invested Enterprises	382	19103	373567.3
国有企业	State-owned Enterprises	14	1698	20054.2
集体企业	Collective-owned Enterprises	1	14	629.7
股份合作企业	Cooperative Enterprises	2	95	1468.2
联营企业	Joint Ownership Enterprises			
有限责任公司	Limited Liability Corporations	55	4194	101047.4
股份有限公司	Share-holding Corporations Ltd.	2	220	3443.4
私营企业	Private Enterprises	306	12846	246141.1
其他企业	Other Enterprises	2	36	783.3
港、澳、台商投资企业	Enterprises with Investment from Hong Kong, Macao and Taiwan	2	3452	37847.9
外商投资企业	Foreign Invested Enterprises	1	36	758.2

其中 of which				客房数（间） Number of Room (room)	床位数（个） Number of Beds (bed)	餐位数（位） Number of Dining-seats (seat)	年末餐饮营业面积（平方米） Business Area of Catering Services at Year-end (sq.m)
客房收入 From Hotel Rooms	餐费收入 From Meals	商品销售收入 Revenue from Commodities	其他收入 Other Revenue				
186481.5	434671.4	13801.3	56109.1	41277	64419	231184	1349063
141325.6	92516.9	6886.8	38160.6	30965	46102	64602	650457
63635.7	72157.8	5449.8	26373.8	9550	15379	51571	283021
68547.4	15856.8	1346.9	11443.8	19725	28151	11822	323166
9142.5	4502.3	90.1	343.0	1690	2572	1209	44270
139433.2	91393.9	6876.3	36481.8	30365	45187	63702	639857
21868.0	28996.6	3487.8	6627.4	2449	4011	8819	86314
1603.2	1673.7		29.5	442	768	2500	7707
962.1	2469.8		120.1	337	660	1600	2400
53387.7	38062.7	2448.7	17519.8	11349	17973	42550	190242
1008.0	192.5	8.0		327	517	236	9146
60604.2	19998.6	931.8	12185.0	15461	21258	7997	344048
1505.1	1087.3		1671.6	470	715	860	7600
387.3	35.7	10.5	7.2	130	200	40	3000
45155.9	342154.5	6914.5	17948.5	10312	18317	166582	698606
45155.9	211684.6	3025.3	15123.9	10312	18317	121991	590725
	105319.5	913.5	2346.6			28804	73158
	5170.2	225.2	17.5			247	1389
	10081.6	2750.5	460.5			3364	9500
	9898.6					12176	23834
45155.9	303701.6	6761.3	17948.5	10312	18317	158623	671724
6901.3	10195.4	15.3	2942.2	1790	3379	6721	72068
582.7	47.0			118	240	500	7000
520.1	931.4	16.7		76	140	414	1180
9449.8	81710.8	3130.8	6756.0	1784	2968	42082	145327
654.1	1257.6	62.9	1468.8	245	320	690	3860
27047.9	208776.1	3535.6	6781.5	6299	11270	108102	441846
	783.3					114	443
	37847.9					7947	26877
	605.0	153.2				12	5

15-8 销售过亿元的商品交易市场一览表 (2020 年)
Summary of Consumer Goods Markets with Annual Transaction Value Above 100 Million Rmb Yuan(2020)

市场名称 Name	市场类别 Category	年末营业面积 (平方米) Operating Area at Year-End (sq.m)	市场总摊位 (个) Number of ooths (unit)	年成交额 (万元) Annual Turnover (10 000 yuan)
济南海鲜大市场	水产品市场	30000	1200	350000
济南市新世界商城	工业消费品综合市场	27850	921	71616
济南西市场小商品批发市场	工业消费品综合市场	26000	620	10120
济南博茗茶叶市场	茶叶市场	82000	680	160000
山东匡山钢材市场	金属材料市场	10000	60	100000
山东匡山农产品综合交易市场	蔬菜市场	21000	910	246751
山东匡山汽车大世界	汽车市场	130000	70	307155
山东老屯汽车配件城	机动车零配件市场	35000	500	28000
山东老屯茶城	茶叶市场	8000	120	11300
槐荫区红旗钢材市场	金属材料市场	35000	112	78590
山东齐鲁鞋城	鞋帽市场	19925	600	91100
济南市堤口路果品批发市场	干鲜果品市场	110000	241	105597
济南中恒商场	工业消费品综合市场	71665	2195	100257
济南红星美凯龙世博家居生活广场	家具市场	128000	427	80000
济南黄台家居广场	家具市场	15000	280	18000
山东东亚金星家居	家具市场	72758	458	28629
济南泺口服装批发市场	服装市场	199000	2760	186919
山东济南重汽配件城	机动车零配件市场	61938	435	223000
七里堡蔬菜综合批发市场	农产品综合市场	150000	2000	329000
山东济南维尔康肉类水产综合批发市场	水产品市场	200000	1000	1230036
济南金田义乌小商品交易市场	小商品市场	45000	1495	104980
济南市章丘区刁镇蔬菜批发市场	蔬菜市场	40600	600	48450
济南曲堤蔬菜销售市场	蔬菜市场	34310	140	37823
商河县富东农贸综合市场	农产品综合市场	27800	585	25739

主要统计指标解释

社会消费品零售总额 指企业（单位、个体户）通过交易直接售给个人、社会集团非生产、非经营用的实物商品金额，以及提供餐饮服务所取得的收入金额。个人包括城乡居民和入境人员，社会集团包括机关、社会团体、部队、学校、企事业单位、居委会或村委会等。

商品销售额 指对本单位以外的单位和个人出售的商品金额（包括售给本单位消费用的商品，含增值税），在批发和零售业中，本指标反映在国内市场上销售商品以及出口商品的总价。

商品销售包括：（1）售给个人和社会集团消费用的商品；（2）售给农业、工业、建筑业、服务业等国民经济各行业用于生产、经营用的商品，包括售予批发和零售业作为转卖或加工后转卖的商品；（3）对国（境）外直接出口的商品。

商品销售不包括：（1）未通过买卖行为付出的商品，如因机构变动移交给其他企业单位的商品、借出的商品、归还受其他单位委托代保管的商品、付出的加工原料和赠送给其他单位的样品等；（2）促销返券所销售的、不计入营业收入的商品；（3）经本单位介绍，由买卖双方直接结算，本单位只收取手续费的业务；（4）未发生所有权转移的商品预付卡销售，如加油卡；（5）汽车维修、电话卡销售等服务性经济活动；（6）购货退回的商品；（7）商品损耗和损失；（8）出售本单位自用的废旧物资；（9）期货交易商品；（10）自来水供应企业、电力企业、天然气供应企业提供的水、电、气。

批发额 指售给国民经济各行业用于生产、经营用的商品金额。

商品批发包括：（1）售给农业、工业、建筑业等行业用于生产的各种机器设备、工具、原料、材料、燃料、建筑材料，售给农民的农业生产资料，售给交通运输、仓储和邮政业用于业务活动的设备、车辆和燃料等；（2）售给信息传输、软件和信息技术服务，科学研究和技术服务业，水利、环境和公共设施管理业等行业用于生产经营、勘察设计、科研试验等业务经营使用的商品，售给批发和零售业、住宿和餐饮业使用的各种设备、工具、原材料、燃料、仓储运输用的商品；（3）售给居民服务、修理和其他服务业各种营业用品，如售给理发业的理发工具、毛巾等，日用品修理业的设备、工具、材料、零配件等，售给民政部门救灾用的商品等；（4）售给批发和零售业作为转卖用的商品；售给餐饮业用于烹饪、调制加工后出售的商品和转卖的商品；售给服务业转卖的商品；（5）出口的商品。

零售额 指售给个人用于生活消费和社会集团用于公共消费的商品金额。

商品零售包括：（1）售给城乡居民和入境外国人、华侨、港澳台同胞的各类生活消费品；（2）售给行政事业单位、社会团体、军队和武警等机构的商品，以及以零售方式售给各类企业的商品。具体包括：用于非生产和社会交往的办公用品，如通讯设备、计算器具和设备、电讯网络设备、文印设备、音像视听器材和设备、纸张、本册、文具及装订文印材料、家具、日用电器、针纺织品、清洁卫生用品、文体用品、奖品、纪念品、礼品等；供内部人员乘坐的交通工具和燃料；用于办公设施修缮的各类配件、材料、工具等；用于取暖和防暑降温的设备、燃料、材料及食品等；专用于教学的用品和设备；非专用的劳动保护用品；不对外营业的内部食堂用的餐具、炊具、设备、清洁卫生工具和食品、燃料等；军队、武警用于其人员生活的衣着品和个人用品；其他各类非生产性设备和用品。

商品零售不包括：（1）售给城乡居民已确知是用于生产、经营的商品；（2）售给各类农业生产者的生产资料类商品，如农机、农药化肥、农膜、种子饲料等商品；（3）售给企业单位生产用具及生产上专用的劳动保护用品；（4）专用于科研的用品和设备；（5）售给医疗机构的中、西药品、中药材和医疗设备器材；（6）以投资为目的商品，如黄金、收藏品等。

住宿餐饮业营业额 指住宿和餐饮业单位在经营活动中，因提供服务或销售商品等取得的全部收入（含增值税），收入主要来源于提供客房、餐费服务、商品销售和其他服务，如商务服务。不包括多产业法人企业附营的其他行业产业活动单位的餐费收入、商品销售收入等各项收入。

Explanatory Notes on Main Statistical Indicators

Total Retail Sales of Consumer Goods refer to the amount obtained by enterprises (units, self–employed individuals) through the direct sales of non–production & non–business physical commodity to individuals, social institutions, and the revenue from providing catering services. Individuals include rural and urban households, population from abroad, social institutions include government agencies, social organizations, military units, schools, institutions. neighborhood or village committees.

Total Sales of Commodities refers to value of commodities sold by the establishments to other establishments and individuals (including commodities sold to their own establishments for consumption, including VAT). This indicator is used to show the total value of sales of commodities at domestic markets and export.

The commodities includes: (1) commodities sold to urban and rural residents and social groups for their consumption; (2) commodities sold to establishments in agriculture, industry, construction, service and various sectors of national economy for their production and operation, including commodities sold to wholesale and retail establishments for re–selling with or without further processing; (3) commodities for directing export to other countries.

Commodities exclude: (1) Commodities given not based on purchase and sale activities, such as commodities handed over to other enterprises due to the change in the institution, commodities lent, commodities which are kept by other unit based on entrustment returned, raw materials for processing given and samples given away to other units; (2) Commodities sold based on promotion coupons and not included into operating income; (3) Businesses introduced by the unit based on direct settlement by the buyer and the seller for which the unit only charges for the service charges; (4) Sales of the prepaid card of commodities without transfer of ownership (such as oil filling card); (5) Service economic activities such as vehicle maintenance and repair and sales of phone card; (6) Commodities returned; (7) Commodity loss and damage; (8) Sale of self–used waste and old materials of the unit; (9) Futures trading commodity; (10) Water, electricity and gas provided by the tap water supply enterprise, the power enterprise and the natural gas supply enterprise.

Wholesale Amount refers to the amount of commodities sold to all industries of national economy for production and operation.

The wholesale includes: (1) Various machines and equipment, tools, raw materials, materials, fuel and building materials sold to agriculture, industry and construction industry, etc. for production as well as equipment, vehicles and fuel sold to transportation, warehousing and mail business for business activities; (2) Commodities sold to information transmission, software and information technology services, scientific research and technological services, water conservancy, environment and public facilities management for production, operation, survey and design, scientific research and test, various equipment, tools, raw materials and fuel sold to the wholesale and retail and accommodation and catering industries for use as well as commodities for warehousing and transportation; (3) Various operating supplies sold to neighborhood services, repair and other service industries, such as barber tools and towels sold to the hairdressing industry; equipment, tools, materials and spare and accessory parts for the commodity repair industry and commodities sold to the civil administration department for relieving the victims of a disaster; (4) Commodities sold to wholesale and retail industries for reselling; commodities sold to the catering industry for cooking, selling after processing and reselling; commodities sold to the service industry for reselling; (5) Exported commodities.

Retail Sales refer to the amount of commodities sold to individuals for living consumption and social groups for public consumption.

Commodity retail includes: (1) Various consumer goods sold to urban and rural residents, inbound foreigners, overseas Chinese and compatriots from Hong Kong, Macao and Taiwan; (2) Commodities sold to such institutions as administrative institution, social organization, army and armed police as well as commodities sold to various enterprises in the form of retails. Specifically include: Office supplies not for production and social interaction, such as communication equipment, calculation appliances and equipment, telecommunication network equipment, printing equipment, audio–visual devices and equipment, paper, books, stationery, binding and printing materials, furniture, household electrical appliance, knitwear and textile, sanitary articles, stationery and sporting goods, prizes, souvenirs and presents; communication media for internal personnel and fuel; various accessories, materials and tools for repair of office facilities; equipment, fuel, materials and food for heating and heatstroke prevention; supplies and equipment for teaching; non–special labor protection appliances; tableware, cooking utensils, equipment, cleaning and sanitation tools, food and fuel for internal canteen only; clothing and personal belongings for personnel from the army and armed police living; all other kinds of nonproductive equipment and supplies.

Commodity retail excludes: (1) Commodities sold to urban and rural residents, having been confirmed to be used for production and operation; (2) Means of production (such as agricultural machinery, pesticide and fertilizer, agricultural film and seed feed) sold to various agricultural producers; (3) Production equipment sold to enterprises and special labor protection articles for production; (4) Supplies and equipment for scientific research; (5) Traditional Chinese and Western medicines, traditional Chinese medicinal materials, and medical equipment and supply sold to medical establishments; (6) Commodities for investment, such as gold and collection.

Sales Revenue of Accommodation and Catering industry refers to the total revenue (included VAT) received by accommodation and catering industries from services provided and goods sold, where the main sources are: guest rooms provided, catering services, goods sold and other services such as business services, other than catering income, goods sold income or income from other activities of other industry activity units additive by multi–industry corporate enterprises.

16

对外贸易与国际旅游

FOREIGN TRADE AND INTERNATIONAL TOURISM

16-1 海关进出口商品总额
Total Value of Imports and Exports by Category of Commodities

单位：万美元　　　　(10 000 USD)

指标	Indicator	2020年进出口总额 Total Value of Imports and Exports in 2020	其中 of which 出口 Export	其中 of which 进口 Import	2019年进出口总额 Total Value of Imports and Exports in 2019	其中 of which 出口 Export	其中 of which 进口 Import
总额	**Total**	1998749	1089426	909323	1630123	935059	695064
按贸易方式分	**By Trade**						
一般贸易	General Trade	1725078	977785	747292	1457574	849750	607824
援助物资	Aid Material	508	508	0	530	530	0
捐赠物资	Donation Material	495	302	192			
补偿贸易	Compensation Trate						
来料加工装配贸易	Processing and Assembling Trade with Sent Materials	11492	6889	4603	2324	1566	758
进料加工贸易	Processing Trade with Imported Materials	46415	34747	11668	54384	42618	11767
对外承包工程出口货物	Export of Contracted projects	18892	18892		10755	10755	0
投资设备	Investment Goods	276		276	252	0	252
出料加工贸易	Export Processing Trate	35	13	22			
海关特殊监管区域进口设备	**Import of Equipment in Special Customs Supervision Area**	2		2	0	0	0
海关特殊监管区域物流货物	**Logistics Freight of Equipment in Special Customs Supervision Area**	101044	20045	80999	43517	10626	32892
易货贸易	Barter Trate						
保税监管场所进出境货物	**Bonded Supervision Entry and Exit Goods**	84554	27269	57285	49387	15078	34309
来料加工装配进口设备	Imported Equipment for Processing Incoming Materials						
租赁贸易	Leasing Trate	5378		5378	2862	0	2862
其他贸易	Other Trate	4582	2976	1606	8538	4136	4402
按运输方式分	**By Ways of Transport**						
水路运输	Waterway Transport	1267202	825059	442143	1117942	774128	343814
铁路运输	Railway Transport	34193	25893	8300	22864	16055	6809
公路运输	Road Transport	338755	45683	293072	286356	47033	239323
航空运输	Air Transport	349862	190450	159412	192414	94118	98296
邮件运输	Mail Transport	2917	2053	864	7504	3586	3918
其他运输	Others	5616	181	5435	3044	139	2904
按企业性质分	**By Natural of Enterprises**						
国有企业	State-owned Enterprises	372105	36545	335560	356339	56857	299483
集体企业	Collective-owned Enterprises	100158	25779	74379	72921	21843	51078
外商投资企业	Foreign Funded Enterprises	353576	259099	94477	327203	248186	79017
中外合资	Joint-venture Enterprises	127583	94178	33406	114539	74860	39679
中外合作	Cooperation Enterprises	466	466	0	1203	1202	2
外商独资	Wholly Foreign-owned Enterprises	225526	164455	61071	211460	172124	39336
其他	Others	2889	2038	852	7606	3539	4067

16-2 主要国别(地区)海关进出口商品总额
Total Value of Imports and Exports of Main Countries or Territories by Categoty of Commodities

单位：万美元 (10 000 USD)

国别(地区)	Country (region)	2020年进出口总额 Total Value of Imports and Exports in 2020	其中 of which 出口 Export	其中 of which 进口 Import	2019年进出口总额 Total Value of Imports and Exports in 2019	其中 of which 出口 Export	其中 of which 进口 Import
总额	Total	1998544	1089319	909225	1630123	935059	695064
亚洲	Asia	932197	496657	435540	766032	432213	333818
香港	Hong kong	21701	21523	178	14771	14614	158
印度	India	48580	35178	13402	54548	40061	14486
印度尼西亚	Indonesia	37621	32827	4794	29840	24735	5105
日本	Japan	97861	55087	42774	80069	49571	30498
马来西亚	Malaysia	138171	23932	114238	117718	23333	94385
巴基斯坦	Pakistan	14435	14355	80	13441	13417	24
菲律宾	Philippines	43533	32606	10927	49009	41799	7209
卡塔尔	Katar	3126	2764	362	2398	2078	320
沙特阿拉伯	Saudi Arabia	16469	10986	5483	15022	8522	6500
新加坡	Singapore	67133	60418	6715	20787	15405	5382
韩国	Repulic of Korea	69279	39390	29889	46904	33242	13662
泰国	Thailand	68239	12954	55285	80849	13367	67482
土耳其	Kurtey	10674	10387	287	8388	8161	226
阿拉伯联合酋长国	The United Arab Emirates	23484	21178	2306	15480	13071	2409
越南	Vietnam	41707	35930	5777	38424	34352	4072
台湾省	Taiwan	94720	15791	78928	40203	13324	26879
非洲	Africa	144905	124208	20698	126353	123112	3241
埃及	Egypt	10332	10322	10	5845	5828	17
南非	South Africa	12556	6988	5568	9028	7908	1120
尼日利亚	Nigeria	15985	15982	3	25614	25614	0

16-2 续表 continued

国别（地区）	Country (region)	2020 年进出口总额 Total Value of Imports and Exports in 2020	其中 of which 出口 Export	其中 of which 进口 Import	2019 年进出口总额 Total Value of Imports and Exports in 2019	其中 of which 出口 Export	其中 of which 进口 Import
欧洲	**Europe**	365097	229887	135210	274920	172065	102854
比利时	Belgium	6872	5715	1157	6670	5466	1204
英国	United Kingdom	23770	15824	7946	19055	14832	4223
德国	Germany	93406	38337	55068	68161	28037	40123
法国	France	30665	26464	4201	17360	10480	6881
意大利	Italy	20474	15012	5462	17635	13038	4597
荷兰	Netherlands	25759	19111	6648	16465	12737	3728
西班牙	Spain	23744	17358	6386	12876	10171	2706
芬兰	Finland	2329	1463	866	2900	2137	762
瑞典	Sweden	7467	2609	4858	10612	3006	7606
瑞士	Switzerland	5782	1591	4191	7199	844	6355
俄罗斯	Russia	47235	38073	9162	32780	29631	3149
拉丁美洲	**Latin America**	180651	74436	106216	141893	71717	70176
阿根廷	Argentina	11600	4247	7353	11334	4523	6811
巴西	Brazil	88100	17062	71038	57719	15352	42367
智利	Chile	19116	6597	12520	17035	6794	10241
墨西哥	Mexico	16040	14541	1500	14820	14296	524
北美洲	**North America**	226942	141360	85582	184269	114435	69834
加拿大	Canada	53849	33888	19961	43451	24333	19119
美国	United States	168289	107451	60838	139115	90079	49036
大洋洲	**Oceanic**	147861	22772	125089	132740	21517	111223
澳大利亚	Australia	134841	17614	117227	120155	15213	104943
新西兰	New Zealand	10450	2588	7863	9765	3488	6277

16-3 海关进出口商品分类金额
Value of Imports and Exports by Category of Commodities

单位：万美元 (10 000 USD)

商品类别	Indicator	2020年 出口 Export	2020年 进口 Import	2019年 出口 Export	2019年 进口 Import
总额	**Total**	1089319	909225	935059	695064
活动物；动物产品	**Live Animals; Animal Products**	705	67378	348	39314
活动物	Live Animals				
肉及食用杂碎	Meat and Edible Met Offal	0	47136		22504
鱼、甲壳动物、软体动物及其他水生无脊椎动物	Fish and Crustacean,Mollusc and Other Aquatic Invertebrates	54	16072	58	11809
乳品；蛋品；天然蜂蜜；其他食用动物产品	Dairy Produce; Birds' Eggs; Natural Honey; Edible Products of Animal Origin, not Elsewhere Specified or Included	49	4068	49	5001
其他动物产品	Products of Animal Origin, not Elsewhere Specified or Included	601	102	241	
植物产品	**Vegetable Products**	75154	15391	59523	11482
活树及其他活植物；鳞茎、根及类似品；插花及装饰用簇叶	Live Tree and Other Plants; Bulbs, Roots and the Like; Cut Flowers and Ornamental Foliage	4	46	9	69
食用蔬菜、根及块茎	Edible Vegetables and Certain Roots and Tubers	38863	66	33551	50
食用水果及坚果；柑桔属水果或甜瓜的果皮	Edible Fruit and Nuts; Peel of Citrus Fruit or Melons	19357	53	14676	156
咖啡、茶、马黛茶及调味香料	Coffee, Tea, Mate and Spices	16697	2892	11175	987
谷物	Cereals	0	5856		6467
制粉工业产品；麦芽；淀粉、菊粉；面筋	Products of The Milling Industry; Malt; Starches; Inulin; Wheat Gluten	49	1736	2	19
含油子仁及果实；杂项子仁及果实；工业用或药用植物；稻草、秸秆及饲料	Oil Seeds and Oleaginous Fruits; Miscellaneous Grains, Seeds and Fruit; Industrial or Medicinal Plants; Straw and Fodder	145	4714	63	3693
虫胶；树胶、树脂及其他植物液、汁	Lac; Gums, Resins And Other Vegetable Saps and Extracts	20	7	39	12
编结用植物材料；其他植物产品	Vegetable Plaiting Materials; Vegetable Products Not Elsewhere Specified or Included	18	22	7	29
动、植物油、脂及其分解产品；精制的食用油脂；动、植物蜡	**Animal or Vegetable Fats and Oils and their Cleavage Products; Prepared Edible Fats; Animal or Vegetable Waxes**	254	2012	181	659
动、植物油、脂及其分解产品；精制的食用油脂；动、植物蜡	Animal or Vegetable Fats and Oils and their Cleavage Products; Prepared Edible Fats; Animal or Vegetable Waxes	254	2012	181	659
食品；饮料、酒及醋；烟草、烟草及烟草用品的制品	**Prepared Foodstuffs; Beverages, Spirits And Vinegar; Tobacco and Manufactured Tobacco Substitutes**	21641	6103	15701	7703
肉、鱼、甲壳动物、软体动物及其他水生无脊椎动物的制品	Preparations of Meat,of Fish or of Crustaceans,Molluscs or other Aquatic Invertebrates	144	0		3
糖及糖食	Sugars and Sugar Confectionery	142	150	104	113
可可及可可制品	Cocoa and Cocoa Preparations	0	253		77
谷物、粮食粉、淀粉或乳的制品；糕饼点心	Preparations of Cereals, Flour, Starch or Milk; Pastry-Cooks' Products	3796	21	3356	9
蔬菜、水果、坚果或植物其他部分的制品	Preparations of Vegetables, Fruit, Nuts or Other Parts of Plants	13509	1158	10126	1879
杂项食品	Miscellaneous Edible Preparations	3273	1627	1722	2282
饮料、酒及醋	Beverages, Spirits and Vinegar	240	2710	44	3104
食品工业的残渣及废料；配制的动物饲料	Residues and Waste from The Food Industries; Prepared Animal Fodder	537	186	349	236
烟草、烟草及烟草代用品的制品	Tobacco and Manufactured Tobacco Substitutes				
矿产品	**Mineral Products**	331	218620	338	166657
盐；硫磺；泥土及石料；石膏料、石灰及水泥	Salt; Sulphur; Earths and Stone; Plastering Materials, Lime and Cement	190	877	310	2307
矿砂、矿渣及矿灰	Ores, Slag and Ash	2	173741	1	147516
矿物燃料、矿物油及其蒸馏产品；沥青物质；矿物蜡	Mineral Fuels, Mineral Oils and Products of Their Distillation; Bituminous Substances; Mineral Waxes	140	44003	27	16833
化学工业及其相关工业的产品	Products of The Chemical or Industries Allied	120322	9957	108608	7745

16-3 续表 1 continued 1

商品类别	Indicator	2020 年		2019 年	
		出口 Export	进口 Import	出口 Export	进口 Import
无机化学品；贵金属、稀土金属、放射性元素及其同位素的有机及无机化合物	Inorganic Chemicals; Organic or Inorganic Compounds of Precious Metals, of Rare-Earth	2191	488	3743	418
有机化学品	Organic Chemicals	56970	2046	50485	2039
药品	Pharmaceutical Products	29587	2607	21836	1242
肥料	Fertilizers	948	0	1465	40
鞣料浸膏及染料浸膏；鞣酸及其衍生物；染料、颜料及其他着色料；油漆及清漆；油灰及其他类似胶粘剂；墨水、油墨	Tanning or Dyeing Extracts; Tannins and Their Derivatives; Dyes, Pigments and Other Colouring Matter; Paints and Varnishes; Putty and Other Mastics; Inks	10753	646	13787	632
精油及香膏；芳香料制品及化妆盥洗品	Essential Oils and Retinoid; Perfumery, Cosmetic or Toilet Preparations	109	177	177	201
肥皂、有机表面活性剂、洗涤剂、润滑剂、人造蜡、调制蜡、光洁剂、蜡烛及类似品、塑型用膏、"牙科 用蜡"及牙科用熟石膏制剂	Soap,Organic Surface-Active Agents,Washing Preparations, Lubricating Preparations, Artificial Waxes, Prepared Waxes, Polishing or Scouring Preparations, Candles and Similar Articles, Modelling Pastes, "Dental Waxes" And Dental Preparations With a Basis of Plast	1198	563	833	318
蛋白类物质；改性淀粉；胶；酶	Albuminoidal Substances; Modified Starches; Glues; Enzymes	1175	570	1344	86
炸药；烟火制品；火柴；引火合金；易燃材料制品	Explosives; Pyrotechnic Products; Matches; Pyrophoric Alloys; Certain Combustible Preparations			0	
照相及电影用品	Photographic or Cinematographic Goods	41	190	11	3
杂项化学产品	Miscellaneous Chemical Products	17349	2670	14926	2766
塑料及其制品；橡胶及其制品	**Plastics and Articles Thereof Rubber and Articles Thereof**			**32576**	**21358**
塑料及其制品	Plastics and Articles Thereof	39144	23257	27317	18314
橡胶及其制品	Rubber and Articles Thereof	33614	20080	5259	3044
生皮、皮革、毛皮及其制品；鞍具及挽具；旅行用品、手提包及类似容器、动物肠线（蚕胶丝除外）制品	**Raw Hides and Skins, Leather, Fur Skins and Articles Thereof; Saddlery and Harness; Travel Goods,Handbags and Similar Containers; Articles of Animal Gut (Other Than Silk-Worm Gut)**	**3943**	**74**	**4531**	**96**
生皮（毛皮除外）及皮革	Raw Hides and Skins(Other Than Fur Skins) and Leather	1	30	15	30
皮革制品；鞍具及挽具；旅行用品、手提包及类似容器；动物肠线（蚕胶丝除外）制品	Articles of Leather; Saddlery and Harness; Travel Goods, Handbags and Similar Containers; Articles of Animal Gut(Other Than Silk-Worm Gut)	1924	43	3199	65
毛皮、人造毛皮及其制品	Fur Skins and Artificial Fur; Manufactures Thereof	2019	0	1316	0
木及木制品；木炭；软木及软木制品；稻草、秸秆、针茅或其他编结材料制品；蓝筐及柳条编结品	**Wood and Articles of Wood; Wood Charcoal;Cork and Articles of Cork; Manufactures of Straw, of Esparto or of Other Plaiting Materials; Basket Ware and Wickerwork**	**8095**	**4186**	**8319**	**1968**
木及木制品；木炭	Wood and Articles of Wood; Wood Charcoal	6371	4186	6466	1968
软木及软木制品	Cork and Articles of Cork	15	0	13	
稻草、秸秆、针茅或其他编结材料制品；蓝筐及柳条编结品	Manufactures of Straw, of Esparto or of Other Plaiting Materials; Basket Ware and Wickerwork	1709	0	1840	1
木浆及其他纤维状纤维素浆；回收（废碎）纸或纸板；纸、纸板及其制品	**Pulp of Wood or of Other Fibrous Cellulosic Material; Waste and Scrap of Paper or Paperboard; Paper and Paperboard and Articles Thereof**	**4054**	**42781**	**4626**	**37442**
木浆及其他纤维状纤维素浆；回收（废碎）纸或纸板	Pulp of Wood or of Other Fibrous Cellulosic Material; Waste and Scrap of Paper or Paperboard	3827	3000	21	34277
纸及纸板；纸浆、纸或纸板制品	Paper and Paperboard; Articles of Paper Pulp, of Paper or Paperboard	194	144	4439	3095
书籍、报纸、印刷图画及其他印刷品；手稿、打字稿及设计图纸	Printed Books, Newspapers, Pictures and Other Products of The Printing Industry; Manuscripts, Typescripts and Plans			166	70
纺织原料及纺织制品	**Textiles and Textile Articles**	**104078**	**3257**	**51026**	**2948**
蚕丝	Silk			0	
羊毛、动物细毛或粗毛；马毛纱线及其机织物	Wool, Fine or Coarse Animal Hair;Horsehair Yarn and Woven Fabric	9	3	156	18
棉花	Cotton	2138	1289	1039	1340

16-3 续表 2 continued 2

商品类别	Indicator	2020 年		2019 年	
		出口 Export	进口 Import	出口 Export	进口 Import
其他植物纺织纤维；纸纱线及其机织物	Other Vegetable Textile Fibres; Paper Yarn and Woven Fabrics of Paper Yarn	5	0	33	4
化学纤维长丝	Man-Made Filaments	4255	168	3460	289
化学纤维短纤	Man-Made Short Fibres	6792	393	6856	465
絮胎、毡呢及无纺织物；特种纱线；线、绳、索、缆及其制品	Wadding, Felt and Nonwoven; Special Yarns; Twine, Cordage, Ropes and Cables and Articles Thereof	7237	429	5911	215
地毯及纺织材料的其他铺地制品	Carpets and Other Textile Floor Coverings	3056	7	3404	21
特种机织物；簇绒织物；花边；装饰毯；装饰带；刺绣品	Special Woven Fabrics; Tufted Textile Fabrics; Lace; Tapestries; Trimmings; Embroidery	335	83	454	102
浸渍、涂布、包覆或层压的纺织物；工业用纺织制品	Impregnated, Coated, Covered or Laminated Textile Fabrics; Textile Articles of a Kind Suitable for Industrial Use	1371	88	1327	57
针织物或钩编织物	Knitted or Crocheted Fabrics	283	76	181	143
针织或钩编的服装及衣着附件	Articles of Apparel and Clothing Accessories, Knitted or Crocheted	7816	95	9610	124
非针织或非钩编的服装及衣着附件	Articles of Apparel and Clothing Accessories, not Knitted or Crocheted	15095	238	9104	40
其他纺织制成品；成套物品；旧衣着及旧纺织品；碎织物	Other Made Up Textile Articles; Sets; Worn Clothing And Worn Textile Articles; Rags Articles; Rags	55682	389	9490	130
鞋、帽、伞、杖、鞭及其零件；已加工的羽毛及其制品；人造花；人发制品	**Footwear, Headgear, Umbrellas, Sun Umbrellas, Walking-Sticks, Seat-Sticks, Whips, Riding-Crops and Parts Thereof; Prepared Feathers and Articles Made Therewith; Artificial Flowers; Articles of Human Hair**	3266	106	3844	32
鞋靴、护腿和类似品及其零件	Footwear, Gaiters and The Like; Parts of Such Articles	693	93	839	32
帽类及其零件	Headgear and Parts Thereof	393	13	808	2
雨伞、阳伞、手杖、鞭子、马鞭及其零件	Umbrellas, Sun Umbrellas, Walking-Sticks, Seat-Sticks, Whips, Riding-Crops And Parts Thereof	43	0	54	0
已加工羽毛、羽绒及其制品；人造花；人发制品	Prepared Feathers and Down and Articles Made of Feathers or of Down; Artificial Flowers; Articles of Human Hair	2137	1	2143	0
石料、石膏、水泥、石棉、云母及类似材料的制品；陶瓷产品；玻璃及其制品	**Articles of Stone, Plaster, Cement, Asbestos, Mica or Similar Materials; Ceramic Products; Glass and Glassware**	26177	2222	25829	1153
石料、石膏、水泥、石棉、云母及类似材料的制品	Articles of Stone, Plaster, Cement, Asbestos, Mica or Similar Materials	6620	103	7862	168
陶瓷产品	Ceramic Products	3728	868	3348	101
玻璃及其制品	Glass and Glassware	15830	1251	14619	884
天然或养殖珍珠、宝石或半宝石、贵金属、包贵金属及其制品；仿手饰；硬币	**Natural or Cultured Pearls, Precious or Semi-Precious Stones, Precious Metals, Metals Clad With Precious Metal and Stones, Precious Metals, Metals Clad With Precious Metal and Articles Thereof; Imitation Jewellery; Coin**	50	14	357	196
天然或养殖珍珠、宝石或半宝石、贵金属、包贵金属及其制品；仿手饰；硬币	Natural or Cultured Pearls, Precious or Semi-Precious Stones, Precious Metals, Metals Clad With Precious Metal and Stones, Precious Metals, Metals Clad With Precious Metal and Articles Thereof; Imitation Jewellery; Coin	50	14	357	196
贱金属及其制品	**Base Metals and Articles of Base Metal**	117428	11235	123862	9866
钢　铁	Iron and Steel	25265	2955	29668	2306
钢铁制品	Articles of Iron or Steel	73701	2590	75662	2400
铜及其制品	Copper and Articles Thereof	2122	2731	2042	2099
镍及其制品	Nickel and Articles Thereof	13	27	8	37
铝及其制品	Aluminium and Articles Thereof	12082	1973	12621	1946

16-3 续表 3 continued 3

商 品 类 别	Indicator	2020 年		2019 年	
		出 口 Export	进 口 Import	出 口 Export	进 口 Import
铅及其制品	Lead and Articles Thereof	6	2	2	5
锌及其制品	Zinc and Articles Thereof	39	21	37	343
锡及其制品	Tin and Articles Thereof	2	0		0
其他贱金属、金属陶瓷及其制品	Other Base Metals; Cermets; Articles Thereof	105	169	67	222
贱金属工具、器具、利口器、餐匙、餐叉及其零件	Tools, Implements, Cutlery, Spoons and Forks, of Base Metal; Parts Thereof of Base Metal	2240	454	2423	325
贱金属杂项制品	Miscellaneous Articles of Base Metal	1853	313	1332	184
机器、机械器具、电气设备及其零件；录音机及放声机、电视图像、声音的录制和重放设备及其零件、附件	**Machinery and Mechanical Appliances; Electrical Equipment; Parts Thereof; Sound Recorders and Reproducers, Television Image and Sound Recorders and Reproducers; and Parts and Accessories of Recorders and Reproducers; and Parts and Accessories of Such Artic**	**355130**	**430736**	**267071**	**331497**
核反应堆、锅炉、机器、机械器具及其零件	Nuclear Reactors, Boilers, Machinery and Mechanical Appliances; Parts Thereof	263456	246488	195412	213531
电机、电气设备及其零件；录音机及放声机、电视图像、声音的录制和重放设备及其零件、附件	Electrical Machinery and Equipment and Parts Thereof; Sound Recorders and Reproducers, Television Image and Sound Recorders and Reproducers, and Parts and Accessories of Such Articles	91674	184248	71658	117966
车辆、航空器、船舶及有关运输设备	**Vehicles, Aircraft, Vessels And Associated Transport Equipment**	**169915**	**11322**	**195151**	**11108**
铁道及电车道机车、车辆及其零件；铁道及电车道轨道固定装置及其零件、附件；各种机械（包括电动机械）交通信号设备	Railway or Tramway Locomotives, Rolling-Stock and Parts Thereof; Railway or Tramway Track Fixtures And Fittings and Parts Thereof; Mechanical(Including Electro-Mechanical) Traffic Signalling Equipment of All Kinds	1896	436	2092	473
车辆及其零件、附件，但铁道及电车道车辆除外	Vehicles Other Than Railway or Tramway Rolling-Stock, and Parts and Accessories Thereof	164016	2115	189357	1879
航空器、航空器及其零件	Aircraft, Spacecraft, and Parts Thereof	3301	8735	2594	8670
船舶及浮动结构体	Ships, Boats and Floating Structures	702	36	1107	86
光学、照相、电影、计量、检验、医疗或外科用仪器及设备、精密仪器及设备；钟表；乐器；上述物品的零件、附件	**Optical, Photographic, Cinematographic, Measuring, Checking, Precision, Medical or Surgical Instruments and Apparatus; Clocks And Watches; Musical Instruments; Parts and Accessories Thereof**	**14337**	**59148**	**11669**	**39012**
光学、照相、计量、检验、医疗或外科用仪器及设备、精密仪器及设备；上述物品的零件、附件	Optical, Photographic, Cinematographic, Measuring, Checking, Precision Medical or Surgical Instruments and Apparatus; Parts and Accessories Thereof	13577	59127	10754	38964
钟表及其零件	Clocks and Watches and Parts Thereof	72	9	76	48
乐器及其零件、附件	Musical Instruments; Parts and Accessories of Such Articles	689	12	839	1
武器、弹药及其零件、附件	**Arms and Ammunition; Parts and Accessories Thereof**			**0**	
武器、弹药及其零件、附件	Arms and Ammunition; Parts and Accessories Thereof				
杂项制品	**Miscellaneous Manufactured Articles**	**22632**	**494**	**17907**	**748**
家具；寝具、褥垫、弹簧床垫、软坐垫及类似的填充制品；	Furniture; Bedding, Mattresses, Mattress Supports, Cushions and Similar Stuffed Furnishings	13724	390	10938	645
玩具、游戏品、运动用品及其零件、附件	Toys, Games and Sports Requisites; Parts and Accessories Thereof	7364	32	1546	57
杂项制品	Miscellaneous Manufactured Articles	1544	73		46
艺术品、收藏品及古物	**Works of Art, Collectors' Pieces and Antiques**	**13**	**54**	**33**	**1**
特殊交易品及未分类商品	**Commodities and Transactions not Classified According to Kind**	**2245**	**877**	**3560**	**4075**

16-4 按企业性质分海关进出口商品总额 (2020 年)

Import and Export Value of Commodities by Ownership(2020)

单位：万美元 (10 000 USD)

指标	Indicator	合计 Total	国有企业 State-owned Enterprises	外商投资企业 Foreign Funded Nterprises 小计 Total	中外合作 Cooperation Enterprises	中外合资 Jointv-enture Enterprises	外商独资 Wholly Foreign-owned	集体企业 Collective-owned Enterprises	其他 Others
进口商品总额	Total Value of Imports	909323	335560	94477	0	33406	61071	74379	852
一般贸易	General Trade		334337	50518					
来料加工装配贸易	Processing and Assembling Trade with Sent Materials		0	4351					
进料加工贸易	Processing Trade with Imported Materials		654	2912					
租赁贸易	Leasing Trate		0	5378					
海关特殊监管区域进口设备	Import of Equipment in Special Customs Supervision Area								
海关特殊监管区域物流货物	Logistics Freight of Equipment in Special Customs Supervision Area								
投资设备	Investment Goods		0	276					
保税监管场所进出境货物	Bonded Supervision Entry and Exit Goods		504	30733					
国际无偿援助和捐赠物资	International Aid and Material Donations		0	0					
其他贸易	Others		65	309					
出口商品总值	Total Value of Exports	1089426	36545	259099	466	94178	164455	25779	2038
一般贸易	General Trade		23531	207937					
国际无偿援助和捐赠物资	International Aid and Material Donations		295	0					
来料加工装配贸易	Processing and Assembling Trade with Sent Materials		0	6361					
进料加工贸易	Processing Trade with Imported Materials		3038	12696					
对外承包工程出口货物	Export of Contracted projects		9292	0					
保税监管场所进出境货物	Bonded Supervision Entry and Exit Goods		234	31791					
海关特殊监管区域物流货物	Logistics Freight of Equipment in Special Customs Supervision Area								
其他贸易	Others		141	314					

16-5 历年海关进出口总额
Total Imports and Exports by Category(Customs Statistics)

单位：万美元 (10 000 USD)

年份 Year	进出口总额 Total Value of Imports and Exports	进口总额 Total Value of Imports	出口总额 Total Value of Exports
1993	27446	21371	6075
1994	41746	23579	18167
1995	66587	29812	36775
1996	91347	48193	43154
1997	104230	52862	51368
1998	79943	45096	34847
1999	96125	60199	35926
2000	143935	86827	57108
2001	150143	90746	59397
2002	149264	79755	69509
2003	201554	117980	83545
2004	304678	167373	137305
2005	376213	198370	177843
2006	438930	194981	243949
2007	621804	278277	343527
2008	802699	342979	459720
2009	565704	260998	304706
2010	743776	338888	404888
2011	1041422	436966	604456
2012	913286	341844	571442
2013	957442	409126	548316
2014	1048867	442950	605917
2015	911424	311763	599661
2016	1086259	352229	734030
2017	1130449	379887	750562
2018	1318209	463119	855090
2019	1630123	695064	935059
2020	1998749	909323	1089426

16-6 利用外资情况
Utilization of Foreign Capital

指标	Indicator	2015 年	2016 年	2017 年	2018 年	2019 年	2020 年
新批外商投资企业个数（个）	Newly established Foreign Investment Enterprises(unit)	104	104	110	239	228	203
外商直接投资	Foreign Direct Investments	104	104	110	239	228	203
合同外资金额（万美元）	Total Amount of Contracted Foreign Capita(10 000 USD)	303100	179479	218692	556119	683441	585244
外商直接投资	Foreign Direct Investments	303100	179479	218692	556119	683441	585244
实际使用外资（万美元）	Total Amount of Foreign Capital Actually Utilized(10 000 USD)	157851	171625	187623	272847	224249	192456
外商直接投资	Foreign Direct Investments	157851	171625	187623	272847	224249	192456

16-7 对外经济技术合作
Technological Cooperation with Foreign Countries or Territories

指标	Indicator	单位 Unit	2015 年	2016 年	2017 年	2018 年	2019 年	2020 年
对外承包和劳务合作合同金额	Foreign Contracted Projects and Service Contrate	万美元 (10 000 USD)	530383	539589	539598	565706	573114	439945
对外承包	Contracted Projects with Foreign Countries or Regions	万美元 (10 000 USD)	530383	539589	539598	565706	573114	439945
对外承包和劳务合作营业额	Foreign Contracted Projects and Service Contrate	万美元 (10 000 USD)	308737	350099	373739	408427	408820	427206
对外承包	Contracted Projects with Foreign Countries or Regions	万美元 (10 000 USD)	308737	350099	373739	408427	408820	427206
外派劳务人数	Number of Persons Sent out	人 (person)	6886	6976	7037	6586	8047	11996
境外投资企业数	Numberof Overseas Investment Enterprises	个 (unit)	50	55	42	50	79	77
中方实际投资额	China Actual Investment	万美元 (10 000 USD)	70052	70175	83760	102434	110798	191321

注："中方实际投资额"，2016 年以前为"中方协议投资额"口径。
Note: "China's actual investment" was the caliber of "agreed investment amount of China" before 2016.

16-8 出口 1000 万美元以上企业一览 (2020 年)
Summary of Enterprises with Annual Exports Value Above 10 Million Dollar(2020)

单位名称 Name of Enterprises	单位名称 Name of Enterprises
中国重汽集团国际有限公司	济南华辰实业有限责任公司
山东浪潮进出口有限公司	莱芜远洋果菜有限公司
山东一达通企业服务有限公司	山东鲁电国际贸易有限公司
山东圣泉化工股份有限公司	山东商龙经贸有限公司
济南玫德铸造有限公司	山东天下鲁商商务有限公司
山东齐鲁医药进出口有限公司	济南海航国际贸易有限公司
莱芜泰丰食品有限公司	齐鲁制药有限公司
山东太古飞机工程有限公司	山东泰山钢铁集团有限公司
山东省万兴食品有限公司	章丘东铁铸锻有限公司
济南澳海炭素有限公司	莱芜英拓进出口有限公司
莱芜泰禾生化有限公司	济南幸福森林食品有限公司
济南裕兴化工有限责任公司	山东臻真然国际贸易有限公司
山东临沃重机有限公司	山东鼎实果蔬有限公司
山东齐发药业有限公司	山东一品农产集团有限公司
山东电力建设第一工程公司	山东立达进出口公司
莱芜万兴果菜食品加工有限公司	山东通翔国际物流有限公司
济南邦德数控设备有限公司	济南秦工国际贸易有限公司
山东莱芜金雷风电科技股份有限公司	博科（济南）国际贸易股份有限公司
济南万方炭素进出口有限公司	山东凯信达工贸有限公司
山东钢铁股份有限公司莱芜分公司	济南华尔重型汽车销售有限公司
济南绿霸化学品有限责任公司	济南丰博进出口贸易有限公司
山东伊莱特重工有限公司	莱芜永保电子有限公司
济南易安达保税物流有限公司	济南诚信通铝业有限公司
济南迈克管道科技股份有限公司	济南维斯尔机械设备有限公司
济南金麒麟刹车系统有限公司	济南轨道交通装备有限责任公司
山东聚德顺电子科技有限公司	济南博意达商贸有限公司
济南金威刻科技发展有限公司	莱芜长荣食品有限公司
济南森峰科技有限公司	济南裕峰生物工程有限公司
山东中农联合生物科技有限公司	济南市冶金科学研究所
济南大自然化学有限公司	莱芜鲁蒙食品股份有限公司
山东鲁航贸易有限公司	济南嘉亚经贸发展有限公司
莱芜市晔霖农产品进出口有限公司	济南瑞泰克制冷设备有限公司
济南尚润通达复合材料有限公司	济南采明木业有限公司
济南四海永联汽车销售有限公司	齐鲁安替制药有限公司
费斯托气动有限公司	济南星辉数控机械科技有限公司
山东润科国际贸易有限公司	斯凯孚（济南）轴承与精密技术产品有限公司
济南圣泉集团股份有限公司	济南尼克焊接技术有限公司

16-8 续表 continued

单位名称 Name of Enterprises	单位名称 Name of Enterprises
济南轻骑标致摩托车有限公司	济南金宝塑业有限公司
莱芜钢铁集团银山型钢有限公司	济南东进皮草有限公司
华熙生物科技股份有限公司	山东月笙果蔬有限公司
迈大食品（山东）有限公司	济南福瑞德纺织品有限公司
山东省永信非织造材料有限公司	山东云缦进出口有限公司
卧龙电气章丘海尔电机有限公司	山东电力设备有限公司
章丘美华进出口贸易有限公司	济南创凯科技有限公司
济南鲁东耐火材料有限公司	山东爱地高分子材料有限公司
山东大鲁阁织染工业有限公司	莱芜泰丰食品有限公司
山东希诺金属材料有限公司	山东欧锐激光科技有限公司
山东冠世时装加工有限公司	济南浩丰进出口有限公司
济南西门子变压器有限公司	济南爱兰德商贸有限公司
济南鸿天国际贸易有限公司	济南特亚国际贸易有限公司
山东华民钢球股份有限公司	济南乐邦贸易有限公司
山东建盛贸易有限公司	济南东耀进出口贸易有限公司
山东电子工程咨询院有限公司	山东威明汽车产品有限公司
济南弘正科技有限公司	山东慧通轮胎有限公司
九阳股份有限公司	山东百利通亚陶科技有限公司
济南二机床集团有限公司	济南圣泉倍进陶瓷过滤器有限公司
山东科赛怡锐化工有限公司	莱芜旭佳经贸有限公司
济南轻骑对外贸易有限责任公司	济南东岳国际贸易有限公司
山东汇金股份有限公司	济南双科国际贸易有限公司
济南力诺玻璃制品有限公司	济南邦和工贸有限公司
山东力诺光伏高科技有限公司	济南东烨国际贸易有限公司
济南台有玻璃制品有限公司	山东洛坤国际贸易有限公司
山东科兴生物制品有限公司	山东信敏惠供应链管理有限公司
中国重汽集团济南港豪保税物流有限公司	莱芜市万鑫经贸有限公司
济南网泽信息技术有限公司	山东博世磨具实业有限公司
山东信久进出口有限公司	福士汽车零部件（济南）有限公司
济南轻骑铃木摩托车有限公司	中铁十四局集团有限公司
中国电建集团核电工程有限公司	山东晋煤日月化工有限公司
山东伊尔曼国际商贸有限公司	济南名祖商业有限公司
山东绿健生命科技股份有限公司	山东三维商贸有限公司
山东源和电站工程技术有限公司	莱芜市金雨地进出口有限公司
济南实达紧固件有限公司	济南宏创博展汽车销售有限公司
济南沃德汽车零部件有限公司	山东宝凯隆供应链管理有限公司

16-9 旅游住宿单位接待入境游客
Received Inbound Tourists by Hotels

指标	Indicator	2015 年	2016 年	2017 年	2018 年	2019 年	2020 年
入境游客人数（人次）	Number of Inbound Tourists(person-time)	332942	351526	375469	398721	456585	108524
外国人	Foreigners	205477	216899	232260	247086	285071	90926
日本	Japan	22154	21972	21967	23123	28653	2674
菲律宾	Philippines	2215	2357	2622	2901	3500	1446
新加坡	Singapore	14837	15586	16588	17503	18092	2729
韩国	Republic of Korea	34238	36137	34695	37432	41390	5536
加拿大	Canada	5697	5558	6445	6970	7859	1836
英国	United Kingdom	9693	10286	10918	11602	12910	7623
德国	Germany	14688	15608	16543	17706	19384	2557
法国	France	6694	7041	7532	8000	8893	1555
意大利	Italy	4086	4330	5190	5524	6069	583
瑞士	Switzerland	986	1051	1119	1216	1348	156
澳大利亚	Australia	8934	9456	10089	10762	12422	3783
新西兰	New Zealand	1625	1825	1958	2078	2113	815
美国	United States	21396	23187	24797	26325	29556	20623
港澳和台湾同胞	Compatriots from Hong Kong Macao and Taiwan	127465	134627	143209	151635	171514	17700
# 台湾同胞	Compatriots from Taiwan	61726	65050	68839	72667	87086	4355
入境游客人天数（人天）	Number of Days on Inbound Tourists(person-day)	786451	829300	878238	1086701	1276852	265436
外国人	Foreigners	460937	483753	513621	683730	806837	187665
港澳和台湾同胞	Compatriots from Hong Kong and Macao	325514	345547	364617	402971	959122	77773
# 台湾同胞	Compatriots from Taiwan	172776	178839	187351	265047	317730	45873
旅游外汇收入（亿美元）	Foreign Exchange Income of Tourism (100 million USD)	1.84	1.96	2.08	2.23	2.75	0.33
# 商品性收入	Commecial Income	0.53	0.51	0.54	0.6	0.7	0.08
附：平均每天来济国际旅游人数（人次）	Number of Tourists Per Day(person-time)	912	963	1029	1092	1251	296.51
星级宾馆客房出租率（%）	Star Hotel Room Rate(%)	61.0	64.5	64.56	63.4	62	47.51

注：2018 年起接待入境游客包含了过夜游客和一日游游客。
Notes: Starting in 2018, inbound tourists include overnight vsitors and day-trippers.

16-10 济南与国外结成友好城市一览表 (2020 年末)
Foreign Friendly Cities of Jinan(End of 2020)

国别	Country	城市	City	缔结日期 Day
日本	Japan	和歌山市（和歌山县首府）	Wakayama	1983.01.14
英国	United Kingdom	考文垂市（英国汽车工业故乡，制造业中心之一）	Coventry	1983.10.03
日本	Japan	山口市（山口县首府）	Yamaguchi	1985.09.20
美国	United States	萨克拉门托市（加利福尼亚州首府）	Sacramento	1985.05.29
加拿大	Canada	里贾纳市（萨斯喀彻温省省会）	Regina	1987.08.10
巴布亚新几内亚	Papua New Guinea	莫尔斯比港（巴布亚新几内亚首都）	Port Moresby	1988.09.28
韩国	Republic of Korea	水原市（京畿道首府）	Suwon	1993.10.27
俄罗斯	Russia	下诺夫哥罗德市（下诺夫哥罗德州首府）	Nizhny novgorod	1994.09.25
芬兰	Finland	万达市（欧洲机场城市、芬兰第四大城市）	Vantaa	2001.08.27
法国	France	雷恩市（布列塔尼大区首府）	Renne	2002.07.17
澳大利亚	Australia	郡德勒普市（西澳洲新兴教育科技中心）	Draper	2004.09.04
德国	Germany	奥格斯堡市（施瓦本地区首府）	Augsburg	2004.10.10
乌克兰	Ukraine	哈尔科夫市（哈尔科夫州首府）	Kharkov	2007.05.23
以色列	Israel	卡法萨巴市（沙龙地区中心城市）	Kafassaba	2009.05.11
白俄罗斯	Belorussia	维捷布斯克市（ 维捷布斯克州首府）	Vitebsk	2009.09.20
佛得角	Cape Verde	普拉亚市（佛得角首都）	Praia	2009.09.22
巴西	Brazil	波多韦柳市（朗多尼亚州首府）	Bothoweri	2011.10.13
土耳其	Turkey	马尔马里斯市（地中海沿岸港口城市和旅游胜地）	Marmaris	2011.10.21
白俄罗斯	The Republic of Belarus	明斯克市苏维埃区（白俄罗斯首都明斯克市历史最悠久的区之一）	Savetski (Soviet) District , Minsk	2012.08.03
印度尼西亚	Indonesia	徐图利祖市（东爪哇省泗水市机场城市、新兴经济城市）	Xu Tzu Chi City	2012.09.21
保加利亚	Bulgaria	卡赞勒格市（保加利亚玫瑰精油生产中心）	Kazanlak	2013.08.29
墨西哥	Mexico	萨博潘市（哈利斯科州经济首府）	Saab Pan	2014.05.20
格鲁吉亚	Georgia	库塔伊西市（格鲁吉亚西部历史名城和第二大工业城市）	Kutaisi	2016.05.26
意大利	Italy	奇维塔韦基亚市（欧洲第三大客运港）	Civitavecchia	2016.06.20
印度	India	那格浦尔市（印度地理中心城市、马哈拉施特拉邦第二首府）	Nagpur	2017.12.08
埃塞俄比亚	Ethiopia	阿尔巴门奇市（埃塞俄比亚西南部重要城镇，格穆戈法州首府）	Arba Minch	2018.09.06
斯洛文尼亚	Slovenia	马里博尔（斯洛文尼亚第二大城市、重要的工业中心）	Maribor	2019.09.26

16-11 济南市与各友好城市交流
Basic Statistics of Transmission Between Foreign Friendly Cities and Jinan

单位：批数、人次 (batch.person-time)

指标	Indicator	2015 年	2016 年	2017 年	2018 年	2019 年	2020 年
因公出访交流考察	Business Trip						
批数	Batch	583	780	747	781	718	7
人次	Number	1444	1907	1906	2107	1798	15
接待来访团组	Receive Visitors						
批数	Batch	123	204	207	206	–	–
人次	Number	1107	1352	1829	1730	–	–

注：本表指标为“–”的，部门相关统计制度中已经不再进行统计。
Notes: The indicator “–” in this table means statistics are no longer in the relevant statistical system of the department.

主要统计指标解释

海关进出口商品总额 指实际进出我国国境的货物总金额。包括对外贸易实际进出口货物，来料加工装配进出口货物，国家间、联合国及国际组织无偿援助物资和赠送品，华侨、港澳台同胞和外籍华人捐赠品，租赁期满归承租人所有的租赁货物，进料加工进出口货物，边境地方贸易及边境地区小额贸易进出口货物（边民互市贸易除外），中外合资企业、中外合作经营企业、外商独资经营企业进出口货物和公用物品，到、离岸价格在规定限额以上的进出口货样和广告品（无商业价值、无使用价值和免费提供出口的除外），从保税仓库提取在中国境内销售的进口货物，以及其他进出口货物。进出口总额用以观察一个国家在对外贸易方面的总规模。我国规定出口货物按离岸价格统计，进口货物按到岸价格统计。

利用外资 指我国各级政府、部门、企业和其他经济组织通过对外借款、吸收外商直接投资以及用其他方式筹措的境外现汇、设备、技术等。

外商直接投资 指外国企业和经济组织或个人（包括华侨、港澳台胞以及我国在境外注册的企业）按我国有关政策、法规，用现汇、实物、技术等在我国境内开办外商独资企业、与我国境内的企业或经济组织共同举办中外合资经营企业、合作经营企业或合作开发资源的投资（包括外商投资收益的再投资）。即“外方投资者的投资股本”和总投资与注册资本差额部分的“外方股东对企业的直接贷款”。

对外承包工程 指各对外承包公司以招标议标承包方式承揽的下列业务：（1）承包国外工程建设项目，（2）承包我国对外经援项目，（3）承包我国驻外机构的工程建设项目，（4）承包我国境内利用外资进行建设的工程项目，（5）与外国承包公司合营或联合承包工程项目时我国公司分包部分，（6）对外承包兼营的房屋开发业务。对外承包工程的营业额是以货币表现的本期内完成的对外承包工程的工作量，包括以前年度签订的合同和本年度新签订的合同在报告期内完成的工作量。

对外劳务合作 指以收取工资的形式向业主或承包商提供技术和劳动服务的活动。我国对外承包公司在境外开办的合营企业，中国公司同时又提供劳务的，其劳务部分也纳入劳务合作统计。劳务合作营业额按报告期内向雇主提交的结算数（包括工资、加班费和奖金等）统计。

入境游客 指报告期内来中国（大陆）观光、度假、探亲访友、就医疗养、购物、参加会议或从事经济、文化、体育、宗教活动的外国人、港澳台同胞等游客（即入境旅游人数）。

外国人 指属外国国籍的人，加入外国国籍的中国血统华人也计入外国人。

旅游外汇收入 入境游客在中国（大陆）境内旅行、游览过程中用于交通、参观游览、住宿、餐饮、购物、娱乐等全部花费。

Explanatory Notes on Main Statistical Indicators

Total Value of Customs Export-import Commodities refers to the total value of cargoes actually importing from and exported to China. It includes cargoes actually imported and exported in the foreign trade; cargoes imported and exported of processing and assembly of supplied materials; free aid and gift between countries, from The United Nations and international organizations; donation of overseas Chinese, Hong Kong, Macao and Taiwan compatriots and Chinese of foreign nationality; lease cargoes belonging to the tenant when the lease term expires; cargoes imported and exported of processing with imported materials; cargoes imported and exported of local border trade and small trade in border areas (except for fair among the inhabitants of border areas); cargoes imported and exported and public objects of Sino-foreign joint venture, Chinese-foreign co-operative enterprise and wholly foreign-owned enterprises; sample goods and advertising samples imported and exported based on cost insurance and freight and FOB above the specified limit (except for export without commercial value or use value and freely provided); import goods extracted from bonded warehouse which are sold in China and other cargoes imported and exported. Total export-import volume is used to observe the total scale of a country in the aspect of foreign trade. China specifies exported goods are subject to statistics as per FOB and import goods are subject to statistics pursuant to cost insurance and freight.

Utilization of Foreign Capital refers to remittance, equipment and technology financed from abroad, by foreign loans, attracting foreign direct investment and other forms undertaken by the Chinese governments at all levels, by various departments, enterprises and other economic organizations.

Foreign Direct Investment refers to investments by exclusively foreign-owned enterprises established by foreign enterprise and economic organization or individual (including overseas Chinese, Hong Kong, Macao and Taiwan compatriots and China's enterprise registered abroad) in China according to related policies and regulations of China based on spot exchange, material object and technology, joint venture with Chinese and foreign investment, cooperative enterprise or cooperative development resources jointly organized by enterprises or economic organizations in China, (including reinvestment of foreign direct investment income), namely "direct loan from foreign shareholders to enterprises" of the balance between "investment capital of foreign investors" and total investment as well as registered capital.

Contract Foreign Projects refer to the following business undertaken by all foreign contract companies based on the method of contract through bidding negotiation: (1) Contracting foreign construction projects, (2) Contracting China's foreign economic assistance projects, (3) Contracting construction projects of China's institution functioning abroad, (4) Contracting projects constructed based on foreign capital in China, (5) Subcontracting part of China's company at the time of joint operation with foreign contracting company or united contracting of the project, and (6) Contracting the housing development business operated concurrently. Turnover of contract foreign projects is the workload of contract foreign projects completed in the current period embodied with currency, including workload of the contract signed in previous year and the contract newly signed in this year which is completed in the reporting period.

Foreign Labor Cooperation refers to the activities of providing technology and labor services for owners or contractors in the forms of receiving salaries and wages. China's foreign contract companies refer to cooperative enterprises established outside the border with labor service provided by Chinese company at the same time whose labor service is included into labor service cooperation statistics as well. The business volume of labor service cooperation shall be counted in accordance with the settlement amount (wages and salaries, overtime pay, bonuses and other remuneration) submitted to the employers during the reporting period.

Entry Visitors refer to foreigners and compatriots from Hong Kong, Macao and Taiwan coming to China (Chinese Mainland) for sightseeing, vacation, visiting relatives and friends, medical treatment, shopping, attending the meeting or engaging in economic, cultural, sports and religious activities in the reporting period (namely the number of inbound travelers).

Foreigners refer to persons with foreign nationality and ethnic Chinese with Chinese descent and foreign nationality is also included into foreigners.

Income from Tourism Foreign Exchange refers to total cost spent by entry visitors on transportation, sightseeing, accommodation, catering, shopping and entertainment, etc. in the process of travelling and sightseeing in China (Chinese Mainland).

17

科 技

SCIENCE AND TECHNOLOGY

17-1 科技综合情况
Basic Statistics on Science and Technology

指标	Indicator	单位 Unit	2012 年	2013 年	2014 年	2015 年	2016 年	2017 年	2018 年	2019 年
R&D 活动单位	R&D Activity Units	个 (unit)	446	573	660	803	890	964	821	1089
R&D 活动全时人员	Full-time R&D Personnel	人年 (man-years)	37824	41643	46796	51297	52395	57506	59995	52153
R&D 活动经费内部支出	Internal Expenditure on R&D	万元 (10 000 yuan)	989528	1111522	1205441.6	1330543.8	1567365	1851538.7	2085980.1	2255264.6
#基础研究	Basic Research	万元 (10 000 yuan)	72717	77918	81092.8	106229	128504.7	152909.2	144105.1	173425.2
#应用研究	Applied Research	万元 (10 000 yuan)	135575	127176	142847.5	136507.2	151841.2	208526.4	246533.3	304343.7
#试验发展	Experimental Development	万元 (10 000 yuan)	781236	906428	981501.4	1087807.6	1287019.1	1490103.1	1695281.7	1777495.7
#日常性支出	Daily Expenditure	万元 (10 000 yuan)	859567	967345	1068380.6	1161517.8	1376837.7	1636821.4	1843653.3	2010202.7
人员劳务费	Staff Service Fee	万元 (10 000 yuan)	277486	320273	376372.8	470989.9	522676.7	616187.2	763134.5	695510.6
#资产性支出	Capital Expenditure	万元 (10 000 yuan)	129961	144177	137061	169026	190527.3	214717.4	242326.8	233015.5
仪器设备	Instrument and Equipment	万元 (10 000 yuan)	123932	135607	126101.9	160989.5	185967.8	188836.8	236760.3	218192.1
R&D 活动经费外部支出	External expenditure on R&D	万元 (10 000 yuan)	38990	46679	57993	42612	62140.8	70569.2	79731.3	107132.1
科技成果情况	Scientific Achievements									
专利申请数	Patent Applications	件 (pieces)	8699	10221	12196	14178	15490	19645		
#发明专利申请数	Inventions	件 (pieces)	3903	4755	6234	8454	9138	12027		
拥有发明专利数	Number of Invention Patents	件 (pieces)	4973	6087	7712	10007	13808	20059		
科技项目（课题）情况	Scientific Projects									
项目（课题）数	Number of Projects	项 (item)	15899	17683	18811	21177	22570	27666		
项目参加人员折合全时当年	Number of Participants	人年 (man-years)	36702	39557	43828.2	46715	44188	46457.1		

注：1. 2018 年数据为行政区划调整前口径，以下各表同。
2. “科技成果情况”2018 年起相关数据，山东省统计局不再反馈。

Note: 1. Data used in 2018 is the statistical scale before the adjustment of administrative division (the same below).
2. "Scientific Achievements" since 2018 have been not reflected by Shandong Provincial Bureau of Statistics.

17–2 科技投入情况 (2019 年)
Basic Statistics on Scientific and Technological Funds(2019)

指标	Indicator	单位 Unit	合计 Total	科研机构 Research Institutions	高等院校 colleges and universities	规模以上工业企业 Industrial Enterprises above Designated Size	其他 Others
有 R&D 活动单位数	Number of Enterprises with R&D Activities	个 (unit)	1089	69	71	711	238
R&D 人员	R&D Personnel	人 (Person)	82024	5439	23976	33952	18657
# 研究人员	Research Personnel	人 (Person)	47230	4035	20967	13089	9139
R&D 人员折合全时人员	Full–time Equivalent of R&D Personnel	人年 (man–years)	50015	4520	11204.2	23282	11009
基础研究	Basic Research	人年 (man–years)	7892	1370	5246.7	18	1258
应用研究	Applied Research	人年 (man–years)	9691	1626	5484.6	839	1742
试验发展	Experimental Development	人年 (man–years)	32431	1524	472.9	22425	8010
R&D 经费内部支出	Internal Expenditure on R&D	万元 (10 000 yuan)	2255265	198553	262284	1295161	499267
基础研究	Basic Research	万元 (10 000 yuan)	173425	43577	106060	216	23573
应用研究	Applied Research	万元 (10 000 yuan)	304344	77647	142254	35556	48887
试验发展	Experimental Development	万元 (10 000 yuan)	1777496	77329	13971	1259389	426806
日常性支出	Routine Expenses	万元 (10 000 yuan)	2010203	136324	226906	1196948	450025
# 人员劳务费	Labor Cost	万元 (10 000 yuan)	695511	77502	41878	389142	186990
资产性支出	Assets Expenditure	万元 (10 000 yuan)	233016	62229	35379	98213	37195
# 仪器和设备	Instrument and Equipment	万元 (10 000 yuan)	218192	53633	32657	95885	36017

17-3 规模以上工业企业科技活动情况(2019年)
Main Indicators of Industrial Enterprises Above Designated Size(2019)

单位:个 (unit)

指标	Indicator	企业数 Number of Industial Enterprises	#有R&D活动的单位数 Number of Units with Research and Development Activities	企业办科技机构数 Number of Technology Institutions Run By Enterprises
总计	**Total**	2153	711	409
按登记注册类型分	**by Status of Registration**			
内资企业	Domestic Funded Enterprises	2005	651	375
国有企业	State-owned Enterprises	12	1	
集体企业	Collective-owned Enterprises	7	1	
股份合作企业	Cooperative Enterprises	4	1	1
有限责任公司	Private Limited Liability Corporations	691	258	175
国有独资公司	State Sole funded Corporations	38	18	23
其他有限责任公司	Other Limited Liability Corporations	653	240	152
股份有限公司	Share-holding Corporations Ltd.	102	67	61
私营企业	Private Enterprises	1188	323	138
私营独资企业	Private-funded Enterprises	32	1	
私营合伙企业	Private Partnership Enterprises			
私营有限责任公司	Private Limited Liability Corporations	1098	288	116
私营股份有限公司	Private Share-holding Corporations Ltd.	58	34	22
港、澳、台商投资企业	Enterprises with Funds from Hong Kong,Macao and Taiwan	62	22	11
合资经营企业(港或澳、台资)	Joint-venture Enterprises	30	12	7
合作经营企业(港或澳、台资)	Cooperative Enterprises	1		
港、澳、台商独资经营企业	Enterprises with Sole Investment	28	8	3
港、澳、台商投资股份有限公司	Share-holding Corporations Ltd.	2	1	1
其他港澳台投资企业	Other Enterprises	1	1	
外商投资企业	Foreign Funded Enterprises	86	38	23
中外合资经营企业	Joint-venture Enterprises	39	20	9
中外合作经营企业	Cooperation Enterprises	3	1	
外资企业	Enterprises with Sole Fund	43	16	9
外商投资股份有限公司	Share-holding Corporations Ltd. with Foreign Investment	1	1	5
按工业行业大类分	**by Sector**			
煤炭开采和洗选业	Mining and Washing of Coal	5	2	
石油和天然气开采业	Extraction of Petroleum and Natural Gas	3		
黑色金属矿采选业	Mining and Processing of Ferrous Metal Ores	12	3	2
非金属矿采选业	Mining and Processing of Nonmetal Ores	9		
农副食品加工业	Processing of Food from Agricultural Products	95	12	10
食品制造业	Manufacture of Foods	67	20	8

17-3 续表 continued

指标	Indicator	企业数 Number of Industial Enterprises	# 有 R&D 活动的单位数 Number of Units with Research and Development Activities	企业办科技机构数 Number of Technology Institutions Run By Enterprises
酒、饮料和精制茶制造业	Manufacture of Wine, Drinks and Refined Tea	21	2	3
烟草制品业	Manufacture of Tobacco	1		
纺织业	Manufacture of Textile	51	11	8
纺织服装、服饰业	Manufacture of Textile Wearing Apparel and Finery	22	2	1
皮革、毛皮、羽毛及其制品和制鞋业	Manufacture of Leather, Fur, Feather & Its Products and Footwear	5	1	
木材加工和木、竹、藤、棕、草制品业	Processing of Timbers, Manufacture of Wood,Bamboo, Rattan, Palm, and Straw Products	14	2	1
家具制造业	Manufacture of Furniture	13	1	
造纸和纸制品业	Manufacture of Paper and Paper Products	33	5	
印刷和记录媒介复制业	Printing, Reproduction of Recording Media	53	12	4
文教、工美、体育和娱乐用品制造业	Manufacture of Culture, Education,Arts and crafts, Sport and Entertainment Goods	24	6	2
石油加工、炼焦和核燃料加工业	Processing of Petroleum, Coking and Nucleus Fuel	14	4	4
化学原料和化学制品制造业	Manufacture of Chemical Raw Material and Chemical Products	105	36	29
医药制造业	Manufacture of Medicines	60	37	47
化学纤维制造业	Manufacture of Chemical Fiber	8	3	1
橡胶和塑料制品业	Manufacture of Rubber and Plastic	61	16	9
非金属矿物制品业	Manufacture of Non-metallic Mineral Products	260	52	35
黑色金属冶炼和压延加工业	Manufacture and Processing of Ferrous Metals	31	11	5
有色金属冶炼和压延加工业	Manufacture & Processing of Non-ferrous Metals	25	6	3
金属制品业	Manufacture of Metal Products	242	68	36
通用设备制造业	Manufacture of General Purpose Machinery	256	103	47
专用设备制造业	Manufacture of Special Purpose Machinery	189	96	37
汽车制造业	Manufacture of Automotive	107	38	15
铁路、船舶、航空航天和其他运输设备制造业	Manufacture of Railroad,Marine,Aerospace and Other Transportation Equipment	27	7	4
电气机械和器材制造业	Manufacture of Electrical Machinery & Equipment	127	56	27
计算机、通信和其他电子设备制造业	Manufacture of Computer, Communications and Other Electronic Equipment	65	40	21
仪器仪表制造业	Manufacture of Measuring Instrument	60	44	43
其他制造业	Other Manufacture	6	3	
废弃资源综合利用业	Comprehensive Utilization of Waste	7		
金属制品、机械和设备修理业	Metal Products, Machinery and Equipment Repair Industry	4	2	5
电力、热力生产和供应业	Production and Supply of Electric Power and Heat Power	39	8	1
燃气生产和供应业	Production and Supply of Gas	19		
水的生产和供应业	Production and Supply of Water	13	2	1

17-4 规模以上工业企业技术改造及引进吸收(2019年)

Innovation and Resorb of Industrial Enterprises Above Designated Size (2019)

单位：万元 (10 000 yuan)

指标	Indicator	技术改造经费支出 Technical Reform Expenditure	引进国外技术经费支出 Acquisition of Foreign Technology Expenditure	引进技术的消化吸收经费支出 Expenditure for Assimilation Technology	购买国内技术经费支出 Expenditure for Purchase Domestic Technology
总计	Total	311487	20	19140	9250
按登记注册类型分	by Status of Registration				
内资企业	Domestic Funded Enterprises	299215	20	12343	9207
国有企业	State-owned Enterprises				
集体企业	Collective-owned Enterprises	1031			
股份合作企业	Cooperative Enterprises				
有限责任公司	Private Limited Liability Corporations	150593	2	11967	7762
国有独资公司	State Sole funded Corporations	31822			
其他有限责任公司	Other Limited Liability Corporations	118770	2	11967	7762
股份有限公司	Share-holding Corporations Ltd.	114800	18	138	562
私营企业	Private Enterprises	32792		238	884
私营独资企业	Private-funded Enterprises				
私营合伙企业	Private Partnership Enterprises				
私营有限责任公司	Private Limited Liability Corporations	19070		238	884
私营股份有限公司	Private Share-holding Corporations Ltd.	13722			
港、澳、台商投资企业	Enterprises with Funds from Hong Kong,Macao and Taiwan	5464			
合资经营企业(港或澳、台资)	Joint-venture Enterprises	2234			
合作经营企业(港或澳、台资)	Cooperative Enterprises				
港、澳、台商独资经营企业	Enterprises with Sole Investment				
港、澳、台商投资股份有限公司	Share-holding Corporations Ltd.	3230			
其他港澳台投资企业	Other Enterprises				
外商投资企业	Foreign Funded Enterprises	6808		6797	43
中外合资经营企业	Joint-venture Enterprises	4344		6191	22
中外合作经营企业	Cooperation Enterprises				
外资企业	Enterprises with Sole Fund			606	
外商投资股份有限公司	Share-holding Corporations Ltd. with Foreign Investment	2465			21
按工业行业大类分	by Sector				
煤炭开采和洗选业	Mining and Washing of Coal				
石油和天然气开采业	Extraction of Petroleum and Natural Gas				
黑色金属矿采选业	Mining of Ferrous Metal Ores	1081			
非金属矿采选业	Mining and Processing of Nonmetal Ores				10
农副食品加工业	Processing of Food from Agricultural Products	153			80
食品制造业	Manufacture of Foods	400			
酒、饮料和精制茶制造业	Manufacture of Wine, Drinks and Refined Tea	91			

17-4 续表 continued

指标	Indicator	技术改造经费支出 Technical Reform Expenditure	引进国外技术经费支出 Acquisition of Foreign Technology Expenditure	引进技术的消化吸收经费支出 Expenditure for Assimilation Technology	购买国内技术经费支出 Expenditure for Purchase Domestic Technology
烟草制品业	Manufacture of Tobacco				
纺织业	Manufacture of Textile	2332			1
纺织服装、服饰业	Manufacture of Textile Wearing Apparel and Finery				
皮革、毛皮、羽毛及其制品和制鞋业	Manufacture of Leather, Fur, Feather & Its Products and Footwear				
木材加工和木、竹、藤、棕、草制品业	Processing of Timbers, Manufacture of Wood, Bamboo, Rattan, Palm, and Straw Products	32			
家具制造业	Manufacture of Furniture				
造纸和纸制品业	Manufacture of Paper and Paper Products				
印刷和记录媒介复制业	Printing, Reproduction of Recording Media	6378			
文教、工美、体育和娱乐用品制造业	Manufacture of Culture, Education,Arts and crafts， Sport and Entertainment Goods				
石油加工、炼焦和核燃料加工业	Processing of Petroleum, Coking and Nucleus Fuel	27307			357
化学原料和化学制品制造业	Manufacture of Chemical Raw Material and Chemical Products	26708			65
医药制造业	Manufacture of Medicines	19868		11508	7682
化学纤维制造业	Manufacture of Chemical Fiber				
橡胶和塑料制品业	Manufacture of Rubber and Plastic	125			
非金属矿物制品业	Manufacture of Non-metallic Mineral Products	39979			1
黑色金属冶炼和压延加工业	Manufacture and Processing of Ferrous Metals	117611			530
有色金属冶炼和压延加工业	Manufacture & Processing of Non-ferrous Metals				
金属制品业	Manufacture of Metal Products	30111			21
通用设备制造业	Manufacture of General Purpose Machinery	18622	18	138	48
专用设备制造业	Manufacture of Special Purpose Machinery	1732		180	126
汽车制造业	Manufacture of Automotive	7295		606	
铁路、船舶、航空航天和其他运输设备制造业	Manufacture of Railroad,Marine,Aerospace and Other Transportation Equipment	5		4017	1
电气机械和器材制造业	Manufacture of Electrical Machinery & Equipment	5369		459	75
计算机、通信和其他电子设备制造业	Manufacture of Computer, Communications and Other Electronic Equipment	2252		2174	252
仪器仪表制造业	Manufacture of Measuring Instrument	875		58	3
其他制造业	Other Manufacture				
废弃资源综合利用业	Comprehensive Utilization of Waste				
金属制品、机械和设备修理业	Metal Products, Machinery and Equipment Repair Industry	1262	2		
电力、热力生产和供应业	Production and Supply of Electric Power and Heat Power	1898			
燃气生产和供应业	Production and Supply of Gas				
水的生产和供应业	Production and Supply of Water				

17-5 规模以上工业企业技术资源 (2019 年)

Technical Resources of Industrial Enterprises Above Desitnated Size (2019)

指标	Indicator	R&D 经费内部支出合计 (万元) Internal Expenditure on R&D (10 000 yuan)	新产品销售收入 (万元) Output Value of New Products (10 000 yuan)	研究与试验发展 (R&D) 人员 (人) R&D Sonnel (Person)	R&D 人员折合全时当量 (人年) R&D Rsonnel Equivalent in Full Time (man-years)
总计	Total	1295161	20671795	33952	23282
按登记注册类型分	by Status of Registration				
内资企业	Domestic Funded Enterprises	1107127	17422656	29231	19850
国有企业	State-owned Enterprises	123	376	10	5
集体企业	Collective-owned Enterprises	162	31774	12	8
股份合作企业	Cooperative Enterprises	894	7106	47	34
有限责任公司	Private Limited Liability Corporations	586780	6474250	14568	10077
国有独资公司	State Sole funded Corporations	74113	530511	2777	1878
其他有限责任公司	Other Limited Liability Corporations	512667	5943739	11791	8199
股份有限公司	Share-holding Corporations Ltd.	342631	8062471	8223	5434
私营企业	Private Enterprises	176538	2846679	6371	4293
私营独资企业	Private-funded Enterprises	326		15	14
私营合伙企业	Private Partnership Enterprises				
私营有限责任公司	Private Limited Liability Corporations	152201	2500996	5544	3784
私营股份有限公司	Private Share-holding Corporations Ltd.	24011	345683	812	496
港、澳、台商投资企业	Enterprises with Funds from Hong Kong,Macao and Taiwan	148914	2596007	3141	2578
合资经营企业(港或澳、台资)	Joint-venture Enterprises	15104	525706	582	433
合作经营企业(港或澳、台资)	Cooperative Enterprises				
港、澳、台商独资经营企业	Enterprises with Sole Investment	132769	2015266	2542	2136
港、澳、台商投资股份有限公司	Share-holding Corporations Ltd.	1030	54945	12	4
其他港澳台投资企业	Other Enterprises	11	90	5	5
外商投资企业	Foreign Funded Enterprises	39119	653131	1580	854
中外合资经营企业	Joint-venture Enterprises	20760	348118	684	439
中外合作经营企业	Cooperation Enterprises	365	386	11	5
外资企业	Enterprises with Sole Fund	8800	153947	740	365
外商投资股份有限公司	Share-holding Corporations Ltd. with Foreign Investment	9195	150680	145	45
按工业行业大类分	by Sector				
煤炭开采和洗选业	Mining and Washing of Coal	2746		151	132
石油和天然气开采业	Extraction of Petroleum and Natural Gas				
黑色金属矿采选业	Mining of Ferrous Metal Ores	8776	95253	185	119
非金属矿采选业	Mining and Processing of Nonmetal Ores				
农副食品加工业	Processing of Food from Agricultural Products	3977	39631	191	103
食品制造业	Manufacture of Foods	10364	56925	698	395
酒、饮料和精制茶制造业	Manufacture of Wine, Drinks and Refined Tea	1421	34751	24	5
烟草制品业	Manufacture of Tobacco				

17-5 续表 continued

指标	Indicator	R&D 经费内部支出合计（万元）Internal Expenditure on R&D (10 000 yuan)	新产品销售收入（万元）Output Value of New Products (10 000 yuan)	研究与试验发展 (R&D) 人员（人）R&D Sonnel (Person)	R&D 人员折合全时当量（人年）R&D Rsonnel Equivalent in Full Time (man-years)
纺织业	Manufacture of Textile	8220	104779	347	188
纺织服装、服饰业	Manufacture of Textile Wearing Apparel and Finery	747	1258	97	66
皮革、毛皮、羽毛及其制品和制鞋业	Manufacture of Leather, Fur, Feather & Its Products and Footwear	118	9686	4	4
木材加工和木、竹、藤、棕、草制品业	Processing of Timbers, Manufacture of Wood,Bamboo, Rattan, Palm, and Straw Products	1342	18442	39	25
家具制造业	Manufacture of Furniture	60	6006	19	8
造纸和纸制品业	Manufacture of Paper and Paper Products	2798	70511	36	23
印刷和记录媒介复制业	Printing, Reproduction of Recording Media	6101	120850	453	316
文教、工美、体育和娱乐用品制造业	Manufacture of Culture, Education,Arts and crafts，Sport and Entertainment Goods	1835	39448	94	56
石油加工、炼焦和核燃料加工业	Processing of Petroleum, Coking and Nucleus Fuel	14158	300263	538	283
化学原料和化学制品制造业	Manufacture of Chemical Raw Material and Chemical Products	66498	980071	1409	837
医药制造业	Manufacture of Medicines	179994	1440070	3351	2810
化学纤维制造业	Manufacture of Chemical Fiber	3409	7372	42	16
橡胶和塑料制品业	Manufacture of Rubber and Plastic	5028	46325	290	204
非金属矿物制品业	Manufacture of Non-metallic Mineral Products	45712	718462	1730	1047
黑色金属冶炼和压延加工业	Manufacture and Processing of Ferrous Metals	197231	2667719	3238	2101
有色金属冶炼和压延加工业	Manufacture & Processing of Non-ferrous Metals	2377	40496	151	125
金属制品业	Manufacture of Metal Products	59302	1000000	2018	1458
通用设备制造业	Manufacture of General Purpose Machinery	99628	1147716	4759	3160
专用设备制造业	Manufacture of Special Purpose Machinery	55653	794637	2158	1394
汽车制造业	Manufacture of Automotive	149522	3724681	3739	2813
铁路、船舶、航空航天和其他运输设备制造业	Manufacture of Railroad,Marine,Aerospace and Other Transportation Equipment	15878	350441	262	166
电气机械和器材制造业	Manufacture of Electrical Machinery & Equipment	102431	1409366	2617	1358
计算机、通信和其他电子设备制造业	Manufacture of Computer, Communications and Other Electronic Equipment	203162	5102410	3179	2616
仪器仪表制造业	Manufacture of Measuring Instrument	30181	240477	1623	1183
其他制造业	Other Manufacture	1108	2257	33	30
废弃资源综合利用业	Comprehensive Utilization of Waste				
金属制品、机械和设备修理业	Metal Products, Machinery and Equipment Repair Industry	5199	48019	186	137
电力、热力生产和供应业	Production and Supply of Electric Power and Heat Power	9143	44942	246	92
燃气生产和供应业	Production and Supply of Gas				
水的生产和供应业	Production and Supply of Water	1043	8532	45	12

17-6 规模以上工业企业科技活动项目（2019 年）
Technology Projict Activities of Industrial Enterprises Above Designated Size(2019)

指标	Indicator	R&D 经费内部支出合计（万元）Internal Expenditure on R&D (10 000 yuan)	新产品开发项目数（项）Number of on New Products Development (unit)	新产品开发经费支出（万元）Expenditure on New Products Development (10 000 yuan)
总计	Total	1295161	6273	1322529
按登记注册类型分	by Status of Registration			
内资企业	Domestic Funded Enterprises	1107127	5619	1079079
国有企业	State-owned Enterprises	123	9	2061
集体企业	Collective-owned Enterprises	162	1	134
股份合作企业	Cooperative Enterprises	894	6	894
有限责任公司	Private Limited Liability Corporations	586780	2643	556794
国有独资公司	State Sole funded Corporations	74113	354	67281
其他有限责任公司	Other Limited Liability Corporations	512667	2289	489514
股份有限公司	Share-holding Corporations Ltd.	342631	780	329879
私营企业	Private Enterprises	176538	2180	189317
私营独资企业	Private-funded Enterprises	326	6	333
私营合伙企业	Private Partnership Enterprises			
私营有限责任公司	Private Limited Liability Corporations	152201	1903	161382
私营股份有限公司	Private Share-holding Corporations Ltd.	24011	271	27603
港、澳、台商投资企业	Enterprises with Funds from Hong Kong,Macao and Taiwan	148914	342	201443
合资经营企业（港或澳、台资）	Joint-venture Enterprises	15104	157	56270
合作经营企业（港或澳、台资）	Cooperative Enterprises			
港、澳、台商独资经营企业	Enterprises with Sole Investment	132769	178	138779
港、澳、台商投资股份有限公司	Share-holding Corporations Ltd.	1030	2	6111
其他港澳台投资企业	Other Enterprises	11	5	284
外商投资企业	Foreign Funded Enterprises	39119	312	42007
中外合资经营企业	Joint-venture Enterprises	20760	200	28972
中外合作经营企业	Cooperation Enterprises	365	5	383
外资企业	Enterprises with Sole Fund	8800	96	9959
外商投资股份有限公司	Share-holding Corporations Ltd. with Foreign Investment	9195	11	2694
按工业行业大类分	by Sector			
煤炭开采和洗选业	Mining and Washing of Coal	2746		
石油和天然气开采业	Extraction of Petroleum and Natural Gas			
黑色金属矿采选业	Mining of Ferrous Metal Ores	8776	1	883
非金属矿采选业	Mining and Processing of Nonmetal Ores			
农副食品加工业	Processing of Food from Agricultural Products	3977	54	5529
食品制造业	Manufacture of Foods	10364	150	11163
酒、饮料和精制茶制造业	Manufacture of Wine, Drinks and Refined Tea	1421	22	2010

17-6 续表 continued

指标	Indicator	R&D 经费内部支出合计（万元）Internal Expenditure on R&D (10 000 yuan)	新产品开发项目数（项）Number of on New Products Development (unit)	新产品开发经费支出（万元）Expenditure on New Products Development (10 000 yuan)
烟草制品业	Manufacture of Tobacco		9	564
纺织业	Manufacture of Textile	8220	76	11246
纺织服装、服饰业	Manufacture of Textile Wearing Apparel and Finery	747	13	805
皮革、毛皮、羽毛及其制品和制鞋业	Manufacture of Leather, Fur, Feather & Its Products and ootwear	118	5	506
木材加工和木、竹、藤、棕、草制品业	Processing of Timbers, Manufacture of Wood,Bamboo, Rattan, Palm, and Straw Products	1342	10	1316
家具制造业	Manufacture of Furniture	60	6	312
造纸和纸制品业	Manufacture of Paper and Paper Products	2798	27	2398
印刷和记录媒介复制业	Printing, Reproduction of Recording Media	6101	64	6958
文教、工美、体育和娱乐用品制造业	Manufacture of Culture, Education,Arts and crafts, Sport and Entertainment Goods	1835	21	2176
石油加工、炼焦和核燃料加工业	Processing of Petroleum, Coking and Nucleus Fuel	14158	20	6008
化学原料和化学制品制造业	Manufacture of Chemical Raw Material and Chemical Products	66498	339	63013
医药制造业	Manufacture of Medicines	179994	781	184030
化学纤维制造业	Manufacture of Chemical Fiber	3409	30	6155
橡胶和塑料制品业	Manufacture of Rubber and Plastic	5028	76	5401
非金属矿物制品业	Manufacture of Non-metallic Mineral Products	45712	370	55897
黑色金属冶炼和压延加工业	Manufacture and Processing of Ferrous Metals	197231	200	132589
有色金属冶炼和压延加工业	Manufacture & Processing of Non-ferrous Metals	2377	24	2458
金属制品业	Manufacture of Metal Products	59302	404	51570
通用设备制造业	Manufacture of General Purpose Machinery	99628	913	108105
专用设备制造业	Manufacture of Special Purpose Machinery	55653	713	71981
汽车制造业	Manufacture of Automotive	149522	387	169434
铁路、船舶、航空航天和其他运输设备制造业	Manufacture of Railroad,Marine,Aerospace and Other Ransportation Quipment	15878	78	19257
电气机械和器材制造业	Manufacture of Electrical Machinery & Equipment	102431	596	108861
计算机、通信和其他电子设备制造业	Manufacture of Computer, Communications and Other Electronic Equipment	203162	382	246549
仪器仪表制造业	Manufacture of Measuring Instrument	30181	434	36036
其他制造业	Other Manufacture	1108	16	469
废弃资源综合利用业	Comprehensive Utilization of Waste			
金属制品、机械和设备修理业	Metal Products, Machinery and Equipment Repair Industry	5199	36	7147
电力、热力生产和供应业	Production and Supply of Electric Power and Heat Power	9143	12	1082
燃气生产和供应业	Production and Supply of Gas			
水的生产和供应业	Production and Supply of Water	1043	4	621

17-7 规模以上工业企业 R&D 经费情况(2019 年)
R&D Funds of Industrial Enterprises Above Designated Size(2019)

单位：万元

指标	Indicator	合计 Total	按支出用途分组 By Object of Expenditure	
			经常费支出 Daily Expenditure	资产性支出 Capital Expenditure
总计	**Total**	1295161	1196948	98213
按登记注册类型分	**by Status of Registration**			
内资企业	Domestic Funded Enterprises	1107127	1023244	83883
国有企业	State-owned Enterprises	123	123	
集体企业	Collective-owned Enterprises	162	162	
股份合作企业	Cooperative Enterprises	894	878	16
有限责任公司	Private Limited Liability Corporations	586780	529414	57366
国有独资公司	State Sole funded Corporations	74113	71904	2209
其他有限责任公司	Other Limited Liability Corporations	512667	457509	55158
股份有限公司	Share-holding Corporations Ltd.	342631	327567	15064
私营企业	Private Enterprises	176538	165102	11436
私营独资企业	Private-funded Enterprises	326	317	9
私营合伙企业	Private Partnership Enterprises			
私营有限责任公司	Private Limited Liability Corporations	152201	142499	9703
私营股份有限公司	Private Share-holding Corporations Ltd.	24011	22286	1725
港、澳、台商投资企业	Enterprises with Funds from Hong Kong,Macao and Taiwan	148914	138275	10639
合资经营企业(港或澳、台资)	Joint-venture Enterprises	15104	14160	944
合作经营企业(港或澳、台资)	Cooperative Enterprises			
港、澳、台商独资经营企业	Enterprises with Sole Investment	132769	123553	9215
港、澳、台商投资股份有限公司	Share-holding Corporations Ltd.	1030	550	480
其他港澳台投资企业	Other Enterprises	11	11	
外商投资企业	Foreign Funded Enterprises	39119	35428	3691
中外合资经营企业	Joint-venture Enterprises	20760	19025	1735
中外合作经营企业	Cooperation Enterprises	365	365	
外资企业	Enterprises with Sole Fund	8800	8456	343
外商投资股份有限公司	Share-holding Corporations Ltd. with Foreign Investment	9195	7582	1613
按工业行业大类分	**by Sector**			
煤炭开采和洗选业	Mining and Washing of Coal	2746	2746	
石油和天然气开采业	Extraction of Petroleum and Natural Gas			
黑色金属矿采选业	Mining of Ferrous Metal Ores	8776	8269	507
非金属矿采选业	Mining and Processing of Nonmetal Ores			
农副食品加工业	Processing of Food from Agricultural Products	3977	3556	421
食品制造业	Manufacture of Foods	10364	9896	468
酒、饮料和精制茶制造业	Manufacture of Wine, Drinks and Refined Tea	1421	1421	0

(10 000 yuan)

R&D 经费内部支出 Internal Expenditure on R&D				R&D 经费外部支出 External Expenditure on R&D
按资金来源分组 By Capital Source				
政府资金 Government Appropriation Funds	企业资金 Self-raised Funds by Enterprises	境外资金 Foreign funds	其他资金 Other Funds	
23556	1271605			59784
21851	1085276			30776
	123			
	162			
78	816			
15490	571290			10389
2517	71596			369
12973	499694			10020
3385	339247			15464
2899	173639			4923
	326			
2242	149960			4499
657	23354			424
1554	147360			28470
1176	13928			9920
378	132391			18550
	1030			
	11			
151	38968			538
130	20630			148
	365			
	8800			390
21	9174			
	2746			
	8776			45
	3977			49
45	10319			113
	1421			5

17–7 续表 continued

指标	Indicator	合计 Total	按支出用途分组 By Object of Expenditure	
			经常费支出 Daily Expenditure	资产性支出 Capital Expenditure
烟草制品业	Manufacture of Tobacco			
纺织业	Manufacture of Textile	8220	7655	564
纺织服装、服饰业	Manufacture of Textile Wearing Apparel and Finery	747	728	20
皮革、毛皮、羽毛及其制品和制鞋业	Manufacture of Leather, Fur, Feather & Its Products and Footwear	118	115	3
木材加工和木、竹、藤、棕、草制品业	Processing of Timbers, Manufacture of Wood,Bamboo, Rattan, Palm, and Straw Products	1342	1316	26
家具制造业	Manufacture of Furniture	60	60	
造纸和纸制品业	Manufacture of Paper and Paper Products	2798	2296	502
印刷和记录媒介复制业	Printing, Reproduction of Recording Media	6101	5905	196
文教、工美、体育和娱乐用品制造业	Manufacture of Culture, Education,Arts and crafts，Sport and Entertainment Goods	1835	1832	3
石油加工、炼焦和核燃料加工业	Processing of Petroleum, Coking and Nucleus Fuel	14158	12912	1246
化学原料和化学制品制造业	Manufacture of Chemical Raw Material and Chemical Products	66498	60859	5639
医药制造业	Manufacture of Medicines	179994	143806	36189
化学纤维制造业	Manufacture of Chemical Fiber	3409	3387	21
橡胶和塑料制品业	Manufacture of Rubber and Plastic	5028	4769	259
非金属矿物制品业	Manufacture of Non–metallic Mineral Products	45712	44509	1202
黑色金属冶炼和压延加工业	Manufacture and Processing of Ferrous Metals	197231	191925	5306
有色金属冶炼和压延加工业	Manufacture & Processing of Non–ferrous Metals	2377	2333	45
金属制品业	Manufacture of Metal Products	59302	54936	4366
通用设备制造业	Manufacture of General Purpose Machinery	99628	95828	3801
专用设备制造业	Manufacture of Special Purpose Machinery	55653	52003	3651
汽车制造业	Manufacture of Automotive	149522	135596	13926
铁路、船舶、航空航天和其他运输设备制造业	Manufacture of Railroad,Marine,Aerospace and Other Transportation Equipment	15878	14617	1261
电气机械和器材制造业	Manufacture of Electrical Machinery & Equipment	102431	100486	1945
计算机、通信和其他电子设备制造业	Manufacture of Computer, Communications and Other Electronic Equipment	203162	191930	11232
仪器仪表制造业	Manufacture of Measuring Instrument	30181	28971	1211
其他制造业	Other Manufacture	1108	1064	44
废弃资源综合利用业	Comprehensive Utilization of Waste			
金属制品、机械和设备修理业	Metal Products, Machinery and Equipment Repair Industry	5199	2215	2984
电力、热力生产和供应业	Production and Supply of Electric Power and Heat Power	9143	8002	1140
燃气生产和供应业	Production and Supply of Gas			
水的生产和供应业	Production and Supply of Water	1043	1006	37

R&D 经费内部支出 Internal Expenditure on R&D				R&D 经费 外部支出 External Expenditure on R&D
按资金来源分组 By Capital Source				
政府资金 Government Appropriation Funds	企业资金 Self-raised Funds by Enterprises	境外资金 Foreign funds	其他资金 Other Funds	
145	8075			164
30	717			
	118			
	1342			
	60			
	2798			
	6101			
	1835			
357	13801			1287
742	65756			1187
10359	169635			7854
	3409			
141	4886			119
113	45599			191
1035	196195			779
	2377			
397	58905			17
4154	95475			1522
1527	54127			1277
697	148825			37128
1	15877			9
258	102173			1665
2534	200627			2260
1022	29160			1957
	1108			
	5199			
	9143			2158
	1043			

17-8 规模以上工业企业办科技机构情况(2019 年)

Science and Technology Institutions of Industrial Enterprises Above Designated Size (2019)

指标	Indicator	机构数(个) Number (unit)	机构人员(人) Research Personnel (Person) 合计 Total	博士毕业 Doctor	硕士毕业 Master	机构经费支出(万元) Agency Expenditure (10 000 yuan)	仪器和设备原价(万元) Original Price of Equipment (10 000 yuan)
总计	Total	409	21029	360	3639	963400	655942
按登记注册类型分	by Status of Registration						
内资企业	Domestic Funded Enterprises	375	17254	315	2991	810343	533053
国有企业	State-owned Enterprises						
集体企业	Collective-owned Enterprises						
股份合作企业	Cooperative Enterprises	1	70		8	908	1408
有限责任公司	Private Limited Liability Corporations	175	9445	206	1896	462002	316580
国有独资公司	State Sole funded Corporations	23	1786	31	340	56078	42833
其他有限责任公司	Other Limited Liability Corporations	152	7659	175	1556	405925	273748
股份有限公司	Share-holding Corporations Ltd.	61	4385	69	818	259802	141658
私营企业	Private Enterprises	138	3354	40	269	87630	73407
私营独资企业	Private-funded Enterprises						
私营合伙企业	Private Partnership Enterprises						
私营有限责任公司	Private Limited Liability Corporations	116	2690	28	182	69627	61175
私营股份有限公司	Private Share-holding Corporations Ltd.	22	664	12	87	18003	12233
港、澳、台商投资企业	Enterprises with Funds from Hong Kong,Macao and Taiwan	11	2685	18	567	123931	79042
合资经营企业(港或澳、台资)	Joint-venture Enterprises	7	967	2	46	21756	16748
合作经营企业(港或澳、台资)	Cooperative Enterprises						
港、澳、台商独资经营企业	Enterprises with Sole Investment	3	1680	16	518	102133	61494
港、澳、台商投资股份有限公司	Share-holding Corporations Ltd.	1	38		3	42	800
其他港澳台投资企业	Other Enterprises						
外商投资企业	Foreign Funded Enterprises	23	1090	27	81	29125	43847
中外合资经营企业	Joint-venture Enterprises	9	481	4	29	11410	14829
中外合作经营企业	Cooperation Enterprises						
外资企业	Enterprises with Sole Fund	9	473	8	48	9380	25648
外商投资股份有限公司	Share-holding Corporations Ltd. with Foreign Investment	5	136	15	4	8336	3370
按工业行业大类分	by Sector						
煤炭开采和洗选业	Mining and Washing of Coal						
石油和天然气开采业	Extraction of Petroleum and Natural Gas						
黑色金属矿采选业	Mining of Ferrous Metal Ores	2	109			10793	10092
非金属矿采选业	Mining and Processing of Nonmetal Ores						
农副食品加工业	Processing of Food from Agricultural Products	10	136	4	26	1246	1804
食品制造业	Manufacture of Foods	8	442	2	9	6219	23174
酒、饮料和精制茶制造业	Manufacture of Wine, Drinks and Refined Tea	3	119	2	6	692	1552

17-8 续表 continued

指标	Indicator	机构数（个）Number (unit)	机构人员（人）Research Personnel (Person) 合计 Total	博士毕业 Doctor	硕士毕业 Master	机构经费支出（万元）Agency Expenditure (10 000 yuan)	仪器和设备原价（万元）Original Price of Equipment (10 000 yuan)
烟草制品业	Manufacture of Tobacco						
纺织业	Manufacture of Textile	8	132	1	6	3643	6232
纺织服装、服饰业	Manufacture of Textile Wearing Apparel and Finery	1	1		1	320	125
皮革、毛皮、羽毛及其制品和制鞋业	Manufacture of Leather, Fur, Feather & Its Products and Footwear						
木材加工和木、竹、藤、棕、草制品业	Processing of Timbers, Manufacture of Wood,Bamboo,Rattan, Palm, and Straw Products	1	12			182	26
家具制造业	Manufacture of Furniture						
造纸和纸制品业	Manufacture of Paper and Paper Products						
印刷和记录媒介复制业	Printing, Reproduction of Recording Media	4	286		3	5718	18544
文教、工美、体育和娱乐用品制造业	Manufacture of Culture, Education,Arts and crafts, Sport and Entertainment Goods	2	22		5	476	957
石油加工、炼焦和核燃料加工业	Processing of Petroleum, Coking and Nucleus Fuel	4	111	1	3	9269	3988
化学原料和化学制品制造业	Manufacture of Chemical Raw Material and Chemical Products	29	1183	19	151	54811	37809
医药制造业	Manufacture of Medicines	47	4034	140	1246	169347	163694
化学纤维制造业	Manufacture of Chemical Fiber	1	15	1	1	180	25
橡胶和塑料制品业	Manufacture of Rubber and Plastic	9	130	1	5	1846	2901
非金属矿物制品业	Manufacture of Non-metallic Mineral Products	35	767	33	87	35283	39388
黑色金属冶炼和压延加工业	Manufacture and Processing of Ferrous Metals	5	1079	32	103	175754	42276
有色金属冶炼和压延加工业	Manufacture & Processing of Non-ferrous Metals	3	153		13	2182	1049
金属制品业	Manufacture of Metal Products	36	919	16	48	28484	22695
通用设备制造业	Manufacture of General Purpose Machinery	47	2591	20	302	52127	57254
专用设备制造业	Manufacture of Special Purpose Machinery	37	1440	20	154	35008	27423
汽车制造业	Manufacture of Automotive	15	2042	31	567	106997	63486
铁路、船舶、航空航天和其他运输设备制造业	Manufacture of Railroad,Marine,Aerospace and Other Transportation Equipment	4	219	1	10	3904	3211
电气机械和器材制造业	Manufacture of Electrical Machinery & Equipment	27	1099	5	229	40647	58365
计算机、通信和其他电子设备制造业	Manufacture of Computer, Communications and Other Electronic Equipment	21	2148	19	499	191336	49057
仪器仪表制造业	Manufacture of Measuring Instrument	43	1363	12	140	21866	12537
其他制造业	Other Manufacture						
废弃资源综合利用业	Comprehensive Utilization of Waste						
金属制品、机械和设备修理业	Metal Products, Machinery and Equipment Repair Industry	5	462		22	4520	6398
电力、热力生产和供应业	Production and Supply of Electric Power and Heat Power	1	2			528	1567
燃气生产和供应业	Production and Supply of Gas						
水的生产和供应业	Production and Supply of Water	1	13		3	23	313

17-9 规模以上工业企业自主知识产权及相关情况(2019年)
Independent Intellectual Property Rights of Industrial Enterprises Above Designated Size(2019)

指标	Indicator	专利申请数(件) Patent Applications (piece)	#发明专利(件) Inventions (piece)
总计	Total	8745	3038
按登记注册类型分	by Status of Registration		
内资企业	Domestic Funded Enterprises	7885	2686
国有企业	State-owned Enterprises	2	
集体企业	Collective-owned Enterprises	3	
股份合作企业	Cooperative Enterprises	8	1
有限责任公司	Private Limited Liability Corporations	2483	1052
国有独资公司	State Sole funded Corporations	290	129
其他有限责任公司	Other Limited Liability Corporations	2193	923
股份有限公司	Share-holding Corporations Ltd.	3232	1064
私营企业	Private Enterprises	2157	569
私营独资企业	Private-funded Enterprises		
私营合伙企业	Private Partnership Enterprises		
私营有限责任公司	Private Limited Liability Corporations	1985	499
私营股份有限公司	Private Share-holding Corporations Ltd.	172	70
港、澳、台商投资企业	Enterprises with Funds from Hong Kong,Macao and Taiwan	602	269
合资经营企业(港或澳、台资)	Joint-venture Enterprises	277	189
合作经营企业(港或澳、台资)	Cooperative Enterprises		
港、澳、台商独资经营企业	Enterprises with Sole Investment	317	80
港、澳、台商投资股份有限公司	Share-holding Corporations Ltd.	8	
其他港澳台投资企业	Other Enterprises		
外商投资企业	Foreign Funded Enterprises	258	83
中外合资经营企业	Joint-venture Enterprises	174	66
中外合作经营企业	Cooperation Enterprises		
外资企业	Enterprises with Sole Fund	67	7
外商投资股份有限公司	Share-holding Corporations Ltd. with Foreign Investment	17	10
按工业行业大类分	by Sector		
煤炭开采和洗选业	Mining and Washing of Coal	2	2
石油和天然气开采业	Extraction of Petroleum and Natural Gas		
黑色金属矿采选业	Mining of Ferrous Metal Ores	6	3
非金属矿采选业	Mining and Processing of Nonmetal Ores		
农副食品加工业	Processing of Food from Agricultural Products	58	28
食品制造业	Manufacture of Foods	44	13
酒、饮料和精制茶制造业	Manufacture of Wine, Drinks and Refined Tea	46	9

有效发明专利数（件）Effective Invention Patent(piece)	拥有注册商标数（件）Registered Trademarks (piece)	#境外注册（件）Overseas Registered (piece)	形成国家或行业标准数（项）Industry or National Standards(unit)
9017	7350		361
8371	6834		318
9	2		
3	1		
1	7		1
3147	3152		173
286	155		17
2861	2997		156
2815	1141		58
2396	2531		86
1893	1843		85
503	688		1
369	349		8
154	319		6
207	28		1
8	2		1
277	167		35
175	140		32
2			
84	10		
16	17		3
13			
4	5		
82	96		
133	176		
36	72		4

17-9 续表 continued

指标	Indicator	专利申请数（件）Patent Applications (piece)	# 发明专利（件）Inventions (piece)
烟草制品业	Manufacture of Tobacco	11	4
纺织业	Manufacture of Textile	77	22
纺织服装、服饰业	Manufacture of Textile Wearing Apparel and Finery		
皮革、毛皮、羽毛及其制品和制鞋业	Manufacture of Leather, Fur, Feather & Its Products and Footwear	19	
木材加工和木、竹、藤、棕、草制品业	Processing of Timbers, Manufacture of Wood,Bamboo, Rattan, Palm, and Straw Products	9	
家具制造业	Manufacture of Furniture	2	
造纸和纸制品业	Manufacture of Paper and Paper Products	25	8
印刷和记录媒介复制业	Printing, Reproduction of Recording Media	44	8
文教、工美、体育和娱乐用品制造业	Manufacture of Culture, Education,Arts and crafts, Sport and Entertain ment Goods	42	10
石油加工、炼焦和核燃料加工业	Processing of Petroleum, Coking and Nucleus Fuel	28	9
化学原料和化学制品制造业	Manufacture of Chemical Raw Material and Chemical Products	208	101
医药制造业	Manufacture of Medicines	393	306
化学纤维制造业	Manufacture of Chemical Fiber	27	7
橡胶和塑料制品业	Manufacture of Rubber and Plastic	98	23
非金属矿物制品业	Manufacture of Non-metallic Mineral Products	366	75
黑色金属冶炼和压延加工业	Manufacture and Processing of Ferrous Metals	594	277
有色金属冶炼和压延加工业	Manufacture & Processing of Non-ferrous Metals	28	7
金属制品业	Manufacture of Metal Products	395	137
通用设备制造业	Manufacture of General Purpose Machinery	995	182
专用设备制造业	Manufacture of Special Purpose Machinery	721	205
汽车制造业	Manufacture of Automotive	510	147
铁路、船舶、航空航天和其他运输设备制造业	Manufacture of Railroad,Marine,Aerospace and Other Transportation Equipment	107	77
电气机械和器材制造业	Manufacture of Electrical Machinery & Equipment	2433	562
计算机、通信和其他电子设备制造业	Manufacture of Computer, Communications and Other Electronic Equip ment	903	668
仪器仪表制造业	Manufacture of Measuring Instrument	459	117
其他制造业	Other Manufacture	11	3
废弃资源综合利用业	Comprehensive Utilization of Waste		
金属制品、机械和设备修理业	Metal Products, Machinery and Equipment Repair Industry	20	12
电力、热力生产和供应业	Production and Supply of Electric Power and Heat Power	58	15
燃气生产和供应业	Production and Supply of Gas		
水的生产和供应业	Production and Supply of Water	6	1

注：境外注册件数 2019 年数据省统计局未反馈。

有效发明专利数（件）Effective Invention Patent(piece)	拥有注册商标数（件）Registered Trademarks (piece)	# 境外注册（件）Overseas Registered (piece)	形成国家或行业标准数（项）Industry or National Standards(unit)
10			
21	10		2
	30		
10	7		1
	4		
3	2		5
17	12		
66	26		
134	9		
29	8		
690	2044		14
787	2829		77
11	8		
40	50		5
512	132		29
764	34		10
3	3		
307	290		27
939	433		33
616	313		22
441	97		7
520	7		2
1347	229		57
1101	237		31
288	184		31
13	1		
11			
38	1		4
30	1		
1			

Note: the offshore registration numbers of 2019 are not released by the provincial bureau.

主要统计指标解释

科技活动 是指在自然科学、农业科学、医药科学、工程与技术科学、人文与社会科学领域（简称科学技术领域）中，与科技知识的产生、发展、传播和应用密切相关的有组织的活动。在企（事）业中只有列入单位工作计划的科技活动才予以统计，而独立发明人等在企（事）业外或计划外进行的科技活动不在统计范围之内。科研活动可分为研究与试验发展（简称 R&D，包括基础研究、应用研究和试验发展）、研究与试验发展（R&D）成果应用及相关的科技服务三类活动。

基础研究 是指为了获得关于现象和可观察事实的基本原理的新知识（揭示客观事物的本质、运动规律，获得新发现、新学说）而进行的实验性或理论性研究。基础研究属于科学研究范畴。从研究目的看，基础研究不以任何专门或特定的应用或使用为目的，它只是通过试验分析或理论性研究对事物的特性、结构和各种关系进行分析，加深对客观事物的认识，解释现象的本质，揭示物质运动的规律或提出和验证各种设想、理论和定律。从研究结果看，基础研究的结果具有一般的或普遍的正确性，通常表现为一般的原则、理论和规律，其成果以科学论文和科学著作为主要形式。

应用研究 是指为获得新知识而进行的创造性研究，主要针对某一特定的目的或目标。应用研究也属于科学研究范畴。从研究目的看，应用研究是探索基础研究成果的可能用途，或是为达到预定的目标探索应采取的新方法（原理性）或新途径，为解决实际问题提供科学依据。从研究结果看，应用研究的成果一般只影响科学技术的某些领域和有限范围，并具有专门的性质，针对具体的领域、问题或情况，其成果形式以科学论文、专著、原理性模型或发明专利等为主。

试验发展 是指利用从基础研究、应用研究和实际经验所获得的现有知识，为产生新的产品、材料和装置，建立新的工艺、系统和服务，以及对已产生和建立的上述各项做实质性的改进而进行的系统性工作。在社会科学领域，试验发展是指通过把基础研究、应用研究获得的知识转变成可以实施的计划（包括为检验和评估实施示范项目）的过程。

专利申请数 指企业在报告期内向国内外知识产权行政部门提出专利申请并被受理的件数。

专利申请数中发明专利 指企业在报告期内向国内外知识产权行政部门提出发明专利申请并被受理的件数。

新产品产值 指报告期企业生产的新产品的产值。新产品是指采用新技术原理、新设计构思研制、生产的全新产品，或在结构、材质、工艺等某一方面比原有产品有明显改进，从而显著提高了产品性能或扩大了使用功能的产品。新产品产值、新产品销售收入既包括经政府有关部门认定并在有效期内的新产品，也包括企业自行研制开发，未经政府有关部门认定，从投产之日起一年之内的新产品。

拥有注册商标 指企业在报告期末拥有的注册商标件数。包括在境内和境外注册的商标件数，一件商标在境内外同时注册时只统计一件。

技术改造经费支出 指企业在报告期进行技术改造而发生的费用支出。技术改造指企业在坚持科技进步的前提下，将科技成果应用于生产的各个领域（产品、设备、工艺等），用先进工艺、设备代替落后工艺、设备，实现以内涵为主的扩大再生产，从而提高产品质量、促进产品更新换代、节约能源、降低消耗，全面提高综合经济效益。

Explanatory Notes on Main Statistical Indicators

Scientific and Technological Activities refer to organized activities closely related to generation, development, dissemination and application of knowledge of science and technology in natural science, agricultural science, pharmaceutical science, engineering and technical science, humanities and social sciences field (called as science and technology field for short). Only scientific and technological activities listed into the work plan of the enterprise (institution) will be included, while scientific and technological activities by independent inventors outside the enterprise (institution) or the plan are out of the statistics scope. Scientific research activities can be divided into three categories -- research and experimental development (called as R&D for short, including fundamental research, application research and experimental development), application of results of research and experimental development (R&D) and related science and technology services.

Fundamental Research refers to empirical or theoretical research aiming at obtaining new knowledge on the fundamental principles of phenomena of observable facts to reveal the nature and law of movement of objects and to acquire new discoveries or new theories. Fundamental research falls into scientific research. From the perspective of research purpose, fundamental research takes no specific or designated application as the aim of the research which only involves analysis on features, structures and various relationships of things by experimental analysis or theoretical research to deepen the understanding of objective things, explain the nature of the phenomenon and reveal the laws of the motion of matter or put forward and verify various assumptions, theories and laws. From the perspective of research result, the result of fundamental research is of general or universal correctness, usually presented as general principle, theory and law. Results of fundamental research are mainly released or disseminated in the form of scientific papers or monographs.

Applied Research refers to creative research aiming at obtaining new knowledge on a specific objective or target. Applied research also falls into scientific research. From the perspective of research purpose, purpose of the applied research is to identify the possible use of results from basic research, or to explore new (fundamental) methods or new approaches as well as provide scientific basis for solving practical problems. From the perspective of research result, achievements of application research only influence some fields and limited scope of science and technology generally and are of a specialized nature and expressed in the form of scientific papers, monographs, fundamental models or invention patents on the basis of specific field, problem or situation.

Experiments and Development refer to systematic activities aiming at using the knowledge from fundamental and applied researches or from practical experience to develop new products, materials and equipment, to establish new production process, systems and services, or to make substantial improvement on the existing products, process or services. In social sciences, experiment and development activities refer to the process of converting the knowledge from or applied researches into feasible programs (including conduct of demonstration projects for assessment and evaluation).

Quantity of Patents Applied refers to the quantity of patents accepted with application for a patent filed by the enterprise to intellectual property administrative departments at the home and abroad in the reporting period.

Quantity of Invention Patent in the Patents Applied refers to the quantity of patents for invention accepted with application for an invention patent filed by the enterprise to intellectual property administrative departments at the home and abroad in the reporting period.

Output Value of New Products refers to output value of new products produced by enterprises in the reporting period. New products refer to new products developed or produced by new know-why and design concept and products with properties of products obviously improved or use function expanded due to the obvious improvement in structure, texture or technology in comparison to those of original products. Output value of new products and sales revenue from new products include new products approved by relevant government departments whose valid term fails to expire and new products developed independently by the enterprise and not approved by relevant government departments which exist for less than one year as of the date of going into operation.

Possession of Registered Trademark refers to the quantity of registered trademarks owned by the enterprise at the end of the reporting period, including quantity of trademark registered at home and abroad. Statistics of a trademark are only conducted once at the moment of being registered at the home and abroad at the same time.

Expenditure on Technological Transformation refers to the expenditure incurred by technological transformation by the enterprise in the reporting period. Technological transformation refers to the enterprise applying scientific and technological achievements to all fields of production (product, equipment and technology, etc.) and replacing backward technology and equipment with advance technology and equipment to realize intention-based expanded reproduction, thus to improve product quality, promote product upgrading, save energy, lower consumption and comprehensively enhance composite economic results in the premise of insisting on scientific and technological progress.

18

教育与文化

EDUCATION AND CULTURE

18-1 教育事业基本情况
Basic Statistics on Education

指标	Indicator	1952 年	1957 年	1962 年	1965 年	1970 年
学校数（所）	Number of Schools(place)	2679	3106	3731	4318	5359
# 驻济高等学校	Colleges and Universities in Ji'nan	5	4	12	8	2
中等教育	Secondary Education	37	67	112	410	1204
# 中等职业学校	Vocational Secondary Education	16	16	15	15	17
普通中学	Regular Junior Secondary Schools	21	51	93	159	1024
小学	Primary Schools	2636	3034	3606	3899	4152
专任教师（人）	Full-time Teachers(person)	8555	13452	19606	26760	32508
# 驻济高等学校	Colleges and Universities in Ji'nan	671	1325	2598	2451	922
中等教育	Secondary Education	1108	2569	3418	5321	9607
# 中等职业学校	Vocational Secondary Education	311	787	765	685	914
普通中学	Regular Junior Secondary Schools	797	1782	2629	3502	8445
小学	Primary Schools	6773	9550	13571	18971	21954
在校学生（万人）	Total Enrollment(10 000 persons)	26.87	31.95	49.82	68.27	80.20
# 驻济高等学校	Colleges and Universities in Ji'nan	0.43	0.82	1.65	1.40	0.30
中等教育	Secondary Education	2.73	5.14	5.80	10.43	18.97
# 中等职业学校	Vocational Secondary Education	0.69	0.93	0.51	0.65	0.12
普通中学	Regular Junior Secondary Schools	2.04	4.21	5.22	7.50	17.81
小学	Primary Schools	23.70	25.98	42.35	56.42	60.91
各类学校毕业生数（万人）	Graduates(10 000 persons)	4.38	8.58	10.60	10.45	12.09
# 驻济高等学校	Colleges and Universities in Ji'nan	0.14	0.11	0.31	0.43	-
中等教育	Secondary Education	0.60	1.14	1.72	1.90	1.02
# 中等职业学校	Vocational Secondary Education	0.13	0.14	0.32	0.03	-
普通中学	Regular Junior Secondary Schools	0.46	1.00	1.40	1.80	0.38
每一教师负担学生数（人）	Each Teacher Burden Number of Students(person)	31.41	23.75	25.41	23.27	24.67
# 驻济高等学校	Colleges and Universities in Ji'nan	6.41	6.19	6.35	5.71	3.25
中等教育	Secondary Education	24.64	20.01	16.97	19.60	19.75
# 中等职业学校	Vocational Secondary Education	22.33	11.84	6.64	9.51	1.36
普通中学	Regular Junior Secondary Schools	25.63	23.64	19.84	21.41	21.09
小学	Primary Schools	34.99	27.20	31.21	29.74	27.74
平均每万人口在校学生（人）	Number of Enrollment Per 10000 Population(person)	843	922	1418	1829	1968
# 大学生	Undergraduate	14	24	47	38	7
中专生	Secondary Students	22	27	14	17	3
中学生	Middle School Students	64	122	150	256	463
小学生	Elementary School Students	743	750	1206	1513	1494

注：1. 驻济高等学校在校生含普通专本科、成人本专科、研究生在校生。
　　2. 驻济高等学校毕业生为普通本专科毕业生。

1975 年	1980 年	1985 年	1990 年	1995 年	2000 年	2005 年	2010 年	2015 年	2018 年	2019 年	2020 年
5412	5066	4511	3924	3360	1725	1251	1025	946	930	1110	1108
4	11	16	16	16	16	59	66	72	51	52	52
922	759	593	529	440	423	348	302	280	304	375	390
21	30	40	39	41	40	91	73	41	34	40	41
783	710	491	417	312	297	247	209	214	251	312	320
4485	4295	3899	3368	2890	1273	832	645	582	575	683	666
42432	49608	46806	55978	58779	62869	77334	83106	88487	101305	118342	121438
2468	3744	4614	7245	7500	8269	24341	29526	31693	37539	40627	42202
15274	19062	17530	21618	23946	26817	27435	28370	30589	33161	41112	42017
985	1338	2367	2890	2941	2916	4738	4511	4068	3711	4058	3642
13571	17294	13572	16065	17621	20585	21915	21943	23643	26588	34177	34796
24654	26775	24579	26922	27417	27417	25201	24801	25795	30605	36067	37219
90.28	83.56	78.38	79.48	91.69	95.79	129.28	144.60	153.71	168.97	182.68	201.27
0.61	1.58	3.02	3.73	5.66	9.30	48.71	64.25	71.40	79.63	76.20	89.85
25.43	20.24	25.34	28.08	36.64	44.99	42.50	41.76	40.77	42.68	52.24	54.41
0.58	0.31	1.92	2.51	4.79	5.75	9.88	8.10	5.93	5.16	5.68	6.28
23.86	19.63	21.49	22.45	27.15	33.82	30.91	30.18	30.16	31.18	39.35	39.84
64.22	61.47	49.98	47.57	49.23	41.40	37.88	38.40	41.44	46.66	54.14	57.01
22.66	18.07	17.31	17.12	20.88	23.65	33.58	38.10	39.83	50.65	55.99	43.89
0.20	0.03	0.45	1.03	1.68	1.55	13.49	17.57	19.48	26.29	17.07	18.37
11.83	8.41	7.36	8.24	10.39	10.80	14.03	13.55	14.22	12.28	16.47	17.12
0.20	0.46	0.52	0.62	1.16	1.84	3.29	3.13	2.75	2.43	2.05	1.73
11.58	7.89	6.39	6.66	7.78	8.16	10.40	9.20	10.23	9.65	12.30	12.97
21.28	16.84	16.75	14.20	15.60	15.24	16.72	17.40	17.37	16.68	15.44	16.58
2.47	4.22	6.55	5.15	7.54	11.25	20.01	21.76	22.53	21.21	18.76	21.29
16.65	10.62	14.46	12.99	15.30	16.78	15.49	14.72	13.33	12.87	12.71	11.00
5.95	2.29	8.12	8.69	16.30	18.84	20.86	17.96	14.58	13.90	14.00	17.24
17.58	11.35	15.83	13.98	15.41	16.43	14.10	13.75	12.76	11.73	11.51	11.45
26.05	22.96	20.33	17.67	18.20	15.10	15.03	15.48	16.07	15.25	15.01	15.32
2062	1822	1605	1518	1691	1702	2177	2395	2465	2600	2505	2510
14	34	62	71	104	165	820	1064	1145	1226	1040	1121
13	7	39	48	88	102	195	192	170	177	178	182
566	429	473	473	553	601	521	500	484	480	542	497
1466	1339	1024	908	908	736	638	636	664	718	745	711

Note: 1. Students under high education in Jinan include regular college students, regular junior college students, adult college students, adult junior students and postgraduate students.

2. Graduates under high education in Jinan are those of regular college and jounior college programme.

18-2 普通高等院校一览（2020年）
Basic Statistics on Institutions of Higher Education(2020)

单位：人 (person)

指标	普通本专科在校学生数 Total Enrollment	普通本专科毕业生数 Graduates	普通本专科招生数 New Enrollment	教职工人数 Teachers and Staff	#专任教师 Full-time Teachers 合计 Total	#正高级 Senior	#副高级 Sub-Senior
总计	687878	183663	204490	59331	40887	5927	12742
综合性大学							
山东大学	41403	9737	10226	8388	4776	1665	1809
济南大学	34513	8615	8588	2879	2165	350	793
山东青年政治学院	15727	3674	5817	903	693	51	205
山东女子学院	14970	3969	4031	781	549	46	187
理工院校							
山东建筑大学	24857	6215	5943	2146	1751	246	650
山东科技大学	34364	8979	7861	3269	2302	344	671
齐鲁工业大学	28762	7062	7350	3522	2150	339	775
山东交通学院	24261	7443	6724	1867	1468	116	480
山东电力高等专科学校	3190	707	1264	324	157	33	36
医药院校							
山东第一医科大学	22027	5363	5311	4601	1659	270	523
山东中医药大学	18694	4367	4276	1482	1253	333	409
山东医学高等专科学校	26699	9105	10308	1147	917	63	200
济南护理职业学院	6030	1568	2256	418	246	27	97
师范院校							
山东师范大学	29064	8314	6585	2718	2016	369	573
齐鲁师范学院	17212	2890	4837	953	798	85	234
济南幼儿师范专科学校	6509	1370	2586	529	306	1	76
财经院校							
山东财经大学	27869	8467	6640	2458	1688	270	639
山东财经大学燕山学院	7271	2107	2292	457	404	48	152
政法院校							
山东警察学院	4925	1486	1483	579	288	22	121
山东司法警官职业学院	7254	1776	2903	259	150	2	39
山东政法学院	11274	3308	2988	935	686	73	157
体育院校							
山东体育学院	8408	2073	2043	726	600	69	213
艺术院校							
山东艺术学院	9253	2914	2349	1067	918	85	281
山东工艺美术学院	7211	1823	1859	770	569	67	168
职业技术学院							
山东协和学院	26248	5485	8814	1399	1253	123	361
山东商业职业技术学院	14959	4751	5266	994	760	51	219
山东劳动职业技术学院	11693	3744	4287	762	596	32	156
山东职业学院	15088	5176	5088	846	654	33	178
山东圣翰财贸职业学院	9397	2634	3034	704	388	13	86
山东艺术设计职业学院	3522	666	1290	291	238	34	38
山东英才学院	20796	5652	5054	1381	1072	96	308
山东旅游职业学院	8960	2510	2903	520	423	14	77
济南工程职业技术学院	12674	3813	5185	689	556	18	149
山东电子职业技术学院	9482	2996	3178	592	448	10	114
济南职业学院	13376	4634	5119	879	641	37	122
山东现代学院	17437	5265	6310	1043	835	75	267
山东工程职业技术大学	15814	1189	6706	933	726	104	179
山东城市建设职业学院	13162	3972	5062	737	589	10	185
山东管理学院	10956	3599	2896	728	601	41	121
齐鲁理工学院	18246	4129	6051	1468	963	158	246
山东农业工程学院	12573	3898	3886	778	565	46	144
山东特殊教育职业学院	1372	282	479	188	132	13	38
山东传媒职业学院	9689	2472	3588	491	405	16	73
莱芜职业技术学院	10687	3464	3774	730	533	29	193

18-3 中等专业学校一览(2020年)
Basic Statistics on Specialized Secondary Schools (2020)

单位：人 (person)

指标	在校学生数 Total Enrollment	毕业生数 Graduates	招生数 New Enrollment	教职工人数 Teachers and Staff	# 专任教师 Full-time Teachers		
					合计 Total	# 副高级 Sub-Senior	# 中级 Middle
总计	12125	3296	4846	1341	974	260	470
工科学校							
济南信息工程学校	3066	886	1206	198	170	54	97
济南电子机械工程学校	2166	584	1104	219	175	42	86
济南铁路学校	178	116	82	43	43	24	14
山东冶金中等专业学校	825	340	363	144	66	35	22
财经学校							
山东省济南商贸学校	1777	394	772	244	196	52	100
体育学校							
济南市体育运动学校	931	231	434	117	50	9	14
济南市第二体育运动学校	242	51	70				
山东体育学院附属中学	1288	473	418				
艺术学校							
山东省文化艺术学校	830	48	162	178	105	10	57
山东工艺美术学院附属中等美术学校	137	48	47	19	17	4	3
济南艺术学校	685	125	188	179	152	30	77

18-4 分县区儿童学前教育基本情况(2020年)
Student Enrollment in Pre-school Education (2020)

单位：人 (person)

指标	Indicator	幼儿园数(所) Number of Kindergartens (unit)	在园人数 Enrolment	入园人数 Entrants	教职工数 Teachers and Staff	# 专任教师 Full-timeTeachers
全市	Total	2204	357320	131440	44211	25163
历下区	Li xia	115	34721	13400	5026	2656
市中区	Shi zhong	187	34479	12385	5248	2793
槐荫区	Huai yin	159	34537	12482	4801	2531
天桥区	Tian qiao	165	30050	10398	4488	2216
历城区	Li cheng	215	46667	19256	6087	3298
长清区	Chang qing	134	17880	6696	1792	1207
章丘区	Zhang qiu	210	29977	10859	3309	1939
济阳区	Ji yang	162	20115	8218	1873	1092
莱芜区	Lai wu	286	29856	9056	3078	2255
钢城区	Gang cheng	79	11088	3277	1201	825
济南高新区	Ji'nan Gao xin	101	19942	7611	2715	1436
莱芜高新区	Lai wu Gao xin	49	8372	3050	758	485
南部山区	Nan shan	58	6998	2674	766	415
平阴县	Ping yin	59	10906	4200	990	712
商河县	Shang he	225	21732	7878	2079	1303

18-5 文化事业机构和人员
Number of Institutions and Persons in Culture

指标	Indicator	2015 年	2016 年	2017 年	2018 年	2019 年	2020 年
机构数(个)	Number(unit)						
电影业	Movies	38	44	52	54	65	64
艺术业	Arts	27	27	27	27	25	27
文物业	Cultural Relics	42	48	48	48	67	64
图书馆业	Libraries	12	12	12	12	14	14
群众文化业	Mass Culture	152	155	153	153	175	174
艺术教育业	Art Education	1	1	1	1	1	1
文艺科研业	Culture Research	1	1	1	1	1	1
从业人员数(人)	Personnel(person)						
电影业	Movies	705	913	936	1380	1075	641
艺术业	Arts	1569	1557	1569	1537	1475	1512
文物业	Cultural Relics	1119	1173	1158	1068	1365	1359
图书馆业	Libraries	431	447	462	472	507	567
群众文化业	Mass Culture	699	710	719	695	745	801
艺术教育业	Art Education	123	164	167	170	175	181
文艺科研业	Culture Research	49	51	49	47	47	50

注：电影业机构、从业人员数据为城市电影院线数据，不含农村。
Notes: The data of the film industry institutions and employees are urban cinema line data, excluding rural areas.

主要统计指标解释

普通高等学校 指按照国家规定的设置标准和审批程序批准举办，通过国家统一招生考试，招收高中毕业生为主要培养对象，实施高等教育的全日制大学、独立设置的学院和高等专科学校、短期职业大学。

文化事业机构 指从事专业文化工作和为专业文化工作服务的独立建制的单位。不包括这些单位另外举办独立核算的其他机构和各部门的业余文化组织。

Explanatory Notes on Main Statistical Indicators

Regular Institutions of Higher Education refer to educational establishments that set up according to the government evaluation and approval procedures, enrolling graduates from senior secondary schools and providing higher education courses and training for senior professionals. They include full time universities, colleges and high professional schools which set up independently as well as short-term vocational colleges.

Cultural Institutions refer to units which have their own organizational system, work on professional culture work and serve the professional culture work, excluding other institutions for independent accounting established by such units separately and amateur cultural organizations of all departments.

19

体育与卫生

SPORTS AND PUBLIC HEALTH

19-1 体育事业
Statistics of Sports Instituons

指标	Indicator	2015 年	2016 年	2017 年	2018 年	2019 年	2020 年
体育部门职工人数（人）	Number of Persons of Physical System(person)	656	724	720	591	672	677
# 业余体育学校	Spare–time Sports School	219	221	9	423	402	410
总计中：教练员	Referees	232	151	231	191	183	181
等级裁判员（人）	Number of Referees in Grades(person)						
一级裁判员	First Grade Referees			7			
二级裁判员	Second Grade Referees	246	122	153	268	344	155
三级裁判员	Third Grade Referees			55			
二级运动员发展人数（人）	Number of Second Grade Sportsmen(person)	359	401	465	279	534	564
少年儿童业余体校在校学生（人）	Enrollment Spare–time Sports School(person)	973	1036	845	1140	1286	1010
业余体校（所）	Spare–time Sports School(unit)	3	5	7	5	10	10
运动员获奖牌数（枚）	Number of Medals Wonby Athletes(unit)	585	1110	1188.5	1186	1353	715.5
# 世界级　金牌	World　Gold Medals	5	12	1	3	13	0
银牌	Silver Medals	3	4	2	1	7	0
铜牌	Copper Medal	0	4	1	2	8	0
# 洲际　金牌	Intercontinental　Gold Medals	5	7	3	3	10	0
银牌	Silver Medals	1	4	3	2	11	0
铜牌	Copper Medal	2	4	0	1	7	0
# 全国　金牌	Country　Gold Medals	48	43	85	50	100	15
银牌	Silver Medals	23	29	61	36	91	7
铜牌	Copper Medal	29	16	100	41	132	10
# 全省　金牌	Province　Gold Medals	215	402	395.5	430	442	285.5
银牌	Silver Medals	119	292	273	319	248	182
铜牌	Copper Medal	135	293	264	288	284	216
体育设施（个）	Sports Facility(unit)						
体育场	Stadium	12	12	6	12	14	14
体育馆	Gymnasium	9	9	17	9	10	11
游泳馆	Natatorium	5	5	11	5	9	10
室内外游泳池	Indoor Swimming Pool	2	2	5	4	10	10
有固定看台的灯光球场	Light Count With Fixed Stand	2	2	7	2	5	5

注：1. 等级裁判员为当年新评定的人数。
2. 2017 年体育设施统计口径为市、区县体育部门主管的设施数量。
3. 2017 年业余体育学校统计口径只指学位，不包括业训网点。

Note: 1.The number of referees is the number of new assessments in the current year.
2.The number of sports facilities in 2017 is the number of facilities in charge of the sports department of the city, district and county.
3.In 2017, the statistical caliber of amateur sports schools only refers to degree, excluding amateur training outlets.

19-2 各时期卫生事业情况
Statistics of Health Institutions in Major Years

年份 Year	卫生机构（个） Number of Health Institutions (unit)		卫生工作人员（人） Medical Technical Personnel (person)		卫生机构床位（张） Number of Health Institutions Beds (set)	
	小计 Total	# 医院及卫生院 Hospitals and Township Hospitals	小计 Total	# 卫生技术人员 Medical Technical Personnel	小计 Total	# 医院及卫生院 Hospitals and Township Hospitals
1952	208	22	6277	4778	3160	1906
1957	708	45	10740	7991	5972	3401
1962	1191	98	13705	9648	7917	5662
1965	1144	114	18885	14881	9035	6438
1970	682	130	13273	10341	7878	6462
1975	934	137	20021	14956	9066	8050
1978	1017	148	24949	19198	11496	9856
1979	1078	152	26385	20110	11902	10781
1980	1091	151	27843	21295	12301	11052
“六五”时期						
1981	1188	152	29597	22559	12428	11436
1982	1159	151	30636	22814	12379	11383
1983	1177	156	31924	23948	12966	11674
1984	1160	157	32967	24502	13728	12960
1985	1175	165	34232	26185	14356	13791
“七五”时期						
1986	1184	167	35803	27360	14757	14165
1987	1137	166	37129	28159	15457	14721
1988	1103	171	38384	29167	16165	15580
1989	1137	180	39926	29878	16698	16176
1990	1300	178	41444	31130	18214	17216
“八五”时期						
1991	1233	177	40957	30815	18439	17538
1992	1331	180	41996	31541	18818	18178
1993	1285	193	43274	32871	20243	19320
1994	1228	213	43630	33007	20001	19064
1995	1185	216	43648	32848	20747	19534

19-2 续表 continued

年份 Year	卫生机构（个） Number of Health Institutions (unit)		卫生工作人员（人） Medical Technical Personnel (person)		卫生机构床位（张） Number of Health Institutions Beds (set)	
	小计 Total	# 医院及卫生院 Hospitals and Township Hospitals	小计 Total	# 卫生技术人员 Medical Technical Personnel	小计 Total	# 医院及卫生院 Hospitals and Township Hospitals
"九五"时期						
1996	1674	214	45765	35219	20428	19716
1997	1567	220	44664	34188	21422	20706
1998	1574	227	45110	34596	21965	21130
1999	1570	226	45121	34000	21735	21086
2000	1414	231	45166	35669	21698	20830
"十五"时期						
2001	1414	231	45296	35790	21906	21033
2002	1708	243	39386	31945	21576	21042
2003	1868	246	41925	33803	22674	22262
2004	1917	243	41625	33998	24044	22588
2005	2138	246	41499	34129	24695	23524
"十一五"时期						
2006	2285	240	43023	35124	27695	26101
2007	2265	243	42513	34579	26055	25328
2008	5092	286	44416	36143	28939	27555
2009	5163	281	46311	37648	30920	28749
2010	5086	277	54711	39366	31947	29844
"十二五"时期						
2011	5159	262	58590	42116	34920	31545
2012	5239	243	60426	44331	38834	35194
2013	5368	255	76955	57700	45465	41287
2014	5784	265	84515	63604	48280	44058
2015	5947	269	89117	71778	49311	45195
"十三五"时期						
2016	6188	270	92060	76447	52191	47524
2017	5770	289	97663	76273	54855	50142
2018	6030	293	104347	82834	57460	51207
2019	7487	351	122370	97532	66623	59697
2020	7514	343	126681	102172	68831	62072

注：2015 年及 2016 年的卫生技术人员为注册卫生技术人员，其他年份为在岗卫生技术人员。
Notes: Health technicians in 2015 and 2016 are registered health technicians, and other years are on-the-job health technicians.

19–3 卫生事业机构及床位
Number of Health Institutions and Beds

指标	Indicator	2015 年	2016 年	2017 年	2018 年	2019 年	2020 年
各类卫生机构数（个）	**Number of Health Institutions (unit)**	5947	6188	5770	6030	7487	7514
医院	Hospital	213	217	238	246	289	284
社区卫生服务中心（站）	Health Service Center for Community	275	286	283	314	352	379
卫生院	Health Centers	56	53	51	47	62	59
门诊部	Outpatient Department	72	89	115	135	156	163
急救中心（站）	First–Aid Center	2	2	1	1	1	1
采血供应机构	Pick and Supply Blood Institution	4	4	2	2	3	2
妇幼保健院（所、站）	Women and Children Care Agencies	12	12	12	12	15	15
专科疾病防治院（所、站）	Specialized Disease Prevention &Treatment Institution	10	10	10	11	13	9
疾病预防控制中心（防疫站）	Center for Disease Control and Prevention	12	12	12	12	15	14
医学科学研究机构	Medical Science Research Institutes	2	2	2	2	2	2
其他卫生机构	Other Medical Institutions	17	18	27	29	39	32
各类卫生机构病床数（张）	**Number of Health Institutions Beds(set)**	49311	52191	54855	57460	66623	68831
医院	Hospital	42204	44526	47575	48843	56315	58790
社区卫生服务中心（站）	Health Service Center for Community	2792	2946	3195	3361	3791	3899
卫生院	Health Centers	2991	2998	2567	2364	3382	3282
门诊部	Outpatient Department	127	112	46	65	33	43
妇幼保健院（所、站）	Women and Children Care Agencies	834	1243	1126	1158	1444	1533
专科疾病防治院（所、站）	Specialized Disease Prevention	360	366	346	1669	1658	1284
千人拥有量（张、人）	**Number Per 1000 Population(set.person)**						
平均每千人拥有病床	Number Of Beds Per 1000 Population	6.91	7.22	7.49	7.70	7.48	7.48
每千人拥有卫生技术人员	Number Of Medical Technical Personnel Per 1000 Population	10.06	10.57	10.42	11.10	10.95	11.10
每千人拥有医生	Number Of Doctors Per 1000 Population	4.60	4.75	3.97	4.31	4.30	4.37
每千人拥有护士	Number Of Nurses Per 1000 Population	5.32	5.82	4.62	5.03	4.91	4.97

19-4 分地区卫生事业机构及床位（2020年）
Number of Health Institutions and Beds by District(2020)

指标	Indicator	全市 Total	市区 Urban	平阴县 Pingyin	商河县 Shanghe
各类卫生机构数（个）	**Number of Institutions(unit)**	7514	6776	263	475
医院	Hospital	284	275	4	5
疗养院	Health Service Center for Community	0	0	0	0
社区卫生服务中心（站）	Health Centers	379	362	8	9
卫生院	Outpatient Department	59	42	6	11
门诊部	Outpatient Department	163	157	1	5
诊所、卫生所、医务室	Infirmaries and Clinics	2852	2687	72	93
急救中心（站）	First-Aid Center	1	1	0	0
采血供应机构	Pick and Supply Blood Institution	2	2	0	0
妇幼保健院（所、站）	Women and Children Care Agencies	15	13	1	1
专科疾病防治院（所、站）	Specialized Disease Prevention &Treatment Institution	9	8	1	0
疾病预防控制中心（防疫站）	Center for Disease Control and Prevention	14	12	1	1
卫生监督所	Medical Supervision Institution	14	12	1	1
医学科学研究机构	Medical Science Research Institutes	2	2	0	0
其他卫生构	Other Medical Institutions	32	32	0	0
各类卫生机构病床数（张）	**Number of Institutions Beds(bed)**	68831	63881	2440	2510
医院	Hospital	58790	55104	1736	1950
疗养院	Sanatorium	0	0	0	0
社区卫生服务中心（站）	Health Service Center for Community	3899	3829	20	50
卫生院	Health Centers	3282	2214	558	510
门诊部	Outpatient Department	43	43	0	0
妇幼保健院（所、站）	Women and Children Care Agencies	1533	1527	6	0
专科疾病防治院（所、站）	Specialized Disease Prevention&Treatment Institution	1284	1164	120	0
千人拥有量（张、人）	**Number Per 1000 Population(set.person)**				
平均每千人拥有病床	Number Of Beds Per 1000 Population	7.48	7.65	7.55	4.76
每千人拥有卫生技术人员	Number Of Medical Technical Personnel Per 1000 Population	11.10	11.59	7.45	5.65
每千人拥有医生	Number Of Doctors Per 1000 Population	4.37	4.55	2.78	2.48
每千人拥有护士	Number Of Nurses Per 1000 Population	4.97	5.20	3.47	2.19

19-5 医疗机构年收入与支出(2020年)
Revenue and Expenditure in Health Insititutions(2020)

单位:万元 (10 000yuan)

机构分类	Institutions	总收入 Total Income			
		合计 Total	财政补助收入 Financial Subsidy Income	上级补助收入 Grant From Higher Authority	业务收入/事业收入 Business Income
合计	**Total**	**5947356.7**	**861409.6**	**41088.3**	**4827599.8**
医院	Hospital	4944988.8	539884.4	13024.1	4276958.1
社区卫生服务中心(站)	Health Service Center for Community	233970.3	72099.7	4602.3	152209.9
卫生院	Health Centers	107210.7	54963.4	2000.6	49244.3
门诊部	Outpatient Department	32077.7	0.0	0.0	23189.3
诊所.卫生所.医务室	Infirmaries and Clinics	65909.5	0.0	0.0	56436.1
急救中心(站)	First-Aid Center	2551.7	2494.7	0.0	57.0
妇幼保健院(所、站)	Women and Children Care Agencies	188383.6	43615.4	432.9	132572.9
专科疾病防治院(所、站)	Specialized Disease revention&Treatment Institution	57914.1	19499.8	300.2	33262.7

19-5 续表 continued

机构分类	Institutions	总费用 Total Expenditure			总费用中:人员费用 Staff Expenditure
		合计 Total	单位管理费 Unit Management Fee	业务活动费 Business Activity Fee	
合计	**Total**	**5449008.9**	**608050.2**	**4524555.0**	**1877250.5**
医院	Hospital	4597279.4	546690.0	3883301.2	1548254.4
社区卫生服务中心(站)	Health Service Center for Community	224777.0	0.0	205039.0	79049.9
卫生院	Health Centers	104028.4	0.0	100089.7	49011.4
门诊部	Outpatient Department	20764.1	0.0	0.0	10357.4
诊所、卫生所、医务室	Infirmaries and Clinics	45937.1	0.0	0.0	25184.3
急救中心(站)	First-Aid Center	3116.4	496.5	2619.9	1602.7
妇幼保健院(所、站)	Women and Children Care Agencies	173786.4	22664.3	147888.0	76027.0
专科疾病防治院(所、站)	Specialized Disease Revention& Treatment Institution	45807.3	5133.6	40679.0	19797.1

注:门诊部及诊所.卫生所.医务室不填报财政补助收入、上级补助收入、单位管理费、业务活动费四项指标。

Notes: Outpatient department and clinic. Health clinic. The medical office does not report four indicators: financial subsidy income, superior subsidy income, Unit Management Fee, Business Activity Fee.

19-6 医院、卫生院工作情况
Basic Statistics on Hospitals and Health Institutions in Rural Areas

指标	Indicator	2015 年	2016 年	2017 年	2018 年	2019 年	2020 年
医院	Hospital						
单位数（个）	Unit Number(unit)	213	217	238	246	289	284
诊疗人次数（万人次）	Visits (10 000 person-times)	2716	2865	3157	3309	3922	3397
#门诊人次数	OutPatients	2446	2570	2779	2960	3449	3018
急诊人次数	Emergency Patients	150	165	207	228	300	235
健康检查人数（万人次）	check-up(10 000 person-times)	131	154	166	201	260	235
入院人数（万人）	Inpatients(10 000 persons)	112.5	127.9	140.4	150.0	182.2	172.3
出院人数（万人）	Discharged(10 000 persons)	112.1	127.3	139.7	149.4	181.5	171.8
平均开放病床数（张）	Average Bed Opened(bed)	39632	41402	44400	45132	52359	54692
病床使用率（%）	Utilization Rate of Beds(%)	82.37	86.12	87.52	87.28	87.27	77.71
病床周转次数（次）	Turnover of Beds(time)	28.30	30.70	31.50	33.10	34.70	31.40
出院者平均住院日（日）	Average Stay Days in Hospital(day)	10.60	10.10	9.90	9.40	9.20	9.10
卫生院	Health Centers						
单位数（个）	Unit Number(unit)	56	53	51	47	62	59
诊疗人次数（万人次）	Visits (10 000 person-times)	211.7	233.4	208.1	195.2	301.9	304.1
#门诊人次数	OutPatients	205.7	224.6	197.6	190.3	292.1	292.7
急诊人次数	Emergency Patients	3.0	3.4	6.5	3.3	3.6	5.0
健康检查人数（万人次）	check-up(10 000 person-times)	23.9	23.0	20.2	20.4	35.8	25.5
入院人数（万人）	Inpatients(10 000 persons)	4.7	6.6	5.3	4.4	7.2	5.8
出院人数（万人）	Discharged(10 000 persons)	4.7	6.5	5.3	4.4	7.2	5.7
平均开放病床数（张）	Average Bed Opened(bed)	2930	2907	2479	2277	3187	3203
病床使用率（%）	Utilization Rate of Beds(%)	38.62	54.54	52.00	54.85	58.03	47.37
病床周转次数（次）	Turnover of Beds(times)	15.90	22.40	21.40	19.40	22.70	17.90
出院者平均住院日（日）	Average Stay Days in Hospital(day)	8.20	8.40	8.30	9.70	7.80	8.50

19-7 分地区卫生技术人员分类情况(2020年)
Medical Technical Personnel by Region(2020)

单位：人 (person)

指标	Indicator	全市 Total	市区 Urban	平阴县 Pingyin	商河县 Shanghe
各类卫生机构工作人员合计	Medical TechnicalPersonnel	126681	119253	3103	4325
#卫生技术人员小计	Medical TechnicalPersonnel	102172	96785	2407	2980
医生	Licensed Doctors	40199	37994	898	1307
注册护士	Registered Nurse	45727	43451	1122	1154
其他	Others	16246	15340	387	519

主要统计指标解释

等级裁判员人数 指经考核正式批准授予等级裁判员称号的人数。裁判员等级分为国际裁判、国家级裁判、一级裁判、二级裁判、三级裁判。

体育场 指有400米跑道(中心含足球场)，有固定道牙，跑道6条以上，并有固定看台的室外田径场地。体育场按看台容纳观众人数分为：甲级25000人以上，乙级15000-25000人，丙级5000-15000人，丁级5000人以下。

体育馆 指有固定看台，可供篮球、排球、羽毛球、乒乓球、体操等项目训练比赛活动用的室内运动场地。体育馆按看台容纳观众人数分为：甲级6000人以上，乙级4000-6000人，丙级2000-4000人，丁级2000人以下。

医院 包括综合医院、中医医院、中西医结合医院、民族医医院、各类专科医院和护理院，不包括专科疾病防治院、妇幼保健院和疗养院，包括医学院校附属医院。

卫生技术人员 包括执业医师、执业助理医师、注册护士、药师(士)、检验及影像技师(士)、卫生监督员和见习医(药、护、技)师(士)等卫生专业人员。

医生 指取得医师执业证书且实际从事临床工作的人。

卫生机构 指从卫生(卫生健康)行政部门取得《医疗机构执业许可证》、《中医诊所备案证》、《计划生育技术服务许可证》或从民政、工商行政、机构编制管理部门取得法人单位登记证书，为社会提供医疗服务、公共卫生服务或从事医学科研和学在职培训等工作的单位。

Explanatory Notes on Main Statistical Indicators

Number of Grade Referees refers to the number of referees formally approved upon evaluation to be granted with the title of grade referee. Referees are divided into international referee, national referee, Level I referee, Level II referee and Level III referee.

Stadium refers to outdoor athletic field with 400m track (football field in the center), fixed kerbs, more than 6 tracks and fixed stands. Stadiums can be divided as follows as per the quantity of spectators contained by the standard: Class A stadium for above 25,000 persons, Class B stadium for 15,000–25,000 persons, Class C stadium for 5,000–15,000 persons and Class D stadium for less than 5,000 persons.

Gymnasium refers to indoor sports ground with fixed stands which can be used for training and competition of basketball, volleyball, badminton, table tennis and gymnastics. Gymnasium can be divided as follows as per the quantity of spectators contained by the standard: Class A gymnasium for above 6,000 persons, Class B gymnasium for 4,000–6,000 persons, Class C gymnasium for 2,000–4,000 persons and Class D gymnasium for less than 2,000 persons.

Hospital includes general hospital, traditional Chinese medicine hospital, hospital of traditional Chinese and Western medicine, ethnic medical hospital, various specialized hospital and nursing home and affiliated hospital of medical college other than specialized disease prevention and maternity and child care center and nursing home.

Medical Technical Personnel refers to health professionals such as medical practitioner, assistant medical practitioner, registered nurse, pharmacist, senior pharmacist (assistant pharmacist), inspection and imaging technician (assistant technician), health supervisor and medical intern (trainee medical assistant), pharmacy intern (probationary pharmacist), trainee nurse (practice nurse) or medical trainee (apprentice technician).

Doctors refer to persons getting the medical practitioner certificate and actually engaging in clinical work.

Health Care Institution refers to units getting Practicing License of Medical Institution, Registration Certificate of TCM Clinic and Family Planning Technical Service License from the administrative department of health (hygiene and health) or getting the registration certificate of legal entity from civil affairs, industrial and commercial administration, institutional establishment management departments, providing the society with medical service and public health service or engaging in medical scientific research and studying on–the–job training.

20

民政、司法和其他

SOCIAL WELFARE CIVIL ADMINISTRATION AND OTHERS

20-1 社会治安主要指标
Main Indicators of Social Offense

指标	Indicator	2015 年	2016 年	2017 年	2018 年	2019 年	2020 年
刑事案件（件）	**Criminal Cases(case)**						
当年全部立案数	Put on Record	35047	21142	19648	18594	25382	32965
破获当年刑事案件数	Cracked the Number of Criminal Cases	20806	7610	8571	7103	9259	18983
治安案件（件）	**Public Security Cases(case)**						
受理数	Cases Accepted	86217	71868	66375	75393	79355	68614
查处数	Cases Punished	81754	68439	63734	73700	72593	60633
城市交通事故	**Traffic Accidents**						
交通事故（起）	Number of Traffic Accidents(case)	2946	2944	3075	3071	3334	3313
伤亡人数（人）	Number of Injuries and Deaths(person)	3885	3573	3219	3618	3925	3747
# 死亡人数（人）	Number of Deathsa(person)	439	403	421	419	472	465
损失折款（万元）	Direct Losses(10 000 yuan)	840	875.2	1020.3	947.4	905.48	1006.2
火灾事故	**Fires**						
火灾起数（起）	Number of Fire Accidents(case)	2609	1825	1752	1539	4577	4319
伤亡人数（人）	Number of Injuries and Deaths(person)	12	15	11	12	12	16
# 死亡人数（人）	Number of Deaths(person)	12	13	10	10	10	13
损失折款（万元）	Direct Losses(10 000 yuan)	1571	1903	599	827	1529	2153

注："破获当年刑事案件数" 2015 年以前为当年全部破案数口径。
Note:"The number of uncovering criminal cases in the year"was the total quantity before 2015.

20-2 分地区社会治安主要指标(2020年)
Main Indicators of Social Offense by District(2020)

指标	Indicator	全市 Total	其中 of which		
			市区 Urban	平阴县 Ping yin	商河县 Shang he
刑事案件(件)	Criminal Cases(case)				
当年全部立案数	Put on Record	32965	31254	784	927
破获当年刑事案件数	Cracked the Number of Criminal Cases	18983	17949	456	578
治安案件(件)	Public Security Cases(case)				
受理数	Cases Accepted	68614	61941	4690	1983
查处数	Cases Punished	60633	54925	4690	1019
城市交通事故	Traffic Accidents				
交通事故(起)	Number of Traffic Accidents(case)	3313	3187	84	42
伤亡人数(人)	Number of Injuries and Deaths(person)	3747	3588	108	51
#死亡人数(人)	Number of Deathsa(person)	465	427	27	11
损失折款(万元)	Direct Losses(10 000 yuan)	1006	992	6	8
火灾事故	Fires				
火灾起数(起)	Number of Fire Accidents(case)	4319	3991	147	181
伤亡人数(人)	Number of Injuries and Deaths(person)	16	15	1	0
#死亡人数(人)	Number of Deaths(person)	13	12	1	0
损失折款(万元)	Direct Losses(10 000 yuan)	2153	1811	184	158

20-3 社会保障和救济
Basic Statistics on Social Security and Receiving Relief Flinds

指标	Indicator	2015 年	2016 年	2017 年	2018 年	2019 年	2020 年
优抚情况（人）	Veteran Benefit and Placement(person)						
享受定期抚恤金人数	Number of Receiving Periodic Pensions	939	907	831	784	914	
在乡复员军人	Demobilized Soldiers in Countryside	2725	2319	1892	1486	1727	
参战退役人员	Veterans	4454	4741	4705	4630	5636	
社会救济情况（人）	Social Relief(person)						
城镇居民最低生活保障人数	Number of Urban Residents for Minimum Livelihood Guarantee	22303	19742	16742	13364	15491	14159
农村居民最低生活保障人数	Number of Rural residents for Minimum Livelihood Guarantee	81215	80147	77121	64271	73305	84209
民政经费（万元）	Civil Affairs Expenditures(10 000 yuan)						
城市居民最低生活保障费	Urban Residents for Minimum Livelihood Guarantee	8585	11573	10966	9563	9657	11030
农村最低生活保障费	Rural residents for Minimum Livelihood Guarantee	13343	24938	26929	26439	26039	39218
其它社会救助费	Other Social Assistance Expenses	11446	6614	5757	3088	1158	1175
社会福利费	Social Welfare Funds	33569	35898	32194	47654	60731	69771
退役安置费（万元）	Decommissioning Costs(10 000 yuan)	89415	96164	134557	12656	13538	
自然灾害生活救助费（万元）	Natural Disaster Assistance Expenses (10 000 yuan)	1646	654	259	69	2450	-
医疗救助费（万元）	Medical Assistance Expenses(10 000 yuan)	4581	7245	8396	7175	3680	9280
社会保障及扶贫（个、元）	Social Security and Poverty Alleviation(unit.yuan)						
建立社会保障服务网络的乡镇数	Number of Towns With Social Security Service Network	48	39	29	29	40	29
城市市区居民最低生活保障金标准	Minimum Living Standards for Urban Residents	550	580	596	616	685	821

注：本表指标为“-”的，部门相关统计制度中已经不再进行统计。
Notes: The indicator “-” in this table means statistics are no longer in the relevant statistical system of the department.

20-4 分地区社会保障和救济(2020 年)
Basic Statistics on Social Security and Receiving Relief Flinds by Region(2020)

指标	Indicator	济南市(汇总) Total	济南市(市本级) Urban	历下区 Li xia	市中区 Shi zhong	槐荫区 Huai yin	天桥区 Tian qiao	历城区 Li cheng	长清区 Chang qing	章丘区 Zhang qiu	济阳区 Ji yang
社会救济情况(人)	Social Relief(person)										
城镇居民最低生活保障人数	Number of Urban Residents for Minimum Livelihood Guarantee	14159		1537	1929	1294	3215	392.0	590	807	92
农村居民最低生活保障人数	Number of Rural residents for Minimum Livelihood Guarantee	84209			1127	360	484	1565.0	10474	18468	6170
民政经费(万元)	Civil Affairs Expenditures (10 000 yuan)										
城市居民最低生活保障费	Urban Residents for Minimum Livelihood Guarantee	11029.7		1381.2	1617.5	1056.9	2708.6	346.7	347.7	570.9	58.8
农村最低生活保障费	Rural residents for Minimum Livelihood Guarantee	39218.1			701.9	225.2	280.0	1035.3	4765.9	8951.3	2517.8
其它社会救助费	Other Social Assistance Expenses	1174.7			265.1	297.7	13.1			519.6	
社会福利费	Social Welfare Funds	69771.2	17991.8	4858.4	2375.7	2455.3	2558.0	2809.5	2142.6	8208.9	3586.0
社会保障及扶贫(个、元)	Social Security and Poverty Alleviation(unit.yuan)										
建立社会保障服务网络的乡镇数	Number of Towns With Social Security Service Network	29							2	1	2
城市市区居民最低生活保障金标准	Minimum Living Standards for Urban Residents	821.0	821.0	821.0	821.0	821.0	821.0	821.0	821.0	821.0	821.0

20-4 续表 continued

指标	Indicator	莱芜区 Lai wu	钢城区 Gang cheng	济南高新区 Ji'nan Gao xin	莱芜高新区 Laiwu Gao xin	济南先行区 JN Pioneer Area	南部山区 Nan shan	平阴县 Ping yin	商河县 Shang he
社会救济情况(人)	Social Relief(person)								
城镇居民最低生活保障人数	Number of Urban Residents for Minimum Livelihood Guarantee	2838	637	20	51	180	52	159	366
农村居民最低生活保障人数	Number of Rural residents for Minimum Livelihood Guarantee	15760	3642	987	524	2426	4639	4116	13467
民政经费(万元)	Civil Affairs Expenditures (10 000 yuan)								
城市居民最低生活保障费	Urban Residents for Minimum Livelihood Guarantee	1866.5	472.5	15.7	33.0	142.5	46.6	131.0	233.6
农村最低生活保障费	Rural residents for Minimum Livelihood Guarantee	6453.7	1686.1	518.0	207.2	1268.6	2679.3	1988.5	5939.3
其它社会救助费	Other Social Assistance Expenses		5.3			73.9			
社会福利费	Social Welfare Funds	4632.5	1616.0	2800.2	197.1	1432.6	1209.1	5246.5	5651.0
社会保障及扶贫(个、元)	Social Security and Poverty Alleviation(unit.yuan)								
建立社会保障服务网络的乡镇数	Number of Towns With Social Security Service Network	7						6	11
城市市区居民最低生活保障金标准	Minimum Living Standards for Urban Residents	821.0	821.0	821.0	821.0	821.0	821.0	821.0	821.0

20-5 律师、公证、司法基本情况（2020 年）
Basic Statistics on Law，Notarizations and Mendiation(2020)

指标	Indicator	单位 Unit	全市 Total	市区 Urban	平阴县 Pingyin	商河县 Shanghe
律师工作	**Lawyers**					
律师事务所	Number of Law Offices	个 (unit)	463	454	7	2
执业律师	Number of Lawyers	人 (person)	7339	7293	33	13
担任常年法律顾问	Permanent Legal Advisor	家 (unit)	9831	9706	94	31
民事诉讼代理	Civil Agent	件 (case)	77528	76316	881	331
刑事诉讼辩护及代理	Criminal Defense and Agent	件 (case)	6776	6344	78	354
行政诉讼代理	Administrative Agent	件 (case)	6151	6135	10	6
非诉讼法律事务	Non-litigation Legal Matters	件 (case)	16659	16643	16	0
公证工作	**Notarization**					
公证处	Number of Notary Offices	个 (unit)	15	13	1	1
公证处人员	Personnel of Notary Offices	人 (person)	486	469	10	7
# 公证员	Notaries	人 (person)	157	151	4	2
办理公证总数	Number of Notarized Affair	件 (case)	163316	158577	1681	3058
# 国内民事公证	Domestic Civil Notarization	件 (case)	103202	102076	927	199
国内经济公证	Domestic Commerce Notarization	件 (case)	39810	36206	754	2850
涉外公证	Foreign-related Notarization	件 (case)	20055	20046	0	9
办理经济公证涉及金额	Money ofCommerce Notarization	亿元 (100 million yuan)	1.20	1.07	0.05	0.08
基层司法行政工作	**Basic Judicical Administration**					
人民调解委员会	People's Mediation Committee	个 (unit)	6608	5260	367	981
人民调解员	People's Mediators	人 (person)	23212	18590	1418	3204
调解纠纷总数	Number of Mediation Disputes	件 (case)	32349	24332	4730	3287
# 调解成功	Success Mediation	件 (case)	30573	24040	3270	3263
法律服务所	Legal Service Office	个 (unit)	151	139	9	3
基层法律工作者	Grassroots Legal Workers	人 (person)	914	865	36	13
担任法律顾问	Legal Advisor	家 (unit)	1636	1399	172	65
民事诉讼代理	Civil Agent	件 (case)	6458	5302	640	516
非诉讼代理	Non-litigation Agent	件 (case)	2854	2452	327	75
法律援助工作	**Legal Aid**					
法律援助机构	Legal Aid Institution	个 (unit)	13	11	1	1
执业人员	Practitioners	人 (person)	91	75	6	10
办理法律援助案件	Legal Aid Cases	件 (case)	15820	14319	864	637

主要统计指标解释

律师 指受聘参加法律顾问处工作，担任法律顾问、刑（民）事代理人、刑事辩护人，办理非诉讼事件、解答法律询问，代写法律事务文书等主要从事律师业务的专职法律工作者和兼职律师。

公证人员 指在国家公证机关依法办理公证事务的司法人员，包括公证员、助理公证员和在公证处工作的其他人员。

调解人员 指在人民调解委员会担负调解民间一般民事纠纷和轻微违法行为引起纠纷的工作人员，包括调解委员会的委员和调解小组的调解员。

立案 指检察机关对犯罪线索进行初步调查后，认为存在职务犯罪事实并需要追究刑事责任时，依法决定作为刑事案件进行侦查的诉讼活动，是追究犯罪的开始。

Explanatory Notes on Main Statistical Indicators

Lawyers refer to full-time legal workers and part-time lawyers hired to work in the legal advisory office, serving as legal adviser, criminal (civil) agent and criminal advocate and mainly engaging in law practice (such as handling non-contentious matter, answering legal questions and ghostwriting legal papers).

Notary Personnel refers to judicial personnel legally handling notarial affairs at the state notary organ, including notary, assistant notary and other personnel working in the notary office.

Mediation Personnel refers to staff taking charge of mediating ordinary civil disputes among the people and disputes arising from minor infraction at the people's mediation committee, including the member of the mediation committee and the mediator of the mediation team.

Case Filing refers to the litigious activity involving investigation of criminal case according to law when existence of duty-related crimes is deemed and it is necessary to investigate the criminal responsibility after preliminary investigation of crime clues by the investigating and prosecuting apparatus. It is the start of the investigation of crime.

附 录

APPENDIX

附录一 山东省十六城市主要经济指标（2020 年）
Main Statistical Indicators of 16 Cities in Shandong(2020)

单位：亿元

城市名称	Region	地区生产总值 Gross Domestic Product	第一产业 Primary Industry	第二产业 Secondary Industry	第三产业 Tertiary Industry	固定资产投资比上年增长（%）Growth Rate Investment in Fixed Assets (%)	房地产开发投资额 Estate Development Investment	一般公共预算收入 General Pubilic Budget Revenue	一般公共预算支出 General Pubilic Budget Expenditure	金融机构本外币存款余额 The Balance of RMB and Foreign Currencies Deposits in Financial Institutions
全省	Total	73129.0	5363.8	28612.2	39153.1	3.6	9450.5	6559.9	11231.2	118349.4
济南市	Ji'nan	10140.9	361.7	3530.7	6248.6	4.0	1707.6	906.1	1288.8	21065.0
青岛市	Qingdao	12400.6	425.4	4361.6	7613.6	3.2	2045.1	1253.8	1584.7	20507.1
淄博市	Zibo	3673.5	157.2	1777.2	1739.2	7.5	366.9	321.5	522.7	5612.6
枣庄市	Zaozhuang	1733.2	165.7	704.1	863.4	3.2	288.2	140.8	270.0	2409.9
东营市	Dongying	2981.2	156.6	1678.5	1146.1	8.9	187.3	249.3	311.3	4122.8
烟台市	Yantai	7816.4	572.7	3192.4	4051.3	2.9	815.2	610.1	845.4	9997.8
潍坊市	Weifang	5872.2	535.6	2308.1	3028.4	4.5	830.8	573.9	793.9	10076.5
济宁市	Jining	4494.3	525.6	1761.7	2207.0	3.2	505.6	411.8	695.9	6568.1
泰安市	Taian	2766.5	299.7	1080.4	1386.4	2.9	264.1	229.2	434.8	4602.7
威海市	Weiha	3017.8	301.7	1162.3	1553.9	2.9	393.5	252.4	350.4	4732.8
日照市	Rizhao	2006.4	171.3	844.2	990.9	3.2	216.3	176.3	286.6	3127.1
临沂市	Linyi	4805.3	440.9	1756.4	2607.9	4.0	634.7	349.8	792.5	8192.6
德州市	Dezhou	3079.0	327.0	1235.9	1516.1	-2.9	410.8	208.5	481.2	4296.3
聊城市	Liaocheng	2316.8	333.3	795.6	1188.0	6.8	303.7	202.0	466.0	4366.3
滨州市	Binzhou	2508.1	243.2	1021.6	1243.4	7.8	166.5	252.8	447.5	3442.6
菏泽市	Heze	3483.1	346.0	1399.6	1737.5	7.5	314.2	237.9	630.8	5039.3
济南位次	Position	2	6	2	2	7	2	2	2	1

注：本表内其他城市数据根据内部资料整理，不做正式发布，仅供参考。各项指标最终数据，敬请关注各城市官方发布机构。

Note: The data regarding other cities in this table is sorted out according to internal data which is for reference only instead of being released officially. As for final data regarding various indicators, refer to official release mechanism in each city.

(100 million yuan)

#住户存款 House--hold Deposits	金融机构本外币贷款余额 The Balance of RMB and Foreign Currencies Loans in Financial Institutions	社会消费品零售总额比上年增长（%）Growth Rate Total Retail Sales of Consumer Goods (%)	货物进出口总额 Total Import & Export	#出口总额 Total Export	实际使用外资（亿美元）Actual Use of Foreign Capital (100 million USD)	城镇居民人均可支配收入（元）Per Capita Disposable Income of Urban Households (yuan)	城镇居民人均消费支出（元）Per Capita Consumption Expenditure of Urban Households (yuan)	农村居民人均可支配收入（元）Per Capita Disposable Income of Rural Households (yuan)	农村居民人均消费支出（元）Per Capita Consumption Expenditure of Rural Households (yuan)	居民消费价格指数（%）Consumer Price Indices (%)
64619.6	97880.6	0.0	22009.4	13054.8	176.5	43726	27291	18753	12660	102.8
7647.5	20720.2	1.1	1382.7	755.0	19.2	53329	34391	20432	12947	102.4
8158.3	21064.8	1.5	6407.0	3876.8	58.5	55905	35936	23656	15138	102.4
3546.6	3879.9	-1.8	887.7	489.2	3.8	46415	29470	20891	14946	102.7
1663.9	1730.2	-2.6	263.8	249.8	3.0	35098	20371	17690	11218	102.2
2155.6	3333.7	-1.8	1344.3	455.3	4.4	52684	31286	20003	14819	102.6
5833.9	6661.9	-0.2	3214.9	1963.1	22.8	49434	31843	22305	15407	102.5
6181.3	7574.2	0.1	1903.9	1215.6	10.8	43085	26466	21651	13669	102.6
4343.1	4783.0	-1.2	545.1	386.1	8.1	38368	22429	18653	11576	102.9
3071.3	3137.4	-3.0	211.9	145.9	6.8	38901	22995	19682	12393	102.6
2907.3	3396.6	0.3	1614.6	1165.8	13.6	50424	31252	23351	13807	102.5
1821.5	2974.3	-3.3	1023.9	343.5	4.7	36752	21950	18274	9383	102.1
5213.1	7008.8	0.2	1167.2	992.2	9.3	39466	18888	15918	9981	102.8
3060.0	2534.9	0.0	386.9	247.2	2.7	29594	17861	16996	13109	103.0
3100.8	2885.8	-3.2	404.2	227.4	2.1	30036	17695	15718	11073	103.1
1996.5	2904.1	1.1	817.5	327.4	3.6	38582	24635	18496	12321	102.4
3916.4	3022.2	1.2	433.8	214.3	2.9	29365	18787	15107	11993	101.7
2	2	3	5	6	3	2	2	6	8	11

附录二 十五副省级城市主要经济指标（2020 年）

Main Statistical Indicators of 15 Vice-provincial Cities(2020)

单位：亿元

城市名称	Region	地区生产总值 Gross Dmoestic Product	第一产业 Primary Industry	第二产业 Secondary Industry	第三产业 Tertiary Industry	固定资产投资比上年增长(%) Growth Rate Investment in Fixed Assets (%)	房地产开发投资比上年增长(%) Growth Rate Estate Development Investment (%)	一般公共预算收入 General Pubilic Budget Revenue	一般公共预算支出 General Pubilic Budget Expenditure	金融机构本外币存款余额 The Balance of RMB and Foreign Currencies Deposits in Financial Institutions
济南	Ji'nan	10140.9	361.7	3530.7	6248.6	4.0	8.3	906.1	1288.8	21065.0
沈阳	Shenyang	6571.6	303.6	2160.4	4107.6	4.1	5.2	736.1	1074.1	19442.5
大连	Dalian	7030.4	459.2	2815.1	3756.0	0.1	5.9	702.7	1002.0	16003.8
长春	Changchun	6638.0	533.8	2758.1	3346.1	8.8	12.4	440.4	1084.1	14230.6
哈尔滨	Harbin	5183.8	615.8	1144.5	3423.5	2.8	0.3	339.6	1162.2	13856.7
南京	Nanjing	14818.0	296.8	5214.4	9306.8	6.6	5.2	1637.7	1754.6	40056.5
杭州	Hangzhou	16106.0	326.0	4821.0	10959.0	6.8	5.3	2093.0	2070.0	54246.0
宁波	Ningbo	12408.7	338.4	5693.9	6376.4	5.5	6.8	1510.8	1742.0	23988.2
厦门	Xiamen	6384.0	28.9	2519.8	3835.3	8.8	17.4	783.9	976.9	13117.1
青岛	Qingdao	12400.6	425.4	4361.6	7613.6	3.2	13.4	1253.8	1584.7	20507.1
武汉	Wuhan	15616.1	402.2	5557.5	9656.4	-11.8	-6.4	1230.3	2407.2	31005.9
广州	Guangzhou	25019.1	288.1	6590.4	18140.6	10.0	6.2	1721.6	2953.0	67798.8
深圳	Shenzhen	27670.2	25.8	10454.0	17190.4	8.2	16.4	3857.4	4177.7	101897.3
成都	Chengdu	17716.9	655.2	5418.5	11643.0	9.9	9.2	1520.4	2158.0	43654.0
西安	Xi'an	10020.4	312.8	3328.3	6379.4	12.8	6.5	724.1	1352.7	26045.9
济南位次	Position	9	7	9	10	11	6	9	10	9

注：1. 为便于排序，厦门、广州、成都实际使用外资数据根据人民币口径和年均汇率推算。
2. 本表内其他城市数据根据内部资料整理，不做正式发布，仅供参考。各项指标最终数据，敬请关注各城市官方发布机构。

Note: 1. To facilitate ranking, the data regarding foreign investment actually used by Xiamen Guangzhou and Chengdu is calculated as per RMB caliber and average annual
2.The data regarding other cities in this table is sorted out according to internal data which is for reference only instead of being released officially. As for final data regarding various indicators, refer to official release mechanism in each city.

(100 million yuan)

金融机构本外币贷款余额 The Balance of RMB and Foreign Currencies Loans in Financial Institutions	社会消费品零售总额 Total Retail Sales of Consumer Goods	货物进出口总额 Total Import & Export	# 出口总额 Total Export	实际使用外资（亿美元）Actual Use of Foreign Capital (100 million USD)	城镇居民人均可支配收入（元）Per Capita Disposable Income of Urban Households (yuan)	农村居民人均可支配收入（元）Per Capita Disposable Income of Rural Households (yuan)	居民消费价格指数(%) Consumer Price Indices (%)
20720.2	4469.1	1382.7	755.0	19.2	53329	20432	102.4
18129.0	3637.6	1028.1	274.4	7.1	47413	19598	102.3
12952.4	–	3854.2	1672.6	6.6	47380	21558	102.1
14535.4	–	1027.6	135.4	3.8	40001	16636	101.9
12653.4	–	255.9	136.9	3.4	39791	19631	101.4
38190.0	7203.0	5340.2	3398.9	45.2	67553	29621	102.4
49799.0	5973.0	5934.2	3693.2	72.0	68666	38700	102.1
25451.6	4238.3	9786.9	6407.0	24.7	68008	39132	101.9
13424.7	2293.9	6915.8	3572.9	24.0	61331	26612	102.5
21064.8	5203.5	6407.0	3876.8	58.5	55905	23656	102.4
36856.0	6149.8	2704.3	1421.7	111.7	50362	24057	102.4
54387.6	9218.7	9530.1	5427.7	71.3	68304	31266	102.6
68020.5	8664.8	30502.5	16972.7	86.8	64878	–	102.3
41148.0	8118.5	7154.2	4106.9	73.7	48593	26432	102.5
25792.9	4989.3	3473.8	1776.0	76.8	43713	15749	102.1
10	9	12	12	11	8	10	6

附录三 二十六省会城市主要经济指标(2020年)
Main Statistical Indicators of 26 Provincial Capitals (2020)

单位：亿元

城市名称	Region	地区生产总值 Gross Dmoestic Product	第一产业 Primary Industry	第二产业 Secondary Industry	第三产业 Tertiary Industry	固定资产投资比上年增长(%) Growth Rate Investment in Fixed Assets (%)	房地产开发投资比上年增长(%) Growth Rate Estate Development Investment (%)	一般公共预算收入 General Pubilic Budget Revenue	一般公共预算支出 General Pubilic Budget Expenditure	金融机构本外币存款余额 The Balance of RMB and Foreign Currencies Deposits in Financial Institutions
济南	**Ji'nan**	**10140.9**	**361.7**	**3530.7**	**6248.6**	**4.0**	**8.3**	**906.1**	**1288.8**	**21065.0**
石家庄	Shijiazhuang	5935.1	498.6	1745.5	3691.0	–18.8	4.4	632.2	1135.3	16611.0
太原	Taiyuan	4153.3	32.2	1504.2	2616.8	11.3	2.4	378.4	647.4	14587.6
呼和浩特	Hohhot	2800.7	126.5	815.7	1858.5	–8.5	40.9	217.1	435.7	6165.5
沈阳	Shenyang	6571.6	303.6	2160.4	4107.6	4.1	5.2	736.1	1074.1	19442.5
长春	Changchun	6638.0	533.8	2758.1	3346.1	8.8	12.4	440.4	1084.1	14230.6
哈尔滨	Harbin	5183.8	615.8	1144.5	3423.5	2.8	0.3	339.6	1162.2	13856.7
南京	Nanjing	14818.0	296.8	5214.4	9306.8	6.6	5.2	1637.7	1754.6	40056.5
杭州	Hangzhou	16106.0	326.0	4821.0	10959.0	6.8	5.3	2093.0	2070.0	54246.0
合肥	Hefei	10045.7	332.3	3579.5	6133.9	4.7	–0.6	762.9	1164.8	18675.3
福州	Fuzhou	10020.0	560.7	3840.8	5618.6	9.6	14.2	675.6	950.2	1980.7
南昌	Nanchang	5745.5	235.3	2676.9	2833.4	8.8	6.4	483.9	838.1	13676.8
郑州	Zhengzhou	12003.0	156.9	4759.5	7086.6	3.6	2.4	1259.2	1721.3	25938.8
武汉	Wuhan	15616.1	402.2	5557.5	9656.4	–11.8	–6.4	1230.3	2407.2	31005.9
长沙	Changsha	12142.5	423.5	4739.3	6979.8	6.2	12.0	1100.1	1480.2	23316.8
广州	Guangzhou	25019.1	288.1	6590.4	18140.6	10.0	6.2	1721.6	2953.0	67798.8
南宁	Nanning	4726.3	534.4	1084.3	3107.7	–2.5	–5.7	263.6	819.9	11498.3
海口	Haikou	1791.6	79.9	269.6	1442.1	9.9	–7.7	186.1	305.4	5164.1
成都	Chengdu	17716.7	655.2	5418.5	11643.0	9.9	9.2	1520.4	2158.0	43654.0
贵阳	Guiyang	4311.7	178.3	1552.6	2580.8	2.7	10.1	398.1	676.4	12523.5
昆明	Kunming	6733.8	312.4	2102.9	4318.5	8.1	8.0	650.5	875.1	–
西安	Xi'an	10020.4	312.8	3328.3	6379.4	12.8	6.5	724.1	1352.7	26045.9
兰州	Lanzhou	2886.7	57.4	933.4	1895.9	3.4	0.1	247.1	485.7	8814.3
西宁	Xining	1373.0	57.2	418.7	897.1	–25.9	–7.1	133.5	329.5	4382.5
银川	Yinchuan	1964.4	75.7	832.6	1056.0	1.1	13.1	157.3	335.8	4500.6
乌鲁木齐	Urumqi	3337.3	27.1	907.9	2402.4	0.3	–2.1	392.6	536.9	9667.2
济南位次	Position	8	9	10	9	15	8	8	9	9

注：1. 为便于排序，昆明进出口总额、出口总额数据根据美元口径和年均汇率推算；福州、广州、成都实际使用外资数据根据人民币口径和年均汇率推算。
2. 本表内其他城市数据根据内部资料整理，不做正式发布，仅供参考。各项指标最终数据，敬请关注各城市官方发布机构。

(100 million yuan)

金融机构本外币贷款余额 The Balance of RMB and Foreign Currencies Loans in Financial Institutions	社会消费品零售总额 Total Retail Sales of Consumer Goods	货物进出口总额 Total Import & Export	# 出口总额 Total Export	实际使用外资（亿美元）Actual Use of Foreign Capital (100 million USD)	城镇居民人均可支配收入（元）Per Capita Disposable Income of Urban Households (yuan)	农村居民人均可支配收入（元）Per Capita Disposable Income of Rural Households (yuan)	居民消费价格指数 (%) Consumer Price Indices (%)
20720.2	4469.1	1382.7	755.0	19.2	53329	20432	102.4
13154.7	2382.7	1341.1	785.6	18.3	40247	16947	102.3
15079.9	1655.1	1211.5	724.7	1.0	38329	19655	102.6
8969.0	1032.9	116.7	72.4	3.9	49789	20489	102.0
18129.0	3637.6	1028.1	274.4	7.1	47413	19598	102.3
14535.4	–	1027.6	135.4	3.8	40001	16636	101.9
12653.4	–	255.9	136.9	3.4	39791	19631	101.4
38190.0	7203.0	5340.2	3398.9	45.2	67553	29621	102.4
49799.0	5973.0	5934.2	3693.2	72.0	68666	38700	102.1
18166.6	4513.8	2597.3	1580.8	36.0	48283	24282	102.3
2207.7	4225.6	2504.8	1786.5	10.9	49300	22669	102.4
16005.6	2452.7	1151.5	713.1	40.6	46796	20921	102.5
29566.3	5076.3	4946.4	2948.8	46.6	42887	24783	102.3
36856.0	6149.8	2704.3	1421.7	111.7	50362	24057	102.4
24261.3	4469.8	2350.5	1548.7	72.8	57971	34754	101.8
54387.6	9218.7	9530.1	5427.7	71.3	68304	31266	102.6
15868.8	2180.4	986.0	470.8	4.4	38542	16130	102.3
6491.0	835.9	368.3	110.3	17.2	40049	17405	101.6
41148.0	8118.5	7154.2	4106.9	73.7	48593	26432	102.5
15861.8	2188.3	231.1	358.0	20.2	40305	18674	101.6
–	3070.4	867.7	524.5	6.6	48018	17719	103.1
25792.9	4989.3	3473.8	1776.0	76.8	43713	15749	102.1
11269.2	1641.2	102.5	32.7	0.6	40152	14652	102.0
5354.4	573.6	16.8	7.1	–	36959	13487	102.7
5733.5	770.9	63.0	45.3	0.9	39416	16428	101.8
8693.4	1043.5	455.9	288.5	2.2	42769	22829	100.9
9	10	11	12	12	5	13	7

Note: 1.To facilitate ranking, total export-import volume and total export of Kunming are calculated pursuant to USD caliber and average annual exchange rate; The data regarding foreign investment actually used by Fuzhou Guangzhou and Chengdu is calculated in terms of RMB caliber and average annual exchange rate.

2.The data regarding other cities in this table is sorted out according to internal data which is for reference only instead of being released officially. As for final data regarding various indicators, refer to official release mechanism in each city.

附录四

中华人民共和国统计法

Statistical Law of The People's Republic of China

（1983年12月8日第六届全国人民代表大会常务委员会第三次会议通过 根据1996年5月15日第八届全国人民代表大会常务委员会第十九次会议《关于修改〈中华人民共和国统计法〉的决定》修正 2009年6月27日第十一届全国人民代表大会常务委员会第九次会议修订）

目 录

第一章 总 则

第一条 为了科学、有效地组织统计工作，保障统计资料的真实性、准确性、完整性和及时性，发挥统计在了解国情国力、服务经济社会发展中的重要作用，促进社会主义现代化建设事业发展，制定本法。

第二条 本法适用于各级人民政府、县级以上人民政府统计机构和有关部门组织实施的统计活动。

统计的基本任务是对经济社会发展情况进行统计调查、统计分析，提供统计资料和统计咨询意见，实行统计监督。

第三条 国家建立集中统一的统计系统，实行统一领导、分级负责的统计管理体制。

第四条 国务院和地方各级人民政府、各有关部门应当加强对统计工作的组织领导，为统计工作提供必要的保障。

第五条 国家加强统计科学研究，健全科学的统计指标体系，不断改进统计调查方法，提高统计的科学性。

国家有计划地加强统计信息化建设，推进统计信息搜集、处理、传输、共享、存储技术和统计数据库体系的现代化。

第六条 统计机构和统计人员依照本法规定独立行使统计调查、统计报告、统计监督的职权，不受侵犯。

地方各级人民政府、政府统计机构和有关部门以及各单位的负责人，不得自行修改统计机构和统计人员依法搜集、整理的统计资料，不得以任何方式要求统计机构、统计人员及其他机构、人员伪造、篡改统计资料，不得对依法履行职责或者拒绝、抵制统计违法行为的统计人员打击报复。

第七条 国家机关、企业事业单位和其他组织以及个体工商户和个人等统计调查对象，必须依照本法和国家有关规定，真实、准确、完整、及时地提供统计调查所需的资料，不得提供不真实或者不完整的统计资料，不得迟报、拒报统计资料。

第八条 统计工作应当接受社会公众的监督。任何单位和个人有权检举统计中弄虚作假等违法行为。对检举有功的单位和个人应当给予表彰和奖励。

第九条 统计机构和统计人员对在统计工作中知悉的国家秘密、商业秘密和个人信息，应当予以保密。

第十条 任何单位和个人不得利用虚假统计资料骗取荣誉称号、物质利益或者职务晋升。

第二章 统计调查管理

第十一条 统计调查项目包括国家统计调查项目、部门统计调查项目和地方统计调查项目。

国家统计调查项目是指全国性基本情况的统计调查项目。部门统计调查项目是指国务院有关部门的专业性统计调查项目。地方统计调查项目是指县级以上地方人民政府及其部门的地方性统计调查项目。

国家统计调查项目、部门统计调查项目、地方统计调查项目应当明确分工，互相衔接，不得重复。

第十二条 国家统计调查项目由国家统计局制定，或者由国家统计局和国务院有关部门共同制定，报国务院备案；重大的国家统计调查项目报国务院审批。

部门统计调查项目由国务院有关部门制定。统计调查对象属于本部门管辖系统的，报国家统计局备案；统计调查对象超出本部门管辖系统的，报国家统计局审批。

地方统计调查项目由县级以上地方人民政府统计机构和有关部门分别制定或者共同制定。其中，由省级人民政府统计机构单独制定或者和有关部门共同制定的，报国家统计局审批；由省级以下人民政府统计机构单独制定或者和有关部门共同制定的，报省级人民政府统计机构审批；由县级以上地方人民政府有关部门制定的，报本级人民政府统计机构审批。

第十三条 统计调查项目的审批机关应当对调查项目的必

要性、可行性、科学性进行审查，对符合法定条件的，作出予以批准的书面决定，并公布；对不符合法定条件的，作出不予批准的书面决定，并说明理由。

第十四条 制定统计调查项目，应当同时制定该项目的统计调查制度，并依照本法第十二条的规定一并报经审批或者备案。

统计调查制度应当对调查目的、调查内容、调查方法、调查对象、调查组织方式、调查表式、统计资料的报送和公布等作出规定。

统计调查应当按照统计调查制度组织实施。变更统计调查制度的内容，应当报经原审批机关批准或者原备案机关备案。

第十五条 统计调查表应当标明表号、制定机关、批准或者备案文号、有效期限等标志。

对未标明前款规定的标志或者超过有效期限的统计调查表，统计调查对象有权拒绝填报；县级以上人民政府统计机构应当依法责令停止有关统计调查活动。

第十六条 搜集、整理统计资料，应当以周期性普查为基础，以经常性抽样调查为主体，综合运用全面调查、重点调查等方法，并充分利用行政记录等资料。

重大国情国力普查由国务院统一领导，国务院和地方人民政府组织统计机构和有关部门共同实施。

第十七条 国家制定统一的统计标准，保障统计调查采用的指标涵义、计算方法、分类目录、调查表式和统计编码等的标准化。

国家统计标准由国家统计局制定，或者由国家统计局和国务院标准化主管部门共同制定。

国务院有关部门可以制定补充性的部门统计标准，报国家统计局审批。部门统计标准不得与国家统计标准相抵触。

第十八条 县级以上人民政府统计机构根据统计任务的需要，可以在统计调查对象中推广使用计算机网络报送统计资料。

第十九条 县级以上人民政府应当将统计工作所需经费列入财政预算。

重大国情国力普查所需经费，由国务院和地方人民政府共同负担，列入相应年度的财政预算，按时拨付，确保到位。

第三章　统计资料的管理和公布

第二十条 县级以上人民政府统计机构和有关部门以及乡、镇人民政府，应当按照国家有关规定建立统计资料的保存、管理制度，建立健全统计信息共享机制。

第二十一条 国家机关、企业事业单位和其他组织等统计调查对象，应当按照国家有关规定设置原始记录、统计台账，建立健全统计资料的审核、签署、交接、归档等管理制度。

统计资料的审核、签署人员应当对其审核、签署的统计资料的真实性、准确性和完整性负责。

第二十二条 县级以上人民政府有关部门应当及时向本级人民政府统计机构提供统计所需的行政记录资料和国民经济核算所需的财务资料、财政资料及其他资料，并按照统计调查制度的规定及时向本级人民政府统计机构报送其组织实施统计调查取得的有关资料。

县级以上人民政府统计机构应当及时向本级人民政府有关部门提供有关统计资料。

第二十三条 县级以上人民政府统计机构按照国家有关规定，定期公布统计资料。

国家统计数据以国家统计局公布的数据为准。

第二十四条 县级以上人民政府有关部门统计调查取得的统计资料，由本部门按照国家有关规定公布。

第二十五条 统计调查中获得的能够识别或者推断单个统计调查对象身份的资料，任何单位和个人不得对外提供、泄露，不得用于统计以外的目的。

第二十六条 县级以上人民政府统计机构和有关部门统计调查取得的统计资料，除依法应当保密的外，应当及时公开，供社会公众查询。

第四章　统计机构和统计人员

第二十七条 国务院设立国家统计局，依法组织领导和协调全国的统计工作。

国家统计局根据工作需要设立的派出调查机构，承担国家统计局布置的统计调查等任务。

县级以上地方人民政府设立独立的统计机构，乡、镇人民政府设置统计工作岗位，配备专职或者兼职统计人员，依法管理、开展统计工作，实施统计调查。

第二十八条 县级以上人民政府有关部门根据统计任务的需要设立统计机构，或者在有关机构中设置统计人员，并指定统计负责人，依法组织、管理本部门职责范围内的统计工作，实施统计调查，在统计业务上受本级人民政府统计机构的指导。

第二十九条 统计机构、统计人员应当依法履行职责，如实搜集、报送统计资料，不得伪造、篡改统计资料，不得以任何方式要求任何单位和个人提供不真实的统计资料，不得有其他违反本法规定的行为。

统计人员应当坚持实事求是，恪守职业道德，对其负责搜集、审核、录入的统计资料与统计调查对象报送的统计资料的一致性负责。

第三十条 统计人员进行统计调查时，有权就与统计有关的问题询问有关人员，要求其如实提供有关情况、资料并改正不真实、不准确的资料。

统计人员进行统计调查时，应当出示县级以上人民政府统计机构或者有关部门颁发的工作证件；未出示的，统计调查对象有权拒绝调查。

第三十一条 国家实行统计专业技术职务资格考试、评聘制度，提高统计人员的专业素质，保障统计队伍的稳定性。

统计人员应当具备与其从事的统计工作相适应的专业知识和业务能力。

县级以上人民政府统计机构和有关部门应当加强对统计人员的专业培训和职业道德教育。

第五章　监督检查

第三十二条　县级以上人民政府及其监察机关对下级人民政府、本级人民政府统计机构和有关部门执行本法的情况，实施监督。

第三十三条　国家统计局组织管理全国统计工作的监督检查，查处重大统计违法行为。

县级以上地方人民政府统计机构依法查处本行政区域内发生的统计违法行为。但是，国家统计局派出的调查机构组织实施的统计调查活动中发生的统计违法行为，由组织实施该项统计调查的调查机构负责查处。

法律、行政法规对有关部门查处统计违法行为另有规定的，从其规定。

第三十四条　县级以上人民政府有关部门应当积极协助本级人民政府统计机构查处统计违法行为，及时向本级人民政府统计机构移送有关统计违法案件材料。

第三十五条　县级以上人民政府统计机构在调查统计违法行为或者核查统计数据时，有权采取下列措施：

（一）发出统计检查查询书，向检查对象查询有关事项；

（二）要求检查对象提供有关原始记录和凭证、统计台账、统计调查表、会计资料及其他相关证明和资料；

（三）就与检查有关的事项询问有关人员；

（四）进入检查对象的业务场所和统计数据处理信息系统进行检查、核对；

（五）经本机构负责人批准，登记保存检查对象的有关原始记录和凭证、统计台账、统计调查表、会计资料及其他相关证明和资料；

（六）对与检查事项有关的情况和资料进行记录、录音、录像、照相和复制。

县级以上人民政府统计机构进行监督检查时，监督检查人员不得少于二人，并应当出示执法证件；未出示的，有关单位和个人有权拒绝检查。

第三十六条　县级以上人民政府统计机构履行监督检查职责时，有关单位和个人应当如实反映情况，提供相关证明和资料，不得拒绝、阻碍检查，不得转移、隐匿、篡改、毁弃原始记录和凭证、统计台账、统计调查表、会计资料及其他相关证明和资料。

第六章　法律责任

第三十七条　地方人民政府、政府统计机构或者有关部门、单位的负责人有下列行为之一的，由任免机关或者监察机关依法给予处分，并由县级以上人民政府统计机构予以通报：

（一）自行修改统计资料、编造虚假统计数据的；

（二）要求统计机构、统计人员或者其他机构、人员伪造、篡改统计资料的；

（三）对依法履行职责或者拒绝、抵制统计违法行为的统计人员打击报复的；

（四）对本地方、本部门、本单位发生的严重统计违法行为失察的。

第三十八条　县级以上人民政府统计机构或者有关部门在组织实施统计调查活动中有下列行为之一的，由本级人民政府、上级人民政府统计机构或者本级人民政府统计机构责令改正，予以通报；对直接负责的主管人员和其他直接责任人员，由任免机关或者监察机关依法给予处分：

（一）未经批准擅自组织实施统计调查的；

（二）未经批准擅自变更统计调查制度的内容的；

（三）伪造、篡改统计资料的；

（四）要求统计调查对象或者其他机构、人员提供不真实的统计资料的；

（五）未按照统计调查制度的规定报送有关资料的。

统计人员有前款第三项至第五项所列行为之一的，责令改正，依法给予处分。

第三十九条　县级以上人民政府统计机构或者有关部门有下列行为之一的，对直接负责的主管人员和其他直接责任人员由任免机关或者监察机关依法给予处分：

（一）违法公布统计资料的；

（二）泄露统计调查对象的商业秘密、个人信息或者提供、泄露在统计调查中获得的能够识别或者推断单个统计调查对象身份的资料的；

（三）违反国家有关规定，造成统计资料毁损、灭失的。

统计人员有前款所列行为之一的，依法给予处分。

第四十条　统计机构、统计人员泄露国家秘密的，依法追究法律责任。

第四十一条　作为统计调查对象的国家机关、企业事业单位或者其他组织有下列行为之一的，由县级以上人民政府统计机构责令改正，给予警告，可以予以通报；其直接负责的主管人员和其他直接责任人员属于国家工作人员的，由任免机关或者监察机关依法给予处分：

（一）拒绝提供统计资料或者经催报后仍未按时提供统计资料的；

（二）提供不真实或者不完整的统计资料的；

（三）拒绝答复或者不如实答复统计检查查询书的；

（四）拒绝、阻碍统计调查、统计检查的；

（五）转移、隐匿、篡改、毁弃或者拒绝提供原始记录和凭证、统计台账、统计调查表及其他相关证明和资料的。

企业事业单位或者其他组织有前款所列行为之一的，可以并处五万元以下的罚款；情节严重的，并处五万元以上二十万元以下的罚款。

个体工商户有本条第一款所列行为之一的，由县级以上人民政府统计机构责令改正，给予警告，可以并处一万元以下的罚款。

第四十二条　作为统计调查对象的国家机关、企业事业单位或者其他组织迟报统计资料，或者未按照国家有关规定设置原始记录、统计台账的，由县级以上人民政府统计机构责令改正，给予警告。

企业事业单位或者其他组织有前款所列行为之一的，可以并处一万元以下的罚款。

个体工商户迟报统计资料的，由县级以上人民政府统计机构责令改正，给予警告，可以并处一千元以下的罚款。

第四十三条 县级以上人民政府统计机构查处统计违法行为时，认为对有关国家工作人员依法应当给予处分的，应当提出给予处分的建议；该国家工作人员的任免机关或者监察机关应当依法及时作出决定，并将结果书面通知县级以上人民政府统计机构。

第四十四条 作为统计调查对象的个人在重大国情国力普查活动中拒绝、阻碍统计调查，或者提供不真实或者不完整的普查资料的，由县级以上人民政府统计机构责令改正，予以批评教育。

第四十五条 违反本法规定，利用虚假统计资料骗取荣誉称号、物质利益或者职务晋升的，除对其编造虚假统计资料或者要求他人编造虚假统计资料的行为依法追究法律责任外，由作出有关决定的单位或者其上级单位、监察机关取消其荣誉称号，追缴获得的物质利益，撤销晋升的职务。

第四十六条 当事人对县级以上人民政府统计机构作出的行政处罚决定不服的，可以依法申请行政复议或者提起行政诉讼。其中，对国家统计局在省、自治区、直辖市派出的调查机构作出的行政处罚决定不服的，向国家统计局申请行政复议；对国家统计局派出的其他调查机构作出的行政处罚决定不服的，向国家统计局在该派出机构所在的省、自治区、直辖市派出的调查机构申请行政复议。

第四十七条 违反本法规定，构成犯罪的，依法追究刑事责任。

第七章 附 则

第四十八条 本法所称县级以上人民政府统计机构，是指国家统计局及其派出的调查机构、县级以上地方人民政府统计机构。

第四十九条 民间统计调查活动的管理办法，由国务院制定。

中华人民共和国境外的组织、个人需要在中华人民共和国境内进行统计调查活动的，应当按照国务院的规定报请审批。

利用统计调查危害国家安全、损害社会公共利益或者进行欺诈活动的，依法追究法律责任。

第五十条 本法自2010年1月1日起施行。

附录五

中华人民共和国统计法实施条例

Regulations for the Implementation of the Statistics Law of the People's Republic of China

中华人民共和国国务院令

第 681 号

《中华人民共和国统计法实施条例》已经 2017 年 4 月 12 日国务院第 168 次常务会议通过，现予公布，自 2017 年 8 月 1 日起施行。

总理　李克强

2017 年 5 月 28 日

中华人民共和国统计法实施条例

第一章　总　则

第一条　根据《中华人民共和国统计法》（以下简称统计法），制定本条例。

第二条　统计资料能够通过行政记录取得的，不得组织实施调查。通过抽样调查、重点调查能够满足统计需要的，不得组织实施全面调查。

第三条　县级以上人民政府统计机构和有关部门应当加强统计规律研究，健全新兴产业等统计，完善经济、社会、科技、资源和环境统计，推进互联网、大数据、云计算等现代信息技术在统计工作中的应用，满足经济社会发展需要。

第四条　地方人民政府、县级以上人民政府统计机构和有关部门应当根据国家有关规定，明确本单位防范和惩治统计造假、弄虚作假的责任主体，严格执行统计法和本条例的规定。

地方人民政府、县级以上人民政府统计机构和有关部门及其负责人应当保障统计活动依法进行，不得侵犯统计机构、统计人员独立行使统计调查、统计报告、统计监督职权，不得非法干预统计调查对象提供统计资料，不得统计造假、弄虚作假。

统计调查对象应当依照统计法和国家有关规定，真实、准确、完整、及时地提供统计资料，拒绝、抵制弄虚作假等违法行为。

第五条　县级以上人民政府统计机构和有关部门不得组织实施营利性统计调查。

国家有计划地推进县级以上人民政府统计机构和有关部门通过向社会购买服务组织实施统计调查和资料开发。

第二章　统计调查项目

第六条　部门统计调查项目、地方统计调查项目的主要内容不得与国家统计调查项目的内容重复、矛盾。

第七条　统计调查项目的制定机关（以下简称制定机关）应当就项目的必要性、可行性、科学性进行论证，征求有关地方、部门、统计调查对象和专家的意见，并由制定机关按照会议制度集体讨论决定。

重要统计调查项目应当进行试点。

第八条　制定机关申请审批统计调查项目，应当以公文形式向审批机关提交统计调查项目审批申请表、项目的统计调查制度和工作经费来源说明。

申请材料不齐全或者不符合法定形式的，审批机关应当一次性告知需要补正的全部内容，制定机关应当按照审批机关的要求予以补正。

申请材料齐全、符合法定形式的，审批机关应当受理。

第九条　统计调查项目符合下列条件的，审批机关应当作出予以批准的书面决定：

（一）具有法定依据或者确为公共管理和服务所必需；

（二）与已批准或者备案的统计调查项目的主要内容不重复、不矛盾；

（三）主要统计指标无法通过行政记录或者已有统计调查资料加工整理取得；

（四）统计调查制度符合统计法律法规规定，科学、合理、

可行;

（五）采用的统计标准符合国家有关规定;

（六）制定机关具备项目执行能力。

不符合前款规定条件的，审批机关应当向制定机关提出修改意见；修改后仍不符合前款规定条件的，审批机关应当作出不予批准的书面决定并说明理由。

第十条 统计调查项目涉及其他部门职责的，审批机关应当在作出审批决定前，征求相关部门的意见。

第十一条 审批机关应当自受理统计调查项目审批申请之日起20日内作出决定。20日内不能作出决定的，经审批机关负责人批准可以延长10日，并应当将延长审批期限的理由告知制定机关。

制定机关修改统计调查项目的时间，不计算在审批期限内。

第十二条 制定机关申请备案统计调查项目，应当以公文形式向备案机关提交统计调查项目备案申请表和项目的统计调查制度。

统计调查项目的调查对象属于制定机关管辖系统，且主要内容与已批准、备案的统计调查项目不重复、不矛盾的，备案机关应当依法给予备案文号。

第十三条 统计调查项目经批准或者备案的，审批机关或者备案机关应当及时公布统计调查项目及其统计调查制度的主要内容。涉及国家秘密的统计调查项目除外。

第十四条 统计调查项目有下列情形之一的，审批机关或者备案机关应当简化审批或者备案程序，缩短期限:

（一）发生突发事件需要迅速实施统计调查;

（二）统计调查制度内容未作变动，统计调查项目有效期届满需要延长期限。

第十五条 统计法第十七条第二款规定的国家统计标准是强制执行标准。各级人民政府、县级以上人民政府统计机构和有关部门组织实施的统计调查活动，应当执行国家统计标准。

制定国家统计标准，应当征求国务院有关部门的意见。

第三章 统计调查的组织实施

第十六条 统计机构、统计人员组织实施统计调查，应当就统计调查对象的法定填报义务、主要指标涵义和有关填报要求等，向统计调查对象作出说明。

第十七条 国家机关、企业事业单位或者其他组织等统计调查对象提供统计资料，应当由填报人员和单位负责人签字，并加盖公章。个人作为统计调查对象提供统计资料，应当由本人签字。统计调查制度规定不需要签字、加盖公章的除外。

统计调查对象使用网络提供统计资料的，按照国家有关规定执行。

第十八条 县级以上人民政府统计机构、有关部门推广使用网络报送统计资料，应当采取有效的网络安全保障措施。

第十九条 县级以上人民政府统计机构、有关部门和乡、镇统计人员，应当对统计调查对象提供的统计资料进行审核。统计资料不完整或者存在明显错误的，应当由统计调查对象依法予以补充或者改正。

第二十条 国家统计局应当建立健全统计数据质量监控和评估制度，加强对各省、自治区、直辖市重要统计数据的监控和评估。

第四章 统计资料的管理和公布

第二十一条 县级以上人民政府统计机构、有关部门和乡、镇人民政府应当妥善保管统计调查中取得的统计资料。

国家建立统计资料灾难备份系统。

第二十二条 统计调查中取得的统计调查对象的原始资料，应当至少保存2年。

汇总性统计资料应当至少保存10年，重要的汇总性统计资料应当永久保存。法律法规另有规定的，从其规定。

第二十三条 统计调查对象按照国家有关规定设置的原始记录和统计台账，应当至少保存2年。

第二十四条 国家统计局统计调查取得的全国性统计数据和分省、自治区、直辖市统计数据，由国家统计局公布或者由国家统计局授权其派出的调查机构或者省级人民政府统计机构公布。

第二十五条 国务院有关部门统计调查取得的统计数据，由国务院有关部门按照国家有关规定和已批准或者备案的统计调查制度公布。

县级以上地方人民政府有关部门公布其统计调查取得的统计数据，比照前款规定执行。

第二十六条 已公布的统计数据按照国家有关规定需要进行修订的，县级以上人民政府统计机构和有关部门应当及时公布修订后的数据，并就修订依据和情况作出说明。

第二十七条 县级以上人民政府统计机构和有关部门应当及时公布主要统计指标涵义、调查范围、调查方法、计算方法、抽样调查样本量等信息，对统计数据进行解释说明。

第二十八条 公布统计资料应当按照国家有关规定进行。公布前，任何单位和个人不得违反国家有关规定对外提供，不得利用尚未公布的统计资料谋取不正当利益。

第二十九条 统计法第二十五条规定的能够识别或者推断单个统计调查对象身份的资料包括:

（一）直接标明单个统计调查对象身份的资料;

（二）虽未直接标明单个统计调查对象身份，但是通过已标明的地址、编码等相关信息可以识别或者推断单个统计调查对象身份的资料;

（三）可以推断单个统计调查对象身份的汇总资料。

第三十条 统计调查中获得的能够识别或者推断单个统计调查对象身份的资料应当依法严格管理，除作为统计执法依据外，不得直接作为对统计调查对象实施行政许可、行政处罚等具体行政行为的依据，不得用于完成统计任务以外的目的。

第三十一条 国家建立健全统计信息共享机制，实现县级以上人民政府统计机构和有关部门统计调查取得的资料共享。制定机关共同制定的统计调查项目，可以共同使用获取的统计资料。

统计调查制度应当对统计信息共享的内容、方式、时限、渠道和责任等作出规定。

第五章　统计机构和统计人员

第三十二条　县级以上地方人民政府统计机构受本级人民政府和上级人民政府统计机构的双重领导，在统计业务上以上级人民政府统计机构的领导为主。

乡、镇人民政府应当设置统计工作岗位，配备专职或者兼职统计人员，履行统计职责，在统计业务上受上级人民政府统计机构领导。乡、镇统计人员的调动，应当征得县级人民政府统计机构的同意。

县级以上人民政府有关部门在统计业务上受本级人民政府统计机构指导。

第三十三条　县级以上人民政府统计机构和有关部门应当完成国家统计调查任务，执行国家统计调查项目的统计调查制度，组织实施本地方、本部门的统计调查活动。

第三十四条　国家机关、企业事业单位和其他组织应当加强统计基础工作，为履行法定的统计资料报送义务提供组织、人员和工作条件保障。

第三十五条　对在统计工作中做出突出贡献、取得显著成绩的单位和个人，按照国家有关规定给予表彰和奖励。

第六章　监督检查

第三十六条　县级以上人民政府统计机构从事统计执法工作的人员，应当具备必要的法律知识和统计业务知识，参加统计执法培训，并取得由国家统计局统一印制的统计执法证。

第三十七条　任何单位和个人不得拒绝、阻碍对统计工作的监督检查和对统计违法行为的查处工作，不得包庇、纵容统计违法行为。

第三十八条　任何单位和个人有权向县级以上人民政府统计机构举报统计违法行为。

县级以上人民政府统计机构应当公布举报统计违法行为的方式和途径，依法受理、核实、处理举报，并为举报人保密。

第三十九条　县级以上人民政府统计机构负责查处统计违法行为；法律、行政法规对有关部门查处统计违法行为另有规定的，从其规定。

第七章　法律责任

第四十条　下列情形属于统计法第三十七条第四项规定的对严重统计违法行为失察，对地方人民政府、政府统计机构或者有关部门、单位的负责人，由任免机关或者监察机关依法给予处分，并由县级以上人民政府统计机构予以通报：

（一）本地方、本部门、本单位大面积发生或者连续发生统计造假、弄虚作假；

（二）本地方、本部门、本单位统计数据严重失实，应当发现而未发现；

（三）发现本地方、本部门、本单位统计数据严重失实不予纠正。

第四十一条　县级以上人民政府统计机构或者有关部门组织实施营利性统计调查的，由本级人民政府、上级人民政府统计机构或者本级人民政府统计机构责令改正，予以通报；有违法所得的，没收违法所得。

第四十二条　地方各级人民政府、县级以上人民政府统计机构或者有关部门及其负责人，侵犯统计机构、统计人员独立行使统计调查、统计报告、统计监督职权，或者采用下发文件、会议布置以及其他方式授意、指使、强令统计调查对象或者其他单位、人员编造虚假统计资料的，由上级人民政府、本级人民政府、上级人民政府统计机构或者本级人民政府统计机构责令改正，予以通报。

第四十三条　县级以上人民政府统计机构或者有关部门在组织实施统计调查活动中有下列行为之一的，由本级人民政府、上级人民政府统计机构或者本级人民政府统计机构责令改正，予以通报：

（一）违法制定、审批或者备案统计调查项目；

（二）未按照规定公布经批准或者备案的统计调查项目及其统计调查制度的主要内容；

（三）未执行国家统计标准；

（四）未执行统计调查制度；

（五）自行修改单个统计调查对象的统计资料。

乡、镇统计人员有前款第三项至第五项所列行为的，责令改正，依法给予处分。

第四十四条　县级以上人民政府统计机构或者有关部门违反本条例第二十四条、第二十五条规定公布统计数据的，由本级人民政府、上级人民政府统计机构或者本级人民政府统计机构责令改正，予以通报。

第四十五条　违反国家有关规定对外提供尚未公布的统计资料或者利用尚未公布的统计资料谋取不正当利益的，由任免机关或者监察机关依法给予处分，并由县级以上人民政府统计机构予以通报。

第四十六条　统计机构及其工作人员有下列行为之一的，由本级人民政府或者上级人民政府统计机构责令改正，予以通报：

（一）拒绝、阻碍对统计工作的监督检查和对统计违法行为的查处工作；

（二）包庇、纵容统计违法行为；

（三）向有统计违法行为的单位或者个人通风报信，帮助其逃避查处；

（四）未依法受理、核实、处理对统计违法行为的举报；

（五）泄露对统计违法行为的举报情况。

第四十七条　地方各级人民政府、县级以上人民政府有关部门拒绝、阻碍统计监督检查或者转移、隐匿、篡改、毁弃原始记录和凭证、统计台账、统计调查表及其他相关证明和资料的，由上级人民政府、上级人民政府统计机构或者本级人民政府统计机构责令改正，予以通报。

第四十八条 地方各级人民政府、县级以上人民政府统计机构和有关部门有本条例第四十一条至第四十七条所列违法行为之一的，对直接负责的主管人员和其他直接责任人员，由任免机关或者监察机关依法给予处分。

第四十九条 乡、镇人民政府有统计法第三十八条第一款、第三十九条第一款所列行为之一的，依照统计法第三十八条、第三十九条的规定追究法律责任。

第五十条 下列情形属于统计法第四十一条第二款规定的情节严重行为：

（一）使用暴力或者威胁方法拒绝、阻碍统计调查、统计监督检查；

（二）拒绝、阻碍统计调查、统计监督检查，严重影响相关工作正常开展；

（三）提供不真实、不完整的统计资料，造成严重后果或者恶劣影响；

（四）有统计法第四十一条第一款所列违法行为之一，1年内被责令改正3次以上。

第五十一条 统计违法行为涉嫌犯罪的，县级以上人民政府统计机构应当将案件移送司法机关处理。

第八章 附 则

第五十二条 中华人民共和国境外的组织、个人需要在中华人民共和国境内进行统计调查活动的，应当委托中华人民共和国境内具有涉外统计调查资格的机构进行。涉外统计调查资格应当依法报经批准。统计调查范围限于省、自治区、直辖市行政区域内的，由省级人民政府统计机构审批；统计调查范围跨省、自治区、直辖市行政区域的，由国家统计局审批。

涉外社会调查项目应当依法报经批准。统计调查范围限于省、自治区、直辖市行政区域内的，由省级人民政府统计机构审批；统计调查范围跨省、自治区、直辖市行政区域的，由国家统计局审批。

第五十三条 国家统计局或者省级人民政府统计机构对涉外统计违法行为进行调查，有权采取统计法第三十五条规定的措施。

第五十四条 对违法从事涉外统计调查活动的单位、个人，由国家统计局或者省级人民政府统计机构责令改正或者责令停止调查，有违法所得的，没收违法所得；违法所得50万元以上的，并处违法所得1倍以上3倍以下的罚款；违法所得不足50万元或者没有违法所得的，处200万元以下的罚款；情节严重的，暂停或者取消涉外统计调查资格，撤销涉外社会调查项目批准决定；构成犯罪的，依法追究刑事责任。

第五十五条 本条例自2017年8月1日起施行。1987年1月19日国务院批准、1987年2月15日国家统计局公布，2000年6月2日国务院批准修订、2000年6月15日国家统计局公布，2005年12月16日国务院修订的《中华人民共和国统计法实施细则》同时废止。

附录六

统计违法违纪行为处分规定

Statistics Regulation Violations of Law

中华人民共和国监察部
中华人民共和国人力资源和社会保障部 令
国家统计局

第 18 号

《统计违法违纪行为处分规定》已经监察部2009年2月9日第一次部长办公会议、人力资源社会保障部2008年12月30日第十六次部务会议、国家统计局2008年11月6日第十八次局务会议审议通过。现予公布，自2009年5月1日起施行。

监察部部长 马 馼
人力资源社会保障部部长 尹蔚民
国家统计局局长 马建堂
二〇〇九年三月二十五日

统计违法违纪行为处分规定

第一条 为了加强统计工作，提高统计数据的准确性和及时性，惩处和预防统计违法违纪行为，促进统计法律法规的贯彻实施，根据《中华人民共和国统计法》、《中华人民共和国行政监察法》、《中华人民共和国公务员法》、《行政机关公务员处分条例》及其他有关法律、行政法规，制定本规定。

第二条 有统计违法违纪行为的单位中负有责任的领导人员和直接责任人员，以及有统计违法违纪行为的个人，应当承担纪律责任。属于下列人员的（以下统称有关责任人员），由任免机关或者监察机关按照管理权限依法给予处分：

（一）行政机关公务员；

（二）法律、法规授权的具有公共事务管理职能的事业单位中经批准参照《中华人民共和国公务员法》管理的工作人员；

（三）行政机关依法委托的组织中除工勤人员以外的工作人员；

（四）企业、事业单位、社会团体中由行政机关任命的人员。

法律、行政法规、国务院决定和国务院监察机关、国务院人力资源社会保障部门制定的处分规章对统计违法违纪行为的处分另有规定的，从其规定。

第三条 地方、部门以及企业、事业单位、社会团体的领导人员有下列行为之一的，给予记过或者记大过处分；情节较重的，给予降级或者撤职处分；情节严重的，给予开除处分：

（一）自行修改统计资料、编造虚假数据的；

（二）强令、授意本地区、本部门、本单位统计机构、统计人员或者其他有关机构、人员拒报、虚报、瞒报或者篡改统计资料、编造虚假数据的；

（三）对拒绝、抵制篡改统计资料或者对拒绝、抵制编造虚假数据的人员进行打击报复的；

（四）对揭发、检举统计违法违纪行为的人员进行打击报复的。

有前款第（三）项、第（四）项规定行为的，应当从重处分。

第四条 地方、部门以及企业、事业单位、社会团体的领导人员，对本地区、本部门、本单位严重失实的统计数据，应当发现而未发现或者发现后不予纠正，造成不良后果的，给予警告或者记过处分；造成严重后果的，给予记大过或者降级处分；造成特别严重后果的，给予撤职或者开除处分。

第五条 各级人民政府统计机构、有关部门及其工作人员在实施统计调查活动中，有下列行为之一的，对有关责任人员，给予记过或者记大过处分；情节较重的，给予降级或者撤职处分；情节严重的，给予开除处分：

（一）强令、授意统计调查对象虚报、瞒报或者伪造、篡改统计资料的；

（二）参与篡改统计资料、编造虚假数据的。

第六条 各级人民政府统计机构、有关部门及其工作人员在实施统计调查活动中，有下列行为之一的，对有关责任人员，给予警告、记过或者记大过处分；情节较重的，给予降级处分；情节严重的，给予撤职处分：

（一）故意拖延或者拒报统计资料的；

（二）明知统计数据不实，不履行职责调查核实，造成不良后果的。

第七条 统计调查对象中的单位有下列行为之一，情节较重的，对有关责任人员，给予警告、记过或者记大过处分；情节严重的，给予降级或者撤职处分；情节特别严重的，给予开除处分：

（一）虚报、瞒报统计资料的；

（二）伪造、篡改统计资料的；

（三）拒报或者屡次迟报统计资料的；

（四）拒绝提供情况、提供虚假情况或者转移、隐匿、毁弃原始统计记录、统计台账、统计报表以及与统计有关的其他资料的。

第八条 违反国家规定的权限和程序公布统计资料，造成不良后果的，对有关责任人员，给予警告或者记过处分；情节较重的，给予记大过或者降级处分；情节严重的，给予撤职处分。

第九条 有下列行为之一，造成不良后果的，对有关责任人员，给予警告、记过或者记大过处分；情节较重的，给予降级或者撤职处分；情节严重的，给予开除处分：

（一）泄露属于国家秘密的统计资料的；

（二）未经本人同意，泄露统计调查对象个人、家庭资料的；

（三）泄露统计调查中知悉的统计调查对象商业秘密的。

第十条 包庇、纵容统计违法违纪行为的，对有关责任人员，给予记过或者记大过处分；情节较重的，给予降级或者撤职处分；情节严重的，给予开除处分。

第十一条 受到处分的人员对处分决定不服的，依照《中华人民共和国行政监察法》、《中华人民共和国公务员法》、《行政机关公务员处分条例》等有关规定，可以申请复核或者申诉。

第十二条 任免机关、监察机关和人民政府统计机构建立案件移送制度。

任免机关、监察机关查处统计违法违纪案件，认为应当由人民政府统计机构给予行政处罚的，应当将有关案件材料移送人民政府统计机构。人民政府统计机构应当依法及时查处，并将处理结果书面告知任免机关、监察机关。

人民政府统计机构查处统计行政违法案件，认为应当由任免机关或者监察机关给予处分的，应当及时将有关案件材料移送任免机关或者监察机关。任免机关或者监察机关应当依法及时查处，并将处理结果书面告知人民政府统计机构。

第十三条 有统计违法违纪行为，应当给予党纪处分的，移送党的纪律检查机关处理。涉嫌犯罪的，移送司法机关依法追究刑事责任。

第十四条 本规定由监察部、人力资源社会保障部、国家统计局负责解释。

第十五条 本规定自 2009 年 5 月 1 日起施行。

附录七

济南市统计局 2020 年统计大事要事

Chronicle of Events of Jinan Statistical Undertaking

1 月 2 日，济南市局组织 8 名志愿者开展文明交通志愿服务活动。济南市统计局党组书记、局长苑子建和执勤带班领导、党组成员、副局长卜繁钢前往执勤路口进行现场指导，了解路口的交通状况，提醒同志们要注意自身安全，同时更要做到文明服务，体现机关干部的精神风貌，引导群众文明出行、依规出行，以身作则为文明城市建设助力加油。

1 月 14 日，济南市统计局党组成员、副局长孙夕良带领相关人员，到莱芜区苗山镇调研协调推进脱贫攻坚工作。

1 月 15 日，济南市统计局党组成员、副局长张兴利带领有关人员到“第一书记”帮扶村莱芜区雪野镇狂山村开展春节前走访慰问活动。莱芜区统计局副局长刘安国、雪野镇政府副镇长岳龙涛等陪同参加活动。

1 月 15 日，济南市局召开近期重点工作会议，安排布署 2019 年统计公报、统计手册编撰工作，以及全市经济社会综合考核数据收集整理工作。会议由济南市统计局党组成员、副局长张谨国主持，济南市统计局党组书记、局长苑子建出席会议并讲话。

1 月 21 日，济南市统计局党组副书记、市社会经济调查中心主任唐军一行 3 人前往历下区姚家街道看望慰问挂职干部。

1 月 22 日，济南市局开展“我们的节日 · 春节”写春联活动，全体干部职工传习中华民族文化艺术，共同分享过年的喜悦，迎接鼠年的到来。

2 月 4 日，济南市统计局党组积极响应市委、市政府决定，成立市统计局下沉社区一线服务疫情防控工作领导小组，主要负责人任组长，分管领导为成员；领导小组下设办公室，分管领导兼任办公室主任，各处室负责人为成员的组织体系。济南市局选派 58 人，下沉一线 29 个社区参加疫情防控工作。

2 月 5 日，济南市统计局党组书记、局长苑子建，党组副书记、市社会经济调查中心主任唐军，代表局党组深入社区，看望下沉一线帮助社区防控工作人员。

2 月 6 日，受济南市统计局党组委托，局党组成员、副局长张兴利深入莱芜高新区鹏泉街道办事处疫情防控服务小组所在社区，看望下沉社区一线服务疫情防控的工作人员，实地了解社区疫情防控工作，并为下沉一线工作人员送去急需物资。莱芜高新区鹏泉街道办事处党工委副书记、主任李传宝陪同。

2 月 21 日，济南市局组织人事处副处长朱效霞荣获济南市疫情防控工作“身边好人”（第 1 批）。

2 月 24 日，受济南市统计局党组书记、局长苑子建委托，局党组成员、副局长孙夕良到济南吉财经贸有限公司进行调研座谈，详细了解企业需求，并就企业当前存在的问题和困难进行了深入交流。

2 月 24 日，济南市局组织召开全市工业统计视频会议。市统计局局长苑子建参加会议并讲话。分管副局长张兴利在莱芜区分会场参加会议。

2 月 25 日，济南市局召开党组（扩大）会议，专题学习习近平总书记在统筹推进新冠肺炎疫情防控和经济社会发展工作部署会议上的重要讲话精神，研究部署疫情防控及当前重点统计工作。济南市统计局党组书记、局长、局新型冠状病毒感染肺炎疫情防控工作领导小组组长苑子建主持会议，局党组成员、其他市管干部、各处室主要负责人参加会议。市纪委派驻第六纪检检查组组长郭尚兰到会指导。

3 月 1 日，济南市局按照市委、市政府安排部署，成立十个下沉小组到企业一线服务疫情防控和企业复工复产工作。

3 月 1 日，济南市局开展“学雷峰　战疫情　助发展”为主题的学雷锋志愿服务月活动。

3 月 2 日 -6 日，济南市局下沉企业工作组实地走访企业，服务企业疫情防控和复工复产工作。

3 月 4 日，济南市局组成进企业工作组，由党组成员、副局长谈友军带队、4 名工作人员参加，开展“进企业、进项目、进乡村、进社区”攻坚行动。

3 月 5 日，济南市局开通了“四上企业”联网直报网络课堂，有效降低新冠肺炎疫情对我市统计业务培训工作带来的影响。

3 月 6 日，济南市局在第 110 个国际劳动妇女节来临之际，采取网络形式举办“抗击疫情，赞颂英雄”主题朗诵活动。

3 月 10 日，济南市统计局党组书记、局长苑子建及工业统计处人员，到浪潮电子信息产业股份有限公司调研企业复工复产情况。

3 月 12 日，济南市局根据省社情民意调查中心《关于疫情期间日常生活必需品保障情况的调查方案》要求，开展网络问卷调查。

3 月 13 日，山东省统计局局长郭训成一行，到济南实地察看疫情防控和企业复工复产情况，市委常委、济南高新区管委会党工委书记、主任王宏志，市委常委、副市长郑德雁，市统计局局长苑子建陪同。

3 月 20 日，济南市三全食品有限公司对济南市局在企业复工复产工作中的帮扶表示感谢并赠送锦旗。

3 月 26 日，济南市局召开第七次全国人口普查工作启动会议，市人口普查领导小组副组长、领导小组办公室主任、市统计局局长苑子建主持会议并作动员讲话，市人口普查办公室副主任、成员，相关人员参加会议。

3 月 26 日，济南市统计局党组成员、副局长李士营及贸易处相关人员到钢城区莱芜钢铁集团有限公司调研，了解企业开工复工、防疫工作及贸易统计工作开展情况，并对企业 2019 年统计年报和 2020 年 2 月份月报数据质量进行了检查。

3月27日，济南市召开季度生产总值统一核算视频培训会，济南市统计局党组书记、局长苑子建主持会议并对季度生产总值统一核算改革进行培训，市直有关部门分管负责同志、业务处室负责人在主会场、各区县政府分管统计负责人、区直部门分管负责同志在各分会场参会。

4月1日，济南市统计局党组书记、局长苑子建参加市委经济运行应急保障指挥部投资运行工作组召开的全市投资项目信息管理和共享专题会并讲话。市统计局党组成员、副局长卜繁钢和投资处相关业务人员参加了此次会议。

4月7日，济南市局召开局长办公会讨论通过并印发《济南市区县级生产总值季度（年度）统一核算工作方案》、《统计专项调查资金使用管理办法》。

4月14日，济南市局被评为全市"迎接省营商环境评价工作"先进单位。

4月14-22日，济南市统计局党组成员、副局长张兴利带领工业统计处到章丘区、莱芜高新区、历城区、平阴县和槐荫区调研并进行数据核查工作。

4月16日，济南市局组织党员志愿服务队进历城区洪北社区开展"双报到"活动，并向社区赠送防疫物品。

4月17日，济南市局印发《2020年济南市统计局精神文明建设工作实施方案》、《中共济南市统计局党组关于开展"让党中央放心让人民群众满意的模范机关"创建工作的实施方案》。

4月22日，济南市局召开全市投资领域统计工作会，济南市统计局党组书记、局长苑子建到会并讲话，市统计局党组成员、副局长卜繁钢出席会议。

4月23日，济南市局召开包容普惠创新工作专班联席会议，济南市统计局党组书记、局长苑子建到会并讲话，市直相关部门分管领导参加会议并交流发言。

4月27日，济南市统计局党组副书记、市社会经济调查中心主任、新闻发言人唐军出席市委市政府举行的新闻发布会，通报一季度全市经济社会运行情况，并现场回答新闻记者的提问。

5月7日，济南市委副书记边祥慧对济南市局撰写的"加快土地流转助力现代农业"的专题调研报告作出批示。

5月7日-11日，济南市局参加全市"四减四增"工作专班评估组赴各区县开展现场评估活动。

5月8日，省统计局陈汉臻副局长一行来济南调研农业产业化龙头企业并召开座谈会，市农业农村局、市发展改革委、市工业和信息化局、济南佳宝乳业有限公司和山东省万兴食品有限公司参加座谈，济南市局副局长孙夕良陪同。

5月8日，济南市局召开党组会专题传达学习市纪委十一届五次全体会议精神，市统计局党组书记、局长苑子建主持会议并讲话。

5月9日，济南市局举办了"爱统计爱生活 我健康我快乐"健步走活动，市统计局党组成员、副局长卜繁钢及全局100余名干部职工参与。

5月10日，济南市局副局长孙夕良及农村统计处一行联合市农业农村局先后到章丘区、历城区开展农业龙头企业调研工作。

5月10日，济南市局志愿者参加山东省暨济南市2020年全国城市节约用水宣传周活动。

5月12日-13日，济南市统计局党组成员、正处级领导干部张秀玲带队赴莱芜区、莱芜高新区开展煤炭消费统计督导工作。

5月14日，济南市局召开全市统计工作暨第四次经济普查总结会议，局市管干部、市纪检第六派驻组负责同志、各区县统计部门主要负责同志、市第四次经济普查先进集体和个人代表、济南市首届基层统计人才培育工程入选人员代表、市统计局副处级以上干部参加会议。

5月14日，济南市局召开全市统计系统2020年度全面从严治党暨党风廉政建设工作会议，市纪委监委派驻第六纪检监察组组长郭尚兰、局市管干部、各区县（含各功能区）统计部门主要负责同志，市统计局副处级以上干部参加会议。

5月15日，省统计局服务业处刘福军处长一行来济南调研服务业企业运行情况，市统计局党组成员、副局长李士营陪同调研。

5月19日-20日，济南市局协同市农业农村局成立联合调研组在莱芜区和南部山区开展农业产业化龙头企业专项调研。

5月21日，济南市局召开党建工作重点任务推进会，机关党委书记唐军同志参加会议并讲话，党委委员、党支部书记、支部委员参加会议。

5月21日，济南市局召开全市第一产业固定资产投资统计部署会，市统计党组成员、副局长卜繁钢参加会议并讲话。

5月26日-27日，省统计局城镇化和人口就业统计处到济南调研劳动工资统计工作，副局长卜繁钢陪同调研。

6月10日，济南市"一次办成"改革领导小组派出督导组到济南市局对包容普惠创新工作专班工作情况进行了专项督导。

6月11日，济南市局召开全市城乡划分业务培训会议，市统计执法监察支队支队长李中亮到会讲话，各区县业务骨干参加培训。

6月15日，济南市委市直机关工委第六调研组到济南市局检查指导机关党建工作。市统计局党组书记、局长苑子建，市统计局党组副书记、市社会经济调查中心主任、机关党委书记唐军参加会议并汇报。

6月17日，济南市统计局党组成员、副局长张兴利带队到济阳区开展调研及数据核查工作。

6月18日，济南市统计局党组理论中心组集中学习习近平总书记关于统计工作重要讲话批示指示精神、《防范和惩治统计造假、弄虚作假督查工作规定》、中纪委《关于加强统计领域数字造假问题监督执纪问责工作的通知》和国家统计局局长宁吉喆文章《开展防惩统计造假、弄虚作假督察，为推动高质量发展提供统计保障》，中心组全体成员参会，处室负责人、局属事业单位负责同志列席会议。

6月19-20日，济南市局召开第七次全国人口普查市级综合试点业务培训会议，市人普办常务副主任、市统计局副局长卜繁钢参加会议，各区县人普办、试点地区街道、普查区"两员"参加培训。

6 月 21 日，济南市第七次全国人口普查综合试点启动仪式在历下区隆重召开，市人口普查领导小组副组长、市统计局局长苑子建出席启动仪式并作动员讲话。

6 月 23 日，济南市局召开全局保密员工作会议，组织保密培训，副局长张兴利参加并提出要求。

6 月 30 日，济南市局举办“数海领航 争当先锋”—市统计局庆“七一”主题党日活动，挂职干部朱效霞做报告，市统计局党组书记、局长苑子建讲党课，全局党员干部参加。

6 月 30 日，济南市召开第七次全国人口普查领导小组暨全市人口普查工作会议，市委常委、副市长、市人口普查领导小组组长郑德雁出席会议并作动员讲话。

7 月 8 日，济南市局组织 40 余名党员干部前往济南美术馆参观“战疫时刻”——全国摄影家作品实录、“文化清风——画说全面从严治党”主题漫画展。市统计局党组副书记、机关党委书记唐军和李士营、卜繁钢、孙夕良、张兴利四位副局长参加了活动。

7 月 6 日 -9 日，市人普办组织各区县收视收听第七次全国人口普查综合业务视频培训会议，市人普办主任、市统计局局长苑子建出席会议。

7 月 14 日，济南市局组织召开 2019 年城市年报和 2020 年《济南统计年鉴》编辑工作会议，对各项编辑任务进行安排部署。局党组成员、副局长张谨国主持会议，党组书记、局长苑子建参加会议并讲话。

7 月 17 日，济南市统计局党组成员、副局长李士营带领服务业处部分人员对济南高新区、历下区的 6 家“临界”纳统企业，开展实地走访调研，为企业牵线搭桥、抒忧解困，助力企业早日“升规纳统”。

7 月 20 日，山东省统计局党组书记、局长辛树人一行，到省统计局联系服务民营企业济南圣泉集团股份有限公司开展调研座谈。济南市政府办公厅党组成员杨传军，章丘区委副书记、区长边祥为，市统计局局长苑子建陪同调研。

7 月 13 日至 24 日，济南市统计执法监察支队支队长李中亮带领统计执法检查组人员，对济南高新区、南山区、新旧动能先行区、莱芜高新区等四个功能区 35 家企业进行了执法检查，对莱芜区、钢城区落实《2020 年度统计执法督查检查方案》开展了督导检查。

7 月 27 日，省统计局人口处（社科处）处长张定新、设管处处长刘东华、核算处二级调研员刘爱芝、设管处二级调研员张圣红等一行 5 人，到济南高新区调研人力资本产业有关情况。市统计局副局长卜繁钢、济南高新区管委会副主任张维国陪同调研。

7 月 28 日，济南市委市政府举行新闻发布会，通报 2020 年上半年全市经济社会运行情况。市统计局党组副书记、市社会经济调查中心主任、新闻发言人唐军出席发布会并回答记者提问。

8 月 6 日，济南市召开第七次全国人口普查领导小组第二次电视电话会议，深入贯彻落实国务院、山东省第七次全国人口普查电视电话会议精神，对全市第七次全国人口普查工作进行再部署、再推动。市第七次全国人口普查领导小组组长、市委常委、副市长郑德雁出席会议并讲话。

8 月 6 日，济南市局组织党组理论学习中心组（扩大）集体学习，专题学习市委十一届十一次全体会议精神，重点传达学习了孙立成同志在市委十一届十一次全体会议上的讲话精神。党组书记、局长苑子建主持会议并就抓好全会精神落实提出具体要求。党组副书记、市社会经济调查中心主任唐军，党组成员、正处级领导干部张秀玲作重点发言。

8 月 10 日，省统计局服务业处副处长邢文一行赴济南调研非公企业人才调查工作。

8 月 17 日，济南市第七次全国人口普查综合业务培训开班。市统计局党组书记、局长苑子建出席开班仪式并讲话。市人普办常务副主任、市统计局副局长卜繁钢主持会议。

8 月 19 日，济南市召开第七次全国人口普查试点总结会议，市人普办常务副主任、市统计局副局长卜繁钢出席会议并讲话，市人普办集中办公人员、各区县分管副主任和业务组组长参加会议。

8 月 25 日，国家统计局核算司副司长吕峰到济南高新区和新旧动能转换先行区考察调研，省统计局党组书记、局长辛树人、省统计局核算处处长彭丽芳、济南市政府办公厅党组成员杨传军、市统计局副局长张谨国、高新区管委会、新旧动能转换先行区相关领导陪同调研。

8 月 26 日，济南市局 8 名志愿者在早晚高峰期间，到经十路奥体西路口疏导交通，值勤带班领导、党组成员、副局长张兴利进行现场指导，了解路口的交通状况，提醒同志们要注意自身安全，同时要做到文明服务，体现机关干部的精神风貌，引导群众文明出行，以身作则为文明城市建设助力加油。

9 月 2 日，济南市委副书记、市长孙述涛对市统计局农村处撰写的统计分析——《上半年全市农民人均可支配收入情况分析》做出重要批示：“请京文同志阅处。要认真分析原因。”

9 月 4 日，济南市局组织党员干部参观“铭记历史 开创未来”纪念中国人民抗日战争胜利暨世界反法西斯胜利 75 周年济南抗战历史图片影像展。在讲解员的详细介绍下，大家认真参观，惦怀抗日英烈，铭记峥嵘抗战史。

9 月 5 日、9 日，济南市统计局党组成员、副局长孙夕良到钢城区、平阴县就重点企业节能降耗情况进行专项调研。

9 月 10 日，山东省统计局党组书记、局长辛树人带领服务业处、数管中心负责人，赴济南调研“四上”企业统计数据联网直报工作流程。市统计局局长苑子建，市中区委常委、副区长程伟等陪同调研。

9 月 10 日，省统计局工业处处长傅相国一行 3 人，到中国重汽集团济南卡车股份有限公司进行调研。济南市统计局副局长张兴利、市中区统计局副局长刘晓然等陪同调研。

9 月 11 日，济南市局参加济南市直机关“广播体操天天做”活动展演，唐军、张兴利、沈桂欣三位局领导带领 40 名同志组队参加展演。

9 月 14 日，济南市统计局党组书记、局长苑子建带队参加济南人民广播电台《作风监督热线》节目，宣传统计工作，与市民互动交流，接受广大市民的咨询，并解答听众关心的热点问题。

9月20日，济南市隆重举办第十一届“中国统计开放日”暨第七次全国人口普查宣传月启动仪式。活动现场市民巡访团团长辛安等7人被聘为济南市第七次全国人口普查“公益形象大使”，并现场颁发了聘书。

9月21日，省统计局服务业处处长刘福军一行3人来济南市调研电信行业发展情况，市统计局副局长李士营、市中区统计局局长丁红梅等陪同调研。

9月22日，济南市统计系统党组理论学习中心组（扩大）读书会暨统计业务骨干培训班举行开班仪式。市统计局党组书记、局长苑子建作动员讲话。党组副书记、市社会经济调查中心主任唐军主持会议。

9月22日至23日，根据《山东省人民政府办公厅关于对全省重点耗能企业煤炭消费情况进行核查的通知》（办公厅便函〔2020〕183号），由省统计局党组成员、副局长周尊考带队的核查组，对济南市煤炭消费压减工作进行核查工作。市统计局党组成员、副局长孙夕良全程陪同。

9月23日，市统计局党组理论学习中心组组织第十五次集体学习，邀请市纪委监委党风政风监督室副主任杨毓永作党风廉政建设专题辅导讲座。党组书记、局长、党组理论学习中心组组长苑子建主持学习会议，市纪委监委派驻第六纪检监察组组长郭尚兰到会指导。

9月23日，按照市统计局党组中心组（扩大）理论学习读书会暨统计业务骨干培训班日程安排，邀请省统计局国民经济核算处处长彭丽芳作GDP核算改革专题辅导讲座，市统计局党组成员、副局长张谨国主持。

9月24日，市统计局组织《习近平谈治国理政》第三卷宣讲活动，邀请市委党校经济学部主任、教授吴学军作专题讲座。党组副书记、市社会经济调查中心主任唐军主持会议。

9月25日，国家统计局贸易外经司副司长刘金钟一行3人，先后来到天下第一泉景区、济南恒隆广场和曲水亭街进行调研考察。省统计局贸易外经处处长王慕然、市统计局副局长李士营、市文化和旅游局二级巡视员刘作宗等陪同调研。

9月29日，济南市人普办联合市委宣传部召开第七次全国人口普查宣传工作会议。市第七次全国人口普查领导小组副组长、市统计局局长苑子建，市委宣传部副部长卞文出席会议并讲话。市人口普查领导小组办公室副主任、市统计局副局长卜繁钢主持会议并解读了《济南市第七次全国人口普查宣传工作实施方案》。

9月29日，省统计局联合济南市局组织部分重点企业开展座谈调研。省统计局总统计师李坤道出席会议。济南坤健钢管有限公司、山东高速信息工程有限公司等8家企业参与座谈。

9月30日，在国庆、中秋佳节和国家第七个扶贫日到来之际，市统计局党组书记、局长苑子建带队到第一书记帮扶村——莱芜区雪野街道狂山村，开展“走进贫困村、共度扶贫日”主题党日暨“我们的节日·中秋”走访慰问活动。市统计局党组副书记、市社会经济调查中心主任唐军，莱芜区统计局党组书记卢诗献，雪野旅游区管委会和街道党工委主要负责同志及相关人员参加活动。

10月12日，省人普办副主任张定新一行对济南市第七次全国人口普查摸底工作进行了督导调研。调研组分别到历下区、历城区采取座谈交流和实地走访入户等形式，深入了解人口普查摸底工作开展情况。市人普办常务副主任、市统计局副局长卜繁钢陪同调研。

10月15日，济南市召开第七次全国人口普查摸底工作推进暨培训会议。市人普办主任、市统计局局长苑子建出席会议并讲话。市人普办副主任、市统计局副局长卜繁钢主持会议并传达了国家、省第七次全国人口普查摸底工作动员视频会议精神。

10月11日至17日，济南市局在山东大学（威海）举办全市统计系统政治与业务素质双提升培训班，全市统计系统55名业务骨干参加培训。

10月21日，在第七次全国人口普查入户摸底工作正式开展的重要节点时刻，济南市人普办主任、市统计局局长苑子建来到天桥区督查指导人口普查工作，并陪同普查员一起深入住户家中进行入户摸底调查。

10月22日，济南市局举行全市统计法治工作和统计执法人员业务培训暨第二批“双随机”执法检查检前培训工作会议。邀请了山东玖相财智管理咨询有限公司董事长史皓光做了题为《读懂财务报表 提升执法能力》的专题辅导讲座。部署了第二批次“双随机”统计执法检查以及涉外统计机构专项检查等工作。市统计执法监察支队支队长李中亮作动员讲话。

10月27日，国家统计局人口司副司长崔红艳一行到我市调研第七次全国人口普查摸底工作，省人普办常务副主任、省统计局一级巡视员刘银田，市人普办主任、市统计局局长苑子建，槐荫区副书记、区长朱玉明和南部山区党委会书记、管委会主任文东河等陪同调研。

10月28日，济南市委市政府召开新闻发布会，通报前三季度全市经济运行情况。市委市政府新闻发言人刘勤介绍了我市前三季度经济社会发展情况，市统计局党组副书记、市社会经济调查中心主任、新闻发言人唐军出席发布会并回答记者提问。

10月29日，济南市委市政府召开新闻发布会，济南市第七次全国人口普查领导小组副组长、办公室主任，济南市统计局党组书记、局长苑子建通报了这次人口普查的目的意义、总体安排和普查工作开展情况。济南市级各主要新闻单位，市第七次全国人口普查领导小组办公室成员参加了新闻发布会。

10月29日，省统计局总经济师官照华、省纪委监委驻省统计局纪检监察组四级主任科员宿福国、省纪委监委驻省统计局纪检监察组干部许文凯、省统计执法监督局四级调研员郑遵昌一行到济南市天桥区调研督导“双随机”工作。市统计执法监察支队支队长李中亮陪同调研督导。

11月1日，省委常委、常务副省长、省第七次全国人口普查领导小组组长王书坚到济南市市中区舜园社区人口普查登记现场视察，慰问一线普查工作人员，并随同普查员入户采集普查数据。省统计局局长、省第七次全国人口普查领导小组副组长辛树人，市委常委、副市长、市第七次全国人口普查领导小组组长郑德雁陪同。

11月1日，省委书记刘家义，省委副书记、省长李干杰在济南以普通公民的身份分别参加了第七次全国人口普查登记。刘家义、李干杰认真接受普查员询问，并逐项作出回答，在仔细核对登记信息后郑重签名。

11月2日，济南市局召开全市统计系统办公室工作培训会议，市统计局党组副书记、市社会经济调查中心主任唐军出席会议并作开班动员，各区县办公室主任、财务人员、业务骨干及市局各处室业务骨干参加会议。

11月5日，济南市统计执法监察支队支队长李中亮同志在济南高新区发展改革和科技经济部作了题为《贯彻决策部署、坚持依法治统，用干干净净的统计数据阐释对党的忠诚》党课辅导讲座。并督导普查登记工作开展情况。

11月6日，济南市统计局党组理论学习中心组组织第17次集体学习，专题学习党的十九届五中全会精神，重点学习了《中国共产党十九届中央委员会第五次全体会议公报》。党组书记、局长苑子建主持学习会议，党组中心组成员参加会议，其他市管干部、部分处室主要负责人及有关同志列席会议。

11月6日，省统计局服务业处刘福军处长一行来到中石油山东天然气管道有限公司进行实地调研。市统计局党组成员、副局长李士营陪同调研。

11月6日，济南市统计局党组副书记、市社会经济调查中心主任唐军到基层党建联系点，以《树立大党建理念，做好与统计工作结合文章》为题，为区统计局党员干部上党课。并督导普查登记工作开展情况。

11月9日，济南市统计局党组理论学习中心组举行第18次集体学习，专题学习习近平总书记在参加第七次全国人口普查登记时的重要讲话精神。党组书记、局长苑子建主持学习会议并讲话。

11月10日，济南市统计局党组成员、副局长孙夕良到基层党建工作联系点章丘区统计局，为区局机关党员干部和普查员代表上了一堂题为《深入学习十九届四中、五中全会精神 积极发挥统计监督职能作用》的专题党课。并督导普查登记工作开展情况。

11月11日，济南市委常委、副市长、市第七次全国人口普查领导小组组长郑德雁到历下区姚家街道办事处汇隆社区，督导第七次全国人口普查工作，看望慰问一线普查工作人员，并对下一步工作开展提出要求。

11月11日，济南市统计局党组成员、副局长张谨国到基层党建联系点槐荫区统计局督导人口普查、上规入库统计工作，同时结合统计工作开展党建调研，以《学习中国共产党十九届五次全会精神 推进统计工作高质量发展》为题，为区统计局的党员干部讲党课。

11月11日，济南市统计局党组成员、副局长谈友军到基层党建联系点平阴县统计局，为党员干部上了一堂以《学习贯彻习近平总书记重要讲话精神 切实做好当前统计重点工作》为题的专题党课。并实地督导调研第七次全国人口普查登记工作。

11月11日，济南市统计局党组成员、副局长张兴利以“以坚强的党性推动统计事业发展”为主题，为历城区统计局和郭店街道办事处党员讲授了一堂精彩生动的党课。并调研督导人口普查登记和“升规直报”等重点工作，到历城区郭店街道办事处调研，看望慰问一线普查工作人员，并听取区统计局和街道工作情况汇报。

11月12日，济南市统计局党组成员、副局长孙夕良带队到济阳区督导普查登记工作开展情况。

11月12日，济南市局召开了全市统计系统综合统计工作培训会议。市统计局党组成员、副局长张谨国出席会议并作开班动员，市统计局党组成员、副局长孙夕良就统计写作进行了授课，各区县（功能区）分管综合统计领导、综合科科长、业务骨干以及市局各处室、直属事业单位相关工作人员参加会议。

11月12日，《济南日报》刊登市统计局党组书记、局长苑子建《做好“升规直报”推动高质量发展》的“升规直报”工作专访，为年度“升规直报”工作对全社会进行了吆喝呐喊。

11月16日，市委宣传部志愿服务工作处处长田建一行来我局检查指导文明单位创建情况。局党组书记、局长苑子建向督导组介绍了我局精神文明建设的亮点工作和显著成果。局党组副书记、市社会经济调查中心主任唐军就我局精神文明创建工作进行了详细汇报。

11月19日，济南市局召开全市农村统计制度培训工作会议。会议学习传达了国家及全省农村统计调查制度布置工作会议精神，布置2020年年报和2021年定期报表制度，安排部署农业农村统计工作，并与市直各有关部门交流座谈。市统计局党组成员、副局长孙夕良出席会议并讲话。

11月23日，济南市召开第七次全国人口普查长表登记和比对复查工作推进会议。市人普办副主任、市统计局副局长卜繁钢出席会议并讲话。

12月1日，市统计局党组成员、副局长卜繁钢赴莱芜区实地督导调研第七次全国人口普查工作。并到基层党建工作联系点莱芜区统计局为区局机关党员干部和普查员代表讲专题党课。莱芜区统计局党组书记卢诗献、羊里街道办事处党工委书记胥会先陪同调研。

12月4日，济南市局组织干部职工开展宪法宣誓，市统计局党组副书记、市社会经济调查中心主任唐军参加活动。

12月7日，济南市档案局测评组一行3人到市统计局进行山东省档案工作业务建设评价测评工作。市统计局党组副书记、市社会经济调查中心主任唐军参加。

12月9日，济南市局召开加强“模范机关”建设工作推进会，市统计局党组副书记、市社会经济调查中心主任唐军同志主持会议。

12月8日，值《统计法》颁布37周年纪念日之际，济南市统计局、国家统计局济南调查队、商河县统计局联合举办2020年统计法治宣传月启动仪式。市统计执法监察支队队长李中亮带队参加启动仪式。

12月10日，按照市委统一部署，市委党的十九届五中全会宣讲团成员，市统计局党组书记、局长苑子建到济南城市建设集团宣讲党的十九届五中全会精神。城市建设集团党委副书记、总经理史海成主持报告会。

12 月 15 日，济南市统计局党组成员、正处级领导干部沈桂欣一行到钢城区统计局调研党建工作并作《发扬斗争精神，提升工作精气神》的专题党课。

12 月 16 日，济南市局举行处级干部党的十九届五中全会精神专题培训班。局党组书记、局长苑子建出席开班式并作动员讲话，党组副书记、市社会经济调查中心主任唐军主持开班式。

12 月 16 日，济南市统计局党组成员、正处级领导干部张秀玲同志到莱芜高新区科技创新部调研经济形势，并作《加强党性修养，筑牢拒腐防变的思想防线》专题党课。

12 月 14 日至 17 日，国家抽查组济南组组长、国家统计局浙江调查总队二级巡视员张祖民一行对济南市人口普查工作开展事后质量抽查。

12 月 18 日，市委党的十九届五中全会宣讲团成员，市统计局党组书记、局长苑子建，到市统计局正在章丘区委党校举办的处级干部党的十九届五中全会精神专题学习班宣讲党的十九届五中全会精神。党组副书记、市社会经济调查中心主任唐军主持辅导报告会。

12 月 22 日，济南市统计局党组理论学习中心组举行第 19 次集体学习，重点学习习近平总书记在党的十九届五中全会第二次全体会议上的重要讲话精神，深入学习《中共中央关于制定国民经济和社会发展第十四个五年规划和二〇三五年远景目标的建议》等有关内容。党组书记、局长苑子建主持会议，市委市直机关工委宣传部部长李军到会巡听并对市统计局党组理论学习中心组年内学习情况进行检查。

12 月 24 日，济南市统计局党组理论学习中心组举行第 20 次集体学习，重点学习中央经济工作会议精神，传达学习习近平总书记在中央政治局 12 月 11 日会议上、在中央政治局第二十六次集体学习时的重要讲话精神等内容。党组书记、局长苑子建主持会议并讲话。

12 月 24 日，市统计局党组成员、副局长谈友军一行到济南高新区宣讲党的十九届五中全会精神，调研调查单位“升规直报”、统计网格化管理等工作。

12 月 24 日，市统计局党组成员、正处级领导干部周光萍一行到历下区统计局调研工作并作《践行新发展理念，服务高质量发展》的专题党课。

12 月 28 日，谈友军、周光萍同志带领一支部党员，到山大路洪北社区走访，并宣讲党的十九届五中全会精神。

12 月 29 日，市统计局参加了由市委、市政府主办，市纪委、市委宣传部承办，济南电视台协办的大型电视问政节目“直面问题 践行承诺”——《作风监督面对面》现场录制，针对社会公众关切的人口普查问题接受问答。

中国统计出版社有限公司最新图书简目

(仅供参考,以实际出版为准)

统计资料

中国统计年鉴　中国统计摘要　中国第三产业统计年鉴
中国第三次全国农业普查综合资料　国际统计年鉴　金砖国家联合统计手册
中国-东盟国家统计手册　中国农村统计年鉴　中国县域统计年鉴
中国农产品价格调查年鉴　中国城市统计年鉴　中国价格统计年鉴
中国贸易外经统计年鉴　中国零售和餐饮连锁企业统计年鉴　中国商品交易市场统计年鉴
大中型批发零售和住宿餐饮企业统计年鉴　中国住户调查年鉴　中国工业统计年鉴
中国环境统计年鉴　中国能源统计年鉴　中国建筑业统计年鉴
中国房地产统计年鉴　中国投资领域统计年鉴　长江经济带发展统计年鉴
中国人口和就业统计年鉴　中国劳动统计年鉴　中国社会统计年鉴
中国科技统计年鉴　中国高技术产业统计年鉴　全国企业创新调查年鉴
中国文化及相关产业统计年鉴　中国妇女儿童状况统计资料　中国青年发展状况统计年鉴
中国基本单位统计年鉴　中国教育统计年鉴　中国教育经费统计年鉴
中国民族统计年鉴　中国残疾人事业统计年鉴　中国电力统计年鉴

省级综合统计年鉴系列

北京 天津 河北 山西 内蒙古 辽宁 吉林 黑龙江 上海 江苏 浙江 安徽 福建 江西 山东 河南 湖北 湖南 广东 广西 海南 重庆 四川 贵州 云南 西藏 陕西 甘肃 青海 宁夏 新疆 新疆生产建设兵团

市(县)级综合统计年鉴系列

滨海新区 石家庄 唐山 邯郸 邢台 保定 承德 沧州 衡水 太原 大同 晋城 晋中 长治 忻州 朔州 临汾 运城 阳泉 吕梁 呼和浩特 包头 鄂尔多斯 赤峰 大连 长春 四平 延吉 延边 哈尔滨 齐齐哈尔 黑龙江垦区 浦东新区 南京 无锡 徐州 常州 苏州 南通 淮安 盐城 扬州 镇江 宿迁 江阴 丹阳 海门 张家港 通州 如东 杭州 宁波 绍兴 台州 温州 金华 嘉兴 湖州 丽水 舟山 合肥 安庆 福州 厦门 漳州 宁德 龙岩 莆田 泉州 三明 南平 思明 南昌 上饶 抚州 赣州 九江 景德镇 宁都 济南 青岛 枣庄 潍坊 聊城 郑州 洛阳 三门峡 南阳 商丘 平顶山 信阳 济源 武汉 宜昌 十堰 荆州 荆门 咸宁 黄冈 长沙 广州 东莞 惠州 深圳 汕尾 珠海 南宁 桂林 柳州 防城港 贵港 梧州 玉林 钦州 海口 三亚 儋州 成都 贵阳 毕节 黔南 昆明 文山 德宏 西安 安康 延安 汉中 渭南 商洛 榆林 银川 兰州 庆阳 乌鲁木齐

调查年鉴系列

天津 内蒙古 上海 河南 湖北 湖南 广西 重庆 四川 云南 甘肃 宁夏 南宁 桂林 贵港 昆明

统计方法应用/实用手册

Python数据分析基础（第二版）　非参数统计（第五版）　现代金融投资统计分析（第四版）
国民经济核算初级教程（第二版）　国民经济核算教程（第五版）　概率统计基础
全国统计专业技术资格考试系列考试用书：统计业务知识（第四版修订版）　统计业务知识学习指导与习题
全国统计专业技术资格考试系列考试用书：统计相关知识（第四版）　统计相关知识学习指导与习题

统计通俗读物/统计科普图书

领导干部统计知识问答（第二版）　统计公文写作及会议办理实用手册　大数据在统计工作中的应用案例汇编
中国国民经济核算知识问答（修订版）　地区生产总值核算国际比较研究　新中国统计制度方法的发展与改革

重点图书

第七次全国人口普查年鉴　第四次全国经济普查地图集　中国经济普查年鉴2018
新编英汉汉英统计大词典　中国国民经济核算体系2016　国民经济行业分类注释
挑大学选专业2020—考研择校指南　挑大学选专业2020—高考志愿填报指南　中华医学统计百科全书